D. W. Griffith's
The Birth of a Nation

D. W. Griffith's
The Birth of a Nation

A History of "The Most Controversial Motion Picture of All Time"

MELVYN STOKES

OXFORD
UNIVERSITY PRESS
2007

OXFORD
UNIVERSITY PRESS

Oxford University Press, Inc., publishes works that further
Oxford University's objective of excellence
in research, scholarship, and education.

Oxford New York
Auckland Cape Town Dar es Salaam Hong Kong Karachi
Kuala Lumpur Madrid Melbourne Mexico City Nairobi
New Delhi Shanghai Taipei Toronto

With offices in
Argentina Austria Brazil Chile Czech Republic France Greece
Guatemala Hungary Italy Japan Poland Portugal Singapore
South Korea Switzerland Thailand Turkey Ukraine Vietnam

Copyright © 2007 by Oxford University Press, Inc.

Published by Oxford University Press, Inc.
198 Madison Avenue, New York, New York 10016

www.oup.com

Oxford is a registered trademark of Oxford University Press

Library of Congress Cataloging-in-Publication Data
Stokes, Melvyn.
D. W. Griffith's The birth of a nation : a history of "the most
controversial motion picture of all time" / Melvyn Stokes.
    p. cm.
ISBN 978-0-19-533678-8
1. Birth of a nation (Motion picture) I. Title.
PN1997.B55S76 2007
791.43'72—dc22   2007022263

Printed in the United States of America
on acid-free paper

Dedicated in loving memory to my parents

Alice Stokes (1906–1983)
Bernard Stokes (1908–1988)

and to Nahed and Sarah
with love

Acknowledgments

It is a pleasure to acknowledge the help I have received in writing this book. Much of the research was accomplished with the aid of a research grant from the British Academy. I would like to thank my friends Dawn and Don Clarke for their hospitality in Washington over many years. Almost half the book itself was written during a period of sabbatical leave I spent in Paris. I am very grateful to François Weil and Francis Bordat for helping to make this possible. I would also like to thank my friends and colleagues in SERCIA (the Societé d'Études et de Recherches sur le Cinéma Anglophone), especially Alain J.-J. Cohen, Raphaëlle Costa de Beauregard, Gilles Ménégaldo, Zeenat Saleh, Dominique Sipière, and Penny Starfield, for listening to perhaps too many papers over the years on *The Birth of a Nation*. For other opportunities to discuss the film and/or for hospitality they offered, I would like to thank Annie Baron, Trudy Bolter, Christopher Clark, Nicole Cloarec, Alain J.-J. Cohen and Denise Warren, Hélène Le Dantec-Lowry, Richard H. King, Marie Liènard, Iwan Morgan, Jacques Portes, Irmengard Rauch, Cornelis A. van Minnen and Sylvia Hilton.

The staff of many libraries have helped greatly toward the writing of this book. I would like to single out especially the Manuscript Division of the Library of Congress, the British Film Institute Library, the British Library, the Bibliothèque Nationale and Bibliothèque du Film in Paris, the University College London Library, and the London University Library for their assistance. I would also like to thank my editor at OUP, Shannon McLachlan, her assistant Christina Gibson, who was particularly helpful over the illustrations, and production editor Keith Faivre. Leigh Priest prepared the index with her usual speed and skill.

Many individuals have also made suggestions or answered research questions that helped along the way. I would especially like to thank Robert C. Allen, Bruce E. Baker, Rhiannon Cain, Nancy Cott, Amy M. Davis, Thomas Doherty, Kathryn H. Fuller-Seeley, Jane Gaines, Arlene Hui, Barbara Klinger, Mark Meigs, Adam Smith, Tom Rice, Gregory A. Waller, and Denise Warren. Richard Maltby kindly became the first reader who was not also the writer. He, the three anonymous readers for Oxford University Press, and copyeditor Patterson Lamb have saved me from many errors. Those that remain are all mine.

Finally, on a more personal note, I would like to thank my parents, who first encouraged the idea of a scholarly career. I owe a huge debt also to Nahed and Sarah, who have provided so much support during the eight years it took to research and write this book.

Contents

D. W. Griffith's
The Birth of a Nation

Introduction

In 1915, a movie was released that changed the history of American cinema. Directed by David W. Griffith, it was originally known as *The Clansman*. Soon after its West Coast première, however, it was renamed *The Birth of a Nation*. This film would bring about a revolution in American moviegoing. *The Birth of a Nation* was the first American film to be twelve reels long and to last around three hours. It was the first to cost $100,000 to produce. It was the first to be shown mainly in regular theaters at the same admission prices of up to $2 that were charged for live performances. It was the first to have a specially compiled musical score to accompany the film's exhibition. It was the first movie to be shown at the White House, the first to be projected for judges of the Supreme Court and members of Congress, the first to be viewed by countless millions of ordinary Americans, some of whom had made long journeys to see it, the first to run in so many places for months at a time, the first to attract viewers who returned to see it, sometimes again and again, and the first to have its existence treated as a story in its own right in local newspapers. Although it was not the first motion picture in the United States to be distributed by means of road shows, it was the first to be shown so extensively this way. The men who advertised and publicized it created ways of promoting movies that would soon become standard across the American movie industry. In many ways, in fact, *Birth of a Nation* was the first "blockbuster": it was the most profitable film of its time (and perhaps, adjusted for inflation, of all time), it helped open up new markets (including South America) for American films, and it may eventually have been seen by worldwide audiences of up to 200,000,000.[1]

To understand the impact of *The Birth of a Nation*, it is necessary to see it in the context of early twentieth-century U.S. cinema. Before *Birth* was made, most American films consisted of one reel. They lasted around fifteen minutes, cost a few hundred dollars to produce, and were mainly shown in the cheap storefront theaters known as nickelodeons. Films of this type were viewed mainly by members of the urban working class. While these short films usually told stories, the stories themselves—given the time constraints on their development—were fairly simplistic. Feature films made up only part of the program of most nickelodeons; other items might include lectures and sing-a-longs. Nickelodeon films were normally accompanied by music (usually from a piano). In the beginning, such music had no particular connection with the film being shown. From around 1909/10 onward, however, film producers—realizing that music could be used to emphasize the film's narrative—began to publish albums of "mood" music and cue sheets.[2] Also from around 1910, movie exhibitors were clearly trying to broaden the audience for their films by attracting middle-class families.[3] This involved building new, more spacious, and comfortable movie theaters, such as the Columbia in Detroit (1911) and the Regent (1913) and Strand (1914) in New York. Yet there were still comparatively few such large movie theaters by 1915 and 300-seat nickelodeons were still being built.[4]

Film critics of 1915 clearly sensed that, in terms of scale and ambition, *The Birth of a Nation* was very different from earlier American productions. W. Stephen Bush complimented "the splendor and magnificence of its spectacles." George D. Proctor hailed it as "the greatest picture yet produced." "Mr. Griffith," observed Mark Vance, "has set such a pace it will take a long time before one [movie] will come along that can top it in point of production, acting, photography, and direction." "W.," the anonymous reviewer in the New York *Dramatic Mirror*, said much the same thing when he wrote skeptically that "If there is to be a greater picture than *The Birth of a Nation*, may we live to see it."[5] Beneath many critics' expressed admiration, however, lay something deeper: a recognition that, with *Birth*, various elements of moviemaking—from acting through editing to the musical accompaniment—had come together so that the picture represented a quantum leap forward in what could be expected from the cinema. Clearly, a number of critics were self-conscious about reviewing films, which they perceived as ephemeral, rather downmarket entertainments designed for the masses—certainly nothing to be compared with more traditional performing arts, such as opera and stage performances. To these men, *The Birth of a Nation* came as a validation and legitimation of their own role and of the possibilities inherent in motion pictures. As a number of them pointed out, it was the first film to challenge the artistic supremacy of live theater, its emotional impact on spectators was much *greater* than that of the theater, and the synthesis of images and music it offered could truly be interpreted as the birth of a new form of art.[6]

Compared to American films produced earlier, it is unsurprising that critics of 1915 should have been impressed by *The Birth of a Nation*. What is much more impressive is that some critics—fully aware of changes that had taken place in movies and the movie industry—continued to praise its aesthetic and technical qualities for many years *after* its first release. "The only film I have seen with any real excitement during the last fortnight," Graham Greene declared in May 1936, "was made in 1915... *The Birth of a Nation*... has hardly dated at all; it is still in advance of the popular film as it exists today." Two years later, Caroline Lejeune compared it to *The Jazz Singer* and *Snow White* as "the sort of film that happens once in a generation." "Nobody could say it had been essentially diminished by the perspective of time," Dilys Powell wrote, after seeing the movie, shown straight through and without any musical accompaniment, in 1945. Leaving the screening, Powell recalled, "one had the sensation of coming out of a thunderstorm." American critic James Agee (Greene, Lejeune, and Powell were all British) reacted in a very similar way. "Among moving pictures it is alone," he insisted in 1948, "as the one great epic, tragic film."[7]

Pioneering historians of American film also paid tribute to the film's vast popularity, its artistic qualities, and its influence both on audiences and later filmmakers. Terry Ramsaye, in *A Million and One Nights* (1926), described it as "the world's greatest motion picture, if greatness is to be measured by fame." Its New York opening demonstrated, he believed, that the movie "had [now] taken its place on a parity with the drama." Benjamin Hampton, in *A History of the Movies* (1929), saw Griffith's film as "an astonishing revelation of camera possibilities." The "first film to be regarded seriously by many intellectuals and sophisticated stage patrons," it had been a major influence in transforming the movies from "a cheap show for cheap people" into entertainment for the entire population. According to Lewis Jacobs, in *The Rise of the American Film* (1939), *Birth of a Nation* "propelled the film into a new artistic level... So rich and profound in organization was this picture that for years thereafter it directly and indirectly influenced film makers everywhere and much of the subsequent filmic progress owes its inspiration to this master achievement."[8]

Historians of film in the second half of the twentieth century continued to write fulsomely about *Birth*'s crucial pioneering role. To Georges Sadoul (1952), its release "marked an outstanding date in the history of American cinema. For the first time in the New World the art of film reached its maturity." Sadoul also emphasized two other consequences of *Birth*: through its great commercial success it helped reconfigure the American movie industry ("the building up of Hollywood could now begin") while simultaneously liberating it from any continuing sense of inferiority vis-à-vis European productions. To Arthur Knight (1957), it was a picture "of extraordinary eloquence and power" that "took its audiences by storm." To both Jean Mitry (1965) and Kevin Brownlow (1968), it was a "masterpiece" that launched the cinema as an art and brought about "revolutions in every field affected by motion pictures."[9] "No one who saw it," Marjorie Rosen (1973) observed, "could deny its potency. With *The Birth of a*

Nation the movies came of age...they became an art." Thomas Cripps (1977) concluded that Griffith's film "in a single stroke synthesized all of the devices and advances developed in the first generation of cinema." It was, remarked William K. Everson (1978), "quite possibly the single most important film of all time."[10]

In spite of the praise it attracted from critics and film scholars, *The Birth of a Nation* also generated intense controversy. Like earlier European-made spectacular films such as *The Fall of Troy* (1911) and *Queen Elizabeth* (1912), it claimed to tell a historical story. What made *Birth* unique was that it was the first such attempt to make a film about *American* history. Set in the United States during the era of the Civil War and Reconstruction, it supposedly told the "true" story of how the white South had been defeated in the war and, during the subsequent Reconstruction era, had been oppressed by a powerful Republican politician attempting to force black rule and full social equality on the region. Encouraged by such policies, black men began to pursue white women in order to marry them. To save Southern whites, and especially Southern women, from this dangerous situation, a new organization emerged: the white-sheeted "knights" of the Ku Klux Klan. Using considerable violence, gallant Klansmen eventually managed to subdue the aggressive Southern blacks, and white supremacy was restored.

Many people at the time of the film's first release attacked its racism and challenged the validity of its claim to represent "history." The National Association for the Advancement of Colored People (NAACP), founded in 1909, and other pro-black organizations organized protests across the country against it. Largely as a result of such pressure, *The Birth of a Nation* was banned for some time by state censorship boards in Ohio and Kansas. Other attempts to suppress it at the time of its first release, however, either through local censorship or political action, invariably failed. The efforts of mayors and police chiefs in a number of American cities to ban it were usually short and fruitless: the film's producers applied to the courts for an injunction to overturn the ban, and such injunctions were usually quickly issued.[11]

The difficulty facing the NAACP and other protest movements was that while demands for the censorship of motion pictures were growing in this period, such demands for the most part grew out of anxieties that movies were encouraging immorality (people of both sexes were sitting in the dark together and many of the films had sexual themes) or stimulating crime (by dealing too closely with matters involving crime and delinquency). Demands for censorship on the whole did not usually—at least before *The Birth of a Nation*—focus on unflattering representations of racial and ethnic minorities.[12] In a sense, therefore, the problem posed by *Birth* was new, and neither local censorship boards nor what was in effect an early attempt at movie industry self-regulation—through the inaccurately named National Board of Censorship—were really able to deal with the issues raised.

Protesting the film, moreover, it could be argued, was doubly countereffective. The controversy generated by the protests themselves in the short run created publicity that may have persuaded more people to see the picture. In the longer term, it made Hollywood extremely wary of dealing with the difficult subject of race. For many years after *The Birth of a Nation*, few blacks appeared in mainstream American films and most of those who did were confined to stereotypical roles as happy servants (mammies, butlers, porters, carriage-drivers) and entertainers.[13] Another long-term effect of Griffith's film was to discourage the representation of interracial relationships on screen. In 1927, the Motion Picture Producers and Distributors of America (MPPDA) issued guidelines to its member studios under the title "Don'ts and Be Carefuls." One of the don'ts was the depiction of miscegenation, described as "sex relationships between the white and black races." The Production Code adopted in 1930 (often known as the "Hays Code") renewed the ban in the same words.[14]

Daniel Lord, the Jesuit priest who played a role in drafting part of the Production Code, had first realized how vast the impact of cinema could be when, as a young man, he saw for the first time *The Birth of a Nation*. "I sat and sensed the beginning of a new era," Lord recalled in his autobiography. Lord left the movie theater convinced that he had witnessed the emergence of a whole new means of communication strong enough to "change our whole attitude toward life, civilization, and established customs."[15] From the beginning of its career, *Birth* was seen as a hugely powerful picture, a triumph in filmmaking art. Yet, to many of those viewing it, it also seemed a deeply controversial movie in terms of its politics.

According to Roy E. Aitken, who helped finance it, *The Birth of a Nation* is indeed "the most controversial motion picture of all time."[16] On the face of it, this seems as outrageous a claim as any of those made by *Birth*'s publicists in selling their movie. Since the beginnings of cinema in the 1890s, many films have caused controversy. "From white slavery films through films noir to adult art films like *Last Tango in Paris*," writes Matthew Bernstein, "movies have provoked multiple interpretations and concerned criticism."[17] In the United States, until the early 1930s, most criticism of home-produced films tended to focus on depictions of sexuality (for instance, *She Done Him Wrong*, 1933) or crime (including *Scarface*, 1932). Occasionally, particular groups in society would be agitated by certain movies, in the way that Jewish Americans were angered by what they saw as the anti-Semitism of Cecil B. DeMille's *The King of Kings* (1927).[18] But with the arrival of the Production Code Administration in 1934, more effective self-regulation of Hollywood's output reduced the number of films that would stir up controversy. A number still remained, however, that provoked the ire of the Catholic Legion of Decency (founded in 1933) and other mainly religious bodies.

The disappearance both of the Production Code and the Legion of Decency in the late 1960s was followed by increasing criticism of—and protests against—certain films or types of films. As Charles Lyons has observed, this was inspired in part by a widespread dislike of movie violence and, in some cases, by the belief that films such as *The Warriors* (1979), *The Program* (1993), *Natural Born Killers* (1994), and *Money Train* (1995) had inspired instances of imitative violence. Other protests were launched by special interest groups and reflected the various "cultural wars" that occurred in the United States in the last decades of the twentieth century. Feminists demonstrated against films depicting violence against women, including *Snuff* (1977) and *Dressed to Kill* (1980).[19] Gays and lesbians increasingly launched protests at films portraying homosexuals "as psychotic and lonely individuals": their targets included *Windows* (1980), *American Gigolo* (1980), and *Basic Instinct* (1992). Ethnic and racial groups carried on the tradition of protest launched by the critics of *The Birth of a Nation*: films targeted in this way included *The Godfather* (1972), *Fort Apache, the Bronx* (1979–80), *Midnight Express* (1981), *Scarface* (1983), and *Year of the Dragon* (1985).[20] Religious groups picked up the torch that had been laid down by the Legion of Decency and criticized such films as *Monty Python's Life of Brian* (1980), Jean-Luc Godard's *Je Vous Salue Marie* (*Hail Mary*, 1985), and Martin Scorsese's *The Last Temptation of Christ* (1988). Angry attacks on the last of these, in fact, began several years before its actual release and culminated in the storming of Universal Studios in Los Angeles by an ecumenical alliance of 25,000 Roman Catholics and Protestant fundamentalists.[21]

There were also, of course, movies made in other countries that created huge controversy on their release. In Europe at times the problem was political: Jean Renoir's *La Régle du jeu* (1939) was criticized as too sympathetic to the left and Leni Riefenstahl's *Triumph of the Will* (1935) as too favorable to the (Nazi) right. In India, the highly successful indigenous movie industry has created controversy from time to time in producing films about mixed Hindu/Muslim relationships (*Dharamputra*, 1961; *Bounty*, 1995; *Zakham*, 1999) or ones that have emphasized sexual themes (*Fire*, 1997; *Bawandar*, 2001).[22] Sex and violence, indeed, either individually or combined together, are the most reliable indicators of why films become controversial. A list of the twenty-five "most controversial films of all time" currently to be found on a commercial website includes one movie that has prompted considerable debate and condemnation over its depiction of the Kennedy assassination (*JFK*, 1991), three that have been heavily criticized on religious grounds (*Monty Python's Life of Brian*, *The Last Temptation of Christ*, and *The Passion of the Christ*, 2004)—and *The Birth of a Nation*. The rest are on the list because of their treatment of sex or violence—or both.[23]

In *The Birth of a Nation*, sex is implicit rather than overt while the violence is omnipresent if, by today's standards, unrealistic (the shots of battlefield corpses are the major exception to this since they still convey very well the bloody effects of war). What effectively justifies Aitken's description of the film as the most controversial of all time is neither of these things. It is the depth of the film's racism and the fact that, far from ending in the aftermath of its initial release, protests against *Birth of a Nation*'s racism would continue until the present day. Many other films have encountered disapproval and protest on their initial release; none but *Birth* has caused as much controversy over so long a period. According to one study, the period from 1915 to 1973 alone saw the film involved in at least 120 censorship controversies. During these years, there were at least fourteen attempts to pass legislation—whether at city, state, or federal level—that related directly to it and at least eight new censorship boards were specifically designed to act against it.[24]

Since it apotheosized the Ku Klux Klan of the Reconstruction period, *Birth* would become closely linked with the new Klan founded by "Colonel" William Simmons in 1915. As the Klan rose and fell in the 1920s, the film functioned as a propaganda and recruitment film. (It would continue to be screened to Klan audiences at least until the 1970s.) By the 1930s, however, argument and protest over the film were starting to develop in new directions. Social scientists argued, as part of the Payne Fund Studies, that *The Birth of a Nation* showed how great an impact films could have in encouraging audiences' racism. Subsequently, Janet Staiger has drawn attention to the ways in which the film came to symbolize divisions on the American left during the 1930s and early '40s.[25] *The Birth of a Nation* was made to look even more racist by the experiences of the Second World War (its invocation of an "Aryan heritage" at one point in its narrative acquired different associations after Hitler and the Nazis).

One factor that helped keep the protests against the film alive was the ever-present possibility that it might be reissued in a different format (a synchronized "sound" version was released in 1930) or that it would be remade. Even David O. Selznick, a few months before he bought the rights to film Margaret Mitchell's novel *Gone With the Wind*, appears to have briefly considered the notion of such a remake. One attempt that appeared to have a good chance of success was made in 1954, when a syndicate formed by financier Ted Thal began to put together the financing for such a movie. After a storm of criticism and adverse publicity, however, the deal fell apart. The idea of such a remake in 1954, the same year in which the U.S. Supreme Court finally—in *Brown v. Board of Education*—began to move toward the desegregation of American schools, is more than a little ironic.

Protests at planned screenings of the film continued. In 1972, a performance at the University of Wisconsin was canceled at the last moment. In March 1978, a showing at the Municipal Museum in Riverside, California—the town in which the film had enjoyed its first previews in 1915—had to be abandoned.[26] In August 1978, violence erupted in Oxnard, California, when the local Klan tried to show *Birth of a Nation*; a communist group, the Progressive Labor Party, demonstrated against the screening, and black and Mexican American organizations became caught up in the conflict. In July 1979, the extreme right once again battled the extreme left over *Birth* at China Grove, North Carolina.

Members of the Communist Workers' Party (CWP) mounted a demonstration outside a local community center where the film was scheduled to be shown to a group of Klansmen. The showing was canceled, and during a brief shoving match between the two sides, the CWP grabbed a Confederate flag from the Klansmen and burned it. Just over three months later, on November 3, Klansmen and Nazis avenged themselves by attacking a CWP rally in a mainly black area of Greensboro. In what would become known as the "Greensboro Massacre," they deliberately shot down several leaders of the CWP: five were killed and one seriously wounded. Though the incident was filmed by several cameramen, all those accused of the crimes were acquitted by an all-white jury. While they were on trial, an attempt to show *The Birth of a Nation* at the nearby University of North Carolina was called off when black students demonstrated against it.[27]

In more recent times, controversy surrounding the film has shown no sign of abating. A planned showing at Brown University in 1989 was called off after local protests. In 1992, when riots broke out in Los Angeles after the acquittal of members of the Los Angeles Police Department (LAPD) for their beating of African American Rodney King, Matthew McDaniel shot a video documentary on the rioting and gave it the ironic title *Birth of a Nation: 4*29*1992*.[28] Later in 1992, when an eighteen-member film board added Griffith's original movie to the Library of Congress's National Registry of Film, black organizations protested. "To honor this film," argued NAACP chair Dr. William Gibson, "is to pay tribute to America's shameful racial history."[29] In 1994, when it was rereleased on video in Britain, the British Film and Video Council decreed that it could be shown only with a 600-word disclaimer emphasizing the movie's racism.[30] In 1995, during the trial of O. J. Simpson, the Turner Classic Movie Channel decided at the last moment to withdraw it from the television schedule lest it provoke racial violence or incidents. In 1998, when the American Film Institute listed *Birth* as one of its "100 best films of all time," the response— declared Jill Jordan Sieder—was "a collective groan...[from] African Americans and film buffs...who consider this early film...the apotheosis of racist, historically haywire Southern mythology."[31]

At the end of 1999, yet another dispute over *Birth of a Nation* erupted when the Directors Guild of America withdrew its prestigious D. W. Griffith award for lifetime achievement since Griffith—although a "brilliant pioneer filmmaker"—had also "helped foster intolerable racial stereotypes." Critics of the decision argued that it was unfair to judge Griffith simply on the basis of *The Birth of a Nation* and that persecuting him for his politically incorrect views was quasi-McCarthyite (one correspondent suggested that to be politically correct, the Guild should name its award after a woman—he facetiously suggested Leni Riefenstahl). Another pro-Griffith correspondent went so far as to argue (apparently with no sense of irony) that by forcing American society to confront racial issues it had otherwise ignored, *Birth* was "a pioneering factor" in what would later become the civil rights movement![32] In contrast, those who supported the Guild's action pointed out that Griffith himself was undeniably racist, that an African American director would find it very difficult to accept an award named after him, and that retiring the award would—rightly—change the standard by which a future director's work would be honored.[33]

As might be expected of a movie that is so controversial—and at the same time so crucial in the history of American cinema—*The Birth of a Nation* has attracted considerable attention from film scholars.[34] Pioneering studies appeared during the 1960s and '70s dealing with the intellectual, social, and cultural influences that went into the making of the film,[35] its status as a "war" movie,[36] its claims to disseminate "history,"[37] the film's reception in particular localities,[38] the black response to the film at the time of its first release,[39] and its role in the reemergence of the Ku Klux Klan.[40] *Birth* also featured prominently in Donald Bogle's study of black representation on screen, Robert M. Henderson's biography of Griffith, and William K. Everson's broader study of silent film.[41] The same era saw the publication of the first shot-by-shot analyses of the film—by Theodore Huff (1961) and John Cuniberti (1979)[42]—and Fred Silva's collection of reviews and essays concerning it.[43]

The first years of the 1980s witnessed published reflections on the film as history,[44] its involvement in censorship controversies,[45] and the attempt of its producers to defuse criticism by adding a short pro-black film at the end of the program.[46] This period also saw the publication of a study by Martin Williams of Griffith's work as filmmaker and a new and definitive biography of Griffith by Richard Schickel.[47]

In 1985, however, Michael Rogin published a seminal article that began to move the debate on the film in new directions. "American movies," Rogin argued, "were born...in a racist epic." Unlike many previous scholars, who had preferred to separate the aesthetic form of the film from its racist content, Rogin insisted on exploring the meaning of the latter by analyzing *Birth* in its social, political, and cultural context.[48] His argument that Griffith's film should be held to account for its racism was echoed in 1991 by Clyde Taylor, who practically blamed the entire discipline of film studies for failing to recognize that by separating *Birth*'s aesthetics from its racism it had effectively colluded in the perpetuation of white racial supremacy.[49] In 1993, in a broader study of Griffith's films, Scott Simmon emphasized *Birth of a Nation*'s fall from grace in the decades since its first release: it had changed over time "into one of the ugliest artifacts of American popular art"—an artifact, moreover, that now failed audiences "on every ethical, emotional, and perhaps even artistic level."[50] In subsequent years, scholars began to analyze *The Birth of a Nation* to lay bare the techniques and mechanisms through which the structures of the film promoted racism. Richard Dyer, in an essay published in 1996, drew attention to the manner in which lighting was used to accentuate the "whiteness" of the principal white female characters.[51] In 2000, Jane Gaines and Neil Lerner wrote of the way in which the original musical score of the film by Joseph Carl Breil greeted the appearance and reappearance of crowds of supposedly primitive blacks by using a theme labeled "The Motif of Barbarism."[52] Also in 2000, Vincent F. Rocchio examined sequences in the film that by showing "the black inability to interact competently with modern Western culture" constructed blackness as synonymous with being "naturally uncivilized."[53]

Rogin's landmark article of 1985, with its analysis of various melodramatic tropes in Griffith's film, also foreshadowed an increasing interest in *Birth of a Nation* as melodrama. James Chandler, in a work first published in 1990, traced back the melodramatic lineage of *Birth* to the fiction of Sir Walter Scott.[54] In an essay of 1996, Jane Gaines compared the melodramatic narrative and structure of *The Birth of a Nation* with those of *Within Our Gates*, a newly rediscovered movie by black filmmaker Oscar Micheaux.[55] In *Playing the Race Card* (2001), Linda Williams argued that in *Birth* Griffith succeeded in blending the appeal of the "Tom" tradition (based on Harriet Beecher Stowe's antebellum novel, *Uncle Tom's Cabin*, and the plays that came to be based on it) with Thomas Dixon's racial melodrama of the post–Civil War period. In 2005, Susan Courtney examined the gender politics underlying the film's preoccupation with what she termed "American cinema's primal fantasy of miscegenation."[56]

The last few years have seen further studies of the film's reception. In an article published in 1987, John Inscoe compared North Carolinian responses to the stage-play *The Clansman* with those to *The Birth of a Nation* a few years later, noting that criticism of the play did not translate for the most part into criticism of the film. In 1992, Janet Staiger compared debates over *Birth* between critics and defenders of the film at the time of its first release with those that broke out among American left-wingers in the late 1930s and early '40s. In a highly original study of the politics of protest (and censorship) relating to *Birth of a Nation*, Jane Gaines noted that "there is the distinct possibility that the film was banned in many towns not because of its ideological message but because of general white distaste for and paranoia about anything black." In *Returning the Gaze* (2001), Anna Everett analyzed some of the intellectual difficulties and ambivalences in the response by black film critics to the film's first release.[57]

Recent scholarship on *Birth of a Nation* has also examined the film from a number of other perspectives. Russell Merritt revisited *Birth* in an essay of 1990 in which he argued, on the basis of a formal reading of one major scene, that Griffith's film at times becomes open to a range of readings. These "spasmodic outbursts of uncontrollability," he concluded, helped keep *Birth* "such a resilient text that defies the banalities and offenses of its source material." In 1994, Robert Lang edited a volume that together with his own excellent introduction to the film, brought together a continuity script, articles, and reviews from the time of *Birth*'s first release; a selection of scholarly articles (including the above-mentioned articles or chapters by Staiger, White, Chandler, and Rogin); and a Griffith filmography. In 2001, Bruce Chadwick devoted three chapters of his book about the representation of the American Civil War on film to *Birth of a Nation*. In 2003, Kris Jozajtis argued that the basis of *Birth's* appeal to 1915 audiences had not been the film's endorsement of white supremacy so much as a series of religious images that attempted "to revitalize the traditions of Protestant America via the modern technology of film." In 2004, Paolo Cherchi Usai edited a volume on Griffith's films of 1914–15 that included a series of short essays on *Birth of a Nation* by Griffith scholars Eileen Bowser, Charlie Keil, Joyce Jesionowski, David Mayer, Philip C. Carli, J. B. Kaufman, and Linda Williams.[58]

Clearly, there is already a voluminous scholarship surrounding *The Birth of a Nation*. Why, it might be asked, is yet another scholarly book on the film needed? There are a number of answers to this. In the first place, so much has been written about *Birth* that there is a considerable need for a synthesis. Second, many false myths and legends have grown up around *Birth of a Nation* and continue to find their way into discussions of it. Many of these had their origins in claims by the film's publicists or D. W. Griffith himself. Joyce Jesionowksi, for example, seems to accept Griffith's claim—a preposterous one—that 4,500 blacks were used in shooting the film.[59] Others can be traced back to the unreliable testimony of self-appointed Griffith "expert" Seymour Stern. Third, most analyses of *Birth* have been grounded in an examination of the movie itself. Film scholars have at times seemed unaware of both historical research relating to aspects of the film's career[60] and the existence of archival materials. In reality, there are many questions about the film that can be answered only by examining manuscript sources, particularly the D. W. Griffith Papers and the papers of the film's main organized opponent, the NAACP. Both Pierre Sorlin and Eileen Bowser, almost a quarter of a century apart, thought it impossible to unravel the details of the film's financing.[61] Yet *The Birth of a Nation* was distributed by a corporation, the Epoch Producing Company, which kept detailed accounts of expenditure and income, and those accounts are available for scholarly investigation.

Because the present volume is based on archival research as well as published sources, it will shed new light on *Birth of a Nation* in a number of crucial areas. The mechanisms by which the film was distributed and exhibited are not, for all the legends, very well known. J. B. Kaufman, for example, remarks that "there was nothing like the systematized road show exhibition of later years."[62] In reality, the distributors of *Birth of a Nation* pioneered such road show exhibitions. Indeed, analyzing the manner in which *Birth* was "sold" to a mass audience underlines its pioneering importance in the development of American cinema. For all the analysis so far published of *Birth of a Nation's* approach to history, there is still little understanding of the role the film played either in the cultural struggle over how Americans remembered the Civil War era or the consequences of that struggle. Finally, with honorable exceptions (Janet Staiger, for example), accounts of the film's reception confine themselves in the main to the Northeast and do not go much beyond its initial release. This means that the full dimensions of the campaign against the film by the NAACP and others have not so far been properly appreciated either in geographical or chronological terms. Examining the film only at the time of its initial release has also created difficulty in understanding the film's wider role in the history of American society and culture—a major theme this volume will address.

The book is divided into eight chapters. Chapter 1 focuses on the West Coast première of the film at Clune's Auditorium in Los Angeles on February 8, 1915. It outlines the movie's plot and explores the reactions of the first-night audience. Chapter 2 analyzes the paths by which Thomas Dixon Jr. came to write the novels and play on which *The Birth of a Nation* was based. It emphasizes the point that Dixon was deliberately trying to create a new "master narrative" of Southern history that would challenge that to be found in Harriet Beecher Stowe's *Uncle Tom's Cabin*. The chapter also covers Dixon's own unsuccessful attempts to bring his work to the screen. Chapter 3 outlines the stage and film career of David W. Griffith, assesses his reputation as a film director, and discusses the reasons for his eventual involvement in the *Birth of a Nation* project. Chapter 4 examines the making of the picture itself, including casting, rehearsals, filming, Griffith's directorial style, and the compilation of a musical score.

Chapter 5 deals with the strategy behind the film's exhibition in "live" theaters by means of road shows, the publicity campaign developed to "sell" the film, and the rapturous response of many spectators. It assesses the role of *The Birth of a Nation* both in altering expectations of the movies and reconfiguring the social composition of the American movie audience. Chapter 6 analyzes the campaign of protest against the film launched by the NAACP. It shows that this campaign, undermined by divisions within the black community as well as legal complexities over censorship, essentially failed. At the same time, however, it helped the NAACP expand in size and establish itself for the first time as a major national force. Chapter 7 contrasts Griffith's attempts to present his film as "history" with its thoroughly biased approaches to slavery, the Civil War, Reconstruction, and the Klan. It sets out to explain why an essentially "Southern" view of these issues also, in 1915, appealed to many Americans living outside the South. Chapter 8 analyzes the film's own long post-1915 history, including the more successful efforts of the NAACP to have the film suppressed during World War I, the 1920s (when the NAACP astutely exploited *Birth*'s association with a revived Ku Klux Klan to broaden the base of opposition to it), and the 1930s. It discusses the relationship between the film and social science research projects, including the Payne Fund Studies. It explains how communists and anti-communists came to fight over *Birth* and shows how the film's producers continued to dream of a remake. It concludes by examining the later careers of those who worked on the *Birth of a Nation* project.

1

Première in Los Angeles

The people who entered Clune's Auditorium in Los Angeles on the evening of Monday, February 8, 1915, were both excited and apprehensive. They almost certainly knew that the earlier, afternoon performance of the film they were about to see, *The Clansman*, had been prohibited by a court injunction obtained by the Los Angeles branch of the National Association for the Advancement of Colored People.[1] Since most of them were connected in some way with the production of the film, they were also worried about reactions to the film at this, its official première.[2] *The Clansman* had taken more time to complete than any other previous American film. It was the longest film so far made. It had cost more than any other film.[3] Consequently, there was a good deal riding on the success of this particular showing. But there was no way of judging the quality of the final production before it was screened.

Once inside the auditorium, the 2,500 members of the audience were greeted by usherettes, all wearing gowns modeled on the fashions of the Civil War era. Many signed the petitions passed round by these usherettes demanding that the Los Angeles City Council take no action to prevent the exhibition of the film.[4]

The first sign that something out of the ordinary might be about to happen came with the unmistakable sound, rising above the noise of the crowd, of a large symphony orchestra tuning up. Then the members of the orchestra made their way, carrying their instruments, through a little doorway under the stage into the orchestra pit. At a little after eight o'clock, the house lights dimmed and a tense silence fell among the audience. The film's title was first projected on to the dark fabric of the curtain. Some in the audience thought that this was a mistake, since all they could see was a flickering faintness; but then the big curtain rose, leaving the title clear on the picture screen. At the same moment Carli Elinor, director of music at Clune's Auditorium, who had compiled a special musical score for the film, raised his baton to inaugurate a huge fanfare from the orchestra.[5]

The audience was first shocked into silence by this musical explosion and then appeared to respond with unusual enthusiasm. They watched the initial titles, which identified the film as a production of D. W. Griffith, listed the players, and expressed the pious aspiration that "If in this work we have conveyed to the mind the ravages of war to the end that *war may be held in abhorrence*, this effort will not have been in vain." The orchestra continued to play quietly until the titles were over and then helped the opening sequences of the film to glide along—in the memory of one audience member—"on a flow of music that seemed to speak for the screen and to interpret every mood."[6]

It is probably impossible to recreate exactly the film that was shown in Los Angeles that night.[7] David Wark Griffith, the director, had been editing the film almost continuously since the last scene had been shot at the end of October 1914. It had already been shown to preview audiences at the Loring Opera House in Riverside, California, on January 1 and 2,[8] and Griffith had afterward continued to edit. Riverside projectionist Carl Douglass would later observe that

> Griffith's cutter was a red-headed woman [Rose Smith], at least six feet tall. She would sit with him and his secretary. He talked while his secretary made notes.
>
> Then the cutter would come into the...projection booth, and the next day I'd see a lot of the film she'd cut on the floor. Then they'd show the picture at the next regular performance, and maybe cut some more and sometimes put back some that had been cut.[9]

Editorial changes continued to be made after the première and also after its East Coast opening.[10] In many states and cities, moreover, a number of cuts were demanded by local politicians and censorship boards before the movie was permitted to open. Even eyewitnesses at the première, including the normally reliable Karl Brown, Griffith's assistant cameraman who had worked on the film, later remembered things being in the film that were not there or became confused over at what point in the film particular sequences occurred.[11] In any case, there is no such thing as a "true print" of the film in existence. The surviving prints of *The Clansman* (which would soon be re-titled *The Birth of a Nation*) suffered not only from Griffith's continual tinkering and censorship demands; they were also, as Robert Lang has pointed out, subject to "careless preservation of the negative...primitive methods of assembling release prints, and inexpert on-the-spot repairing done by projectionists after film breakage."[12]

Yet, on the balance of probability, the film screened at Clune's that night was broadly similar to a 16mm copy of a 35mm nitrate print that is preserved in the Library of Congress.[13] In this print, the first sequence of the film is preceded by a title asserting that "The bringing of the African to America planted the first seed of disunion." It shows a minister praying over manacled slaves on the point of being auctioned in a town square.[14] The second shot of the film is of abolitionists demanding the freeing of the slaves (though it is plain that this shot originally also implied that slaves were extremely malodorous, with a female abolitionist being repulsed by a young black boy).[15] After these short references to slavery, the film begins to introduce the main characters of the two families around whom the narrative will be built: the Northern Stonemans and the Southern Camerons.

Austin Stoneman is presented as "a great parliamentary leader" in the House of Representatives. He has three children: Elsie, Phil, and Tod. The brothers have promised Ben, the oldest son of the Camerons, to visit him on his family plantation in Piedmont, South Carolina. Ben has two sisters, Margaret and the much younger Flora, and two brothers, Duke and Wade. After the Stoneman boys arrive on the plantation, they meet the entire Cameron family, including Dr. and Mrs. Cameron. A close and tender relationship develops between Phil Stoneman and Margaret Cameron. Meanwhile, Tod Stoneman and Duke Cameron become prankish chums and Ben Cameron falls in love with a portrait of Elsie that her brother Phil is carrying.

Into this idyllic world, the film introduces the looming threat of the Civil War. Dr. Cameron is shown reading a newspaper proclaiming that "If the North carries the election, the South will secede." The scene then switches to the Stoneman library in Washington, where the congressman is shown receiving Republican senator Charles Sumner—and cherishing a strong passion for his mulatto housekeeper, Lydia.[16] Again, the film returns to Piedmont, where the younger Camerons and Stonemans are taking their sad leave of one another.

The Civil War is shown breaking out, as newly elected President Lincoln calls for volunteers and the Stoneman brothers set out to join their regiment. Ben Cameron is depicted as present at a ball in Piedmont in honor of the departure of its quota of troops to fight in the Confederate Army (the South, it is pointed out, has just won the battle of Bull Run). At dawn, Ben leads the troops (including Wade and Duke) off to the war. In the North, less colorfully, Elsie tells her father of Phil and Tod's departure for the front.

The movie then jumps two and a half years by means of a title, to show Ben Cameron in the field reading a letter from Flora, followed by Flora reading one of her brother's own letters providing news from the front. Immediately afterward, a mainly black force of guerrillas is shown attacking Piedmont. While Dr. Cameron tries to resist, and is knocked down for his pains, his wife, Margaret and Flora hide in a cellar. The black soldiers, under a white officer, engage in a riot of looting and destruction. The Cameron family, however, are rescued by the arrival of a company of Confederate troops, who drive off the guerrillas.

Action in the film then switches to the main conflict in the war. Tod Stoneman and Duke Cameron had earlier promised to see each other again. Duke is wounded in a charge and, as he lies on the ground, Tod prepares to kill him with his bayonet. At the last moment, however, he recognizes his old chum. As he stands over the Southerner with a smile of recognition, he is shot in the back and collapses on top of Tod. The two boys die in each other's arms. The Cameron family and Austin and Elsie Stoneman are shown learning of the deaths of the boys.

The war continues and the South is shown increasingly hard-pressed. General Sherman's army is pictured marching through Georgia to the sea. The siege of Atlanta follows—and the death of Wayne, the second Cameron son. The Confederate forces at Petersburg are shown eating their only food: parched corn. In an attempt to rescue a stranded food train, General Robert E. Lee orders his forces forward. An artillery bombardment commences and "Little Colonel" Ben Cameron leads a final desperate attack on the Union lines, commanded by Phil Stoneman. (As the Confederates charge, an inset shows

A terrified Flora Cameron during the raid by black "guerrillas" on Piedmont. (Epoch/The Kobal Collection)

the Cameron family praying.)[17] The Southern forces take two entrenchments but in the process lose almost all their men. "The Little Colonel" pauses before the final, suicidal assault to offer his water bottle to a wounded Union soldier, and is cheered for his heroism by the Union men. Cameron leads the Confederate remnant into a charge. When the man carrying the regimental standard is hit, Cameron picks up the standard and—though wounded—continues the advance. Phil Stoneman orders his men to stop firing, and as Cameron rams the standard into the mouth of a cannon and collapses, Stoneman protects his friend and drags his now limp body into the trench. The battle continues.[18] Dead soldiers are shown lying in a heap. The North is finally victorious.

The Camerons now learn that their second son is dead and their eldest is badly injured in a Washington hospital. At this point, "The Little Colonel" meets Elsie Stoneman, who is working in the hospital as a nurse. He shows her the portrait of her he has taken from Phil Stoneman. Mrs. Cameron arrives at the hospital to visit her wounded boy. At this point, an army doctor tells Mrs. Cameron and Elsie that Ben Cameron has been sentenced to be hanged as a guerrilla. Elsie and Mrs. Cameron together call on President Lincoln to ask for clemency and, after initially refusing, Lincoln finally gives in to the mother's

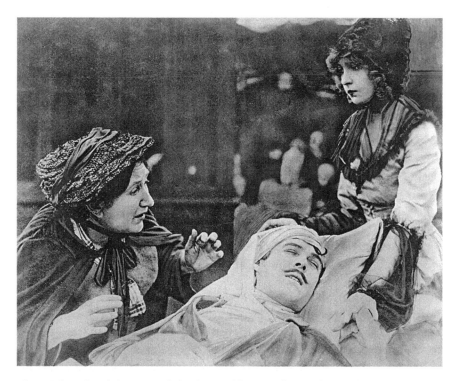

The "Little Colonel" lies wounded in hospital between his mother and his nurse, Elsie Stoneman. (Epoch/The Kobal Collection)

plea and signs a pardon. Her mission accomplished, Mrs. Cameron leaves her now-convalescent son to return home.

Lee's surrender to Grant at Appomattox Court House is then shown, and the same day, Colonel Cameron is discharged from the hospital and leaves for home.[19] On arrival in Piedmont, he is met by Flora wearing strips of cotton wool ("Southern ermine") to hide the raggedness of her dress.

Back in Washington, Austin Stoneman meets Lincoln to protest the president's policy of clemency for the ex-Confederate states but is rebuffed. The South, encouraged by Lincoln, begins to rebuild. Then the film reconstructs the events of the evening of April 14 as, with Elsie and Phil Stoneman in the audience, Lincoln goes to Ford's Theatre. When his bodyguard deserts his post to get a better view of the play, Lincoln is shot by John Wilkes Booth. With the very different reception of the news of the assassination in the Stoneman household ("You are now the greatest power in America") and by the Camerons ("Our best friend is gone. What is to become of us now!"), the first part of the film comes to an end.

For much of the first part of the film at its première, the vast bulk of the audience at Clune's had seemed entranced. Helped by the music, but perhaps most of all by skilful editing, the film flowed from shot to shot without any real sense of discontinuity. To one skeptical observer, Karl Brown, who had worried about the fragmentation and even the triteness of the sequences he had watched being shot, the finished film came as a revelation. He would later recall feeling "hot and cold," with a series of "tingling electric shocks" running through him, as the film unfolded. The battle scenes, he noted, were especially powerful, aided by the special effects of explosions created by a backstage crew and the musical score. As the "Little Colonel" charged the Union guns and rammed his flag into the cannon's mouth, "bombs" burst in the air and orchestral trumpets sounded. By that stage, Brown remembered, every man in the audience was on his feet cheering Cameron on.[20]

The more sentimental scenes, however, seemed equally effective: Brown remembered the women in the audience (his mother included) weeping openly as the "Little Colonel" returns after the war to his ruined home. There were also moments of intense humor: when a guard at the hospital looks at Elsie (Lillian Gish), realizes she is unattainable, and sighs, that sigh was greeted by "gales of laughter" from the audience.[21]

When the intertitle came on reading "Intermission," Brown and his father made their way into the lobby where they eavesdropped on the conversations around them. Many people were expressing their enthusiasm for the film. Some were arguing that it was an authentic recreation of the Civil War and its character. But there were also a number of voices warning that director Griffith had crowded all the best scenes into the first half of the picture and that the remainder of the film was likely to be an anticlimax. (Brown also shared this anxiety.) When chimes from inside the auditorium announced the end of the intermission, Brown went back to his seat "with a sense of cold foreboding." The second part of the film, he thought, had passages of "long, dull, do-nothing stuff" before the final action shots, which essentially only repeated scenes from earlier films such as Griffith's *The Battle of Elderbush Gulch* (1913). Brown believed that the audience was likely to become restive and bored with the slow pace and common clichés.[22]

The second part of the film begins with a succession of titles introducing the notion of the "agony" suffered by the South during the period of Reconstruction that immediately followed the ending of the war. (Some of these are made up of quotations from Woodrow Wilson's *History of the American People*.) According to these, congressional leaders set out to crush the white South under the rule of blacks and Northern adventurers. With Lincoln's death, Austin Stoneman has become "the uncrowned king" of the United States. He has a protégé, Silas Lynch, a mulatto who has become a black leader. Stoneman announces his intention to make Lynch the equal of any white man. (Lydia, his mulatto mistress, hearing this cannot contain her sense of triumph.) Senator Sumner calls to try to persuade Stoneman to moderate his policy of extending power to blacks, but Stoneman refuses (again to Lydia's joy and excitement).

Stoneman, ill in Washington, sends Lynch to the South to help Northern carpetbaggers[23] organize black voters. Lynch decides to make the Camerons' town of Piedmont his headquarters and sets about persuading blacks to stop work in order to celebrate their freedom. His message is aided by the distribution of free supplies by the Freedmen's Bureau, which encourages the blacks in the delusion that they are to be given "Forty Acres and a Mule" by the federal government. When Ben and Flora Cameron are temporarily prevented from passing into the street by a squad of marching black soldiers, Lynch reprimands the "Little Colonel" for not accepting that African Americans now have an equal right to walk on the sidewalk.

Stoneman, partly for health reasons and partly to see at firsthand the working out of his policies, leaves for South Carolina where—on the advice of his children—he will also live at Piedmont. He and his family visit the Camerons' home. Lynch arrives and greets Elsie Stoneman (to whom, it has already been made clear, he is attracted). When Lynch holds out his hand for Ben Cameron to shake, the "Little Colonel" (to Stoneman's great annoyance) refuses it by turning away.

At a Union League meeting held before the elections, there are signs demanding "Equality" and "Forty Acres and Mule." Stoneman is the guest of honor and Lynch speaks. Outside the Freedmen's Bureau, a white official is shown registering black voters. In the meantime, Ben Cameron and Elsie Stoneman have fallen in love. Although Margaret Cameron and Phil Stoneman are plainly attracted to each other, Margaret's memories of her dead brothers will not allow the relationship to develop.

On election day, all the blacks vote (some more than once) while the whites are disfranchised and physically prevented from voting. The blacks and carpetbaggers, therefore, sweep the state. Lynch is elected lieutenant-governor. Black soldiers in the street fire their rifles in the air and Lynch is carried in celebration by his cheering supporters.

In the aftermath of the election, Ben Cameron relates to his father and three other men a series of outrages that have taken place. A white family has lost a legal case tried by a black judge in front of an exclusively black jury. African American soldiers have pushed a white man and his two children off the sidewalk into the street. A white family has been dispossessed and driven out of their home. Even while Cameron is speaking, his loyal African American servant, Jake, is being beaten by a black soldier for not voting with the Union League and carpetbaggers. When an elderly black man tries to stop the beating, he is shot and killed.

The movie then presents a re-creation of the black-dominated State House of Representatives in 1871. African American members are eating, surreptitiously drinking alcohol, and taking their shoes off. The speaker is obliged to rule that all members must wear shoes. The house passes a resolution insisting that all whites must salute black officers on the streets and a law allowing the intermarriage of blacks and whites. Inspired by such ideas, a black soldier, Gus, begins to covet Flora Cameron. When he is reprimanded by Ben Cameron for skulking so close to Cameron Hall, Lynch protests.

The "Little Colonel," brooding by the riverbank on the fate of his people, sees two white children sitting on the ground who cover themselves with a sheet. Four black children are frightened by them and run away. The incident gives Cameron the germ of the idea for the Ku Klux Klan. The white-hooded night riders are shown terrorizing two blacks. But first blood goes to the supporters of Lynch, who ambush three Klansmen. Stoneman tells Elsie that Ben Cameron is a Klansman, and when she confronts him with the accusation, he drops what is clearly a Klan uniform to the ground. Her suspicions confirmed, she breaks off their engagement.

Young Flora Cameron, against the advice of her brother, goes alone to the spring to fetch water. She is followed by Gus. Meanwhile, the "Little Colonel" arrives home and, alarmed that Flora has gone off alone, sets off in pursuit. At the spring, Gus confronts Flora and tells her he wants to marry her. Flora panics and runs off. Not knowing that Ben is on his way, she climbs a rocky slope to get away from Gus, who still follows her. Finally, at the top of the hill, with Gus still following her, she jumps off the rocks and is fatally injured. Gus runs away and the dying Flora is found by Ben Cameron.[24] While the Cameron family (and their black servants Mammy and Jake) mourn Flora, Gus takes refuge in a black saloon.

Whites search the town for Gus. The blacksmith, Jeff, goes to the saloon where Gus is hiding. When confronted by several blacks, he fights and beats them, throwing several out of the window. He is then shot in the back. Gus runs away from the saloon and tries to escape on a horse, but he is cornered. Tried by the Klan, he is found guilty and killed.[25] His body is left on the steps of the lieutenant-governor's house with a sign bearing a skull and crossbones and the letters "K.K.K." It is found there in the morning by Lynch, who orders black militiamen into the streets to take up the challenge laid down by the Klan.

The Klans prepare for action and that night make the decision to disarm all blacks. In the meantime, black spies set out to uncover whites in possession of Klan uniforms so they can be killed. One such spy catches sight of Margaret Cameron hiding one of the uniforms and Lynch orders the arrest of Dr. Cameron. Margaret runs to the Stoneman house to plead with Elsie to have her father intervene. The white scalawag[26] captain who has arrested Dr. Cameron parades him in chains before his former slaves, who jeer him. Mammy and Jake, black but "faithful souls," mount an attempt to rescue Dr. Cameron, which is observed by Mrs. Cameron, Margaret, and Phil Stoneman. To complete the rescue, Phil punches the captain in the face and shoots one of the black soldiers. Mr. and Mrs. Cameron, Margaret, Phil, Mammy, and Jake all

Gus's "trial" by the Klan. (Epoch/The Kobal Collection)

escape in a wagon. When the wagon loses a wheel, they take refuge in a log cabin occupied by two Union veterans.

Elsie Stoneman, in her father's temporary absence, goes to Lynch to ask for help. Lynch, who has been hosting a party, clears the room to be alone with her. He proposes marriage and Elsie, shocked, threatens to have him whipped. Lynch, with black soldiers thronging the streets, dreams of carving out a black empire for himself with Elsie as his consort. Drunk and besotted with this dream, he orders his servants to rush preparations for a "forced marriage." The Klans, in the meantime, begin to assemble, led by the "Little Colonel."

Stoneman returns to Piedmont. He approves when Lynch says he wants to marry a white woman but then angrily rejects the idea after Lynch informs him that Elsie is the objection of his affections. Stoneman is restrained by force. The town is taken over by rioting blacks, brought in by Lynch to overawe the whites.[27] Elsie manages to smash the window of the room in which she is imprisoned. Her call for help is heard by two mounted white spies.

When black soldiers surround the log cabin in which the Camerons, their servants, and Phil Stoneman have taken refuge, the Union veterans refuse to allow Dr. Cameron to give himself up. As black soldiers attack the cabin, the veterans join in its defense. In the town, black mobs riot in the streets while helpless whites look on. Finally, the massed ranks of Klansmen reach the town, attack the black soldiers, and force them to flee. Lynch is captured and Elsie is rescued by Ben Cameron.[28]

Meanwhile, things are growing desperate in the little cabin. Their plight, however, has reconciled Margaret Cameron and Phil Stoneman. Just as the black soldiers are about to take the cabin—and Dr. Cameron plans to kill Margaret to prevent her falling into black hands—the Klansmen arrive and drive off the attackers. The blacks are all disarmed. Led by Margaret, Elsie, and Ben, the Klansmen parade through the town. Whites celebrate as blacks slink away. At the next election, blacks are prevented from voting by a line of armed, mounted Klansmen.

In the aftermath, first Margaret and Phil, then Elsie and Ben, are seen on a "double honeymoon." An image of the God of War surrounded by broken bodies is followed by that of Christ, then that of a celestial city. Elsie and Ben are shown looking toward the city. The final title appears: "Liberty and Union, one and inseparable, now and forever!"[29]

The predictions of the doomsayers at the intermission proved inaccurate and Karl Brown's fears unnecessary. The audience at the première remained intent during the second part of the picture, completely caught up in the drama. At times, they reacted strongly to particular sequences.[30] One critic would later note that audiences "invariably" applauded the scene in which the "Little Colonel" re-

The victorious Klan parade in Piedmont. (Epoch/The Kobal Collection)

fused to shake hands with Lynch.[31] The audience at the première probably did the same. Brown recalled that as the Klansmen began to ride,

> The cheers began to rise from all over that packed house. This was not a ride to save Little Sister but to avenge her death, and every soul in that audience was in the saddle with the clansmen and pounding hell-for-leather on an errand of stern justice, lighted on their way by the holy flames of a burning cross.

Brown also remembered one special sequence "that made the audience duck and scream," as it seemed that the horses of the clansmen were heading straight for the audience.[32]

When "The End" appeared on the screen, the audience, according to Brown, "didn't just sit there and applaud, but they stood up and cheered and yelled and stamped feet until Griffith finally made an appearance." The director stepped out a few feet from the left of the stage. He did not bow or raise his hands, but simply stood there, a tiny figure against the backdrop of the great proscenium arch, as wave after wave of cheers and applause engulfed him.[33] We shall never know what Griffith thought as he stood in front of the enthusiastic crowd. It was quite possibly the greatest moment of his life. It seemingly justified his attempt to make a film longer than anyone else in the United States had so far done and the time and effort required to bring the project to a successful conclusion. It held out the promise that *The Clansman* would make a return on the very large sum it had cost to make.

Above all, perhaps, it justified Griffith's own decision to become a film-maker. It may be, standing on the stage of Clune's Auditorium, that Griffith was reflecting on the route by which he had arrived at that night. If so, he may well have spared a thought for his fellow Southerner, Thomas Dixon Jr. Though *The Clansman*, like all films, was a collaborative enterprise, the roles of two men had been absolutely crucial in leading up to this screening: those of Griffith and Dixon.

2

Thomas Dixon Jr.

The essential narrative and the principal fictional characters of *The Birth of a Nation* were originally created by Thomas Dixon Jr. Any attempt to understand the genesis of the film, therefore, must start with Dixon. Successively lawyer, politician, minister, lecturer, novelist, dramatist, actor, theatrical and motion picture producer, and real estate entrepreneur, he was a man of tremendous energy, considerable versatility, and enormous ambition. Almost forgotten nowadays, he was a significant figure in early twentieth-century American culture. He was a highly successful minister and popular lecturer. His novels, frequently addressing racial issues, enjoyed huge sales. He also wrote a number of plays that attracted large, enthusiastic audiences. The popularity of Dixon's novels and plays, indeed, suggests that the issues he addressed struck a responsive chord among many Americans of his time.

Childhood and Youth

Dixon was born on January 11, 1864, on a farm near Shelby, North Carolina. Both the time and the place would heavily influence his later career. It was the third year of the Civil War, and North Carolina was one of the slave states fighting for independent nationhood as part of the Southern Confederacy.[1] Though the Dixon family had deep roots in North Carolina going back to the eighteenth century, it was because of the impact of the Civil War that Dixon was born there. His father, Thomas Dixon Sr., had moved west with his family in 1862 to establish a farm near Little Rock, Arkansas. One reason for this change may have been to help his wife, Amanda, overcome depression brought about by the deaths of two of her four children. It may also have seemed to the slave-owning

Thomas Dixon Jr. (1864–1946). (Library of Congress, Prints and Photographs Division, LC-USZ62-110941)

Dixons that Arkansas was less likely to be occupied by advancing Union forces. If these were indeed the main reasons for their move, nothing worked out as the Dixons hoped. A few months after their arrival in Arkansas, the younger of their two surviving sons died.[2] Shortly thereafter, with Amanda pregnant again, the couple realized that the advance of Grant's Union Army southward along the Mississippi toward Vicksburg (which surrendered on July 4, 1863) was effectively cutting the Confederacy in two and leaving Arkansas detached from Confederate states to the west. They set off home, with their slaves, on an epic journey that—to avoid battle lines and hostile Union troops—would ultimately cover more than 2,000 miles. Finally, in August 1863, their caravan halted twelve miles away from Thomas Dixon Sr.'s boyhood home, at King's Mountain in North Carolina, where he bought a farm. Five months later, Amanda gave birth there to a boy, whom they named after his father.[3]

While it was not yet clear in January 1864 that the South had lost the Civil War, its prospects had become increasing grim by the summer. Those prospects would get no brighter in the ensuing months. Grant had pinned Lee down at Petersburg, twenty miles from the Confederate capital of Richmond, Virginia. Meanwhile, Sherman captured Atlanta on September 2, marched to the Georgia seacoast in December, and then swung north into the Carolinas. He sealed off Wilmington, North Carolina, the Confederacy's last remaining major seaport, in February 1865 and drove Confederate forces north through the state before him. In April, the two main Southern armies surrendered. Although Sherman's route had taken him to the east of Shelby, the area around Dixon's birthplace had also suffered from the depredations of the Union army. A force of 7,000 men, led by General George Stoneman (whose surname many years later would be appropriated by Thomas Dixon for the white villain of his novel and play *The Clansman*), invaded North Carolina from Tennessee in early April, stealing or destroying property in a score of western counties.[4] When the war ended a few days later, the Shelby area was also obliged to deal with the economic and social consequences of the South's defeat. The Dixon family found itself hovering on the verge of destitution. An endless procession of soldiers passed by their farm on their way home to the Deep South, begging food, taking the wooden fences for campfires, and eating any remaining livestock. His former slaves begged Thomas Dixon Sr. for employment, but he was unable to help them. He had just enough money to help himself. On his return from Arkansas, he had carefully buried a cache of a hundred dollars in gold in a secluded place on his farm. Now he dug up this money, moved into a house in Shelby, and opened a small store.[5]

Politically, from March 1867 onward, North Carolina, in common with most of the ex-Confederate South, experienced a period of "radical" Reconstruction.[6] The South was temporarily reorganized into five military districts, each under the command of an army general. To be readmitted to the Union, each state was required to draft a new state constitution providing for black suffrage and the disfranchisement of ex-Confederates disqualified under the terms of the Fourteenth Amendment to the Constitution proposed by Congress. It was also necessary for the new state legislatures elected under these arrangements to ratify the amendment itself.[7] In many Southern states, the new legislatures had sizable numbers of black members. However, in only one state, South Carolina, did the legislature have a majority of black members. Dixon would later remember, as a small boy, being taken by his uncle, Colonel Lee Roy McAfee, to the state capital, Columbia, to see the South Carolina legislature in action. It contained, he would later write, "ninety-four Negroes, seven native scalawags, and twenty-three white men [Conservatives or Democrats who were hostile to the Reconstruction process]."[8]

In 1868, William W. Holden was elected the first Republican governor of North Carolina with the help of a small number of scalawags, carpetbaggers, and large numbers of newly enfranchised African Americans. Holden, proprietor of the *North Carolina Standard* and a former Democrat, was opposed both before and after his election by the Ku Klux Klan. The Klan, which first appeared in North Carolina in 1867, was probably the most effective weapon in the hands of the whites opposed to the whole process of radical Reconstruction. At its peak, it may have had 40,000 members in the state. Through intimidation, whippings, and occasional murders, it set out to defeat the Republican Party and reestablish "white supremacy" in North Carolina. The Klan was particularly strong in western areas of the state, including the region around Shelby. By 1870, Holden, realizing that he and the Republicans faced political defeat unless the activities of the Klan were checked, attempted to combat it by using the state militia to arrest local supporters. In the elections that followed, native whites (known as Conservatives) carried both houses of the legislature. In 1871, they succeeded in impeaching Governor Holden and in convicting him and removing him from office—the first state governor in American history to be ousted in this way. Subsequently, the Klan gradually declined, partly as a result of more effective federal legislation and partly because it had achieved its main aim, the restoration of white supremacy.[9]

Living in the South as a child during the era of radical Reconstruction affected Thomas Dixon Jr.'s outlook throughout his life. He would always look back on Reconstruction as a "tragic era" in which the white South had been unjustly treated by the North. Much of his later career was spent trying to tell the "true story" of what had happened. He would later claim that some of his earliest memories dealt with the Ku Klux Klan, one of which was watching the hanging of a black convict accused of raping a white woman. In the beginning, the Klan was led by respectable members of the social elite, including Dixon's uncle, Colonel Lee Roy McAfee, and his own father. It liked to see itself as a "law and order" organization attempting to mitigate the chaos of the Reconstruction period. Over time, however, the Klan was effectively taken over by more unruly elements—particularly working-class white men who, seeing free black men as their competitors, set out to harass them by violent means. On one occasion, young Dixon and his father encountered a group of drunken, swearing men on their way to beat up an "insolent nigger." Trying to enlist the help of Colonel McAfee (the local Klan leader) in preventing this, Thomas Dixon Sr. drove his horse so hard that it died of exhaustion outside the entrance to McAfee's home.[10]

In 1872, the Dixons' house in Shelby burned down. Faced with this disaster and the still-depressed state of the local economy, Thomas Dixon Sr. concluded that a return to farming offered the best hope of survival for his growing family (another son had been born in 1866 and a daughter early in 1872). On Christmas Eve, the Dixons moved to a farm on Buffalo Creek, some six miles from Shelby. Thomas Dixon Jr. would remember the next three years as unpleasant and difficult. With his elder brother, Clarence, away studying at Wake Forest College, he was obliged to take on many duties around the farm. Dixon hated the monotony and drudgery of farm life. "The deeper I buried my feet in the soil," he would write many years later, "the clearer became my conviction that the beastly toil of it de-humanized its people."[11]

While Dixon respected his father, there were tensions between them during his childhood. Dixon Sr. was a strong-minded man who functioned not merely as a farmer but also as a Baptist preacher. As he had been self-educated, he was determined that his children should have the chance for a higher education. On matters of behavior, however, he was inflexible and stern. His children were prohibited from fighting. When an argument between Thomas Jr. and another minister's son (over Reconstruction) deteriorated into fisticuffs, he gave his son a sound whipping. The elder Dixon was even more opposed to drinking than fighting since he thought the early death of his father had been caused by alcohol. His mother, who had moved in with the family on the farm, did not share his temperance views. She persuaded young Thomas to buy her some whiskey. Once his father found out about it, Thomas received another whipping. This time, the punishment had dramatic consequences for the whole Dixon family. Grandma Dixon, equally inflexible in her own way, went off to live with another of her children and never returned. Young Thomas's mother was so furious over the whipping that she insisted on moving the rest of the family back to Shelby immediately. Amanda, pregnant again at the age of forty-three, was also adamant that the family live in her mother's home while a house was built for them.[12]

Education

Returning to the town not only released Thomas Dixon Jr. from the drudgery of farm labor but it also allowed him to attend school more regularly than he had done before. At Shelby Academy, he did so well that in 1879—only three years after his arrival and at the age of fifteen—his teachers considered him good enough at mathematics, Latin, and Greek to begin college that fall. His older brother Clarence had already graduated from Wake Forest College and, after further training at the Southern Baptist Theological Seminary, had embarked on a career as a minister. His father probably expected Thomas to follow a similar path yet also seems to have cherished some doubts about the strength of his younger son's faith. He suggested that Thomas attend a series of revival meetings he was about to conduct. Despite his initial skepticism, Dixon, caught up in the emotionalism of the revival, experienced what was in essence a religious conversion.[13]

Like most Southern colleges in the years immediately following the Civil War, Wake Forest College was an impoverished and threadbare institution. Thomas Dixon was disappointed on his arrival in September 1879 to realize that it was much smaller and its buildings less impressive than he had anticipated. Soon, however, he settled down to his academic work and started to build up what, by the time he gained his master of arts degree in 1883, would be the best student record ever achieved at Wake Forest. Dixon also plunged energetically into extracurricular activities. He was an accomplished orator. He additionally wrote for the college newspaper (the first story he ever published dealt with the organization of the Ku Klux Klan). In one respect only can he have been a disappointment to his father and older brother: in his final year at Wake Forest, he developed a great interest in science and, his religious faith undermined by reading the work of evolutionists such as Darwin, Huxley, and Spencer, abandoned the church.[14]

After graduating from Wake Forest, Dixon was offered a scholarship to do graduate work in political science at the Johns Hopkins University in Baltimore. Johns Hopkins, opened only in 1876, was a new kind of university. "For the first time in an American university," wrote Richard T. Ely, who taught political economy there from 1881, "the graduate and professionals schools constituted the center of its activities, and the undergraduate school was but an appendage."[15] With its stress on research, scientific seminars, and laboratories; scholarships for promising graduate students; and the new Ph.D. program it offered, Johns Hopkins was much closer in spirit to the universities of Germany than to any contemporary American institution. Dixon attended the seminar run by Ely and historian Herbert Baxter Adams, both of them German trained. It is likely that Dixon gained much of his later belief in the superiority of white "Anglo-Saxons" from Adams, who was convinced of the special genius of the "Teutonic" peoples for self-government and whose "germ" theory of political development led him to believe that the roots of American democracy could be traced back to the primitive arrangements of medieval German tribes. Albert Shaw, later a well-known expert on municipal reform and long-serving magazine editor, sat to the left of Dixon during his first Hopkins seminar. A few months earlier, Shaw had recorded his "intense interest" in a lecture given by Adams in which he traced the office of New England town constable "back to the ancient Saxon titheing-man"—a characteristic example of the historical approach associated with the germ theory.[16]

Sitting on the right side of Dixon at his first seminar at Johns Hopkins was another young man, Woodrow Wilson, who would have a distinguished academic career after which he would become twenty-eighth president of the United States. Dixon and Wilson became close friends who would, at crucial moments in their lives, help each other with favors. Their friendship would later have some impact on *The Birth of a Nation* story. As young graduate students, however, they were both interested in politics and political theory—and in the stage. Wilson, at some point in the first term, introduced Dixon to the editor of the Baltimore *Mirror*, who was so impressed with Dixon's enthusiasm and apparent knowledge of the theater that he hired him to be the paper's drama critic. As his obsession with the stage grew, Dixon began to think that he should abandon his studies at Johns Hopkins in order to enroll as a drama student in New York. When Wilson tried to dissuade him, he remained obdurate and, in January 1884, he left Johns Hopkins for good.[17]

On his arrival in New York, Dixon entered the Frobisher School of Drama, threw himself with his usual commitment into his studies, and went to see as many plays as he could afford. He took what he thought was the first step on the road to becoming an important actor when he was invited to join a company about to tour with Shakespeare's *Richard III*. Being inexperienced, he did not think it at all odd that the manager of the company financed it by requiring each of the actors to invest in the production (Dixon's contribution was $300, which he borrowed from his father and brother Clarence). Predictably, after a performance in upstate New York, the manager absconded with all the money and the company disbanded. Dixon now sought work with another company, but the director, looking at his tall, gangling frame, prophetically suggested that he might be more suited to writing plays than acting in them. Humiliated and disappointed, Dixon abandoned his hopes for a stage career and set off back to North Carolina.[18]

Just as acting had been a false start (as well as perhaps a youthful rebellion), Dixon now found himself pursuing two other lines of activity that proved of almost equally short duration. Looking for a way to make a living, he entered the law school at Greensboro, North Carolina. Shortly thereafter, his father, perhaps intending to wean him away even further from his interest in the stage, suggested that he run for the state legislature. His two opponents, one of them a cousin, were experienced politicians. But Dixon, mobilizing the oratorical gifts he had first shown in college, defeated them both with ease. Someone then suggested that he run for Speaker of the House; he seemed a serious possibility for election until it was pointed out that he was not yet twenty-one.

When the legislature met, Dixon proved himself a skillful lawmaker. One successful bill he introduced was the first in the South to provide pensions for Confederate veterans. (Dixon's speech on his bill was covered in a highly flattering way by Walter Hines Page, then editor of the Raleigh *State Chronicle* and later the publisher of Dixon's best-known novels.) In spite of such successes, the young legislator rapidly became disenchanted with the corruption and wheeler-dealing that characterized politics and did not seek reelection.[19]

Dixon as Minister

In 1885, Dixon gained his law degree and started to practice. Yet law gave him no more satisfaction than politics had done. His forensic skills helped him to a number of courtroom victories, but they left him with little sense of personal fulfillment. After one case, in which he had successfully prosecuted a man for burning a mill, Dixon publicly confessed that the prosecution had been a mistake and led a campaign for the man's release. The one bright spot during this period was his attraction to a minister's daughter, Harriet Bussey. When her father opposed the match, the couple eloped to Montgomery, Alabama, where they were married in March 1886. Now Dixon had someone with whom to share his doubts over a legal career. Sometime that summer, standing on the beach at Wilmington, he had a mystical experience somewhat reminiscent of his earlier "conversion." This time, interpreting it as a call to a new way of life, he told his father that he intended to enter the ministry.[20]

In October 1886, Dixon received his first call to a Baptist church in Goldsboro, North Carolina. His reputation as a minister grew rapidly: six months later he accepted a call to a church in Raleigh, and six months after that to a church in Boston, Massachusetts. While in Boston, he was invited to deliver the commencement address at Wake Forest College. He used the opportunity to persuade the board of trustees to offer an honorary degree to Woodrow Wilson. A journalist, hearing Dixon's praise of Wilson, reported it to the national wire services. The publicity that ensued gave Wilson his first taste of the limelight and helped launch his career. Later, as president of the United States, he would repay Dixon's assistance by granting his old friend's request to show *The Birth of a Nation* in the White House.[21]

After less than three years as a minister, Dixon received a call to the Twenty-Third Street Church in New York City. On his arrival in New York in August 1889, he was at first depressed by the seeming alienation of city dwellers from the churches. By focusing on local issues in his own sermons, however, and making sure his preaching was fresh and relevant, he was able to attract increasing numbers to his own services. His success drew him to the attention of John D. Rockefeller, a fellow Baptist. Rockefeller went to hear Dixon preach, was impressed, and invited him to dinner. Dixon by this stage was dreaming of a great temple in Manhattan with a huge auditorium that would allow him to reach the masses of the city. When he confessed this, Rockefeller offered to pay half the cost of building such a temple (which Dixon estimated at a million dollars) if Dixon could raise the balance. Dixon hoped to raise much of this money from his own congregation, but found them too cautious and conservative. His scheme, moreover, was opposed by other Baptist churches, which were jealous of the large sum Rockefeller had promised. The whole experience seems to have convinced Dixon that to reach the masses, he would have to establish a new church that would be attached to no single denomination. In March 1895, he resigned from the Twenty-Third Street Church and in April inaugurated his "People's Church" in New York in the huge hall of the Academy of Music.[22]

As a preacher and speaker, Dixon had the ability to play on the emotions of his hearers. He did not shrink from controversial issues: he adopted clear political stances, attacking both the corrupt Tammany Hall machine in New York and William Jennings Bryan, the Democratic and Populist parties' candidate for president in 1896. He was in favor of Cuban independence from Spain and supported the war with Spain in 1898. Subsequently, he supported

Theodore Roosevelt, now a war hero, in his successful campaign to become governor of New York. Dixon campaigned constantly against the saloons—and on behalf of the poorest members of society. He produced three books dealing with religion that combined social sympathies with a fervent defense of conservative religious values. He also found himself in increasing demand as a lecturer. Eventually, his health broke down, and on the advice of his doctor, Dixon moved away from New York. He bought a house on the coast of Virginia and settled there with his wife and three children. For a time, he commuted back to New York on weekends to preach or speak. It became increasingly clear to him, however, that the People's Church was never going to fulfill the hopes he had entertained for it and he resigned his ministry there early in 1899.[23] If Dixon's health had not been undermined and he had remained a successful minister and guest speaker, it is likely that he would never have written the novels and play that would become the basis of *The Birth of a Nation*.

Dixon as Novelist

After his retirement from the ministry, Dixon earned a considerable income from lecturing all over the United States. During one of his lecture tours, in 1901, he attended a stage production of Harriet Beecher Stowe's novel, *Uncle Tom's Cabin* (1852). Shortly after his arrival in Boston, fourteen years earlier, Dixon had listened to a lecture on the "Southern problem" at Tremont Temple. Offended by the speaker's description of the South as an enduring threat to the nation, Dixon had jumped to his feet and attacked both the accuser and the accusation, coming close in the process to causing a riot. After this incident, he later claimed, he had studied the Civil War and the Reconstruction period with the hope, at some stage, of telling the true story of the South.[24] Seeing *Uncle Tom's Cabin* acted as the catalyst for this ambition. Angered by what he perceived as its unjust view of white Southerners and its misapprehension of the true nature of blacks, Dixon left the theater resolved to tell the "true story" of the South's postwar history. The best way of doing this, he thought, would be in a novel.[25]

Dixon's previous careers—as actor, lawyer, politician, minister, and lecturer— had focused, with varying degrees of success, on reaching and influencing people. The novel he planned and researched in the remaining months of 1901 was intended to do this on a broader scale. Dixon hoped to convince Americans generally that the view of the South and of race relations presented in *Uncle Tom's Cabin* was completely ill founded. In the process, he was attacking one of the best-known icons of American culture. Blending a fervent critique of slavery with sentimental romanticism, Harriet Beecher Stowe's novel was a best seller almost as soon as it was published.[26] It probably had a major effect in turning Northern opinion against slavery during the 1850s and thus helped drive the sections further apart (Lincoln supposedly once greeted Mrs. Stowe as "the little lady who made this great war"). The popularity of *Uncle Tom's Cabin* as a novel, however, endured long after the Civil War and the final abolition of slavery. It was still, as late as 1899, the book that was most frequently checked out of the New York Public Library. A year earlier, novelist and critic William Dean Howells had hailed it as "the great American novel."[27]

The number of people reached by *Uncle Tom's Cabin* as a novel, however, was greatly exceeded by those who saw it as a play. For each individual who read the novel, perhaps fifty would eventually attend the play. Shortly after the book was first published, stage adaptations began to appear. Because of the absence of copyright law, directors, writers, and actors could make whatever changes they wanted to Mrs. Stowe's story. Some adaptations changed or omitted characters; others modified the plot to produce a conventional melodrama. At times, the book's antislavery line was softened. Yet the play proved a landmark in the history of the American theater. It attracted members of the middle class who had hitherto, for religious and moral reasons, looked down on the theater. It also appears to have presented antislavery views to working-class theatergoers, in many cases for the first time.[28]

The popularity of *Uncle Tom's Cabin* as a play grew in the decades after the Civil War. As it became more and more distanced from the reality of slavery, formally ended by the Thirteenth Amendment in 1865, it took on increasingly the character of a history lesson (children made up a rising proportion of the audiences). Already, by the early 1880s, large numbers of companies were touring the United States, exclusively devoted to what were coming to be known as "Tommer shows." (One Detroit newspaper in 1881 complained of being "tortured with an invasion of Uncle Toms!!!!!") This, however, proved only a prelude to what was to come. By the 1890s, there were around five hundred touring companies producing Tommer shows. As the twentieth century dawned, what had become a craze showed no sign of diminishing: one 1902 reviewer estimated that in that year alone, the play would be seen by one in every thirty-five Americans.[29]

There is now no way of establishing which version of the play Dixon saw in 1901. To reach the play's position at the very heart of American popular culture, the antislavery critique of the novel had been steadily weakened. "Uncle Tom" and "Topsy" survived as signifiers whose signifieds had long since disappeared, the former as a dignified, stoical, rather elderly victim, the latter as a source of vulgar comedy. Since most of the audiences for the play were still in the North and West, many of these productions made the villainous Simon Legree into a Southerner instead of a Yankee. Inevitably, the most melodramatic aspects of the book found themselves emphasized: Eliza's flight across the Ohio River, jumping from ice floe to ice floe with little Harry in her arms, was dealt with in the novel in two brief paragraphs. Toward the end of the nineteenth century, theatrical versions would have her chased by packs of dogs (in Tombstone, Arizona, in 1888, one drunken member of the audience shot one of the pursuing dogs).[30] It may have been the *success* of the play even more than its bias that angered Dixon. Stowe's book had become the "greatest popular hit in American dramatic history."[31] In the process, over half a century, it had established a master narrative that had succeeded in demonizing the white South and privileging the sufferings of black slaves.

Dixon remembered his response to *Uncle Tom's Cabin* as virtually akin to his earlier "conversion" experiences. It changed his life and gave it new focus and direction. For several months afterward, while still lecturing across the country, he assembled around a thousand pages of notes on Reconstruction and plotted his novel. The actual writing took only two months, and early in 1902, Dixon sent off the unrevised manuscript to Walter Hines Page, an old North Carolina friend who had recently gone into publishing as part of the firm of Doubleday, Page and Company. According to Dixon's later account in his unpublished autobiography, Page became so absorbed in the story that continuing to read it on the way to his office, he was knocked down by a cab. Picking up the dirty, crumpled manuscript, he carried on reading. When he was finished, he sent a telegram to Dixon inviting him to New York to sign a contract. The book, entitled *The Leopard's Spots: A Romance of the White Man's Burden*, was published in March 1902. In the first few months after its appearance, it sold over 100,000 copies.[32]

Dixon consciously framed his first novel as a "sequel" to *Uncle Tom's Cabin* as well as a refutation of it. One character, Simon Legree, appears in both books, changing in the process from an evil slave owner into a local Republican politician. He is elected governor of North Carolina, making a fortune from corruption. On his final defeat, he flees to New York and buys a seat on the stock exchange. Tim Shelby, formerly a black slave on the plantation of Mr. Shelby in *Uncle Tom's Cabin*, reemerges as a leader of the Union League. He is chosen as majority leader of the state House of Representatives, and serving also as school commissioner, functions as an important cog in Legree's corrupt regime.[33] Alec Haley, a slave trader in *Uncle Tom's Cabin*, also now belongs to the Republican machine.[34] One minor character, Bob St. Clare, the son of a Democratic congressman and former slave owner, probably belongs to the same family as another of Tom's former owners.[35] Other characters in *The Leopard's Spots* are clearly identified as the children of those created by Mrs. Stowe. George Harris, the son of Eliza and George Harris, is the well-educated mulatto protégé of Everett Lowell, an important congressman from Boston. When he aspires to marry Lowell's daughter, Helen, he is disowned by his patron. Finding it impossible, as a black man, to find work in the North, he turns for assistance to union official Hugh Halliday, the son of the Quaker couple who had originally helped his parents escape from slavery.[36]

Yet if some characters are the same in the two books—or those in *The Leopard's Spots* are descendants of those created by Mrs. Stowe—Dixon's novel is different in many ways from *Uncle Tom's Cabin*. It begins in the immediate aftermath of the Civil War, with defeated Southerners making their way home. While the South is physically ruined, the principal concern of white Southerners is with the threat posed by the freed blacks.[37] Encouraged by the Union League, which gives them arms, blacks engage in violent acts and look forward to revenge on the whites. In the first election after "radical" Reconstruction begins in 1867, using fraud and intimidation they win control of the government of North Carolina.[38] In the aftermath of the election, the new regime taxes the homes of whites so severely that a high proportion have to be auctioned to pay off tax debts.[39] Dixon had already hinted that black men lusted after white women: Tim Shelby at one point refers to "Desdemonas" who would soon "be fascinated again by an Othello," and after the elections, he proposes (and is persuaded to withdraw since his colleagues see it as inexpedient) a bill dissolving the marriages of all those who fought for the Confederacy. Yet black soldiers in the Union army have no similar inhibitions: seven of them, drunk, arrive at the house of one-legged Confederate veteran Tom Camp; his young daughter, Annie, has just been married, and they try to carry her off. In the mêlée that follows, Annie is shot dead. Another incident, shortly afterward, leads to the emergence of organized white resistance. Shelby, encouraged by a military order allowing the marriage of blacks and white women, dreams of "a fair white bride." When a white girl, Mollie Graham, visits him in his capacity as schools commissioner to apply for a teaching post, he offers her the job in exchange for a kiss. The next night the Ku Klux Klan appears on the scene, and Shelby is hung for his affront to white womanhood. The union League is suppressed, and at the ensuing elections, white supremacy is restored.[40]

Eighteen years pass and it seems that the "mistakes" of the Reconstruction period are to be repeated. The rule of the Democratic Party is challenged and then overthrown, as blacks combine with the state's disgruntled white farmers. Against this background, Charles Gaston, a boy in the first part of the book, now falls in love with and courts Sallie Worth, the daughter of a prominent Southern businessman. Despite Gaston's attempts to stop them, the Republicans carry the state elections. For the first time since Reconstruction ended, black officeholders return. Law and order begin to break down as many blacks roam the countryside stealing and committing other crimes. Matters come to a head when Tom Camp's remaining daughter, eleven-year-old Flora, is raped and left for dead. Despite the best efforts to save her, Flora is hysterical at the memory of what has happened to her and finally dies. A crowd of whites identifies her killer as a black man, Dick, who has been Charles Gaston's boyhood friend; ignoring Gaston's plea for a fair trial, the mob lynches Dick by burning him alive. A year later, with crime and disorder still increasing, Gaston leads a movement called the Red Shirts that overthrows black rule for a second time. He is briefly arrested by the Republicans (and finally marries Sallie, over her father's opposition, while he is in jail). Finally, in a great speech to the

Democratic convention, he adopts the policy—urged throughout the book by the Reverend John Durham—of eliminating blacks completely from public life. With Gaston's landslide election to the governorship, white supremacy returns and all black voters are disfranchised.[41]

In common with most first novels, Dixon's book was heavily autobiographical. The great-grandfather of Charles Gaston had fought the British (as had Dixon's) at King's Mountain, North Carolina, during the War of Independence.[42] Like Dixon, young Gaston sits up at night with his sick and delirious mother, is immensely proud of his first medal won as a student, and (at least temporarily) abandons religion while away at college.[43] Like Dixon, also, Gaston marries despite the strong opposition of his wife's father.[44] But Gaston is not the only *doppelgänger* for Dixon in the book. John Durham, like Dixon, has graduated at the top of his class at Wake Forrest and gone on to become a successful Baptist minister. Unlike Dixon, however, Durham has refused a call from a wealthy church in Boston to stay in the South with his own people.[45] He is obsessed by the threat posed by blacks both to Southern society and, more generally, to the future of the American Republic. The United States is an "Anglo-Saxon" civilization, the product of 2,000 years of historical development. If race lines are abandoned and blacks allowed intermarriage with whites, that civilization will inevitably regress to the level of "African barbarism." According to Durham, "One drop of Negro blood makes a negro. It kinks the hair, flattens the nose, thickens the lip, puts out the light of intellect, and lights the fires of brutal passions." To safeguard the future of Anglo-Saxon America, equality of any kind between the races is impossible, since political equality will inevitably lead to social equality. "You cannot seek the Negro vote without asking him to your home sooner or later," Durham maintains. "If you ask him to your house, he will break bread with you...And if you seat him at your table, he has the right to ask your daughter's hand in marriage." But to create a nation from two entirely separate, unequal, and antagonistic races is in the end unimaginable. Ultimately, therefore, Durham believes it will be necessary for blacks to be removed from the United States.[46]

The extreme racial philosophy articulated in *The Leopard's Spots* represented an important change in Dixon's earlier outlook. Although he would remember, as a child, arming against an attack from a crowd of threatening blacks during the Reconstruction era (an attack that never materialized), he was not initially anti-black. At one stage of his boyhood, his closest friend was an African American boy called Dick, and he would recall this friendship even decades later with "nostalgic tenderness."[47] Dixon also had an affectionate memory of his "dear old nurse...at whose feet I sat and heard the sad story of the life of a slave until I learned to hate slavery." In a book of religious essays published in 1896, he celebrated the demise of slavery, arguing that while it may have had its benevolent aspects, "democracy is the destiny of the race, because all men are bound together in the bonds of fraternal equality with one common father above." "Race prejudice," he observed later in the same volume, "is a terrible fact."[48]

Sometime around the turn of the century, however, Dixon became obsessed with racial fears. One catalyst for this change may have been the Spanish-American War. The outbreak of war seemed to promote a new mood of national unity. In *The Leopard's Spots*, indeed, Dixon would look back on the war of 1898 as the moment when the Anglo-Saxon race became reunified.[49] But the war, in destroying Spanish power, also raised the issue of what to do with the native inhabitants of the former Spanish colonies, including the Filipinos. Dixon, together with other fervent imperialists, thought that the United States had a moral duty to help such backward peoples. At the same time, he did not believe that they had the necessary judgement and self-control to govern themselves, making it necessary for the United States to manage them without their consent. Having supported white supremacy in the colonies gained from Spain, Dixon may subsequently have begun to rethink his views on race relations at home.[50]

A second possible influence on Dixon's thinking was the growing significance of racial "Radicalism." Joel Williamson has distinguished three main varieties of Southern thinking about race at the end of the nineteenth century and beginning of the twentieth. "Liberals" were open minded on the potentialities of blacks and believed that by absorbing aspects of white culture they might improve. "Conservatives" regarded them as inferiors who should be assigned a fixed place in American society. "Radicals" were convinced that African Americans were swiftly retrogressing to their primitive roots (a major symptom of this being the alleged increasing frequency of black sexual assaults on white women) and that they would soon be eliminated from American society, either through racial decline leading to extinction or mass deportation. Radicalism had its political roots in the elections of 1888, when the Republicans not only elected a president but also gained a majority in both houses of Congress. For a time, it seemed likely that they would pass bills giving federal aid to the education of blacks as well as whites and introduce federal election supervisors, thus beginning a second period of Reconstruction. The economic origins of Radicalism lay in the problems faced by Southern farmers, especially during the depression years of the 1890s. Williamson suggests that for some whites, an assault on "the black beast rapist" offered "psychic compensation" for being unable to provide for their families in material terms.[51]

Other Southern farmers, moving from the Farmers' Alliance protest movement into the Populist Party (formed in 1892), unwittingly encouraged the eventual growth of Radicalism by allying themselves with the Republican Party (and its mainly black voters) in an attempt to secure their economic aims through political means.[52] In some Southern states, fusion tickets of Populists and Republicans succeeded in ousting the Democratic Party and gaining power: North

Carolina, for example, as Dixon observes in *The Leopard's Spots*, was ruled by an alliance of Populists and Republicans between 1894 and 1898. With the collapse of the Populist Party in and after 1896, many vengeful Southern Democrats (supported by a number of former Populists) became converts to the Radical position. They set out—through tighter legal disfranchisement and segregation—to weaken the position of blacks (especially black men), to make them insecure "and ultimately less aggressive," and to induce them to take "with minimal resistance the inevitable path to racial extinction." By 1902, radicalism was thriving in many parts of the South, including Virginia. While Dixon was writing *The Leopard's Spots*, a constitutional convention was meeting in Richmond and debating the issue of whether blacks should be able to vote. Delegates from the east of the state (where Dixon lived) were passionately in favor of complete black disfranchisement.[53]

At one point in Dixon's novel, there is a reference to Harriet Beecher Stowe. "The history of the world is made up of the individuality of a few men," argues Mrs. Durham, the preacher's wife. "A little Yankee woman wrote a crude book. The single act of that woman's will caused a war, killed a million men, desolated and ruined the South and changed the history of the world." While Dixon may have exaggerated the political impact of *Uncle Tom's Cabin*, he clearly hoped that *The Leopard's Spots* would have an equally drastic impact on American public opinion. A number of critics commented on the similarity between the two novels. When they compared them, Dixon's often came off the best. "It is an epoch-making book," one critic declared, "and a worthy successor to 'Uncle Tom's Cabin.' It is superior in power of thought and graphic description."[54] Few observers appreciated that Dixon intended quite consciously to supplant the images in *Uncle Tom's Cabin* with impressions of his own. One who did was Max Nordau, the German writer and physician. "You have deliberately undone the work of Harriet Beecher Stowe," Nordau wrote to Dixon in the summer of 1902.[55]

In place of the victimized blacks of Stowe's creation—saintly Tom, homely Aunt Chloe, anxious Eliza Harris, her exploited husband George, devious Topsy, and bitter Cassy—Dixon offered either "faithful souls" (Nelse and Eva) or, more usually, aggressive men intent on sexual relations with white women (Tim Shelby, the anonymous troopers at Annie Camp's wedding, and Dick). The white men of *Uncle Tom's Cabin* are nearly all flawed in some way: Shelby is impractical and cowardly, St. Clare skeptical and fond of procrastination, Harris and Legree (together with more minor characters such as Tom Loker, the slave catcher) cruel, violent, and narrow-minded. By contrast, the Southern white men described by Dixon, especially the Klan leader Stuart Dameron, John Durham, and Charles Gaston, are in the main heroic figures battling in defense of their civilization. The Southern white women in *Uncle Tom's Cabin* are marginalized for most of the book: Mrs. Shelby, though sensitive and businesslike, is sidelined from the affairs of the plantation while her husband is alive. Marie St. Clare is selfish, self-absorbed, and, when afforded the chance, cruel to her slaves. Dixon's white female characters, by contrast, are idealized and made appropriate symbols of threatened white civilization.[56] Young Flora, in particular, has an innate goodness and innocence that reminds one forcibly of little Eva. But instead of dying of tuberculosis like Eva, she is a victim of black lust.

If Mrs. Stowe's book foregrounded the sufferings of black slaves at the hands of whites, Dixon's focused on the later anguish of whites, supposedly at the hands of free blacks. There are a number of similarities between the two novels. Both are structured around a racial division between "Anglo-Saxons" and "Africans."[57] Both agree that there was racial prejudice in the North as well as the South: St. Clare's sister Ophelia from Vermont, while trying to help Topsy, cannot bear to touch her, and Dixon's Congressmen Lowell, a fervent advocate of political equality between the races, hysterically rejects the possibility of George Harris marrying his daughter.[58] Both, confronting the realities of entrenched racial prejudice on the part of whites, support plans for ultimately colonizing blacks back to Africa.[59] Both accept that blacks often behave in ways that are deceitful, dishonest, and brutal; yet they part company over why this should have been the case. To Dixon, American blacks are descendants of the ancient tribes of Africa who, over thousands of years, had failed to make any progress toward building a true civilization. Slavery, however blameworthy in moral terms, had succeeded in civilizing them to some limited degree. With slavery gone, blacks had swiftly regressed to their earlier, primitive state. Dixon, disagreeing with the leading advocates of black education of his time (including Booker T. Washington), saw no point in educating blacks. It would only persuade them to believe in ideas of political and social equality that would eventually destroy Anglo-Saxon civilization by promoting miscegenation. According to Stowe, in contrast, the defects of character supposedly displayed by many blacks were a consequence not of their African heritage, but of the brutalizing effects of slavery. She believed it perfectly possible for them to be civilized and morally uplifted by means of education.[60]

The first edition of 15,000 copies of *The Leopard's Spots* was exhausted on publication. The book eventually sold over a million copies, helped establish Doubleday, Page as a major publisher, and made Dixon several hundred thousand dollars in royalties.[61] What Dixon had essentially done with his novel was to dramatize the black problem as a national rather than merely sectional issue,[62] to encourage Northern whites to redefine themselves as "non-blacks," and introduce to Northern readers radical Southern ideas on how blacks should be treated.

Shortly after *The Leopard's Spots* appeared, Dixon began to research the second novel of a proposed trilogy in which he hoped to tell the "true" story of Reconstruction. In the process of sifting through vast numbers of books and pamphlets, he found time to write another novel on a very different theme.

The One Woman, published in 1903, was in essence an anti-socialist polemic. It deals with the career of Frank Gordon, a minister with socialist sympathies who hopes to create a new, independent church. A wealthy young woman, Kate Ransom, encourages his ambition with a gift of one million dollars. Gordon later divorces his wife and marries Kate. But having undermined the family (which Dixon regarded as a crucial bulwark of civilization), they are not left to enjoy their "shared wealth" for very long. Gordon's best friend, Mark Overman, falls in love with Kate and wins her. When she leaves him, Gordon kills Overman. He is twice sentenced to death for murder but finally reprieved by the governor of New York, coincidentally a former boyfriend of Gordon's first wife. Despite—or perhaps because of—the fact that it was criticized as being of "doubtful propriety," *The One Woman* sold almost as well as *The Leopard's Spots*.[63]

In 1905, Dixon published a third novel—his second dealing with the Reconstruction period—under the title *The Clansman: An Historical Romance of the Ku Klux Klan*. Although the book is the first Dixon novel *not* to have a preacher as a main character, many of the other characters are clearly derived from *The Leopard's Spots*. Everett Lowell becomes Austin Stoneman and Lowell's daughter, Helen, becomes Elsie Stoneman. Lowell's protégé, George Harris, is transformed into Stoneman's protégé, Silas Lynch. Flora is now Marion Lenoir and will be sexually pursued not by Dick but by Gus. Major Stuart Dameron, John Durham, and Charles Gaston have all been combined into the single character of Ben Cameron. The faithful souls are no longer Nelse and Eva, but Mammy and Jake. Because much of the story will revolve around the two families, the Camerons and the Stonemans, additional characters include Ben Cameron's parents, Dr. and Mrs. Richard Cameron, and his sister, Margaret, together with Elsie Stoneman's brother, Phil.

Book I of *The Clansman* begins in a Washington hospital. Elsie Stoneman is playing the banjo and singing to wounded soldiers when she is interrupted by news of the ending of the Civil War. One of the wounded soldiers is Ben Cameron, a young Confederate colonel captured at Petersburg. Phil Stoneman, who had been with the Union army there, has earlier written to his sister describing Cameron's heroism and asking her to look after him.[64] Although Cameron is recovering from his wounds, Elsie is told by the doctor that he has been condemned to be hung as a guerrilla. Colonel Cameron's mother arrives at the hospital and on being notified of the threat to her son's life, she and Elsie determine to seek a pardon from President Lincoln. Even though Lincoln agrees to spare Ben Cameron's life, Secretary of War Stanton refuses to implement the order, emphasizing that there is political pressure from Austin Stoneman, Elsie's father and leader of the House of Representatives, for Cameron's swift execution. The president insists on having his way and prepares the pardon. At this point, Austin Stoneman arrives at the White House and he and Lincoln have a long argument over the treatment of the former Confederate states. Stoneman demands that they be treated as "conquered provinces," with rebels exiled and disfranchised and blacks given the vote. Lincoln, by contrast, insists that he will show clemency to the defeated South, argues that it will not be possible for whites and blacks to live together permanently on terms of political and social equality, and supports the colonization or expulsion of all blacks from America as his ultimate solution to the race question.[65] Elsie, leaving the White House, delivers the pardon to Ben Cameron's mother and sister, Margaret, whom she finds at the hospital. Later that day, Elsie and her brother Phil call upon the Camerons, and Phil is immediately impressed with Margaret Cameron. He invites her to join him and Elsie at Ford's Theatre that evening. All three, therefore, are present when President Lincoln is assassinated. Lincoln's death provokes cries for vengeance and many Southerners are arrested. One of them is Ben Cameron's father, Richard, who, having once given medical treatment to Jefferson Davis, president of the Confederacy, is charged with complicity in Lincoln's murder and placed in jail in Washington.[66]

Book II starts with the aftermath of the assassination. The main focus of political power in the nation has now shifted to Stoneman's Washington home, presided over by his mulatto housekeeper, Lydia Brown. At a dinner with his two principal assistants, Colonel Howle and Silas Lynch, a mulatto protégé, Stoneman discusses what is to become of the South now that Lincoln is no more.[67] To safeguard the future of both the Republican Party and the nation itself, he asserts, it will be necessary to confiscate the land of former Confederates and divide it between blacks and loyal Unionists. Howle and Lynch are sent off on a secret mission to the South. Meanwhile, under pressure from Secretary of War Stanton, a military court finds several suspects guilty of complicity in Lincoln's assassination and they are executed. Mrs. Cameron, worried the same fate may be in store for her husband, pleads with Elsie to ask her father to use his influence with Andrew Johnson, the new president, to let her visit Dr. Cameron in jail. Stoneman accedes to the request of his daughter, whom he adores, and President Johnson agrees to see Mrs. Cameron. Though reluctant at first, the president finally allows her to see her husband. While Dr. Cameron is convinced that he is destined to be executed, he makes light of his situation to his wife and persuades her to return home to South Carolina, where there are many people in need of help. Two weeks after Mrs. Cameron and Margaret leave, Ben is finally discharged from hospital. During his convalescence, his relationship with Elsie grows steadily. When they go for a sail on the river together, he pays court to her but at the same time explains that slavery was the fault of the North as well as the South and points to the earlier existence of antislavery sentiment in the South. He then tells Elsie that he loves her, and she confesses that she returns his love. Subsequently, the two lovers attend the first meeting of Congress since the Civil War and watch it refuse to seat the newly elected representatives from the South. Austin Stoneman then successfully moves the appointment of a Congressional Committee on

Reconstruction to take over the government of the "conquered provinces" of the South. Elsie makes it plain to Ben, who almost despite himself has been impressed by Stoneman's performance, that she loves her father and is not prepared to marry without his approval.[68]

The next few chapters deal primarily with the duel between Andrew Johnson, Lincoln's successor as president, and Stoneman. Johnson vetoes the first bill attempting to give the suffrage to Southern blacks, and since black suffrage is unpopular in the North, Stoneman is unable to find the two-thirds majority in Congress necessary to override the presidential veto. He consequently launches a publicity campaign about the "barbarism" of Southerners, and in the following elections, the North sends many new radicals to support his policies. To weaken the president, Stoneman introduces a bill that will take away his power to remove cabinet officers. Although the bill is an attempt to protect the position of Stanton, the radical secretary of war, it is also carefully designed to provide the grounds for Johnson's impeachment and removal from office if he violates it. Stoneman now reintroduces his black suffrage bill. When he finds that he is one vote short of being able to pass the bill over Johnson's veto, he is so furious that he decides to expel sufficient Democrats from the House and Senate to give the Republicans a clear two-thirds majority. With this done, Stoneman is finally able to pass the acts to protect Stanton, give blacks the vote, and impose military Reconstruction on the South. When Johnson attempts a futile veto of the Reconstruction bill, Stoneman introduces a bill for his impeachment. Meanwhile, Elsie Stoneman and Ben Cameron are growing steadily closer, though Elsie is disturbed by what her father is trying to do to the white people of the South and dreads the day when he and Ben will come into conflict with each other. Phil Stoneman is also critical of Austin Stoneman's Southern policies, suspicious of the influence of Lydia Brown. His father, however, perceiving Johnson's removal as vital to his plan to give confiscated land to Southern blacks, presses on with the impeachment and trial of the president. So great is the strain, however, that Stoneman's health collapses and he is obliged to remain in bed. Though he rallies for one final appeal to the senators trying Johnson, the radicals fail by one vote to convict the president. In the aftermath of the trial, Stanton resigns as Secretary of War and Dr. Cameron is at last released from prison. He and Ben return to their home in Piedmont, South Carolina. Partly because he needs a warmer climate for the sake of his health and partly to further his plans for the South, Stoneman also decides to move to Piedmont.[69]

At the beginning of Book III, the scene changes from Washington to Piedmont.[70] Elsie and Phil Stoneman, together with their father, rent the cottage of Jeannie Lenoir and her fifteen-year-old daughter, Marion (Ben Cameron's childhood sweetheart). Both the Lenoirs and Camerons are suffering from the tax placed by Congress on cotton on top of the disastrous economic consequences of the war. Elsie hears Silas Lynch telling Gus, a former slave of the

Camerons, that he should no longer be ordered around by any white man. Lynch then reports to Stoneman that his strategy of encouraging blacks to join the Union League, and thus controlling them, is going according to plan. When Lynch (who plainly admires Elsie) leaves, she finds her father has had a stroke. Phil, now in love with Margaret Cameron, is frustrated by the amount of time she spends with a young local minister. He himself spends time talking with Dr. Cameron, whom he is surprised to discover uses hypnosis in his practice. He also sympathizes with Dr. Cameron's view of the sufferings now being experienced by Southern whites. Ben Cameron comes home, finds Gus loitering outside it, and orders him to move away. When Gus insolently refuses, Ben strikes him with a wooden paling. Ben is arrested and taken to the state capital, Columbia. Phil follows to try to secure his release, but instead discovers a plot to frame his friend for murder and succeeds in rescuing him. Dr. Cameron writes an article in the local paper condemning Ben's arrest but is then himself arrested by the local military commander; he is led in chains down the main street of Piedmont and past the old slave-quarters. To avoid heedless friction before the state elections, however, he is quickly released.

When the elections take place, a combination of white disfranchisement, intimidation of loyal black voters such as Jake, and ballot-stuffing lead to a Republican triumph. The new radical state constitution is approved, the legislature has a large black majority, and Silas Lynch is elected lieutenant-governor. In the aftermath of the election, bills are introduced into the legislature to put into force the radical program, including permitting the intermarriage of whites and blacks. Meanwhile, Austin Stoneman recovers from his stroke. Although his political views have not changed, he has grown to adore young Marion Lenoir, and on discovering that the Lenoirs' farm is about to be sold, he buys it from them at a generous price. Marion and her mother move back into their home, but during the first night after their return, Gus and three other blacks break into the house and rape Marion. To hide the shame of what has happened, and at Marion's urging, she and her mother commit suicide by jumping off a cliff.[71]

When the bodies are found, Dr. Cameron examines them and—peering with a microscope—claims to be able to see the image of Gus still printed on the mother's retina. Gus is apprehended by members of the Ku Klux Klan and taken to the cave that has become the rendezvous for the Piedmont branch of the organization. In front of the other Klansmen, Dr. Cameron hypnotizes Gus and makes him relive the crime. The local Grand Dragon (Ben Cameron) then steps forward and orders that Gus be executed and his body left on the lawn of Lieutenant-Governor Silas Lynch's house. He also summons the Klans from adjoining counties to join him in revolt against black rule. The discovery of Gus's body, with the letters "K.K.K." written in red on a paper attached to his chest, is the first public evidence that the Klan exists in Piedmont. It is followed, shortly afterward, by the Grand Dragon's order to the black militia to surrender their weapons. Stoneman now asks Phil to break off all ties with the Camerons, who are the main suspects in Gus's murder, but Phil refuses to do so. He is more successful with Elsie, who promises to give up Ben if she finds he is responsible for an ultimatum telling Stoneman to leave. Ben meets Elsie wearing his Klansman's uniform, and though she realizes how much this demonstrates his trust in her, she threatens never to see him again if the Klan commits another crime.[72]

That night, according to Ben's instructions, Klansmen disarm all blacks in the county. Ben leads a Klan attack on the black armory in Piedmont. After ten minutes, the black militia surrenders and all but three men are permitted to go home. These three, who were with Gus in his assault on the Lenoirs' home, are shot. The Klansmen in other South Carolina counties soon also disarm blacks and the Union League starts to collapse. Stoneman, seeing his plans for the South falling in ruins, resolves in revenge to hang Ben Cameron. Since no one else can be found to do so, he determines (over Elsie's protests) to conduct the prosecution himself. No witnesses can be found, however, and he is obliged to discharge Ben when he (finally) appears. Stoneman then sends a telegram to the White House, and the new president, Ulysses S. Grant, declares the South Carolina counties in a state of insurrection and imposes martial law. Thus encouraged, black insolence revives. When two black troopers insult Margaret Cameron, however, Phil Stoneman shoots one of them dead. Ben succeeds in getting Phil out of town but is then himself arrested for the murder, quickly tried, and sentenced to death. Phil races to the jail where he is held and, changing clothes with Ben, takes his place. Ben sends Margaret, his sister, to explain the situation to Stoneman and the two set off in a race to prevent Phil's execution. Yet it is the Klan that finally rescues Phil, not his father. At midnight of that day, Ben and Elsie see the fiery crosses burning across the mountains to celebrate the elections in which the Southern states have been "redeemed" from black rule and white civilization finally saved.[73]

The Clansman as a Play

The Clansman was even more successful as a novel than The Leopard's Spots and The One Woman. The book had a number of critics, but within a relatively short time, it had sold more than a million copies.[74] This "immediate and tremendous popularity" encouraged Dixon to adapt his novel into a play. Raymond Cook, Dixon's biographer, suggests that he had already decided to have a second attempt at theatrical success *before* the publication of The Clansman, and that the favorable reception of the novel provided him with the solution on how to do so.[75] Dixon was aware that far more people had seen Uncle Tom's Cabin as a play than had read it as a novel, and part and parcel of his cultural war with the earlier novel was his determination to do for his own work what others had done for Mrs. Stowe's.[76] Aided by a course on dramatic technique in the spring of 1905, he completed the play and sent it off to theatrical agent Alice Kauser in New York. Crosby Gaige, a member of Kauser's staff, read the play, liked it, and submitted it to George H. Brennan, a former newspaperman who had just set himself up as a theatrical producer. Brennan invited Dixon to New York and together the two established a new corporation, the Southern Amusement Company, to produce the play. Much to Brennan's surprise, Dixon bought a half interest in the play.[77]

Dixon's first play includes elements from both his earlier books on Reconstruction. Nelse and Eva from *The Leopard's Spots* reappear as the "faithful souls." Helen Lowell, also from *The Leopard's Spots*, is now a friend of Elsie Stoneman, and Dick reemerges as a minor character. Flora Camp has been transformed in the play into Flora Cameron, Ben's much younger sister. Although some of the major characters from *The Clansman* as a novel (Dr. Cameron, Ben Cameron, Austin and Elsie Stoneman, Silas Lynch, and Gus) have crucial roles in the play, others (including Jeannie and Marion Lenoir, Phil Stoneman, Margaret Cameron, Mrs. Cameron, and Lydia Brown) are omitted entirely. Yet the play also introduces several new characters, including Nellie Graham, a friend of the Camerons who is given some of the lines and qualities of Marion Lenoir; General Nathan Bedford Forrest, the Grand Wizard of the Ku Klux Klan; and William Pitt Shrimp, the governor of South Carolina. Other principal differences between *The Clansman* as novel and play revolve around chronology and setting. Whereas the novel starts with the ending of the Civil War and its action takes place both in Washington (Books I and II) and Piedmont (Books III and IV), the play does not commence until election day 1867 and its action takes place entirely in Piedmont.

Act I of the play focuses on the election. Blacks are drinking and voting repeatedly, while most of the whites are disfranchised. Austin Stoneman appears. While he is pretending to be in the South for the sake of his health, he is really the commander of the Black League. Because of the election and the excited state of the blacks, young Flora Cameron is told by her father and brother to stay close to her home. Ben Cameron meets Elsie Stoneman, who has nursed him back to health after his injuries in the war. While the two of them argue—for example, over slavery and the fact that Elsie treats Silas Lynch, her father's black protégé, as a social equal—it is evident that they are in love. Elsie is determined, however, that she will not marry without her father's approval. Austin Stoneman reappears, together with Lynch (who covertly admires Elsie). Ben, deliberately ignoring Lynch, goes off to vote, and Elsie also leaves. Left alone with his acolyte, Stoneman explains that he plans to recruit Ben Cameron as the white leader of the Black League and asks why Lynch has not yet posted the order of the commanding general permitting the intermarriage of whites and blacks. When Lynch objects that doing so would be a dangerous act, Stoneman takes the proclamation and pins it to the bulletin board outside the

Camerons' house, which is now operating as a hotel. Once all the blacks have voted, Alex, a rascally if naïve black election official, closes the polls, ignoring the protest of Dr. Cameron. Ben Cameron is concerned, if the blacks carry the whole state, that the whites will no longer have any form of protection. He suggests to his father that the only answer to the secret nighttime meetings of the Black League is a similarly secret white organization, the Ku Klux Klan, but Dr. Cameron makes him promise never to resort to violence without first seeking his father's advice. Stoneman returns, and confessing that he is the leader of the Black League, he invites Ben to join him at its head. Ben asserts that he cannot accept social equality with blacks, and Stoneman, who has guessed that Ben loves Elsie, asks him to prove himself worthy of her. At this point, the election results are announced: Shrimp has won the governorship and Lynch the lieutenant-governorship by a landslide, and the new Legislature will consist mostly of blacks. For the sake of Elsie, Ben agrees to continue listening to Stoneman's arguments but refuses to meet with Lynch under any circumstances. His father now points out the proclamation about intermarriage posted by Stoneman outside the Camerons' house, and Ben demonstrates his rejection of Stoneman's offer (and outlook) by tearing it down.[78]

Act II begins six months later. The Camerons' house is about to be sold to pay taxes. The faithful Nelse tries to prevent this by chasing away Gus, one of the Camerons' former slaves who is now an army officer, and seizing the "Auction Sale Today" flag Gus has been trying to attach to the house. Ben tells his father that he has received a telegram from Governor Shrimp booking every room in Cameron House. Silas Lynch is also coming to Piedmont and it seems obvious to the Camerons that he is intent on forcing the sale of the house. Ben mentions to Dr. Cameron that General Forrest is in Piedmont and the night before he had asked if Ben would become the chief of the Ku Klux Klan in South Carolina. Shrimp and Lynch arrive and Lynch admits that he aims to buy Cameron House at the auction for himself and a white bride. To forestall opposition to his plans, Lynch asks Shrimp for a proclamation disarming the state's six white military companies (one of which is led by Ben Cameron). Although initially reluctant, Shrimp agrees to issue the proclamation when Lynch offers to support his candidacy for the U.S. Senate. The auction begins, and just as Lynch is about to succeed in winning the house, Elsie Stoneman arrives and outbids him. Elsie and Ben are reconciled, but she still insists that Ben must win her father's approval for their marriage. Elsie leaves to meet her father at the station. General Forrest now appears, and Nellie Graham is excited to meet him, though Dr. Cameron makes it plain to the head of the Ku Klux Klan that he is opposed to any further violence. At this point, however, Shrimp and Lynch arrive with an escort of soldiers and Shrimp announces his decision to disband the six white military companies. When Ben and his father object, they are both arrested.[79]

At the beginning of Act III, Flora Cameron has just come to the end of her thirteenth birthday party. Gus is watching her stealthily from behind a fence.

When Ben appears, Flora tells him that Gus has given her a box of candy. Ben angrily throws the box away and warns her not to allow someone like Gus near her again. He tells his father that the blacks are growing bolder and to save white womanhood he and others may have to use force. Dr. Cameron, however, believes that a reaction against radical rule has already set in. After he and Ben had been released after their first arrest, Shrimp had not dared interfere with them again. Flora, however, paying no attention to Ben's warning, sets off to go down to the spring to feed her tame squirrel. She is followed by Gus. In the meantime, Stoneman arrives, passes on to Elsie his discovery that Ben is the leader of the Klan in the state, and asks her to give him up. Elsie promises her father that if what he says is true, she will certainly do so. When she confronts Ben, however, he shows his complete trust in her by admitting that he is the Grand Dragon of the Klan. Elsie, while flattered by that trust, tells him that he must choose between the Klan and her. Nelse's wife, Eve, now appears, looking for Flora, and Ben sends her to bring Flora back from the spring. But Eve is soon back, panicky and holding Flora's bonnet. Flora has disappeared. A crowd gathers to search for her. They are to signal once she is found: one shot if she is alive, two shots if she is dead. A neighbor mentions that he has seen Gus sneaking along the river bank. Then two shots are heard. The Klan meets, to try Gus. He denies committing the crime but is mesmerized by Dr. Cameron and relives what has happened. He sprang out at Flora and in her desperate attempt to escape him, she jumped over the cliff and drowned in the river. Ben, believing that the time has come to disarm all blacks, summons the Klan to assemble. He also orders that Gus be hanged from the balcony of the Court House until dead and his body left on Lynch's doorstep.[80]

Act IV begins with Lynch planning to take the offensive. Intending to hang Ben Cameron, he attempts to blackmail Governor Shrimp into temporarily leaving the state and appointing Lynch acting governor. In the meantime, Stoneman has been provided by the president with a proclamation of martial law, to be used when he wishes. A civil warrant is issued for Ben's arrest and in the absence of any other lawyer, Stoneman volunteers to prosecute him for treason and conspiracy. When Ben arrives for his trial, Stoneman tries to persuade Elsie to testify that he is a member of the Klan, but she refuses and declares her love for the accused man and his people. Stoneman responds by using the president's proclamation to establish martial law and sets off for Washington. Ben is arrested by the military and Lynch arranges an immediate court-martial. Elsie is staggered to learn that the court-martial has already sentenced Ben to be shot. Lynch delays the execution of the sentence and offers to commute it completely. In return, he obviously hopes that Elsie will be his wife. When he touches her, however, she becomes hysterical and faints. Lynch has two of his black assistants carry her to an adjoining room. At this point, Stoneman returns, having convinced himself that he must intercede on Ben's behalf for the sake of his daughter. But when Lynch tells him that a court-martial has already ordered Ben's execution, he is quickly reconciled to what seems a fait accompli. Buoyed up by the feeling of camaraderie between them, Lynch confesses that he is in love with a white girl. Stoneman encourages him in this until he learns that Elsie is the object of Lynch's affections. He is furious and informs Lynch that their relationship is over. Hearing Elsie scream, however, he draws his revolver. Lynch draws his own gun and instructs one of his minions to shoot Elsie if he hears a struggle or shot from the room in which he and Stoneman are confronting one another. He then sends for a minister to marry him and Elsie. Stoneman raises his revolver to fire the shot that will save his daughter from Lynch by leading to her own death. Before he can fire, the door is flung open and Klansmen burst into the room. Ben (who has been rescued first) takes off his costume and Elsie falls into his arms. Stoneman, having finally seen the light, promises Ben that the army will be withdrawn and normality restored.[81]

The Clansman was an immediate hit as a play. It opened in Norfolk, Virginia, on September 22, 1905, and made a profit of $50,000 during its first week. It toured much of the South in the next few weeks, performing in cities from Richmond to New Orleans. Although it met opposition in some places (part of the audience booed and hissed in Columbia, South Carolina), most of those who saw the play were highly enthusiastic.[82] It was particularly successful in Dixon's home state of North Carolina. In Winston-Salem, "men fought madly for choice seats" and in Raleigh audiences proved "wildly enthusiastic."[83] Local newspapers in a number of places, however, were quite critical. "What a pity there is no way to suppress *The Clansman*," mourned the *Montgomery Advertiser*. In the view of the Charleston *News and Courier*, it was "one of the most remarkable exhibitions of hysterics to which we have been treated." Another South Carolina paper, the Columbia *State*, summarized Dixon's message as "Hate the negro; he is a beast; his intention is to rob and murder and pollute; he should be transported or annihilated."[84]

From the beginning, fears were expressed that the play would provoke conflict between the races. It was "hazardous to the peace of whites and blacks," commented a Norfolk newspaper, predicting that its tour of the South would be "like a runaway car loaded with dynamite." "We shall be agreeably surprised," declared a Winston-Salem editor, "if innocent blood is not upon the head of the Reverend Thomas Dixon Junior before he reaches New Orleans," and a Charlotte commentator feared "it will leave behind a new trail of lynchings." To the *Chattanooga Daily Times*, it was simply "a riot breeder...designed to excite rage and race hatred."[85] The violence foretold by many came close to breaking out when the play was performed in Atlanta. Tensions between the whites in the stalls and blacks in the balcony prompted the theater's management to keep the lights on throughout the performance and suspend the sales of soda pop to prevent the bottles from being used as missiles. Eventually, the police stormed the balcony and made a number of arrests.[86] More crucially, argues Pete Daniel, Dixon's play was a factor contributing to the later outbreak of the

Atlanta race riot (September 22–24, 1906), which left up to forty blacks dead. Walter White, subsequently executive secretary of the NAACP, who as a boy observed the riot firsthand, would also in his autobiography blame Dixon for helping to provoke such violence.[87]

Criticism and controversy, however, did not deter the crowds who flocked to see the play: by the time it reached New Orleans in December, it was being hailed as "the greatest theatrical triumph in the history of the South." The fact that many white Southerners should have greeted the play—with its open advocacy of white supremacy—with such warmth is unsurprising. More remarkable (and revealing), when *The Clansman* moved on from New Orleans into the Midwest, it continued to attract overflowing crowds. Partway through the Midwestern tour, Dixon returned to New York to help rehearse another cast for the New York opening. Although there were many objections and protests before the play started its run at the Liberty Theater (where *The Birth of a Nation* would be exhibited nine years later) in January 1906, New York audiences reacted enthusiastically. The cast also worried about the possibility of violent protest when the play opened at the Wheiting Opera House in Syracuse—once a staging post on the Underground Railroad helping escaped slaves to reach Canada—but theatergoers responded favorably to the production. Only in Philadelphia was there any real trouble: four weeks into its run at the Walnut Street Theater, a riot broke out during a performance and the play was banned.[88]

While audiences declined to some extent after the first enthusiastic year, the two *Clansman* companies continued to perform across the country for several more years.[89] Encouraged by the success of the play, Dixon also adapted his anti-socialist novel *The One Woman* for the stage. In October 1906, as director-producer-author, he began to tour with the new production. The lead role of Frank Gordon was initially played by Lawrence Griffith, the stage name of a young actor from Kentucky whose real name was David Wark Griffith. The company also included Griffith's then wife, Linda Arvidson. After two months on the road, Dixon discharged the Griffiths (Arvidson later claimed that he had engaged a leading man at half the salary paid her husband).[90]

Through his three novels and two stage plays, Dixon had made a considerable fortune. Living in New York again since 1905, however, he allowed himself to be tempted by speculations on Wall Street and lost everything in the stock market "panic" of October 1907. Fortunately for Dixon, the last of his trilogy of Reconstruction novels, dealing with the dissolution of the Klan, had been published in July before the crash. Selling almost a million copies, *The Traitor* made it possible for him to save his home and begin to rebuild his fortune.[91] During the next few years, Dixon completed a second trilogy of novels, this time on socialism: *The One Woman* was followed by *Comrades* (1909) and *The Root of Evil* (1911). Yet from 1907 onward he gave more and more of his attention to the theater. A stage adaptation of *The Traitor* in 1908 was followed a year later by *The Sins of the Father*, the first play written by Dixon that was not based on one of his novels.[92] It revolved around a theme very close to Dixon's heart: the dangers of miscegenation. It also led to yet another twist in Dixon's enormously versatile career. The day after a performance in Wilmington, North Carolina, he went with the cast to the beach. According to Dixon's biographer, while they were swimming, the actor playing the lead role was killed by a shark. Since Dixon was the only one who knew the lead actor's lines, he took over the role, and when reviewers praised his performance he toured with the company for almost a year as an actor. He then returned to New York where he spent the next two years following his various occupations as novelist, playwright, producer, director, and actor.[93]

Failure as a Movie

At some point, Dixon also decided to try his luck in the new motion picture industry. Large audiences were flocking to the nickelodeons in New York and other cities. The thought of involvement in something so new must have been an important attraction to so restless and ambitious a man as Dixon. He was probably also aware that *Uncle Tom's Cabin* had already been filmed three times.[94] Dixon may have felt that it was necessary to carry his cultural war with Mrs. Stowe into the new medium. On September 26, 1911, George H. Brennan of the Southern Amusement Company (the company formed to produce *The Clansman* as a play) signed a contract with Charles E. Ford of the Kinemacolor Company to create a new company, to be known as the Kinemacolor-Clansman Corporation. The objective of the new company, as its name implied, was to produce a motion picture based on Dixon's play.[95]

Many people assume that there were no attempts to use sound in films until the late 1920s and color until the 1930s. In reality, there were many earlier attempts to introduce both.[96] The British company Kinemacolor had produced two color films, *The Royal Visit to India* and *The Durbar at Delhi*, which had caused something of a sensation. Kinemacolor of America, a separate but allied company, set out to import the color process into the United States. At first they encountered opposition from the Motion Picture Patents Company, a powerful association of production companies that was trying to monopolize the movie market. Kinemacolor was consequently forced to set up its own studios, first at Allentown, Pennsylvania, then at Whitestone Landing, New York, and finally, in 1912, in Hollywood, California.[97] The fact that Dixon obviously wanted his play to be filmed at the cutting edge of film technology was thoroughly consistent with his insatiable ambition. *The Clansman*, after the success (and controversy) of its initial production, had survived to become a popular play with traveling stock companies. Brennan had apparently sold the management of Kinemacolor on the idea that the actors with one of these companies, the Campbell MacCullough Players, would repeat their roles on film.

As the company moved across the South, scenes could be shot on location in former antebellum plantations or on battlefields. Yet William Haddock, the man assigned by Brennan to direct, found it very hard to do much shooting with the company constantly on the road. Although he persuaded MacCullough to remain for two weeks in Natchez, Mississippi, where several scenes were shot, McCullough then insisted on returning to the tour. At that point, with $25,000 supposedly spent and with little more than a reel of film to show for it, Kinemacolor halted production. Several explanations were later advanced for the failure of the project: the photography was so poor that there was never a print that could be used, Haddock's direction was inadequate, the acting by the stock company was inappropriate to the medium of film, the script needed continual revision to transform Dixon's original play into a workable motion picture. Since the film has long vanished and no records apparently survive, it is impossible to establish the actual reasons for its abandonment.[98] After the failure of the Kinemacolor project, Dixon seems to have approached a number of other film companies. No one showed any interest in what Dixon referred to as his "historical beeswax."[99]

Born in a Confederate state during the last months of the Civil War, Thomas Dixon Jr. had passed his early childhood during the Reconstruction era. While his later career involved a succession of jobs, and considerable periods spent living in the North, Dixon never forgot the North Carolina of his youth. Increasingly obsessed, by the early twentieth century, with what he saw as the dangers of interracial relationships and the threat they supposedly posed to the future of the Anglo-Saxon race, Dixon wrote several novels set in the South that warned against such racial admixture. Deliberately, in fact, Dixon set out to create a master narrative of Southern history and race relations that would challenge and replace that associated with Harriet Beecher Stowe's novel, *Uncle Tom's Cabin*. Whereas Mrs. Stowe had focused attention on the sufferings of black slaves at the hands of antebellum whites, Dixon depicted the "anguish" of Southern whites at the hands of free postwar blacks. The Ku Klux Klan (in which several members of Dixon's family had once been involved) provided the main heroes of his fiction. The cultural impact of *Uncle Tom's Cabin* had been greatly increased by its transformation into a play; Dixon set out to do the same by converting his novel *The Clansman* into a successful theatrical production. Yet Dixon had apparently failed to emulate Mrs. Stowe's legacy in one crucial respect: he had not succeeded in having a film (or films) based on his work. But his luck began to change in 1914. Film director D. W. Griffith developed an interest in *The Clansman* project. The eventual result of the collaboration of Dixon and Griffith would be *The Birth of a Nation*.

3

David Wark Griffith

In 1914, when his path crossed that of Thomas Dixon Jr. for the second time in their lives, David Wark Griffith was already a commanding figure in American cinema. The principal director for the Biograph company since 1908, Griffith had produced more than four hundred motion pictures before quitting Biograph in late 1913 to produce longer films. Griffith's interest in using Dixon's story of *The Clansman* as the basis for a film was to lead to the release of *The Birth of a Nation*. It was also in many ways to transform the American film industry. To appreciate Griffith's part in making *The Birth of a Nation* as well as his creative role in early American cinema, it is necessary to know something of the man himself.

Family Background and Youth

Griffith was born on January 22, 1875, at a farm known as Lofty Green, located in the north of Kentucky about twenty miles east of Louisville. He was the sixth of the seven Griffith children to survive into adulthood. His family claimed that their roots in the New World could be traced back to the early eighteenth century, when a man with the title of "Lord Brayington" had been exiled from England, apparently for political reasons. Settling in Somerset County, Maryland, he abandoned his title and took his wife's maiden name, Griffith, as his own. His son, Salathiel Griffith, served in the Revolutionary War, afterward being appointed sheriff of Somerset County. Salathiel's son, Daniel Wetherby Griffith, carried on the family's military tradition by fighting with the Virginia militia as a corporal during the War of 1812. His own son, Jacob Wark Griffith, was born in October 1819.[1]

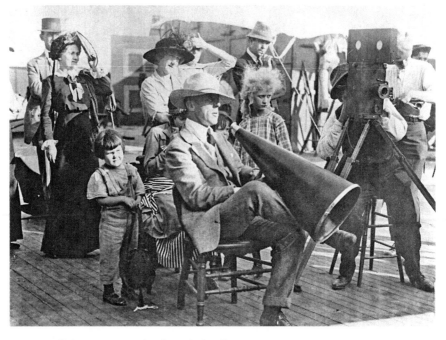

D. W. Griffith on Set. (Epoch/The Kobal Collection)

When Jacob reached the age of twenty-one, he decided to become a doctor and apprenticed himself to two medical practitioners in Shelby County, Kentucky, where his father was farming. Eventually, he set up in practice on his own and in 1845 bought a horse to bear him on his rounds. Life as a country doctor, however, could not have proved very satisfying to the young man. A year later, revealing a restlessness that would dog him for much of his life, he went off to fight in the Mexican War. Jacob served for a year with the First Regiment of the Kentucky Cavalry, mainly as a surgeon, and saw action at the battles of Buena Vista and Saltillo. In September 1848, a year after leaving the army, he married Mary P. Oglesby. From Jacob's point of view, the match was a good one: Mary's father, Thomas Oglesby, was one of the wealthiest men in Oldham County, which adjoined Shelby County. The young couple moved into a five-room house given them by her father and Jacob returned to the practice of medicine.[2]

Very little is known about Mary Oglesby Griffith. Surviving photographs of her in middle and old age show a rather sad-faced, severe-looking woman, but this may have been because years of hard work and disappointment had etched themselves on her features. She was apparently intensely religious and her devotion to Methodism, already strong, only deepened as a result of her family's later economic misfortunes. She was clearly very reserved and, outwardly at least, cold and detached in personal relationships. A fairly grim and silent personality, however, may actually have been a mask for her true nature. David W. Griffith would later remember the shock of finally discovering, when she was around seventy years old, that her "stern, cold, hard exterior covered a tremendous emotional and an affectionate nature that was terrible in its intensity."[3]

Certainly, Mary's earnest appeal was not strong enough to keep Jacob at home. Dissatisfied with the rewards of medicine—or frustrated at his economic dependence on his father-in-law—he jumped at the opportunity offered by the California gold rush to try to make a fortune of his own. In May 1850, he set off, together with some Oglesby relations, on a large wagon train heading for the West Coast. For a time, indeed, until dismissed for his bad temper, he seems to have acted as captain of the train. But his wider ambitions appeared to be realized. After two years of hard work prospecting, Jacob set off homeward with $16,000 in his pocket. The journey went well until he reached Louisville, just a few miles from home, where he managed to lose everything he had through gambling.[4]

Compelled to return to medicine and helping out at times on his father-in-law's farm, Jacob seems to have hidden his frustrations by developing a gift for oratory (this may be the origin of his nickname as "Roaring Jake" Griffith) and involving himself in politics. In 1854, the year when American politics was transformed by the Kansas-Nebraska Act, bringing about the birth of the Republican Party, he was elected to a term in the Kentucky legislature. Jacob was not particularly distinguished as a politician (there is no evidence that he was affected by the intense battles of his time) and he served only one term. Richard Schickel suggests, however, that his political career may have been cut short by his father-in-law's death in 1856, leaving him for the first time in his life with considerable property to manage. His wife's inheritance included part of the Lofty Green farm (the rest going to her brother), the main house, five slaves, and numerous herds of livestock.[5]

Superficially, during the next few years, Jacob's life became more settled. He ran his farm and Mary bore him two sons and two daughters (a son had earlier died during infancy). Neither farming nor family life seems to have satisfied him permanently, however. When the Civil War broke out in 1861, though now forty-two years old, he set off to raise a company of cavalry to fight under his command for the Confederacy.[6] In many respects, this was a quixotic thing to do. Kentucky was one of the four border states whose position crucially influenced the course of the war ("I hope I have God on my side," Abraham Lincoln remarked, "but I must have Kentucky"). Though it had not followed the Upper South into the Confederacy, Kentucky opposed the idea of coercion and refused Lincoln's call for troops. Initially, it tried to stay neutral in the conflict. But in September 1861, responding to a Confederate invasion, the Kentucky legislature finally declared for the Union. Therefore, in the following month when Jacob Griffith was sworn in to the Confederate Army, he could not claim that he was joining out of loyalty to his state. His motivation may have had something to do with the slavery issue (Jacob and his wife owned slaves and Oldham county was a center of pro-slavery sentiment). Yet it is hard to escape the conclusion that what truly motivated Jacob to volunteer were his endemic restlessness and his instinctive desire for action and adventure.

In going off to fight for the Confederacy, Jacob left his wife with four very young children. Perhaps he found, in the war, refuge from his failures as husband, father, and provider. At last, in the army, he discovered a way of life and a challenge that suited him. For all his weaknesses and faults, he was a brave man. He participated in many of the crucial battles of the war, including Shiloh, Corinth, and Chickamauga; was wounded at least twice; and was mentioned as "distinguished for gallantry" in dispatches. More surprisingly, perhaps, he turned out to be an able military leader: in March 1863, he was appointed lieutenant-colonel of the Kentucky Brigade. Thereafter, he would often command his own regiment, fighting under General Joe Wheeler (the two got on so well that they agreed to name their first postwar children after each other, condemning one of D. W. Griffith's sisters to go through life with the unlikely Christian name of Wheeler). In 1865, after Lee's surrender, Jacob was apparently commanding the escort to Confederate President Jefferson Davis (who was trying to reach the last two small Southern armies still fighting) when the entire group was captured by Union cavalry.[7]

After the war, nothing was quite the same. Jacob returned home with an injured arm, some useless Confederate money, and several souvenirs taken from the enemy. He found most of his slaves gone, debts piling up, and his wife in poor health. A few weeks after the war's end, the Lofty Green farmhouse was destroyed by a fire. Although no one was injured (the Griffith family had prudently spent the Civil War years living in the neighboring town of Floydsburg), most of the house's furnishings were destroyed. It would have taken a good deal of hard work and commitment to rebuild the farm and make it economically successful. Jacob lacked both the energy and determination—and perhaps even the motivation—to do so. He built a (much smaller) house for his family but was incapable of restoring the farm to its earlier prosperity. He started to sell the land off piecemeal and began to borrow money against the security of the farm itself (eventually taking out no fewer than three mortgages).[8]

Apart from producing three other children, David Wark Griffith being the second, Jacob did very little with the rest of his life. He was fond of reading aloud from Shakespeare and other literary classics. He was also something of an orator (and was elected again to the state legislature for a single term in 1877). He enjoyed dancing, gambling, and drinking. Above all, it seems, he liked to reminisce about his experiences during the Civil War. His son would later recall Jacob claiming that he was wounded five times in all, including once when he was "virtually disemboweled" and had to be sown together by an army surgeon on the battlefield. In another of his stories, unable to ride a horse as a result of his wounds he led his men in a charge on the enemy from a buggy. Jacob's stories not only turned him into a hero in the eyes of his son, but many would later find their way in some form into *The Birth of a Nation*. That picture, his son would later confess, owed "more to my father than it does to me."[9]

In 1885, Jacob died suddenly and unexpectedly. His son would later blame that death on the "wounds and crude dressings" suffered by his father during the war. In reality, Richard Schickel notes, it may just as well have been from Jacob's over-indulgence in food and alcohol.[10] Whatever its cause, his father's death when D. W. Griffith was only ten meant that the son would never see his father as he really was: a lazy, unsuccessful braggart who gambled and drank away his income. "Roaring Jake" would be remembered by his son through the uncritical eyes of childhood. He did not live long enough for D. W. Griffith to begin to appreciate that his father had feet of clay.

Griffith would later remember that his father had been particularly close to one ex-slave. This man, Griffith recalled shortly after making *The Birth of a Nation*, together "with the heads of four other families refused to leave the plantation; those four families were four important factors in keeping the Griffith family poor." Griffith, deeply hurt by the criticism of his attitude toward blacks after the release of *Birth*, was obviously determined to disprove any charge of racism by demonstrating the benign paternalism with which African Americans had been treated by the Griffith family. He may, of course, have remembered only what he wanted to remember and what would create the best impression; it required a major imaginative leap to transform the small Griffith farm into a "plantation," and in his unfinished autobiography, Griffith later reduced the four families of former slaves to two. Although he was probably right concerning "the peculiarly close relationship between the whites and Negroes" that existed in the Kentucky of his boyhood, it was also true that for many whites, probably including the Griffiths, this paternalist closeness was firmly grounded on, and ultimately limited by, the assumption of white superiority.[11]

The Experience of Poverty

Jacob's death left the Griffith family in an extremely precarious financial situation. They now discovered that he had been paying high interest rates on several mortgages. To settle his debts, his widow was obliged to sell his personal effects, part of the land making up the farm, and eventually Lofty Green itself. D. W. Griffith would remember the family's intense poverty in the first months after his father's death: his school lunch consisted of a few slices of bread and an "apple butter" made in the fall that became increasingly sour as the winter progressed. With the sale of their home, most of the family moved to the farm bought by David's eldest brother, Will, in nearby Shelby County. The move brought no change in their fortunes. Griffith would later describe this as "the most useless farm in the entire world" and retain unpleasant memories of their long and "losing fight against rocks, roots, bugs, and worn-out soil."[12]

From his new home, Griffith went each day to a school that was even farther away than the one he had attended while living at Lofty Green (two and a half miles rather than one and a half). He would later recall being bullied there—and falling in love for the first time with a young girl with curly chestnut hair. Each day, before setting off for school, he got up before daylight to help milk the cows and perform other farmyard chores. (Like Thomas Dixon Jr., Griffith loathed farm labor.) There is no evidence that he did very well at school (Griffith would later confess that he "did not grow up overly bright").[13] He probably learned more in his earliest years from his eldest sister, Mattie, who after the sale of Lofty Green went off to Louisville to work as a teacher.

The Griffith family struggled hard to make the Shelby County farm work. The burdens must have been especially heavy on Mary Griffith who, as her son remembered, had "never done work of any kind" before the Civil War. Now she tried to keep the family together by working endless hours. She even made all the clothes worn by David (and presumably the other children as well). Yet financial success eluded the family. Perversely, far from appreciating her sacrifice (and placing the blame on his father as the real cause of the family's impoverishment), Griffith would later criticize his mother for her lack of business sense and compare her unfavourably with his aunt, Becky Oglesby, a shrewd farmer who put six children through college with her sales of butter and eggs.[14]

Finally, in 1889, Mary had had enough of farm life. Giving in to the urgings of Mattie and another sister Ruth, who had joined her in the city, she decided to move with her three youngest children to Louisville. If David Griffith is to be believed, the children greeted the prospect of a move to the city with great enthusiasm. It would mean the end of "back-breaking toil in the tobacco patch," of milking, of plowing, and of "tediously long farm chores." So, in midwinter, the family loaded all their possessions onto a two-horse wagon and with D. W. Griffith on top of the pile of furniture, drove to Louisville. When they reached the city and slowly made their way toward their new home, Griffith later remembered, they were met with cries of "Country jakes!" from jeering street urchins.[15]

Louisville

In 1889, Louisville was a prosperous and expanding city with a population of around 200,000. The Griffith family had no real share in that prosperity. They would have seven homes there over the next decade, and at each of them Mary would take in boarders. Nothing seemed to go right for the family. Mattie died of tuberculosis soon after the family arrived. And although David was able finally to attend a good high school, he left after one year to try to help solve the family's financial crisis by taking a full-time job. For two and a half years, he worked in the J. C. Lewis Dry Goods Store, first as a cash boy and later as an elevator operator. In 1893, he left to take a position as clerk at Flexner's Book Store. Not only was Flexner's the main bookshop in Louisville at that time, but it was also a major focus of the city's intellectual life. Louisville's intelligentsia often gathered in the back room of the store after closing time to discuss literature and other "mighty subjects."[16]

Griffith's own interest in reading considerably antedated his employment at Flexner's. It probably stemmed in the beginning from his father's fascination with literature, especially Shakespearian plays, romantic poets, and novelists. When "Roaring Jake" died, although the county court directed that his personal effects be auctioned to settle his debts, it allowed his widow and her children to keep some of his books. Almost certainly, Griffith became familiar with these. Later, after his arrival in Louisville, he would spend a high proportion of his spare time at the public library. One of his friends from that time, Edward Rucker, would remember him reading Browning—and perhaps Tolstoy and Hardy—as well as histories of the Civil War. At some stage, then or earlier, he developed what would remain a lifetime passion for Dickens. Working at Flexner's bookstore left him free to indulge his growing interest in literature; on one occasion, he was gently reproved by the head of the store, Bernard Flexner, for spending too much time reading when he should have been working.[17]

Louisville also made it possible for Griffith to develop the other great interest of his youth. He saw his first play—*America's National Game* starring Pete Baker—at Macauley's Theater, which specialized in "quality" drama and light opera. A few weeks later, he watched Julia Marlowe in *Romeo and Juliet*. After that, he would much later claim, "the die was cast" and he knew that he wanted to become an actor. In practice, it is unlikely that his ambition crystallized so quickly. For the moment, he tried to attend as many theatrical performances as his slender means allowed, including inexpensive melodramas and burlesque shows. At some point while he was with the Lewis store, he went on stage for the first time, performing as "the dunce" in an amateur production of *The District School*. He had only one line. He also took singing lessons with Mrs. Annie H. Baustead, a popular local music teacher. From time to time, he found temporary "suping" jobs as a non-speaking actor with touring stock companies. When Sarah Bernhardt came to Louisville at the beginning of 1896, for example, he was one of the extras in *Gismonda* and *The Lady of the Camellias*.[18]

Becoming an Actor

Shortly thereafter, Griffith finally committed himself to a stage career. His decision may have had something to do with losing his job at Flexner's; the Flexners had sold out and the new owner finally asked him to leave. Sometime in the spring of 1896, Griffith signed on with a traveling stock company. He would later recall that his family, and his mother in particular, were firmly opposed to this decision.[19] Not only was the theater perceived by the Methodist church as sinful, but Griffith was also regarded as letting down the family tradition by embracing an occupation that was far from respectable. (Mary Griffith, something of a snob, apparently really wanted her son to become a minister.[20]) Yet while Griffith would not allow himself to be dissuaded from his new career, he did at least conceal his identity to some degree by performing throughout his acting career under a variety of stage names. Although he would become best known as "Lawrence Griffith," from time to time he would also use other professional names.[21]

Between spring 1896 and spring 1897, Griffith traveled through Indiana, Ohio, Michigan, Minnesota, and North Dakota playing a range of roles with several companies. Returning to Louisville in May 1897, he was offered a small part in David Belasco's *Men and Women* at the Temple Theater. The production was by the Meffert Stock Company, which was a cut above the other companies Griffith had toured with (he would describe them later as "a real company" that "actually paid their actors salaries"). Unhappily for Griffith, he was dismissed by the manager after the first matinée performance. There followed a curious episode in which Griffith was engaged by a new company called the Twilight Revellers. Organized by Irishman Ned Risley, "a sort of steamboat comedian and small-town barnstormer," and bankrolled by a stage-struck blacksmith, Jim White, the Revellers tried to bring plays such as *Pygmalion and Galatea* and *The Arabian Nights* to small towns in Indiana and Kentucky. Their money ran out in the fourth town and they were caught by the landlord of their boarding house attempting to escape without paying. Risley managed to persuade the man that what he really wanted to do was to join the company (Griffith, whose description of the Revellers is probably the most affectionate of all his theatrical reminiscences, asserted that in the end there were no less than five landlords involved in a doomed attempt to keep the show on the road). When the company disbanded, Griffith probably found a temporary job or jobs to see him through the summer.[22]

In the fall season of 1897, the Meffert Stock Company acquired new management in the form of Oscar Eagle and his wife, Esther Lyon. The two, who acted in as well as directed their own productions, had a high reputation and were determined to offer a considerable range of plays, including some premièred only recently in Europe. Although it is not clear who first suggested Griffith to the new managers, by October 1897 he had become a full member of the company. While he played mainly minor roles during his first year, he gained much from the experience of regular acting as part of a highly professional acting troupe. When Eagle left Louisville temporarily in 1898 to direct a summer season at the Alhambra Theater in Chicago, he took Griffith with him. Performing in a number of plays that were new to him, Griffith scored a major personal triumph with his depiction of Abraham Lincoln in William Haworth's play, *The Ensign*. He seems subsequently to have reproduced the role at an Elk's Club minstrel show in Indiana where, according to the trade press, he "made his famous Lincoln pose in the tableau finale and received deserved praise."[23]

Between September 1898 and March 1899, he acted with another company that toured Iowa, Minnesota, Indiana, Ohio, and Michigan. At the end of this period, he returned for one last time to the Meffert Company. His parts were now much more important, reflecting his growing reputation as an actor. He played Athos in the adaptation of *The Three Musketeers* that closed the season. During the summer of 1899, perhaps while working in a temporary job as a stringer for the Louisville *Courier-Journal*, Griffith must have been thinking deeply about his future. He probably sensed that his career was at a turning point. He was twenty-four years old. His stature as an actor had increased and he had been in virtually continuous employment for the previous two years. He may also have known that Eagle and Lyon, his main local patrons, were not coming back to Louisville for the next season. Griffith was ambitious: he obviously felt the time had arrived to test his theatrical skills on a wider stage. Drawing out his savings, he paid $19 for a round-trip ticket to Atlantic City. On his arrival in the New Jersey resort, he cashed in the return part of the ticket and bought another, this time to New York.[24]

Griffith's arrival in New York was inauspicious. He lived for three days in a cheap flophouse under the Brooklyn Bridge, under the delusion that he was in New York proper, before moving on to even worse accommodation near the Bowery. He "haunted" (his word) the main theatrical agencies. Eventually, he was rewarded with the lead role, as "Happy Jack" Ferrers, in a popular melodrama called *London Life*. The show toured New York State, Ontario, Ohio, Michigan, Indiana, Illinois, Tennessee, Georgia, Alabama, Mississippi, Texas, Arkansas, Wisconsin, and Minnesota, with Griffith receiving "generally good" reviews. In Minneapolis, however, he left the show for reasons that are unclear. It was midwinter and he had no money for train fare. Imitating (and sometimes traveling with) hoboes, he "hopped freights" or "grabbed the blinds" of baggage cars on passengers trains to Louisville, where he was able to scrape up enough money to pay for his return to New York. On another occasion, when a melodrama he was performing in folded in upstate New York, Griffith was forced to become "an ore shoveler and puddler" for the Tonawanda Iron and Steel Company to earn the cost of his train fare back to New York.[25] It seems, indeed, that Griffith frequently turned to manual labor to survive financially when acting roles were scarce. He claimed to have worked, at various times, shoveling concrete and scraping rust from the iron supports in the New York subway. This, together with his experience of the cheapest form of accommodation and his acquired knowledge of tramps and hoboes, would help give him the sense of identification with the poor that characterized many of his early films and probably helped account for a good deal of their success with nickelodeon audiences.[26]

Between 1899 and 1904, although he regarded New York as his home base, Griffith did not by any means spend all his time there. He worked with several touring companies. Early 1901 found him on the West Coast for the first time. A year later, he joined a company formed by his old friend, Oscar Eagle, which toured from Troy, New York, to Indianapolis. Over the next two years, he belonged to several companies that toured the Midwest, the East Coast, and New England. In 1904, however, perhaps seduced by the notion of higher earnings or the possibility of greater acting achievements, he decided to move to San Francisco, then second only to New York as a major theatrical hub.[27]

Soon after his arrival in the city, Griffith found work playing Rupert of Hentzau in *The Prisoner of Zenda* at the Central Theater. As soon as that run finished, he did six weeks of repertory with Melbourne MacDowell at the Opera House on Mission Street. It was during this period that he met Linda Arvidson Johnson, an aspiring young actress. Hired as an extra in *Fedora*, Linda was initially terrified by Griffith's "deep stern voice" as the police inspector in the play, but the two rapidly became romantically involved. When the MacDowell company moved on to Portland, Griffith was dismissed (MacDowell, he would later remember, "grew prosperous and particular. I got fired"). Returning to San Francisco and finding no theatrical work immediately available, he took a temporary job as a hop-picker. In January 1905, he played the lead (as John the Baptist) in *The Holy City* in San Francisco. Next month, he went to Los Angeles to take a role in an adaptation of Helen Hunt Jackson's novel *Ramona*, which focused on the story of a Spanish mission girl persecuted for bearing the child of an Indian (Griffith played the part of the Indian outcast, Alessandro). When *Ramona* finished its two-month tour, he played a comic detective for three months. In early 1906, he joined the repertory company run by Nance O'Neill, which was a highly professional troupe offering an excellent range of old classics and new plays. (The latter included *Judith of Bethulia*, which, a few years later, Griffith would use as the basis for his move to longer films.) Griffith, taking on more and more important roles, traveled with Miss O'Neill and her company in a tour that would eventually embrace ten states and four Canadian provinces. While the company was in Minneapolis in April 1906, he received a telegram from Linda with news of the San Francisco earthquake. Thinking over the matter for a few days, he wrote inviting her to join him in Boston toward the end of the tour. Leaving San Francisco on a refugee train, carrying a lunch box and clothes provided by the Red Cross, she took several days to cross the country. The couple were married on May 14, 1906, in Boston's Old North Church. The marriage license gave his age as thirty (he was actually thirty-one) and his occupation as "writing."[28]

Griffith's Writing

Griffith would later claim to have "been writing more or less all my life." One of his stage directors remembered him as "forever writing or reading from a manuscript which he carried with him" and Linda was deeply impressed in the early days of their relationship by the fact that he traveled with "a trunk full" of writings. Yet Griffith at first had entertained little hope of profiting financially from his hobby.[29] He apparently once sold the *New York World* for $5 an article he had written about Southern cooking. His first real success as a writer was a short vaudeville play set during the American Revolution and called *In Washington's Time*. After opening in Springfield, Massachusetts, in early 1901, it was also staged in Worcester, Washington, D.C., and New York. Four years later, it had a brief run in San Francisco, with Griffith and Linda Arvidson (her stage name) in the cast. It was, indeed, during his years in California that Griffith, encouraged by Linda, began to think more seriously about becoming a playwright. While working as a hop-picker, he began to gather material for a play he proposed to write. During the summer of 1906, living with his new wife in an apartment on New York's West Fifty-sixth Street, he finished that play, a romantic melodrama he called *A Fool and a Girl*. With the play finished, he set out both to sell it and—to stay financially afloat in the meantime—to find work as an actor. In retrospect, what then happened was a first step on the road to *The Birth of a Nation*, for Thomas Dixon Jr. had turned his anti-socialist novel *The One Woman* into a stage-play he hoped would enjoy the same theatrical success as *The Clansman*. When the play (like *The Clansman*) opened in Norfolk, Virginia, it had Griffith playing the lead role and his wife in the cast.[30]

Many years later, Griffith would use the climactic scene of the play—the main character being sent to the gallows as the first wife and the governor race in a car to reprieve him—in the ending of *Intolerance*. In the early fall of 1906, however, all that Dixon's adaptation of his novel seemed to hold out to Griffith and his wife was the hope of a long engagement. That hope, however, was not to be: after two months of touring with the play in Virginia, West Virginia, and the Carolinas, both Griffith and Linda received two weeks' notice.[31] In the long run, Griffith's firing by Dixon does not seem to have affected the relationship of the two men, and it was with Griffith's help that Dixon would finally be able to see his novel and play *The Clansman* transformed into a film.

Out of work, Griffith went back to the dreary daily round of theatrical agents and producers. Just before Christmas, his luck seemed to have changed. Actor/producer James K. Hackett bought the rights to *A Fool and a Girl* for $700 (according to Mrs. Griffith) or £1,000 (Griffith's own later recollection). Whatever the amount, it was the most money Griffith had ever had. He decided to stop touring for a while and devote himself to writing. For a time, it seemed that his gamble was paying off. The editor of *Cosmopolitan* paid him three cents a word for a story (Linda remembered $75), though he did not finally publish it in the magazine. *Leslie's Weekly*, by contrast, printed in early January 1907 a poem by Griffith called "The Wild Duck," for which they paid $15 (Griffith's recollection) or $6 (Linda's). Despite his best efforts, however, Griffith was unable to sell anything else and the summer of 1907 found him back in Norfolk, Virginia, pounding the boards in a historical pageant called *Pocahontas*. In the early fall, *A Fool and a Girl* opened in Washington. Constant changes were made to the play itself at the request of the cast during rehearsal (Griffith later remembered many occasions on which he was "ejected into the alley behind the theatre for objecting to changes in the script"). On opening night, a high proportion of the audience walked out. The critics savaged the play (prompting Griffith to publish a detailed rebuttal of one accusation that it offended propriety by mimicking "the art of Zola"). The controversy meant that the last performance of the week's run in Washington played to a full house, but after another week in Baltimore the play folded. Far from discouraged, Griffith promptly researched and wrote a four-act play, set in the era of the American Revolution, which he called *War*. When it was finished, however, it failed to find a producer. What must have seemed a complete disaster to Griffith at the time seems retrospectively the best thing that could have happened to him. For near the end of 1907, looking for work to see him through a difficult winter, he turned to the movies.[32]

Griffith and the Movies

Griffith claimed that he saw his first motion picture at a Fourteenth Street nickelodeon after he returned to New York from Washington in 1907. Richard Schickel, by contrast, suggests that this may have happened as early as 1898 while he was acting in Chicago.[33] But like most stage actors, Griffith looked down on movies and felt his reputation would be undermined if people saw him in one. *Writing* for the movies, however, was something different: it was anonymous and also paid comparatively well (from $5 to $30 for a scenario). There are differing accounts of who first recommended that he try his hand at the American Mutoscope and Biograph Company, usually known as the Biograph. Linda Arvidson remembered the suggestion coming from Max Davidson, an old acquaintance from the days of the Twilight Revellers who later graduated from the Yiddish theatre to silent film comedy.[34] Griffith would subsequently attribute it to the advice of a gloomy looking actor named Harry Salter. Sometime in December 1907, however, he presented himself with "an armful of hurriedly written scenarios" at the Biograph studio on 11 East Fourteenth Street. Interviewed by George McCutcheon, Biograph's only director, he also indicated his availability for acting roles.[35] It was, indeed, as an extra at $5 a day that Griffith began his relationship with the Biograph Company. His first small role was in *Falsely Accused!*, filmed in late December 1907.[36]

Although later writers would associate Griffith only with the Biograph, he also approached the Edison Studio in the Bronx hoping to sell a scenario (loosely based on *Tosca*). The studio was uninterested in the script but hired him to play the lead role in *Rescued from the Eagle's Nest*, filmed in early January. For a short time, Griffith alternated between the two studios: he was an extra for Biograph in *Classmates* in mid-January and for Edison in *Cupid's Pranks* around three weeks later.[37] But from mid-February, he seems to have worked exclusively for the Biograph Company. He had a principal role in *The Princess in the Vase*, made in February, and wrote the scenario for *Old Isaacs the Pawnbroker*, filmed in March. He had a leading role in *The Music Master* and was an extra in *The Sculptor's Nightmare*, both of them produced in April. In the same month, he appeared in *When Knights Were Bold* with Linda Arvidson, whom he had also encouraged to look for work at the studio (no one there knew until much later that the pair were married). During May and June, he acted in six more Biograph films, some based on his own scenarios, and seems increasingly to have specialized in villain roles.[38]

As a screen actor, Griffith was far from outstanding. He had a tendency to wave his arms about too much—G. W. "Billy" Bitzer, who photographed several of the films in which he appeared, was told off by the Biograph management for making it seem, in one of them, that Griffith had three or four arms. Bitzer also subsequently recalled advising him not to overact when playing a minor role as a bartender.[39] It did not matter very much because Griffith's rather brief career before the camera was already almost at an end. During the summer of 1908, McCutcheon became too ill to work. By this stage, Griffith had apparently already spoken of his desire to direct. After experimenting with a number of stopgap solutions (including McCutcheon's son, Wallace), the studio offered the job to Griffith. After a little hesitation (he was worried that he would cease to be employable as an actor), he accepted.[40]

The Adventures of Dollie, Griffith's first film as director, was a brief melodrama about a child stolen by gypsies, who is enclosed in a barrel and floats down a river until she is rescued by some boys out fishing. After studying other Biograph films, he offered the role of the anguished mother to his wife, whom he found (rather to his surprise) to be rather good at conveying emotion on screen. Unimpressed with the studio's leading men, he took a tour of theatrical agencies and hired Arthur Johnson, whom he met coming out of one of them, as the father. Charles Inslee, an actor Griffith had known on the West Coast, was asked to play the leader of the gypsies. The cameraman on the picture was Arthur Marvin, but Griffith apparently turned frequently for advice (though he did not always take it) to Bitzer, the other Biograph cinematographer. The film itself, Griffith later recalled, was made in two days at a total cost of $65. When it was completed, he moved on to other films: Griffith had already begun work on his sixth motion picture when *Dollie* opened. Linda Griffith remembered the favorable reaction of the audience at the Union Square nickelodeon to the single-reel, 713-foot film and subsequent demands for the film greatly exceeded that of any previous Biograph release. The company, quickly realizing that it had found its man, offered Griffith a permanent contract as its principal director.[41]

Griffith directed all Biograph films made between June 1908 and December 1909, as well as all the important ones over the next four years. During the 1908–1913 period, he directed in all more than 450 films, averaging around two every week.[42] Many of these were fairly short and simple. Griffith recalled that the pictures he had been making in 1909 and 1910 "ran about six or seven minutes on the screen and their cost averaged...about $150."[43] The films offered a vast range of stories. Griffith was fond of adapting classical or modern literature into motion pictures, and this tendency would increase over the years. He also directed Westerns, sea stories, and comedies. He was adept at producing urban crime melodramas, including *The Musketeers of Pig Alley* (1912), seen by one expert as introducing the principal themes and settings that would characterize "crime" films until today.[44] While the great bulk of his films had contemporary urban or rural settings, some were set in foreign parts and historical circumstances. One such circumstance, of course, would be of major importance for the future. Early American cinema, according to Jack Spears, regarded dramas played out against a Civil War background as a staple product.[45] Given his Kentucky background and recollections of his father, it is unsurprising that no less than eleven of Griffith's Biograph movies dealt with Civil War themes: *The Guerrilla* (1908), *In Old Kentucky* (1909), *The Honor of His Family* (1910), *In the Border States, or A Little Heroine of the Civil War* (1910), *The House with Closed Shutters* (1910), *The Fugitive* (1910), *His Trust* and *His Trust Fulfilled* (1911), *Swords and Hearts* (1911), *The Battle* (1911), and *The Informer* (1912).[46] These films, as Robert Lang has pointed out, often introduced "themes and scenes that would appear later in *The Birth of a Nation*."[47] The shot of the "Little Colonel's" homecoming in *Birth*, for example, was prefigured in *In Old Kentucky*. Elements of *Birth of a Nation* can be discerned in *Swords and Hearts* (the story of two families, one Northern and one Southern), *His Trust* and *His Trust Fulfilled* (loyal, faithful slaves) and *The Battle* (for the battlefield sequences).[48]

Griffith's arrival at the Biograph Company as a director coincided with a time of great change in the American film industry. The boom in nickelodeons and the move to changing films daily had created a demand for films that American producers were failing to meet: of the 1,200 motion pictures of one reel or less released in the United States in 1907, only around 400 were American-made.[49] Film exchanges had emerged; these greatly increased the number of films available as films could now be bought from manufacturers and rented to many exhibitors. American film manufacturers were competing among themselves for preeminence. One in particular, the Edison Company, was engaged in the latest stage of a long-running battle to control film production on the basis of its legal ownership of patents for the motion picture camera and film. Edison had no desire to drive its competitors out of business: it preferred to license them to make films, in the process exacting considerable royalty payments for the use of its patents. The company intended, once it had acquired a stranglehold on film production, to use its near-monopoly position to regulate the exchanges (and reduce their profits). By 1908, the main obstacle to the attempt to rationalize film production launched by the Edison Manufacturing Company was the American Mutoscope and Biograph Company, aided by a number of dissatisfied exchanges and importers of foreign films whom Edison was attempting to exclude from the market. Biograph, as it would come to be known, had two principal advantages that enabled it to survive the Edison campaign. Its camera did not infringe the Edison patents (indeed, it had been designed—by a former Edison employee —specifically *not* to do so). Moreover, it had Wall Street backing. Its main investor was the Empire Trust which, in the summer of 1907, engineered the appointment of one of its own men, businessmen Jeremiah J. Kennedy, as head of the Biograph Company.[50]

Kennedy rapidly proved himself an able leader in the battle with Edison. Under his leadership, Biograph began to acquire its own patents with which to threaten the Edison Combine. Each company filed numerous suits against the other. Meanwhile, to help beat Edison, Biograph expanded its film production, making two films a week to try to meet the demands of the exchanges. It was in the midst of this major attempt to boost production that the company found itself without a full-time director. According to Tom Gunning, it was "probably in near panic" when it offered Griffith the job.[51] Over the next few weeks and months, Griffith showed that he could produce films of sufficient quality to compete with those of the Edison Combine. Richard Schickel suggests that the manner in which Griffith's films were accepted "by exhibitors and public" was a factor in Edison's decision to abandon his battle with Biograph in favor of collaboration. This is unlikely: the new Motion Picture Patents Company [MPPC], integrating together the two combines, was incorporated on September 9, less than three months after the release of *The Adventures of Dollie*. For most of 1908, while battling each other publicly and in the courts, Edison and Biograph had been quietly negotiating behind the scenes for an accommodation. When the existence of the MPPC was officially announced in December, although Frank Dyer of the Edison Company was president, his vice-president was Henry N. Marvin, general manager of Biograph, and his secretary Jeremiah Kennedy, who remained president of the Biograph Company.[52]

The advent of the MPPC established the broad context within which Griffith worked. Those production companies, including the Biograph, that were part of the new combine found their position far stronger in relation to exchanges and exhibitors. Exchanges were now licensed and required to return films to producers after a fixed period of exploitation, encouraging the production of new films. In a more stable and secure environment, producers could invest more money in their films: Marvin raised Griffith's budget per film from $300 to $500.[53] The MPPC, responding to growing criticism of the moral impact of the movies by middle-class "progressive" reformers, declared its intention to produce "Moral, Educational, and Cleanly Amusing" motion pictures. At the back of this lay a general strategy of repositioning the film industry as a "higher class" (and therefore more expensive) form of entertainment that would appeal to "respectable" audiences. The MPPC swiftly realized that the new Board of Censorship (soon to be called the National Board of Censorship) set up in New York in March 1909 could be a useful instrument toward achieving this objective. It provided the Board with financial support and a screening room, and announced that all films made by MPPC members would be submitted to it for approval. As Tom Gunning points out, the necessity of submitting his films to the Board "certainly encouraged Griffith's use of moral discourse." (One of the very first films approved by the new Board was his prohibitionist attack on the saloon, *A Drunkard's Reformation*.) But things could sometimes go wrong: objecting to the sexual themes in the film and its excessive violence, the Board refused to approve Griffith's *The Heart of an Outlaw* (1909) without extensive cuts. Biograph objected, and since the Board refused to give way, the film was never released.[54]

The contract Griffith signed with Biograph in the summer of 1908 committed him to work for the company for one year at a salary of $50 a week. He was also to receive a royalty of one-twentieth of a cent on each foot of film sold—an encouragement, if one was needed, to produce as many films as possible.[55] Griffith settled into a schedule of producing two one-reeler movies each week. Many were shot in the Biograph studio inside an old brownstone house at 11 East Fourteenth Street, New York. Others were filmed wholly or partly on location at Fort Lee, New Jersey. Beginning in the summer of 1909, Griffith found another location site at Cuddebackville, a five-hour journey away in New York's Orange Mountains. In January 1910, searching for better weather, the sunshine that would permit longer hours of shooting in the open air, and new background locations, Griffith made the first of what would become annual winter trips to California.

During his years at Biograph, Griffith recruited a large and talented group of actors and actresses. The actors included Arthur Johnson, Owen Moore, Michael Sinnott (who would become better known as Mack Sennett), James Kirkwood, Henry Walthall, and Bobby Harron (a prop boy when Griffith arrived, Harron rapidly became Biograph's leading juvenile actor). Griffith's first actresses were Linda Arvidson (his wife), Marion Leonard, and Florence Lawrence. His later "discoveries" included Mary Pickford, Blanche Sweet, Mae Marsh, and the Gish sisters, Dorothy and Lillian. Griffith modeled the organization he created at Biograph on the theatrical stock companies he had known in his own acting career. He kept his actors up to speed by means of competition: everyone knew that a leading role in one production was likely to be followed by a supporting role only in the next. The repertory model, as well as being familiar to Griffith, had the great advantage of ensuring that he remained the sole focus of artistic power at the studio. At the same time, of course, it helped encourage the eventual defection of those with wider ambitions: Florence Lawrence, advertised as the "Biograph Girl," left the company in 1909 for the higher wages and personal star billing offered by Carl Laemmle's Independent Motion Picture Company.[56]

Griffith also either inherited or was able to recruit an accomplished group of technical and editorial assistants. Billy Bitzer, who had begun to work for the American Mutoscope Company (predecessor to Biograph) as a motion-picture cameraman at the end of 1895, shot almost all of Griffith's pictures. Bitzer had managed to employ Abe Sholtz, "the most skilled lab man in the business," as the developer for the films he made. It was the painstaking work of Sholtz, assisted by Joe Aller, a fellow Russian Jew, which helped turn Bitzer from an extremely good cameraman into a great one. James Edwards ("Jimmie") Smith, also already at Biograph when Griffith arrived, was soon promoted from working in the shipping room to editing his films—a skilled and very difficult task since, as Richard Schickel comments, Griffith hardly ever worked according to a script.[57] When Griffith first arrived at Biograph, the story department was headed by a former newspaperman, Lee "Doc" Dougherty, who had hired as chief scenarist Stanner E. V. Taylor, another sometime journalist and failed playwright. They were soon joined by Frank E. Woods, who had begun his career as a journalist on a small newspaper in Erie, Pennsylvania. After his move to New York, Woods became a pioneering film critic for *The Dramatic Mirror*. While continuing to write his "Spectator" column, however, he also began to submit scenarios. Soon he and Taylor were providing Griffith with most of the stories for his films.[58] A few years later, Woods would play a crucial role in the genesis of *The Birth of a Nation*.

At first, there was apparently little conflict between Griffith and the management of the Biograph Company. The president, Jeremiah J. Kennedy, was initially very much preoccupied with the battle against Edison and the formation of the MPPC. The vice-president and general manager, Henry Marvin, left Griffith much to his own devices. When Kennedy and Marvin occasionally visited the studio, they did so in such a discreet way as not to interfere with Griffith's filmmaking.[59] Although Griffith was worried during the negotiations for a new contract in the summer of 1909, the company eventually recognized his contribution by raising his salary and doubling his commission on each foot of film sold. His 1910 contract (on which he signed his real name instead of "Lawrence Griffith" for the first time) raised his commission once more, as did its successor of 1911.[60] However, royalty increases and the semi-autonomy enjoyed by Griffith—more or less complete control over his company of actors, the choice of scenarios to film, and the production of the films themselves—could not permanently conceal the fact that the Biograph management and Griffith approached film in very different ways. Kennedy and Marvin were businessmen; like Henry Ford, they were intent on producing a single, standardized product for a mass market (they coincidentally hired Griffith as a director in the same year as the first Model T cars were manufactured). The more one-reel films produced for nickelodeon audiences, the greater the profits for Biograph (hence the strategy of paying Griffith a royalty for each foot of film). Any expression of difference or individuality was firmly discouraged. Biograph films were company products, and the company refused to give credits to individuals, whether actors/actresses or the director himself (leading players became known as the "Biograph Man" or "Biograph Girl," with the films themselves simply referred to as "Biographs"). Having found a successful formula, moreover, the management of Biograph resisted change, especially when such innovations would threaten profits by increasing production costs. In the end, such conservatism would play a major role in Griffith's departure from the company and the ultimate demise of the Biograph company itself.

As a film director, Griffith was ambitious both for himself and his medium. Over the years, his aspirations came increasingly into conflict with what the Biograph management regarded as sound commercial practice. As Griffith refined his technique, shooting more and more film, the costs of filming rose.[61] He became frustrated, moreover, with Biograph's insistence that the maximum length of a film should be one 1,000-foot reel. Griffith was almost certainly aware that the Vitagraph Company, another member of the MPPC, had produced four longer films during 1909: *The Life of Napoleon* and *The Life of George Washington* (both two-reelers), *Les Misérables* (four reels), and *The Life of Moses* (five reels). In accordance with the policy of the Trust, these films were released one reel at a time, each to be shown separately. Yet by 1910, they were being shown together as multireel features in some places.[62] In November 1910, Griffith shot his own 2,000 foot film, *His Trust*. Instead of agreeing that it should be cut down to one-reel size, Griffith fought for his film and, as a compromise, it was finally released in two parts.[63] His second two-reeler, *Enoch Arden*, was released in June 1911. Again, Biograph insisted that it be issued as a serial, but when public demand compelled exhibitors to show the parts on consecutive days, the company finally gave in and allowed both reels to be shown on the same program.[64] During the next twenty-one months, almost all of the films Griffith produced were of the one reel or one half-reel length preferred by the company. Of the three exceptions, *A Temporary Truce* (released in June 1912) did not make up two reels and could consequently be shown as an ordinary part of a Biograph program. The company also accepted *Brutality*, a two-reel film exhibited for the first time in December 1912. But it drew the line at *The Massacre*, a 2,097-foot Western completed by Griffith in May 1912. Although *The Massacre* was released in Europe, which was largely untroubled by restraints on the length of films, the Biograph management refused to show it to American audiences. It was not released until February 1914 in the United States, and by that time Griffith had left the company.[65]

During 1912 and 1913 Griffith's relations with Biograph deteriorated over a number of matters. The company's management, at least at first, seemed to be offering movement on two issues: the attribution of credit and the length of films. In 1912, they finally agreed to identify Griffith and his leading actors by name, though only in publicity material and not credits on the films themselves. Before he left for California in December 1912, moreover, Griffith was also told that he might make a small number of two-reel films, though only after approval by the company's management in New York.

In reality, Kennedy and Marvin had probably already decided to move toward the production of longer films but not in a way Griffith would approve. Biograph had earlier assisted with the exhibition and promotion of the four-reel French import *Queen Elizabeth*, a filmed stage-play starring Sarah Bernhardt. To some shrewd observers, films of this kind represented the next step in the evolution of the motion picture industry. Adolph Zukor, who had also been involved in the distribution of *Queen Elizabeth*, had the idea of organizing "Famous Players in Famous Plays" as a direct consequence. In the spring of 1913, without the knowledge of Griffith, who was still in California, the Biograph company signed an agreement with theatrical producers Klaw and Erlanger to film some of their plays as five-reel motion pictures and show them in legitimate theaters.[66]

Griffith himself saw *Queen Elizabeth* as a step backward in cinematographic terms. Robert M. Henderson notes that it had only twelve shots on all four reels, compared to sixty-eight in Griffith's one-reeler *The Sands of Dee* (1912), and no close or medium shots.[67] A more accurate indication of the direction in which cinema was going was the very successful run of *Quo Vadis*, an eight-reel Italian spectacle, in New York. Although Griffith was unable to see it until his return from California, he almost certainly read reviews of *Quo Vadis* in the trade press and may have been encouraged to try to emulate it.[68] Of the thirty-two films Griffith is believed to have directed in California in 1913,[69] seven were of more than one reel. Some of these, including *The Little Tease*, were stretched versions of what started out as one-reelers; others, such as *The Yaqui Cur*, were approved as two-reelers in advance by the Biograph management. Two, however, must have disturbed Marvin and Kennedy considerably. For the shooting of *The Battle at Elderbush Gulch*, Griffith (without bothering to explain why to the company) had a mock-up of an entire Western town built in the San Fernando Valley. His plans for *Judith of Bethulia*, based on the play he had originally been introduced to while acting for Nance O'Neill's company, involved the construction of even more elaborate sets. *Judith* was clearly seen by Griffith as his answer to films such as *Quo Vadis*.[70] Released eventually in both four- and six-reel versions, it represented a major step forward in Griffith's artistry, bringing together all the skills—including the contrast between the personal and the spectacular—he had honed in his shorter films. Because of Griffith's insistence on large sets and expensive rehearsals, however, *Judith* cost twice as much as the $18,000 budgeted for it and seems to have been the final straw for the Biograph front office.[71] The company's management was appalled by the film's cost, its length, and some of its scenes, including the gruesome beheading of Holofernes by Judith.[72]

In July 1913, when Griffith returned from California, it was no longer to his old workplace on 11 East 14th Street but to a new and expensive studio at 175th Street in the Bronx that was a symbol of the prosperity of the Biograph company. Griffith could, with some justice, have seen himself as the principal architect of that prosperity. In the summer of 1912, he had asked J. J. Kennedy for stock in the Biograph Company or for 10 percent of the company's profits. There is no evidence that his demands were ever taken seriously. Kennedy simply regarded Griffith as "a small cog in the big wheel" that was Biograph. Moreover, a year later, he moved to clip the wings of his over-mighty director. At a meeting with Kennedy and Marvin, Griffith was informed that he must give up his control over budgets and expenditure. He was promised that additional directors would be hired and that he would be able to supervise their work. So far as *Judith* was concerned, he would finish shooting the final, interior scenes and edit it down to usable size (preferably as a serial with four episodes) but would not straightaway be assigned a new film to direct. At a subsequent meeting, Kennedy finally informed him that, though the company was about to embark on the production of longer films, as a result of the deal with Klaw and Erlanger, Griffith would have no part to play in directing them. If he remained with the company, he would be confined to directing traditional one-reelers. Once Griffith declined this humiliating proposition, his career with Biograph came abruptly to an end.[73]

Griffith's Reputation

On December 3, 1913, a one-page advertisement appeared in *The New York Dramatic Mirror*, placed there by Griffith's new personal attorney, Albert H. T. Banzhaf.[74] At one level, it was intended to rescue the work Griffith had done at Biograph from the anonymity to which company policy had habitually condemned it. The ad identified Griffith as the "producer of all great Biograph successes" and listed 147 he had directed (around a third of the actual total). It also laid claim to the longer films he had done but which Biograph had not yet released, including *The Massacre* and films he had shot earlier in the year in California: *Judith of Bethulia*, *The Battle of Elderbush Gulch*, and *Wars of the Primal Tribes*.[75] At another level, the ad was a skillful exercise in self-promotion, formulating and disseminating the idea of Griffith as the great director who had succeeded in "revolutionizing Motion Picture drama and founding the modern technique of the art." Among the innovations he had been responsible for, it was claimed, were the "large or close-up figures, distant views as represented first in Ramona, the 'switchback,' sustained suspense, the 'fade out,' and restraint in expression, raising motion picture acting to the higher plane which has won for it recognition as a genuine art."

Because *The New York Dramatic Mirror* ad was a crucial moment in the later construction of the Griffith legend, it is important to give the claims it made some consideration.[76] Griffith was not, of course, the first to use close-ups: Edwin S. Porter, for example, ended his early 1903 film *The Life of an American Fireman* with a close-range shot of a hand opening a fire-alarm box and pulling the alarm.[77] Porter also employed close-ups in the sense in which the ad in the *Dramatic Mirror* used the term: *The Great Train Robbery* (1903) included such a shot of the outlaw leader. Griffith, notes Edward Wagenknecht, had "been photographed in close-up in films made by others before he became a director."[78] Billy Bitzer, Griffith's principal cameraman, would later confess that the invention of the "fade out" or dissolve ought "really" to be credited to French filmmaker George Méliès.[79] The "distant" (or long or panoramic) shot also preceded the making of *Ramona*. It was often used in early Westerns. Griffith had made many of these, using locations at Fort Lee or Cuddebackville in the east.[80] By 1909, however, notes Eileen Bowser, he was producing fewer such films, in part because "the authentic western scenery appearing in Selig and Essanay films was making eastern landscape less acceptable."[81] Moreover, while Griffith's experiences in California in the early months of 1910 had a liberating effect on his filmmaking—Ramona proved only the first of a series of films in which the California landscape was used to accentuate the "spectacular" in filmic terms—he was not the first filmmaker to arrive in the state nor the first to see the possibilities it offered for location shooting.[82]

While Griffith, in collaboration with Bitzer, was not as pioneering as the ad in the *Dramatic Mirror* claimed, the films he made for the Biograph were distinguished by continual experimentation. In August 1908, shooting *For the Love of Gold*, for example, Griffith demanded something almost unheard of until then: a change of camera angle in the middle of a scene.[83] There were also many experiments with lighting, such as the firelight effects produced in *The Drunkard's Reformation* (1909) and *The Cricket on the Hearth* (1909).[84] Complicated patterns of lighting were also used in *Pippa Passes* (1909) to create the impression of a day as it progressed from sunrise to evening (so striking were these effects that *The New York Times* compared the film's deployment of light and shade to the work of the contemporary Secessionist photographers).[85] It is not clear from the record whether Griffith or Bitzer was primarily responsible for such effects (both would later independently claim the credit, for example, for the discovery of reverse or back-lighting).[86] The two worked extremely closely together for sixteen years. "If Mr. Griffith asked for some effect," Bitzer would later recall, "I tried one way or another to produce what he wanted. When it worked successfully, we were hailed as inventors."[87]

Griffith was one of a new group of film directors that included Ralph and Thomas Ince. Eileen Bowser points out that unlike the previous generation of filmmakers, most of whom had been "businessmen, technicians, cameramen with some variety-show people," most of these new directors had a background in road show drama or legitimate theater.[88] There were two main consequences of this change. The first was that the new directors often insisted on overseeing every aspect of their productions, including the composition of shots, lighting, and the makeup of the actors. In this sense, they were closer to successful contemporary stage directors such as David Belasco than to earlier filmmakers.[89] The second consequence was that they perceived cinema, like the theater, above all as a means of telling stories. To Griffith, the tricks and illusions that the camera could be made to perform were of significance only if they helped support this narrative function. As Tom Gunning has pointed out, while Griffith did not invent devices such as the close-up and the fade-out, he used them primarily to express characterization and help develop the story.[90] Filming *After Many Years* (based on Tennyson's "Enoch Arden" poem about a sailor supposedly lost at sea) in late October 1908, he asked Bitzer for a close-up of the grieving face of the wife. Bitzer was reluctant at first, not because close-ups were new (he had shot several himself) "but because they were virtually unheard of as a dramatic device in a narrative film."[91] Unlike the earlier close-up of the outlaw in Porter's *The Great Train Robbery*, which had no narrative significance (exhibitors were informed that it could go either at the start or the end of the film), Griffith's close-ups were designed to help audiences follow the story line by observing the emotional reactions of the characters at crucial dramatic moments.[92]

The close-up, of course, required greater restraint from actors: small gestures and slight changes in facial expression were usually a more effective way of conveying emotion than broader, more melodramatic movements and gestures. Acting in Griffith Biographs generally, in fact, was sometimes praised for being more restrained in style than that in other American productions of the time. One contemporary critic praised the fact that in *The Welcome Burglar* (1908), "characters act naturally, as real people."[93] It may well be, therefore, that Griffith's claim for "restraint in expression" in his *Dramatic Mirror* ad was more justified than some of the others he made. Roberta E. Pearson sees Griffith as playing a crucial role in the transformation of performance style in American film between 1909 and 1912, with the original "histrionic" style—heavily influenced by theatrical melodrama—giving way to a more "verisimilar" style, allied to the "realist" movements in literature and theater.[94] Ironically, during his brief career before the cameras, Griffith seems to have been a highly histrionic actor (assessing his acting performance, director Wallace McCutcheon succinctly commented that "He stinks!"). Confronted with McCutcheon's disapproval, however, and told off by Bitzer for waving his arms about, Griffith obviously learned from his own mistakes and was able, once he became a director, to pass on these lessons to his own actors.[95]

The claims made in The Dramatic Mirror ad that the "switchback" and "sustained suspense" were first introduced by Griffith are less justifiable. The "switchback" involved alternating scenes showing what takes place simultaneously in two or more locations, frequently building suspense until the various lines of action are brought together in the film's resolution. Half a decade before Griffith directed his first film, Edwin S. Porter had employed what Iris Barry termed "a rough form of cross-cutting" to display parallel action of this kind.[96] Griffith was quick, however, to embrace the technique; only a month into his directorial career, he used alternate shots as a means of increasing suspense in The Fatal Hour.[97] He was not, of course, the only moviemaker to use shots of this type: they appeared from 1908 onward in movies produced by a variety of companies, including Selig and Vitagraph.[98] But his skill at the kind of parallel editing required to stitch such shots together into a fast-moving narrative soon became clear.[99] It was a skill, moreover, that developed further over time; a comparison between The Lonely Villa (1909) and The Lonedale Operator (1911) shows Griffith's growing ability to inject suspense into a story by terse, highly selective editing.[100]

Clearly, Griffith's ad in The Dramatic Mirror claimed far too much. He had not been responsible for "revolutionizing Motion Picture drama," although one modern scholar, Tom Gunning, assigns him a major role in reorienting American cinema from being a "cinema of attractions" into a "cinema of narrative integration."[101] Nor had he really succeeded in turning film by 1913 into a "genuine art," even if he encouraged writer Louis Reeves Harrison to construct a myth of him as a "dreamer-artist" forced to leave Biograph in the face of opposition from "practical businessmen who tried to hold him back."[102] His claims to have invented new cinematic techniques were false; it is more accurate, as Eileen Bowser notes, to see his role as being "to consolidate what had been done sporadically by earlier filmmakers."[103] In retrospect, the most crucial part of the ad was the list of Biograph films Griffith had directed. Within a few months, he had made Biograph into the leading brand among American film-producers, an advantage it retained during the rest of his time with the company. As a consequence of Griffith's work as director, writes William K. Everson, "Biograph films became the yardstick by which all others were measured, critics referring to competing films as being 'up to' or 'below' Biograph standards."[104]

A New Commitment

Whatever the precise purpose of Griffith's December ad in the Dramatic Mirror, Richard Schickel points out that it was not a personal advertisement for work. Two days after the ad was published, the trade press announced that Griffith had signed a deal with Harry Aitken of Reliance-Majestic.[105] Aitken, born in Wisconsin in 1877, had worked in the insurance business before founding the Western Film Exchange in Milwaukee. He and his brother, Roy, subsequently built up a chain of film exchanges in the Middle West. Attempting to move into film production, they were effectively "frozen out" by the MPPC. Trying to find enough films to keep their exchanges operating, they turned first to independent companies outside the MPPC and then to importing European films. Within six months, however, it became obvious to the two that to satisfy demand, they would have to produce films of their own. In the fall of 1911, they formed the Majestic Film Company in Los Angeles, mainly to produce pictures starring Mary Pickford and her husband, Owen Moore, whom the Aitkens had persuaded to defect from Adolph Zukor's Famous Players. Soon afterward, they also acquired the Reliance Company and its studios in Yonkers, New York. The films produced by these studios, as well as a number of independents, were distributed through another Aitken company, the Mutual. Gaining the services of Griffith—a prominent director with a well-established reputation for productivity—made good business sense for the Aitkens. From the point of view of Griffith, the connection with the Aitkens was less immediately advantageous: his contract with the Majestic Company guaranteed him a salary of $300 a week (Zukor had apparently offered $50,000 a year). But it also removed two of his main grievances against the Biograph management. It guaranteed him stock in the company, and while committing him to direct and supervise the regular program features made by both Majestic and Reliance, it also allowed him to make two longer, independent films each year.[106]

While he would later deny it, there can be little doubt that Griffith was greatly impressed by the European "historical-spectacle" films, particularly *Dante's Inferno, Quo Vadis* and *Cabiria,* shown in the United States in 1912–13. His *Judith of Bethulia* may be seen, in part, as an answer to this European "invasion."[107] Filming in California since early 1910, moreover, he was aware that the scenery of the state offered a means of providing spectacle without the large and expensive sets used in such Italian productions as *Quo Vadis*.[108] Yet however much Griffith might dream of an *American* spectacle to rival such European imports, there was no immediate opportunity of making one. Griffith's own first independent film would have to wait until he had satisfied his contractual obligations to the Reliance-Majestic syndicate.

Almost all of the Griffith team of actors and technicians went with him to Majestic. "None of us," Lillian Gish later recalled, "felt that we were working for Biograph. Our ties were with Mr. Griffith." The hardest person to persuade to leave, in the end, was Bitzer, who believed that the new company was just as likely to be critical of Griffith's profligacy over film and money than was the old one.[109] Conscious of the need to impress—and raise money for—his new company bosses, Griffith improvised a studio in a loft near New York's Union Square, and quickly turned out a five-reel "potboiler," *The Battle of the Sexes*. He then transferred his company to California, where he successively produced *The Escape*, an early film about the consequences of a social disease; *Home Sweet Home*, a fictional version of the life of songwriter John Howard Payne; and *The Avenging Conscience*, loosely based on "The Tell-Tale Heart," a story by Edgar Allan Poe.[110] But by the spring of 1914, Griffith was increasingly preoccupied with what would be his first independent production and most ambitious project to date.

It was almost certainly Frank Woods who suggested *The Clansman* as the basis for a film.[111] Woods had been among several writers engaged in the doomed Kinemacolor project. He was apparently paid $200 for his efforts. Woods had not only returned to Biograph in late 1912, but he followed Griffith to Majestic a year later as scenario editor. When Griffith began to look for the story that could be the basis for his first really major film, Woods apparently showed him the version of the script of *The Clansman* he had written for Kinemacolor and suggested a new version of Dixon's play.[112] The story appealed to Griffith for all kinds of reasons, including his Southern background and the memories of his father. He probably read both novels by Dixon, *The Leopard's Spots* and *The Clansman*, at this point. According to Griffith's later recollection, the visual qualities of the stories appealed to him immediately: "I could just see these Klansmen in a movie with their white robes flying." He also saw Dixon's work as the basis for the "chase" movie to end all chase movies:

> We had had all sorts of runs-to-the-rescue in pictures and horse operas. The old United States cavalry would gallop to the rescue—East, one week; West the next. It was always a hit...the most surefire gag in the business...Now I could see a chance to do this ride-to-the-rescue on a grand scale. Instead of saving one poor little Nell of the Plains, this ride would be to save a nation.[113]

To clear the way to make the film, Griffith and the Aitkens set out to buy the rights to use both of his novels from Dixon himself. Negotiations did not run easily. When the four met together for the first time, Dixon apparently demanded $25,000.[114] He later came down to $10,000, possibly because—as Raymond Cook comments—his own plans to turn *The Clansman* story into a film had now been turned down by several production companies.[115] On top of the $40,000 Griffith estimated the filming was likely to cost, it was still too much for the Aitkens to consider (Roy would later recall that the "going rate" for a two- to four-reel script at the time was between $75 and $125). Dixon, who may have lost money in the Kinemacolor fiasco and was certain he needed cash up front, continued to demand $10,000 for the rights (Griffith remembered him as endlessly harassing the other three for this sum).[116] Finally, however, he was persuaded to accept $2,000 in cash and a quarter-share of the profits of the forthcoming film.[117] While he probably grumbled a good deal at the time, the deal in the end may have eventually earned him anything from one to several million dollars.[118]

With Dixon's agreement reluctantly secured, one major financial problem remained to be resolved. When Harry Aitken presented the plans to make *The Clansman* to the Majestic board of directors, they turned the project down. Even bankers Felix Kahn and Crawford Livingston, whom the Aitkens had counted on for support, argued that Griffith's film would cost too much and be too big a risk. Finally, the Aitken brothers, with much difficulty, put together a syndicate to finance the picture. At some stage of the early summer of 1914, they wired Griffith that $25,000 had been raised. A week later, they managed to find the additional funding to bring the total up to the $40,000 Griffith thought would be necessary to produce his film.[119]

To the task of making the new film, Griffith brought all the skills he had acquired during his twelve years as an actor and six as a film director. He had already made eleven films about the Civil War era; there was no reason to suspect at least initially that the twelfth would be any more controversial. Opinions differ concerning the racism of Griffith's earlier films. Daniel Bernardi argues that Griffith's own racism was inextricably bound up with his mastery of cinematic form: that the narrative and stylistic techniques he used in his Biograph movies were deployed to help establish a hierarchy of races with the whites on top and non-whites beneath them.[120] Yet Griffith also gave a degree of agency to some of his non-white characters—the black "hero" of *His Trust* and *His Trust Fulfilled*, for example—and certain film scholars have seen his portrayal of Native Americans, in some films, as unusually liberal for his time.[121] What he plainly did not foresee was that in seeking to make a spectacular film that would be seen by millions, he was also inaugurating a new struggle over the representations of racial and other groups in the new mass media.

4

Making *The Birth of a Nation*

The Story

If there ever was a scenario for shooting *The Birth of a Nation*, it disappeared a long time ago. Raymond Allen Cook claims that sometime in early 1914, Dixon and Griffith spent several weeks working on such a scenario in a loft in New York's Union Square.[1] This *may* be true, although Dixon's demands for financial compensation for the rights to his work (and dissatisfaction when the full amount was not forthcoming) make it unlikely. In any case, there was probably already a scenario of sorts, the one prepared by Frank E. Woods in 1912 for the unsuccessful Kinemacolor version of *The Clansman*. Early prints of *The Birth of a Nation* contain a credit for a "Story by D. W. Griffith and Frank E. Woods." The film's copyright also jointly credited the scenario to Griffith and Woods.[2] What appears most likely is that Griffith and Woods worked closely together as they had at Biograph to refashion Dixon's novels (with some additional material from his play) into a narrative treatment that could be used at the start of filming. The fate of that original scenario (as well as his improvised way of working) was suggested by Griffith in an article he published in 1917:

> At an early stage of the work, after the rough outlines have been filled in, the scenario is thrown away. The building and rebuilding of the story, the piecing of the intimate bits and the discarding of the useless go right on ... from day to day.[3]

For the characters in the story, Griffith and Woods seem to have decided to use Dixon's novel *The Clansman*—rather than the play of the same name—as

81

the basis for their scenario. Some characters, of course, had been common to both novel and play (Dr. Cameron, Ben Cameron, Austin Stoneman, Elsie Stoneman, Silas Lynch, and Gus) and naturally went into the film. Other characters from the novel who had failed to make it into the play were now reinstated: Mrs. Cameron, Margaret Cameron, Stoneman's housekeeper/mistress Lydia Brown, and his son Phil. Griffith had a liking for "family" stories, and most of the additions to the cast list of the play were clearly intended to build the film fundamentally around the struggle between (and within) two families by establishing a counterpoint between the Southern Camerons and the Northern Stonemans.[4] Thus, in the film, Phil Stoneman acquired a younger brother, Tod, and Ben Cameron two such brothers, Wade and Duke. Moreover, Gus's victim, Marion Lenoir in the play, became Flora, youngest daughter of the Camerons, in the movie.[5] The Camerons' faithful black servants reappeared under the names (Mammy and Jake) accorded them in the novel rather than the play (which, oddly, revived the names Nelse and Eva, originally given by Dixon to the "faithful souls" in *The Leopard's Spots*).

As well as building up the "family" angle for the film, Griffith and Woods probably determined at an early stage to simplify the story line by cutting minor characters from the play (Helen Lowell, Nellie Graham, Dick, and General Nathan Bedford Forrest, the Imperial Wizard of the Ku Klux Klan). They almost certainly decided to remove most of the national "political" struggles of the novel (Lincoln and Andrew Johnson, his successor as president, versus "radicals" Secretary of War Stanton and Congressman Stoneman) and the local political struggles (involving Lynch and Governor Shrimp) of the play. Lincoln still appeared in several scenes of the film, and there was one sequence showing a confrontation between Lincoln and Stoneman over the form postwar Reconstruction should take; but otherwise the film would largely turn its back on political drama to favor a combination of spectacular drama and familial melodrama.

Perhaps the most crucial difference between Dixon's work and the film planned by Griffith and Woods was its starting point. Whereas the novel began in the final days of the Civil War and the play with the South Carolina elections of 1867, the film expanded Dixon's story backward to the eve of the war. For the family stories the film was telling, this shift allowed Griffith to flesh out the Civil War as a conflict between "kith and kin" who were divided by very little apart from geography. It also made much sense in terms of the commemorations of the Civil War that were then taking place. Griffith, who had himself made eleven Civil War films, was hardly unaware that the year in which he planned to release his first really major "spectacular" picture was likely to see perhaps the biggest celebration of all: the fiftieth anniversary of the ending of the war.

The Clansman, therefore, would be both a "family" film and a Civil War film. Moreover, as Griffith's later comments made plain, he visualized the picture from the beginning as a melodramatic "chase" movie with the Klansmen riding to the rescue. In the end, there are actually *two* chase sequences: the Klan rides first to rescue Elsie Stoneman from Silas Lynch, and subsequently (in a virtual recreation of the climactic scene of *The Battle of Elderbush Gulch*) to save assorted Camerons and Stonemans from the attack by black soldiers on the log cabin in which they have taken refuge.

Casting the Film

One afternoon in spring 1914, Lillian Gish later remembered, Griffith took her aside from the set of *Home Sweet Home* which was then being filmed on the Reliance-Majestic lot in California and asked her to stay on after the end of the working day. It was a typical thing for Griffith to do in the early stages of a new film project. Later, with most of the eventual cast of *The Birth of a Nation* assembled, Griffith broke the news of his plans to turn Dixon's story into a film and swore everyone to secrecy.[6]

The subsequent process of assigning roles in the new film was not always a simple one. One of those Gish remembered as present when Griffith announced his project was Henry B. Walthall. A Southerner (born in Alabama) who had started, like Griffith, as a stage actor, Walthall had been a member of the Griffith company for five years. With his "patrician's face—coal-black hair waving off a splendid forehead," the director thought him in many ways ideal for the leading role of Ben Cameron. But Griffith also ideally wanted an actor who would somehow "epitomize all the heroes of The Lost Cause" and would have preferred someone "at least six feet tall with a powerful physique." Walthall was too much on the small side ("about five feet six"), slightly too old for the part (he was in his late thirties), and though Griffith charitably never mentioned it, had a drinking problem. But no younger, physically more imposing actor was ever identified, so Griffith finally resolved to give Walthall the role (trying to head off possible criticism of his size by giving him the affectionate label "The Little Colonel" in intertitles and attempting to make him look younger by wearing wide-brimmed hats to soften the light on his face).[7]

If Walthall, as the male lead, was a little old for the role, the striking thing about the actresses playing the female leads is how amazingly *young* they all were. Lillian Gish, who played Elsie Stoneman, was only twenty in the summer of 1914; Mae Marsh, acting the part of Flora Cameron ("Little Sister") was eighteen; and Margaret Cooper, cast as the oldest Cameron sister, Margaret, was only nineteen. All three, as they would acknowledge in their later interviews and writings, were essentially Griffith "creations," and all had become movie actresses to some extent by accident.

Lillian Gish and her younger sister, Dorothy, came from a theatrical background. Their father had deserted the family, and their mother, to make ends meet, had turned to the stage. Both Lillian and Dorothy were child actresses and toured the country for several years with stock companies. At some point, the Gishes became friendly with a similar all-female theatrical family, the Smiths. Later, Lillian's mother attempted to abandon the touring lifestyle for a time by opening an ice-cream parlor in East St. Louis. There was a nickelodeon next door showing a film called *Lena and the Geese*. When Lillian went to see it, she realized that the girl playing Lena was none other than young Gladys Smith. Shortly after this, both the nickelodeon and the Gish ice-cream parlor were destroyed by fire. Abandoning St. Louis, the family traveled to New York in search of work on the stage. Sometime in the summer of 1912, Lillian and Dorothy set off to visit Gladys Smith at the Biograph studio. After some initial confusion (Gladys Smith was now known as Mary Pickford), they met their friend, who introduced them to D. W. Griffith. What began as a social visit quickly turned professional: Griffith was impressed by the sisters, especially Lillian, and was in need of two young girls for roles in a melodramatic chase film, *An Unseen Enemy*. Ignoring their protests, he swept them off into an instant rehearsal with other members of the Biograph company, including Walthall, Lionel Barrymore, Elmer Booth, Harry Carey, and Bobby Harron. Lillian remembered Griffith firing an actual gun to induce the expressions of real fright he wanted on the girls' faces. The next day, they reported back to the studio for the shooting of the film itself.[8]

Lillian Gish and D. W. Griffith. Gish would entitle her autobiography *The Movies, Mr. Griffith and Me*. (Epoch/The Kobal Collection)

Mary Warne Marsh—renamed Mae Marsh by Griffith, perhaps to avoid having two Marys in his company—also had a sister, in this case an elder one, who was an actress. Marguerite Marsh had begun her career on the New York stage. After rejoining her family in Los Angeles, she started to make films. In January 1912, Mae, wanting to follow in her sister's footsteps, persuaded Marguerite to take her along to the Biograph studio. There she met Griffith, who seems to have been impressed. Mae Marsh was later given a role in *A Siren of Impulse*, released in March 1912. Her first starring role, in *Man's Genesis*, came about because neither Blanche Sweet nor Mary Pickford would appear in a film wearing a grass skirt that showed their bare legs. Partly because he liked rotating his company and probably partly because he was still annoyed at their behavior, Griffith subsequently ignored the resentment of Pickford and Sweet to give the leading female role in *The Sands of Dee* to Marsh. When Griffith and his company returned to New York, Mae Marsh remained in Los Angeles, where she appeared in two Kalem productions. After Pickford decided to leave Biograph, however, Griffith wired her to come and join his company on a permanent basis. She also followed him to Majestic, appearing in several of his 1914 releases.[9]

Anthony Slide points out that unlike other Griffith actress, such as Gish and Marsh, Miriam Cooper "was not a delicate beauty." Dark-haired and athletic, she had been educated first at convent schools and then at the Arts Students League and the Cooper Union High School in New York. She became a model while still in school for well-known painter and photographer Harrison Fisher. She seems to have done a day's work around 1910 as an extra on a Griffith film, but most of her early film work—again as an extra—was with the Kalem Company. Kalem, indeed, invited her to join their stock company in Florida, and with the reluctant consent of her mother, she accepted. In 1912 and 1913 she appeared in over 100 Kalem pictures, sometimes as a leading lady, at other times as an extra. In December 1913, Griffith invited her to become a member of his company at Majestic. His reasons for doing this are unclear. He may have seen and observed something special in her Kalem productions (he was an enthusiastic moviegoer),[10] or Mae Marsh, who appeared in two Kalem pictures in 1912, may have met and recommended Cooper to him. Her first film for Griffith (which also featured Marsh and Gish) was *Home Sweet Home*.[11]

Separated from Linda Arvidson since 1911, there is little doubt that Griffith was attracted to many of the young actresses in his company. Years later, Cooper remembered being told by Marsh that she sometimes (behind his back) called Griffith "Mr. Heinz" because he liked to be surrounded by "57 Varieties" of girls.[12] It would be a graceless and pointless task to speculate on the precise nature of the relationship between Griffith and his young female stars. Almost none of them ever commented on the subject (though Miriam Cooper did later claim to have rebuffed the director when he tried to kiss her).[13] What is important is that Griffith, in his films, associated blondeness with innocence and frailty, which perhaps helps to explain why Lillian Gish was given the part of Elsie Stoneman.

Because Gish and her sister had joined the Griffith company comparatively recently, Lillian suspected that she might only be an extra in the big film Griffith planned. But during an early rehearsal, Blanche Sweet, whom Gish and many others assumed would be given the role of Elsie Stoneman, was absent. Griffith, pointing at Gish, said "Come on, Miss Damnyankee, let's see what you can do with Elsie." The scene being rehearsed was the "near-rape" one in which Silas Lynch, the mulatto leader, proposes to Elsie and, when she rebuffs him, chases her round the room intent on forcing his attentions on her. Gish recalled that in the excitement of the chase (and her desire to impress Griffith), the pins came out of her very long blonde hair so that it tumbled down below her waist. When she finally "fainted," Lynch held her in such a way that her hair and feet "almost touched the floor on both sides of him." Gish believed she appeared "very blonde and fragile-looking," in comparison to the dark Lynch (played by Griffith's assistant George Siegmann in black-face), and watching Griffith's reaction, began to feel that the role might be hers.[14]

Certainly, from Griffith's point of view, the slender Gish could appear more vulnerable in the role of Elsie than could Sweet, with her fuller, more mature figure. Gish had already demonstrated her aptitude for playing innocent victims, most notably as the woman who loses both her unfaithful husband and her baby in *The Mothering Heart* (Biograph, 1913). Moreover, as Richard Dyer has pointed out, she offered an ethereal whiteness on screen that both underlined the feminine purity of Elsie and emphasized the miscegenational contrast with the black and threatening Lynch.[15] Finally, in considering Griffith's selection of Gish for the role of Elsie, it is worth remembering that, as Richard Schickel notes, he "was beginning to be romantically taken with her."[16]

If who would play Elsie was unclear at first, there seems to have been little doubt in Griffith's mind who would be the other white female leads. The part of Flora Cameron was by no means an easy one since, as Griffith remarked, it ran "the gamut from comedy to the height of tragedy." Moreover, the actress playing Flora would have to age five years or so in the movie. While Griffith claimed to have rehearsed Mae Marsh in the part to make sure she could do it, there is no evidence that he ever seriously considered anyone else. Marsh would remember being virtually type-cast for the role. "You remind me so much of my little sister. You are a little sister," Griffith said when offering her the part.[17] Moreover, he explained to *Photoplay* (October 1916), Miriam Cooper was the obvious choice for Flora's elder sister because she—despite her Northern upbringing—"was a perfect type of the beauty prevalent below the Mason and Dixon line." Indeed, Griffith insisted, he had kept Cooper "in the company for all the months between the idea that I might make the picture until the work began, because I knew she would be an exact 'Cameron' girl."[18]

The other members of the Cameron family were played by Spottiswoode Aitken (Dr. Cameron) and Josephine Crowell (Mrs. Cameron), both established members of the Griffith company, with Maxfield Stanley as Wade, the second son, and J. A. Beringer as Duke, the youngest.[19] Ralph Lewis, who would soon become stereotyped as a screen villain, had the role of Elsie's father, the Honorable Austin Stoneman. Elmer Clifton played the eldest Stoneman boy, Phil, and Bobby Harron assumed the role of Tod, the youngest. The colored servants of both families were played by white actors and actresses wearing blackface: Jennie Lee was the Cameron's Mammy and William de Vaull was Jake, with Mary Alden as Lydia Brown, Stoneman's housekeeper, and Tom Wilson as the other Stoneman servant. Elsie's white maid was played by Miriam Cooper's sister, Lenore.

The decision to have no black actors in major roles in the film would later be one of the many grounds on which Griffith would be criticized. He himself declared that "on careful weighing of every detail concerned, the decision was to have no black blood among the principals; it was only in the legislative scene that Negroes were used, and then only as 'extra people.' "[20] This was a remarkable statement, both for what it did say and what it did not. It minimized the role of African Americans in *The Birth of a Nation*. In reality, quite a number of black extras were used: they were housed in separate "barracks" near the Griffith lot.[21] They appeared much more often than Griffith suggested: Gish, for example, remembered their presence in the scene in which the visiting Stoneman boys were taken out to visit the cotton fields and the plantation, and blacks can also be identified in the closing stages of the film in the battle for Piedmont.[22] (One black actress, Madame Sul-Te-Wan, who would remain close to Griffith for the rest of his life, was visible in at least three shots.)[23] Instead of defending his decision not to use black actors in major roles in terms of their unavailability in California, or the expense of bringing them from the East Coast, or his preference for working with the actors from his own company (some or all of which Griffith and his defenders would later argue),[24] it is highly revealing that the director's attempt to explain himself was initially couched in terms of straightforward racism: the desirability of excluding "black blood."

Since there were no makeup men or women, Mary Alden (as Lydia Brown), George Siegmann (as Silas Lynch), and Walter Long (as Gus) had to make themselves up as mulattoes (Alden and Siegmann) or as a pure black (Gus) by using burned cork. They must all have known that especially in close-up, there was no chance of being mistaken for the real thing. As Karl Brown, Bitzer's assistant, would later recall, Long "made no effort to look like a real Negro. He put on the regular minstrel-man blackface makeup, so there could be no mistake about who and what he was."[25] Wearing minstrel makeup, of course, associated *The Clansman* as a film with the codes of another form of popular entertainment.[26] It may also have created the freedom (even the expectation) that the character concerned would behave more histrionically than would otherwise have been the norm. Besides the fact that the three principal characters who were "colored" were clearly labelled as villains, they were also the only characters in the film to show anything in the way of real passion—as when Lydia Brown has a fit of frustration over her treatment by Charles Sumner, Lynch plans to rule a "Black Empire" with Elsie as his queen, and Gus chases Flora while literally (thanks to the help of a bottle of hydrogen peroxide) foaming at the mouth.[27]

If the fictional villains of the film (including Stoneman) were presented as grotesques—figures drawn from the melodramatic imagination—they were balanced by nonfictional characters who looked at least to a degree like their counterparts of the Civil War era. Joseph E. Henabery, who in the end played Abraham Lincoln, later speculated that if there had not been financial problems over making *The Clansman* Griffith might have preferred to have hired an actor such as Benjamin Chapin, already well known for his Lincoln impersonations on stage. Henabery, having watched several actors dressed as Lincoln appear at the studio, did some research of his own at the Los Angeles Public Library on Lincoln's appearance. Convinced that with makeup he could do a better job than the actors he had seen, he asked Robert Woods to speak to Griffith on his behalf. Invited by the director to make up and try out the Lincoln costume for the role, he spent much of the next two days, complete with wig, padding, and heavy makeup, broiling under the hot Californian sun while Griffith never spoke to him once. Having given up in discouragement on both days (and twice being told off for leaving the set without permission), he was finally, to his surprise, told to report early the next day and to put on his makeup for the Lincoln role.[28] Gish later recalled that the search for Mary Todd Lincoln "ended when we found a woman with an uncanny similarity to the First Lady working in wardrobe" and that "Members of Mr. Lincoln's cabinet were chosen on the basis of facial resemblance to the historical characters."[29] Raoul Walsh, playing John Wilkes Booth, had the dark intense good looks of Lincoln's assassin.[30] Finally, Donald Crisp, Howard Gaye, and Sam de Grasse, all wearing full makeup, created reasonably good impressions (respectively) of Grant, Lee, and Charles Sumner.

When he was not playing Silas Lynch, George Siegmann functioned as Griffith's main assistant on *The Clansman*. Despite his forbidding exterior, he was a warm-hearted and much-loved man, yet also one who was "sensitive to Griffith's every whim" and "powerful enough to bend everyone else to his will."[31] Other members of Griffith's company who also doubled as assistant directors were Elmer Clifton, Donald Crisp, Bobby Harron, and Raoul Walsh. With the exception of Harron, all would eventually become well-known directors in their own right, as would Griffith's "Lincoln," Joseph Henabery. One of the bit-part players, who fell off the roof of a building during the raid on Piedmont, was Erich von Stroheim, who subsequently took the first step on the road to his own directorial career by being promoted to assistant director.[32]

Lillian Gish remembered that to economize as much as possible, members of the regular Griffith company often played several different roles.[33] Joseph Henabery, who became a full member of the company while *Birth of a Nation* was being made, later recalled that through careful makeup he was able to appear in the film as thirteen entirely different characters. In one sequence, by the use of cross-cutting, he appeared both as a black man fleeing white soldiers and one of the pursuing whites.[34]

There were also far fewer extras than the later publicity for the film would claim. The battlefield sequences probably had no more than 300 to 500 at most. Griffith created the impression of large armies, according to Gish, by beginning with a close-up and then moving the camera farther away from the scene, thus creating an "illusion of depth and distance," and having the same soldiers run around to make a second entrance.[35] Extras were hired by the day for $1.10 or $2.00 (depending on the authority) and a free lunch.[36] They remained, for the most part, entirely anonymous. One exception was the man playing the Union soldier guarding the entrance to the military hospital where the "Little Colonel" was recuperating, who made plain—to the audience's amusement—both his attraction to Elsie Stoneman and his awareness of her unattainability. Twenty-five years later, William Freeman, the man who had played the "mooning sentry," introduced himself to Lillian Gish at the 1939 World's Fair in New York.[37]

Rehearsals

While finishing *The Avenging Conscience* in May, Griffith began rehearsals for *The Clansman* that would continue for two months before shooting began, bringing his cast together in "a makeshift building of cheap rough pine." A small hall served as makeup room for the extras and there were only "hard kitchen chairs" to sit on (Griffith believed that more comfortable seating would loosen his players' concentration). Once roles had been assigned (and some of the early rehearsals were intended to try out performers in different parts), each player got to know very thoroughly the scenes in which he or she was to play.[38] According to Karl Brown, Bitzer's assistant, Griffith directed these rehearsals as

> strictly ad-lib, off-the-cuff improvisations to see what would work and what would not. He started with a central idea from which the story grew and took shape and came to life through his manipulation of these living characters. It was his way of writing... Instead of working with a pen or pencil, or through the mind and artistry of a professional writer, however skilled, he sculptured his thoughts in living flesh, to see and feel and sense what could be achieved and what could not, and

to know in advance what scenes would "play" and which would not. This called for a sort of cut-and-try, or trial-and-error procedure.[39]

Joseph Henabery, who participated in many of these rehearsals, also emphasized their experimental quality, with Griffith and his company beginning "to unravel the story and translate it into action, rather crude at first, but gradually bits of business were conceived and developed... Difficult situations were simplified or smoothed out and made plausible." According to Henabery, Griffith kept an open mind and was receptive to suggestions from the cast, although this was rather contradicted by his account of the shocked reaction of other actors when he disagreed with the director over how a particular shot of Lincoln should be taken.[40]

The rehearsal of a simple scene, Brown remembered, might be tried two, three, five, or a dozen different ways. After a number of such rehearsals, Bitzer recalled, Griffith had the habit of disappearing for a while to his otherwise rarely used office and lying down on a couch. Bitzer came to believe that rather than planning the mechanics of the scene he was rehearsing, Griffith was really "giving his people a chance to get into the mood or attitude of what he expected of them."[41] And rehearsals were not just for the actors. Everyone involved in the production—whether responsible for settings, props, costumes, or photography—also attended with notebooks and sketch pads ready as "everything was not only worked out but *thought* out to the finest detail." The need for doors, windows, drapes, and props became clear as rehearsal followed rehearsal. It became apparent to Griffith's chief carpenter, Frank ("Huck") Wortman, "what sets to build and how to build them." Rehearsals demonstrated to Ralph DeLacey, the props man, what would be needed so that he could start "rummaging in secondhand shops, pawnshops, or even cellars and attics of old-timers." Finally, they showed Bitzer the scenes he would have to shoot and helped him plan how to do it.[42] It was through Bitzer that the cast eventually learned when Griffith was satisfied that a particular scene was ready to be shot. Since the director timed a scene only when it was pretty much in its final form, when Bitzer appeared with a scratch pad and took out his watch it signaled that the rehearsal process for that scene was almost over.[43]

This rehearsal method was common in the early American movie industry, but it had never been used before for so long and complicated a film as *The Clansman*. The lack of any kind of systematic shooting script still appears startling to modern commentators.[44] Yet, as Joseph Henabery later commented, "Either with or without a script, there has to be planning."[45] Sets had to be built, props acquired, and costumes ordered. As preparations for the film increased in tempo, Gish recalled that sets began to go up, costumes arrived, and "mysterious crates, evidently filled with military equipment, were delivered."[46] The construction of sets was the responsibility of "Huck" Wortman, then a "down-to-earth," rather solid man in his forties who chewed tobacco incessantly.[47]

A carpenter and self-taught designer, Wortman could build anything Griffith wanted. Gish remembered the director consulting him on the sets to be built even *before* rehearsals began for *The Clansman*:

> He would show Huck a photograph that he wanted copied, or point out changes to be made in the reproduction. They would decide how the sun would hit a particular building three, four, even five weeks from then.[48]

If Gish's memory is correct, of course, it would mean that Griffith—while he may have had no shooting script—had the scenes he planned to shoot (and possibly the order in which he planned to shoot them) visualized from a very early stage.[49]

According to Karl Brown, there was a vacant lot just opposite the Griffith studio at the point where Sunset Boulevard curved to the west and Hollywood Boulevard began. Once this had been leased, Wortman and his crew of former stage carpenters built a whole Southern street on it in "violated" or forced perspective (with the buildings farthest from the camera's position being smaller so that the street would look longer and more imposing when photographed).[50] The Camerons' house, Brown would later recall, "was built on the studio grounds, just inside the gate at the western end, along with Piedmont Street, which ran back to where the dressing rooms were hidden by a return piece that blocked the camera vision."[51]

Gish insisted that Griffith did "meticulous research" for *The Clansman*. At least as far as the outward appearance of things was concerned, there was some truth in this. Several of the historical scenes and tableaux were based on Matthew Brady photographs from the war period. Moreover, the director telegraphed a South Carolina newspaper for photographs of the interior of the state house and had Wortman construct the set of the state legislature to correspond with the pictures. To build the largest interior set for the film, intended to represent Ford's Theatre where Lincoln was assassinated, Wortman and his crew also "had authentic still pictures of the real theater to guide them."[52] It was not merely sets that Wortman had to provide. There were no authentic cannons from the Civil War era available in the West, so the construction crew also had to create guns, carriages, and caissons. Their "bible" in this respect was *Battles and Leaders of the Civil War*, a classic work originally published by the Century Company in 1894 but reprinted in a very cheap edition by a New York newspaper in 1912. The detailed pictures of guns and other military equipment allowed Wortman and his team to make realistic-looking simulations.[53] The same book also helped the Goldstein costume house provide uniforms for both Northern and Southern armies. The firm made no real effort to produce uniforms that fit well, but, according to Karl Brown, that too added to the "authentic" look of the film ("one glance at a Brady picture proved that the real uniforms had been turned out in quantity far from the field of action and that nothing fit anybody").[54] There was one area, however, in which authenticity had to take a back seat: while Civil War muskets were easily obtainable from a firm called Bannerman's in New York, they had all been converted to fire metallic cartridges loaded through the breech. Given the limitations of the "army" of extras who would do the film's "fighting," there was no real possibility—even if the money could have been found to convert the guns back again—of training them how to load muskets with ramrods through the muzzle.[55]

Shooting *The Birth of a Nation*

Griffith chose to begin shooting his film on a symbolically important date: July 4, Independence Day. His biographer speculates that he may have decided to do this as a means of "announcing his own independence not only from the niggling [financial] concerns of the Aitkens back East, but of all the conventions that had ruled American films in their infancy."[56] It is unclear what scenes were shot this first day. According to Karl Brown, they focused on the election near the beginning of Reconstruction in South Carolina. Carpetbaggers were photographed plying newly freed slaves with alcohol and supplying each of them with multiple marked ballots for the elections. There followed a celebration with a lot of dancing.[57] Brown's recollection was contradicted by Billy Bitzer and Raoul Walsh, each of whom insisted that the first scene shot was the battle of Petersburg.[58] On the face of it, Petersburg seems the likelier possibility. It made sense for Griffith to shoot the large-scale scenes first—the battle of Petersburg, the Klan's ride to the rescue—while he had the money to pay the extras and the time to reshoot if he thought it necessary.

Considerable preparation had already been made for shooting the battlefield sequences. In common with most of the other location shots, they were filmed in relatively close proximity to the studio. Griffith, who had studied maps of the battle, recreated the field of Petersburg, with the help of a number of Civil War veterans he had recruited, just below Cahuenga Park in the San Fernando valley, in an area that is now part of Forest Lawn Memorial Park.[59] In filming the battle, Gish claimed, he directed both armies by shouting through a megaphone from the top of a forty-foot tower. When the din of the battle made it no longer possible to hear him even with a megaphone, a system of magnifying mirrors let him pass on instructions round the battlefield.[60] In reality, Griffith seems to have used a system of flags to communicate with groups of extras: Raoul Walsh remembered a white flag being used to start the action and Karl Brown recalled flags of different colors being used to tell particular groups to advance or retreat.[61] Each group of extras was controlled by one of Griffith's many assistant directors. Since every sequence shot was preceded by a meeting in which Griffith outlined in general terms the action that was to follow, the assistants' job once shooting began was to watch from the middle of their group (where they wore uniforms and also acted as extras) for signals telling them to move forward, pull back, or stop and fight in accordance with the director's master plan.[62] The battle sequences took around three days to shoot, with most extras being needed on the first day.[63] To take advantage of the cross light from the right in the morning and the left in the afternoon, all filming was done from camera placements facing north. Gish recalled that Griffith, to help audiences distinguish further between the armies with their differently colored uniforms, arranged things so that the Confederate forces always entered from the left of the camera and the Union army from the right.[64]

Other shots were done on location in the surrounding hills (the Little Colonel's inspiration for the Ku Klux Klan), the area near Whittier between southern Los Angeles County and Orange County (the Klan rides), and the Ojai Valley in Ventura County (once Griffith discovered that it was cheaper to bring actors to the horses than vice versa for the Klan shots). Seymour Stern later maintained that some group shots of the Klan, and in particular the shot of Klan riders against the sky on a hilltop, had been taken in Calabassas and the Agoura Trading Post.[65] The sequences in the cotton fields were shot at Calexico, one of the few areas in California below sea level (Margaret Cooper would recall experiencing several days of 100 degree heat there, with most of her suffering for nothing since much of the footage taken was later edited out).[66] The most distant location shoot, Gus's chase of Little Sister, was in the pine forest around Big Bear Lake. Not only was the journey long and often dangerous for Griffith and his team, but when they got back to Los Angeles Griffith realized that he also needed a simulated shot of Little Sister jumping from the rock. Bitzer and Brown were consequently sent back to Big Bear Lake so Bitzer could photograph the dummy Brown threw (with difficulty) off the top.[67]

With the exception of these shots, *The Clansman* was made on or next to the Griffith lot. Henabery recalled that "all interior scenes were shot on open stages, which were level floors or platforms with movable overhead diffusers and with no side walls." To prevent damage from rain or fog, all dressings and properties had to be removed and stored at night and set up again the next day.[68] For exterior shots, space on the back lot was at a premium: Bitzer remembered it as being "terribly crowded" with the consequence that, bit by bit, the filmmakers encroached on the property next door, owned by a Mrs. Thorsen, renting more and more land from her until finally it was all in use.[69]

Once filming began, days began early and continued until there was no longer sufficient sunlight to shoot by. According to Lillian Gish:

> sunlight controlled the shooting schedule. Preparations began at five or six in the morning. The actors rose at five in order to be ready at seven, when it was bright enough for filming. Important scenes were

played in the hard noon sun. I remember that we used to beg to have our closeups taken just after dawn or before sunset, as the soft yellow glow was easier to work in and much more flattering.[70]

By the standards of a later day, the actors and actresses worked very long hours and were far from cosseted. They had no one to help with their makeup, which Miriam Cooper recalled as

difficult. The harsh California sunlight was hard on our faces. Billy Bitzer, the cameraman, blended a brown powder for us to wear over pink grease paint. He showed us how to do it the first time, then we were on our own.[71]

There were no continuity people: players had to remember for themselves what they had worn earlier and, in the case of actresses, what their hair had looked like. There was no one to help them with their costumes: because there was no time between takes to return to the dressing rooms, they became used to carrying various changes of clothes with them around the set.[72] Sometimes there was a break for lunch; often, as Gish remembered it, there was not.[73]

Billy Bitzer, who had been Griffith's principal cameraman since 1908, later claimed to have shot every single foot of *The Birth of a Nation*. The camera he used was the hand-cranked Pathé model on which, according to Jean Mitry, a high proportion of the movies made in the world were then filmed. Known as the "crackerbox" in the United States because of its wooden frame, the Pathé camera was inexpensive (only $300) and light to carry (it could easily be picked up and moved forward for a close-up, back for a longer shot, giving Griffith "the opportunity of directing every detail of every scene personally").[74] Besides its cheapness and mobility, the Pathé camera appealed to Bitzer because of the effects, such as washboarding, he could create with it. In his autobiography, Bitzer asserted that the film had been shot with two lenses—one 2.52 inches, the other wide-angle—each of which, when needed, had to be screwed into the camera thread mount.[75] The camera was focused using a small lens on the back. Footage and stop numbers could be read from little dials that were also located on the camera's back. Turning the camera by hand at a constant pace to three-quarters waltz time—first with one arm, then with the other—had become so much a part of him by 1914 that Bitzer later confessed "that I felt I could do it in my sleep."[76]

Two important cinematographic effects produced with the Pathé camera were fades and dissolves. Fades were used both to begin and to end shots; Billy Bitzer's assistant, Karl Brown, would later recall that Griffith always used the terms "fade in" and "fade out" rather than the "camera" and "cut" commonly used by other directors.[77] To accomplish a fade, Bitzer had to continue cranking the camera with his right hand, while simultaneously using his left hand to loosen the lock knob on the stop lever and pushing it forward to open the lens (fade in) or back to stop down the lens (fade out).[78] Another shot Griffith was particularly fond of—the "iris" shot seemingly taken through a round eye-hole—had been developed by Bitzer during his long career at the Biograph Company. When he tried to create a lens shade from an old glue can, he discovered that this improvised shade darkened the corners of the frame. Later, looking for different-sized openings for different lenses, he used a larger can to which he attached a diaphragm from an old still camera. Attached to the lens and operated by an ordinary electrical switch, this diaphragm could be closed or opened to create an "iris in" or "iris out" effect.[79]

Bitzer insisted in his autobiography that *The Birth of a Nation* had been shot only in sunlight, with the only exception being "the carpenter-made model of the burning of Atlanta, which had to have special lighting to make it look real." Gish, by contrast, remembered that, overriding Bitzer's pessimistic objections, "Mr. Griffith would order bonfires lit and film some amazing night scenes."[80] While both Bitzer and Gish agreed that *most* photography was done during the daylight hours, and Bitzer's recollection that there was no electric light equipment in the California studio appears to have been correct,[81] there clearly was more night photography, lit by bonfires and/or flares, than Bitzer later recalled. Scenes shot in this way included the celebrations (themselves around a bonfire) in Piedmont before the Confederate troops set off for war, the refugees fleeing from a burning Atlanta, and the later stages of the battle of Petersburg (intitled "the battle goes on into the night," shot 438).[82]

Thirty years after he had photographed *The Birth of a Nation*, Bitzer wrote about the experience, and at that time his hand still showed faded blue powder specks from shooting the battlefield scenes. Not only had the men in the trenches being firing their guns straight at him, but to have them within camera range, the fireworks men had exploded their smoke bombs (representing bursting artillery and mortar shells) close to Bitzer himself.[83] Photographing the Klan rides also had its hazardous side. Griffith insisted on shooting these chases from every angle. Sometimes this involved Bitzer and Griffith careering ahead of the white-robed Klansmen in a fast automobile.[84] On another occasion, Griffith had Bitzer and his camera positioned in a ditch to photograph the Klansmen and their horses leaping overhead. Although some of the cast (Walthall in particular) were superb horsemen and the Klan rides were led by expert riders, the horses that had been rented were mostly not of very high quality. At one point, Griffith, "waving his arms and yelling madly" had to intervene to save Bitzer from being trampled underfoot. One horse, blinded by a Klansman's sheet, still managed to kick in the side of the camera, which Bitzer had to repair with tape before he could use it again.[85]

Without electric lights, Bitzer at times had to resort to improvisation: shooting the scene of Lincoln's assassination in broad sunlight, he faced the problem of picking out from other people the black-clad figure of John Wilkes Booth (Raoul Walsh) as he crept along the wall. His simple solution, according to Karl Brown, was to use a full-length mirror to focus the sun's reflected rays on Booth and "follow him wherever he went, just like a spotlight in a theater."[86] In later years, Bitzer argued that the very technological limitations he had faced in shooting *The Birth of a Nation*—the lack of electric lights, his "practically one lense[d]" Pathé camera, and "the old slow emulsion orthochromatic film"—had combined to produce an impression of historical "realism" in shots of battles, Lincoln's assassination, and Lee's surrender.[87] In effect, the "limited half tones" of the film stock gave such shots an "antique, or period" look that effectively reproduced the "hard brilliant quality" of what were commonly perceived by Americans as the most accurate and authentic visual records of the Civil War era: the photographs of Matthew Brady.[88]

The set of Ford's Theatre before the filming of Lincoln's assassination. Natural light only was used for this sequence. The man in the white suit is Griffith. (Epoch/The Kobal Collection)

Continuing Financial Problems

Griffith had originally estimated that *The Clansman* could be made for $40,000. He actually scheduled production of the picture—renting land for shooting the battle sequences and placing orders for essential items—*before* receiving the final assurance from the Aitkens that they had succeeded in raising the first $25,000. Once that assurance was forthcoming, of course, Griffith had the Aitken brothers where he wanted them. As the costs of the movie began to spiral out of control, they had only two choices: to cancel the whole project and lose completely the money already invested, or to continue to bankroll what at times must have seemed to them the director's mad folly. In the short term, however, the news that the film was now in production made it easier to raise the remaining $15,000 of the promised $40,000.[89]

As production accelerated, it rapidly became clear that $40,000 had been a considerable underestimate. Griffith was far from cost conscious; Billy Bitzer remembered him acting "as if the budget we were supposed to follow did not exist." At one point, Griffith apparently planned to end his film with a flock of angels suspended over a battlefield. He was sublimely unconcerned over the cost needed to achieve this effect, and with fifty telegraph poles (each costing $60) already being erected for shooting the scene, decided to drop the idea in favor of a different ending.[90] When Harry and Roy Aitken came out to Los Angeles in late summer 1914, Griffith broke the news to them that he needed more money to finish the film. While his initial reaction was to tell Griffith to finish the film for the $40,000 already provided, Harry later relented and raised a further $19,000. At the same time, he made it very clear that there would be no more money from the Aitken brothers and that Griffith ought to complete and market the film on the basis of the $59,000 already advanced.[91]

In addition to directing the film, Griffith now found himself having to raise the money to finish it. Gish and other members of Griffith's regular company were reasonably happy to do without paychecks for several weeks, confident (or at least hopeful) that they would be paid in the end.[92] But raising the money to pay extras was a recurring problem: Adela Rogers St. John would later remember Griffith, with the support of the paper's drama editor, passing the hat around the city room of the *Los Angeles Herald* to meet one payroll bill. On another occasion Bitzer was persuaded to dip into his own savings to pay the wages for the extras.[93] Eventually, to cover these and other costs, Griffith adopted the policy of selling stock in the film itself. His biggest coup was persuading William Clune, owner of Clune's Auditorium in Los Angeles, to advance $15,000 in return for stock, the California rights to the film, and Griffith's promise to have the West Coast première in Clune's theater. Bitzer eventually invested $7,000 in the film.[94] Robert J. Goldstein, whose firm provided most of the costumes and uniforms used in the movie, accepted $3,000 of stock in lieu of payment and invested a further $3,000 of his own money.[95] Other investors included O. Wimpenny, who ran a small restaurant near the studio ($3,000), Dr. E. J. Banzhof, the brother of Griffith's lawyer ($5,000), L. Hampton ($5,000), Mrs. Mae B. Ranger ($5,000), R. J. Huntingdon ($3,000), and J. Harrison (£1,000).[96] The offer of stock in return for money or services became so common that Bitzer at one point was authorized to offer an interest in the picture to one of the studio's neighbors "for the use of our overflow negro mob scenes."[97]

In effect, therefore, there were *two* syndicates at work in financing the film: the one originally put together by the Aitken brothers and the one assembled by Griffith. Harry Aitken, informed by accountant J. C. Epping that Griffith was offering investors stock in the picture, was far from pleased. It complicated the business of who owned *The Clansman*. Griffith, moreover, now formed the David W. Griffith Corporation and when the film was completed he copyrighted it in the name of this company. From Aitken's point of view, the director had "no monetary interest" in the movie, so his right to do this was at best questionable.[98] Aitken, however, had an ace up his sleeve: Griffith would need him and his contacts to distribute and exhibit the completed film. Because the Majestic studio, despite having been founded by the Aitkens, had turned down the opportunity of making the film, Harry Aitken decided not to distribute it through his regular company, the Mutual, but instead to organize a new company specifically for *The Clansman*.[99] On February 8, 1915, the day of *The Clansman*'s West Coast premi̇ère, the Epoch Producing Corporation was incorporated at Eddyville, Ulster County, New York. On March 2, the day before the East Coast opening at the Liberty Theater in New York, Harry Aitken became president of the new company and Griffith vice-president. The Epoch Producing Company was not simply a vehicle for distributing Griffith's film. It was also, from the Aitkens' point of view, a means of regularizing the issues of financing and ownership surrounding the picture. All the investors surrendered their rights in *The Clansman* to Epoch, receiving in return stock proportionate to the size of their investment. (As part of the deal, the Aitkens and other shareholders agreed to surrender $5,000 of stock so that Griffith could purchase it.) All investors were to be reimbursed for the amounts actually invested from the movie's first receipts. After that, 25 percent of the receipts were to be paid to Thomas Dixon with the balance to be divided between the David W. Griffith Corporation and the remaining investors.[100]

Griffith as Director

There is a good deal of evidence that Griffith found work on *The Clansman* project a liberating experience. Bitzer noted that his "directorial personality" changed completely: "Where heretofore he was wont to refer to films as sausages, he now seemed to say, 'We have something worthwhile and valuable in this drama of the Civil War.'"[101] Clearly, Griffith sensed that the film offered the opportunity for a great step forward in cinematic art. Bitzer, having worked closely with Griffith for so long, was well able to "see and feel his eagerness." But others who knew him less well, including Joseph Henabery and Karl Brown, would also recall that he seemed energetic and full of delight.[102] The fact that the movie was about the Civil War era was also crucial. Griffith, passionately interested in the period, virtually "*lived*" every minute of the saga during shooting. He was at times obsessive over the accuracy of details, insisting, for example, that the horse playing Robert E. Lee's famous horse "Traveller" be exactly the same kind of dappled gray as the original. "You'd think we were back in 1864–5," commented Bitzer. "Of course, in Griffith's mind we were."[103]

Griffith was thirty-nine years old when he began filming *The Clansman*. He was a tall man (almost six feet in height). His most prominent physical feature, according to Joseph Henabery, was his "large, hooked nose" although this became really apparent only in profile.[104] He habitually wore wide-brimmed hats, partly to protect himself from the sun on location and partly to balance "his jutting nose and strong chin." He was, however, beginning to lose his hair and someone had told him that hats were bad for the scalp, so his hats had their tops sliced off. (Lillian Gish would remember him watching the filming, one leg crossed over the other, unconsciously massaging the top of his head.)[105] Griffith habitually dressed in street clothes, Henabery recalled, normally "rather casual-looking tweeds, in a color that would be suitable if he had to work in dirty surroundings." He always wore a jacket, never appearing shirt-sleeved.[106]

The formality with which the director dressed was also visible in his relationships with others on set. He used Christian names only with Billy Bitzer and Joe Aller. Lillian Gish was always "Miss Geeesh," in Griffith's idiosyncratic pronunciation (he also said "boom" for bomb and "gell" for girl).[107] He had "a strong, deep voice" and usually spoke slowly and with assurance. At times, however, when he wanted to encourage a degree of overstatement in a scene, he could "become histrionic, almost hammy in his utterances." For the most part, Griffith seemed very much in control of himself, seldom displaying anger or exasperation; this made his rare "blow-ups" (as Bitzer termed them) even more startling.[108] On these occasions, he might explode with rage against all his actors or even set out to subdue a misbehaving extra with his fists. But in the main, he avoided such temperamental excess.[109]

To cope with the daytime pressures of filming, the long hours of the night spent sitting without moving in the projection room, and the constant financial anxieties, Griffith resorted to a variety of stratagems. One was physical activity. He repeatedly shadow-boxed on his own, throwing a series of punches at a phantom opponent. At other times, according to Karl Brown, he would dance with Lillian Gish or challenge a member of the working crew to a footrace. Although he carefully maintained his authority, Griffith was not above helping with the physical labor involved in filming, including the creation of sets. Finally, as a means of letting off steam, he would declaim poetry, sing loudly, or give vent (especially during the shooting of the Klan sequences) to his own version of the rebel yell.[110]

Most days, during the filming of *The Birth of a Nation*, Bitzer collected Griffith from the Alexandria Hotel at seven-thirty in the morning in a chauffeured company car. It was only a short ride to the studio and Griffith, impeccably dressed as always, was on the set before eight. By this stage, Bitzer's assistant, Karl Brown, had prepared all the necessary equipment. Griffith now gave Bitzer his instructions and he set up the camera in the proper position for the scene to be shot. Under Bitzer's guidance, Brown put down the lines, marking the area within which the actors could move and still be viewed by the camera. While these preparations were being made, Griffith often shadow-boxed by himself. The cast, already rehearsed and now in costume, waited. Once everything was ready, Griffith took his seat, in an ordinary kitchen chair, usually directly in front of Bitzer's camera. There was a final rehearsal of the scene to be shot and then Griffith would call "fade in" to start shooting. From time to time, as filming progressed, he would call out directions, using a large megaphone with big scenes, such as the ball on the eve of war.[111]

Griffith, with no apparent shooting script, worked out complete scenes in advance in his mind. The film as a whole was to have a balance between large "action" sequences (the battle scenes, the Klan rides) and smaller, domestic scenes. One of the most successful of the latter was the "Little Colonel's" homecoming at the end of the war. It was introduced by a shot of Flora arranging little strips of raw cotton ("Southern ermine") on top of her dress. As Joseph Henabery later commented,

> The childish idea of self-adornment provided a bit of pathetic humor because the scene conveyed the idea that a once affluent family was in dire straits...It developed a degree of sympathy for the plight of the family. It [also] told of a young girl's desire to appear at her best before her brother, that they were dear to each other, which made the hurt of the brother most intense when the little sister met her tragic end.[112]

Griffith wanted the actual shot of the "Little Colonel's" return to be played very slowly, to build up the emotional intensity.[113] Once he meets Little Sister, they inspect each other's clothes and twice embrace. When Ben finally reaches the door of his home, all that can be seen is his back and two arms that draw him into the house. Because of the discretion of this shot, much is left to the audience's imagination. The "Little Colonel's" return, indeed, becomes generalized, perhaps even mythologized. "Instead of it being one woman," Karl Brown noted, "it was every woman welcoming her returning hero."[114]

While Griffith had worked out much of the film in his mind before shooting began, he was also able to improvise. According to Lillian Gish, "whenever he saw a spontaneous gesture that looked good—like the soldier's leaning on his gun and looking at me during the hospital scene—he would call Billy over to film it." On another occasion, when the cannons and their crews from the Artillery Corps in Los Angeles, hired for the sequence dealing with Sherman's march to the sea, were late in arriving, Griffith noticed "a little family group (the Burns family) on a hill near us [—] a mother and some children who were really eating what I suppose was a thin breakfast." On his instructions, Bitzer later wrote,

> I inched the camera unobtrusively up to them, all the while pretending we were after shots of the valley below. Later, the combined scenes, edited by Jimmy and Rose Smith, would vary the long panorama shot [of the march] with this little intimate picture of a mother and her children caught in the grip of war. It was one of the touches that made *The Birth* so real and convincing.[115]

Griffith discussed his ideas on important scenes with most members of the cast, making them feel involved. He also emphasized the need to develop distinct, and also contrasting, characterizations. An ex-actor himself, he knew how to handle actors and secure the best possible performance from them. Naturally, his tactics varied according to the age and experience of the actor concerned. Dealing with young, untrained players, he gave them instructions "almost like an elementary school teacher." He would sometimes act out the part for them, usually in an exaggerated way. With the more experienced actors, none of this was necessary. Dealing with Henry Walthall, for example, Griffith "would simply tell him the substance of the scene without telling him how to act."[116] Occasionally, he would scold particular actors, but he would offer real praise when their work improved. According to Gish, when an actor did well in a scene, Griffith would hug him and insist—in his own, highly personal language—"That's a darb!"[117]

Developing and Editing

At the end of each day's shooting, the film was delivered to a laboratory built at the studio, where Abe Scholtz and Joe Aller, two Jewish refugees from Tsarist Russia, developed it with enormous, painstaking skill.[118] Since each scene was usually shot only once, there was only one negative.[119] That negative, at least by the standards of a later day, was treated in a most cavalier fashion. To verify details of plot and continuity, Griffith and Bitzer needed to be in a position to make continual reference to film already shot. Because Bitzer had been dissatisfied with the quality of the test prints he had done (the local Los Angeles water, he believed, contained too much alkali to wash the prints properly), the positive prints were processed and printed in New York.[120] Rather than risk delaying shots or making mistakes over continuity while they awaited these prints' arrival, Griffith and Bitzer developed the habit of carrying sections of the negative with them for constant consultation. These negatives, Karl Brown recalled many years later, were passed "from hand to hand to check costume [continuity]...and such things. Seems strange, these days, to think of a negative like that being stacked away in loose rolls, in cans, to be gone through by anybody who wanted to find out something. No gloves, no anything."[121]

Editing work on the film began immediately after shooting got under way. At the end of each day's filming, Griffith went to the projection room to look at the previous day's rushes. Two projectionists—Billy Fildew and George Teague—divided the work between them. Each, as he hand-ground the projector, had to be ready to stick a slip of paper into the uptake reel whenever Griffith's buzzer sounded. The slip told Griffith's expert editors, Jimmy Smith and his wife Rose, where to begin or end a cut in the film.[122] Since there was no shooting script, the scenes were numbered consecutively as they had been shot. As Bitzer's assistant, Karl Brown had the job of chalking the numbers on a slate to be photographed by the camera at the very beginning of the take. Cleaning the slate well enough to show the number clearly was difficult, so Brown invented the plywood board with inset numbers that would soon come into general use with moviemakers (who would continue, as a result of its origins, to refer to it as a "slate"). It was Brown's job also to record in a book the date of the shooting, scene number, characters involved, some hints as to the action, the space involved (Interior, Exterior, etc.), the camera stop number, and the amount of footage.[123]

Once shooting finished, Gish remembered that Griffith spent three months "on cutting, editing and working on the musical score." During this time, a third projectionist, George Richter, was added as Griffith "did his editing on a day and night schedule."[124] Everything shot had been developed and printed—150,000 feet in all.[125] Griffith had to cut this down to manageable proportions (around 12,000 feet in the version finally released) and edit the film actually used into a coherent and absorbing narrative.[126] It was, as Richard Schickel comments, a "brutal task."[127] Even to those closely involved in the film's production, it seemed "one long disjointed puzzle." Brown, who had watched every scene being shot, observed that "nothing seemed to go together, nothing seemed to fit." Gish, who often watched the rushes, remarked that seeing "these snatches of film was like trying to read a book whose pages had been shuffled. There was neither order nor continuity."[128]

Working endless hours in the projection room, Griffith slowly constructed the final version of his monumental film. As A. R. Fulton observed, "only he knew how the parts were to be fitted together."[129] Yet this was true only in the most general sense: Griffith knew roughly the narrative *order* that underpinned the movie, the approximate sequence of events that would characterize its story line. When editing started, he did *not* know the combination of shots that would compose particular sequences. It took endless hours in the projection room, running segments of film over and over again, taking short sections from several takes and assembling them together, continually altering and changing before the "final" version of such scenes began to emerge.[130]

The sequence dealing with Lincoln's assassination is a case in point. As Karl Brown recalled, this "took so long to shoot, with so many individual shots from so many different angles, that I couldn't see how they could possibly be put together in anything much better than a series of set pieces."[131] After its editing by Griffith, the sequence eventually incorporated more than fifty shots.[132] These varied spatially, with eighteen long shots (with the human figures occupying around half the frame), twenty-four medium long shots (entire bodies occupying the frame), four medium shots (a human figure from the knees up filling the frame), ten medium close-ups (of the human figure from the waist up), and one extreme close-up (the face of Lincoln's assassin, John Wilkes Booth). They also differed in duration as well. But in general, as Fulton notes, the ultimate effect of Griffith's editing of this scene is to create a coherent and convincing narrative through the establishment of relationships

> between Lincoln and Booth—showing Lincoln's unconsciousness of danger and Booth's intention; between Lincoln and the play—showing where Lincoln's attention is directed; between the bodyguard and the play—showing why the bodyguard leaves his post; and even between Lincoln and the audience in Ford's Theater, particularly Elsie and Phil—showing that the audience too is unconscious of the terrible deed about to be committed.[133]

The première at Clune's Auditorium on February 8, 1915, did not mean the end of Griffith's editing of the film. As Karl Brown pointed out, he "depended absolutely, even slavishly, upon audience reactions."[134] Griffith had unquestionably changed parts of the film in response to the reaction of the preview audiences at Riverside on January 1 and 2. He continued to alter the movie based on the reaction of the audience at Clune's. Also, over the next few weeks and months, he was asked, or compelled, to cut scenes by political authorities and censorship boards. The scale of these cuts is open to question. Seymour Stern argued in 1965 that *The Birth of a Nation* was composed of 1,544 shots in its original form and later cuts reduced this to 1,375. Although he gave no source for his initial estimate of 1,544 shots, the later figure was clearly derived from Theodore Huff's shot-by-shot analysis of the film, published posthumously in 1961.[135] More recently, John Cuniberti and Robert Lang have agreed that the best surviving prints of the film contain in all 1,610 scenes, with Cuniberti emphasizing that this was only thirty-one scenes fewer than the number recorded for copyright purposes five days after the Clune's opening.[136]

Although this suggests the possibility of fewer cuts being made in the film after its Los Angeles première than previously thought, some scenes had either never been shot or else were later removed. The budget for the film in the Griffith papers includes provision for an interior scene showing the area below deck on a slave ship. "Exteriors" listed include slaves in Africa, shipping slaves at the dock, the ship at sea, slaves on sale in a Southern market place, and a cavalcade effect for the two and a half year chronological break that occurs during the Civil War. An autograph list of scenes in Griffith's own hand suggests that the original plan was to include initial scenes of a proclamation against slavery and men receiving money for the slaves. Further shots were to include the Northern reaction to Lincoln's election, Southern congressmen in the House of Representatives, Northern soldiers marching off to war, a scene in the middle of the battle sequence cryptically referred to as "Nigger in the jungle," speeches on the franchise in the House of Representatives, a sick Stoneman being carried in to vote, a Union League picnic, and martial law being introduced in South Carolina.[137] None of these shots survive in available prints of the film. Corroborative evidence exists, however, for at least one of them: a review in the *Nashville Banner* commented that the film opened with a scene of slaves being sold, and Karl Brown later remembered seeing a scene of this type being filmed.[138]

There is evidence with varying degrees of reliability of sequences that may have been seen by the film's first audiences. In a March 1915 review, W. Stephen Bush mentioned a shot of an old lady at an abolitionist meeting recoiling in disgust from the odor of a young black boy. This was one of the highly racist scenes that New York Mayor John Purroy Mitchell insisted must be removed.[139] Bush's review also supported Seymour Stern's insistence that the opening sequences of the film linked the rise of the abolitionist movement to the hypocrisy of the descendants of the original slave traders who had "no further use for the slaves." Stern also claimed that there had originally been a shot of black men abducting screaming white women into the back streets of Piedmont and that toward the end of the film, an intertitle of "Lincoln's solution" had been followed by shots of the mass deportation of blacks; these claims also found substantiation in contemporary reviews.[140] Stern's most controversial assertion, however—that Griffith had filmed the actual rape of Flora by Gus on the rock—has no evidence whatever to back it up. In a letter of 1974, Karl Brown specifically denied that such a sequence had ever been shot.[141]

While Griffith was editing the film, he was also supervising the production of the intertitles. These were first written by Frank Woods and printed at a downtown shop. They were then filmed by Brown who had developed a complicated technique of his own to achieve maximum definition (clear white lettering on an all-black background). This obliged him to "shoot on lantern plates, print the plates on more lantern plates, then shoot the result on positive film stock, which became the negative for the picture." Once the intertitles written by Woods and photographed by Brown were inserted in the film, Griffith viewed them and suggested revisions, at which point the entire cumbersome process began again. Since Griffith was a perfectionist and intertitles were relatively cheap to produce, deciding on the final titles was a lengthy process.[142]

Much if not all of the film was also tinted, although when this was done is uncertain. Gish remembered that Griffith used tinting "to achieve dramatic results and to create mood." She gave as an illustration of this the scene of the battle of Petersburg where "the shots of Union and Confederate troops rushing in to replace the dead and wounded are tinted red, and the subtitle reads "In the red lane of death others take their places." Karl Brown maintained, in an interview in 1975, that "no sequences were in black and white, that everything carried some sort of tint to offset the visible electric blue of the projector's arc."[143] Certainly, the statement of receipts and disbursements for the film prepared for the Epoch Producing Company includes the sum of $621.65 for the cost of tinting ($371.22 for labor, $250.43 for materials). Who actually did the tinting is unclear, although Brown recalled being given the "endless" task of coloring the final shot of Elsie Stoneman and Ben Cameron. The two were on a bluff overlooking the ocean with a double-exposed celestial city also visible on the left; Brown had to turn this scene into "a roseat dream" by hand-tinting the whole sequence "with a fine brush and a solution of... Erythrosine."[144]

The Musical Score

As Russell Lack has commented, Griffith was one of the very small number of filmmakers who took music seriously and tried to improve the musical accompaniment of their films.[145] From the recollections of his co-workers, including Lillian Gish and Karl Brown, it is clear that he knew a lot about music. He often sang operatic arias on set during filming (Brown recalled extracts from *I Pagliacci* and *Tosca* and his attempts to model himself on Titta Ruffo's style of singing in preference to that of the more famous Caruso).[146] Some of the plots of his films were "borrowed" from operas: *A Fool's Revenge* (1909) was based on *Rigoletto*.

During the early years of his career, however, Griffith had no control whatsoever over the music that accompanied his films. He was probably aware, however, of comments by critics suggesting that if the local nickelodeon manager insisted on good music, then his own films were more successful. *A Fool's Revenge*, noted the *Moving Picture World*, was a film that

> made a deep impression on the audience...A pleasant variation from the eternal ragtime was a refined deliverance of classical music corresponding to the character of the picture, including Schumann's "Träumerei" and Beethoven's "Moonlight Sonata." The first time, indeed, we ever heard Beethoven in a five-cent theater.[147]

A few months later, a critic writing in the New York *Dramatic Mirror* commented:

> When the Biograph film *In Old Kentucky* [directed by Griffith] was ex-
> hibited at the [Keith and Procter movie house on Union Square]...the
> applause was more frequent throughout the reel than at the other
> houses where the same subject was shown, and the difference is attrib-
> uted to the excellent musical selections that were used.[148]

Although attempts were made by some studios to improve the quality of the music in movie houses during this period—around 1909, for example, Edison and Vitagraph began to furnish exhibitors with "musical suggestion sheets" (later known as cue sheets) of suitable music for particular films—it was the arrival of the *film d'art* from France that signaled the start of a new relationship between movies and music.[149] The pioneering French *film d'art*, *L'Assassinat du Duc de Guise* (1908), had been produced together with a full score by Camille Saint-Saëns, then probably France's most distinguished com- poser. Yet *L'Assassinat*, edited down and probably without its accompanying score, made little impact in the United States when it was released there (for just five weeks) in 1909. It took until 1911–12 for the type of "art films" produced by Pathé to begin to attract sizable American audiences—and for American producers to learn how to "sell" such films with music. One successful 1912 import was *Queen Elizabeth*, the filmed version of a French play starring Sarah Bernhardt that was distributed in America by Adolph Zukor's new Famous Players Film Company.[150]

Plays on screen, however, suffered greatly by comparison with plays per- formed on stage. Of necessity, they were much briefer, being reduced to pre- senting what was essentially a series of tableaux. In addition, they were unable to use the principal instrument of stage drama: speech. Producers of these plays consequently turned to music (which had itself long been associated with "live" theater) to help convey moods and emotion. Zukor accordingly commissioned Joseph Carl Breil to write a special score for the opening of *Queen Elizabeth* in July 1912 at the Lyceum Theater in New York. Breil, who had first made his name composing incidental music for the theater, may have provided scores for two earlier examples of French *film d'art*, *Camille* (also featuring Bernhardt) and *Mme. Sans-Gêne* (starring another famous French actress, Réjane). After the success of *Queen Elizabeth*, he composed scores for three American films pro- duced by Famous Players in 1913 (*The Prisoner of Zenda*, *Tess of the d'Urbervilles* and *In the Bishop's Carriage*). He also could have compiled (and certainly fre- quently conducted) the music for *Cabiria* (1914), the long and spectacular Italian film that enjoyed a highly successful American run.[151]

At some point of early 1914, after his arrival in California, Griffith saw a performance of *Cabiria*. Breil would later claim that the experience gave him the idea of a complete musical score for his own film and simultaneously brought Breil himself to Griffith's notice.[152] Once the shooting of *The Clansman* was completed in early November 1914, Breil was asked to begin work on a score. He would not do so completely alone, however, because Griffith took an active role in the scoring, helping to choose the music and match it up to the images. "Mr. Breil would play bits and pieces," Lillian Gish remembered, "and he and Mr. Griffith would then decide on how they were to be used." As Charles Berg comments, this was "the first time that a director had personally undertaken control over the musical accompaniment of a major film."[153]

Approximately half the music in the final score was composed by Breil. There were two other types of music making up the other half of the score. First, there were borrowed tunes, from "Auld Lang Syne" to "Dixie." According to Martin Marks, twenty-six of these have been identified. They were all derived "from the standard repertoire for home and community singing" and their words, though not actually heard, helped underpin the film's action: "Auld Lang Syne," for example, was used to emphasize the sequence in which most of the Cameron family take refuge in a cabin owned by some former enemies from the North ("old acquaintance").[154] Second, the score included ten excerpts from symphonic music. All except one were taken from the nineteenth-century tradition of romantic music, including works by Beethoven, Grieg, Weber, Tchaikovsky, and Wagner.[155] Many of these excerpts were probably unfamiliar to most of the American public. Concertgoing was still rather rare in much of the United States (only in 1915, for example, did Beethoven's Ninth Symphony have its first performance west of the Mississippi). Some of the pieces had been made available in printed form only relatively recently: Tchaikovsky's "1812 Overture" in 1882 and Grieg's "In the Hall of the Mountain King" in 1888.[156] Both Breil and Griffith may have felt that by using pieces from celebrated composers, they were helping to legitimate their film in cultural terms. At the same time, they arranged and adapted such music to meet the needs of the action. Even Wagner's "Ride of the Valkyries," used to accompany the ride of the Ku Klux Klan in the final stages of the film, had been reworked in this way.[157]

While Breil's score included two excerpts from different works by Wagner—the only composer to be treated in this way—it is possible that the debt to Wagner on the part of Breil and Griffith may actually have been considerably greater.[158] Wagner's dislike of traditional forms of opera, which he saw as tending to exalt the music at the expense of the drama, had led him to develop the idea of a "Gesamtkunstwerk" [total art work] to be produced through the combination of several single arts. Applied to opera, such a theory implied that music should be composed in relation to the drama, that it should be played continuously, and that a number of recurring themes or "leitmotifs" should be used to integrate music and drama.[159] There was widespread interest in Wagner's music and his ideas in late nineteenth-century and early twentieth-century America.[160] Early writers on film quickly realized that his theorizing on the unity of music and drama could also be applied to cinema. A *Moving Picture World* editorial of 1910 hoped that "just as Wagner fitted his music to the emotions, expressed by words in his operas, so in the course of time, no doubt, the same thing will be done with regard to the moving picture." A year later, critic W. Stephen Bush observed that "Every man or woman in charge of [the] music of a moving picture theatre is, consciously or unconsciously, a disciple of Richard Wagner."[161]

In 1910, *Moving Picture World* also began to publish a regular column by Clarence Sinn entitled "Music for the Pictures." In 1911, Sinn fell under the spell of Wagnerian ideas and summarized them in these terms:

> Boiled down, it amounts to something like this: To each important character, to each important action, motif, or idea, and to each important object...was attached a suggestive musical theme. Whenever the action brought into prominence any of the characters, motifs, or objects, its theme or motif was sung or played...Such a method of applying music to the pictures is the ideally perfect one.[162]

Breil seems to have been convinced in the same manner as Sinn (and perhaps as a consequence of reading him) that leitmotifs were just as important for movies as for operas. The score he created for *Queen Elizabeth* assigned a "motif" to each of the film's characters. Both Breil and Griffith agreed that it was necessary to have similar motifs for *The Clansman*.[163]

Although *The Birth of a Nation* would be heavily criticized, both at the time of its release and later, for the racial bias it displayed, it was also widely recognized as an aesthetic masterpiece. It signaled, as Jean Mitry would later assert, the birth of cinema *"as an art."*[164] If not a "total art work" in the Wagnerian sense, *The Birth of a Nation* at least emphasized the *synthetic* nature of cinema, combining together a filmed drama with highly appropriate and effective music. As Martin Marks notes, the film represented "a spectacular, moving, and deeply troubling marriage of image and music."[165] The musical score arranged or composed for it by Breil, under Griffith's supervision, was conceived as an integral part of the film. It was intended to help in the development of both narrative and characterization, to preserve continuity, to create mood and, perhaps not least, to help maintain the interest of audiences in a film that lasted more than three hours. So successful was this blending of music and cinema that after *Birth*, it became harder and harder to think of producing a major film without a musical score.

The key decision made by Griffith in the very beginning was to extend the chronology of Dixon's story by devoting the first part of his film to the Civil War period.[166] He also pared down the "political" aspects of Dixon's story and increased the emphasis on two intersectional families. Griffith made *The Birth of a Nation* using methods he had worked out as a Biograph director: he shot each scene after prolonged rehearsals by his company of actors and actresses. The actual shooting involved few innovations (though nighttime cinematography was used for some sequences). As a director, Griffith proved equally adept at handling large, set-piece battle sequences and more intimate moments (and was also successful at raising the money to finish filming). Yet what were perhaps his greatest contributions to *The Birth of a Nation* came after shooting was over. He edited 150,000 feet of film down to around 12,000 to produce an absorbing narrative and, conscious that music could be a major source of the film's impact on audiences, commissioned Joseph Carl Breil to compile a full accompanying musical score.

5

Transforming the American
Movie Audience

On February 18, 1915, *The Birth of a Nation* became the first motion picture ever
to be shown in the White House. Operators wearing full evening dress utilized
two Simplex machines to project the film onto the white wooden panels of the
East Room. The screening was a personal favor by President Woodrow Wilson
to Thomas Dixon Jr., a former classmate and longtime friend. Invited by Dixon
to view Griffith's film, the president had only one objection, and that was practical: he could not accept social invitations because he was still officially in mourn-
ing for his wife, Ellen Axson Wilson, who had died a few months earlier. To get
around this difficulty, Dixon suggested exhibiting the film at the White House,
where the president, his daughters, and some members of the cabinet would
be able to view it.[1] There is a legend (one of many that would grow up around
this movie) that at the end of the showing, Wilson remarked: "It is like writing
history with lightning. And my only regret is that it is all so terribly true."[2] He
may have said this. After all, the film's view of the Civil War and Reconstruction
periods was not too different from Wilson's own (his historical writings were
several times quoted in the film's intertitles). Moreover, it is unlikely that the
Southern-born Wilson (who, as president, had extended segregation to all departments of the federal government) was bothered by the film's rampant racism.[3] But there seems to be no contemporary reference for the remark. In 1977,
when the only survivor of the White House screening was interviewed, she
recalled that the president "seemed lost in thought during the showing" and
"walked out of the room without saying a word when the movie was over."[4]

Griffith may have presented his film personally at the White House screening: both a preview program and a subsequent letter from him to the president
expressing his gratitude for the opportunity imply that he did.[5] Certainly, on the

Woodrow Wilson, twenty-eighth president of the United States (1913–1921). (Library of Congress, Prints and Photographs Division, LC-USZ62-111452)

following evening, he and Dixon were reported as sitting together at a screening of *The Birth of a Nation* in the grand ballroom of the Raleigh Hotel in Washington. At this private exhibition, organized under the auspices of the National Press Club, the guest of honor was Chief Justice of the Supreme Court Edward White. (Dixon would later claim that White, who had never seen a motion picture before, finally agreed to attend because he had once been a Klansman and wanted to see the "true story" of the Ku Klux Klan.)[6] In addition to White and his wife, other guests included "Secretary of the Navy [Josephus P.] Daniels, thirty-eight U.S. senators and about fifty members of the House of Representatives." Many had brought their wives along. The large invited audience also included "a sprinkling of members of the Diplomatic Corps [and] scores of high [government] officials" as well as many journalists. One newspaper described this elite gathering (which "showered" Griffith with congratulations once the film was over) as "doubtless the mo[st] [dis]tinguished that ever saw motion picture reels unraveled."[7]

On February 20, *The Birth of a Nation* was scheduled to be shown at a preview in New York. Reports of its racism had already been transmitted to the East Coast from the Los Angeles branch of the National Association for the Advancement of Colored People (NAACP), so it seemed very likely that this and subsequent New York screenings would be controversial.[8] It was probably for this reason that the film made its detour to Washington. Although the two Washington showings had been arranged on the basis of no publicity,[9] Dixon and Griffith obviously intended, when protests from the NAACP and other black rights organizations arrived, to defend themselves against demands for censorship by citing the enthusiastic approval of the Washington establishment. The Washington screenings, however, can also be regarded as part of a wider strategy aimed at attracting a vast popular audience to *The Birth of a Nation*. That strategy, indeed, aimed at nothing less than a major reconfiguration of the American movie audience.

Escaping the Nickelodeons

In the first years after the April 1896 showing of moving pictures at Koster and Bial's Music Hall in New York City demonstrated that they might be commercially viable, films were screened in vaudeville theaters, music halls, opera houses, cafés, storefronts, department stores, local fairs and schools, Chautauquas, YMCAs, churches, and church halls. Audiences for early film, reflecting such different locations, were socially heterogeneous. This situation began to change in 1905 with the advent of the store-front movie theater or "nickelodeon." The nickelodeon, with its cheap seats, one-reel films, and musical accompaniment, demonstrated that there was a mass market for the movies. At least in the large cities that made up the biggest and most profitable market for films, that audience was primarily working class and often of immigrant origin. As the number of nickelodeons increased—there were 3,000 in the United States by 1907 and more than 10,000 by 1910[10]—the type of viewers they attracted became a source of dissatisfaction to two critical groups in American society: the middle class and the nickelodeon proprietors. Many native-born members of the middle class, seeing only that the nickelodeon was a new form of entertainment, that it took place in the dark, and that its patrons were drawn mainly from the lower classes, embarked on attempts to regulate and control nickelodeons through various forms of censorship and safety regulations. While this generated a whole new public discourse concerning the nickelodeon and helped transform both the physical environment of the store-front movie theater and the nature of the filmic experience it offered, it was probably in the end less influential in terms of the evolution of cinema than actions of the other group: the movie exhibitors and nickelodeon proprietors themselves.

As Russell Merritt argued, nickelodeon proprietors and movie exhibitors often looked down on their working-class patrons and sought to appeal to a better class of clientele.[11] Ambitious and upwardly mobile, they sought to attract the middle-class family trade. By broadening the audience for movies to bring in the middle class, they sought to secure for movie entertainment a greater cultural legitimation, something they believed that would eventually generate higher profits. This strategy had two main strands. One was to improve the quality of the films shown. Between 1896 and the early stages of the nickelodeon era, most of the motion pictures on offer in the United States have been categorized by Tom Gunning as part of a "cinema of attractions" that concentrated its attention on showing views, often illusory, to audiences rather than attempting to focus on stories. The advent of the nickelodeons encouraged a shift to the chase films and "sequential farces" that quickly became the staples of movie entertainment. With more emphasis on storytelling, the "cinema of attractions" gave way to what Gunning refers to as a "cinema of narrative integration."[12] Griffith, of course, was a major pioneer in this shift. As he and other filmmakers became increasingly proficient in telling "stories," through the use of continuity editing and other practices, films tended to become longer. Griffith himself quit the Biography Company in 1913 to make longer movies. By 1913–14, indeed, other film producers—including Kalem, Selig and Vitagraph—were producing multireel films.[13] With the rise of the longer feature film as the characteristic product of the American film industry, the concept emerged of watching movies as an evening's entertainment in their own right. (Nickelodeons had often varied their diet of short films with vaudeville acts and popular "sing-alongs"— the latter, according to one contemporary commentator, often led by a "breed of 'singers' in the cheaper theaters that in many cases [called] for suppression by either the police or the board of health, or both.")[14]

A second strand in the strategy designed to appeal to middle-class moviegoers concentrated on improving the exhibition environment. Better, more comfortable theaters with higher prices of admission began to appear in cities such as Los Angeles (where Clune's Theater—later Auditorium—opened in 1910), Milwaukee, and New Orleans. By 1914, this trend had reached New York, with the transformation of the old Criterion Theater into a movie house and the opening of the purpose-built Strand Theater.[15] By now it was beginning to become clear that the nickelodeon era of cheap moviegoing was coming to a close and the future lay with the picture palace.[16] The Strand, in particular, located in the heart of the theatrical district on Broadway, symbolized the "new breed of movie houses...designed for comfort and deliberately situated in more prosperous parts of town in order to attract a more middle-class audience." Closer in its facilities to existing theaters than to the nickelodeons, it boasted a thirty-piece orchestra to accompany the films it showed. "If anyone had told me two years ago," observed the theater critic of the *New York Times*, "that the time would come when the finest looking people in town would be going to the biggest and newest theater on Broadway for the purpose of seeing motion pictures, I would have sent them down to...Bellevue Hospital."[17] An alternative to this approach, increasingly adopted for the longer French *film d'art* productions and Italian spectacles, was to book the film into a regular theater. Thus, *Queen Elizabeth* (1912) began its American run at the Lyceum Theater in New York. *Les Misérables* (1913), *Quo Vadis* (1913), *The Last Days of Pompeii* (1913), and *Cabiria* (1914) were also exhibited mainly in legitimate theaters.[18]

Griffith and the Aitken brothers must have had these changes in exhibition practice in the forefront of their minds when planning the New York première of *The Birth of a Nation*. In the end, probably the closest parallel with their own film was *Cabiria*, a twelve-reel Italian spectacle whose distributors made "extravagant" claims for its cost and scale (a budget of $250,000, a cast of 5,000), touted its vast length and popularity, and charged admission ranging from 25 cents to $2.[19] In his account of the making of *The Birth of a Nation*, Roy E. Aitken credited his brother Harry with the decisions to open the picture at the Liberty Theater, to hold a private matinée for drama critics and other influential New Yorkers in advance of the public première, and (over the initial resistance of Griffith and Dixon) to charge up to $2 for a seat.[20] The Liberty Theater on West 42nd Street was familiar territory for Dixon: his original play, *The Clansman*, had opened there nine years earlier for its New York run.[21] The theater was owned by the Klaw and Erlanger syndicate (ironically the same organization that had signed the deal with the Biograph Company to produce filmed plays that had prompted Griffith, feeling himself by-passed and excluded, to leave Biograph in the first place). According to the New York *World*, the syndicate did not want to lease the theater to Griffith and his partners "on the usual percentage basis" as they believed his film "would not attract patronage at two dollar prices." The Aitkens, Griffith, and their partners were consequently obliged to lease the theater outright, taking on their shoulders all the burden of financial risk should the film fail. By the same token, of course, they guaranteed themselves nearly all the profits should the film succeed.[22]

Selling *The Birth of a Nation*

Between February 13, when Harry Aitken announced the leasing of the Liberty Theater, and March 3, when the film officially opened in New York, a series of private screenings occurred. It was at one of these, according to legend, that Thomas Dixon—impressed by the enthusiastic response of the audience—suggested to Griffith that *The Clansman* be renamed *The Birth of a Nation*.[23] Even more crucially, perhaps, after considerable persuasion from Harry Aitken, Theodore Mitchell agreed to attend one of the previews. Mitchell, a publicity man for the Schubert Theater, was deeply skeptical of motion pictures. Yet he was simply overwhelmed by the experience of watching *The Clansman*. Within a matter of hours, Mitchell and J. R. McCarthy, another Schubert publicity man, had signed a contract with Harry Aitken to handle all the publicity and promotion for the film. Over the next few months, they would launch a deeply imaginative array of stunts and promotional devices. In many ways they pioneered most of the major methods that would later be used by the Hollywood studios and their chains of theaters to "sell" moving pictures.[24]

The main problem facing Mitchell and McCarthy in the beginning was how to attract a large audience willing to pay "live" theater prices to see what was still "only" a film. In their initial advertising, they attempted to draw a distinction between *The Birth of a Nation* and previous movies of the one- or two-reel variety by emphasizing the spectacular scale of the production. Truth became the first casualty of this attempt at "boosting" their film. They claimed that *The Birth of a Nation* had cost $500,000 to bring to the screen, and that 18,000 people and 3,000 horses had been involved—claims that were endlessly reproduced in the months that followed.[25] The publicists also endeavored to make a distinction between *Birth* and previous imported epics from Italy and France. Ads presented it as "the mightiest spectacle ever produced," "a colossal production" that was simply "too great for comparisons." But they also appealed to American nationalism by describing it as "a red blooded tale of true American spirit" dealing with "national figures" and "stirring events in the development of our country." They stressed that *Birth* had been "conceived, inspired and created in America." While it was a film that offered sensational entertainment—"gripping heart interest and soul stirring emotions"—it was also one "rich in historical value." Presenting the film as history, however, was only one means of trying to legitimate it in cultural terms. Another was the attempt to depict Griffith as a brilliant cinematic *auteur*: *The Birth of a Nation* was described as "the expression of genius in a new realm of art." Finally, to remove the objections of anyone whose perceptions of motion pictures had been molded through watching out-of-focus movies with a honky-tonk piano accompaniment in a seedy nickelodeon, the publicity campaign emphasized that the Liberty Theater had been "remodeled according to scientific adjustment of focal requirements" and that music to accompany the film would be provided by a "symphony orchestra of 40."[26]

Mitchell and McCarthy seem to have organized a series of private viewings for journalists.[27] Their efforts in advance of the official opening culminated in a special preview with an invited audience on the afternoon of Monday, March 1. The guest list was drawn from New York's social and literary elite. It included financiers and society ladies; actors such as Douglas Fairbanks and his wife; writers such as Rex Beach, Richard Harding Davis, and Booth Tarkington; and illustrators such as Charles Dana Gibson.[28] Two nights later, the film opened to a capacity audience, greeted by female ushers wearing 1870s-style dresses and male ushers dressed in Union blue and Confederate gray uniforms of the kind worn by the armies during the Civil War. Spectators began to applaud even during the early shots of the streets of Piedmont, and during the Civil War sequences, their applause was "nearly incessant for a full half-hour." They showed so much enthusiasm for the film that by the intermission they were already calling for Dixon and Griffith to speak. Dixon responded first. Asserting that the film was superior to his own book and play, he declared that only some-one who was both the son of a soldier and a Southerner could have made such a picture. He then introduced Griffith as "the greatest director in the world." Griffith spoke briefly, claiming that his objective was to place moving pictures "on a par with the spoken word as a medium for artistic expression" and thank-ing the audience for the reception being accorded his film.[29]

"The drama critics of all of the New York newspapers attended the pre-miere," reported *The Moving Picture World* a few days later, "and in almost every instance the picture was reported at length and in glowing terms." The anonymous reviewer for the *New York Times* was one of relatively few to display any ambivalence toward the subject matter of the film, and even he described *Birth* as "an impressive new illustration of the scope of the motion picture cam-era." Others were not so circumspect. "The mind falters and the typewriter baulks before an attempt to either measure or describe D. W. Griffith's crowning achievement in screen drama," wrote Burns Mantle of the *Evening Mail*. "Judged by all the photo dramas New York has given," declared the *Standard Union*, "this new film spectacle is the greatest and largest ever produced."[30] "Never before has such a whirlwind combination of story, spectacle, and tense drama been unrolled before New Yorkers," commented *The Sun*'s critic. To Louis Sherwin of the *Evening Globe* it was "beyond question the most extraordinary picture that has been made—or seen—in America so far." C. F. Zittel's highly enthusiastic review in the *Evening American* must have overjoyed anyone connected with the film: it was less a critical appraisal than a spirited panegyric. "'The Birth of a Na-tion,'" Zittel assured his readers, "will thrill you, startle you, make you hold on to your seats. It will make you laugh. It will make you cry. It will make you angry. It will make you glad. It will make you hate. It will make you love. It is not only worth riding miles to see, but it is worth walking miles to see."[31]

The combination of ecstatic reviews, publicity, and word-of-mouth reports assured the film's success. "There has not been a vacant seat in the house since the opening performance," commented the *New York Commercial* a few days later, "and crowds have been turned away at every presentation." Anxious about his investment in the picture, Billy Bitzer kept returning to watch the lines forming in front of the box office. He need not have worried: as the days went by, the queue of those wanting to see *The Birth of a Nation* only grew longer.[32] Even in the first few days, newspapers were noting that the film was "doing the biggest business" ever known at the Liberty Theater and predicting a long run.[33] Over the next few months, doubtless prompted by Mitchell and McCarthy, they would hail the various landmarks of what would become a record-breaking run. "Even Holy Week seemed to have no effect upon attendance at the Liberty Theater," commented the *Journal of Commerce* on April 3, "and the house was crowded at every performance." With two showings a day, at 2:10 in the afternoon and 8:05 in the evening, the total number of performances grew rapidly. In mid-May, the film had its 150th performance. At the 200th performance in early June, souvenir programs bound in vellum were distributed to moviegoers. On August 9, the *New York Press* estimated that more than 400,000 people had seen *Birth* at the Liberty Theater, where it was now in the sixth month of its run.[34] Thanks to the installation of new cooling equipment in the Liberty, the film ran steadily throughout the summer months.[35] It continued throughout the fall and into early winter: the final performance of its unprecedented run of nearly forty-four weeks at the Liberty came on January 2, 1916.[36]

Originally, Griffith and the Aitkens had intended to charge $2 just for box seats, with the remaining prices varying between 25 cents and $1 for evening performances and 25 cents and 50 cents for matinées. The huge demand for seats and the movie's "wonderful send-off...in the papers," *Variety* noted on March 12, had persuaded them to charge $2 for most of the lower floor. In the same issue, *Variety* made an early estimate of the film's profitability. With the Liberty's 1,200 seats filled at each performance, *The Birth of a Nation* would be making $14,000 a week. With an exceptional $14,000 having been spent on advertising in the first week, the total expenses had now settled down to $4,500 a week, including $1,250 rent for the theater.[37] While *Variety*'s estimate of income actually earned was pretty accurate (total receipts at the Liberty Theater for the week ending March 13—the first full week of the film's run—were $13,320.25), the actual cost of showing *Birth* (including publicity, rent, and salaries for staff and orchestra) was much higher than suggested: $13,317.79 for the same week. Even by the end of April, the profits from the New York engagement were small: $12,455.90 on receipts totaling $99,455.10.[38] Yet reports in newspapers and the trade press of the film's great popularity and commercial success prompted a flood of offers either from theater owners wishing to book it or of businessmen wanting to purchase the right to distribute the film in particular areas (future M-G-M mogul Louis B. Mayer apparently telephoned the Aitkens as early as March 1, the night of the private preview, to offer $50,000 for the New England rights). According to reports in the New York newspapers, during the first three weeks of its run at the Liberty Theater some 2,138 offers for bookings or the cash purchase of territorial rights had already been received.[39]

Distributing *The Birth of a Nation*

When the board of the Epoch Producing Company met in mid-March to decide how to distribute the film, the atmosphere, as Roy Aitken recalled, was "tense."

On the one hand, the members of the board (including both Aitken brothers, Griffith, and Griffith's lawyer, Albert J. Banzhof) were aware that what seemed startlingly large offers for the film were being made. After the months of financial uncertainty surrounding the film's production, and the risks that had been taken, there must have been a strong incentive to accept such offers. The Aitkens had borrowed most of the $59,000 they had invested in the picture and were now being pressed by their creditors for payment—another argument for acceptance. So, too, were the uncertainties surrounding the film in relation to censorship problems and possible boycotts. On the other hand, members of the board knew that the greatest profits were likely to come from organizing "road show" companies themselves to exhibit the film both in the United States and abroad. Organizing such road shows, however, would require further infusions of capital at a time when, Roy Aitken later remembered, "most of Epoch's stockholders were tired of the tension of shoestring financing" and yearning "to pay debts and reward ourselves with a few luxuries." The end result was a compromise: the board decided to organize road companies to show *The Birth of a Nation* in selected major cities, hoping thereby to cream off the most profitable section of the potential market. To help create the money to do this, they sold off distribution rights in some areas. The California rights went to William H. Clune and Griffith himself. Harry Sherman of Minneapolis acquired for $100,000 the rights to show the film in sixteen Western states. Louis B. Mayer's syndicate received for $50,000 the rights to New England (excluding Boston, which—at least initially—was reserved for an Epoch road show).[40]

Each road show company was established with its own manager, publicity chief, projectionists, electricians and other technicians, sound effects staff, porters and stage hands, and an orchestra of twenty to forty performers.[41] It resembled in many ways the theatrical and musical comedy companies that had toured the country in previous decades.[42] Made up of fifty to a hundred people, each road show took time to organize. They were also expensive, and the money from the sale of state and city rights was slow to arrive: by June 30, only $36,500.00 had been received.[43] While most accounts of *The Birth of a Nation* emphasize how *quickly* it became a financial success, in reality that success came relatively slowly. As late as July 1915, there were still only four road show companies in existence; by September, the figure had reached eight; by January 1916, there were twelve. By the end of February 1916, the total gross income for all the road shows had reached $2,226,885.42. During the same period, their outlays came to $1,131,633.68, making a total profit of $1,095,251.74.[44] This figure did not represent the *total* profit on the film to that point. It did not include the income from the rights distributors, derived both from the sale of rights and the subsequent percentage paid of the box office take.[45] Nor did it cover any returns from the road show companies that by this stage were operating in England, Australia, and South America.[46] But it was Epoch's largest and certainly best-regulated source of income during *Birth's* first run

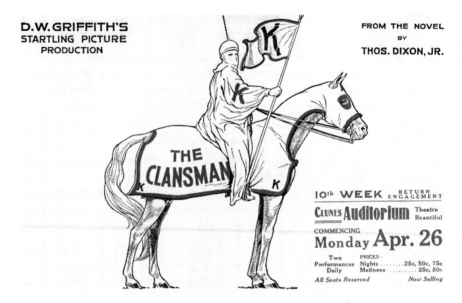

D.W. GRIFFITH'S
STARTLING PICTURE
PRODUCTION

FROM THE NOVEL
BY
THOS. DIXON, JR.

THE CLANSMAN

10th WEEK RETURN ENGAGEMENT

Clunes Auditorium Theatre Beautiful

COMMENCING
Monday Apr. 26

Two Performances Daily

PRICES—
Nights 25c, 50c, 75c
Matinees 25c, 50c

All Seats Reserved   Now Selling

The Birth of a Nation, under its original title of *The Clansman,* continued to run profitably at Clune's Auditorium in Los Angeles. (Epoch/The Kobal Collection)

(there is considerable evidence that states' rights distributors, including Mayer, minimized the percentages they were supposed to pay through underreporting box-office grosses).[47]

The success that attended the showings in Los Angeles, Washington, and New York had convinced Griffith and the Aitkens that they had a hit on their hands. Yet in the circumstances, their commitment to a road show strategy was quite brave. It depended on a series of assumptions: that *The Birth of a Nation* would appeal to audiences from different regions and classes, that enough people would be prepared to pay "live" theater prices of up to $2 to see what was after all still just a motion picture, and that long runs in one place would not quickly exhaust the novelty value of the film (nickelodeons sold themselves in part on their frequent changes of program).[48] If the road show was not an entirely new phenomenon (George Kleine, for example, had exhibited *Quo Vadis* and other imported spectacular films on a similar basis), it had certainly never been tried before on such a scale.[49] There was also the problem of how to communicate the character and appeal of the film—and the enthusiastic reception by its earliest audiences—to people across the country. The only national media existing in the United States in 1915 were the monthly magazines, and these rarely commented on motion pictures except in the context of censorship debates. Epoch, no doubt advised by Mitchell and McCarthy, set out to publicize their film by feeding "news" and selective information to local newspapers across the country through press agencies and wire services.

The Press Campaign

Since *The Birth of a Nation* was advertised as the first "$2 picture," much of this publicity campaign was aimed at showing the ways in which it differed from previous, shorter movies. Griffith was quoted as saying that the public "is alert to values. They have shown themselves willing to pay five cents to see a film that cost $500 to produce, 50 cents to see one that cost $50,000 and $2 for one that cost half a million."[50] By implication, therefore, charging up to $2 a seat for *Birth of a Nation* could be justified by the cost of producing the film and its vast scale: the original claims made before the Liberty Theater showings that *Birth* had cost $500,000 to make and that 18,000 people and 3,000 horses had been involved were constantly repeated in local newspapers.[51] Such claims, of course, were highly exaggerated. But many newspapers also reported items of information about the film that were completely fictional. These so-called "facts," entirely created by *Birth*'s publicity department, included the assertions that all the "history" in the movie had been verified by three college professors, that the "town" of Piedmont (in reality, just a set) had been found only through a patient search in several Southern states, that five other towns had been specially built and three of them destroyed, and that the film had been shot on location in five states and "partly in Mexico."[52] Various myths also accumulated in relation to the battle scenes: that 18,000 actors "encamped for months in the picturesque hills of Virginia," that the action sequences involved a fifty-mile march over rough country, that an organized corps of surgeons and nurses accompanied the "troops," that roads were specially built for the production, and that the battle-front trenches extended for five miles. It was claimed that Griffith directed the battlefield sequences from a sixty-foot tower, using an elaborate telephone system (with its cables hidden underground) and that real shells costing $80 apiece were fired from the cannons.[53] All these claims, of course, were false—as was the declaration that 500 costumers and seamstresses had worked for three months to produce all the uniforms, Klan robes, and women's frocks.[54]

Overwhelmingly, the local American press greeted *The Birth of a Nation* with enthusiastic endorsements.[55] "Only once in a lifetime is such a magnificent production produced," noted the Baltimore *American*. Griffith's movie, editorialized the Huntsville, Alabama, *Daily Times*, "is so far out of the ordinary that we do not hesitate to commend it and urge all who can to see it." "The spectacular effects, the breadth of conception and the skill of execution with which the picture has been made differentiate it from all previous attempts at photospectacle," commented the *Washington Herald*. "Not even Nero ever gazed upon so magnificent a spectacle," observed the Akron, Ohio, *Paragraph*. "Never has such a photographic spectacle been shown in this city," declared the Quincy, Illinois, *Daily Journal*, "and it far surpasses those spectacular foreign photo

plays, *Cabir[i]a* and *Quo Vadis*, shown here last winter."[56] Several other reviewers drew attention to the parallels between *Cabiria* and *The Birth of a Nation*.
On the whole, they found Griffith's production at the very least equal to that of
Giovanni Pastrone.[57] One newspaper, the Philadelphia *Evening Ledger*, printed
a thoughtful comparison of the two films by its "dramatic editor." *Cabiria*, he
argued, was better than *Birth of a Nation* on a number of technical points, especially the lighting. Griffith, however, excelled in action and fire scenes, and with
the use of "cut-backs" (parallel editing) brought the second part of his film to a
dramatic and engrossing climax.[58] Other than on racial and historical grounds,
there was remarkably little direct criticism of *Birth*: the film critic of the New
York *Mail* thought the editing at times a little clumsy, was unimpressed by the
footage taken from a camera moving rapidly in front of the Ku Klux Klan ("It
absolutely kills the illusion"), and disliked the allegorical ending.[59] Most critics,
however, dealt only in superlatives: the aesthetics of the film, many believed,
were such an advance on what had gone before that *Birth of a Nation* signified
little less than the emergence of the motion picture as a new form of art.[60]

If *Birth* was art, whose art was it? In Germany before the First World War,
the term *"autorenfilm"* (author's film) had been coined to denote the claim
of the scenarist (rather than the director) to be the principal creative source
in making movies.[61] The film reviewer of the New York *Mail*, however, had an
alternative suggestion. "The producer of a film (by producer, I mean the man
who actually directs the making of the production) either makes or breaks the
effort," he wrote in March 1915. "Yet the producer has never, to date, had the
credit he deserves. This is especially true so far as the public is concerned."[62]
Griffith, as pointed out in Chapter 3, was a classic example of this unnamed
producer during his Biograph years.[63] But in terms of *The Birth of a Nation*
(which the *Mail* reviewer saw as a pioneering demonstration of the new possibilities of film), critics had no hesitation in identifying him as the movie's principal creator. Some hailed him as an artistic genius: one reviewer classed him
with Homer, Herodotus, Phidias, Michelangelo, Titian, and Wagner; another
saw him as "the modern Shakespeare."[64]

Mitchell and McCarthy's publicity team must have been delighted with
such unsolicited compliments. They were busy trying to build up the reputa-
tions of Griffith and his players by passing on tidbits of information (usually
fictional) about them to the newspapers. The hoary old claims about Griffith as
the originator of various new cinematic techniques were revived;[65] even more
far-fetched stories (including that Griffith had inspired the introduction of the
foxtrot as a dance) found their way into some newspaper reports.[66] Sometimes,
"planted" stories made the actors in the film seem even more fascinating and
exotic. According to one paper in Pennsylvania, the part of the lovesick sentry
gazing at Elsie Stoneman in the hospital scene was played by Paul LeBlanc, a
New Orleans Creole who had played comedy roles with Sarah Bernhardt before
going to Los Angeles, where Griffith discovered him. In spite of the convincing

level of detail provided, the story was false: the actual part of the lovesick sentry was played by William Freeman.[67]

One of the most influential things the publicity team did was to furnish the press with statistics on the length of the runs *Birth* was enjoying in major cities. It was not the first motion picture to enjoy a long run in a "live" theater; Herbert Brenon's seven-reel *Neptune's Daughter* held the pre-*Birth of a Nation* record with a half-year engagement at the Globe Theater in New York.[68] But it was the first to run for so long, to so much acclaim, in so many places at once. "The production starts in to-morrow upon its third month," observed one New York paper, anticipating somewhat, "and is going as strong as ever. Its success has been duplicated in Boston, Los Angeles and San Francisco and plans are now shaping for a Chicago production. Nearly 125,000 people have seen the picture...in this city."[69] "There have been over 500 performances at the Liberty theater, New York; 300 at the Tremont theater, Boston, and over 850 performances at the Illinois theater, Chicago," noted the Akron *Paragraph* in mid-September, "and it is still showing in these cities."[70] A few weeks later, the *Kansas City Star* reported (prematurely as it turned out) that *Birth* would close at the Liberty Theater in New York on November 27 after a run of 725 performances, and on the same day, its record-breaking runs of thirteen weeks in Philadelphia, St. Louis, and Pittsburgh (where the previous longest run—*Ben Hur*—had lasted five weeks) would also end. In Boston, it was noted, the film had opened on April 10 and closed on October 30, a twenty-nine week run that exceeded by 100 performances the record of any previous engagement.[71] By emphasizing the length and success of the film's runs in major metropolitan centers, local newspapers whetted the appetite of envious potential viewers in the rest of America. Reports of the controversy swirling around the film also made people outside the big cities eager to see what all the fuss was about.[72] There must also have been increasing numbers of word-of-mouth recommendations from neighbors and relatives who had seen the film on visits to one of the cities where it was showing.

As the number of available road companies grew, the publicity machine reversed itself. In the beginning, it had justified the film's few exhibition outlets by the difficulties of showing it. "Only in New York and two or three other large cities is 'The Birth of a Nation' on view," one newspaper explained. "The elaborateness of the mounting and accessories forbids its multitudinous reproduction."[73] After road shows made it possible to take the production on tour to smaller-sized communities, Mitchell and McCarthy realized that they would meet resistance in many localities to paying the same top price of $2 for admission as big city audiences had done. "It is hardly feasible to expect the smaller cities to contribute that amount of money to see it," commented a local newspaper in Fitchburg, Massachusetts. "With New York 1,934 miles to the east of us," observed one Western paper, "it seems probable the $2 admission price will have a long, slow, tedious and tiresome time reaching Denver."[74] To justify charging the higher prices that spelled bigger profits, publicists began to put across the message that *The Birth of a Nation* would be shown in only the highest-quality legitimate theaters "at prices charged for the best theatrical attractions."[75] They emphasized that the theaters concerned would need several days of preparation before they could show the film: a booth housing two projecting machines and various other pieces of electrical equipment would need to be installed at the correct distance from the screen and the stage and orchestra pit rearranged to accommodate the apparatus necessary to produce realistic battle and other sound effects.[76] While the film was actually being shown, a large number of operators, electricians, and effect men would be required, as would a full symphony orchestra to play the musical score. As a result of all these additions, road company managers such as Howard Herrick could try to justify the higher prices charged for admission by claiming that the film was being exhibited in some much smaller community "exactly as in New York and Chicago."[77]

There had, of course, been music at many theatrical performances; one reviewer referred rather disparagingly to the moment in *Uncle Tom's Cabin* when Eliza crossed the ice over the Ohio River to the sound of "three scrapy [sic] fiddles," and early movies were frequently screened to musical accompaniment, though often this was dependent on the whim and the skill (or lack of skill) of a single pianist.[78] Newspapers made it plain that the music written and performed for *The Birth of a Nation* was of a very different order. Some asserted (falsely) that the film's score was "the first significant accompaniment written for photo-drama."[79] They emphasized the degree to which it actually corresponded with the action taking place on the screen: *Birth's* music, remarked the St. Louis *Globe-Democrat*, "synchronised almost perfectly with the reel and added considerably to the enjoyment."[80] That the accompaniment was provided by a full orchestra—though its size varied from place to place[81]—was also the basis of much comment. Given the length of the film, for example, it was noted that the orchestra was required to play for nearly six hours a day. Sometimes musically aware film critics successfully identified the original melodies in Breil's score and assessed their effectiveness in relation to the particular sequences of the film they accompanied.[82]

So successful was the manipulation of the local press by the film's publicity department that paid advertisements for the movie were often almost undistinguishable from so-called news material (the latter often simply a reprint of press releases issued by Mitchell and McCarthy). Newspapers treated the presence of *Birth of a Nation* in their locality as an event. They emphasized that seeing it was a unique "once-in-a-lifetime" experience, that it had already enjoyed long runs and played to capacity houses in major cities, that the local engagement would be a comparatively brief one, and that seats would need to be reserved in advance.[83] Once the film started running, they reported that many people had traveled from miles around to see the show (sometimes, indeed, they published the names of such prominent "out-of-towners"), that there had been enormous queues at the box office and ticket sales had been spectacular, and that demand had been so great that additional performances had been scheduled or the film held over.[84] Almost everything connected with *Birth of a Nation* was news: the cost to exhibitors of securing the film for their theater, the parades held in many places before the first performance (later some of these would be organized by a revived Ku Klux Klan), the presence of local dignitaries at opening night, the 1870s uniforms and dresses worn by the ushers, and the special trains arranged to bring viewers from neighboring towns and cities.[85] In many places, theater owners invited certain groups—Northern and Southern veterans of the Civil War, visiting conventioneers, schoolchildren, newsboys, and orphans—to attend particular screenings for free, a tactic that led to much favorable comment in the local press.[86]

Changing the American Movie Audience

An innovative and effective publicity machine, enthusiastic reports in local newspapers, favorable word-of-mouth recommendations ("Each person who views the great film," observed a writer in the St. Louis *Star*, "becomes immediately a 'booster' for it"),[87] and the campaign to have the film banned or censored (which almost certainly persuaded many to view it mainly to see what was causing all the controversy) combined to make *The Birth of a Nation* the most successful movie of its time in the United States. Local newspapers made approximate estimates of the audiences who had seen the film toward the end of its run in particular cities: 185,000 in Boston, 100,000 in Kansas City, 100,000 in New Orleans, and 200,000 in Baltimore.[88] There were differing estimates of how many people in total saw it after its first release: one source suggested that, from its first performance at Clune's Auditorium in Los Angeles to the end of its ten-month run at New York's Liberty Theater, it had been viewed by a total audience of 5 million. *The Brooklyn Eagle* guessed that 10 million had seen it by June 1917. According to *The Columbus Dispatch*, one in every nine American adults had viewed it.[89] Through its success, *The Birth of a Nation* helped mold the future course of American cinema. Even if the trend toward bigger and better movie theaters actually preceded the release of *Birth*, Griffith's film greatly accelerated it. According to Roy Aitken, the road shows for *Birth of a Nation* "did much to convince many men with money that it could be a profitable venture for them to erect large theaters for the showing of outstanding motion pictures."[90]

Another effect of the success of *The Birth of a Nation* was further to encourage the construction of a new type of cinemagoer, closer in many ways to traditional theatergoers than patrons of nickelodeons. This new spectator would be prepared to pay the same price (up to $2) as for a live stage performance, to devote a whole evening to watching a single film, to book seats well in advance and, if necessary, to queue for them, even—*in extremis*—to pay the extortionate prices demanded by ticket speculators.[91] He or she would expect to watch a film in reasonable comfort and have it accompanied by music of greater standard and sophistication than that played in the nickelodeons. These viewers would also be ready to see a movie they liked more than once; commentators of the time noted with surprise just how many people had been to see *The Birth of a Nation* two, three, or more times.[92] To make such repeat viewing possible, of course, the films concerned would need to have longer runs.

Clearly, spectators of *The Birth of a Nation* differed in a number of crucial respects from previous American moviegoers. First, because of the road show character of the film's early distribution, they often had to travel considerable distances to see it at all. Journeys of sixty to a hundred miles and including an overnight stay in the city or town where the film was showing were relatively common.[93] Second, spectators of *Birth* were almost invariably far from passive in their response to the movie. "No play ever produced," observed one early critic, "has the gripping power of this picture. All the women were crying and not a few men." "People sit quietly and make no demonstration at ordinary motion pictures," observed another writer, but "not at 'The Birth of a Nation.'"[94] Many people who saw *Birth* became sufficiently emotionally engaged with the story as to lose their natural inhibitions. They found themselves, perhaps for the first time in their lives, caught up in the enthusiasm of "an audience that cheered and wept and sung."[95] Sometimes, old war shouts were heard in the theater, as Civil War veterans relived the conflict.[96] It is probable that audiences in different sections of the country reacted in different ways to particular sequences of the film: an audience in Terre Haute, Indiana, for example, applauded Lee's surrender to Grant. It is hard to see Southern audiences reacting in the same way, though they may have shared the enthusiasm of the Terre Haute audience for other scenes in the film, including the "Little Colonel's" refusal to shake the hand of the mulatto leader or the blacksmith's single-handed struggle against a gang of blacks in the saloon.[97] Wherever the film was shown, however, observers agree that storms of applause greeted the climax of the film—the Klan rides—and that such applause was virtually continuous for the rest of the movie.[98] Third, spectators' engagement with *The Birth of a Nation* did not always end when the screening did. Viewers continued to talk about it with family members, neighbors, and friends (one commentator, probably exaggerating somewhat, noted that "as a tea table topic" it had "quite eclipsed the European imbroglio"). Many also later sent glowing letters of appreciation for the film to the manager of the theater.[99]

Reconfiguring the American movie audience did not begin with *The Birth of a Nation*. Previous films—"spectaculars" or historical films, usually of European origin—had been longer than basic nickelodeon fare, had been booked into real theaters, and had been accompanied by orchestral music. They had attracted middle-class moviegoers, who were ready to pay more to see them than the five or ten cents required for entrance to the nickelodeons. The five years before *Birth*'s release had also seen an increasing trend toward longer films by some American producers and, as a corollary to the idea of the movies as an evening's entertainment, the opening of a number of larger, more comfortable movie theaters. What *Birth* succeeded in doing was greatly to accelerate these trends. It accustomed millions of people to the idea of watching a film lasting almost three hours in what had formerly been a "live" theater and paying up to $2 for a seat. It habituated them to the ideas that a film, like a play, had timed performances (nickelodeon programs tended to be continuous), that it would normally have a full musical score and orchestral accompaniment, that it could run at the same theater for long periods making repeated viewings possible, and that it might be necessary to reserve seats well in advance.

The Birth of a Nation was the first American-made film to be seen by a heterogeneous (if largely white) national audience. "Old and young, rich and poor, in the gallery and in the choice seats, united in the heartiest cheers and shouts of applause and often wept together," noted a New Orleans newspaper. According to a Baltimore reporter, the movie possessed "a peculiar sway over the emotions of all classes and degrees of men." When *Birth* was completed, there were two major doubts surrounding its release. "It was feared," remarked one commentator, "that this play was so strongly pro-Southern that it would not take with Northern audiences." In reality, Northern spectators cheered the Klan on just as enthusiastically as Southerners did.[100] The other uncertainty related to the social composition of the audience: would the film appeal to middle-class Americans who rarely attended movies as well as to the mainly working-class audiences of the nickelodeons? The previews held at the White House and the Raleigh Hotel in Washington suggested that it would, and this was later confirmed once the film opened in New York.[101]

The movie was able to construct such a large and socially heterogeneous audience for four main reasons. First, it was impressive in scale and highly entertaining. Second, *Birth* was the first domestically produced film to deal in truly spectacular fashion with American history. It encouraged Americans to engage with it by offering them a particular view of their past. Third, the film (as discussed in Chapter 7) was in many ways a response to and commentary on the state of the country itself and some of the problems facing American society in the mid-1910s. For audiences of the time, it offered many contemporary parallels and resonances. Fourth, the film was associated with the most expensive and ambitious publicity campaign that had ever been launched in connection with any motion picture.

6

Fighting a Vicious Film

The long war over *The Birth of a Nation* began quietly.[1] On January 20, 1915, a small subcommittee of the National Board of Censorship of Motion Pictures met in New York to watch *The Clansman* (soon to be renamed). The subcommittee was made up of ten people, including two members of the board's general committee.[2] It is impossible to identify the members of this group—the board insisted on the anonymity of its viewing committees.[3] It was certainly all white and in all likelihood predominantly female: in the spring of 1915, the board had a general pool, the so-called Censoring Committee, of 116 censors, of whom 95 were women.[4] All that is known about the committee for certain is that it approved Griffith's film for general exhibition.[5] The producers of *The Clansman* must have been pleased; the board's decision seemed to suggest that the film would not be greatly troubled by censorship difficulties. Over the next few days and weeks, they would come to realize that this was an illusory impression.

The first hints of trouble came from Los Angeles, where by late January *The Clansman* was being advertised as a forthcoming attraction at Clune's Auditorium. The local branch of the National Association for the Advancement of Colored People (NAACP), together with other Los Angeles organizations, approached the city's own censor board to try to have the film banned. The censor board itself arranged for a committee from the NAACP and its allies to see the film on the afternoon of January 29. Ignoring their protests, however, it then passed the film. The NAACP subsequently appealed to both the mayor and chief of police of Los Angeles to stop the film, but both declined on the grounds, as the NAACP branch secretary explained, that "the Censor Board had jurisdiction...and that they were powerless." Next, on February 2, the NAACP protested to the city council. On the morning of February 3, the council passed a resolution asking the board of censors to ban the film and demanding an emergency city ordinance to forbid its exhibition. However, with no sign that the board of censors was prepared to change its mind and no additional evidence of action on the part of the city council, the NAACP—with the February 8 première looming—as a last resort went to court to obtain an injunction to stop the film. Their grounds, as Richard Schickel points out, were the same as those later used by other branches of the NAACP: that showing the film created a threat to public safety since it encouraged racial tensions that might well lead to violence. Although the injunction was granted, it was narrowly drawn, forbidding the matinée screening on February 8 but not the actual evening première (or any later performance).[6]

In protesting against *The Clansman* and attempting to have it suppressed, the small local branch of the NAACP in Los Angeles had fired the first shots in a very long campaign. Moreover, in its appeal to the city council, it foreshadowed many of the arguments against the film that would subsequently be made by its opponents. The Los Angeles NAACP objected to the film on five grounds: that it revived the issues of the Civil War period, simultaneously belittling the North and the cause of liberty; that it made the black man "look hideous" and invested him "with the most repulsive habits and depraved passions"; that it was immoral in suggesting an illicit relationship between Stoneman and his mulatto servant; that the confrontation between the "Little Colonel" and black soldiers encouraged the perception that differences between the races might best be solved through violence; and that the scene of the meeting of Silas Lynch, the mulatto politician, and the "Little Colonel" was "calculated to excite feelings of animosity between the races."[7] While the authors of the protest were prepared to concede that Griffith's film had been "prepared with elaborate care" and displayed "some artistic qualities, particularly in the first half," they saw these as "wasted on a bad cause." Attempting "to commercialize the evil passions of man," the filmmakers had encouraged "bitterness and strife between the races" by portraying the black man as "a hideous monster." Their movie, alleged the NAACP, was both "historically inaccurate and, with subtle genius, designed to palliate and excuse the lynchings and other deeds of violence committed against the Negro."[8]

The members of the Los Angeles branch of the NAACP who saw the film on January 29 recognized both the danger the film posed to the position and reputation of American blacks and its hugely seductive power. Highly conscious of their own numerical weakness and lack of local organization (their secretary confessed that they had "accomplished so little" and apologized for being unable to send a delegate to the NAACP's annual conference), they made it clear from the first that the campaign against *The Clansman* should be led by the *national* organization. According to branch secretary E. Burton Ceruti, the film posed "a larger question [of racial friction] and concerns the whole country." Aware that the National Board of Censorship had already approved the film, he urged the NAACP's national headquarters in New York to devote its best efforts to persuading the board to think again and withdraw its approval—a strategy he deemed far preferable to "the waging of local fights wherever the 'Clansman' is introduced."[9]

On the face of it, this was good advice. The United States, in early 1915, offered a crazy-quilt pattern of local film censorships. Three states had so far passed censorship laws: Pennsylvania in 1912 and Ohio and Kansas, both in 1913. But many towns and cities had also established censor boards. Progressive reformers all over the country were anxious to discourage the exhibition of films encouraging immorality, violence, or crime. In 1914, Congress held hearings to consider the establishment of a federal censor board.[10] The main line of defense of the film industry against official censorships of this kind was the National Board of Censorship. Despite its grandiose title, the National Board of Censorship was neither national in character nor an effective instrument of censorship. Inaugurated in March 1909 as a private initiative of the People's Institute of New York, a progressive body dedicated to fighting for social welfare, it had quickly been adopted by a movie industry that preferred (and would continue to prefer) informal modes of self-regulation to legal censorship. In 1914, progressive reformer Frederic C. Howe, who directed the People's Institute and chaired the National Board of Censorship, managed to persuade the House of Representatives to let the board (whose decisions, he claimed, were respected by 80 percent of film exhibitors) continue its work in place of federal supervision of movies.[11] If the NAACP nationally *was* going to try to suppress the film, trying to persuade the National Board to revoke its approval would be a sensible initial strategy. Apart from anything else, both the National Board of Censorship and the headquarters of the NAACP were located in the same building: 70 Fifth Avenue, New York.

But was the NAACP ready and able to launch a fight against the film? Founded, like the National Board of Censorship, in 1909, it had a total membership in January 1915 of 5,000.[12] Most of its energies during early 1915 were absorbed by the struggle against discriminatory legislation. "Never has Congress...so engrossed the attention of our Association as during the last two months," observed *The Crisis*, official organ of the NAACP, in March 1915. As part of what the national NAACP chairman referred to as "an orgy of Negro-baiting," the Southern-dominated 63rd Congress had tried to include a complete ban on black immigration as part of a general immigration bill and was still considering bills for Washington, D.C., that banned racial intermarriage and introduced segregated streetcars.[13] As well as combating Congressional legislation, the NAACP was also heavily involved in fighting discriminatory state laws, such as a second attempt by Michigan to prohibit miscegenation (the first had been defeated a year earlier).[14] Another part of the strategy of the NAACP involved the attempt to overturn existing anti-black legislation in the courts. In May 1915, this campaign celebrated an important victory when, in the case of *Guinn v. United States,* the Supreme Court unanimously struck down Oklahoma's "grandfather" clause restricting blacks from voting.[15] To launch a campaign against *The Birth of a Nation* would involve the association in a new struggle at a time when its resources were already stretched.

If, on the other hand, one of the aims of the NAACP was to try, by means of agitation and protest, to arouse the moral conscience of Northern whites, could it continue to ignore the impact of cinema?[16] As early as 1910, the American *Review of Reviews* had hailed the motion picture as "probably the greatest single force in shaping the American character."[17] The rising tide of demands for censorship underlined this perception. Yet African Americans, confronted by a highly unfavorable and stereotypical view of themselves in many early films, had apparently only rarely complained.[18] Lester Walton, the movie critic of the New York *Age,* had tried and failed to mobilize fellow blacks to protest at a lynching movie that claimed to be "educational" and foregrounded the experience of the victim ("Hear His Moans and Groans"). It may have been the case, as Thomas Cripps suggests, that some blacks realized that the growing number of Southern-biased films about the Civil War was making it more and more difficult to think of representing African Americans more favorably on the screen.[19] Yet not until *The Birth of a Nation*—if then—would the relative complacency of blacks toward the cinema be shattered.

To dislike a film intensely was one thing, but preventing its exhibition was quite another. Although by 1915 many films had been cut or suppressed by censorship boards, this had normally been for the ways in which they treated issues such as sexual relationships, violence, and crime. The only films banned for racial reasons (though this was not usually openly avowed) were the pictures of famous black boxer Jack Johnson defeating his "white hope" opponent, Jim Jeffries, at Reno in 1910. In 1912, Congress made this policy official when it passed the Sims Act banning the interstate transportation of fight films, a piece of legislation directed almost exclusively at Johnson himself.[20] Only a tiny minority of localities in the United States had laws against racial discrimination that could be employed against the film. For the most part, attempts to stop the movie from being shown would have to focus on the danger it presented to public order through the incitement to racial violence. The most useful precedent here was not a film but Dixon's original play, *The Clansman,* which had been banned in a number of places, including Philadelphia where it had caused several riots.[21] There had also been vigorous black protests over the play in New York, where, according to Sylvester Russell in the *Chicago Defender,* "the Negro race had raved over the coming production [in 1906] and wanted it stopped."[22]

Attempts to suppress *The Birth of a Nation* through censorship, however, inevitably confronted many hurdles. Just over a week before the film opened in New York, the U.S. Supreme Court delivered its decision in the celebrated *Mutual Film Corporation v. Industrial Commission of Ohio* case, in which it created the legal framework for the censorship of motion pictures that would hold for the next thirty-six years by refusing to extend to movies the free speech protections of the First Amendment.[23] Despite this apparently promising start, however, spokesmen for *Birth of a Nation,* led by Griffith, fought back, making a very effective defense of the right to freedom of expression where cinema was concerned. On the afternoon before the New York première, Griffith addressed a meeting of the League for Political Education at the Cort Theater, attacking the attempt to censor any art form.[24] The director also inserted a new intertitle in his film immediately after the title sequence. In words that were designed to protect *Birth* and at the same time critique the *Mutual* decision, Griffith sought to claim the same rights of free expression "for the art of the motion picture" as had traditionally been conceded to more traditional arts, especially literature.[25] Over the next few months, he would effectively act as perhaps the leading publicist for the motion picture industry in its struggle against censorship, defending the right to freedom of expression on the part of filmmakers in speeches, interviews, and his 1916 pamphlet "The Rise and Fall of Free Speech in America."

Many white liberals would find themselves torn between their dislike of *The Birth of a Nation* and their dislike of censorship.[26] This was true even among the national leadership of the NAACP. As one perceptive Chicago journalist commented, the organization's demand that the film be suppressed

> must have embarrassed those members of the association who, like Charles T. Hallinan, have always fought censorship of any kind. Liberals are torn between two desires. They hate injustice to the negro and they hate a bureaucratic control of thought.[27]

The struggle over Griffith's film emphasized tensions and divisions within the board of directors of the NAACP itself. Some, as suggested above, were opposed to censorship on principle. Others felt the fight was simply not worthwhile. "Several of the members of the Board," wrote NAACP national secretary May Childs Nerney in spring 1915, "doubt if 'The Birth of a Nation' is doing the harm that many of us feel it is." And even those most publicly committed to the campaign against the film at times wondered if their efforts might be counterproductive. "One always fears," Mary White Ovington confessed, "that publicity will only aid a show."[28]

The release of *The Birth of a Nation* proved very revealing about the state of the NAACP generally in 1915. It threw the problems of the organization—from a divided board of directors to the limitations of some branches—into sharp relief. Many local branches maintained a tenuous existence: R. W. Stewart of Newark, New Jersey, attempting to form a committee to lobby the mayor against *The Birth of a Nation,* sadly admitted that he "could never get enough of us together after several attempts."[29] Other branches, as in Louisville and Pittsburgh, were threatened by factionalism.[30] Some, as in Kansas City, were so divided that they collapsed.[31] The distribution of branches was very uneven across the country as a whole and tended to be concentrated in major cities such as New York, Philadelphia, Pittsburgh, Chicago, and Washington, D.C. (where the local members acted as the main shock troops in the fight to prevent Congress from passing discriminatory legislation). In some places, the local leadership had its own priorities: the president of the branch in Alton, Illinois, for example, was apparently totally uninterested in protesting at *The Birth of a Nation*. Other branches, such as in Pittsburgh, were slow to respond to requests for information from the national organization.[32] Both locally and nationally, the NAACP was a sometimes uneasy coalition of whites and blacks (with whites dominating on the board of directors). Moreover, those blacks involved were normally from the relatively small educated elite. "The masses of the colored people know nothing of the association," it was reported to the board in January 1916; "the Crisis [the NAACP journal] does not reach them; often they do not read."[33]

The National Board of Censorship

At the beginning of February 1915, the national leadership of the NAACP, though far from unanimously, started to fight for the suppression of *The Birth of a Nation*. May Childs Nerney, the NAACP's national secretary, visited the offices of the National Board of Censorship to ask for four things: the names of the members of the committee that had approved the picture, the addresses of all the members of the board of censorship, a list of the cities where the film had already been released, and the opportunity for a committee of the NAACP's National Board to view the film at an advance performance. W. D. McGuire, the executive secretary of the National Board of Censorship, told her that the film had so far been released only in Los Angeles and advised her that "it would be impossible for anything to be done about it now since it had been approved by the Board of Censorship." Temporarily balked, Nerney wrote a courteous letter to D. W. Griffith asking that a committee from the NAACP be permitted to attend an advance performance.[34] Griffith, who must have known very well why the request was being made, does not seem to have replied. Instead, the NAACP turned to Frederic C. Howe, chairman of the National Board of Censorship. Howe, a well-known urban reformer, had been an ally of progressive mayor Tom L. Johnson of Cleveland, Ohio, until Johnson lost power after eight years in office in 1909. Author of several books on municipal reform, Howe had first become head of the People's Institute in New York and later, in 1914, U.S. Commissioner of Immigration. Already, by February 25, Nerney claimed that Howe and his wife were "strongly partisan in our favor." Although Howe did not attempt to arrange a special screening of *The Birth of a Nation*, he did ask that the entire General Committee of the National Board of Censorship be permitted to be present at the private viewing of the film on March 1. He also requested McGuire to arrange for twelve tickets to be made available for members of the NAACP at the same screening. While Nerney was drawing up a list of those to be given tickets, the assistant secretary of the National Board of Censorship, W. A. Barrett, came to her office and told her that no colored people would be admitted. A few moments later, McGuire telephoned to say that the number of seats had been reduced from twelve to two.[35] In reality, three members of the NAACP's board seem to have been present at the March 1 showing: chairman J. E. Spingarn and directors Paul Kennaday and the Reverend John Haynes Holmes.[36]

Later, on March 1, with the screening over, Howe convened a meeting of the General Committee. Spingarn was invited to attend part of this meeting to present the NAACP case against the film but apparently was allowed only a few minutes to speak. Howe seems to have believed "that the picture portrayed the Negro in such a brutal and degrading way that half of it, or the second part, should be either eliminated or cut so completely that but little of it would be left." In a triumph of wishful thinking, he and another member of the executive committee, Dr. Warbasse, seem to have convinced themselves that the General Committee as a whole shared this view. Accordingly, once the meeting was over, they informed the NAACP that the National Board of Censorship had repudiated its former view and had now disapproved the film.[37]

For the next few days, Nerney and the NAACP leadership basked in the apparent satisfaction of a job well done. Although by now they had clearly given up the notion of suppressing the film completely, they believed that The Birth of a Nation would not be shown until the most controversial features had been cut. "Association has scored great triumph in New York," Nerney telegraphed the Los Angeles branch on March 2. "National Board of Censorship...unanimously voted last evening to disapprove entire second part of film and to cut out all objectionable race allusions."[38] In a flood of wishful thinking, the NAACP leadership convinced itself that not only had its campaign persuaded the National Board of Censorship to change its mind about the film but also that both organizations were now working together to make the film acceptable. Believing that the board of censorship had changed direction, the NAACP set out to publicize the board's disapproval of the film to ministers (in the hope that they would preach against it),[39] film production companies,[40] and the New York Commissioner of Licenses (in the hope that he would stop the performance of The Birth of a Nation as a "public nuisance").[41] Conscious, however, that an as yet unannounced decision by the National Board of Censorship would not be enough to stop its first public exhibition, on the morning of March 3 the NAACP tried and failed in the police court to have the première at the Liberty Theater canceled because it constituted a threat to public order.[42]

Meanwhile, the National Board of Censorship pursued a path very different from the one imagined by the NAACP. After the criticism of the film offered by several members of the General Committee at the meeting on March 1, a conference was held between the National Board of Censorship, represented by its chairman, Frederic Howe, and executive secretary, W. D. McGuire, and the film's producers. At this conference, the producers "at once offered to modify certain scenes and re-submit the picture to the General Committee." A further viewing of the film, followed by a meeting of the General Committee, was held on March 12. At this meeting, the committee voted by a majority of twelve to nine to pass the film, subject to two additional changes that the producers quickly agreed to make. It was reported, to the great dismay of the NAACP, that the committee had actually cheered Griffith when he appeared before them.[43]

Still Fighting in New York

There were many consequences for the NAACP of the National Board of Censorship's decision. Leaders of the fight against Griffith's film like Nerney, already exhausted by their efforts, were heartbroken. The NAACP decided to put more efforts into the legal battle against *Birth of a Nation* and hired as its counsel James M. Osborne, perhaps the leading trial attorney in New York.[44] It also called a special board meeting for March 23 to ratify Osborne's appointment. The date for the hearing of the NAACP case against Aitken and Griffith was set for March 19. On March 18, however, the NAACP was informed that the case had been postponed indefinitely. On the same day as the canceled hearing, therefore, the NAACP switched tactics: nine members of the organization's leadership wrote to John Purroy Mitchel, mayor of New York, asking him to suppress the film "as an offense against public decency and as endangering public morals."[45]

Henceforth, the fight against the film would be primarily political, with New York as the starting gun in this new campaign. "Our experience in New York where we tried everything," commented May Childs Nerney a few weeks later, "indicates that the only hope [of suppressing the film] is with the city authorities."[46] Yet having failed to prevent the film's acceptance by the one national institution capable of either suppressing it or ensuring the removal of its more controversial features, the NAACP now became involved in a war of attrition in which it depended on local branches to discover when the film was due to open and to take the lead in the fight against it.[47] In places where the local organization was numerous and determined, the battle was often fierce. In other towns and cities, however, where branches were weak or nonexistent, the film was shown with little or no protest.

With the postponement of the NAACP's legal case in New York—something that would be repeated on several occasions[48]—the board meeting of the NAACP on March 23 was mainly a discussion of the tactics to be employed in preparation for the meeting with the mayor. Social worker Lillian Wald suggested that "a dignified procession" representing all the local organizations interested in helping colored people march to the mayor's office to protest against the film; this idea was accepted and a committee set up to organize the march.[49] The original plan called for as large a delegation as possible to assemble in Union Square and proceed down Broadway to the mayor's office, but this idea was foiled by the police commissioner's insistence that such parades could take place only on business streets "on Saturdays and holidays." The NAACP was obliged to concentrate most attention on organizing speakers for the meeting with the mayor, finally set for March 30. These speakers included the chair of the National Board of Censorship Frederic Howe (who had refused to allow the use of his name in the board's approval of *The Birth of a Nation*);[50] Dr. William H. Brooks, pastor of St. Mark's Methodist-Episcopal Church; W. E. B. Du Bois, editor of *The Crisis*, the NAACP journal; Fred R. Moore, editor of the New York *Age*; Oswald Garrison Villard, editor of the New York *Evening Post* and vice-president of the NAACP; Lillian Wald; Rabbi Stephen S. Wise; and George E. Wibecan, president of the Brooklyn Citizens' Club.[51] Altogether, about 500 people attended the hearing before the Mayor at City Hall. They were drawn from many organizations with an interest in promoting

W. E. B. Du Bois (1868–1963), editor of the NAACP journal *The Crisis*. (Library of Congress, Prints and Photographs Division, LC-DIG-ggbain-07435)

racial harmony, and—for the first and last time during the New York campaign against the film—the majority seem to have been African Americans. According to Fred Moore, the "neat personal appearance" of the black clergymen, businessmen, and professional people "was in itself a strong denial to the slurs made against the Negro in 'The Birth of a Nation.'"[52]

Until the meeting with the mayor, the battle against Griffith's film had been very largely an NAACP affair. It had tried to put pressure on the National Board of Censorship to ban the film. To further its legal suit, it had gathered signed affidavits criticizing the film from individuals such as scientist Jacques Loeb. It had orchestrated celebrated social worker Jane Addams' opposition to the film, culminating in her highly critical interview with the New York *Post* on March 13.[53] While not responsible for Francis Hackett's searing indictment of *The Birth of a Nation* in *The New Republic* on March 20, it had effectively publicized his view by purchasing off-prints of the article and posting them to many newspapers across the country.[54] But when the NAACP opted to become involved in New York politics, it felt obliged to seek allies outside its own immediate circle. Du Bois put the best possible gloss on this when he insisted, in *The Crisis*, that all colored groups had worked well together in the lead-up to the meeting with Mayor Mitchel.[55] In reality, this was untrue. The NAACP's intervention in New York politics underlined the differences existing within the black community in 1915. Booker T. Washington, regarded by many whites as the principal black leader of the time, disliked the NAACP and wanted to preserve his own influence. Outgoing federal officeholder Charles W. Anderson,[56] who was close to Booker T. Washington and his "Tuskegee machine," managed to reach the New York mayor during the week *before* the meeting on March 30 with the suggestion that he see the film and act at once. NAACP representatives who did attend the meeting with the mayor on March 30 were dumbfounded when Mitchel told them "that he had seen the play and had informed the producers that...two objectionable scenes must be eliminated and they had promised to comply with his wishes." Washington himself was delighted with the whole affair, congratulating Anderson on "forestalling that crowd [the NAACP]" and taking "some of the wind out of their sails."[57]

The NAACP, having expected help—which it failed to get—from the National Board of Censorship, was much warier of the mayor's assurances. It did, the next day, temporarily adjourn its legal case against the film but made clear that the action would be renewed if the changes promised by the film's producers had not been made.[58] The day after the hearing with the mayor, several members of the NAACP saw *The Birth of a Nation* again and reported that while some small changes had been made the two main scenes the mayor had objected to (Gus's chasing Flora Cameron to her death and Lynch's attempt to arrange a "forced marriage" with Elsie Stoneman) had not been removed. NAACP Chairman J. E. Spingarn wrote to the mayor to inform him of this on April 1.[59] That same day, Mayor Mitchel met with D. W. Griffith, Thomas Dixon,

Black leader Booker T. Washington (1856–1915). (Library of Congress, Prints and Photographs Division, LC-USZ62-119897)

and their lawyer and told them of his objections to the scenes concerned. The Griffith team, conscious that these particular sequences were vital to the narrative of the second part of the film, dissimulated. They promised to make the suggested cuts and arranged to meet Commissioner of Licenses Bell and Deputy Commissioner Kaufmann at the Liberty Theater to discuss what should be removed. It seems clear that Griffith and his colleagues had no intention of making more than minor, cosmetic changes to the film.[60] On April 6, Spingarn again wrote to Mitchel pointing out that, although some cuts had been made, the two offensive scenes remained. The mayor asked Commissioner Bell for a report, and on April 9, May C. Nerney wrote to Bell pointing out that both controversial scenes were still being screened, although the one of Gus chasing Flora had been shortened. And there, in essence, the matter rested.[61]

Reflecting on the NAACP's New York campaign in mid-April, Nerney confessed that the whole experience had been "a most liberal education."

"I have ceased to worry about it," she told a Chicago correspondent, "and if I seem disinterested, kindly remember that we have put six weeks of constant effort on this thing and have gotten nowhere."[62] Having failed to persuade the National Board of Censorship either to suppress *The Birth of a Nation* completely or to have the most controversial sequences cut, the NAACP had also failed to persuade the mayor of New York to live up to the promises he had made at the hearing on March 30.[63] It was left with a not very convincing lawsuit that tried to have the film banned as a danger to public order. Because the Liberty Theater was careful to avoid admitting blacks to the film—and had a group of private detectives on hand to forestall any hint of trouble—there was little danger of any real threat to social peace.[64] The closest to an actual disturbance inside the theater came on April 14, when a white member of the Industrial Workers of the World, Howard Schaeffle, threw eggs at the screen and African American Cleveland G. Allen, the head of a black news agency, shouted a protest at the inappropriateness of showing a film like *Birth* on the fiftieth anniversary of Lincoln's assassination. Both men were promptly hustled out by detectives and ushers.[65] There was a brief flicker of hope on the part of the NAACP in late April and early May; an ordinance was introduced in a meeting of the Board of Aldermen supposedly to extend the authority of the Commissioner of Licenses to make it possible for him to suppress movies (both Mayor Mitchel and Commissioner Bell were uncertain over the precise limits of their authority), but when the NAACP realized that the draft ordinance had no such provisions it lost interest.[66] Finally, in late May, the legal suit against *Birth of a Nation* was dismissed and the NAACP's campaign against the film in New York finally came to an end.[67]

In retrospect, it was never likely that the NAACP could have won. The struggle against *The Birth of a Nation* was a war fought to defend blacks but waged primarily by whites. Even when it came to organizing clergy to oppose the movie, it was primarily white ministers who became involved. Yet, there was always only a tiny minority of whites involved in fighting the film. Even men and women who were usually supporters of the NAACP found it hard to understand what all the fuss was about: S. S. Frissell went to see *Birth* and found it largely unobjectionable.[68] Most white audiences who watched the film became enthusiasts for it. The white press concentrated on printing favorable reviews and advertisements for the film; the only real criticism came from Oswald Garrison Villard's *Post*, which printed Jane Addams's critical interview on March 13, and radical papers such as the *Call*.[69] It was in vain that the NAACP leadership tried to accumulate evidence of the ways in which the film fostered racial prejudice against African Americans.[70] Most of the black population of New York seem to have reacted to *The Birth of a Nation* with "utter indifference." Lester Walton, the black film critic of the *New York Age* and a convinced opponent of Griffith's film, accused other African Americans of lacking racial solidarity because of their failure to protest against it.[71]

The Boston Campaign

In early April, as its campaign against *The Birth of a Nation* in New York was starting to wind down, the NAACP found itself involved in a second major fight to have the film suppressed, this time in Boston where it was advertised to have its first public performance at the Tremont Theater on April 10. In theory, Boston offered far more fertile ground for such an attempt than New York. It had a strong antislavery tradition. Boston was the home city of William Lloyd Garrison and his supporters, such as William Ellery Channing, Theodore Parker, Wendell Phillips, and John Greenleaf Whittier. Black voters made up a significant part of the Democratic coalition of minorities and the disadvantaged assembled by James Michael Curley, then in the early stages of his long career as the city's mayor.[72] Finally, the press had a record of being more sympathetic toward black anxieties and preoccupations in Boston than in New York. But if the NAACP expected to exercise uncontested leadership of the Boston campaign, they reckoned without the bullish figure of William Monroe Trotter. Editor of the black newspaper *The Guardian*, Trotter—in common with another Harvard-trained African American, W. E. B. Du Bois of the NAACP—was a severe critic of what he saw as the compromising and accommodating approach to race relations of Booker T. Washington. Trotter, as a result of his outspokenness, had managed to alienate President Wilson at a meeting at the White House in November 1914 when he had led a delegation protesting the continuing segregation in Washington.[73] In some ways, however, this was symptomatic of the Trotter style. Whereas the NAACP preferred discreet background pressure and lobbying, Trotter was a pioneer of direct action and confrontation.[74]

Trotter was away from Boston when the city's branch of the NAACP, together with the radical Boston Literary and Historical Association, requested that Mayor Curley hold hearings to consider whether *The Birth of a Nation* should be banned. But he rushed back for the meeting on April 7. In the days leading up to it, the film's critics and its defenders had already staked out their positions. Moorfield Storey, president of the NAACP's board of directors, wrote a letter attacking the film that was published in the Boston *Herald*. Storey argued that *The Birth of a Nation* distorted history, offered "a caricature of the negro," and incited racial prejudice. He quoted from Jane Addams's critique of the film. J. J. McCarthy, business manager for the film, replied in a letter published in the *Herald* on the day scheduled for the mayoral hearings. McCarthy argued that the NAACP was intent on fomenting racial prejudice and violence and that the historical "truth" of the film was attested to by such authorities as James Ford Rhodes, Woodrow Wilson, and Walter L. Fleming. Indeed, he said, Griffith was so certain of the film's accuracy that he had offered $10,000 to anyone who could demonstrate that any part of it was historically untrue. McCarthy further claimed that the director should be credited with inventing a whole new art. He suggested that Addams's comments on *Birth* were vitiated because she had viewed only half the film, and he queried whether Storey had actually seen the movie or was acting on hearsay alone. McCarthy finished by declaring that the film had the support of many distinguished Americans, including banker and philanthropist George Foster Peabody; ministers Charles H. Parkhurst and Thomas B. Gregory; Congressman Claude Kitchen, the new majority leader of the House of Representatives; Senators Martine, Fletcher, Myers, Walsh, and Jones; Governor Hiram Johnson of California; and several eminent writers.[75]

The hearing before Mayor Curley was held in the afternoon of April 7. Curley was genial and clearly enjoyed the opportunity for grandstanding. He interrupted the anti-film speakers with questions and, equally, allowed them to interrupt him. Mary White Ovington, the first witness, thought him "a democratic and very kindly Irishman." Curley was clearly more worried about hints of sexual immorality than anything else, questioning Ovington over whether Flora Cameron in her scenes with Gus was "unsufficiently dressed." Ovington was honest enough to answer in the negative, but she tried (unavailingly) to persuade him that the "sensuous look" on Gus's face would inevitably have suggested immorality to audiences. From the end of Ovington's testimony onward, things went steadily downhill for the NAACP contingent. Curley dismissed the evidence of Storey, who spoke next, because he had not himself seen the film. Neither, apparently, had the rector of Trinity Church, Alexander Mann, who attempted to suggest that the film should be suppressed because it was based on Thomas Dixon's play, *The Clansman*, which had been banned in Boston by Curley's mayoral predecessor (and great rival), John F. Fitzgerald. Then architect Joseph P. Loud made some comments on the film in a "very shaky" voice. At that point, the NAACP's formal role in the proceedings came to an end. The next speaker, Trotter, who was also the last to attack the film, proved far better: Ovington described him as "eloquent" and thought he had made "a very fine impression." Knowing Curley well, Trotter knew just how to appeal to the mayor: he reminded him that blacks had supported him in the past, but asserted that future support would depend on how Curley responded to *The Birth of a Nation*.[76]

After Trotter had finished, the defenders of the film were permitted half an hour to make their case. John F. Cusick, the attorney for Epoch, argued that the film demonstrated the racial progress that had been made since the Civil War and mentioned the formal approval for the film by the National Board of Censorship. When Cusick commented, however, that the film had been seen by President Wilson, a "tremendous hissing" became audible from the mainly black audience. Griffith was then given a chance to speak in defense of his film. He insisted on his right to film history as he saw it, but—asked by Curley if he would cut the scene of Gus pursuing Flora—assured the mayor he would if the Boston authorities required such a change. After the hearing was over, Storey asked Griffith (in relation to his promise to pay $10,000 to anyone who could

James Michael Curley (1874–1958), long-serving mayor of Boston. (Library of Congress, Prints and Photographs Division, LC-USZ62-62918)

prove that the film presented an untrue version of history) if it was true that a mulatto lieutenant-governor of South Carolina had locked up a white girl to force her into marriage. Griffith made no direct reply, only asking Storey to go and see the film. He then offered to shake hands with Storey who, in an ironic echo of the scene in the film in which Ben Cameron declines to shake the hand of Silas Lynch, drew back and refused.[77]

While Curley had seemed sympathetic to critics of the film, he made no immediate move to prevent its exhibition. Indeed, he declared that he had no right to stop it from being shown unless it tended "to injure the morals of the community" or was "immoral or obscene." Yet he asked to have municipal censor John S. Casey and a representative of the police commissioner present at a private showing of the film on April 9. In their reports, both asserted that there were no legal grounds for banning the film. Curley, however, had attended the same preview and become convinced that a number of racially inflammatory sequences should be cut. While the mayor had no legal power to *require* this, the film's producers obviously felt it would be politically sensible to have him on their side. The film officially opened on April 10, therefore, with a number of cuts in addition to those made in New York. According to Curley, these included the intertitle that said bringing the African to America planted the first seed of disunion, Charles Sumner's meeting with Lydia Brown, Austin Stoneman's mulatto housekeeper [Sumner, an opponent of slavery, had been a senator from Massachusetts], "certain scenes" between Lydia Brown and Stoneman and Lydia and Silas Lynch, sequences set in the South Carolina House of Representatives showing a man removing his shoes and the assembly discussing a motion that all members must wear shoes, and parts of the sequence in which Gus chases Flora, including at least five shots of Gus's facial expressions.[78]

To the annoyance of the film's opponents, *The Birth of a Nation* opened in Boston to a fanfare of praise from the press and clear audience approval. "The picture, an unusual and admirable entertainment," remarked the Boston *Herald*, "deserves every success." Its reception by the opening night audience, Harry Aitken noted, had equaled the warmth of that in Los Angeles or New York.[79] Efforts to have the film suppressed continued. On Monday, April 12, Trotter and a delegation of around twenty-five black men and women called on the mayor to reiterate their demand that *Birth* be banned. Trotter argued that colored people were being denied tickets by the management of the Tremont Theater and thus that a Southern-style segregationist color line was being drawn in Boston. Curley appeared to be sympathetic (Joseph P. Loud of the NAACP would accuse him later that week of "playing to the colored galleries"). He condemned the film as "an outrage on the negro race" but insisted that he had no power to prevent its being shown.[80]

The first week of *The Birth of a Nation*'s run in Boston saw the Griffith forces go on the offensive. As well as claiming that many prominent Americans endorsed the film, they also took out advertisements in all the newspapers in an attempt to discredit as "agitators" those who were protesting against the film. The film's producers may also have had a hand in ensuring that many of the leading protestors were followed for several days by detectives. "They certainly have employed every possible means money will buy to force the play upon Boston," declared Joseph P. Loud on April 15.[81] That same day, the Boston press reported that Griffith had begun work on a new film that would balance the account of the black role in the era of the Civil War described in *Birth of a Nation* with a supplementary film that would show the progress achieved by African Americans since that time.[82] There was a considerable element of dissimulation involved in this news; it seems to have been simply a trial balloon. The new film was already complete and had its first airing at the Tremont Theater the next day, April 16.[83] This chronology undermines the assumption that Griffith first thought of basing such a film on the Tuskegee Institute in Alabama, directed by Booker T. Washington. He had actually suggested this to Philip J. Allston and Dr. Alexander Cox of the Negro National Business League after the April 10 première.[84] But the film itself, shot at the Hampton Institute, the industrial school in Virginia from which Washington had graduated, must have been ready or nearly ready at that point.

Little specific evidence is available on how what became known as the "Hampton Epilogue" came to be in the possession of the producers of *Birth*. Nicki Fleener observes that the relationship may have had its origins in a suggestion made by members of the National Board of Censorship to Hollis B. Frissell, principal of the Hampton Institute, that showing a more hopeful picture about black progress would help counter the impression left by *Birth of a Nation*. One of the Hampton trustees, William J. Schieffelin, also seems to have advocated the idea.[85] The film appears to have been made by Hampton itself; it may already have been traveling around with a Hampton singing quartet in early 1915. Although it no longer exists, contemporary reports indicate that it lasted about five or six minutes and included both scenes of students of Hampton at work and statistics on black economic progress in the previous half-century. Clearly, Griffith and his colleagues jumped at the idea of trying to undermine African American protest over *Birth* by adding the epilogue. Frissell, by contrast, was attempting to weaken the film's racism through more positive images of blacks and also to publicize the work of his school to the new mass audience created by *Birth*.[86] One important by-product of the screening of the Hampton Epilogue was that it altered the trajectory of *Birth*: instead of concluding with the shot of blacks awaiting transport back to Africa (as Dixon and Griffith had originally planned), the film program now ended with a brief suggestion that the race problem would be solved as blacks made progress within American society. Whatever impact the showing of the epilogue had, however, was probably diminished by its brevity and the fact that it was not screened in many places. As a correspondent of Booker T. Washington observed, "the film people do not regularly show the Hampton picture, but only...when the spirit moves."[87]

On April 17, one week after *Birth*'s official première in Boston, May Childs Nerney confessed to an NAACP colleague that "I never believed myself that this thing could be shown in Abolition Boston. When I heard that it was to be shown there without any demonstration whatsoever against it, I lay down like Jack Johnson. I do not know whether I want to get up again or not."[88] Later that same day, a "demonstration" finally did occur in Boston. It was led, however, not by the NAACP but by William Monroe Trotter. Before the evening performance, Trotter and a group of blacks entered the lobby of the Tremont Theater and attempted to buy tickets. They were refused (though a white man was allowed to buy tickets). The theater management had been expecting trouble that evening—there were rumors of an African American plan to pack the house and perhaps destroy the film—and many plainclothes police were inside the theater with other uniformed police outside. When Trotter and his friends were ordered out of the lobby and refused to obey (protesting that they were being discriminated against), the police moved in, clearing the lobby with their clubs. Trotter, who had been struck by a policeman, and ten others were arrested. Inside the theater (where, despite security, some blacks had managed to gain admittance) there were occasional jeers. At the point when Flora was about to leap to her death to escape the pursuing Gus, one African American threw a well-aimed egg at the center of the screen. Shortly afterward, stink bombs were set off. After the performance ended at eleven, the audience went out into the streets where there were more arguments, fistfights, and arrests. "It was," according to Trotter's biographer, "the most ominous racial incident in Boston in anyone's memory, probably the most ominous since the Civil War era."[89]

On the afternoon of the next day, Sunday April 18, a mass meeting took place at Faneuil Hall. While the great majority of those who attended were black, most speakers, including eighty-five-year-old veteran abolitionist Frank B. Sanborn who presided, were white. They included Michael J. Jordan of the United Irish League and Rolfe Cobleigh, assistant editor of *The Congregationalist*. But the audience saved its warmest applause for Trotter, one of three African Americans who spoke. Charged the previous evening with disturbing the peace and then released on bail, Trotter criticized Curley for refusing to ban the film.[90] Then, encouraged by the decision of the state police to prevent *The Birth of a Nation* from being shown anywhere in Massachusetts on Sundays,[91] the meeting endorsed a new strategy: to appeal to the state government to stop the film, effectively by-passing Curley and the city authorities. It was decided that all those present at the meeting should march to the State House on Monday morning to lobby Governor David I. Walsh in the hope that he would suppress the film. Walsh, a Democrat, facing a critical reelection campaign, probably saw the issue raised by *Birth* as a means of seducing the black voters of Massachusetts away from their traditional Republican allegiance. As early as April 14, he had met with Boston Police Commissioner Stephen O'Meara to see if there was any legal way of suppressing the film.[92] Yet he had no desire to be seen as acting solely at the behest of militants led by Trotter. Instead, he consulted with William H. Lewis, once a black football star and sometime assistant attorney-general of the United States, and white lawyer Butler R. Wilson. Lewis had close links to Booker T. Washington and the Tuskegee machine; Wilson was a member of the NAACP. Together with these moderates and a small number of their colleagues, Walsh worked out a way of defusing the situation. He would instruct the attorney-general of Massachusetts to prosecute the management of the Tremont Theater under a law of 1910 that banned performances that were "lewd, obscene, indecent, immoral or impure" or even merely suggestive of such things. He would also seek from the legislature a new state censorship law.[93]

On Monday morning, a large crowd of up to 2,000 people marched along Beacon Street to the State House, where they saw Trotter and sixty of his closest supporters admitted to meet with the governor. Inside, Trotter and his group were presented with the deal Walsh had worked out with the moderates.

Though this was effectively a fait accompli, Trotter was permitted to save face by announcing the governor's plans to the waiting crowd. The crowd subsequently dispersed in an orderly fashion; so promising did these developments seem that a further demonstration at the theater was called off.[94] Up to this point, the Boston campaign against the film seemed far more successful than that in New York. The black community had become increasingly involved and the protests more numerous and organized. "It is said," Samuel Edward Courtney wrote to Booker T. Washington from Boston on April 19, "[that] not since Civil War times have such demonstrations been seen here in Boston."[95] In retrospect, however, April 19 marked the peak of the struggle against *Birth*. Afterward, it was mostly downhill. The hope of successful legal action proved chimerical. While Judge Thomas H. Dowd of the Municipal Court refused the request of lawyers for the Tremont Theater and Griffith that the case be delayed, in his judgement (delivered on April 21) he made it clear that the law of 1910 under which the suit had been brought did not apply to the arousal of racial prejudice but only to expressions of immorality. Dowd accordingly demanded that the scene in which Gus spies on Little Sister and then chases her be cut out, and the theater management announced that it would comply with this demand. As Richard Schickel points out, this was in itself an odd decision since Dowd, in focusing exclusively on Gus, ignored "the much more erotic forced marriage sequence." Moreover, as Joseph Loud noted, though the actual chase sequence was eliminated, audiences were still free to draw the inference of rape. But with Dowd's decision, the attempt to have the judicial system ban *Birth* in Boston ground to a halt.[96]

Opponents of the film were now left with but a single option: to take up Governor Walsh's suggestion of passing a new censorship law. On Tuesday, April 20, Representative Lewis J. Sullivan of Boston had filed a bill that would extend the provisions of the 1910 law to include a ban on "any show or entertainment which tends to excite racial or religious prejudice or tends to a breach of the public peace." Supported by the governor and Lieutenant-Governor Grafton D. Cushing, hearings on the proposed new law were scheduled for the end of the same week. Black and pro-black groups launched a vigorous campaign to secure acceptance of the new law.[97] Even during the first few days, however, it became clear that the struggle over censorship would be complex and difficult. Representative Bates offered an alternative to the Sullivan bill that sought to tighten up the regulation of movies by transferring responsibility for it from the state police to the Massachusetts board of labor and industries.[98] Several other bills would be proposed over the next few weeks, confusing the issue yet further.[99] On principle, censorship was opposed by many newspapers as an undesirable restriction on freedom of expression. The Boston *Herald* conceded that the Sullivan bill had been framed "to secure an end [the banning of *Birth of a Nation*] for which just now there is much popular demand" but cautioned that its enactment would represent a major threat to "the freedom of the individual, of the theatre, and of the church and the press." The *Transcript* pointed out that banning any show or entertainment that threatened the public peace would encourage violence since, if two men engaged in a fight in the lobby of a theater, the authorities might find themselves obliged to step in and stop the show concerned.[100] Thomas Dixon, seeing the proposed bill as the work of "a few negro agitators," attacked it in a letter to the *Journal* as a means of suppressing "two-thirds of all the serious drama at present running."[101]

While Dixon, Griffith, and their supporters in the press continued to protest at the threat to freedom represented by the potential new law, it seemed as if the current was running against them. The NAACP, applying itself seriously for the first time to Massachusetts politics, helped put together a bipartisan coalition: the censorship bill was supported by Governor Walsh (a Democrat) and the two leading contenders for the Republican gubernatorial nomination: Lieutenant-Governor Cushing and Samuel W. McCall.[102] A steady drumbeat of meetings and protests emphasized the engagement of Boston's black community with the attempt to ban *The Birth of a Nation* under a new censorship regime. Two mass meetings were held in churches on Sunday, April 25, one (addressed by Charles W. Eliot, former president of Harvard University) in Cambridge and the other predominantly of black women (but attended by Trotter) in Roxbury. The following day, April 26, a lively, largely black crowd of 500 attended the hearings on the new censorship bill.[103]

At the end of the week, the joint committee on the judiciary of the Massachusetts legislature reported favorably on a revised version of the Sullivan bill. In essence, it proposed a new censorship board for Boston made up of the mayor, the chief justice of the Municipal Court, and the chief of police. Since there was no provision for any appeal against a decision by the board to revoke the license of an offending theater, this was unpopular both with theater managers and the *Birth of a Nation* forces (who would organize a special showing of the film to all members of the legislature on Monday, May 3).[104] At the same time, it was unsatisfactory to the NAACP because it required unanimity among the censors. Over the next few days, the organization tried to have the bill amended to allow decisions by majority vote. As Joseph Loud pointed out, this would increase the chance of suppressing *The Birth of a Nation* since both the mayor and the chief of police had already asserted that "the film should be stopped if the law made it possible." Although the NAACP did not abandon the strategy of public meetings—it organized a big one at Tremont Temple on Sunday, May 2—it threw most of its effort now into lobbying members of the legislature in support of its proposal for majority voting on the new board.[105] Although the House rejected this on May 10 and the Senate on May 13, the Senate reversed itself on May 17 and the censorship bill signed into law by Governor Walsh on May 21 included the NAACP amendment.[106] So far as Boston was concerned, *The Birth of a Nation* now seemed doomed.

While the struggle to ban the film in Boston was taking place, its producers' strategy of defending *Birth of a Nation* against critics by citing the prominent officeholders and other public figures who approved it effectively collapsed. Edward D. White, chief justice of the Supreme Court, led the way by threatening to denounce *Birth* if Dixon continued to claim that he had endorsed it.[107] President Wilson was obviously embarrassed to be associated with it. When Margaret Blaine Damrosch, the wife of the conductor of the New York Symphony Orchestra, wrote in late March to Wilson's secretary, Joseph P. Tumulty, to discover whether the president really did see "nothing objectionable" in the film, Wilson denied expressing any opinion over it. As the Boston fight developed, pressure on Wilson intensified. Former Massachusetts Democratic congressman Thomas C. Thacher wrote to Tumulty on April 17, enclosing reports of the hearing before Mayor Curley on April 7 at which the film's producers claimed that Wilson had approved the film. Another correspondent sent Tumulty a press clipping describing the same meeting. Tumulty suggested that Wilson write "some sort of letter" indicating "that he did not approve of the 'Birth of a Nation,'" and the president agreed in principle, though he did not wish to be seen as responding to pressure from the agitation against the film, especially since one of the agitators was "that unspeakable fellow [Trotter]." Finally, on April 28, Tumulty replied to Thacher (in words drafted by Wilson himself) acknowledging that *Birth* had been screened at the White House as "a courtesy extended to an old acquaintance," but insisting that the president had been "entirely unaware of the character of the play" beforehand and had "at no time expressed his approbation of it."[108] In the last days of April, under pressure from the NAACP, other well-known figures cited by McCarthy and the film's publicity machine as having approved it—philanthropist George Peabody, Washington senator Wesley L. Jones, and writer Walter P. Eaton—either qualified or distanced themselves from their earlier comments.[109]

With the passage of the new censorship law, the campaign against *Birth of a Nation* in Boston now entered its final phase. On the same day that the governor signed the censorship bill, Trotter demanded that Curley and his new board act immediately to ban the film. Next day, the Boston NAACP petitioned the board for a hearing. This was clearly not to be a united struggle: Joseph Loud warned NAACP national secretary May Nerney that the "chief danger" was now "the possibly hasty and ill advised action of our friends but not associates—Trotter and his crowd." Trotter, however, for the moment seemed relatively conciliatory: at a meeting on May 23, he tried to stop one of the black speakers attacking Curley, insisting that the mayor be given time to feel himself into his new job as a censor.[110] Curley had so far shown himself willing to make encouraging noises about banning the film but had taken refuge behind the (debatable) insistence that as mayor he had no power to do so. Clearly, he was interested in including as many blacks as possible in his coalition of supporters. Yet he can hardly have been unaware that by the end of May, 100,000 or so white Bostonians had watched (and often expressed enthusiasm for) the movie and that African Americans still made up only a small percentage of the total population of the city. Most newspapers had favored the film (and attacked the idea of censorship). From his first involvement with the film, at the hearing on April 7, Curley had emphasized that his real concern with it related to matters of sexual morality. He had suggested the removal of the sequence in which Gus chased "Little Sister" even *before* this had been demanded by Judge Dowd.[111] The mayor and the other two members of the censorship board went, at differing times, to see *The Birth of a Nation*. Then, on June 2, they held public hearings on the film. The case against it was put by two blacks, William L. Lewis and Butler R. Wilson, and one white, J. Mott Hallowell. Trotter was not permitted to appear. The case for the film was argued, as at the first hearing on April 7, by John F. Cusick. At the end of the hearing, the censors met together briefly and announced that they had decided not to revoke the license of the Tremont Theater.[112]

With this announcement, the Boston struggle to suppress the film really ended. A small number of protests occurred—including one outside the Tremont Theater on the night of June 7 that resulted in eight arrests. But *The Birth of a Nation* itself, observed Steven R. Fox, was now "impregnable." After changing theaters in September, it would continue its record-breaking Boston run until late October, when it finally closed after 360 performances.[113] Locally, the NAACP criticized the "enormous capital" invested in the film, the lavish advertising in newspapers that had declined to become involved in the controversy, and the "extraordinary" police measures that had prevented demonstrations at the theater. It drew attention to the increased interest in "human rights" that had been generated by the campaign. Nationally, it insisted that the removal of the Gus chase sequence and the other cuts made had so mutilated the film that it had become "almost unintelligible."[114] Certainly, Bostonian whites and blacks had collaborated together in the fight against *Birth* in a way that had not happened since the era of the Civil War. The campaign against the film, however, had been weakened by personality conflicts. "The movement," complained Albert E. Pillsbury (a nephew of abolitionist Parker Pillsbury), "has suffered severely from too much Trotter."[115] Most impressive of all, in retrospect, was the engagement of a considerable proportion of the African American population of Boston in the struggle. Whereas the campaign against *Birth* in New York had been conducted primarily by whites with comparatively little black support, the opposite was true in Boston.[116] The willingness of black Bostonians to organize, lobby, attend mass meetings (at least eighteen of these were held), and sign petitions suggests that the *Birth of a Nation* controversy had a major impact locally in terms of the promotion of racial solidarity.

Chicago

While major battles against *The Birth of a Nation* were being fought in New York and Boston, the national NAACP was always on the alert to try to prevent it from being shown in other places. In mid-March, May C. Nerney wrote to Dr. Charles E. Bentley to ask if the film had yet been advertised in Chicago. In April, after local rumor and a notice in one of the Chicago dailies seemed to suggest that its arrival in the city was imminent, she several times urged Bentley and the local branch to oppose it.[117] The NAACP quickly discovered both that an official permit had been issued allowing the film to be shown in Chicago and that the permit itself had been acquired in a way that was highly irregular. Normally, permits for motion pictures in the city were granted by the Second Deputy Superintendent of Police, on the advice of a three-person Board of Censors chaired by the formidable Major Lucius C. Funkhouser. In the case of *Birth of a Nation*, a screening was arranged by Charles Fitzmorris, secretary of the lame-duck mayor of Chicago, Carter H. Harrison. The only other person present at the screening appears to have been Mrs. Carter Harrison, the mayor's wife, a writer of film scenarios who had been born and brought up in the South. When the screening was over, Fitzmorris apparently informed Funkhouser that the film was acceptable and—without either the deputy police superintendent or any member of the Board of Censors actually having seen it—a permit to show the film at the Illinois Theater was granted.[118] Once the local NAACP became aware of the circumstances under which the permit had been issued, it launched a campaign to persuade the incoming mayor, Republican William H. Thompson, to rescind it.

Thompson, Chicago's mayor from 1915 to 1923 and again from 1927 to 1931, was a machine politician almost as legendary as Curley in Boston. It was later asserted that he owed a particular debt of gratitude to Chicago African Americans who, by voting decisively for him in the primaries, had helped him win the Republican nomination and thus launch his mayoral career.[119] For whatever reason, Thompson seemed open to persuasion where *The Birth of a Nation* was concerned. On May 4, Charles Bentley of the Chicago NAACP asserted that if the new mayor found the film "as offensive as has been represented," he would not hesitate to rescind its permit.[120] Both the NAACP and local representatives of Booker T. Washington's Tuskegee machine seem to have been both active and effective in putting pressure on Thompson.[121] In mid-May, with the battle against the film in New York virtually over and the struggle to pass a new censorship bill in Boston in its final climactic week, the Chicago mayor handed the opponents of the film what must have seemed their first clear-cut victory: he summarily revoked the film's permit, thereby effectively banning it from being shown in his city. While Thompson gave no immediate explanation for his decision, he appears to have relied on a section of the Chicago City Code preventing the issuance of a permit to any film tending "to create contempt for any class of law-abiding citizens."[122]

While critics of the film hastened to congratulate Mayor Thompson on his decision,[123] the producers of *The Birth of a Nation* began to mount their counterattack. In contrast with the battles over the film in New York and Boston, the political struggle in Chicago took place well *before* the film was due to open. Most of the attempts to suppress or cut *Birth* in New York and Boston had been weakened because it was already running in those cities and was supported by a groundswell of audience enthusiasm and critical acclaim.[124] To set the ball rolling toward the creation of a similar sentiment in Chicago, the film's producers began to arrange private showings for the city's opinion makers.[125] Moreover, although there was no evidence to back up their fears, opponents of the film suspected the Griffith forces, a few days after the permit for the film was withdrawn, of attempting to get a bill through the state legislature that would have inaugurated a state system of film censorship. "From what I know of Griffith," May Nerney wrote to Charles Bentley on May 21, "I think he may be back of this...[I]f he thought a State censorship which he might be able to bribe would enable him to put on this photo play, I am sure he would work for one." Nerney urged the Chicago NAACP to get involved in the fight against the censorship bill, lest it prove a means of allowing *The Birth of a Nation* to be shown in the Windy City after all.[126] In reality, both the censorship bill and an alternative measure—sponsored by R. R. Jackson, a black member of the Illinois legislature—designed to ban any film that might encourage race hatred by showing "a lynching or unlawful hanging" were essentially distractions from the real battle over Griffith's film.[127] For on June 5, to the dismay of *Birth*'s opponents, an injunction was issued preventing the city from interfering with the movie's exhibition.[128]

Thompson's revocation of the permit to show *Birth* brought the issue of censoring films to the forefront of political debate in Chicago. The mayor's decision was criticized by the *Tribune* and the *Examiner* and supported by the *Herald*.[129] Under pressure from the producers of the film and in response to the furor that had now broken out, Thompson apparently began to weaken: he first offered to view the film himself, then to abide by the advice of a "delegation of colored ministers" once they had seen it.[130] The mayor, however, was about to lose his principal role in the drama. On June 2, Joseph J. McCarthy, acting on behalf of the film's producers, filed a petition in the Superior Court of Cook County asking for an injunction to restrain the city authorities from interfering with the exhibition of *The Birth of a Nation* in Chicago.[131] A hearing, presided over by Judge William Fenimore Cooper, was speedily arranged for June 4. That hearing did not go well for the NAACP forces (who were unhappy at having to go to trial with only twenty hours notice). While Nerney had provided them with a good deal of newspaper material, none of the NAACP witnesses had actually seen the film. *Birth*'s producers fielded four witnesses who were familiar with the film in addition to Griffith, whom even the hostile Charles E. Bentley judged as "suave."[132] In delivering his opinion, Judge Cooper mocked the argument of the city's lawyers that exhibiting the film would promote racial animosity against African Americans. This would be true, he argued, only if those seeing the play were "so stupid" that they were incapable of understanding that the people represented on screen "were of two to three generations ago" and, partly as a consequence, did not appreciate that in the years since "the negro race has advanced almost immeasurably." He also insisted that the film dealt as much with good black men and bad white men as with bad black men. It was, the judge insisted, the duty of the legal system to protect property rights. The producers and lessee of *The Birth of a Nation*, having properly secured a permit and paid a fee, were now the possessors of such a property right in the film and could not be arbitrarily deprived of it without due process of law. In drawing up his opinion, Cooper clearly relied heavily (though this was not directly acknowledged) on the Fourteenth Amendment.[133]

The producers of *The Birth of a Nation* were jubilant when the injunction was issued on June 5. That same night, the film began its run at the Illinois Theater and at the end of the performance, Griffith appeared on stage to plead for "a square deal for the motion picture." He publicly thanked Judge Cooper, who was in the audience, for his courage in allowing the film to be shown.[134] But the city authorities were not yet prepared to concede defeat. Four municipal censors were ordered to view the film and compile a report, which counsel for the mayor proposed to use in asking that the injunction be overturned.[135] In the meantime, the censors harassed the film by refusing to allow the "Hampton epilogue" to be shown with it (on the grounds it had not been included in the original application for a permit) and insisting that no one younger than twenty-one be admitted to screenings.[136] When Cooper declined to set aside his injunction, lawyers acting on behalf of the city filed an appeal. The local branch of the NAACP began to gather witnesses who had seen the film and were ready to testify against it. They were hopeful that the judicial system would permit the suppression of the film. But national secretary Nerney, conscious of earlier legal failures in New York and Boston, was much less confident.[137] Her pessimism was justified. On July 15, the suit to set aside Cooper's injunction was held over until the fall term of the Appellate Court. In effect, with the film now free to run over the summer to packed houses, *Birth*'s Chicago critics had lost. Thomas W. Allinson, secretary of the local NAACP, consoled himself with the thought that some of the most objectionable scenes—including that of Gus chasing Flora—had been cut and some intertitles modified.[138] Clearly, however, the forces fighting to have the film suppressed had experienced yet another major defeat.

Kansas, Ohio, Pennsylvania

At the beginning of 1915, three states had their own censorship boards: Kansas, Ohio, and Pennsylvania. The Pennsylvania board approved *The Birth of a Nation* very quickly. The quality of the film may have been one reason for the decision (the chairman of the censorship board, J. Louis Breitinger, described it as "the highest development of motion picture production" at a special showing organized for members of the state legislature). But with the board under attack from independent filmmakers for being in the pocket of the General Film Company (the distributing arm of Edison's attempted movie monopoly, the Motion Picture Patents Company) and with a bill for its abolition already before the legislature, approving a film such as *Birth*—made and distributed by independents—may also have been a sensible political move for the censors.[139] Their endorsement of Griffith's film, however, made the task of fighting it considerably harder in Pennsylvania. Although the NAACP at times floated the idea of asking the state board to reconsider its decision,[140] their efforts to suppress *Birth* focused mainly on city authorities. As soon as the movie was announced as a forthcoming attraction in Pittsburgh, for example, a committee from the NAACP and other organizations called on Mayor Joseph G. Armstrong in protest. At the same time, a new ordinance prepared by the president of the city's NAACP branch was introduced to the city council to ban any entertainment "which incites to riot or tends to disturb the public peace; or prejudice the public mind against any class of law-abiding citizens." In late August, lobbied by a delegation of over one hundred African Americans, Armstrong announced that he would not permit the forthcoming presentation of *The Birth of a Nation* "unless forced by [the] courts to do so." The mayor's afterthought was prophetic: lawyers acting on behalf of the film's producers quickly secured an injunction to prevent him from interfering with its exhibition.[141]

In Philadelphia, there was more reason to anticipate disorder than in most other cities and also, perhaps, more reason to anticipate that *Birth* would be suppressed. When Dixon's play *The Clansman* had been performed there in 1911, there had there been serious riots and the mayor at the time had insisted that such performances be stopped. Perhaps most encouraging of all for the NAACP, an attempt to mount a legal challenge to his decision had failed.[142] *The Birth of a Nation* was advertised to open in Philadelphia on September 4. In the days running up to this, the NAACP and other organizations concentrated much of their attention on lobbying Director of Public Safety Porter. There were "overwhelming protests" from black groups, including one claiming to represent 20,000 African American "Knights of Pythias," and Porter was also informed that "many negroes had purchased tickets for the opening performance." The director of public safety traveled outside the state to see the film, emerging from the screening with the conviction that "it was not a proper subject for Philadelphia with a larger negro population than any other Northern city." In the end, Porter "ordered the production stopped, claiming the possibility of serious disturbance if the play was allowed to go on." This time, however, the ban was not sustained in the courts: Judge Ferguson of Court Number Four in Philadelphia had also viewed the film and had seen nothing in it likely to provoke "disturbances or riots." Consequently, he was happy to issue an injunction to stop the authorities from interfering with the production.[143]

In the days that followed, black Philadelphians tried hard to have the injunction vacated. When their efforts failed, they began to plan for more direct action against the film. On September 20, printed cards were distributed across the city calling African Americans and white sympathizers to a protest meeting that night outside the Forrest Theater, where *Birth* was showing. The organizers of the demonstration were a group of black clergymen of various denominations. During the day, two meetings were held in Philadelphia churches that were attended by "nearly all negro ministers in the city"; they listened to a series of "fiery addresses" denouncing Griffith's film and calling for its suppression.[144] Almost certainly, the planned demonstration was intended to be peaceable. But since the film's opening, Director of Public Safety Porter had ensured that a large force of police was present, both inside and outside the theater, to prevent trouble. The police presence, together with the inflamed passions of the black community, made some kind of confrontation at the theater almost inevitable. At first, the demonstration, involving around 500 black men and women, was quiet enough. But at some point, a brick was thrown through the plateglass window at the entrance to the theater, and around 150 police charged the protestors, using their night sticks freely to break up the demonstration. At one point a revolver was fired, though it was unclear whether this was done by a policeman or a demonstrator. Several arrests were made, although only one man—a nineteen-year-old black youth—was charged (with "inciting a riot"). Many demonstrators were hurt and needed medical treatment for head injuries. The "respectable" character of the demonstration may be judged from the social profile of those arrested or injured: according to a local newspaper, they were all drawn from "the educated classes, a lawyer, two ministers and several doctors and institutional heads being among the number."[145] The day after the demonstration, a group of five prominent African Americans met with Mayor Blankenburg to ask that he suppress the film and to demand a hearing at which they could voice their protests against it; one member of the delegation— variously reported as Dr. W. A. Sinclair, who worked for the Douglass Hospital, or Dr. Martin—had a bandage on his head because of the injuries he had received the previous evening. Blakenburg (shades of James Michael Curley) told the committee that he was not certain he had the power to stop the film and insisted that the planned hearing also include the "film's manager."[146] Nothing came of the hearing, and apart from an attempt by black ministers to exploit the issue by asking candidates in that fall's municipal elections to state where they stood on *The Birth of a Nation*,[147] the campaign against the film in Philadelphia— and, indeed, in Pennsylvania generally—came abruptly to an end.[148]

In Ohio, the story was very different as the Cleveland NAACP had already flexed its political muscles. In combination with figures such as former politician Harry C. Smith, editor of the Cleveland *Gazette*, and allies in the

Ministers' Association, the NAACP had convinced the State Board of Censorship to withdraw its approval for *The Nigger*, a film about miscegenation based on a play by Edward Sheldon. This victory was apparently secured by persuading Republican governor Frank B. Willis to exert pressure on the board.[149] When NAACP national secretary May C. Nerney suggested, therefore, that the Cleveland branch protest to the mayor concerning the impending exhibition of *The Birth of a Nation* in the city, the local secretary pointed out that the successful struggle against *The Nigger* "shows we can accomplish more by an appeal to Gov. Frank B. Willis."[150] Sometime in early April, the Cleveland NAACP wrote to the governor protesting the possibility that *Birth* should be exhibited, and Willis passed on their comments to the board of censors. There were then several weeks of major confusion, with Nerney trying on the part of the national organization to discover whether the Board of Censors had actually refused permission for *Birth of a Nation* to be shown in Ohio and some of her correspondents in the state apparently not appreciating that *The Nigger* and *The Birth of a Nation* were two different films. In late May, the NAACP finally learned from Charles B. Williams, chairman of the Ohio Board of Censors, that *Birth* had not yet been submitted to the board for its decision.[151] Perhaps, as some NAACP members thought, the withdrawal of the permit for *The Nigger* had discouraged *Birth*'s producers from applying for one. Or perhaps Epoch was waiting for the result of the Ohio film exhibitors' campaign to have the board of censors eliminated.[152]

During the summer, however, a revised version of *The Nigger*, with many scenes cut, was finally approved by the Ohio censors and began screenings under a new title, *The Mystery of Morrow's Rest*; also, the attempt to eliminate the censorship board failed. There was no point in waiting any longer, so *Birth of a Nation* was finally submitted to the censorship board. The NAACP and its allies sprang into action and the board received "numerous" letters of protest from African Americans. They were delighted when the censors, in late September, rejected the film on the grounds that it might arouse prejudice against blacks and also between North and South.[153] The politics behind this decision would be made clear a few weeks later by May C. Nerney, who visited Columbus, Ohio, as part of a tour of Midwest NAACP branches. The chairman of the Ohio censors, Charles B. Williams, had been "all right" and had opposed the film. Another member of the board, W. R. Wilson had been "wobbly." The last member of the three-person board, Maude Murray Miller, had been rabidly in favor of Griffith's film. Miller, Nerney reported, was "'a Southern woman,' the worst Bourbon I ever met." She apparently believed that *Birth of a Nation* "was a great education to the North" and that after "a few slight changes" to the intertitles, it "must be shown in Ohio." (Miller would also inform an aghast Nerney "that if it was not for us Northerners she would still be living on her plantation like a lady instead of working for a living.") In order to bring the "wobbly" members of the board into line, the black Robert B. Barcus, attorney for the Columbus

NAACP, and the white former Secretary of State Ryan had persuaded the Ohio Civil Service Commission to make it clear that members of the board of censors who voted to approve Griffith's film would lose their jobs.[154] It is probable that Frank B. Willis, who promised Nerney that *Birth* would not be shown in Ohio as long as he remained governor, exerted similar pressure.[155]

While the struggle against *Birth of a Nation* in Ohio was successful (the ban on the film by the board of censors was upheld by the Ohio Supreme Court in October, renewed by a majority vote of the censorship board in January 1916, and once again upheld by the Supreme Court a few months later),[156] Nerney's visit to the state during the course of the fight shed a good deal of light on the local problems that at times hampered the NAACP campaign. Local leaders were sometimes unreliable: Robert B. Barcus apparently wanted to take all the credit for the struggle against the film, and until he was stopped by Nerney, was attempting to raise his own personal "defense fund" from the various NAACP branches in Ohio. Moreover, the producers of the film adopted a "divide and rule" strategy toward the black community. They had paid for Wilbur King (according to Nerney "probably the brightest and most unscrupulous colored man in Columbus") to go to Pittsburgh to see *Birth* with the expectation that he would find the film acceptable if a few minor cuts were made. Nerney, while in Ohio, held a number of mass meetings, one of which King attended. This gave her the opportunity to ask him point-blank if he thought "the play should be shown with eliminations." Put on the spot like this, King had little option but to answer negatively. At this and other meetings, Nerney also underlined the danger of blacks being offered financial inducements by *Birth*'s agents to support the film. Her exposure of this strategy was deliberately intended to undercut its effectiveness since, as Nerney observed, "anyone now standing for the play in any form here will practically be saying he has been bought."[157]

Although there was at least one attempt to exhibit *Birth of a Nation* in Ohio in early 1916—attempting to get round the prohibition on public performance, Shriners in Cincinnati tried to arrange a private showing[158]—the ban on the film issued by the state board of censors seems to have been effective. Two months after *Birth* was refused a permit in Ohio, it was also suppressed in Kansas. In both states, given the growing size of the black vote as the black population generally was inflated by migration from the South, it made good politics for Republican governors to oppose the film.[159] Kansas seemed particularly fertile ground for opponents of the film since the new governor, Arthur Capper, was both a member of the state board of censors and president of the Topeka branch of the NAACP. Requested by Nerney to help keep *Birth of a Nation* out of his state, Capper assured her that the film "with its objectionable features" would get into Kansas only "over my strongest protests." Yet he also observed that if the producers eliminated "the features which tend to intensify race prejudice," this would throw "a very different light" on the movie. When Nerney appealed to him, however, as "President of Our Branch as well as Governor...to protect colored people against this play," Capper finally acted more decisively. *The Birth of a Nation*, he assured her, would not be shown in Kansas during his governorship: "I informed those interested in it that I would not stand for it in this state and the company has announced that they will not come here."[160]

Local Campaigns

Attempts were made to have other state governors take a position against Griffith's film, but these proved unsuccessful.[161] The fight against *The Birth of a Nation* therefore became very much a local one, fought out in cities of varying size across the United States. It was banned, after protests, by the city authorities in places such as Gary (Indiana), St. Louis (Missouri), Oakland (California), Atlantic City (New Jersey), New Haven (Connecticut), Providence (Rhode Island), Springfield (Massachusetts), Boise (Idaho), and Minneapolis (Minnesota).[162] Normally, bans of this type did not survive for very long: the film's producers were quick to appeal to the courts for injunctions preventing such interference. In Oakland, the attempt of Mayor J. L. Davie to suppress the film lasted for one night only; the suppression was overturned by the Superior Court the next day.[163] As the NAACP quickly realized, it was easier to keep *Birth of a Nation* out of a city if there was already an ordinance prohibiting entertainments that stimulated racial prejudice. Des Moines, Iowa, had led the way here: attorney S. Joe Brown, president of the local Afro-American Council, had drawn up such an ordinance and secured its adoption by the city council in 1907. "It may be," May Childs Nerney informed Brown, "that we can get ordinances of this character introduced in cities where we have branches and thus keep ahead of this moving picture." Nerney circulated copies of the Des Moines ordinances to many of the local NAACP branches that were fighting the film.[164] As a tactic, it had decidedly mixed results: adopting such an ordinance helped keep *Birth* out of Tacoma (Washington) and Wilmington (Delaware), but in Lansing (Michigan), the censorship board ignored the new ordinance and allowed the film to run uncut. Moreover, the unsuccessful struggle to pass such an ordinance in Detroit may actually have weakened the fight against the film by helping unite the theatrical opponents of censorship and by dissipating campaigning energies that needed concentration for their success.[165]

Across the United States as a whole, the NAACP and its allies suffered a considerable number of defeats. In Washington, D.C., Congressman Emerson tried and failed to have a joint resolution passed by the House and Senate instructing the commissioners of the district to prevent exhibition of *Birth of a Nation* on the grounds that the film "has a tendency to, and does engender prejudice against colored people."[166] The city authorities in Terre Haute (Indiana), Louisville (Kentucky), and Spokane (Washington) decided to allow the film to be exhibited in spite of the protests made because they saw nothing objectionable in it.[167] In many other places, including Sacramento (California), Milwaukee (Wisconsin), and St. Paul (Minnesota), Birth of a Nation was shown after only minor cuts were made.[168] There were at least two attempts—almost certainly born of frustration, rather than hope—to prosecute the managers of the theaters where the film was playing. Walter Sanford, manager of the Olympic Theater in St. Louis, was found not guilty by a jury of showing a "lewd, indecent and immoral" picture, and attorney William A. Heck's ingenious attempt to arrest Anson O. Bigelow, manager of Macauley's Theater in Louisville, under an old "master and slave" law that forbade the performance of any play that excited racial prejudice, was thrown out by a judge on procedural grounds.[169]

The fight against The Birth of a Nation shed considerable light on the social changes taking place in the North and West in the early years of the twentieth century. Beginning in the years after the Civil War, African Americans had begun to leave the South in search of job opportunities in Northern cities. By 1910, many Northern and Western cities had sizable black communities: New York, for example, had over 90,000 black residents, Philadelphia 84,000, Chicago 44,000, Pittsburgh 25,000, Cleveland 8,000, and Detroit 5,000. In the decade between 1910 and 1920, the African American population of some of these cities increased dramatically: New York by 66 percent, Philadelphia by 59 percent, Pittsburgh by 47 percent, Chicago by 148 percent, Cleveland by 308 percent, and Detroit by 611 percent.[170] More and more, as black competition for jobs and housing grew, whites adopted discriminatory practices that encouraged the growth of urban African American ghettoes. The appearance of African American communities in Northern and Western cities had political effects. The black vote, small but growing, came to be seen as an important element in urban elections. The emergence of ghettoes also prompted white fears of the potential threat they posed to social peace and stability. The campaign against The Birth of a Nation intersected with these trends. Some supporters of the film suggested that the struggle against it was essentially a means of organizing and controlling the colored vote.[171] Fears of social disorder lay behind the actions against the film taken by some city authorities. For example, the film was banned in Atlantic City after police found that in "the black belt" of the city, where 10,000 African Americans had their homes,

> men, women and children [were] congregating in the streets to talk about the film and the attack upon their race they claim it carries. Threats of violence were made freely in the saloons patronized by colored men. The detectives heard proposals to attack the Boardwalk playhouse.[172]

In many places, the arrival of Birth of a Nation forced local leaders to address—perhaps for the first time—the state of race relations in their community. In some places (such as St. Joseph, Missouri), there were fears that the film would undermine the good relations that currently existed.[173] In other cities there were real anxieties that the film might make a bad situation worse. In Evansville, Kentucky, for example, critics of the film argued that it would encourage the kind of racial hatred and violence that had recently led to the lynching of a black man in the neighboring town of Henderson.[174]

The Campaign in the South

Concern on the part of the NAACP that showing *The Birth of a Nation* would provoke violent racial incidents intensified from August 1915 onward, as the producers of the film revealed their plans for showing it in the South. The racial situation in many states was already tense—May Nerney observed in mid-September that there had been "a record of forty lynchings already...this year"—and the inflammatory potential of the film was very plain (Nerney wrote in the same letter of a young Southern man who remarked, after viewing *Birth*, that "I should like to kill every nigger I know").[175] One of the reasons the original chairman of the National Board of Censorship, Frederic C. Howe, had opposed the film was that he feared it "might lead to serious race riots and assaults" and that this was "particularly true" in the South. For several months, the NAACP forces had allowed themselves to believe an assurance given by one of the film's producers that "they would not think of taking it South for fear of race riots." By September, with the film already booked for West Virginia, Virginia, and Texas, that assurance had been shown to be false and the NAACP began gearing up to fight the film across the South.[176]

The campaign against *The Birth of a Nation* in the Southern states would obviously be very different from elsewhere in the nation. With no network of branches to rely on, the NAACP had to depend on the initiative of local people. The national NAACP organization first learned that the film was to be shown in Bluefield, West Virginia, from P. A. Goines of the North and West Railway YMCA Colored Department. Goines had organized a meeting of black physicians, ministers, and schoolteachers to protest plans to show *Birth*. He wrote to W. E. B. Du Bois as editor of the NAACP journal *The Crisis* to ask for information and advice on how to carry the campaign further (he also confessed that he hoped "to use this occasion to influence the organizing of a Branch of the N.A.A.C.P."). Learning that Griffith's film was to be shown in Bluefield clearly disturbed the national NAACP: the lynching of "an absolutely innocent colored man" named Robert Johnson there three years earlier had become something of a cause célèbre in the North.[177] In reply to Goines, May Nerney informed him that anti-*Birth* literature was being sent to him by the Boston branch and described the NAACP fight against the film in other places. She offered to write to anybody Goines thought might be able to help, but at the same time she showed her awareness of Southern regional susceptibilities by questioning "the advisability of outside interference." Nerney insisted that the "best Southern sentiment" was against the picture but it is noticeable that with one exception, all the Southerners she cited in support of this proposition now lived *outside* the South. She finished by informing Goines that the "whole hope" for local protestors lay "in fighting the matter on the ground that it may lead to race riots."[178]

The campaign against *The Birth of a Nation* in the South suffered from many weaknesses and disadvantages. Although the black population in many Southern cities was far higher than in centers of the North and West, it was almost completely disfranchised and could consequently cause little difficulty for politicians. Mayor George Ainslie of Richmond, Virginia, while aware that blacks made up "about thirty-eight per centum" of the population of his city, had no difficulty in brushing aside the protest of a delegation of African Americans against exhibiting the film there. Ainslie also refused to order cuts in the film, assuring the manager of the theater that "I have not heard the slightest unfavorable comment on 'The Birth of a Nation.'...[O]n the contrary, those who have been fortunate enough to have seen it, and who have related their impressions to me, have given it unstinted praise."[179] As Ainslie's remark indicates, the popular reception of Griffith's film in the South was even more ecstatic than that in the North: the movie treated the history of the South of the Civil War era in a deeply sympathetic way. For white Southerners, it mythologized and justified their past. As the Baltimore *Afro-American* sadly but accurately noted a few months later, "there is hardly a theater audience from Maine to Florida that does not applaud the orchestra when it plays 'Dixie,' and the intensity of the applause increases to an uproar as you pass the Mason and Dixon's line going South."[180] It was harder for individuals and groups to protest against the film in the South than in the North because Southern whites liked the movie even more than their Northern compatriots. Opponents of the film were also hampered by the constraints of segregation. In much of the South, there was no possibility, as had been the case in Boston and other Northern cities, of blacks and whites joining together publicly against the film. When a correspondent in Dallas, Texas, wrote to the NAACP asking it to try to influence the City Welfare Board (which supervised the film censors), he requested that it write separately to the white and colored departments of the Board. Moreover, May Nerney, in a letter to the African American head of the colored department, clearly recognized the realities of the racial situation in the South when she advised him "that the only way to accomplish anything is to work through influential white people."[181]

For the opponents of Griffith's film, efforts to prevent its exhibition in the South were even more difficult and frustrating than they were in other parts of the country. There was a "hard fight" against it in Norfolk, Virginia, the first Southern city in which it was shown, but in the end the city authorities took no action to prevent its exhibition.[182] During subsequent weeks, similar unsuccessful protests occurred in Bluefield (West Virginia), Dallas (Texas), Asheville (North Carolina),

Columbia (South Carolina), Birmingham (Alabama), and Richmond (Virginia).[183] Only in December did the forces opposed to *Birth* finally score a success, when the film was banned in Charleston, West Virginia. But hopes of repeating this victory two weeks later in Hot Springs, Arkansas, were dashed when the city council—which had initially seemed critical of the film—reversed itself.[184] The defeat of those opposing the film was especially galling in Birmingham, since Dixon's play *The Clansman* had been "about frozen out" of the city the year before. But the producers of *Birth of a Nation* had taken their own precautions, arranging for the city engineer and a "popular lady writer" to view the film in New York. When the city commissioners held a hearing, they ignored protests against the movie and accepted the assurance of these two "that the pictures were O.K."[185]

The advance agents of Griffith's film were clearly skillful in helping deflect criticism of it. Yet the differences in many areas of the South between the reception of Dixon's play and Griffith's film are very striking. Dixon's stage-play had been booed and hissed when it opened in Columbia, state capital of South Carolina. There does not seem to have been any such response to *Birth*. Indeed, studying the reception of *Birth of a Nation* in South Carolina as a whole, John Hammond Moore found "almost unanimous approval" instead of the controversy and criticism that had accompanied Dixon's play.[186] Much the same change, John C. Inscoe observes, had taken place in Dixon's native North Carolina. Reviewers tended to emphasize that the events recounted in the film had occurred a long time in the past and that African Americans were now playing a full part in the progress of the nation. Fearing a racial crisis provoked by the rapid retrogression of blacks seemed, by 1915, absurd. The racial radicalism advocated by Dixon in the early twentieth century now appeared deeply anachronistic. It had begun to recede in 1907, partly because of the embarrassment of many Southern whites over the Atlanta race riot. The very success of black disfranchisement and segregation in North Carolina, Inscoe points out, had brought with it a liberalization of white attitudes. White fear of blacks had diminished sharply. By 1915, not only were there far fewer lynchings in the state than in the opening years of the century, but Confederate memorials were beginning to appear commemorating the faithfulness of slaves during the Civil War.[187] While part of the reason for the lack of controversy associated with *Birth of a Nation*'s reception in the South may have stemmed from the entertaining qualities and high production values of the film itself, it is probable—based on the experience of North and South Carolina—that a major part also had to do with the more stable race relations that followed the attainment of complete white supremacy.

Fighting Film with Film

While most of the NAACP's energy went into fighting the film at a political level (trying to have it suppressed or cut), some of its leaders saw clearly that they would have to engage in a cultural battle as well. *The Birth of a Nation* encouraged—and considerably worsened—stereotypes of American blacks that were already deeply ingrained in American popular culture. During the earliest years of cinema, motion pictures offered unflattering and highly clichéd representations of blacks. "Black women," comments Dan Leab, "were either fat, asexual, servile, and dark, or promiscuously attractive and lightskinned. Black men were...supposedly born 'hoofing on the levee to the strumming of the old banjo.'" To this complement of often-ludicrous "toms," "coons," "mulattoes," and "mammies [sic]," as Donald Bogle points out, *The Birth of a Nation* added a new and more sinister figure: the ambitious and sexually rapacious "black buck."[188]

Although the origin of the idea is unclear, sometime in spring 1915 Carl Laemmle's Universal Film Manufacturing Company began to consider making a movie to contradict the unflattering stereotypes of blacks that had apparently reached an apogee with *Birth*. Two days after Griffith's film opened in New York, Laemmle and much of his staff boarded a train at Grand Central Station to begin the long journey that would move the company's headquarters from New York to its new studio at Universal City in the San Fernando Valley, California. As Richard Koszarski notes, Laemmle may or may not have seen *The Birth of a Nation* before he left, but he could hardly have missed the reviews "which suggested a revolution in motion-picture content and style."[189] While Universal was still committed to producing the short films on which its prosperity was based, Laemmle, shrewd showman that he was, may well have speculated about producing a film that would simultaneously challenge *Birth* and profit from the publicity that was beginning to surround its exhibition. By mid-April, Rose Janowitz, head of Universal's Educational Department, and writer Elaine Sterne were working on a scenario dealing with the same themes as *Birth of a Nation* (slavery, Civil War, and Reconstruction) but aiming to "show the important and often heroic part that the Negro played during these difficult times."[190]

Universal may have been "cash-poor" at this time because of acquiring the large amount of real estate making up Universal City, and to produce a film to rival *Birth* was so far outside the studio's experience that Laemmle seems to have decided to approach the NAACP in search of financial angels. May Nerney reported that Universal was proposing to make a four-reel picture which, she commented, would "probably be lost in obscurity." If, however, the NAACP could raise $50,000, the studio would undertake to raise a further $150,000 and make a picture on a scale similar to that of *The Birth of a Nation*. It also offered to publicize the NAACP in the film.[191] The Universal offer created a major dilemma for the NAACP leadership. They could see the advantages of such an imaginative riposte to Griffith's film and also of the publicity it would create for their own organization. On the other hand, they were aware that the NAACP did not have the resources to finance such a project and were doubtful of the propriety of recommending it to others as a speculative investment venture. May Nerney, in particular, had a clear-eyed view of the motivation of the studio people. They were, she wrote, "hard-headed business men" who "care only for money and have no sentiment about the race question." The NAACP also worried that it was perhaps being too naive in its relations with Universal. "It has occurred to us," Nerney declared, "that in asking us to raise $50,000 this moving picture company may intend to use that sum and advance nothing themselves. Dramatic people are proverbially unreliable in matters of this kind."[192]

Whatever the suspicions of the NAACP leadership, they seem to have recognized that this was an opportunity that was simply too good to ignore. "No one knows better than yourself the effect of this play [*The Birth of a Nation*] on the public," Nerney wrote to Frederic C. Howe, former chairman of the National Board of Censorship. "If it goes unchallenged it will take years to overcome the harm it is doing. The entire country will acquiesce in the Southern program of segregation, disfranchisement and lynching. If we do challenge it it must be done in some telling way, that is, by a spectacular photo-play."[193] Nerney wrote to Howe after weeks of negotiation with Universal Pictures, who revised their proposition several times. Their final proposal (a scaled-down version of the first) was that if the NAACP could raise $10,000, the studio would agree to commit sufficient resources "to insure the production of a twelve-reel film on a scale as large as 'The Birth of a Nation.'" Universal also clarified what it was prepared to offer in terms of publicity: it would permit the NAACP to assist in writing the intertitles, which would include a reference to the organization as approving the film, together with "a brief statement of the program of the Association" and the names of some of its most prominent members, such as social worker and progressive reformer Jane Addams.[194] Most seductive of all, from the point of view of the NAACP, the studio (or at least Jane Janowitz and Elaine Sterne) gave the leadership of the association the impression that they would have an active role in shaping the scenario for the film and, consequently, the nature of the film itself.

In late April, Janowitz and Sterne attended a meeting in Nerney's office at which a number of suggestions were made for improving the draft scenario that Sterne had prepared. Among other things, the proposed changes related to an African scene, a slave ship, a slave auction, cotton picking, Frederick Douglass, the Emancipation Proclamation, and the possibility of footage from black educational institutions such as Hampton and Tuskegee. Nerney also provided Sterne, as she had requested, with the address of John R. Lynch, who had written an eye-witness account of Reconstruction from a black perspective.[195] A little more than two weeks later, the NAACP Board of Directors voted to establish a small committee to hear the scenario and recommend whether the association should collaborate further with the project. This "Scenario Committee" consisted of Mary White Ovington, then a vice-president of the NAACP; William English Walling, one of the directors; and playwright John G. Under-hill (who replaced the original choice, *Crisis* editor W. E. B. Du Bois, when Du Bois refused to serve).[196] It met on the evening of May 14 and approved the scenario. This was not the end of the story, however. When Nerney reported the decision of the committee to Joseph P. Loud, requesting his assistance in iden-tifying potential investors, Loud advised them to submit the scenario also to a committee in Boston "before we can interest people financially in it." Sterne, who had already made numerous changes to her scenario at the request of the NAACP, must have been dismayed by the thought of further revisions. Nevertheless, she agreed to travel to Boston to read the scenario to "a small group of people," though she requested that Professor Albert Bushnell Hart of Harvard be present at the meeting to give his advice on historical facts and interpretations.[197]

Despite's Sterne's efforts to please the NAACP, she became increasingly frustrated at the inability of the NAACP to raise money—or identify any con-vincing sources of money—for the project. Some NAACP leaders were op-posed to the idea from the beginning. Charles E. Bentley of Chicago expressed himself "doubtful as to its being a paying investment." Even among those who supported the scheme, there was sometimes little sense of urgency. "I fear it will be very difficult to get anyone interested financially just at this crisis," Mary Hallowell Loud wrote on May 19, twelve days after the sinking of the *Lusitania* provoked a crisis in German-American relations and anxieties over possible American involvement in the war. "I think myself it would be better to wait until we see how things are going in our foreign relations—and wait a year or so before putting a 'rival' [to *Birth of a Nation*] on the stage." National secretary May Nerney sharply disagreed. "It must be pushed through imme-diately or dropped," she declared on May 17. Very conscious that a good deal of the publicity from the NAACP fight against *Birth* had actually helped the movie, she believed that the best chance of countering it was to produce an opposing film immediately "so as to get the full benefit of all this publicity and strife."[198] But even Nerney, despite her enthusiasm for the project, was aware that Booker T. Washington and the Tuskegee machine had a far better exist-ing network of philanthropic supporters than the NAACP. "I suppose," she remarked, "[Sears, Roebuck president Julius] Rosenwald would be hopeless because of the B.T.W. influence." Moreover, Nerney did not want to approach people who would put money into the film project rather than contribute to the NAACP itself. "My idea," she wrote, "would be to interest people who have not contributed much to us and would never be interested except in a venture of this kind."[199]

By mid-June, however, the NAACP's "Scenario Committee" had failed to persuade anyone to invest in the proposed film.[200] Feeling she had no alternative in the circumstances, Sterne now adopted a two-track strategy: while she took care to maintain good relations with Nerney (who was starting to refer to her as "my friend"), she also opened negotiations through Rose Janowitz and Booker T. Washington's secretary, Emmett J. Scott, with the Tuskegeeans.[201] Washington and Scott in turn made overtures to producer-director Thomas H. Ince, to see if he would be interested in a filmed response to *Birth of a Nation*. Once Ince declined (he was already at work on his pacifist epic, *Civilization*, and in July 1915 joined Griffith and Mack Sennett in the Harry Aitken-designed Triangle distribution company), the Tuskegeeans turned back to Universal. In late September, Harry C. Oppenheimer, acting as their agent, had a meeting with Joe Brandt, general manager of Universal. When Brandt informed him that Sterne's script had "been accepted in a more or less indefinite manner" and was currently "undergoing certain changes before being produced," Oppenheimer argued that the crucial thing to Tuskegee was countering Griffith's depiction of the Reconstruction period, either by demonstrating that whites were as much responsible for the "Scally Wag" legislation of the time as blacks or by "showing the activities at the present time, of some of the Colored Race." He finally reached a tentative deal with Brandt: the Sterne scenario would now be submitted to Washington and Scott for their approval and assuming that approval was forthcoming, the scenario would be remodeled to include scenes of the Tuskegee Institute. (At the same time, Oppenheimer muddied the waters by suggesting to Brandt that since the Sterne picture was not yet in production, Universal might instead like to consider making a movie based on Washington's autobiography, *Up from Slavery*.)[202]

In the early fall of 1915, the NAACP and the Tuskegee Machine—neither apparently aware of the other's role—were both involved in the effort to bring Sterne's scenario, now known as *Lincoln's Dream*, to the screen.[203] The NAACP Scenario Committee continued to report on its attempts to persuade the studio to put the film into production. Its chair, Mary White Ovington, became concerned at rumors that Universal was cutting "parts favorable to the Negro" from the now much-revised scenario as a consequence of "the prejudice of the Southern members" of the company. Yet by this point, there was little the NAACP could do. They had failed to persuade anyone to invest in the film, and finally, with no outside funding in prospect, Universal shelved the whole project.[204] The NAACP appears to have accepted this decision; Tuskegee, however, continued trying to fight film with film. Emmett Scott wrote to Edwin L. Barker of the Chicago-based Advance Motion Picture Company reviving the idea of a filmed version of Washington's *Up from Slavery*. As well as the rights to the autobiography, Scott offered both the support of the National Negro Business League and his own services as screenwriter-consultant to ensure that the proposed film would embody "that indefatigable something which I shall call *the colored man's viewpoint*."[205] Unfortunately for the proposed film, Washington died in November 1915, and although Scott persisted with his efforts, the film that was eventually released three years later under the title *The Birth of a Race* could not realistically be seen as any kind of answer to Griffith's movie. The original notion of a film celebrating black progress had been jettisoned (along with Scott) in favor of a mishmash that apparently included (most of the film was later lost) scenes of the Jews fleeing from Ancient Egypt, the preaching of Jesus, Columbus's discovery of the New World, Paul Revere's ride, the Philadelphia Constitutional Convention of 1787, Lincoln freeing the slaves, modern armies marching, and a German-American family battling with its divided loyalties during World War I.[206]

The fate of *Lincoln's Dream* and *The Birth of a Race* underscored the problematic nature of trying to make favorable films about blacks within a system of movie production that was dominated by whites.[207] Years earlier, in *The Souls of Black Folk* (1903), W. E. B. Du Bois had written of the difficulties facing the black man confronting "a world which yields him no true self-consciousness, but only lets him see himself through the revelation of the other world." It was, Du Bois insisted, "a peculiar sensation, this double-consciousness, this sense of always looking at one's self through the eyes of others, of measuring one's soul by the tape of a world that looks on in amused contempt and pity."[208] Du Bois had been writing in general terms of American culture, but his words applied with particular aptness to cinema. Very few blacks had so far tried, like Will Foster or Hunter C. Haynes, to challenge the dominance of the condescending and derogatory depictions of African Americans offered by white moviemakers.[209] It may have been Du Bois's own consciousness of just how hard it would be to escape the manner in which the hegemonic white cinematic culture constructed blackness that prompted him to turn down membership on the NAACP Scenario Committee. Writing to whites Joel Spingarn and May Nerney, however, he diplomatically preferred to explain that he was mainly "interested in a pageant of Negro history and some plays of my own and in moving pictures based upon them."[210]

Although the plays and films did not materialize, Du Bois *was* responsible for producing a pageant, *The Star of Ethiopia*, that offered a broader, alternative view of African American history to the one offered in *The Birth of a Nation*. Originally written in 1911, the pageant had already been seen by 30,000 spectators in 1913 as part of New York's commemoration of the fiftieth anniversary of the Emancipation Proclamation. To Du Bois, who had grown increasingly doubtful of the value of political protest in connection with *Birth*, *The Star of Ethiopia* was essentially a cultural weapon. It advanced an alternative historical and aesthetic tradition emphasizing the roots of American blacks in an African civilization that—at least until the initial contacts with whites—had been as "advanced morally and intellectually" as most Europeans. Du Bois's much-expanded pageant was performed with considerable success to large audiences in Washington, D.C., in October 1915 and Philadelphia in May 1916.[211]

Assessing the Fight

At the beginning of January 1916, May Nerney summarized the efforts of the NAACP's New York headquarters in the campaign against *The Birth of a Nation*:

> in addition to its sixty-three branches and locals, to which several hundred letters were sent, the Association reached twenty-four towns and sent out over 200 individual letters and 12,000 pieces of literature. A conservative estimate of the time the National Office devoted to the fight against this play is at least two months. This included work with the National Board of Censorship, the effort to influence individual members of the Board, an attempt to persuade film corporations to boycott the play, hearings in the Police Court and before the Mayor, time consumed in bringing legal proceedings, securing witnesses, and in our effort to have a scenario produced in reply.

The fight had been carried on in spite of continuous political battles taking place among the organization's directors (Spingarn and Villard had submitted their resignations in December 1915 after losing a power struggle with Du Bois, though both were subsequently persuaded to reconsider; Nerney surprised everybody by resigning as secretary a few weeks later).[212] It had been waged in the face of widespread indifference on the part of some blacks (especially in New York) who could not see what all the fuss was about and deep-seated opposition to censorship on the part of many white liberals, both in New York and across the country.

All the statistics of letters written and literature distributed, indeed, could not disguise an uncomfortable fact: the NAACP's campaign against *The Birth of a Nation* had essentially failed. Beginning as an attempt to have the film suppressed, it had rapidly evolved into a damage-limitation exercise focusing on having the most controversial scenes cut. Only in Ohio and Kansas had the film been banned for any length of time; elsewhere, attempts on the part of local authorities to suppress the film were usually rapidly circumvented by the courts. Mayors and censorship boards were on firmer ground when it came to ordering cuts; scenes that were favorite candidates for censorship included the so-called "smell" incident when a female abolitionist recoils in disgust from an African American boy, the scene between Stoneman and Lydia after she has torn her clothing, the brutality of the guerrilla attack on Piedmont, the unflattering shots of the black-dominated South Carolina legislature, Gus's pursuit of Flora, the struggle between Lynch and Elsie Stoneman, and scenes of black men grabbing white women before the arrival of the Klan.[213] Most cuts were made, however, in a way that did not destroy the narrative trajectory of the film: Boston was exceptional, for example, in requiring the complete elimination of the Gus chase sequence.[214] From the NAACP's point of view, the record of delayed showings and cut scenes did little to justify the time and effort involved in fighting the film. If anything, some leaders of the NAACP came to wonder whether their campaign had actually contributed to *Birth*'s success: Du Bois himself noted that the struggle had "probably succeeded in advertising it even beyond its admittedly notable merits."[215] Corroboration that controversy was widely regarded as being good for the film's prospects came from exhibitors in Oakland, California (who paid one group of blacks to create publicity by boycotting it), and a trade journal, the *Motion Picture News*, which blamed the low box office in Seattle, Washington, on the absence of protest there.[216]

The campaign launched by the NAACP against *Birth* may actually have helped the film become a success. Many must have gone to see the film because of the controversy surrounding it or because they were curious to see what had incited the protests against it. Conversely, argues Jane Gaines, the NAACP focus on *Birth of a Nation* came "at the expense of focus on films produced by African Americans themselves."[217] But the NAACP benefited from the campaign as well. When the fight began, it was a small organization, not very well known and highly dependent on the initiative of its uneven network of local branches. The campaign against *Birth of a Nation* gave it much-needed publicity: as one member wrote, it would "help to place the name of the Association before a great many persons who did not know that there is such an organization at work for the good of the race."[218] The struggle also encouraged the NAACP to think in national rather than local terms. Moreover, despite the personal disputes and rivalries that often characterized it, to outsiders the NAACP appeared united and with a clear identity: it was the one organization that consistently attacked Griffith's movie. Even those who were not members found themselves looking to it for advice and leadership.[219] The fight against *Birth* helped the NAACP to double in size. At the beginning of 1915, it had a total membership of 5,000. By early May, this had grown to over 7,000; almost 700 new members joined in April alone, probably as a result of the organization's greatly increased visibility resulting from its battles against *Birth* in New York and Boston. In early November, membership was 8,500 and by December, it had reached "nearly 10,000."[220] Thomas Cripps sees a major transformation taking place in the African American community during the early twentieth century: "leadership passed from that of Booker T. Washington's sort of rural self-help to an urban activism."[221] Two events of 1915—Washington's death (in November) and the NAACP's fight against Griffith's film—marked crucial tipping points in this change.

Additionally, in the heat of the struggle, the NAACP also found itself moving beyond its early emphasis on private protest and legal action toward the tactics of more militant public protest (including demonstrations, marches, and meetings) that would characterize the civil rights movement later in the twentieth century. While the NAACP failed in its main objective, which was the immediate suppression of *The Birth of a Nation*, it emerged stronger from the struggle. What soon became clear, however, was that the battles of 1915 and early 1916 against the film were only the first shots in what would be a very long campaign.

7

Griffith's View of History

A few days before Griffith gathered his cast together to announce his intention of filming *The Clansman*, Lillian Gish noticed that "his pockets were crammed with papers and pamphlets." Unusual for a Griffith film, the director felt obliged to consult printed source materials before embarking on rehearsals and shooting. Even after shooting began, Gish recalled, he still carried around with him pamphlets, maps, and books "which he read during meals and the rare breaks in his hectic schedule."[1] Although Griffith had already made films based on historical events before *The Clansman*, including several "Civil War" pictures, clearly there were crucial differences between them and his new project. Like Dixon, who also claimed to have mastered huge amounts of reading before writing his two novels about the Klan and consequently justified his fiction in terms of its "historical accuracy," Griffith defended his greatest movie as a faithful representation of the events of the Civil War and Reconstruction eras.[2]

When Griffith set out to turn *The Clansman* into a film, the loyalties of the Civil War and Reconstruction eras were still very much a part of the American political and cultural scene. Despite his own personal engagement with the "Southern" point of view represented in Dixon's novels and play, the director must have known that many Northerners and some Southerners would reject it as biased and inaccurate. He consequently set out to demonstrate that the version of history offered in *The Clansman* was carefully researched, factually based, and accepted by most contemporary American historians. Whether Griffith realized this possibility from the beginning, the claim that his film represented *history* would later become a powerful argument in resisting attempts at censorship. But seeing himself as involved in showing history on screen also mirrored both the director's aspirations so far as the status of cinema was concerned and his idiosyncratic view of how history would soon come to be constructed and understood.

Griffith believed that associating cinema with history would help legitimate it as an art form. "The foremost educators of the country," he noted, "have urged upon motion picture producers to put away the slapstick comedies, the ridiculous sentimental 'mush' stories, the imitation of the fiction of the cheap magazines and go into the fields of history for our subjects." Griffith went further in articulating ambitions for his medium. "The time will come...," he declared in an interview in March 1915, "when the children in the public schools will be taught practically everything by moving pictures. Certainly they will never be obliged to read history again." He foresaw a time when public libraries would have viewing booths. Anyone interested in learning about an episode in Napoleon's life, he maintained, would no longer be faced with "consulting all the authorities, wading laboriously through a host of books, and ending bewildered,...confused at every point by conflicting opinions about what did happen." Instead, Griffith believed, the curious investigator would be able to approach the subject through the medium of film. She or he would receive "a vivid and complete expression" of the episode concerned, having been "present at the making of history."[3]

Griffith appears to have perceived filmed re-creations as a more objective alternative to written history. "All the work of writing, research, collating, and reproducing," he argued, "will have been carefully attended to by a corps of recognized experts." Like many political reformers during the so-called "Progressive Era," Griffith thought that judgments and decisions were best left in the hands of impartial experts. He apparently believed that there was some essential core of "truth" about the past waiting to be found and disseminated. Academic historians only confused the issue by their disagreements, and in any case, their teachings reached only a small elite. "The truths of history today," Griffith declared in a pamphlet attacking censorship of the movies, "are restricted to the limited few attending our colleges and universities; the motion picture can carry these truths to the entire world, without cost, while at the same time bringing diversion to the masses."[4] In interviews, he argued that the camera was "the instrument with which history is beginning to be written" and that "in time it [would]...be used exclusively in place of typewriters." Having predicted screening rooms in libraries, Griffith went on effectively to foresee the advent of domestic access to "historical" films (the equivalent of today's videocassettes, DVDs, and history channels on cable TV) by suggesting that "when one wants to refresh one's mind about a historical incident," each house would have a "receptacle" for the films concerned and a screen to show them on.[5]

Griffith's defense of film as history itself formed part of an ongoing struggle that, as Lee Grieveson has shown, began toward the end of 1906 and pitted those who regarded cinema as a dangerous, subversive influence that required careful monitoring and policing against those who defended it as a positive, educational force. Griffith had been a consistent advocate of the idea that cinema could have a useful social role. For example, he had made several films foregrounding the dangers of alcohol, and in his 1916 pamphlet attacking film censorship, he claimed that motion pictures—by offering an alternative form of entertainment—"keep men away from saloons and drink." Yet between *The Birth of a Nation*'s Los Angeles première on February 8, 1915, and its New York opening at the beginning of March, the U.S. Supreme Court (on February 23) had come down firmly on the side of critics of the movies when it decided, in the case of *Mutual Film Corporation v. Industrial Commission of Ohio*, that motion pictures had no educational or informative function. They were, in fact, "a business pure and simple, originated and conducted for profit," and, in consequence, could not protect themselves from censorship by claiming the free speech protections of the First Amendment to the Constitution.[6]

It was because of the wording of this decision that Griffith reacted so strongly to an editorial of the New York *Globe* that claimed on April 6 that his film had revived "the passions of the Civil War period," rekindled sectional animosities, and fomented racial hatred "for purely sordid reasons": to "make a few dirty dollars." In an angry response, published on April 10, Griffith complained that these allegations damaged his reputation and insisted that his film portrayed "historic events" and, firmly grounded "upon the authenticated history of the period," told "a story which is based upon truth in every vital detail."[7] Griffith did, of course, protest too much: *The Birth of a Nation* might have endeavored to put across a particular view of history, one with which the director sympathized, but it was essentially an entertainment made "for profit," as the Supreme Court had suggested. By claiming to be representing history, Griffith was attempting to conceal this—in much the same way as, by wrapping himself in the cloak of free speech, he covered up the fact that he wanted this freedom in order to express racist sentiments.

Michael Rogin, defining history in terms of "contingencies and conflicting interpretations," believed that Griffith's idea of depicting the past on film offered "not an avenue to history but its replacement."[8] However, Griffith's consistent faith in what he variously called "the pictorializing of an epoch" or the "picturization of history as it happens"[9] was in some ways only a visual variant of the declared aim of Leopold von Ranke—founder of the school of scientific "history" that emerged in the nineteenth century—to see the past *Wie es eigentlich gewesen* (how it essentially was). To achieve this objective, Ranke and other scholars had sought to examine the most authentic primary source materials—referred to by Ranke as the "purest, most immediate documents" from the period concerned—"to understand the past as the people who lived in it understood it."[10] Ranke's belief that an objective "truth" could be gained from the exhaustive exploration of primary documents was mirrored in Griffith''s perception that "truth" could be established by thorough investigations into the past by "recognized experts." Once this was accomplished, Griffith assumed, historical events and personalities could accurately be represented on film, opening up the possibility of popular access to history.

In taking aim at those who taught American history in higher education, Griffith—even though he probably did not know this—was criticizing a vulnerable target. In the last years of the nineteenth century, under the influence of German ideas on specialized research, the breakdown of the old classical curriculum in higher education, and the emergence of modern universities, history had become increasingly professionalized. This was symbolized by the growing dominance of university teachers within the American Historical Association (founded in 1884) from the mid-1890s onward. In American history, the steady professionalization of the discipline was demonstrated by the publication of the twenty-six-volume "American Nation Series" (almost all by authors with graduate training) between 1904 and 1907 and the organization of the Mississippi Valley Historical Association in 1907.[11] Yet the professionalization of history was paralleled by the virtual collapse of the once-lucrative general market for history books. More and more, historical scholars teaching in universities found the books they wrote being read only by colleagues or students. In this, they differed from the amateur (or at least more literary) "gentlemen-historians" of the nineteenth century whose works had circulated also among nonspecialists.[12]

With professional historians reaching only a small minority of the population, Griffith apparently believed that the path was clear for motion pictures to bring history to the masses and entertain them at the same time. In making *The Birth of a Nation*, he went to considerable lengths to establish it as a "historical" film. *Birth* was characterized by what Mimi White has termed an "insistent historical referentiality."[13] Some of the characters in the film are drawn from history (Abraham Lincoln, Charles Sumner, Ulysses S. Grant, Robert E. Lee, John Wilkes Booth) or resemble a real figure. Austin Stoneman, for example, was fairly closely based on Republican congressman Thaddeus A. Stevens of Pennsylvania. Like the real Stevens, Stoneman has a club foot. Also like the real Stevens, he has a mulatto housekeeper named Lydia.[14] The other mulatto in the film, Silas Lynch, was also based to some degree on fact: South Carolina had not one but two mulatto lieutenant-governors: Alonzo J. Ransier (1870–1872) and Richard H. Gleaves (1872–1876). Apart from their mixed-race background, neither had anything else in common with Lynch.[15] In physical terms, the actors representing historical figures were chosen because they resembled their real counterparts: Joseph Henabery (Lincoln), Howard Gage (Lee), Donald Crisp (Grant), and Raoul Walsh (Booth) seemed, in the opinion of Jack Spears, to have stepped straight from the pages of "a book of Civil War daguerrotypes by [Matthew] Brady."[16]

The story of the Camerons and Stonemans plays out against the chronological background of the Civil War period. The personal drama is closely tied to the historical context by the interactions between the fictional (or semifictional) characters in the film and actual events or real people. Stoneman is seen conferring with both Senator Sumner and President Lincoln. Both the "Little Colonel" and Phil Stoneman command opposing units at the battle of Petersburg. Mrs. Cameron and Elsie Stoneman visit Lincoln to ask for a pardon for Ben Cameron, who has wrongly been condemned to death as a "guerrilla." Both Elsie and Phil Stoneman are present in the audience at Ford's Theatre on the night of Lincoln's assassination. It is noticeable, however, that the link to real people largely vanishes in the second part of the film. Lincoln, of course, is dead and there is no further reference to Sumner after his early visit to Stoneman to urge a less radical policy than full power and equality for blacks.[17]

Reference is continually made in intertitles to actual events (the first battle of Bull Run, the siege of Atlanta) and to real organizations (the Freedmen's Bureau, the Union Leagues, and the Ku Klux Klan).[18] Griffith also offered "historical facsimiles" or tableaux of some of the most crucial moments: Lincoln's call for 75,000 volunteers at the start of the war, the surrender of Lee to Grant at Appomattox Court House, Ford's Theatre on the night of April 14, 1865, and the appearance of the black-dominated House of Representatives in South Carolina in 1871.[19] Each of these, the intertitles claimed, was based on a historical source.[20] He also included elaborate historical reconstructions of the battle of Petersburg and Lincoln's assassination. Finally, to emphasize yet further that his film was—as one intertitle claimed—"an historical presentation of the Civil War and Reconstruction period (shot 621)," Griffith began the second part of *Birth* with three extracts from the *History of the American People* by Woodrow Wilson, the former scholar who was now president of the United States. Later, he referred to another historical assessment by Albion W. Tourgée.

The film's publicists helped "sell" *The Birth of a Nation* by emphasizing the amount of "research" that had gone into verifying the "history" the film supposedly covered. "With the selection of the theme finally agreed," noted the *Kansas City Journal*, "came the primary work of research to establish the historical truth of the narrative. Several professors of history from different universities worked three months compiling this data. Actual measurements of the battle ground [of Petersburg] were made and surveyors and engineers of military experience laid out an exact reproduction of these scenes." Besides producing this farrago of nonsense, the Mitchell/McCarthy advertising team also spread many other fictions that helped legitimate the film in terms of history. Readers of the New York *Sun*, for example, were told that Griffith had "dug up many little known facts" in preparing his picture, one of which was that the Ku Klux Klan was "an indirect outgrowth of the Highland clans of Scotland."[21]

For Griffith's reconstruction of crucial historical episodes, the film's publicity machine went into overdrive. "Many of the scenes," commented the Baltimore *Star*, "[including] President Lincoln signing the order for 75,000 troops and the surrender of General Lee at Appomattox, are historically accurate even to the chairs in the rooms and the pictures on the walls." "Great accuracy and attention to detail and historical accuracy was given in the making of the picture," noted the Waco *Herald*. "For instance, in the scene at Appomattox Courthouse, Gen. Grant is correctly represented in his fatigues uniform, dusty and travel-stained, whilst Gen. Lee is shown in the complete panoply of military dress." The reconstruction of Lincoln's assassination was perhaps the most significant in establishing the film's "historical" credentials. "The incident," declared the Milwaukee *Sentinel*, "was the product of many months of research in museums and historical libraries. Persons…who participated in the event, in one way or another, were interviewed." Such detailed research, observed the Chicago *Post*, had disclosed that "the temperature fell just before the assassination," so that Griffith asked "his Lincoln to…slip a warm cape over his shoulders" immediately before Booth's fatal shot. Both Lee's surrender and Lincoln's assassination, the Kansas City *Labor Herald* observed, "are depicted by Mr. Griffith in so realistic a manner as to startle with their realism even that fast-scattering few who were themselves a part of what was done in those momentous days."[22]

Considerable effort went into making *The Birth of a Nation* seem visually accurate so far as the Civil War sequences were concerned. A variety of reference works were consulted, including photographs by Matthew Brady and books including *Harper's Pictorial History of the Civil War*, *The Soldier in*

Lee surrenders to Grant at Appomattox. (Epoch/The Kobal Collection)

Our Civil War by Paul F. Mottelay and T. Campbell-Copeland, and *Battles and Leaders of the Civil War*.[23] The uniforms and frocks provided by Robert Goldstein's company of theatrical costumiers were mainly successful in conveying the "look" of the period. Genuine muskets of the Civil War era were purchased from a New York firm called Bannerman's. "Huck" Wortman and his crew of carpenters set out to make copies of guns and their carriages that would appear genuine enough to viewers of the picture. Karl Brown recalled that even though "the gun carriages, and especially the trails of the cannon, were made of thin plywood, and the rivets were merely rounded wooden buttons glued in place,...they had been painted with a black paint containing graphite, so that they gleamed with the authentic sheen of polished iron."[24] Billy Bitzer, Griffith's chief cameraman, would argue later that even the manner in which the film was shot gave *The Birth of a Nation* the same visual appearance as Brady's Civil War photographs.[25]

There were several reasons that Griffith and his publicists went to such lengths to convince audiences that they were watching "history." First, it would help attract the wider, middle-class audience for motion pictures that Griffith hoped to reach. It was part of the same strategy that called for *Birth* to be shown in "first-class" theaters at the same prices as "live" productions. Second, it would legitimate the film for both spectators and critics. There was very little direct point in having the actors in the assassination scene reading the play that Lincoln was actually watching at the time of his murder—or in timing the assassination at just the right moment in the play[26]—since, as *Birth* was a silent film, audiences would never hear the lines spoken. But there was an *indirect* point: spectators informed by newspaper reviews of the accuracy with which the film had been made would have been more inclined to accept its historical authenticity. Third, if *Birth of a Nation* could be established as "history" through the re-creation of historical incidents in the first part, the credibility of the second part, largely based on Dixon's extravagant fiction, would be greatly enhanced.

Rather than being a historical film, *Birth of a Nation*, as some of its shrewdest observers noted, was essentially a romance set against a historical backcloth. "These historical scenes," declared the Muncie *Post* "are all shown in a way that links history to romance." "The story," corroborated the Evansville *Courier*, "is one of romance and adventure linked to the most vital periods of American history."[27] *Birth* consequently echoed the very popular genre of live plays based on the Civil War. It even borrowed many of the conventions associated with such stage melodramas: the intersectional love affair, with its subjects initially separated by their regional loyalties but reconciled once the war was over, and the outcast motivated "simply by the desire to do evil."[28] According to Linda Williams, "what this film does is what melodrama does: it stages a recognition of virtue through the visible suffering of the endangered white woman." It also offers a "uniquely American yoking of melodramatic form to a dialectic of racial pathos and antipathy."[29] Part of the second part of the film, indeed, echoed an even older cultural form: Gus's chase of "Little Sister," evoking the idea of the Beast in the Forest, is quite close to a fairy tale. Partly because of his Southern background and partly because of the criticisms made of himself and his film, Griffith could never accept that *Birth of a Nation* was primarily fiction. He had to insist it was true. In reality, however, his fiction was built on—and also helped nurture—a series of historical myths that had grown up around the Civil War and its after-effects: the myth of the "Lost Cause"; of a saintly, compassionate Abraham Lincoln; of a "Tragic era" of "Black Reconstruction"; and of the Ku Klux Klan as the chivalrous saviors of white civilization. Each of these myths deserves examination in its own right.

The "Lost Cause"

The Birth of a Nation, released in the semicentennial of the ending of the American Civil War, would become a major factor in the political struggle taking place over the control of American memory relating to the war itself. That struggle began almost as soon as the war ended. On April 9, 1865, the principal Southern military commander, Robert E. Lee, surrendered the main confederate army to Union commander Ulysses S. Grant at Appomattox Court House in Virginia. For four years, the North had prosecuted a war and had now achieved what in the twentieth century would be referred to as total victory. Or had it? In the years after the war, politicians, especially Southern politicians, began to blur the issues surrounding why the war had been fought and what its consequences had been. By the 1880s, former Confederate general—now Georgia senator—John B. Gordon was habitually introduced (and vociferously applauded) at political rallies as "the hero of Appomattox."[30] In the topsy-turvy world of the postwar South, it was beginning to seem as if the Confederates had won a battle in the place where they had actually surrendered.[31] Symbolically, perhaps, they had. For the end of military conflict between North and South was followed by a political and cultural struggle that lasted for many decades. And if the North had won decisively on the battlefield, the South would emerge equally triumphant from this later conflict.

The main centerpiece of the second war was the attempt to control the public memory of the Civil War through what would come to be known as the myth of the "Lost Cause."[32] That myth, as Thomas Connelly and Barbara Bellows have pointed out, can be divided into two distinct parts. The first, the inner Lost Cause, was initially constructed by the Confederate generation that had fought and lost the Civil War. Led by men such as former president of the Confederacy Jefferson Davis and southern military leaders, such as General Jubal Early, it published partisan memoirs and favorable accounts of the Confederacy, organized veterans' associations, built monuments, turned Robert E. Lee into a romantic folk hero, and generally, in the words of David W. Blight, "sought justification for their cause and explanations for their defeat."[33] One explanation, of course, was that the Confederacy never *had* been defeated: it had simply been overwhelmed by the larger population and industrial capacity of the North. Later, the defense of the Confederacy was taken up by larger and more powerful organizations of Southern veterans and their supporters (the 1890s, for example, would see the emergence of the United Confederate Veterans, the magazine entitled *Confederate Veteran*, and the United Daughters of the Confederacy).[34]

The national Lost Cause emerged in the 1880s and '90s, encouraged by mass-circulation magazines and their primarily Northern readership. It was for the most part a creation of Southern literature. Writers such as John Esten Cooke, William Alexander Carruthers, Mary Johnston, John Pendleton Kennedy, Sara Pryor and—above all—Thomas Nelson Page wrote at one remove from the experiences of the Civil War. For the most part, they ignored the subjects of the Confederacy and Southern defeat. Instead, they opted to create a nostalgic portrait of the antebellum South, the "Old South" of legend. In this artificially constructed world, dominated by the great plantations, romance and chivalry ruled. White society was gracious and cultivated. It was willingly served by black slaves who, as Bruce Chadwick notes, "were typically shown as helpful mammies, obliging butlers, smiling carriage-drivers, joyful cotton-pickers and tap-dancing entertainers."[35] Slavery in these stories was usually associated with "laughter, music, and contentment."[36] The "Old South" myth, rooted in an imaginative, stable preindustrial world, appealed to many Northerners in the final decades of the nineteenth century, as they became more and more conscious of the impact of urbanization, industrialization, labor unrest, and immigration on their own fast-changing society.

Northern readers, when they read about the "Old South," were not being asked to sympathize with the Confederacy. All that was being requested of them, as David Blight remarks, was "to recognize the South's place in national heritage and to enjoy sentimental journeys into a nostalgic past of happy race relations, often narrated in the dialect of a faithful slave."[37] But paralleling the increasing acceptance of a largely mythical view of the South's antebellum past was the growing trend toward intersectional reconciliation, apparent in both the North and the South, during the 1880s and '90s. The end of Reconstruction in 1877, when Republican president Rutherford B. Hayes withdrew the last federal troops from the South as the price of his accession to the presidency, established the political ground for this rapprochement, which can be traced in the increasing number of veterans' reunions that brought former Union and Confederate soldiers together. The first tentative signs of such reconciliation came in 1875, when Confederate veterans marched in a commemorative parade in Boston. Massachusetts veterans accepted a similar offer to march in New Orleans in 1881. In 1882, the Grand Army of the Republic marched together with thousands of Confederate veterans in a commemorative parade. When Union commander (and former president) Ulysses S. Grant died in 1885, several Confederate generals acted as his pallbearers. One of them was Joseph E. Johnston, who also performed the same service for William T. Sherman in 1891, with sad consequences for Johnston himself: bare-headed on a bitterly cold day, he caught pneumonia and died shortly afterward.[38] In 1888, there were intersectional celebrations for the twenty-fifth anniversary of the battle of Gettysburg. Another sign of intersectional reconciliation was the growing observance of Memorial Day, first officially introduced in 1868. By 1891, most states were celebrating it, honoring in the process *both* sides in the conflict. In the Spanish-American War of 1898 President William McKinley was careful to ensure that two of the four American commanders against the Spanish were ex-Confederates.[39]

The reunion of the sections by the end of the nineteenth century was based on a reinterpretation of the Civil War that celebrated the valor and sacrifice of the men on both sides (who were, of course, in this view invariably white). The war became a focus of mutual respect between Union and Confederate veterans in which its ideological attributes—particularly slavery, secession, and emancipation—were set aside and forgotten. If the white North and South were to be members of the same metaphorical family, neither could be blamed for the Civil War. Both had fought with equal heroism on behalf of their section. In historical terms, slavery was thoroughly sidelined as a basic cause of the war. Blacks were presented as happy and content under the benign system of slavery. African Americans, indeed, were the main victims of this rewriting of history and the wider sectional reconciliation it expressed. Instead of being regarded as actors in the drama of the struggle for their own freedom, they were largely ignored or, on screen, reduced to a passive stereotype—what Thomas Cripps refers to as the "loyal slave, the sacrificial goat in the ritual of the reunion of the sections."[40]

The "Lost Cause" legend flourished against this background of sectional reconciliation. As Alan T. Nolan has observed, it incorporated many different elements. According to the "Lost Cause," slavery was not the primary cause of the war; that dubious honor went to the actions of trouble-making abolitionists. Slaves were content with their status (although, rather paradoxically, the South would ultimately have given up slavery). Southern plantation society (which really meant *white* society) was marked by superior grace and gentility. It had descended from the Norman cavaliers who had once conquered the Anglo-Saxon tribes (predictably, perhaps, Northerners were seen as having "Anglo-Saxon" origins). In the end, Southerners were compelled to exercise their lawful right to secede from the Union to protect their liberty, independence, and states' rights. Led by remarkable, saintly figures such as Robert E. Lee, Confederate soldiers had proved themselves gallant and heroic. Confronted with a North superior in both material and manpower, it was inevitable that the South would lose in the end, and after four years of courageous resistance, it was finally overwhelmed.[41]

By the first decade of the twentieth century, therefore, when feature films telling (however poorly) a story became the characteristic product of the American movie industry, there was already a culturally dominant view of the Civil War based on a rereading of the era that was deeply sympathetic to the South. However, since most of the early feature films produced by companies such as Biograph were made in the North for primarily Northern and Western audiences, when they began to deal with the Civil War as a theme, they did so at first from a Northern perspective. An exhibitor in Charleston, South Carolina, indeed, wrote to the *Moving Picture World* in 1910 in complaint: "Why do all civil war pictures have the Northern army come out ahead?... Everyone knows the South won some battles...and a picture [like that] would simply set 'em up down here." The exhibitor had obviously not heard of the *The Old Soldier's Story*, made by the Kalem Company in its new Florida studio and released in the previous year, when it had been hailed by the *Moving Picture World* as the "first [film] ever made that represents the Southern side." Also in 1909, Kalem inaugurated its series devoted to the exploits of Nan, the Southern "girl spy," and Biograph released Griffith's *In Old Kentucky*, with Henry Walthall in the part of the Southern hero. Producers, indeed, quickly discovered that what Eileen Bowser calls "the more romantic, noble, and heroic ideals to be found in the defeated South" appealed to moviegoers in the North as well as in the South. In consequence, from 1911 onward, films reflecting the Southern point of view became twice as numerous as films with a Northern bias.[42]

The fact that Lost Cause ideas and assumptions began to disseminate themselves through film was of major importance in terms of their general impact on American popular culture. The Civil War movie, according to Bowser, was almost as popular as the Western or the Indian film at this time. According to copyright records (which may not present a complete picture), at least twelve Civil War pictures had been made in 1908, twenty-three in 1909, thirty-two in 1910, seventy-four in 1911, fifty-eight in 1912, ninety-eight in 1913, and twenty-nine in 1914. The peaks of production (1911 and 1913) probably had a good deal to do with moviemakers' awareness of the major anniversary celebrations held in those years.[43] Many of these early films were produced either by Thomas H. Ince, a Northern-born Civil War buff, or by D. W. Griffith. It was only natural, therefore, when he set out to adapt Thomas Dixon's novel and play *The Clansman* into a film, that Griffith would extend Dixon's story backward in chronological terms to include the Civil War years. And in *The Clansman* (soon to acquire the more grandiose title *The Birth of a Nation*), Griffith would give the Lost Cause myth probably its most popular and influential expression.

While *The Birth of a Nation* does cover many aspects of the Lost Cause myth, however, it does not cover them all. There is no character like Ashley Wilkes, in *Gone With the Wind*, to claim that the South would have freed its slaves if the Civil War had not freed them already. Eventually, the cultural/ nationalist division between North and South becomes rather confused; in the second part of the film, an intertitle speaks of white Northern and Southern veterans coming together against African Americans "in common defense of their Ayran birthright" (shot 1287). Moreover, given the general atmosphere of sectional reconciliation by 1915, while the Confederate officer, Ben Cameron, is shown to be brave and gallant, so too is Phil Stoneman, his Union adversary. Equally, neither the Confederate nor the Union Army is shown unfavorably. In the one wartime action that might seem discreditable—the attack on private homes in Piedmont by Northern soldiers who seem eager only to loot, destroy, and burn (and possibly rape?) —it is emphasized that the men involved are not part of the proper Union Army. They are, in fact, variously described as either "an irregular force of guerillas [sic]" (shot 232) or a "negro militia" heavily influenced by a white "scalawag" captain (shot 249).

In four main areas, however, the film followed—and helped publicize—central tenets of the "Lost Cause" point of view. In the "Lost Cause" interpretation of the Civil War era, the war had been brought about primarily by abolitionists. *The Birth of a Nation* broadly followed this pathway. The intertitle introducing the first real scene of the film—a minister praying over manacled slaves about to be auctioned—observed that "The bringing of the African to America planted the first seed of disunion" (shots 7–8).[44] The second scene, also introduced by an intertitle, was of a meeting of nineteenth-century abolitionists demanding an end to slavery (shots 9–15). There is evidence that this short scene focusing on abolitionists was originally longer and more critical. At least two sections seem to have been cut from the version of the film that comes down to us: both underlined the insincerity of the abolitionists. One blamed the rise of the abolitionist movement on the hypocrisy of descendants of Northern slave traders who had "no further use of the slaves."[45] The other, already mentioned above, showed an old lady at the abolitionist meeting holding out her arms toward a black boy, but then recoiling from him because of the child's bodily odor.[46]

The Birth of a Nation also endorsed "Lost Cause" notions concerning the superiority of Southern white society and the benign, even uncontroversial, nature of slavery. It is evident from their first appearance in the film that the Camerons belong to the planter class. We see their white-painted house with columns. Clearly, they typify the Old South: an intertitle describes their home as a place "where life runs in a quaintly way that is to be no more." They seem genteel (their daughter, Margaret, is introduced as "a daughter of the South, trained in the manners of the old school.") Above all, perhaps, they are benevolent: Dr. Cameron, described as "the kindly master of Cameron Hall," sits reading a newspaper surrounded by pets (shots 33–34, 41, 47–50). How could such a man, the film appears to suggest, be unkind to his slaves?

The main sequence involving slavery occurs when Phil Stoneman, and Ben, Margaret and Flora Cameron, and a small boy set off to visit the slave quarters. Black workers are shown picking cotton in the background, but the main emphasis of the film at this point is on the burgeoning romance between Phil and Margaret, and on Ben's falling in love with a portrait of Elsie Stoneman carried by Phil (shots 78–96). This pastoral idyll is followed by a shot of the space in front of the slaves' cabins (located geographically by means of an intertitle). The following title makes it plain that the visitors (who by now also include Tod Stoneman and Duke Cameron) have arrived at midday and that the slaves are well treated. It speaks of "the two-hour interval given for dinner, out of their working day from six till six." While the title does not say how many days a week the slaves work, the general impression is that the allotted time for the main meal of the day is generous and that the working day is not excessively long. So little tired, indeed, are the slaves by their work that they put on an impromptu dance to entertain the Camerons and their guests. One reviewer later praised the film for showing "the fun and frolic of plantation days."[47] Finally, as the visitors begin to leave, two old slaves approach Ben: he shakes hands with one, and rests his other hand on the second man's shoulder. As he leaves to follow the rest of the party, the two slaves nod approvingly in his direction. Clearly, the slaves are well treated by white "massa" (or his son) and respond with affection to such care (shots 100–106).[48] Later, they will demonstrate in support of Ben Cameron's regiment as it goes off to fight for the Confederacy (shots 200, 207, 209, 215). The enthusiasm of the whole Southern community, including slaves, for the war effort demonstrates an acceptance of the existing state of society, including slavery. Not only is slavery *not* a repressive system of labor, but it is far from being a major bone of contention between Northerners and Southerners: there is no sign during their visit to the slave quarters that Phil and Tod Stoneman, despite being the sons of a radical Northern politician, are in any meaningful sense offended by their exposure to the slave system.

In explaining why the South fought, *The Birth of a Nation* adopted the same approach as the advocates of the Lost Cause. The film begins to sketch out the states' rights argument for war with an intertitle insisting that "The power of the sovereign states, established when Lord Cornwallis surrendered to the individual colonies in 1781, is threatened by the new administration." Dr. Cameron is subsequently shown reading a newspaper with the headline "If the North carries the election, the South will secede" (shots 107, 109). No attempt is made to provide a political context by explaining why Lincoln's election in 1860 is such a threat to the South. When Lincoln calls for troops, he is said to be using "the Presidential office for the first time in history to call for volunteers to enforce the rule of the coming nation over the individual states" (shot 146). Later, the South Carolina state flag is referred to as "the spirit of the South." The flag carries the motto "CONQUER WE MUST—VICTORY OR DEATH— FOR OUR CAUSE IS JUST." Once the war ends, Lee's surrender to Grant is depicted as "The end of state sovereignty" (shots 196, 198, 507).

Like the Lost Cause, *The Birth of a Nation* depicted the South as clearly the underdog: hence the treatment of time in the first part of the film which, as

Pierre Sorlin has noted, is "confused."[49] It seems primarily designed to ensure that the South is seen as victim and to suggest that the North was eventually bound to win the Civil War. The first overt mention of the war comes with the first tableau in the film: a facsimile of Lincoln signing the first call for 75,000 volunteers, allegedly taken from the biography of Lincoln by Nicolay and Hay. In reality, of course, the first act in the conflict had been the Confederate firing on Fort Sumter on April 12, 1861. To have mentioned this, however, would have made it clear that the South, far from being a victim, was the real aggressor in the conflict.

The farewell ball for the men of Piedmont who are going off to fight is also a celebration of the Confederate victory at the first battle of Bull Run (July 21, 1861). After the shots of the men of Piedmont marching off and a much more low-key reference to Northern Congressman Stoneman's learning, indirectly, from Elsie of his two sons' departure for the front, there is a strange hiatus (suggested by an intertitle) of "two and a half years" (shots 160, 174, 181–222). Clearly, much has gone wrong for the South during this period. The Southern economy has collapsed and standards of living have fallen: Flora Cameron "wears her last good dress" to give a touch of ceremony to the reading of one of Ben's letter from the front. Northern forces appear to be roaming the South almost at will: a group of mostly black guerrillas attacks Piedmont and General Sherman begins to march and burn his way to the sea, taking Atlanta in the process. In the meantime, the Camerons sell the "last of their dearest possessions...for the failing cause." Finally, in the "last grey days of the Confederacy," Southern soldiers in besieged Petersburg, Virginia, are reduced to eating nothing but "parched corn" (shots 226, 232–91, 317–38, 313, 339).

In reality, as historians have shown in the last thirty years, none of the principal "Lost Cause" myths enshrined in the film was true. To say that the South was the victim of a war forced on it by abolitionists ignores both the fact that the abolitionists were correct in identifying slavery as a major evil *and* the aggressive, expansionist ambitions of many Southerners between the Missouri Compromise of 1820 and secession in 1860–61.[50] To see the South as victim means setting aside Southern attempts to expand slavery into central America and the Caribbean and the attitudes of Southerners and their politicians to such major 1850s issues as popular sovereignty and "Bleeding Kansas." The so-called superiority of the Southern whites depends on ignoring both the appallingly low educational standards throughout the South as a whole and the fact that the planter class, properly defined, was only a minuscule proportion of Southern society. If white masters were so benevolent and slaves so happy, it becomes very difficult to explain why so many ran away or ended up fighting for the Union forces. In reality, slavery was a brutal system of labor. The states' rights case for Southern secession depends on a highly dubious assumption of constitutional rights: Lincoln, who asserted that the union was perpetual and, in any case, could be dissolved only with the consent of all the contracting

The devastating march through Georgia of General Sherman—a burning house in the background. (Epoch/The Kobal Collection)

parties, had distinctly the better of the argument here. Finally, although the South certainly had fewer men than the North, it managed to keep its armies supplied with sufficient arms and munitions until the end of the conflict. It only had to keep protecting its own territory until the North became tired and, at least in the view of a number of recent historians, could have won the war at several points until the late summer of 1864.[51]

The Birth of a Nation—despite, or perhaps partly because of, the campaign waged against it by the NAACP and other pro-black organizations—was an enormous popular success. It spread the myth of the "Lost Cause" to a mass, popular national audience and in the process helped ensure that it would re-main the way most Americans would think of the Civil War era for decades to come. In terms of national memory, it became a popular substitute for the his-tory of the war.[52] But as the editors of Cahiers du cinéma argued more than thirty years ago, even films that seem to articulate the most hegemonic collections of myths and ideas at times contain contradictions that undermine the myths they ostensibly express.[53] Whatever Griffith's broader intentions, The Birth of a Nation has sequences that draw attention to the inaccuracies and contradic-tions that made up the myth of the Lost Cause. One of the most obvious is that while Griffith emphasizes in intertitles how poor and ill-equipped Southern soldiers are by the end of the war, as a showman he cannot resist showing Confederate artillery endlessly bombarding enemy lines. The idea that the Civil War was mainly a conflict between heroic and gallant white men is undercut by the scenes of hand-to-hand combat in the trenches at Petersburg (shots 402, 404) and in particular by the scene in which Tod and Duke Cameron meet on the battlefield. Tod is about to bayonet Duke, who is already lying wounded on the ground, when he recognizes him and lowers his gun; he is then shot in the back by a Confederate soldier hiding in the bushes behind, leaving the two to die embracing each other (shots 299–308). Finally, the myth of the benevolent master and loyal slaves is exploded in the second part of the film when Dr. Cameron is brought, chained, before his former slaves and taunted and abused by two African American women (shots 1231–32). Ironically, this part of the film revolves around the apparent threat posed by black men to white women. Under slavery, however, the reality of miscegenation—as this scene possibly suggests—had been white slave owners, together with their sons and overseers, preying on black female slaves.

Lincoln as a Symbol of Reconciliation

To many people today, Abraham Lincoln—the so-called Great Emancipator, immortalized since 1922 in Daniel Chester French's giant sculpture in Washington's Lincoln Memorial, and one of the four presidents whose features are carved on Mount Rushmore—is perhaps the greatest of all American presidents. The reputation of the martyred fourteenth president, however, is in many ways a construction, created by different people in different ways at different times.[54] The portrayal of Lincoln in *The Birth of a Nation* both reflected and influenced that process of construction.

In contrast to his twentieth-century successor John F. Kennedy, Lincoln did not experience an immediate apotheosis after his assassination. "Although the subject [at the time of his death] of a great deal of immediate sentimentality," remarked Eric F. Goldman, "[he] did not become the unassailable Abraham Lincoln of the schoolbooks until two decades after his murder."[55] The first major architects of Lincoln's reputation were John Nicolay, formerly Lincoln's secretary, and John Hay. *The Century* magazine published their biography of Lincoln over two and a half years at the end of the 1880s, and, in 1890 with the serial ended, as a book in ten volumes.[56] Not only was the Nicolay and Hay study of monumental size but it encapsulated a particular view of Lincoln as an ideal hero and semi-mythical character. In contrast to the Nicolay and Hay study, the three-volume life of Lincoln by his friend and former law partner William Henry Herndon, published in 1889, took a determinedly critical view of Lincoln as heroic legend to focus on his personal qualities as a characteristic

Westerner.[57] But Herndon's debunking of the now-expanding Lincoln myth did not attract many readers, and his book was either reviled, or, perhaps worse, ignored.

For an alternative view of Lincoln to emerge required a major change in American cultural formations. *The Century*, the magazine that had published the biography by Nicolay and Hay, was one of the four most important magazines of the Gilded Age (the others being *Harper's Monthly*, *Atlantic Monthly*, and *Scribners*). The members of this "sedate quartet," as Cornelius Regier once described them, were primarily literary magazines.[58] Patrician in tone, belle-lettristic in character, they sold for either twenty-five or thirty-five cents and reached an audience largely drawn from the American upper-middle class. The decade of the 1890s, however, saw the emergence of a group of new, cheap, popular "monthlies." While some of these, including *Munsey's* and *Cosmopolitan*, had first been published in the late '80s or early '90s, they had not immediately caught on. This situation altered with the first publication of *McClure's Magazine* in June 1893. The appearance of *McClure's*, which was initially sold for just fifteen cents, provoked a price war among the newer magazines that finally resulted in the emergence of the ten-cent magazine. With the arrival of the cheap "monthly," the United States acquired its first truly national media and took a crucial step toward the popularization of culture in general. Vast numbers of people now began to buy and read magazines; Frank Munsey, one of the founders of the new medium, estimated that between 1893 and 1899 "the ten-cent magazine increased the magazine-buying public from 250,000 to 750,000."[59]

One of the most crucial reasons for the success of the new magazines, *McClure's* in particular, was the importance they accorded biography. A biography of Napoleon by Ida M. Tarbell ran as an illustrated serial in *McClure's* from November 1894 to April 1895, and during this period, circulation of the magazine doubled. Sam McClure, flying in the face of the conventional wisdom that the publication of the Nicolay and Hay biography had exhausted popular interest in Lincoln, then assigned Tarbell to write a new and more popular life of him. Within ten days of the first installment of Tarbell's Lincoln biography, *McClure's Magazine* added 40,000 fresh subscribers; within three months, the figure had reached 100,000.[60]

Tarbell's work on Lincoln, which started publication in November 1897, took an approach to its subject that was very different to that of Nicolay and Hay. Like Herndon, in some respects, Tarbell's life focused on Lincoln as a Westerner. But whereas Herndon had projected a realistic image of a man who was plain, frank, and at times crude, Tarbell presented him as a great man not so much *despite* his background as *because* of it. In essence, Tarbell created a folk myth of Lincoln as the conscious descendant of generations of pioneers. This representation of him as an illustration of "indigenous greatness" obviously caught the imagination of large numbers of Americans of the late 1890s. Buffeted by the economic depression of 1893–97 and highly conscious of the changes in their society as a result of industrialization, urbanization, and immigration, many native-born Americans saw the character of Lincoln (as constructed by Ida Tarbell) as a reaffirmation of the values of an older America at a time when those values seemed very much under attack.

The popular view of Lincoln advanced, especially by Tarbell, in the popular magazines was echoed in another form of mass media to emerge in the 1890s: the movies. Motion pictures often presented to mass audiences a perception of the martyred president that emphasized his democratic and accessible qualities. He was usually represented as a homely and compassionate figure, happy to make time to see ordinary citizens and discuss their concerns. In many of these early motion pictures, including *The Reprieve* (1908), *Abraham Lincoln's Clemency* (1910), *One Flag at Last* (1911), *The Seventh Son* (1912), *When Lincoln Was President* (1913), and *The Songbird of the North* (1913), the on-screen Lincoln saved the life of a sentry who had fallen asleep at his post or a convicted spy by issuing a presidential pardon. Maybe the most fanciful of all these films was *The Toll of War* (1913), in which Lincoln freed a Southern girl sentenced to death for spying against the North. After her release, she saw the assassination of Lincoln at Ford's Theatre. The president was carried to her nearby room and died in her bed while she knelt beside him in prayer.[61] *The Man Who Knew Lincoln* (1914), with Ralph Ince, Thomas H. Ince's brother, playing Lincoln, was directly based on Ida Tarbell's story, "He Knew Lincoln."[62]

With the release of *The Birth of a Nation* in 1915, the popular view of Lincoln reached a much wider audience. In some respects, *Birth* offered the by-then conventional view of a humane and merciful Lincoln. After he signs the call for volunteers to subdue the South's rebellion, for example, he is shown wiping away tears with a handkerchief (shots 144–45, 147). When Colonel Cameron is unjustly condemned to be hanged, as a guerrilla, his mother and Elsie Stoneman visit Lincoln to plead for a presidential pardon. After some hesitation, the compassionate Lincoln—described as "Great Heart" in an intertitle—agrees. Mrs. Cameron, resisting with some difficulty the urge to embrace the president, returns to the hospital and tells Ben that "Mr. Lincoln has given back your life to me" (shots 476–95, 497). One curious feature of Griffith's Lincoln, however, as Robert Lang notes, is his strangely "androgynous" quality. He combines masculine *and* feminine qualities. He is a bearded man, but is sensitive to his own feelings and those of others. He is ready to make war on the South, but he cries after signing the proclamation calling for volunteers. He angrily dismisses the man speaking to him before his meeting with Elsie and Mrs. Cameron, but finally gives in to the emotional persuasions of the Little Colonel's mother to save her son's life. In the last moments before he is shot, Lincoln draws a shawl around his shoulders, perhaps symbolizing his awareness of the chill of impending death (shots 586, 588). As a gesture, however, Lang points out, it is "coded culturally as feminine."[63] In *The Birth of a Nation*, Lincoln is both a father *and* mother to his people.

The film also depicts Lincoln as a Moses figure: he will never reach the promised land of the "coming nation" he has done so much to create. That nation will be born only after Reconstruction has ended and Southern whites have succeeded in subordinating all blacks and excluding them from power.[64] *Birth of a Nation* encouraged the perception that if Lincoln had lived, this new (white) American nation would have been born much sooner. Though a Southerner, Griffith (like Dixon) admired Lincoln for his magnanimity and believed that if he had not been murdered, Reconstruction generally (and the radical Reconstruction after 1867 in particular) would not have happened.[65] With the war over, Griffith depicts a confrontation between Lincoln and Austin Stoneman, the leader of the radicals. Stoneman protests Lincoln's policy of clemency for the South, insisting that "their leaders must be hanged and their states treated as conquered provinces." (The "conquered provinces" phrase was actually used by Thaddeus Stevens, the radical congressional leader on whom Stoneman's fictional character was based.) But Lincoln lives up to the spirit of his second inaugural on March 4, 1865 ("with malice toward none; with charity for all") and tells Stoneman he will deal with the seceded states "as though they had never been away." Encouraged by this liberal attitude on the part of the president, the South begins rebuilding itself (shots 529–35), but this process is interrupted by Lincoln's death.

The treatment of Lincoln's assassination at Ford's Theatre—including 55 shots and 9 intertitles, and lasting almost five minutes—is one of the longest sequences in *The Birth of a Nation*. It also ties the film's fictional story line effectively to a major historical event (both Phil and Elsie Stoneman are in the audience and enthusiastically applaud Lincoln when he arrives to take his seat. Later, Elsie is the first person to notice, and point with her fan at, assassin John Wilkes Booth [shots 545–46, 559, 578–84]).[66] The intertitles emphasize the essential truthfulness of the reconstruction by giving a series of historical details: the play being presented is *Our American Cousin*, starring Laura Keene; the presidential party arrives at 8:30; Lincoln's bodyguard deserts his post outside the presidential box to have a better view; the shooting takes places at 10:13, during Act III, Scene 2; and Booth, having fired the fatal shot, leaps onto the stage shouting "Sic semper tyrannis!" (shots 547, 554, 570–71, 576, 596–98). Lincoln's assassination is important for the narrative development of *Birth of a Nation*: it sets the scene for the second half of the film. On hearing the news, Stoneman's mistress Lydia informs him that he is "now the greatest power in America" (shot 611). The path is open to a much more radical kind of postwar Reconstruction than Lincoln would ever have countenanced.

In practice, of course, what we see is a further development and refinement of the Lincoln legend. While Lincoln did indeed hope to treat the South with considerable leniency, he never had the time to develop a truly coherent policy. The war effectively ended with Lee's surrender on April 9, 1865, and Lincoln was assassinated just five days later. The South generally had very little

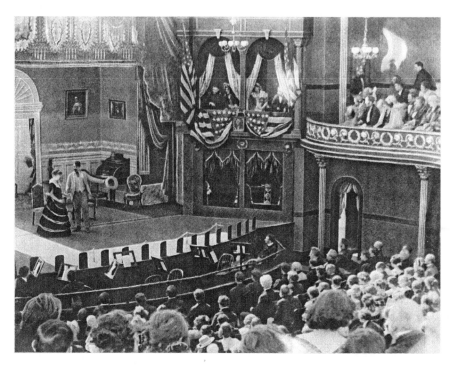

Shot of Ford's Theatre just before the assassination sequence. (Epoch/The Kobal Collection)

of "Lincoln's fostering hand" to encourage it, and the reaction of Dr. Cameron to the news of Lincoln's assassination ("Our best friend is gone. What is to become of us now?") is frankly absurd (shot 617). What Griffith was doing was in essence displacing the notion of Lincoln as a unifying national figure—a perception many Southerners had also come to share by 1915—onto the closing moments of the Civil War.[67] "His" Lincoln, ironically, is presented as a hero to the hostile Southerners he has spent the last four years trying to subdue.

The "Tragic Era" Legend of Reconstruction

Most of the controversy surrounding *The Birth of a Nation* both at the time of its initial release and later did not have to do with its depictions of slavery and the origins of the Civil War, the war itself, or Lincoln's leadership. It arose from the second part of the film dealing with the era of Reconstruction in the South and the rise of the Ku Klux Klan.

In its spring 1947 issue, the British film journal *Sight and Sound* published a letter from D. W. Griffith. The director was writing in response to a hostile article by Peter Noble, criticizing Griffith as a "pioneer of prejudice" who, in

The Birth of a Nation, had produced a film that had viciously distorted the facts, caricatured blacks, and made heroes of the Klansmen who had invented the horrors of lynching. Historians, Noble observed, had been "quick to point out the many inaccuracies in the film." Griffith rejected the idea that he was anti-black: his attitude toward African Americans, he insisted, had "always been one of affection and brotherly feeling." But it was the accusation that his greatest film was historically inaccurate that seemed to anger him most. In *Birth of a Nation,* Griffith argued,

> I gave to my best knowledge the proven facts, and presented the known truth, about the Reconstruction period in the American South. These facts are based on an overwhelming compilation of authentic evidence and testimony. My picturization of history as it happens requires, therefore, no apology, no defence, no "explanations."[68]

The fact that Griffith referred *only* to his treatment of the Reconstruction period (in a film that spanned the antebellum and Civil War years) showed how aware he was of the controversy attached to the second part of his film. Yet at the time *The Birth of a Nation* had been made, the view it offered of the Reconstruction era after the Civil War had not been very different from the dominant "Dunningite" view among professional historians. The term "Dunningite" referred to the followers of William Archibald Dunning of Columbia University who in his books—*Essays on the Civil War and Reconstruction and Related Topics* (1897) and *Reconstruction, Political and Economic, 1865–1877* (1907)—had argued that the Reconstruction process after the Civil War had been a mistake. Radical Republicans, motivated by hatred of the white South, had imposed the corrupt rule of blacks, scalawags, and carpetbaggers on the states of the old Confederacy. In the end, that rule had been brought to an end, sometimes peacefully and sometimes violently, by decent Southern whites. Dunning's many graduate students, including Walter L. Fleming, James W. Garner, J. G. de Roulac Hamilton, Charles W. Ramsdell, and C. Mildred Thompson, had reaffirmed his critical view of the Reconstruction era. In 1929, Claude G. Bowers would recapitulate the arguments of the Dunningites for a popular audience in his highly critical best seller, *The Tragic Era.*[69] Even in 1947, Griffith was by no means the only Southerner still to be defending what had come to be known as the critical "Dunningite" or "Tragic Era" interpretation of Reconstruction. Writing in the introduction to the volume he published that year on the history of the South after the Civil War, Georgia historian E. Merton Coulter declared in a phrase strikingly similar to Griffith's that "there can be no sensible departure from the well-known facts of the Reconstruction program as it was applied to the South."[70]

In January 1948, six months before his death, Griffith began to dispose of his library. He gave much of it away to his acolyte and supposed biographer, Seymour Stern, with the suggestion, which Stern acted on, that the books he could not store be donated to the Hollywood Public Library. Among the works now given to him, Stern identified five that Griffith had used in researching the Reconstruction period: Woodrow Wilson, *A History of the American People*, Vol. V, *Reunion and Nationalization*; Albion Winegar Tourgée, *A Fool's Errand and The Invisible Empire*; J. C. Lester and D. L. Wilson, *Ku Klux Klan—Its Origins, Growth and Disbandment*; John S. Reynolds, *Reconstruction in South Carolina, 1865–1877*; and *Testimony Taken by the Joint Committee on Reconstruction to Inquire into the Condition of Affairs in the Late Insurrectionary States* (the volume on North Carolina). [71] Stern also listed a pamphlet entitled *The Prescript of [the] Ku Klux Klan* by West Virginia history professor Walter L. Fleming, an unpublished paper on the uniform of the Klan by Elizabeth M. Howe, and a collection of "original documents" on the Klan, including handbills, notices, and warnings that had been given to Griffith by Dixon. [72] In a letter of 1915, J. J. McCarthy, a leading publicist for Griffith's film, also cited Walter L. Fleming's "Reconstruction in South Carolina" [73] and James S. Pike's *The Prostrate State: South Carolina under Negro Government* as the sources for Griffith's film. [74]

What is intriguing about the works Griffith apparently used in his preparation for shooting *Birth* is that not all of them were favorable to or romanticized the Klan. *Testimony Taken by the Joint Committee*—unofficially known as the "Ku Klux Report"—was published by Congress in 1872 as a justification for the Federal Force Acts of 1870 and 1871, which had been used effectively to destroy the Klan. The report reprinted testimony from countless victims of Klan outrages. Anyone reading it objectively would surely have reached the conclusion that the Klan was a brutal, violent, and degraded organization.

Even more interesting, in some ways, was the inclusion of Tourgée's *The Invisible Empire*. Besides Woodrow Wilson, he was the only writer to be mentioned by name in the second part of *The Birth of a Nation*. Immediately after the "Little Colonel" has the inspiration for the Ku Klux Klan, the Klan is described in an intertitle as "the organization that saved the South from the anarchy of black rule, but not without the shedding of more blood than at Gettysburg, according to Judge Tourgée of the carpet-baggers" (shot 925). The intertitle does not make clear whether Tourgée is being cited as the source both for the assertion that the Klan had rescued the South and the assessment of the human cost ("more blood than at Gettysburg"), or only for the latter. It brings together in the same phrase two deeply untrue propositions: that there was ever "black rule" in the South and that it had produced "anarchy." It exaggerates the casualties involved in the Klan campaign [75] while leaving unclear precisely just *whose* blood has been spilt—that of the Klansmen or blacks or both—and whether Tourgée approves or disproves of the Klan's actions. Indeed, the only reasonably accurate parts of the intertitle were the identification of Tourgée as a judge and as belonging to the "carpetbaggers" (as mentioned above, this was the term of opprobrium applied by native white Southerners to all Northerners who arrived in the South during Reconstruction).

Tourgée, a one-eyed Ohioan of French Huguenot stock, had enlisted in the Union Army at the start of the war. In July 1861, he was seriously injured at the first battle of Bull Run. Although discharged from the army as a result, he reenlisted as a lieutenant in July 1862. At the battle of Perryville, Kentucky, in October 1862 he was again injured. He recovered quickly, only to be captured by the enemy in January 1863. Tourgée remained a prisoner in Tennessee until May, when he was exchanged. He went back briefly to Ohio, where he married, before returning to duty. He fought in many battles over the next few months. Resigning from the army in December 1863, he returned to Ohio where he was admitted to the bar. Still suffering the effects of his wartime injuries, he began to dream of a place where he could both recover his health and make his fortune. In October 1865, he settled with his wife in North Carolina. He did not, as John Hope Franklin pointed out, fit the Southern stereotype of the impecunious carpetbagger, since he arrived with $5,000 which he invested, and eventually lost, in a farming business.[76] Over the next two years, Tourgée became deeply involved in Reconstruction politics. He organized the Union League in his county and for six months edited a newspaper that campaigned for a more sweeping approach to the Reconstruction of the South. Tourgée got his wish in March 1867 when Congress passed the first of a series of Reconstruction Acts. Existing state governments across the South were dissolved and conventions, elected on the basis of black suffrage, were called to draw up new state constitutions. Tourgée was elected to the North Carolina constitutional convention of 1868 and appears to have played a major part in its deliberations. Soon afterward, he was elected to the Superior Court, on which he served for six years. From the bench he attacked white North Carolinians, and especially the Klan, for their treatment of African Americans. After 1870, when the Democrats came back into power in the state, bringing the Reconstruction process there effectively to an end, Tourgée came under increasing pressure from his enemies. In 1876, he was given a federal job as a pension agent by President Ulysses S. Grant. Three years later, he finally gave up the idea of living in the South and moved back North with his family.[77]

In November 1879, Tourgée published *A Fool's Errand: By One of the Fools*, a semifictionalized account of the failure of Reconstruction in North Carolina. Although not in the strict sense autobiographical, the main character, Comfort Servosse, the fool of the title, is plainly modeled on Tourgée. Many of the incidents in the book closely paralleled Tourgée's own experiences, including the threats made by the Klan against Servosse and his family and the story of a failed murder plot.[78] Throughout the book, Tourgée described the activities of the Klan in detail. Much of this material was based on a systematic record of the activities of the Klan he had made during his time as a judge.[79] In 1880, when *A Fool's Errand* was republished, Tourgee added a second part to the book, an appendix entitled "The Invisible Empire." It was this edition that Dixon had given to Griffith as he started work on what became *The Birth of a Nation*.

Griffith's use of Tourgée in an intertitle suggests that he was familiar with the book. Seymour Stern also asserted that he used material from "A New Institution" (Chapter 27 of *A Fool's Errand*) and "The Invisible Empire" "both in scenes and in *subtitles* of the unabridged version" of *Birth*.[80] Since whatever longer version of the film he referred to has long disappeared, it is difficult to assess the accuracy of the claim. Moreover, because the view of the Klan in *Birth* was so different from that in Tourgée's writing, it is plain that ideas derived from the book would need considerable transformation before they could be included in the film. The chapter of *A Fool's Errand* entitled "A New Institution," for example, is about an attack on a muscular African American blacksmith, Bob Martin, by the Klan. During the course of the attack, Martin's one-year-old son is killed. Martin himself is tied to a tree and whipped. A coura-geous man (he fought in the 54th Massachusetts regiment during the war), he dismisses the mythology surrounding the Klan ("I didn't 'bleve any nonsense about ther comin' straight from hell, an' drinkin' the rivers dry").[81] Griffith takes elements from this chapter and inverts them totally to fit his own perspec-tive. The black man tied to a tree and whipped in *Birth* is Jake, the Camerons' "faithful soul," and he is beaten not by the Klan but by other blacks who want to punish him for not voting for the radical regime (shots 824–30). Two blacks, one identified as a "barn burner," clearly *are* terrified by three Klansmen, one of whom endlessly drinks water from a bucket (927–37). And Bob, the power-fully built black blacksmith, is reincarnated in *Birth of a Nation* as Jeff, the brave *white* blacksmith who dies trying to apprehend the evil Gus, the black soldier who has driven Flora Cameron to her fate (shots 1104–33).

In "The Invisible Empire," Tourgée insisted that *A Fool's Errand* had been closely based on fact—drawn "either [from his] personal cognizance or authen-tic information." "The Invisible Empire" set out to show that the Klan really *had* been as evil as the novel had suggested. It republished voluminous extracts from the 1872 majority report by the congressional committee of inquiry into the Klan.[82] Although most of the testimony included related to Alabama and Georgia, it offered glimpses into the workings of the Klan that Griffith could use (in suitably refashioned form) in his film. Tourgée stressed the importance of threats and warnings issued by the Klan to groups and individuals, and the attempt to exploit superstition by suggesting that the ghostly figures menacing blacks were the spirits of Confederates who had been killed in battle.[83] These themes were echoed in the above-mentioned shot of the Klansmen threatening the "barn-burner." Three other points made by Tourgée were also reflected in the film. He noted that Klansmen were almost invariably mounted on horses (which Tourgée believed emphasized that they "had the co-operation and approval of the better classes").[84] He underlined the importance the Klan attached to disarming African Americans.[85] In the film, this is the first thing done by Klans-men once Elsie Stoneman and the party in the cabin have been rescued (shots 1578–79). Finally Tourgée commented on how easily the Klan disguise could be carried around; it was worn only for Klan meetings and rides.[86] (In *Birth of a Nation*, the costume is initially carried by the "Little Colonel" in a paper bundle to a meeting with Elsie, and then hidden under his coat. Later, Margaret Cameron hides it under her skirt and both she and Flora are shown concealing the robe inside a pillowcase [shots 954–59, 983, 1186, 1188]).

If Tourgée's book influenced a number of features of the Klan's portrayal in *Birth of a Nation*, it does not appear to have affected the actual *appearance* of Klansmen in the film. Tourgée, citing testimony given to the "Ku Klux" committee, claimed that the actual Klan's disguise differed from state to state. Walter L. Fleming, in a reprint of Lester and Wilson's 1884 book on the Klan, included lithographic prints that supported this idea. Klansmen from Mississippi and west Alabama were shown to have worn much darker and more elaborate costumes than those from Tennessee and northern Alabama. The common factor was that all were wearing white hoods on top of darker, floor-length gowns.[87] Griffith seems to have rejected these uniforms (and the one described in Elizabeth Howe's eyewitness account[88]) in favor of his own design (perhaps influenced by recollections of the Klan passed on to him by Thomas Dixon). Almost all the Klansmen in *Birth of a Nation* wear long white gowns decorated with crosses on an oval dark patch across the chest (Ben Cameron has two patches, other Klansmen only one). Some (again including Ben) have smaller crosses on their sleeves. Klansmen wear either a rounded white helmet with a spike and a face mask or a conical hat. The horses they ride are similarly dressed all in white and often seem (because of the holes cut for their eyes and ears) to have crosses on their foreheads. Some display other crosses or the emblem "K.K.K." on their sides.[89]

Although unlike Tourgée he was not mentioned in an intertitle, James Shepherd Pike was perhaps the most influential writer on Reconstruction so far as *Birth of a Nation* was concerned. Born in Maine, Pike had by the 1850s become a leading Republican champion of antislavery and a writer for Horace Greeley's New York *Tribune*. As his biographer observes, however, Pike's dislike of slavery "was accompanied by a strange indifference, even hostility" to blacks. Nevertheless, by the end of the Civil War (which he spent as American minister to Holland), he had become convinced of the necessity for the new freedmen to be given the vote. During the late 1860s, Pike was associated with the radical Republican position on Reconstruction, but by the early 1870s he had become far more skeptical. In the 1872 election, he supported the Liberal Republican movement which, among other things, proposed to end Reconstruction in the South. In January 1873, he traveled south to write the series of articles for the *Tribune* that would become *The Prostrate State*.[90] Characterized by an intense and virulent racism—it sought to defend white "Anglo-Saxons" against "black barbarism" or "Africanization"—Pike's book foregrounded what he saw as the manifest evils of Reconstruction in South Carolina.[91] A key text in the development of the Dunningite or "Tragic Era" legend of Reconstruction,[92]

The Prostrate State affected *Birth of a Nation* both indirectly and directly. The indirect influence came through Thomas Dixon, who claimed to have researched *The Clansman* for a year. Clearly, *The Prostrate State* was one of his sources since parts of the novel bore a very close (if unacknowledged) relationship to Pike's work.[93] The direct influence came via Griffith, who seems to have used it both to confirm and to elaborate on Dixon"s story.

In South Carolina, according to *The Birth of a Nation*, the process of Reconstruction begins after Stoneman "sends Lynch South to aid the carpetbaggers in organizing and wielding the power of the negro vote" (shot 668). Once he arrives in the state, Lynch and his helpers try to persuade blacks to stop work and join in the celebrations. What African Americans can now hope to receive is painted as a legend on a billboard: "Forty Acres and a Mule" (shots 680–88). The Freedmen's Bureau is shown distributing free supplies to clamorous blacks, confirming the idea that they can now expect to live without working ("The charity of a generous North misused to delude the ignorant," as an intertitle expresses it) (shots 689–90). A squad of black soldiers, accompanied by Lynch, dominates the sidewalk, preventing Ben and Flora Cameron from entering the street (shots 691–93). Before the planned elections, the Union League holds a rally with Stoneman as the guest of honor. Signs in the hall demand "Equality" in rights, politics, and marriage, and again, "FORTY ACRES AND A MULE for every colored citizen" (shots 722–740). All blacks are enrolled to vote, though many clearly have no idea what this means: one elderly man refuses to register to vote "Ef I doan' get 'nuf franchise to fill mah bucket" (shots 741–44). Election day dawns: blacks vote early and often (one man is shown stuffing extra ballots into the box) and "leading whites," including Dr. Cameron, are physically prevented from voting by armed black soldiers (shots 784–87). Unsurprisingly, "negroes and carpetbaggers sweep the state," Lynch is elected lieutenant-governor, and—as a large crowd of blacks celebrate—he is borne away by cheering supporters (shots 788–92, 794–95, 797, 806–809). In the aftermath of the election, the "Little Colonel" describes a series of outrages that have taken place: a black man has been acquitted by a black magistrate and jury, black soldiers have pushed a white man and his two children off the sidewalk, and a dispossessed white family have been pushed and jeered by soldiers as they abandon their former home. While he is speaking, his loyal black servant, Jake, is being tied up and whipped by black soldiers for refusing to vote "with the Union League and Carpetbaggers." An elderly man who tries to rescue him is killed (shots 811–34). *The Prostate State* provided justification for many of these incidents. For example, Pike had written about black dreams of equality, the promises made by the Union League to provide land for the freedmen, corruption in South Carolina elections (including repeat voting), the intimidation of blacks who had not supported Republican candidates, and the unfairness toward whites of a judicial system increasingly dominated by African Americans.[94]

In many scenes in the second part of the film, it is possible to trace the influence of Pike or Dixon or, commonly, both. One of the most revealing sequences is the succession of shots claiming to represent the South Carolina House of Representatives in 1871.[95] In *The Prostrate State*, Pike had described the atmosphere in the black-dominated House as "the slave rioting in the halls of his master." Dixon took over this idea in *The Clansman*, calling his chapter on the House "The Riot in the Master's Hall," and Griffith appropriated Dixon's title as the introduction to this section of *Birth* (shot 839).[96] Pike's assumption, in discussing the legislature, was that most black members were freed slaves who had no real idea how to behave in a deliberative body.[97] They dressed in odd and eccentric ways; both Pike and Dixon had them wearing "second-hand...frock coats," "stove-pipe hats" of many different styles, and "coarse...garments of the field."[98] This eccentricity of dress was also foregrounded by Griffith, notably in his depiction of the black politician with the check suit (shots 848, 850, 855). Some perceptions migrate more-or-less unaltered across the three works. All three mention the dignified but impotent group of twenty-three white representatives who opposed Radical Reconstruction (shots 839, 859–60).[99] Pike has the members of the legislature chewing peanuts, Dixon describes the same scene, and Griffith has a shot of two legislators also eating peanuts (shot 844).[100]

Other ideas transform and evolve over time. Pike wrote in general terms of the black man's fondness for whiskey, of the garrulousness of African American members of the House ("Sambo can talk"), of the "heavy brogans" many wore on their feet, and the black member protesting at being called to order by the Speaker by putting his feet on his desk. Dixon personalized some of these issues in the form of Ulster county representative "Old Aleck," the talkative ex-slave, who tries to go barefooted until the speaker rules that all members must wear shoes (brogans in Aleck's case) and shows his annoyance with the Speaker for calling him to order by placing his feet (clad only in socks) on top of his desk. Elsewhere, Dixon wrote of the "reek...of stale whiskey" in the chamber and the floor "strewn with corks...and picked bones." Griffith eliminated the character of Uncle Aleck from his film but used an intertitle to introduce "The honorable member from Ulster," a black man who is shown drinking surreptitiously from a bottle of whiskey. He also showed a black legislator taking off his shoes and putting his feet on his desk, prompting the Speaker's ruling that shoes must be worn. Griffith gave a visual connotation to Dixon's reference to "picked bones": he has another African American member eating a chicken leg (almost a cliché in the American cinematic depiction of blacks by 1915) (shots 845–47, 849–54).[101] On one major issue only is there no linkage between the three: Dixon and Griffith both refer to the passage of a bill permitting the intermarriage of blacks and whites, but since no such law was actually passed Pike does not mention it.[102] Finally, what Griffith thought of as "research" was sometimes done rather sloppily. Pike identified

101 Republicans in the House in 1871, this group being composed of ninety-four blacks and their white allies. Dixon wrote of ninety-four blacks and seven "scallawags [South Carolina-born collaborators] who claimed to be white." Griffith seems to have ignored Pike on this point and clearly misread Dixon: his intertitle in *Birth* (shot 839) erroneously asserted that the majority of the House was made up of 101 blacks.[103]

The scholar referred to most in the intertitles of *The Birth of a Nation* probably influenced Griffith least. The second part of the film began with the word "Reconstruction," immediately defined as "The agony which the South endured that a nation might be born." It was suggested that the "blight" of Civil War did not end with the coming of peace. An intertitle followed that attempted to disarm contemporary critics of the film by claiming that "This is an historical presentation of the Civil War and Reconstruction period, and is not meant to reflect on any race or people of today" (shots 620–21). The next three intertitles were all described as "excerpts" from Woodrow Wilson's *History of the American People* (shots 622–24). Clearly, Griffith believed it in his interest to have the president appear to legitimate the "history" in *Birth*. This explains both the special showing of the film at the White House and the quotations from Wilson's earlier historical work. An examination of the intertitles and what Wilson had actually written suggests, however, that Griffith was at the very least rather inexact in the quotations he used and that, in each case, his selective excerpts altered to a degree the original meaning (see table 7.1).

In the first extract from Wilson, Griffith removed the sentence immediately preceding the start of his quotation. This implied that while African Americans had enjoyed a numerical majority in three states, they had never *really* held power themselves in any of them. The idea of a politically dominant "black" South, therefore, as suggested in the second Wilson quotation, was little more than a figure of speech. The second quotation, by ignoring the preceding sentence in the original text, made it appear as if the "overthrow of civilization" that Wilson had perceived as most evident in the villages had, in fact, been virtually universal across the South. Griffith's third quotation also made it seem that the Klan was the *only* response by Southern whites to the threat posed by blacks (and specifically, as his film asserted, by black men to white women). In fact, Wilson believed that the Klan itself was only part of the wider determination of white Southerners ("by fair means or foul") to get rid of corrupt carpetbag regimes that clung to power by means of black votes.

Although Wilson plainly sympathized to a considerable degree with the South (he had grown up in Virginia), his *History* was in reality much more balanced in its discussion of Reconstruction than Griffith would have wished. According to Wilson, it was the passage of the Thirteenth Amendment abolishing slavery by the House of Representatives, not the restoration of white supremacy in the South, that marked the real beginnings of American nationhood ("Men

TABLE 7.1. A comparison of Griffith's intertitles with Wilson's text

Intertitles from *Birth of a Nation*	Woodrow Wilson, *A History of the American People, Vol. 5, Reunion and Nationalization*
1. "Adventurers swarmed out of the North, as much enemies of the one race as of the other, to cozen, beguile, and use the negroes…In the villages the negroes were the office holders, men who knew none of the uses of authority, except its insolences" (shot 622).	1. "Negroes constituted the majority of…[the] electorates [in South Carolina, Louisiana, and Florida]; but political power gave them no advantage of their own. Adventurers swarmed out of the North to cozen, beguile, and use them" (p. 46). "[In the villages and country-sides] the negroes themselves were the office-holders, men who could not so much as write their names and who knew none of the uses of authority except its insolence" (p. 49).
2. "The policy of the congressional leaders wrought…a veritable overthrow of civilization in the South…in their determination to *'put the white South under the heel of the black South'*" (shot 623).	2. "It was there [in the villages] that the policy of the congressional leaders wrought its perfect work of fear, demoralization, disgust, and social revolution. No one who thought justly or tolerantly could think that this veritable overthrow of civilization in the South had been foreseen or desired by the men who had followed Mr. Stevens and Mr. Wade and Mr. Morton in their policy of rule or ruin. That handful of leaders…were proof against both fact and reason in their determination to 'put the white South under the heel of the black South'" (pp. 49–50).
3. "The white men were roused by a mere instinct of self-preservation…until at last there had sprung into existence a great Ku Klux Klan, a veritable empire of the South, to protect the Southern country" (shot 624).	3. "The white men of the South were aroused by the mere instinct of self-preservation to rid themselves, by fair means or foul, of the intolerable burden of governments sustained by the votes of ignorant negroes and conducted in the interest of adventurers; governments whose incredible debts were incurred that thieves might be enriched…" (p. 58). "Year by year the organization spread… Every countryside wished to have its own Ku Klux, founded in secrecy and mystery like the mother "Den" at Pulaski [Tennessee], until at last there had sprung into existence a great *Ku Klux Klan*, an 'Invisible Empire of the South,' bound together in loose organization to protect the southern country from some of the ugliest hazards of a time of revolution" (p. 60).

dreamed...that they had that day seen a new nation born"). He blamed the early difficulties facing the freedmen on the fact that slavery had encouraged their habits of dependence. To Wilson, the establishment of the Freedmen's Bureau in March 1865 had been unavoidable: the plight of former slaves, many of them refugees, meant that it had become "obviously necessary that, for a time at least, Congress should take the care of the negroes under the direct supervision and care of the government."[104] Wilson agreed that most Southern states were mismanaged by corrupt radical governments—his statistics on South Carolina's fallen taxable values and rising taxes were taken straight from Pike[105]—and that huge debts were accumulated. But he also anticipated later "revisionist" arguments by emphasizing that corruption in the South was in no sense unique: there were many comparable scandals (Credit Mobilier, the Whiskey Ring) in the North.[106] Wilson was also surprisingly understanding toward the motives of members of the Republican Party who imposed Reconstruction on the defeated South; he pointed out that some supported the radical program despite their misgivings because they felt it necessary to do something to protect African Americans and to prevent the old leaders of the South from returning to power, and he also absolved the Republicans from implementing a deliberate plan to ruin the South.[107]

Where Wilson differed most from Griffith was in his treatment of the Ku Klux Klan. The Klan had been, Wilson observed, "a very tempting and dangerous instrument of power for days of disorder and social upheaval." In the beginning, "sober men" had advised upon and curbed the activities of the hooded order. As time went on, however, such control proved increasingly impossible to exercise as the Klan was drawn deeper and deeper "into the ways of violence and outlawry." "Men of hot passions who could not always be restrained," Wilson commented, "carried their plans into effect. Reckless men not of their order, malicious fellows of the baser sort who did not feel the compulsions of honor and who had private grudges to satisfy, imitated their disguises and borrowed their methods." The number of abuses grew: "Brutal crimes were committed; the innocent suffered with the guilty; a reign of terror was brought on, and society was infinitely more disturbed than defended." In contrast with Griffith's later film, which depicted the Klan as rescuing white women from the threat posed by black men, Wilson made it clear that the Klan itself attacked female targets. "The more ardent regulators," he wrote, "made no nice discriminations. All northern white men or women who came into the South to work among the negroes, though they were but school teachers, were in danger of their enmity and silent onset." According to Wilson, the Klan was deeply unchivalrous. It was also short-lived and relatively unsuccessful. Instead of overthrowing Radical regimes and triumphantly restoring white supremacy by force, as *The Birth of a Nation* suggested, the original Klan had been effectively destroyed by new federal laws of 1870 and 1871 and the determined actions of President Grant.[108]

The Ku Klux Klan

The Birth of a Nation began as a film based on Thomas Dixon's novel about the Ku Klux Klan. Although Dixon would later claim that some of his earliest memories dealt with the Klan (including watching the hanging of a black convict convicted of raping a white women), it is impossible to established the correctness of his assertions. What is clear, however, is that Dixon's uncle, Colonel Le Roy McAfee, had been one of the Klan's local leaders in North Carolina and that Dixon's father had been a member of the hooded organization. Dixon, whatever the accuracy of his childhood recollections, belonged to a family that looked favorably on the Klan.[109] Griffith's view of the Klan seems to have been more complicated. By the time he was born in 1875, the Klan had largely ceased to exist. It had been active for some time in Kentucky, and when Griffith started reading *The Clansman*, he began to remember the stories his cousin, Thurston Griffith, had once told him of the Klan.[110] Yet the reputation of the Klan was at best equivocal in Griffith's home state. Kentucky had the dubious distinction of having been the only state outside the old Confederacy in which the Klan had been of importance. But since the state had never undergone Reconstruction, the Klan there had not been able to present itself as a protest against "Black" Republicanism (the Democratic Party never lost its control of the state in the postwar period). While the state had contributed more men to the Union side than to the Confederates, many communities had been deeply divided, and the Klan was a continuing symptom of that division.[111] Before he began to consider making *The Clansman*, indeed, Griffith himself had shown a degree of hostility to Klan-type organizations. In 1911, he had made *The Rose of Kentucky*, a one-reel film criticizing contemporary Klan-style night riders.

Two factors seem to have been crucial in persuading the director of the viability of *The Clansman* project. The first was the visual possibilities he could see in the story. As Griffith later confessed, on first reading Dixon's novel he "skipped quickly through the book until I got to the part about the Klansmen...I could just see these Klansmen in a movie with their white robes flying."[112] The second was the continuing influence of Griffith's adored father. Although Lieutenant-Colonel Griffith had never been a Klansman, he had been a cavalry officer. Reincarnated as the "Little Colonel," he led the charges of the Klan in his son's greatest film. Some of his stories of the Civil War period were incorporated into *Birth;* for example, the attempt to rescue a stranded Confederate food train (shots 344–54), which acts as the opening act of the battle of Petersburg in the film, was probably inspired by the attack led by "Roaring Jake" Griffith on a Union supply train.[113] In making a "spectacular" film about the Civil War and Reconstruction, D. W. Griffith was also expressing filial loyalty. As he would later confess: "Underneath the robes and costumes of the actors playing the soldiers *and night riders* [my italics], rode my father."[114]

Reflecting his own priorities, Griffith's Klan in *The Birth of a Nation* differed considerably from the Klan of Dixon's novels. Dixon's Klan was organized—in some ways, as Russell Merritt observes, "over-organized, too much like a corporation to be an authentic folk movement."[115] Griffith localized the Klan; it is born when the Little Colonel, agonizing over the oppression of his people, sees some black children frightened by white children with a sheet over their heads (shots 913–24).[116] The uniforms the Klansmen wear are loyally produced—all 400,000 of them—by the women of the South, and not a single member's identity is betrayed (shot 970). Much of the ritual Dixon lovingly recounted (as, for example, in his account of Gus's trial)[117] is removed from the film; what ritual remains revolves around the Little Colonel's reaction to the death of Flora Cameron, when he takes the small, now bloodstained Confederate flag Flora has been wearing as a belt around her waist and holds it up while simultaneously raising the standard of revolt, "the fiery cross of old Scotland's hills."[118] He then quenches the flames of the cross in Flora's blood (shots 1172–75).

By simplifying the Klan described by Dixon, Griffith's *Birth of a Nation* encouraged false impressions of the organization in a number of crucial respects. Far from having its origins in the imagination of the fictional Ben Cameron in South Carolina, the Klan was actually founded in Tennessee in December 1865 by former officers in the Confederate Army looking for high-spirited entertainment.[119] It did not spread to South Carolina until 1867, when R. J. Brunson, one of the original founders, organized dens in the state.[120] The Klan as a whole was especially active after March 1867 when the dominant congressional Republicans brushed aside the protests of President Andrew Johnson to impose "Radical" Reconstruction on the defeated South. In April 1867, representatives of the Klan from several states met in Nashville to draw up a prescript or constitution.[121] As time passed (and as Wilson later suggested), there were signs that the Klan was losing its support among the white social elite and becoming increasingly a fraternity for poorer whites. It correspondingly became a more and more brutal organization. In 1869, its Imperial Grand Wizard, ex-Confederate cavalry commander Nathan Bedford Forrest, formally disbanded it. Embers of the Klan still glowed, however, and those embers were finally extinguished by the Force Acts of 1870 and 1871, which provided that Klansmen could be tried for their crimes in federal courts. While the old Klan disappeared, its place was taken by a plenitude of other organizations dedicated to overthrowing the radical Republican regimes in the South, organizations with such whimsical names as the "First Baptist Church Sewing Circle" and "Mother's Little Helpers."[122]

In addition to its mythologized account of the Klan's origins and rise, *The Birth of a Nation* was inaccurate in other significant ways. In South Carolina, the courts were never dominated by blacks as the film implied, and ex-Confederates experienced only "partial and temporary disfranchisement."[123] While blacks were in a numerical majority in the state legislature, they never really controlled the state. There was no real attempt by black leaders to make intermarriage between the races more acceptable. The rape of white women by black men, the nightmare of many white Southerners, was never a widespread occurrence.[124] While law and order *did* collapse in many areas of South Carolina, this had much more to do with the aggressiveness of whites toward blacks than the other way around. Most of the justifications advanced by the film for Klan activity, therefore, were fallacious. On a more minor factual note, the burning of crosses was not a part of the ritual of the Reconstruction-era Klan. It was imagined by Thomas Dixon Jr., who in turn may have plagiarized it from the work of Sir Walter Scott, especially *The Lady of the Lake* (1810).[125]

On the other hand, some aspects of the portrayal of the Klan in the film were rooted in historical fact. The Klan *did* justify itself (however unreasonably) as a response to black criminality; the first shot of Klansmen is accompanied by an intertitle (shot 927) stating that they are terrorizing "a Negro disturber and barn burner."[126] The same scene emphasizes the belief of Klansmen in the superstition and credulity of blacks: a Klansman is shown drinking from a bucket, a direct reference to the legend (promoted by the Klan) that its members were the ghosts of former members of the Confederate Army who had not had a drink since they were killed at the battle of Shiloh (shots 929–30, 932, 934–35).[127] The name given to the Camerons' hometown—Piedmont—accurately suggests

The Klan attacks the black militia in Piedmont. (Epoch/The Kobal Collection)

that the main strength of the Klan in South Carolina was in the "up country" or "piedmont" area of the state.[128]

Unlikely, moreover, as the pitched battles between the Klan and the black militia shown in the film appear, they came close to happening on several occasions in Reconstruction-era South Carolina. The state legislature in 1869 passed a law permitting the organization of a militia and radical governor Robert K. Scott, to prevent his Republican regime from being defeated by white force and intimidation during the elections of 1870, organized and armed fourteen regiments of black militiamen. Although most violence and intimidation continued to come from anti-radical whites, including Klansmen, armed black militiamen drilled, moved in groups around towns, and may in some places have pushed white people out of their way. There were a number of incidents, including the so-called "Laurens riot" on the day after the 1870 election. Armed blacks confronted around 2,500 whites, mainly Klansmen, in the town of Laurens. The blacks were finally disarmed by the sheriff and a white posse of around a hundred men, though only after several of the militiamen had been killed.[129] In Unionville, where black militia shot and killed a one-armed Confederate veteran, the Klan mounted two successive raids on the town jail to seize and execute the men thought responsible.[130] Moreover, in an incident that could have provoked a violent confrontation, the Klan in Yorkville attempted to fight incendiarism by issuing a proclamation that it would execute ten leading blacks if there were any further arson attacks. With black militia patrolling the town, there were more fires on the night of January 25, 1871. Many armed Klansmen arrived in the town and conflict was averted only when the black militia withdrew from the streets.[131] In each of these cases, as in *The Birth of a Nation*, Klansmen were summoned by courier from neighboring counties.[132] In each case, however, the black militia, when confronted with the possibility of the kind of armed conflict shown in the film, preferred to back down instead of continuing the kind of organized resistance shown in *Birth*. Finally, the sequence (later removed) in the earliest versions of *The Birth of a Nation* titled "Lincoln's Solution" and showing blacks ready to be sent back to Africa had a small basis in fact. Led by Elias Hill, a crippled black minister who had been harassed by the Klan, 136 blacks left South Carolina in 1872 to settle in Liberia.[133]

The Debate over "History"

To many of those who saw it in 1915, *The Birth of a Nation* was quite simply a history lesson. "The great historical value of this picture," commented the Baltimore *Sun*, "is shown by the large number of school classes that have been attending the performances in a body." Children, C. F. Zittel of the *Evening Journal* insisted, "must be sent to see this masterpiece. Any parent who neglects this advice is committing an educational offense, for no film has ever produced more educational points than Griffith's latest achievement." Dorothy Dix was just as certain of the film's merits, regarding it as "history vitalized." "Go and see it," she urged her readers, "for it will make a better American of you."[134] Some of the film's supporters in its struggle against censorship insisted on the accuracy of its representation of the past. The Reverend Dr. Charles H. Parkhurst, a leading New York clergyman and progressive reformer, commented that it was "exactly true to history." "A boy can learn more true history and get more of the atmosphere of the period," Parkhurst added, "by sitting down for three hours before the film which Mr. Griffith has produced with such artistic skill than by weeks or months of study in the classroom."[135] Griffith, confident in the reconstructions of actual events he had included in the film as well as the numerous references to historical works in the credits, had offered $10,000 if anyone could point to some incident in the film that was not true.

As previously shown, there were, in reality, many historical errors in *The Birth of a Nation*. The intertitle (shot 232) asserting that "The first Negro regiments of the war were raised in South Carolina" was wrong.[136] Other scenes created false impressions. As Robert Lang points out, the shot of a minister praying over manacled slaves and the preceding title ("The bringing of the African to America planted the first seed of disunion" [shots 7–8]) suggests that "an America without Africans was a harmonious Eden." In reality, the first blacks arrived in America soon after the earliest white settlers.[137] Dr. Cameron, who had not served the Confederacy directly, would almost certainly not have been prevented from voting in the South Carolina election of 1868. There was no period of corrupt black rule or black terror in South Carolina or anywhere else.[138] The Klan, which was formally disbanded in 1869 and practically dead by 1871, played no role in the final overthrow of the radical regime in South Carolina. The character of Austin Stoneman was really a caricature of Thaddeus Stevens, the radical Republican politician from Pennsylvania.[139] As already noted, Stoneman—like the real Stevens—had a club foot and a mulatto housekeeper called Lydia.[140] *The Birth of a Nation* faithfully reproduced Thomas Dixon's almost obsessive dislike of Stevens.[141] It maintained, wrongly, that Stevens's harsh attitude toward the defeated South was simply a product of his sexual infatuation with Lydia ("The great leader's weakness that is to blight a nation," shots 133–34). There are many other distortions. John Hope Franklin points out that the real Stevens "never went to South Carolina and had, indeed, died [in 1868]...several years before the high drama of South Carolina Reconstruction actually began."[142] In suggesting, moreover, that Stoneman favored full equality for blacks until Lynch expressed the wish to marry his daughter (the real Stevens had no children), and consequently that his racial beliefs were insincere, *Birth* was deeply unfair to Stevens who insisted on being buried in a cemetery that did not discriminate against colored occupants and left the bulk of his estate to endow an orphanage open to the children of all races.[143]

Such instances of bias could be multiplied almost indefinitely. *The Birth of a Nation* was not an objective presentation of history. Even those who praised the film as spectacular entertainment often conceded this. "Nothing on record has ever been produced in history, novel or play," declared one reviewer, "that could begin to tell the South's side of the Civil War so clearly as this photo-drama."[144] Griffith, in an explanatory "talkie" issued with the new synchronized version of *Birth* in 1930, admitted "that the film is a little one-sided in its approach to historical truth."[145] *Birth*, of course, was more than "a little one-sided." In its account of the Civil War and Reconstruction period, it was thoroughly biased in favor of the South. The problem for critics of the film who recognized this was that most of the academic and popular history of the day could be seen to endorse the "history" recounted in the film. The perception of slavery as a benign institution was supported in the contemporary work of Ulrich B. Phillips.[146] Presenting Reconstruction as a tragic mistake—with Southern blacks and Northern "radical" politicians as the villains of the piece—was at the core of the dominant "Dunningite" school of history. But whereas Dunningite history reached only a comparatively small audience, *The Birth of a Nation* disseminated critical views of Reconstruction to a popular audience made up of millions of Americans. In an essay published as late as 1979, black scholar John Hope Franklin assessed its influence "on the current view of Reconstruction" as "greater than any other single force."[147]

A counter-tradition to the Dunningites had started to emerge and could be traced back to the work of Tourgée in the late 1870s. In 1910, W. E. B. Du Bois published an article defending Reconstruction in the prestigious *American Historical Review*.[148] Three years later, black former U.S. senator John R. Lynch published a book emphasizing Reconstruction's achievements.[149] But these were only the very beginnings of the attempt to revise the "Dunningite" view of history, a revisionism that would become truly successful only from the 1950s and 1960s onward. If one thing more than any other underscored the fact that Griffith could afford to ignore contemporary critics of his film about Reconstruction, it was the fact that he was able—with almost no protest—to appropriate Lynch's name for *Birth*'s principal villain.[150]

The Appeal of *Birth* to Contemporary Audiences

One crucial reason for the appeal of Griffith's film to audiences of 1915 was that it raised issues and took positions that were of relevance to such audiences. While allegedly a film about the past, *The Birth of a Nation* spoke to contemporary political, social, and cultural concerns. At an early screening in New York of *The Clansman*, Thomas W. Dixon, author of the melodramatic novels and play on which the second part of the film was based, was allegedly so impressed by the audience's enthusiasm for the film that he proposed changing the title to something more in keeping with what he perceived to be the film's significance: *The Birth of a Nation*. The story is appealing but, as film scholars have demonstrated, probably apochrypal. The new name had already appeared in the film's pre-release publicity as a secondary or alternative title.[151] As it happened, *The Birth of a Nation* did prove an excellent title, though for reasons largely irrelevant to Dixon's and Griffith's thinking: it emphasized the salience of issues of nationality and nationhood in the United States in 1915.

In essence, *Birth* told the story of how North and South had moved beyond their differences of the Civil War era to unite together in a new nation. In reality, there was little evidence of such general reconciliation at the end of the Reconstruction era. Nor, despite the smattering of North–South commemorations and ceremonies that began to take place, can it truly be said to have happened until the second half of the 1890s. Interviewed by the press in 1915, Griffith maintained that no such national unity could exist "without sympathy and oneness of sentiment," something that he thought had "only existed [in] the last fifteen or twenty years."[152] If Griffith's chronology is correct (and it seems to have been), it is possible to delimit the progress of sectional reconciliation through a series of particular events. The Spanish-American War of May–June 1898 was one of the first and most significant of these. It was a commonplace for newspapers at the time to observe that "the blue and the gray" were marching together for the first time in decades against a common foe.[153] In subsequent years, more evidence of sectional unity appeared. In 1909, President William Howard Taft visited (and was filmed addressing) a joint encampment of Northern and Southern veterans at Petersburg, Virginia.[154] In 1912, Woodrow Wilson became the first president originating in the South to be elected since Zachary Taylor in 1848. Perhaps most crucial of all, the celebration of the fiftieth anniversary of the end of the Civil War loomed as Griffith began preparations to shoot his movie. In making that film, of course, he would displace the growing sectional amity of the late nineteenth and early twentieth centuries onto the much earlier period of Reconstruction.

The circumstances in which *Birth of a Nation* was released, moreover, gave its foregrounding of national unity and harmony special appeal. One of the consequences of the outbreak of the First World War was to underline the ethnic diversity of the United States. President Wilson's appeal, in August 1914, for Americans to be "impartial in thought as well as in deed" was unlikely to have much effect since so many residents of the United States retained residual loyalties (or antipathies) to the nation from which they or their ancestors had originated. One-third of all U.S. residents were either immigrants or the children of immigrants.[155] Consequently, long before actual American involvement in the conflict in April 1917, the war had made Americans only too conscious of their own disunity. The fact that there were so many "hyphenated" Americans—for example, German-Americans, Irish-Americans, Polish-Americans and Italian-Americans—would lead later in the war to demands for

"100 per cent Americanization."[156] To concerned American audiences of 1915, *The Birth of a Nation* offered a reassuring vision of national unity. By depicting Lincoln as a symbol of reconciliation and unity, the film provided a fragmented and increasingly insecure society with an iconic hero.

One week before filming began on *The Birth of a Nation*, Archduke Franz Ferdinand had been assassinated in Sarajevo, setting in motion the train of events that would lead to the outbreak of the First World War. Shortly after Griffith started reconstructing the Civil War in California, real battles were being fought in east Prussia (Tannenberg, August 26–29) and France (the Marne, September 5–8). The European war, therefore, formed an inescapable backdrop to the making of *Birth*. "I desired the peace idea to be uppermost," Griffith told an interviewer; "I feel that is what the world needs just now."[157] Griffith's film, indeed, was a pioneering war film, and, as Norman Kagan noted, "like almost all war films" it "professed anti-war sentiments."[158] *Birth* foregrounds the illusions with which most wars begin. The Camerons are shown self-consciously wearing their new uniforms, the captured battle flag from Bull Run is proudly displayed, young people dance the night away before the young men set off for war, and the population celebrates as Piedmont's regiment marches out the next day. Yet there are also signs of sadness and anxiety, as women wait, and the war—it is quickly shown—touches everybody. Many of the scenes of war actually shot by Griffith, especially the guerrilla raid on Piedmont and the burning of Atlanta, offer no purposeful, victorious view of the war. Even the climactic charge led by the Little Colonel against the Union emplacements at Petersburg, according to Michael Rogin, "is mock-heroic and fails."[159]

Griffith certainly meant to demonstrate the futility of the Civil War. He may also, however, have been intent on driving home a different message, cautioning Americans against the dangers of involvement in the First World War. The antiwar tone of his film becomes particularly evident in the intertitles, which Griffith had written and rewritten to make them say just what he wanted. At the very beginning of the film, immediately after the title and credits, an intertitle observes, "If in this work we have conveyed to the mind the ravages of war to the end that <u>war may be held in abhorrence</u>, this effort will not have been in vain" (shot 6). A fight between a dog and a cat, introduced by a one-word intertitle, "Hostilities," also suggests that "war is a mindless, accidental business men should outgrow" (shots 53–54).[160] The shot in which the two "chums," Duke Cameron and Tod Stoneman, meet again on the battlefield, only to die in each other's arms, is preceded by an intertitle claiming that "War claims its <u>bitter, useless sacrifice</u>" (shot 296). Elsie and Austin Stoneman, learning of the death of Tod, are introduced as reading <u>"war's sad page"</u> (shot 311). The effects of war on the civilian population are emphasized by a printed comment on an unidentified General Sherman: "While the women and children weep, a great conqueror marches to the sea" (shot 317). Young Flora Cameron, reading of the death of her second brother and the injury to the "Little Colonel," is shown clenching her fists and holding out her arms in despair after a caption reading "War, the breeder of hate" (shot 450). But perhaps the most savagely antiwar of all Griffith's intertitles was the appearance of the ironic words "War's peace" before a shot of bodies lying chaotically in a trench (shot 440). The film moves toward its end with an intertitle referring to "a golden day when the bestial War shall rule no more," followed by a metaphorical scene in which Christ ("the gentle Prince in the Hall of Brotherly Love in the City of Peace") supplants the God of War (shots 1603–1605). This philosophizing about peace is both preceded and followed by shots of romantic, intersectional couples. Intersectional romances, representing what Tara McPherson calls "a regained familial nationalism," were a staple of the early Civil War movie genre. The unusual thing about *Birth* is how *long* it took for such romances to come to fruition, and then only under the stress of the black "threat."[161] Finally, Ben Cameron and Elsie Stoneman are shown looking at the vision of a celestial city ("the City of Peace") and the link between peace and American nationhood is driven home by the words of Daniel Webster: "Liberty and Union, one and inseparable, now and forever!" (shots 1608–1609).

Nations, of course, as Benedict Anderson has argued, are "imagined communities."[162] Nationhood itself resists closure. It is always being formed. It is constantly open for contestation, development, and debate. The crucial point about the "nation" constructed in *Birth* is that it was founded on exclusion: a white North joined together with a white South at the expense of African Americans.[163] *The Birth of a Nation* thus inflected—and contributed to—contemporary debates on the nature of American citizenship by couching them in terms of *whiteness*. As David Roediger, Alexander Saxton, and others have shown, whiteness is a constructed category. Some groups are born white; others have to acquire whiteness. The Irish immigrants of the mid-nineteenth century, for example, were not initially constructed as white.[164] Paradoxically, the Treaty of Guadalupe Hidalgo, which ended the Mexican War, defined Hispanics as white.[165]

The whiteness constructed in *The Birth of a Nation* was not simply based on region, however. It also had its roots in contemporary theories dealing with race and the origins of American democracy. When most of the surviving Cameron family (and Phil Stoneman) attempt to escape the pursuing black militia, they are given refuge by two Union veterans in their cabin. An intertitle asserts that "The former enemies of North and South are united again in common defence of their Aryan birthright (shot 1287)." That title still has the power to shock a modern audience, since nowadays the word "Aryan" is most closely associated with the belief in German racial superiority advanced by Hitler.

In its original sense, however, the idea of an Aryan race grew out of the work of pioneering philologists such as Sir William Jones, who suggested in a 1786 paper that Sanskrit, Latin, and Greek all developed from the same original language, and that old Persian, Gothic (German), and Celtic belonged to the same linguistic family. Jones's paper had a major impact, especially in Germany (Hegel hailed it as the discovery of a new world). It inspired further research into language systems, research that rapidly became inextricably intertwined with two other ideas: that the human race had originated in an Asiatic home-land and that, as population migrated westward, a vigorous Germanic people had arrived in Europe to revivify the declining Roman Empire. The second of these ideas, based on a fallacious identification of race with language, was particularly associated with the work of Friedrich von Schlegel and August F. Pott. By the 1840s, it had become widely accepted among German schol-ars. Initially, the languages spoken by the migratory population were referred to as "Indo-European" or "Indo-Germanic," but by the second half of the nineteenth century, as the notion of Europe being peopled by former Asians migrating west came to be propagated outside Germany, the term "Aryan" or "Arian" began to be used more frequently as a way of denoting both the lan-guages and those who used them. In 1851, for example, the *Edinburgh Review* noted that "the Arian nations...carried the germs of civilisation from a com-mon centre." Later, the expression "Aryan" was publicized in the work of Max Müller, a German-born Oxford philologist and orientalist.[166]

The second half of the nineteenth century saw further refinements in the usage of the term "Aryan." A Frenchman, Count Joseph de Gobineau, who had been heavily influenced by the work of German philologists (including Pott and Schlegel) published a four-volume *Essai sur l'inégalité des races humaines* (1853–55) in which he fixed the Aryan at the top of a hierarchy of races. Accord-ing to Gobineau, the white race was destined to conquer the other two races (the yellow and the black) because it displayed more forcefulness and intel-ligence. Although the white race also included Celts and Slavs, Aryans made up the "cream." Gobineau clearly identified who he thought Aryans were ("the German race"). He also for the first time described them in terms of physical appearance: Aryans were "blond, blue-eyed giants of great muscular force and physical beauty." His work, as Richard Hofstadter would later remark, was "a landmark in the history of Aryanism."[167] Another approach to Aryanism in this period focused on the attempt by British and American scholars to discern threads of unity in Aryan political institutions or to identify the unique capacity of Aryans in matters of political organization.[168]

Despite the spread of Aryan ideas to America, Aryanism would never be so pervasive an influence as another cluster of ideas it overlapped with during the nineteenth century: what came to be known as "Anglo-Saxonism." It is pos-sible, even probable, that Griffith's reference to Aryanism in the intertitle was a mistake: what he may have had in mind was an *Anglo-Saxon* heritage. Anglo-Saxonism had its roots in England where, in the sixteenth century, religious reformers created a myth of a pure Anglo-Saxon church, and in the seventeenth century, parliamentarians cited the supposed liberties of pre-Conquest times in their struggles with the king. Anglo-Saxonism was consequently associated from the beginning with notions of religious and political liberty. In the eighteenth century, it was used by American colonists, Jefferson in particular, to argue for a return to the rights and freedoms they saw as characteristic of the Anglo-Saxon period.[169] Also during the eighteenth century, colonists, like Englishmen before them, came increasingly to view the Anglo-Saxons as a branch of the wider race of freedom-loving Germans or "Teutons." The origins of this idea go back as far as the *History of the Germanic People* by Tacitus. Montesquieu, in *De l'esprit des lois* (1748), used Tacitus as the basis for his argument that the British political system had its roots in German forests. Montesquieu's writings were well received in the American colonies, along with works by French and British authors contending that liberty and parliamentary government had moved from Germany to England as a result of the Anglo-Saxon migration.[170]

The publication of Sharon Turner's four-volume *History of the Anglo-Saxons* (1799–1805) signaled a growing interest in the Anglo-Saxon idea. It would receive a major boost through the romantic medievalism of Sir Walter Scott's novel *Ivanhoe* (1819). Throughout the nineteenth century, it was publicized by British historians such as John M. Kemble (*The Saxons in England*, 1849) and Edward A. Freeman (*History of the Norman Conquest*, 1867–76). In these decades, some members of the American elite began to regard themselves not only as sharing the same descent from Anglo-Saxon roots as the English but also as members of the same Anglo-Saxon *race*, whose virtues they apotheosized. Such views were reflected in the works of American historians William H. Prescott, George Bancroft, John Lothrop Motley, and Francis Parkman.[171] They reached their peak in many ways with the appointment of historian Herbert Baxter Adams to Johns Hopkins University in 1881. Adams believed that people of "Anglo-Saxon" descent had a particular genius for self-government and that the roots of American democracy could be traced back to the primitive collectivism of Teutonic tribes during the early Middle Ages.[172] A German-trained scholar, Adams established his famous historical seminar at Johns Hopkins "with the official blessing of Freeman."[173] Members of the seminar over the years included Woodrow Wilson, whose *History of the American People* had frequent references to ideas of Anglo-Saxonism and Teutonic origins, and—more briefly—Thomas Dixon Jr., who also sprinkled Anglo-Saxon ideas liberally throughout his work.[174]

Both Dixon's *Clansman* and Griffith's *The Birth of a Nation* reflected a febrile fear that the ascendancy of the white Anglo-Saxon race was under threat: its political dominance was in question and its racial purity at stake. While the threat was couched in historical terms and displaced onto the Reconstruction period several decades earlier, what strikes the historian is the resonance such ideas had in the social world of early twentieth-century America. How did the confident belief in an Anglo-Saxon racial superiority give way to insecurities of this kind? Part of the answer lies in intellectual changes brought by the nineteenth century. In the first decades of the century, comparative studies of race established "scientific" reasons why some were superior and others inferior. By 1850, supporters of the Anglo-Saxon myth on both sides of the Atlantic were depicting Anglo-Saxons as forming a distinct elite within a Caucasian race that was itself superior and justifying that elitism in terms of inherited blood.[175] In what was increasingly perceived as a hierarchy of races, blacks and Indians were at the bottom, joined there during the 1830s and 1840s by Mexicans, a "mongrel race" allegedly weakened by interbreeding with Indians.[176] This hierarchy clearly was not going to change: even antislavery writers such as Theodore Parker accepted that blacks and Indians were unlikely to improve their position.[177] The emergence of Darwinian ideas of "natural selection" and the "survival of the fittest" did not at first affect this notion. It was assumed that inferior races would be outbred by the superior Anglo-Saxons and disappear. More and more, proponents of the Anglo-Saxon point of view believed it was the destiny of the Anglo-Saxon race to take over much of the world. The degree to which this had already been achieved in the second half of the nineteenth century, according to Richard Hofstadter, appeared to prove the Anglo-Saxon the "fittest" of all races, and it seemed likely that the movement toward Anglo-Saxon supremacy was destined to continue. A number of Republican politicians (including Theodore Roosevelt, Henry C. Lodge, John Hay, and Albert J. Beveridge) defended the war with Spain in 1898 and the annexation of the Philippines, Hawaii, and Puerto Rico which followed as part of such a movement.[178]

In retrospect, the expansionism of 1898–99 marked the peak of confidence in the notion of Anglo-Saxonism. Some "Anglo-Saxons" did not approve of expansionism: many Southern politicians, with a racial problem on their own doorstep, opposed the idea of acquiring overseas colonies with unassimilable populations drawn from different races.[179] The idealism of the war with Spain was rapidly succeeded by the realities of a brutal colonial revolt, as Filipinos resisted having the blessings of American democracy forced upon them.[180] (It was ironic that the other main branch of the Anglo-Saxon "race," the British, was simultaneously fighting to suppress a similar revolt in South Africa.) At home, moreover, the confident Anglo-Saxonism of the last years of the nineteenth century rapidly gave way to a gloomier sense that the continuing domination of the world by Anglo-Saxon stock was not assured. In a world ruled by the principles of Social Darwinism, dominant races could also decline. In a few short years, indeed, the conviction of effortless "Anglo-Saxon" racial superiority gave place to pronounced feelings of anxiety in America that "Anglo-Saxons" might lose their pole position on the evolutionary scale. Already, in 1894, conscious of the consequences of the economic depression for the world of Western whites, Henry Adams had written of his belief "that the dark races are gaining on us."[181] By the final years of the century, other Americans had begun to share his concern.

Such anxieties and insecurities reached their height in the decade and a half before *Birth* was released. Many native-born, upper-class Americans of the early twentieth century became convinced that their own, superior white race was in danger of being displaced by "inferior" races. In 1901, sociologist Edward A. Ross coined the term "race suicide" to denote what was happening: the "best" American stock—people of north European origin—were simply not breeding as fast as their immigrant counterparts from Asia. President Theodore Roosevelt appropriated Ross's term and gave it greater publicity in a speech of 1903, arguing that white Anglo-Saxons in the United States were (partly through using birth control) simply not keeping up in terms of fertility with immigrants and minorities. In 1909, Homer Lea published a book warning of the danger posed by an emergent Japan to Anglo-Saxon ambitions and arguing that the current pattern of European immigration, by undermining the strength and unity of Anglo-Saxons, was aiding Japanese ambitions. In 1914, another West Coast writer, Jack London, argued that Anglo-Saxons in the United States were being swamped by southern and eastern European "half-castes" and "mongrel-bloods."[182] Later, in 1916, Madison Grant published *The Passing of the Great Race*, a book in which he similarly underscored the danger posed to the traditionally dominant "Nordic" strain in the American population by blacks and nontraditional immigrants.[183]

Among them, Ross, Roosevelt, Lea, London, and Grant identified "threats" from three particular social groups to the dominant position of white Anglo-Saxons. The oldest in historical terms was represented by American blacks. Slavery had in reality been a vicious system of economic and sexual exploitation. If full-scale revolts against it, such as Denmark Vesey's in South Carolina in 1822 or Nat Turner's in Virginia in 1831, had been very rare, slaveholders were often anxious that violence might break out. Indeed, as John Blassingame has noted, "the white man's fear of the slave was so deep and pervasive that it was sometimes pathological."[184] The abolition of slavery and the myth of the "Old South" that developed in subsequent decades changed the perspective of Southern whites. Anxieties about slavery and possible slave violence were forgotten. In the rosy glow of hindsight, slavery seemed a benign institution. It had worked as a system because the whites had been in control and because it precisely defined the nature of the relationship between both races. In the generation or more after the ending of the Civil War, white fears of black slaves were displaced onto freed blacks. *The Birth of a Nation* faithfully reflected this shift. "In Griffith's film," observes Natalie Zemon Davis, "black people were laughing and happy when slaves, trusting and supportive of their masters; once freed, they were violent, deceptive, and sexually predatory."[185] The film supported the view of many members of the Southern white elite that after the ending of slavery, the Reconstruction experiment, and the attempt of "poor white" Southern Populists in the 1890s to construct a coalition between the disadvantaged of both races, it was time to put in place new controls over blacks to replace those of slavery.[186]

This process actually began in 1887, when the first segregationist or Jim Crow law was passed in Alabama requiring separate accommodations for whites and blacks on trains. Other states followed the Alabama lead and in 1896, in *Plessy v. Ferguson*, the U.S. Supreme Court accepted the principle of legal segregation in relation to transportation provided (at least in theory) that the facilities provided for both races were equal. By 1907, what Joel Williamson perceives as two waves of segregationist legislation had been enacted to separate the races in restaurants, hotels, and streetcars as well as trains.[187] While laws were being passed rendering blacks socially invisible, action was also taken to remove them totally from politics. Starting in 1890 but gathering pace with the collapse of the Populist movement after the débâcle of the 1896 election, Southern states had excluded blacks from voting by a series of legal stratagems: "grandfather" clauses, poll taxes, and literacy tests.[188] A third, extralegal device for keeping blacks under control was lynching: in the early years of the twentieth century, around sixty blacks were lynched each year.[189]

Given the social and legal subordination of Southern blacks by 1915, the manner in which *The Birth of a Nation* depicted aggressive, lascivious African Americans during the Reconstruction period might seem unduly hysterical. Pierre Sorlin argues that there was no domestic crisis apparent when *Birth* was being made, making the film's "alarmist tone...somewhat surprising."[190] Yet segregation and disfranchisement had not enabled the white South completely to overcome its insecurities. Many whites continued to believe that blacks were dangerous. It was an unusual Southern newspaper, as Edward Ayers has pointed out, that did not include some stories of black wrongdoing.[191] Segregation had failed to identify the exact space African Americans should occupy. Segregated streetcars, for example, were usually supposed to have whites at the front and coloreds at the back, but there was no distinct line of demarcation. To progressive journalist Ray Stannard Baker in 1908, this uncertainty seemed symbolic: the existence of a color line which neither race was able precisely to define provided "a fertile source of friction and bitterness."[192] Additional problems arose from the growing tendency of Southern blacks to leave the land in search of jobs in towns and cities. This migration increased the potential for racial conflict in such communities and led to a further wave of legislation between 1913 and 1915 that segregated facilities in factories and attempted to impose segregation in urban housing.[193] But African Americans not only migrated within the South; the growing movement of blacks to Northern industrial cities meant that these communities were faced with racial problems for the first time. It was a race riot in Springfield, Illinois, in August 1908 that provided the catalyst for the organization, a year later, of the NAACP.[194]

The second oldest threat to the position of white Anglo-Saxons was associated with Oriental immigrants. The boom conditions of the 1840s—the California "Gold Rush" of 1849 in particular—brought thousands of immigrants from China. Later, gangs of Chinese laborers played a major role in building the western section of the Union Pacific railroad. But anti-Chinese feeling in California had led, in 1882, to the passage of the first of a series of Chinese

Exclusion Acts that effectively brought Chinese immigration to an end. By the early twentieth century, the Japanese had replaced the Chinese as the main group of oriental immigrants to the West Coast. The influx of around 100,000 Japanese into California prompted hysterical talk of a "yellow peril" and demands for Japanese exclusion. In October 1906, the San Francisco school board inflamed American relations with Japan by ordering that Japanese children attend the already segregated Chinese school. Fearing the expression of this kind of prejudice might drag the United States into a war with Japan, President Theodore Roosevelt persuaded the board to rescind the segregation order in return for a promise to cut Japanese immigration. This was achieved through the "Gentleman's Agreement," an exchange of diplomatic notes in 1907 and 1908 in which the Japanese government agreed not to issue passports in future to workers wishing to emigrate to the United States. The Gentleman's Agreement, however, did nothing to end prejudice or discrimination against California's existing Japanese population. In 1913, the state legislature tried to ban Japanese residents from acquiring the ownership of any more land.[195]

The third and most recent "threat" came from a shift in the pattern of immigration from Europe. Until the 1880s, most immigrants came from northern and western Europe. Thereafter, an increasing proportion (85 percent by 1914) originated in southern and eastern Europe.[196] The largest streams among what came to be known as this "new" immigration (to distinguish it from the "old") were composed of Italians and Polish or Russian Jews. From the point of view of many native-born, white Americans, the new immigrants were very much inferior to the old: they were less literate, less skilled, and poorer than their predecessors. Rather than being easy to Americanize, they persisted with the habits of the countries from which they had come, including religion (the growing influx of Catholics and Jews appeared to threaten traditional American Protestantism) and sometimes dress. They had little or no experience of democracy or representative government. In 1911, the forty-one-volume report of the Dillingham Commission confirmed that through the rising tide of "new" immigration the Anglo-Saxon element in the American population was in danger of being marginalized.

The years leading up to the First World War had effectively witnessed a nationalization of insecurities arising from the threat to white Anglo-Saxons posed by "other" races and ethnicities. The sections of the country drew together in their estimate of the danger posed by blacks, Orientals, and Jews. "Mr. White American," cautioned a pamphlet published in San Francisco in 1914, "if you have any race pride or patriotism, you will organize for the protection of your race." Propaganda of this kind, as John Higham pointed out, had hitherto been mainly aimed at Orientals in California. In this case, it was directed primarily against African Americans and Jews.[197] "In every section," Higham noted, "the Negro, the Oriental, and the southern European appeared more and more in a common light."[198] In the period before the outbreak of the

war, while the South slowly became converted to the notion of restricting immigration, in part at least because "new" immigrants (particularly Italians) appeared too ready to fraternize with blacks,[199] parts of the North, facing an influx
of black migrants, began to demonstrate growing sympathy for the racial outlook of the South. With all sections united on the need to reduce the "new" immigration, bills calling for all immigrants to take a literacy test passed Congress
in 1913 and 1915.[200] During the debate on the second of these bills, a strong but
ultimately unsuccessful attempt was made to insert a clause that would have
brought together the campaigns against "new" immigrants and blacks by specifically banning those of African descent from entry into the United States.[201]
Whiteness seemed very much under threat in the United States in 1915, and
this perception created the perfect environment for the successful release of
The Birth of a Nation. Looking back on *Birth,* Cedric J. Robinson perceptively
notes that "what Griffith had inadvertently served as midwife for was the birth
of a new, virile American whiteness."[202]

The Issue of Miscegenation

In the early twentieth century, white Americans tried to shore up the ascendancy of their race by introducing immigration restrictions, first on Oriental
entry to the United States, later on the supposedly inferior "new" immigrants
from southern and eastern Europe. They also endeavored to preserve the purity of their own race by passing laws against miscegenation:[203] between 1887
and 1930 at least forty-one attempts were made to ban interracial marriage in
Mid-Atlantic and East North Central states.[204] In the South, laws of this type
were mainly designed to prevent marriage between blacks and whites. In some
Western states, however, they were much more complex, at times banning
marriage between whites and Orientals, Indians, and Mexicans.[205]

    The idea of a pure white race can be traced back at least as far as Tacitus.
"In the peoples of Germany," maintained the Roman historian, "there has been
given to the world a race untainted by intermarriage with other races...pure,
like no one but themselves."[206] Gobineau had also declared his opposition to
racial mixing to protect the purity of the "Aryan" race. In the United States
during the first half of the nineteenth century, as previously noted, those who
regarded themselves as pure-bred Anglo-Saxons had a tendency to look down
on Mexicans, whom they regarded as a "mongrel" race through intermarriage
with Indians and blacks.[207] Yet in the final decades of the century, the confidence
of those who regarded themselves as "Anglo-Saxons" was such that for most of
the time they could view with equanimity the arrival of European immigrants
from a wide variety of national and ethnic origins. So vague was the concept of
an Anglo-Saxon race and so confident in its powers of assimilation were those
who regarded themselves as members that they regarded the "Melting Pot" as

principally a means of producing future Anglo-Saxon citizens. Moreover, so great was their faith in the reproductive powers of the white Anglo-Saxons that some were prepared to argue that relationships between white men and black women would succeed in "white-washing" their descendants and finally erasing all trace of the black race.[208]

Confidence such as this had been replaced, by the early years of the twentieth century, with feelings of anxiety and trepidation. *The Birth of a Nation* both shaped and reflected contemporary concerns over racial intermingling. Of the three irredeemably evil characters in *The Birth of a Nation*, two, as mulattoes, symbolized the dangers of racial mixing: Lydia, the "housekeeper" of Austin Stoneman, whose passion for her is suggested to be the basis for his attempt to impose racial equality on the defeated South; and Silas Lynch, the black lieutenant-governor who attempts to create a black empire of his own and arrange a "forced marriage" with Stoneman's daughter, Elsie (shots 133–34, 1322, 1346).[209] The third villain is Gus, a black, who first tells the white Flora Cameron that he would like to marry her and then, when she runs away, chases her until, panicking, she jumps to her death to escape him (shots 1024–82).

The issue of sexual relationships across racial lines, of course, was a particularly salient issue at the time of the film's release, as a result of the efforts

Silas Lynch attempts to trap Elsie Stoneman into a "forced marriage." (Epoch/The Kobal Collection)

of many states to pass laws forbidding intermarriage. The NAACP fought hard against such legislation, for the most part successfully.[210] It also managed to fight off the attempts of Southern Democrats, using to the hilt their party's majority in the final weeks of the 63rd Congress, to pass a bill forbidding racial intermarriage in the District of Columbia.[211] That *The Birth of a Nation* foregrounded the whole intermarriage issue so emphatically—blacks are seen with placards demanding "equal marriage"; the South Carolina legislature is pictured passing a bill acceding to this demand; and both Lynch and the other black villain, Gus, want to marry their white female victims (shots 732, 866, 1026, 1309)—had very little to do with what actually happened during Reconstruction days and everything to do with the sexual obsessions of Thomas Dixon, reinforced by contemporary racial concerns at the time the film was made.

What happens to Gus after Flora's death also sheds considerable light on the tangled relationship between race, sexuality, and alcohol that existed in American culture in 1914–15. As the Klan organizes, the whites of Piedmont go looking for Gus. One such searcher is the town's blacksmith (played by Wallace Reid), a large and powerful white man. When he arrives at the saloon, he meets another, equally powerful black man (played by Eugene Pallette wearing makeup). The two confront one another. A fight breaks out and the blacksmith defeats his opponent. He then fights (and beats) another six or seven black men who are present in the saloon, throwing some of them out of the window (shots 1100–29). At its simplest, this is a racist depiction of how a single strong white (Aryan) man can take on, in a reasonably fair fight, a crowd of perhaps eight black men. The blacksmith is beaten only when he is shot in the back by one of the few blacks remaining in the saloon and then finally killed by Gus, using the same gun (shots 1130–33).[212]

Analysis of this single scene must start from the effort to contextualize it. Many popular assumptions of the time were embodied in the scene and may have accounted for the way it was interpreted by contemporary viewers. The scene reflects the racial attitudes of Thomas Dixon Jr. and perhaps those of much of the white South (including Griffith).[213] The idea of the black man as threatening rapist haunted the imagination of the white South in the closing years of the nineteenth century and the first years of the twentieth. It was used to justify the extreme prevalence of lynching, perceived as a necessary means of "keeping the black man in his place."[214] Accompanying this was the image of blacks as innately weak, childlike, and cowardly creatures fostered by a vast array of Southern writers, together with historians (usually Northerners) of the Dunningite school. The two images, of course, were inconsistent. The weak, cowardly black male was turned into a brutal, sex-crazed rapist, so this interpretation ran, by either sudden opportunity (the availability of unprotected white females) or alcohol (encouraging the black man to slough off his veneer of civilization and return to his bestial origins), or both.

It seems no accident, therefore, that Gus, after Flora has killed herself, takes refuge in "White-arm Joe's gin-mill" (shots 1101–1103), or that Silas Lynch, the black lieutenant-governor, gives instructions to his henchmen to prepare for his "forced marriage" to Elsie Stoneman while "drunk with wine and power" (shot 1346). *The Birth of a Nation* appeared while the movement to prohibit alcohol was gaining strength. A period of reverses in which eight states had voted to reject statewide prohibition came to an end in November 1913 when the Anti-Saloon League committed itself to pushing for nationwide prohibition.[215] The crusade for prohibition was something that appealed to Griffith, who came from a Methodist background and had already made at least three films—*A Drunkard's Reformation* (1909), *What Drink Did* (1909), and *Drink's Lure* (1912)—emphasizing the threat of alcohol. *The Birth of a Nation*, a film made by a Southerner about the South, tied alcohol irretrievably to the issue of race. In part, this simply reflected the outlook of the time. White Southern progressives often linked black crime to the effects of alcohol; reformer Alexander J. McKelway, for instance, argued that "if drunkenness caused three-fourths of the crime ascribed to it, whiskey must be taken out of the Negro's hands."[216] Yet by establishing a link between black men desiring white women and alcohol, it also helped justify the more repugnant methods (including lynching) often employed by Southern whites to discipline black males.

The fight in the saloon had a number of other cultural referents, however. One of the first types of film to emerge in the 1890s was the so-called fight film, depicting either a real or, more commonly, reproduced prizefight. Many commentators at the time noted that a large proportion of the audience for such boxing films was made up of women. According to one estimate, women constituted 60 percent of the Chicago audience for the Corbett-Fitzsimmons fight of 1897.[217] On the one hand, women were taking possession of a new public sphere, the cinema, and in so doing asserting their own independence. On the other hand, they were outflanking established conventions of what women were able to do in terms of sexual propriety. Few of the women in these audiences were likely to have seen a man naked before—apart from, if married, their husbands. Now they were being introduced to the erotic possibilities inherent in the sight of semi-naked, large, fit men on film.

To this assault on conventions of gender would soon be added an even more combustible element: race. In 1908, black prize-fighter Jack Johnson became the heavyweight champion of the world after defeating a white opponent in Australia. He successfully defended his title against white fighters Stanley Ketchum (October 16, 1909) and Jim Jeffreys (July 4, 1910). Films of the fights were widely shown in the United States, though they were also banned in some states, especially in the South.[218] What these films did was not only to allow white women the possibility of watching a half-naked black sportsman in action, but also to undermine established perceptions of racial hierarchy by having a black man defeat an opponent who was white. As retired boxer Jim Corbett wrote to the *Chicago Tribune* emphasizing this point, "the white man has succumbed to a type which in the past was conceded to be his inferior in physical and mental prowess."[219] The white male response to the Johnson phenomenon was perhaps inevitable. In July 1912, hastened by Johnson's defeat earlier that month of Jim Flynn, yet another "Great White Hope," Congress passed the Sims Act forbidding the transport of fight films across state lines.[220]

The irony of this law, of course, was that when Johnson finally *was* beaten by a white boxer, Jess Willard, in a fight staged in Cuba in April 1915, the film of his defeat could not be shown anywhere in the United States. The only white man fighting African Americans with his fists to be depicted in a major film in 1915 was the blacksmith in *The Birth of a Nation*, and it is probable that many contemporary spectators viewed this sequence in the context of the popular, press-inspired search for a "Great White Hope."[221]

More than any other single factor, Johnson was responsible for making miscegenation an issue in the United States in the early 1910s. His role must be seen against the context of the time. A combination of sensational journalistic investigations, inaugurated by three major magazine articles by George Kibbe Turner[222] and public anxieties over the fate of young girls arriving in the city, had prompted a "white slave" panic in the United States; many people apparently believed that crime rings were abducting young girls, either from Europe or the American countryside, and forcing them to become urban prostitutes.[223] In 1910, Congress, which had earlier tried to limit the migration of prostitutes from abroad by tightening the immigration laws, passed the Mann Act, which sought to undercut the supposed "white slave trade" by prohibiting the transportation of women across state lines for "immoral purposes." The difficulty was that the notion of white slavery, while it exempted the women concerned from blame (and may also have made it possible for rural and small-town America to avoid confronting the reality of rebellious and runaway daughters), perpetuated the myth that women were usually forced into prostitution. The actual administration of the Mann Act weakened the credibility of that myth: as David J. Langum has pointed out, the vast majority of prosecutions under the act would always involve the transportation of "adult, willing prostitutes."[224]

Perhaps the most famous case brought under the Mann Act during the first years of its existence was that involving Jack Johnson. The main agency involved in the enforcement of the Mann Act was the Bureau of Investigation (later to become the Federal Bureau of Investigation) formed within the Department of Justice in 1908.[225] In October 1912, Johnson was arrested and charged with abducting Lucille Cameron, a white girl and former prostitute in Minneapolis, who had had a sexual relationship with Johnson after she came to Chicago. The accusation of abduction was originally made by Cameron's mother. But though Lucille admitted she had been a prostitute, she adamantly refused to implicate Johnson in her move to Chicago. While Johnson was still being tried for abduction, on November 7 he was charged by agents of the Bureau of Investigation with breaking the Mann Act. The "white slave" in this case was Belle Schreiber, a prostitute who had traveled around the United States with Johnson on an intermittent basis for a year and a half. On November 20, Johnson was acquitted of abducting Lucille Cameron and two weeks later, on December 4, he and Lucille were married.[226] In his private life, Johnson appeared to be mounting a direct attack on the contemporary white prejudice against miscegenation. The result was almost preordained. In May 1913, Johnson was found guilty of transporting Schreiber across state lines for the purposes of prostitution and sentenced to a year and a day in jail (the federal prosecutor later ill-advisedly told the press that Johnson "as an individual" had "perhaps" been unjustly "persecuted" but that it had been "his misfortune to be the foremost example of the evil in permitting the intermarriage of whites and blacks.")[227] The publicity accorded Johnson's marriage to a white girl and the Johnson case itself appears to have given a powerful fillip to the contemporary movement to ban miscegenation by legal means. In 1913, in the wake of Johnson's marriage and trial, "[anti-]miscegenation bills were introduced in half of the twenty states that [still] permitted interracial marriages." In Congress, in the aftermath of the Johnson case, at least twenty-one miscegenation bills were introduced, though none was finally passed.[228]

Legislation prohibiting miscegenation was designed to contain a possible threat from non-white men and to protect white women. The representation of white women in The Birth of a Nation underlined the need for such protection. The film's white women are weak and fluttery creatures who need to be rescued from or defended against the threat from colored men (as shown by Flora's fate and Elsie's imprisonment by Lynch). The final act of such male protectionism is to save them from the "fate worse than death": in the climactic scene in the log cabin, when the black militiamen are on the point of breaking in, both Dr. Cameron and one of the Union veterans—all bullets spent—prepare to beat their daughters to death with guns rather than see them fall into the hands of the victorious African Americans (shots 1558, 1561–63, 1565). White women in Birth of a Nation represent an ideal type of womanhood: Ben Cameron, according to an intertitle, "finds the ideal of his dreams in the picture of Elsie Stoneman…whom he has never seen" (shot 93). They are decorative rather than productive. The closest any white woman comes to real work in The Birth of a Nation is to take in boarders; with the Civil War over and the South beginning to rebuild itself, Mrs. Cameron and Margaret put up a "Boarding" sign outside the Cameron mansion (shot 536). Otherwise, all they seem good for is strumming a banjo, stitching costumes for Klansmen, or fetching water in a bucket from the spring (shots 455–62, 466, 970, 984–85). The only truly independent act committed by a white woman in the film is Mrs. Cameron's visit to Washington to plead with the president to pardon her son, and that is simply an extension of her maternal role.

This lack of agency on the part of white women contrasts with the relative activism of those who are mulatto or black: Lydia Brown is clearly identified as the source of Stoneman's radical policies ("The great leader's weakness that is to blight a nation"—shot 133); Mammy twice knocks down a man who is jeering the arrest of Dr. Cameron and plays a major part in her former master's subsequent rescue (shots 1221–24, 1226, 1242–50). Such ascription of agency to mulatto or black women, while white women were presented as passive, may simultaneously have reflected Griffith's racism (black women were consigned to the periphery of society in early twentieth-century America, so what they did could be discounted) and his traditional gender assumptions. Essentially, the film's white women simply wait around to react to news from the public sphere dominated by men ("The woman's part," shot 452) or to wear pretty clothes to meet male preconceptions, as when Flora attempts to dress up for her eldest brother's homecoming (shots 514–17). There is no suggestion that they have either the willpower or the ability to take their place in the political or economic sphere. Although *The Birth of a Nation* was set in the past, it is difficult to contradict the notion that Griffith was using the film as propaganda for his own paternalistic view of women—that he was, at least implicitly, criticizing the "New Woman" of the early twentieth century who campaigned for the same legal and civil rights as men, including the vote.

In *The Birth of a Nation*, Griffith created a largely fictional view of the past that both commented on and critiqued existing American society. Most crucially, his film constructed a (supposedly historical) narrative of national unity based on an ideal of whiteness. The new element in *Birth of a Nation*, argues Linda Williams, "is that it links new feelings about race to equally new feelings of national identity, based on an overt celebration of white supremacy." It demonstrated that movies were now "capable of forging a myth of national origin grounded in race to spectacular effect."[229] The problem, of course, is that it was a myth essentially based on error and exclusion.

The Reaction of Black Spectators to *The Birth of a Nation*

While many historians and film writers have addressed the campaign against *Birth of a Nation* launched by both black and white critics of the film, no one has so far attempted to assess the reaction of the movie's black spectators. The whole area of black silent era spectatorship is itself comparatively unexplored.[230] One problem faced by many black spectators was that they belonged to a community in which the most significant formal institution—the church—tended to disapprove of the cinema generally as frivolous and materialistic entertainment.[231] With *The Birth of a Nation*, there were problems specific to that particular production. Given the amount of heat generated by the campaign against the film, most African Americans must have been aware of the film's racism.

On the other hand, it was clearly a film of considerable technical and aesthetic merit. Many blacks probably went to see it just to find out why it had generated so much controversy. One who did was black actor William Walker, who watched the film in a segregated African America movie house in 1916. Walker later recalled the reaction of the audience:

> Some people were crying. You could hear people saying, "Oh, God." And some said "Damn."...You could hear them because [of] the reaction of the people. You had the worst feeling in the world. You just felt like you were not counted. You were out of existence...I just felt like killing all the white people in the world.[232]

Walker's memory suggests two things: first, that to a racial audience rendered almost socially invisible by segregation, it was now made to appear historically marginal as well; second, that the film not only encouraged hostile, aggressive attitudes to blacks on the parts of whites but it also prompted some blacks to dream of violent revenge on whites. This, of course, was probably principally a *male* response; the author is unaware of compelling evidence about the response of African American female spectators to *Birth of a Nation* (although it might be conjectured that black women were among the "people" Walker heard crying during the film's exhibition).[233] Black women viewers almost certainly found no echo of themselves on the screen. At one extreme was the passionate mulatto, Lydia Brown, eager to seduce Stoneman to bask in his reflected glory (but who disappears from the second half of the film); at the other was the loyal but often comical figure of Mammy. Black women were as marginalized in *Birth* as they were in segregated Southern society. White women were the focus of the film's attention, its heroines—and its real and potential victims. The achievement of Griffith's film, suggests bell hooks, was to inscribe a "politics of race and gender...into mainstream cinematic narrative...As a seminal work, this film identified what the place and function of White womanhood would be in cinema. There was clearly no place for Black women." Although Black female spectators who were "not duped by mainstream cinema" might well "develop an oppositional gaze," hooks insists that there is no clear empirical proof of this happening in relation to *Birth*.[234]

Many African Americans either avoided or were repelled by the film, but there is evidence that some responded in a very different manner. According to Samuel Edward Courtney, reporting to Booker T. Washington in the spring of 1915, two Boston blacks, druggist Phillip J. Allston and lawyer/dentist Dr. Alexander W. Cox, had not only endorsed the film themselves but had attempted to push an endorsement of it through the executive committee of the local branch of the National Business League [an African American organization].[235] In July 1915, one black Ohio newspaper noted that "we saw a Negro newspaper the other day which endorsed *The Birth of a Nation*."[236] The *Philadelphia Tribune*, one of the oldest black papers in the country, thought it unlikely "to increase race hatred" and declared that "on the whole it was not so bad."[237] Several reasons may be advanced for such a stance. Not all imply approval of the film. The black community in 1915 was split by internal rivalries, including the struggle between Booker T. Washington's supporters and the NAACP over who should lead the community. Some of these rivalries (such as the initiative of Allston and Cox in Boston) were expressed in the varied responses to *Birth*. Additionally, a number of blacks believed that the strategy of protest as a whole was misconceived. By providing the film with priceless free publicity, it greatly aided its commercial success.[238]

It may be that some blacks, however, probably actually *did* enjoy the film. In explaining how and why this could have happened, the first and most obvious explanation is the film's power. Karl Brown, Griffith's assistant cameraman, testified to the dramatic effect of the Klan ride on the Los Angeles audience at the première: "every soul...was in the saddle with the clansmen and pounding hell-for-leather on an errand of stern justice." According to Richard Schickel, even some members of the NAACP would later confess that while viewing the film, they had been caught up in the excitement and carried along with the rest of the audience.[239]

Some blacks, including George L. Knox, publisher of a black newspaper, the Indianapolis *Freeman*, and A. E. Manning, publisher of a sister publication, the Indianapolis *World*, seem to have adopted a public stance in favor of the film. The two men spoke on behalf of *Birth* before the City Censors of Dayton, Ohio, apparently persuading them not to ban the film. According to the *Forum*, a local black newspaper, Knox "stated that he had seen the film three times, that it was all right, as it showed the love of the Negro for his master and the love the black 'mammies' had for the young white soldiers."[240] In contrast to Knox, other African Americans may have enjoyed the film because they did not in any sense see themselves or their ancestors on the screen. All the major characters who were both bad and black—Lydia Brown, Silas Lynch, and Gus—were played (and very obviously) by whites. "The transparent whiteness of those blacks," observes Maurice Yacowar, "is a reminder that we see not the black man *per se* but a white man's projection of a black man, an artist's deployment of an image in a poetic fiction."[241] The use of burned cork, a traditional trope associated with minstrel shows, may have served to emphasize the film's character as fictionalized entertainment.

If African American spectators were distanced from the blacks portrayed in the film by the recognition that most were really white, a further distancing may also have occurred because of time. The events represented in the film had all happened several decades earlier. It was entirely possible for those watching the film to regard it as an accurate reconstruction of history while simultaneously considering it irrelevant to the racial situation of the United States in 1915. The so-called Hampton Epilogue—the short film made at the

Hampton Institute in Virginia and sometimes shown after *Birth of a Nation* had ended—emphasized the point that Griffith's movie was concerned solely with the past. The makers of this short film (almost certainly themselves black) implicitly accepted the idea that African Americans had been accurately represented in *The Birth of a Nation* by advancing the view that *Birth* had failed to take account of the progress made by American blacks since Reconstruction.[242]

Also, African Americans viewing the film may have created meanings from the experience that had comparatively little to do with the narrative white audiences saw on screen. Traditional film theory regards the theoretical spectator as essentially passive, positioned by the filmic text and the modes of signification with which it is associated but, in recent years, scholars have challenged this view. Researching how "real" spectators (especially women) respond to certain expressions of popular culture, they have often seen them actively involved—through interactions between their own social and cultural identities and textual practices—in constructing a variety of possible meanings.[243] The incentive to construct counter-hegemonic meanings may, of course, be especially great among viewers who are marginalized both on screen and in their own lives. While bell hooks writes of the "oppositional gaze" developed by black female moviegoers, Manthia Diawara regards the terms "Black spectator" and "resisting spectator" as interchangeable.[244] If white audiences watching *Birth of a Nation* saw blacks depicted on screen as uncouth, aggressive, sexually rapacious, and corrupt, African American viewers may have read the film in a thoroughly oppositional or resistant way to construct meanings very different from those of white spectators. Above all, perhaps, to the disfranchised and persecuted blacks of 1915, the film may have appealed because it portrayed a time when African Americans had not only voted but had managed to elected both a lieutenant-governor and a distinct majority of the members of a state legislature from their own race, when they had dominated the judicial process, and—perhaps most important of all—when they had actually fought back against white oppression with guns in their hands.

8

After *Birth*

The NAACP Campaign from 1916

By the beginning of 1916, apart from statewide bans on the exhibition of *The Birth of a Nation* in Ohio and Kansas, the campaign to suppress the film run by the NAACP had largely failed. Over the next few years, however, the organization's efforts to prevent screenings proved considerably more successful. Part of the reason for this success was that events encouraged the NAACP to adopt a new and more convincing argument. "The day may come," observed Elijah Hodges with prophetic foresight in July 1915, "when we shall need the colored man's help to defend the flag."[1] Black soldiers played a major part in the American expeditionary force led by Brigadier-General John J. Pershing that invaded Mexico in March 1916 in an attempt to capture Mexican revolutionary leader Francisco ("Pancho") Villa, who had killed Americans on both sides of the border in an attempt to embroil the existing Mexican government in a war with the United States. The participation of these black soldiers was obviously very much in the mind of W. E. B. Du Bois a few months later when a proposal was made to show *The Birth of a Nation* at theaters patronized by soldiers in the Canal Zone in Panama. "Colored troops," argued Du Bois, "have been giving too good an account of themselves recently to deserve having this vicious attack on their race in military posts."[2] Once the United States entered the First World War,[3] and African American soldiers formed part of the American army fighting in France, arguments such as these were deployed with increasing strength and frequency.

American involvement in the war brought huge pressures for social and political conformity. George Creel's Committee on Public Information encouraged national unity and helped whip up popular dislike of German sympathizers and pacifists—anyone, indeed, who seemed to threaten the war effort. Soon, the NAACP found, the emphasis on patriotism and unity in public discourses could be exploited and redirected into its own campaign against *Birth*. "Especially at the present time," wrote NAACP national secretary John R. Shillady to Mayor John F. Hylan of New York in February 1918, "when nearly a hundred thousand colored men are enlisted in the service of their country..., it would be damaging to the national unity upon which our success in the war with Germany depends to permit anything which would accentuate class feeling as between the white people and the Negroes." Black critics of the film now represented it as an unprovoked assault on a section of the community that loyally supported the war. "The colored people," reported a local newspaper in Juneau, Alaska, "declare it an insult to their race and unfair at this time when the colored population is fighting with their white brothers on the battlefields of France, as well as supporting all patriotic efforts such as the Red Cross, Liberty Loans, etc."[4] The appeal of such wartime arguments was demonstrated in June 1918 when the West Virginia State Council of Defense, responding to a request from a largely African American county, prohibited the showing of *Birth of a Nation* in the state for as long as the war continued. The resolution imposing the ban paid tribute to West Virginia blacks (who, it was said, were "loyal and patriotic" and had "cheerfully responded to all demands"). It also insisted that showing *Birth* would create tensions between the races that would prevent them "from working together in peace and harmony in...producing the best results for our national defense." This success in West Virginia was followed by the decision of the film's exhibitors in Ohio, at the request of Governor James M. Cox, to withdraw it from circulation after October 1.[5]

The last few months of the world conflict saw the exhibitors of *The Birth of a Nation* increasingly wrong-footed by arguments focusing on the ways the film weakened the patriotism and social solidarity required for a successful prosecution of the war. In February, opponents of the film in Springfield, Ohio, gained a partial victory by having its showing on Sundays prohibited. In May, a local black organization in Texas launched an attempt to have the War Department ban the film from military bases. Also in May, William Monroe Trotter and his Equal Rights League managed to have *Birth* suppressed in Lynn, Massachusetts. In June, Nebraska attorney general Willis E. Reed successfully applied for an injunction to bar the showing of the film in Lincoln lest it "stir up strife and dissension at a time when harmony should prevail and hence was a hindrance to the successful prosecution of the war."[6] At the beginning of October, the governor of Alaska and the mayor of Juneau both acted to ensure that *Birth* was not screened in the capital city of the Alaska Territory.[7] At almost exactly the same time as the Alaskan ban (which they may not as yet have known about), the NAACP launched a nationwide campaign to persuade state governors and state councils of defense to prevent the showing of *The Birth of a Nation* as long as hostilities lasted. It could have been that the NAACP wanted to re-assert its own leadership in the campaign against the film. But the precedent of *Birth*'s suppression in West Virginia and perhaps, above all, Ohio, also suggested that the time was ripe to press for the film's banning or withdrawal in other states for the duration of the war.[8]

Because critics of *The Birth of a Nation* could now reframe their opposition to the film in the new dominant tropes of patriotism and national unity, the campaign of 1918 had a much broader reach at the state level than had been enjoyed by that of 1915–16. A number of governors sympathized with the NAACP's point of view. The governor of Kansas insisted that the film "has not exhibited and will not exhibit" in his state "so long as I have anything to say about it." The governor of Oregon claimed that he had managed to secure "the partial suppression of it in this State." The governors of Minnesota and Rhode Island claimed that if *Birth* was advertised for exhibition in their states, they would take action against it. The governor of North Dakota wrote to the Griffith Corporation requesting that the film not be shown in his state. Revealingly perhaps, the governor of North Carolina, Thomas Dixon's home state, observed that the local authorities in Winston-Salem "for the reasons mentioned in your letter" had stopped an advertised screening of the film and "I do not think it will be shown here during the war."[9]

Even in 1918, however, opposition to *The Birth of a Nation* was far from unanimous. Some governors saw no problem with it (Mississippi), avoided the issue completely by insisting it was being shown nowhere in their state (Maine), argued that they had no power to interfere (New Jersey and Florida), or simply passed the whole problem over to the state council of defense (Michigan, Utah, and Wisconsin).[10] The state councils themselves, principally composed of prominent businessmen and politicians, embraced a wide range of views. At one extreme was Utah, which expressed "full sympathy" with the NAACP's stance and promised to use "whatever influence" it had to suppress films such as *Birth*. At the other was Connecticut, which disclaimed all interest in the matter since the film was not being shown there and, in any case, the subject was "not...distinctively of a war character." Interestingly, the State Council of California mentioned that "some time ago" the exhibitors of the picture had voluntarily agreed to withdraw it from the state for six months. Because it appeared likely that this agreement had now lapsed, the council informed the NAACP that it was once again "taking the subject up with them [the exhibitors of *Birth*] as suggested in your letter."[11]

So successful was the NAACP at mobilizing the discourses of wartime patriotism and national unity in aid of its once-faltering campaign against *The Birth of a Nation* that the momentum of its campaign persisted for a while after the armistice was signed on November 11, 1918. Only a few days into the peace, *Birth* was supposed to run for a week in Louisville, Kentucky. Confronted with NAACP protests, and conscious that with demobilization beginning a victory parade was about to be held in his city, Mayor George W. Smith decided to ban the film's exhibition by executive order.[12] At the end of November, the film was scheduled for the Alhambra and Opera House in Richmond, Virginia, which had just re-opened after closing down for six weeks because of the influenza epidemic. The manager of the theater was clearly looking to *Birth* as a proven money-spinner to make good the losses caused by this closure. However, protests were made by black and white committees to Mayor Evans "that the picture is inclined to incite race prejudice among the lower classes of both races." A conference of Richmond ministers also passed a resolution opposing any attempt "to stir up hatred between the negroes and whites ..., particularly when...they have so recently fought with equal devotion the world's battle for liberty and justice." Perceiving the film as a means of encouraging friction between the poorer, less educated members of both races—and being particularly concerned by such friction at a time "when so many forces are contributing to the drift towards Bolshevism or anarchy"—Evans finally (and successfully) asked that the movie be withdrawn.[13]

Mayor Evans's concern over Bolshevism underlines the fact that new issues and discourses were beginning to dominate public attention in the immediate postwar period. The momentum acquired by the campaign against *The Birth of a Nation* during the last months of the war was sufficient to keep it going at least until February 1919. The NAACP fought hard to prevent the film from being shown at New Castle, Pennsylvania, on February 7 and 8. "As colored people," Robert J. Nelson, the secretary of the Harrisburg NAACP, wrote to Pennsylvania governor William C. Sproul, "we have performed our duty in giving patriotic service in the fighting forces of the nation both at home and abroad and we feel that now, above all times, national unity should be maintained." Sproul apparently agreed, passing on Nelson's letter to the state censorship board "with an opinion on my part that the pictures in question are not only provocative of dissension and trouble but are unjust to our colored citizens."[14] Toward the end of February, the West Virginia legislature effectively made permanent the wartime ban on *Birth of a Nation* when it passed a bill drafted by H. J. Capehart, a colored member of the lower house, prohibiting the showing of any picture "calculated to result in arousing the prejudice...of one race or class of citizens against any other race or class of citizens."[15]

During the remainder of 1919 and 1920, *The Birth of a Nation* appeared far less frequently in newspaper headlines and NAACP reports. The fear of Bolshevism mentioned in November 1918 by Mayor Evans of Richmond crystallized into the "Red Scare" of 1919, with left-wingers of all kinds being persecuted. In this atmosphere, NAACP activists fighting for racial equality could easily be identified—and dismissed—as "radicals." The rapid demobilization after the war together with the abandonment of price controls led to a combination of growing unemployment and rising inflation. A wave of industrial unrest, beginning with a five-day general strike in Seattle in February, contributed to fears of revolution, as did the posting of homemade bombs to businessmen and politicians and a number of simultaneous explosions in major cities. The summer and early fall of 1919 also saw a sharp increase in racial tensions. This was especially pronounced in the cities of the North, which had recently experienced a great influx of black Southerners eager to escape the poverty and backwardness of their own region and find employment in booming wartime industries. The return to peacetime conditions meant that blacks and whites were frequently competing for the same jobs. As friction between the races grew, there was an explosion of race riots; more than twenty-five took place, with the most notorious occurring in Chicago (July 27–August 2). When more than 200 African Americans were murdered in Elaine, Arkansas, in early October, the NAACP sent assistant secretary Walter F. White to investigate the circumstances underpinning the riot.[16]

Consequently, the NAACP had enough to do in 1919 and 1920 without worrying as much as it had previously about the impact of The Birth of a Nation.[17] When it relaunched its campaign against the film in 1921, it would do so in very different circumstances. Anxieties over the content of movies, coupled with a series of "Hollywood" scandals peaking in Roscoe "Fatty" Arbuckle's arrest for the murder of Virginia Rappe, had led to greatly increased demands for movie censorship at all levels (federal, state, and local).[18] By 1921, the NAACP would not simply be fighting what it perceived as a vicious film; it would also be attacking the apparent link between Birth of a Nation and a revived Ku Klux Klan.

The Birth of a Nation and the New Klan

There had been few references to the Ku Klux Klan in American cinema before the release of The Birth of a Nation in 1915. In 1905, the Edison Company produced The White Caps, a favorable view of a band of Klan-like vigilantes protecting helpless women (they are shown attacking a wife beater who is tied up and tarred and feathered). The White Caps, on whom the movie was based, were a group dedicated to maintaining moral values in the mountain communities of Indiana and Kentucky early in the twentieth century. Unlike the Klan of the Reconstruction period, they do not appear to have been concerned with racial matters.[19] Six years later, Griffith directed The Rose of Kentucky, which presented contemporary night riders in his home state in a very unflattering way. Although race was referred to (the main male character is the owner of a tobacco plantation with what Scott Simmon refers to as an "integrated work force"), the Klan-type riders attack him not because of this but apparently because he has refused to join them.[20] Until 1915, the only film dealing with the *real* Klan of the Reconstruction era appears to have been Kalem's The Northern Schoolteacher (1909), showing the Klan persecuting a white Yankee schoolteacher in a Southern town. This portrait of the post–Civil War Klan as an evil, violent organization would not be challenged on screen until 1915, when Griffith presented the Klan as the heroes of *Birth of a Nation*, saving white civilization from the threat posed by armed and aggressive blacks. By mythologizing as "good" the violent Klan of former times, Griffith not only distorted history but inadvertently contributed to the reappearance of an organization that—away from the historical context of the 1860s and 1870s—even Thomas Dixon would dismiss as "evil."[21]

The new Klan came into existence as the result of a series of factors and events. On April 27, 1913, thirteen-year-old Mary Phagan was found raped and murdered in the basement of the factory where she worked in Atlanta, Georgia. Her employer, Leo M. Frank, was tried and convicted for the murder. Sentenced to death on evidence that was both sparse and confused, Frank, a Texas-born Jew raised in New York, was temporarily spared from execution when the governor commuted his sentence to life imprisonment. Tom Watson was a prominent Georgia politician of the day who during the Populist revolt of the 1890s had supported the idea that poor whites should cooperate with African Americans. Over time, however, his views had shifted toward a virulent hatred of blacks, Catholics, and Jews, and he exhorted his fellow Georgians to redress the injustice of Frank's commuted sentence. On the night of August 16–17, 1915, responding to Watson's call, a team of twenty-five men who referred to themselves as the "Knights of Mary Phagan" abducted Frank from the prison farm where he was incarcerated, took him to Marietta, Georgia, near Phagan's birthplace, and hanged him.[22] Precisely two months later, according to Wyn Craig Wade, the members of this lynch party climbed Stone Mountain, eighteen miles from Atlanta, and burned a huge cross that was "visible throughout the city."[23]

Two weeks after the lynching of Frank, Watson, in applauding the lynching itself, had suggested in one of the periodicals he published that "another Ku Klux Klan" be organized "to restore HOME RULE."[24] It was not Watson, however, but another Southerner—William J. Simmons—who effectively relaunched the Klan in 1915. Born in central Alabama in 1880, Simmons was too young to have personal memories of the original Klan. His father, however, had been a member in the 1860s and Simmons grew up "fascinated by Klan stories." Seeking adventure on his own account, Simmons volunteered to fight as a private in the Spanish-American War. Once the war was over, he became a Methodist circuit rider in the backwoods of Florida and Alabama. Simmons was not a very good minister, outraged many Methodists by his fondness for whiskey, and sank deeper and deeper into debt. In 1912, he was suspended for inefficiency by the annual conference of his church. For a time, he wandered from job to job before finally finding his niche as an organizer for a fraternal order, the Woodmen of the World. In 1914, he moved to Atlanta as district manager. Early in 1915, he was injured by an automobile and spent three months in bed. During this time, he began to dream obsessively of founding a fraternal order of his own, based on the model of the Ku Klux Klan of Reconstruction days.[25]

The way Georgians had reacted to the Frank lynching convinced "Colonel" Simmons (his honorary rank in the Woodmen) that reestablishing the Klan was a timely idea. Gathering together thirty-four men, including some supposedly drawn from the Knights of Mary Phagan[26] and two who had ridden as Klansmen during the Reconstruction era, he applied on October 26, 1915, to the State of Georgia for a charter for the Knights of the Ku Klux Klan as a fraternal order. A month later, on Thanksgiving Day, Simmons told his charter members that he planned to revive "the ancient glories" of the Klan by lighting another fiery cross on Stone Mountain. Since it was a cold night, only fifteen of the original thirty-four agreed to go with him to the mountain in the sightseeing bus he had chartered. On arrival, Simmons filled his canteen from a spring of sparkling water (making "a few remarks on purity and honor" in the process). He and his colleagues then gathered together some boulders to make a rough altar and covered it with an old American flag, laying a Bible on top of the flag. Simmons lighted the cross with a match and while it burned, administered the oath of membership. "And thus," he would later assert, "on the mountain top that night at the midnight hour... bathed in the sacred glow of the fiery cross, the Invisible Empire was called from its slumber of half a century to take up a new task and fulfill a new mission for humanity's good."[27]

Simmons was well aware at the time of his improvised ceremony of the existence of *The Birth of a Nation*. The film and the saturation publicity associated with it had already helped mold both fashion and social life in the North. Manufacturers produced "Ku-Klux hats" modeled after those worn by the riders in *Birth* and "KK" kitchen aprons. New York society ladies organized K-Klux balls and on Halloween, 2,000 University of Chicago students partied in Klan costumes.[28] By late November 1915, the film had already been shown very successfully in several Southern cities and its first showing in Atlanta was due. Simmons realized that this offered an opportunity too great to be missed to publicize his new organization, which finally received its charter from the state of Georgia on December 4. Consequently, the same edition of the *Atlanta Constitution* that announced the opening of *The Birth of a Nation* in Atlanta on December 6, 1915, also carried an advertisement of the Klan's rebirth as a "HIGH CLASS ORDER FOR MEN OF INTELLIGENCE AND CHARACTER." The actual première was preceded by a parade in which Simmons and his first recruits rode down Peachtree Street wearing bedsheets and fired rifle salutes in front of the large queues of people waiting to enter the Atlanta Theater. It was, as Wyn Craig Wade has commented, "an enormously effective stunt."[29] Simmons understood the vital importance of rapid publicity for his new order, and fearing that *The Birth of a Nation* would encourage the emergence of rival Klan fraternities, he insisted that his own Klan was the true descendant of the original one.[30]

As both film and revived Klan spread across the South, they became locked in a marriage of publicity-oriented convenience. Ushers in some states alternated between wearing Confederate uniforms and the sheets of the Klan. In many towns, Klansmen rode through the streets in full regalia in advance of screenings of the film. Newspapers published advertisements by the Klan endorsing the movie. Members of the organization distributed Klan literature outside movie houses in which it was being shown.[31] By the early 1920s, as the Klan spread beyond its base in the South—where, as David Chalmers comments, "Georgia was its citadel and Atlanta its holy city"—it continued to exploit *The Birth of a Nation* as part of its recruitment and propaganda drive. In 1921, for example, the film was shown to two local Klan branches in Virginia and one in Portland, Oregon. In February 1922, the film was screened at two New York theaters, and according to critics, this helped the local Klan in its campaign to increase membership. Two years later, the U.S. Grant Klan of Chicago, Illinois, showed the film successfully over two weeks at the Auditorium Theatre.[32] By 1925, when 40,000 invited Klansman paraded in Washington, D.C., the Klan was strong in many states of the North and West, including Maine, Massachusetts, Rhode Island, New York, New Jersey, Pennsylvania, Ohio, Indiana, Illinois, Wisconsin, Kansas, Oklahoma, Colorado, California, and Oregon. The new Klan, at least outside the South, was no longer simply anti-black. Reflecting changing social circumstances, it was also critical of Catholics, Jews, Orientals, and recent immigrants—in fact, of all who were considered to challenge traditional American social hierarchies and values. Besides giving the new Klan an idealized view of its predecessor and important propaganda symbols (the figure of a Klansman on a rearing horse holding a fiery cross, copied from the film's publicity stills, became the principal insignia of the order), Griffith's film may also have appealed to Klan recruits for its clear endorsement of white supremacy and intense hostility to interracial relationships ("mongrelization").[33]

Despite the use by the Klan of *The Birth of a Nation* as a means of attracting and keeping its members, it is difficult to estimate the precise influence of the film on the expansion of the order in the early years after its reemergence in 1915. Certainly, as a contributor to the *Confederate Veteran* observed in April 1916, the film had "done more in a few months' time to arouse interest" in the original Klan "than all the articles written on the subject during the last forty years." "No one who has seen the film," declared journalist Walter Lippmann in 1922, "will ever hear the [Klan's] name again without seeing those white horsemen." Asked in 1928 whether the Klan would have grown as quickly without the film, "Colonel" Simmons answered "no... *The Birth of a Nation* helped the Klan tremendously."[34] On the other hand, the really rapid growth of the Klan did *not* occur in the early years when *The Birth of a Nation* was at the peak of its influence and availability. By 1919, the Klan had only a few thousand members. Not until the summer of 1920, with the hiring of publicity agents Edward Young

Clarke and Mrs. Elizabeth Tyler, did the real expansion of the Klan begin. By the summer of 1921, it had around 100,000 members. The further expansion of the Klan was aided by a series of critical articles about the organization and the violence with which it was associated that were published by the New York *World* and other newspapers in the closing months of 1921 (most Americans in rural areas were quick to support what New Yorkers condemned). It was also helped by the favorable impression created by Colonel Simmons when he testified before Congress in October 1921. By the middle years of the 1920s, the Klan, according to Nancy Maclean, may have reached a peak of 5 million members spread across the nation in almost 4,000 local chapters.[35] It is impossible to say with any certainty what the precise role of *The Birth of a Nation* was in encouraging this increase; but as African American scholar Lawrence Reddick noted in 1944, "its glorification of the Ku Klux Klan was at least one factor which enabled the Klan to enter upon its period of greatest expansion."[36]

Fighting Both Klan and Film

When the NAACP campaign against *The Birth of a Nation* resumed in 1921, the principal flashpoints in the struggle—New York, Boston, and Los Angeles—were much the same as in early 1915. What was new was the relative effectiveness of the campaign and the fact that the fight was no longer simply against the film but also against the revived Klan. Moreover, since the Klan was no longer just anti-black, the NAACP began to find new allies among those whom the Klan attacked.

On April 26, 1921, Walter F. White, assistant secretary of the NAACP, wrote to the manager of New York's Capitol Theater, the largest picture palace in the country, asking him to cancel the screening of *The Birth of a Nation* for a week from May 1. White argued that the film presented "in most erroneous fashion" the history of the Civil War, threatened to undermine the relatively good race relations then existing in New York by portraying the black man "as a vicious, lustful and horrible being," and idealized the Ku Klux Klan. In reply, S. F. "Roxy" Rothapfel contended that some of the objectionable scenes in the film had been removed, that audiences were unlikely to be stirred to hatred by the depiction "of history of sixty years ago," and that Griffith's movie was both "a purely American production" and "a master picture." The NAACP initially reacted to Rothapfel's refusal to withdraw the picture in time-honored ways. As in 1915, it lobbied the mayor, police commissioner, and commissioner of licenses, only to be informed (again as in 1915) "that the city authorities were without jurisdiction in stopping the film."[37] It also sent a telegram to the governor of New York suggesting he use the "revival [of] this vicious and dangerous film as [an] additional argument for [the] enactment [of the] Lusk Censorship Bill into law." Governor Miller may have taken the advice. Certainly, the Lusk bill, creating a state board of censorship for motion pictures in New York, became law in mid-May.[38] But this was too late to affect the showing of *Birth of a Nation* at the Capitol. With no hope of redress from politics, the NAACP turned to direct action—action aimed more against the Klan than against the film. It arranged for a peaceful demonstration outside the movie theater, with around thirty black ex-servicemen in uniform (often wearing foreign decorations) handing out leaflets attacking the Ku Klux Klan for its "activities...today and in the past." They were accompanied by three African American women in the uniform of the Y.W.C.A. who carried placards saying "We Represented America in France, Why Should 'The Birth of a Nation' Misrepresent Us Here?" When asked by the police to move on and not obstruct the sidewalk, they refused and five demonstrators (including the three women) were arrested.[39]

The NAACP picket of the Capitol Theater in May 1921 underlined the changes which had taken place since *The Birth of a Nation* had first been shown in New York in 1915. The demonstrators, about a dozen in all, wore uniforms and decorations to draw attention to the experience of the war, a war in which blacks had served loyally and patriotically. Women played a prominent role in the protest since after the ratification of the Twentieth Amendment in the previous year, female suffrage was now a reality. The leaflet distributed by the protestors was essentially an attack on the Klan: it criticized *Birth* for supporting the Klan by distorting and falsifying history. It also critiqued the activities of the revived Klan in Georgia, Florida, and North Carolina and sought to broaden the base of opposition to it by asking readers if they knew "that the Ku Klux Klan is not only anti-Negro but anti-Jewish and anti-Catholic?" Finally, it raised the issue of censorship: readers were asked if they were prepared "to allow Ku Klux Klan propaganda to be displayed in the movies in New York City."[40]

So far as the NAACP was concerned, the arrest of the demonstrators and their prosecution under a city ordinance banning the distribution of "any handbill, circular, card or other advertising matter" was an obvious threat to freedom of speech. When the five people arrested first appeared before Magistrate Douros in the Night Court, their NAACP counsel argued that they intended "to stop the Ku Klux Klan from inciting dissension and riot between two peace loving people who fought side by side in France." Douros, acidly commenting that he wanted "no stump speeches here," adjourned the case to the magistrates' court and released the women on parole while setting bail for the men at $200. Preparations for the case were made, including the calling of Griffith himself as a witness. But when the defendants actually appeared in court on May 12, it was clear that the judicial system was deeply embarrassed by the whole process. First, before the case began, Magistrate Robert E. Ten Eyck apparently ordered (though he later denied this) that numerous "well-dressed" black men and women be expelled from the part of the court reserved for spectators. Second, he was apparently intimidated by what he termed the "authority" of the defendants (by which he probably meant their war service, but also perhaps that one of the women was the wife of a former American minister to Liberia). Trying to dispose of the case quickly, Ten Eyck offered to dismiss the case if those accused promised to discontinue the protest. When they refused, he found them guilty of a misdemeanor but suspended sentence. NAACP lawyers promptly launched an appeal and six months later, Judge Tulley of the Court of General Sessions overturned the conviction on the grounds that the ordinance under which the five had been prosecuted "was never intended to prevent the lawful distribution of anything other than commercial and business advertising matter."[41]

Although the NAACP publicized the campaign ending with Tulley's decision as a major victory for free speech and the right of peaceful protest, it was clear that not everyone in the black community and its allies approved of the NAACP's tactics. Alone among New York papers, both white and black, Fred R. Moore's *Age* published no account of the original protest against the movie. "Personally," wrote Lester Walton, the *Age*'s film critic, writing a few days later to NAACP Secretary James Weldon Johnson, "I do not see what good was accomplished by the demonstration you staged before the Capitol theater. You were playing into the hands of the enemy by giving them valuable advertising. Certainly you did not bring about the desired results: have the picture taken off." Walton believed "that the best way to prevent the presentation of such pictures as the 'Birth of a Nation'" was "to stop them in advance."[42] Walton was being unfair: he was writing with the knowledge that the existence of a city censorship board in Boston had made it possible to mount a campaign against the film before it opened, and that New York state had just adopted a censorship law that would affect the treatment of *Birth* in the future. But no such censorship board had existed in New York at the beginning of May 1921, and the NAACP had first lobbied the civil authorities before engaging in direct protest. Moreover, the new strategy adopted by the NAACP—their concentration on associating the film with the reborn Klan and looking for new allies against both—had (at the time Walton wrote) just been vindicated in Boston.

The Birth of a Nation was advertised for a new run in Boston, starting May 16, 1921. On the morning of May 15, a large delegation of African Americans and their allies attended a hearing at city hall where they lobbied and testified against the showing of the film. One of those involved was R. Butler Wilson, secretary of the Boston branch of the NAACP. "In our protest," Wilson explained to James Weldon Johnson, "we coupled the propaganda of the play with the new Ku Klux Klan organization and the barbarous crime of lynching." During the afternoon, the three-man Boston Board of Censors, set up partly as a result of the struggle against *Birth* in 1915, met to watch the film. At the end of the screening, Mayor Andrew J. Peters met with the two other members of the board and announced that the license of the Shubert Theater, where the film was to be played, had been suspended indefinitely (though the mayor also explained that the board would not prevent the theater from presenting an alternative film or play).[43] It is probable that in highly Catholic Boston, the hostility displayed by the revived Klan toward the Catholic Church may have been a crucial factor in Peters's decision: one of the organizations represented at the hearing had been the Knights of Columbus, an influential body among Irish Catholics.[44] The NAACP's decision to foreground the relationship between *Birth* and the new Klan was a shrewd one. "I think we made no mistake," R. Butler Wilson declared two days after the mayor's announcement, "in hitching up the film with the Ku Klux Klan."[45] Where the NAACP *did* make a mistake was in claiming the lion's share of the credit for the film's suppression. A press release announced that the hearing before the mayor had been the result of the NAACP protest and that R. Butler Wilson had "acted as attorney for the protestants against the film." A sharply worded letter from the president and secretary of the National Equal Rights League claimed that the League "had an equal and co-ordinate role in the protest"; that even if the NAACP had got here first, the League had also pressed the mayor for a hearing; and that the NAACP's account omitted "perhaps the most prominent figure in the hearing ..., a man who went to the lock-up fighting the film in 1915": William Monroe Trotter. In reality, Trotter and the nine witnesses he introduced had been allotted exactly the same amount of time as the NAACP's Wilson to make the League's case against *Birth*.[46] Therefore, while the Boston campaign of 1921 against *The Birth of a Nation* succeeded while the one six years earlier had failed, both, as well as the unsuccessful New York struggle of 1921, served to emphasize divisions within the pro-African American community.

The success in Boston seemed to open the door to bans on the film in other places. In August 1921, declaring himself "opposed to any exhibition which has a tendency to incite race prejudice," Mayor George E. Leach of Minneapolis, a strong opponent of the Klan, followed the example set by Mayor Peters and refused to allow *The Birth of a Nation* to be shown in his city.[47] In California, a long campaign waged by attorney E. Burton Ceruti seemingly reached a triumphant conclusion at a conference called by Los Angeles Mayor M. P. Snyder when William Clune, co-owner of exhibition rights in the state, promised not only to withdraw *Birth* from the market in that state but also to destroy the film. This must have seemed to many in the NAACP as a (more successful) repetition of the struggle of January/February 1915, when Ceruti had been among the film's very first critics and Clune had held its première in his theater. But more was at stake by the summer of 1921 than the fate of just one film. The main issue in Los Angeles and the reason many movie executives attended the conference organized by the mayor was the growing demand for censorship of the film industry in its home state. It was not so much the racism of *The Birth of a Nation* or its links with the new Klan that made it a target in California as its general propensity to rouse controversy. The movie industry, feeling very vulnerable, not only sought to avoid such controversy but it also tried to enlist the aid of the NAACP in defeating the supporters of censorship. In other places, the NAACP supported censorship as a means of suppressing *Birth*: in Los Angeles, it seems to have agreed to fight censorship in alliance with film producers and exhibitors, on condition that *The Birth of a Nation* be withdrawn.[48]

On November 24, 1922, advertisements in the New York press proclaimed that *The Birth of a Nation* was to be shown at the Selwyn Theater, on 42nd Street, for a week beginning December 4. Three days later, the press reported that the Reverend Oscar Haywood, a Klan lecturer and organizer, had announced that the Klan was beginning a drive to expand its membership in New York City. The coincidence of the two things, as NAACP assistant secretary Walter F. White and two New York politicians explained in a joint letter to the state Motion Picture Commission, suggested that *Birth* was "being reproduced in New York City again as a part of the campaign of the Ku Klux Klan to recruit members." As in its recent campaigns in New York and Boston, therefore, the NAACP tried to strengthen its case against the film by associating it with the modern Klan. It also reached out to other opponents of the Klan, particularly Catholics and Jews. What was new, however, was the understanding that public protest and demonstrations might well be counterproductive, creating advertising for the film. "We are trying," White wrote to the state director of the Knights of Columbus, "to prevent the showing of the picture without any publicity because that is exactly what the Ku Klux Klan and the producers of the picture want."[49] As in 1921, the NAACP protested privately to the mayor, the police commissioner, and the license commissioner of New York as well as the state governor. It also lobbied Will Hays, chairman of the Motion Picture Producers and Distributors of America (MPPDA) established earlier in 1922, and Joseph Levenson, secretary of the state Motion Picture Commission.[50] There was considerable irony in the NAACP's approaching both Hays and Levenson, since Hays (a former postmaster general in Harding's cabinet) had been appointed by the movie industry to make sure there would be no further censorship of films of the type adopted by New York in 1921.[51] It was by no means clear what Hays, only a few months in office and—as his autobiography published many years later would reveal—an admirer of Griffith, could possibly have done.[52] Inevitably, therefore, the main hopes of those who wished to stop the film came to rest with the new Motion Picture Commission.

The NAACP, at Levenson's suggestion, filed a formal protest with the commission against the exhibition of *Birth*. This group held formal hearings on the morning of December 2. At either this four-hour session or two further sessions on December 4, Griffith, Dixon, and their lawyers tried very hard "to prove that there is no connection between the original Ku Klux Klan of Reconstruction days and the modern organisation of that name." The film's producers seem to have offered to add an intertitle to this effect and to have the same point made verbally before each showing. For its part, the NAACP argued that the film glorified the Klan, encouraged "racial and religious prejudices," and fostered "a spirit of antagonism" toward blacks.[53] At the end of the final hearing on December 4, the members of the commission viewed the film and by a majority of two to one (Levenson wanted to suppress the film completely) decided not to ban it. On December 20, the commission insisted that for screening of the film to continue in New York state substantial cuts would have to be made. These focused mainly on the scenes in which miscegenation was referred to, as in the representation of Lydia Brown's relationship with Austin Stoneman, Gus's chase of Flora Cameron, and Lynch's pursuit of Elsie Stoneman.[54] Later, the NAACP would express concern that the required cuts, or at least some of them, had not been made.[55] But for the moment, they could only watch in frustration as the original, unedited film opened at the Selwyn Theater as scheduled. Much of the audience, the New York *World* reported the next day, appeared to be composed of members of the modern Klan who cheered each time a Klansman appeared on the screen.[56] The only success the NAACP could point to (apart from the cuts to the film ordered by the censors) was that at a meeting on December 22, the 750-strong New York City Theater Owners' Association went on record as opposing both the Klan and any further showing of *The Birth of a Nation*.[57]

Another state in which attempts to show the film and the Klan would become linked was Kansas. *The Birth of a Nation* had been kept out of the state by governors Arthur Capper (1915–1919) and Henry J. Allen (1919–1923). Allen was a strong opponent of the Klan, which first appeared in Kansas in 1922. Under his successor, Jonathan M. Davis, attempts were made to lift the ban on *Birth*. A first appeal to the governor in June 1923 to permit the showing of the film was met by vigorous protests from the NAACP and the Topeka *Daily Capital*, published by former governor (now U.S. senator) Arthur Capper.[58] At the beginning of December, however, the NAACP was informed that the state censorship board, presumably with Davis's prior sanction, had reversed its earlier stance and given its approval to the picture.[59] NAACP committees lobbied the governor both before and after the board's decision, presenting him at the second meeting with a copy of one of Dixon's books on the Klan and pointing out "several paragraphs" that were clearly there to discourage "inter-racial feeling." C. W. Comagor, chairman of the Kansas City branch of the NAACP, reported that Attorney General Charles B. Griffith, a staunch critic of the Klan, had apparently hinted that if screening the film caused "disturbance, rioting or trouble," he would ask for an injunction to ban it. Comagor also suggested that the national NAACP launch an appeal to all Christians in Kansas against the film. In his reply, Walter F. White warned that "such a move would be exactly what the producers of the film would want. They would get a tremendous amount of free advertising and Klansmen in every city of the state…would immediately want the picture brought to their city." Instead, White advised that NAACP branches fight to have ordinances adopted excluding the film from their locality. He also recommended making clear to the governor that support for *The Birth of a Nation* could well cost him the black vote that might help swing a close election. Finally, since it was "undoubtedly true" that the Klan was behind the movement to show the picture so as to help its recruitment efforts in the state, White proposed seeking allies against the film from other Klan victims, notably Catholics, Jews, and organized labor.[60]

At its peak in 1924, the Klan may have had 100,000 members in Kansas. Yet it also had powerful opponents there, including Governor Allen, Attorney General Griffith, and William Allen White, editor of the *Emporia Gazette*, who got almost 150,000 votes running independently for governor in 1924 on an anti-Klan platform. In early 1925, the Klan was refused a charter and thereafter started to decline in the state.[61] The history of the Klan in Kansas paralleled that in other areas of the United States, where there was a popular revulsion against the persecutions and violence with which the organization had become associated. To advance its agenda, in many states the Klan had become involved in politics and it subsequently began to be torn apart by factionalism and disputes over patronage. There were also several scandals, perhaps the worst being the 1925 conviction of the head of the Indiana Klan, David C. Stephenson, for the kidnap and rape of a secretary. Even the unsuccessful campaign of Democrat Alfred E. Smith, a Roman Catholic, for the presidency in 1928 failed to ignite anything in the way of a real revival. As David M. Chalmers remarks, "by the beginning of the great Depression, the Klan's power and glory were almost gone." The Depression further undermined its efforts at recruitment. As the Memphis *Commercial-Appeal* correctly observed, "Not many persons have $10 to throw away on an oversized nightshirt."[62]

The decline of the Klan probably also accelerated the decline of the film with which it had become most closely associated. The peak earning power of *The Birth of a Nation* was from 1915 to 1922. In 1922, the president of United Artists, Hiram Abrams, was granted permission by the Epoch Company to distribute the film to cheaper theaters, where the admission price would be around fifty cents rather than the $2 that had formerly been the case for the best seats. Until 1926, with the film playing in many theaters and communities it had not previously reached, United Artists had been happy to handle *Birth*'s distribution worldwide. However, in 1926, with receipts falling fast, they handed the task of distributing it back to Epoch.[63] NAACP campaigns against the film continued until 1926: it was banned in Camden, New Jersey, in December 1923; West Newton, Massachusetts, and Montclair, New Jersey, in July 1924; New Britain, Connecticut, in August 1924; and Hartford, Connecticut, in March 1925.[64] In April 1925, the Supreme Court of West Virginia upheld the legislation passed in 1919 to bar the film from the state. Two months later, the Supreme Court of Ohio upheld the ban in that state, and in March 1926 Attorney General Crabbe ruled that the ban also covered private showings of *Birth* to Klansmen and their friends.[65] After 1926, as showings of the film diminished, the NAACP campaign against it wound down. It would spring to life again with the release of a sound version of *Birth* in 1930.

Protesting the Sound Version

After 1922, *The Birth of a Nation* suffered from being shown in less luxurious theaters. One reason for the success of the original road show strategy had been the impressive sound effects and musical score, as played by a full orchestra. In cheaper movie houses, the film's exhibitors were obliged to depend on whatever musical arrangements the management had to offer—an organ or perhaps a small band. The actual *effect* of the film on its spectators must have been considerably less. The innovation of sound across much of the movie industry between 1927 and 1929 probably made *Birth* seem even more passé. But in August 1929, Griffith watched with great interest the effects of a revival of *The Birth of a Nation* (together with *Intolerance* and *Broken Blossoms*) at a Los Angeles theater. Spectators queued for several blocks to see the films. The demand was so great that the screenings were repeated a week later, with equal success. While the movie house involved had done the best it could by having its organ provide a musical accompaniment to the screening of *Birth*, there had been no attempt to use Breil's score. "I think there is no doubt," Griffith wrote to his lawyer and fellow Epoch director Albert H. T. Banzhaf, "that if the *Birth of a Nation* were synchronized, so the small towns could hear the music, you could get a lot of money."[66]

At a meeting of Griffith, Dixon, and Harry and Roy Aitken at New York's Algonquin Hotel, it became clear that neither Dixon nor Griffith had sufficient cash to invest in a synchronized version of the film to incorporate the musical score and sound effects. Once again, as in 1915, the Aitkens agreed to try to raise the money. In some ways, it proved an even harder task: the long campaign against the film by the NAACP and other groups made potential investors leery. At last, George Kemble, who came from a theatrical background in Brooklyn and was a "fan" of the film, managed to raise the $150,000 that was needed and Griffith was asked to edit *The Birth of a Nation* down so that it could be synchronized. Kemble and Griffith collaborated together over the synchronization process, which was carried out by the Western Electric Company and took just under a year.[67]

Opponents of *The Birth of a Nation* were disturbed by press reports that a sound version of the film was in preparation. The director of the Atlanta-based Commission on Interracial Cooperation, a mainly religious organization founded in 1919 to fight lynching and other racial abuses, wrote to Will Hays of the MPPDA in July 1930:

> It would be particularly unfortunate to give this picture a new lease on life at the present time. Because of the financial depression and the political situation, race feeling in the South is very acute. Lynchings this year have gone beyond what they have been in previous years

and we are having almost weekly outbreaks of racial antagonism. The injection of a talking version of "The Birth of a Nation" would greatly intensify this.[68]

In reply to this and a later letter, Hays's secretary Carl Milliken made three essential points. First, *Birth* had "become one of the classics of the motion picture industry." Second, at issue was not a new version of the film but merely the addition of sound to the old print, to which he could see no reasonable objection. Third, with the arrival of the Production Code of 1930, if *Birth of a Nation* was really to be remade, "some changes would undoubtedly be indicated." "My private opinion," Milliken shrewdly added, "is that nothing much will happen and the revived picture will not get much circulation unless a controversy should develop."[69]

A number of members of the NAACP clearly shared Milliken's view. "There are some here," Walter White wrote to the president of the San Francisco branch, "who feel that it might be the part of wisdom not to help advertise the film." White, however, was also conscious that *The Birth of a Nation* "by its very excellence of photography and staging, to which is now added sound effects, make it…a most vicious and dangerous thing."[70] The question of what to do about the new synchronized version of *Birth* was discussed by the NAACP Board of Directors in New York on September 8. In the end, White reported to all branches, it was agreed "that open protest against the picture would only serve to draw public attention to the revival of the film…If the revival does not meet with the necessary financial success it undoubtedly will quietly be withdrawn." The national NAACP consequently recommended that branches approach local authorities and request them to recommend that local movie houses not show the film. It also sought to enlist Jewish and Catholic organizations and various "church bodies" in its strategy of "quiet opposition" to the film.[71]

Over the next fourteen months, the new version of *The Birth of a Nation* was banned in many places: Detroit (Michigan), Portland (Oregon), Omaha (Nebraska), St. Paul (Minnesota), Glen Cove (New York), Montclair (New Jersey), Jersey City (New Jersey), and Philadelphia (Pennsylvania). The statewide bans in Kansas and Ohio were reimposed.[72] Discreet protests were also made in New Castle (Pennsylvania), New Kensington (Pennsylvania), and New York (where Walter White attempted to persuade the police commissioner to suppress it "to prevent its possible use as the means of recruiting or securing followers for a fast dying Ku Klux Klan").[73] No one from the NAACP ever admitted that the organization had perhaps made a mistake by giving so much free publicity to the fight against the film on its initial release. Yet the much quieter 1930–31 campaign proved far more successful in the number of suppressions secured.

Although the synchronized version of the film gained "quite a few bookings" in the first months after its appearance, those involved in its production soon realized that it would be nothing like the money-spinner the original film had been. Kemble ran into financial difficulties distributing the sound version, and the Aitkens, to protect themselves, were forced to cancel their contract with him. The 1930 version, by comparison with its predecessor, may have suffered from the lack of controversy—and thus publicity—attending its release. But the absence of crowd reaction at the première in San Francisco underlined what may have been the real problem: the movies in general had moved on, and what had seemed new and impressive to 1915 spectators was now not just familiar but rather staid and old-fashioned. Audiences of the synchronized version, according to the *New York Times*, liked the action sequences but laughed openly

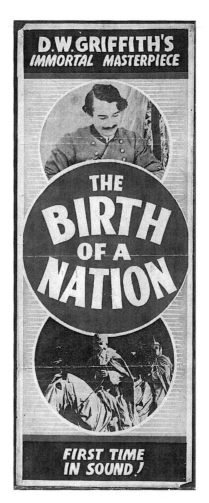

A 1936 advertisement for the sound version of the film. (Library of Congress, Prints and Photographs Division, LC-USZC4-2427)

at the film's archaic sentiments. "Today," claimed the *Outlook*, "it carries but little of its old punch." Because of the addition of the soundtrack, the film had to be speeded up from seventy to ninety frames a minute, and this may also have contributed to *Birth*'s declining appeal. The faster movement gave an air of unreality to the Klan rides. As the *Outlook*'s critic commented, the new speed made the movie appear "jerky, erratic, and ruinous to the eyes."[74]

For the remainder of the 1930s, the new version of *Birth of a Nation* was shown sporadically in a variety of locations. Wherever it appeared, commented one newspaper, it was "militantly picketed by groups of fearless young—and sometimes not so young—white and Negro men and women."[75] As the decade wore on, the NAACP especially became increasingly concerned at attempts to legitimize the film by showing it in nontheatrical venues. In 1935, for example, the New York Young Men's Hebrew Association voted to include it on the basis of "its artistic merit" in a program of evening films. After a brisk letter from Walter White, pointing out that "this notorious picture...more than any other one thing, was responsible for the revival a few years back of the Ku Klux Klan," the screening was canceled.[76] Less successful was the NAACP's attempt to stop the showing of *Birth* to a class taking an adult education course at New York University in the fall semester of 1937. On August 29, Dean Ned H. Dearborn announced that this pioneering course in film studies, aiming "to make possible a comprehensive history and appreciation of the cinema," would include the showing of thirty "film classics," including *Birth*. On September 8, Walter White wrote to Dean Dearborn objecting to the plan to show Griffith's movie. While conceding that *Birth of a Nation* "was one of the pioneers in certain techniques of the film," White argued that it distorted the history of the Reconstruction era, treated blacks in a "vicious" way, had helped revive the Klan, and spread "racial and religious hatreds" which expressed themselves in lynchings and...movements like the Black Legion."[77] Initially, the NAACP campaign to persuade the university to abandon the scheduled showing of the film seemed to be going well. As one sympathetic university figure observed, *Birth*, "regardless of its artistic view," was "one of the most outrageous [films] that has ever been produced from the social point of view." It may have helped that the Klan was in the headlines in mid-September 1937 through the revelations that former senator Hugo Black of Alabama, nominated to the Supreme Court by President Roosevelt, had once been a Klansman.[78] On September 24, a draft NAACP press release claimed that the film had been withdrawn, citing a statement by Dean Dearborn that "a substitute film will be used." Six days later, however, course director Robert R. Gessner wrote to White informing him that such a substitution had not been possible. He went on to emphasize that the film was being shown only because of its "technical and historical importance." But he also promised in his own introductory lecture to point out Griffith's "racial unfairness" and assured White "that the injustice of the picture will be relentlessly scored." Gessner, himself a writer on racial minorities (including Indians and Jews), was clearly embarrassed by *The Birth of a Nation*. But in defending his right to show it, he pioneered the strategy that would be used by most future teachers of the film: while praising *Birth*'s artistic qualities and technical innovations, he simultaneously deplored the racist values it expressed.[79]

For the NAACP, of course, this was not enough. Although many, from Du Bois to White, had been prepared to acknowledge that the movie represented a technical, even an artistic, achievement, they still wanted it suppressed because of its anti-black character and capacity for harm. NAACP spokesmen must have been dismayed in the 1930s to find *Birth of a Nation* beginning to acquire a new form of legitimacy through being presented by film scholars as a huge step forward in the history of American cinema. Even realizing that aspects of the film's racism had become ludicrous over time—one reviewer who watched the October 4 screening at NYU observed "that some of the anti-Negro episodes drew laughs from the audience"—did not weaken their opposition to the film's exhibition "under any circumstances." Thus, the NAACP quickly found itself fighting new screenings at the DeWitt Clinton high school in New York (as part of an adult education course) and at Wesleyan University.[80] It also learned, early in 1938, that the Stone Film Library had addressed a circular to many schools offering them the chance of renting "this film classic of the Civil War." The NAACP, which earlier had managed to persuade the New York Board of Education not to show the film at the DeWitt Clinton school, now managed to convince the board to ban the film throughout the New York school system.[81] In its wider efforts to prevent the Stone Company from exhibiting *Birth*, the NAACP also acquired a most unlikely ally: in July 1938, Thomas Dixon brought suit against the Stone Film Library and its associates, whom he accused of having pirated their copy of the film, to restrain them from any further exhibition of *The Birth of a Nation*.[82] Even more serious, from the NAACP's point of view, was its discovery in early 1939 that the Association of School Film Libraries had included *Birth* among the range of films it offered. Since the new association had been created by the General Education Board, itself set up through the Rockefeller Foundation to improve the standards of black education in the South, this endorsement of *The Birth of a Nation* must have seemed to the NAACP like a slap in the face from a sister organization.[83]

At each stage of its struggle against *The Birth of a Nation*, the NAACP had used different tactics. In 1915, it had tried to put pressure on public authorities to have the film banned. Where it thought such moves might help, it had supported the introduction of censorship. It had also publicized its protest as much as possible. After American intervention in the First World War, it had tried, with more success, to put pressure on state governors and councils of national defense to suppress the film as a wartime measure. From 1923 onward, the NAACP had learned to rely less on public protests and demonstrations and more on the discreet pressuring of public officials. It continued this strategy with considerable success in the fight against the sound version of the film, released in 1930. At the end of the 1930s, however, it found this approach criticized from an unexpected quarter.

In April 1939, Robert E. Allan, proprietor of the Jewel Theater in Denver, Colorado, was arrested for exhibiting *The Birth of a Nation*. The local branch of the NAACP made the original complaint against him: by showing *Birth*, Allen had broken the city ordinance banning motion pictures "which tend to stir up or engender race prejudice." The trial dragged on by means of continuances for several months. Finally, in February 1940, Allen pleaded guilty and was fined $200, with half suspended for sixty days. The importance of the case to the NAACP was that Allen was defended by the American Council of Civil Liberties (ACLU), which argued that the Denver ordinance was unconstitutional and violated the right of free speech. Reviewing simultaneous NAACP attempts to suppress the film in both Denver and Milwaukee, Roger Baldwin emphasized the ACLU's opposition to film censorship per se. "Of course," he wrote to Walter White, "there can be no objection to protests to motion picture distributors nor to picketing. But when appeal is made to the public authorities to take action, it crosses the line of legitimate pressure, and invades the field of censorship."[84] A few days later, when it seemed that the police censors of Detroit might follow the advice of the city's Corporation Counsel and ban *The Birth of a Nation* on the grounds that it was "obscene and indecent," the ACLU's Arthur Garfield Hays wrote promising that "any exhibitor, who is prevented from showing the film on that ground, will have our support in a contest in the courts." Making it plain that "we hold no brief for the kind of intolerance represented by this particular film," Hays at the same time insisted that giving police officials the right to bar films in this way could open the door to all kinds of pressure and prejudice.[85]

The libertarian argument against censoring *Birth* was spelled out in more detail by Roger Baldwin in a letter to *The Crisis* several months later. The drawback with film censorship, Baldwin explained, was that if an anti-black film could be suppressed, so could a pro-black one. Laws designed to protect one minority "always stir up more prejudice than they prevent." He cited the case of the law passed by New Jersey in 1935 to protect Jews by curbing Nazi propaganda—a law that had actually been used by Catholics to persecute Jehovah's Witnesses. (Baldwin was too tactful, or perhaps too politic, to mention that eleven months earlier, Adolph J. Rettig, manager of the Ormont Theater in Orange, New Jersey, had been arrested and charged under the same law with exhibiting "the race-hating film 'The Birth of a Nation.'")[86] The essential point made by Baldwin and the ACLU was that any "machinery of public suppression" necessarily threatened civil liberties. Those who opposed *The Birth of a Nation*, Baldwin argued, "have in their hands the means of boycott, picketing, demonstration, letters of protest to motion picture proprietors—and they should use them. Calling the police or prosecutor into action is quite a different matter. It creates bad legal precedents that can be turned as easily against Negroes as for them."[87]

By the spring of 1939, the NAACP Board of Directors was once again rethinking its strategy in fighting *Birth*. The ACLU's hostility to censorship may have been a major factor in this, but it was not the only one. There were signs, even before the Allan case, that some censorship boards were reluctant to act against a film that was now so old. "In view of the long history of the exhibition of this picture... covering a period of so many years," wrote the director of the New York state censorship board in October 1938, "I do not think that I would be justified in taking action for the cancellation of the [exhibition] permit."[88] At its meeting on May 8, 1939, the board discussed both Roger Baldwin's letter of April 25, outlining the ACLU's opposition to the involvement of public authorities, and a letter from Dr. James J. McClennon, president of the Detroit branch of the NAACP, suggesting an attempt to get Will Hays and the MPPDA to withdraw *The Birth of a Nation* from circulation. It decided both to write to Hays and to "use every means in its power to prevent the showing of the film." The bravado of the second part of the resolution did not prevent some anxiety over how the ACLU might react to the first: Walter White wrote to Roger Baldwin asking for clarification on this point. Baldwin reassured the NAACP on June 17: "We have no complaint about the use of pressure on private agencies such as the Will Hays organization to prevent the showing of 'The Birth of a Nation,' but we do object to the use of police power to stop a film."[89]

Over the next few months, the NAACP and its supporters wrote to Hays protesting the continuing circulation of existing prints of *Birth* and suggestions in some quarters that a new sound version of the film was planned. Hays replied to Rabbi Stephen Wise in March 1940, reassuring him on both points:

> You realize, of course, that the picture mentioned has been on exhibition for twenty-five years. It will doubtless continue to be booked by unaffiliated [to the MPPDA] theatres here and there. Unless a new controversy in the press should develop, which would call attention to it anew, it is my belief that no special public interest in or demand for a remake of this picture is likely to develop.[90]

So far as the NAACP was concerned, the MPPDA proved woefully unmoved by the danger the existing film represented. Its secretary, Carl Milliken, responded to Walter White's insistence "that the... showing THE BIRTH OF A NATION in any form would be disastrous" with the bland assurance that recently "the circulation of the film has not been great, and we have had practically no comment from the public."[91]

Hays and the MPPDA would not act to prevent *Birth*'s continuing distribution, the ACLU remained completely opposed to banning the film through state or local censorship, and the NAACP no longer believed it helpful to generate publicity for the film by mass protest; therefore, the only tactics left in the fight against the film involved trying to persuade theater managers not to show it or attempting to discourage people from attending performances by picketing outside the theater concerned. The latter tactic seems to have been the most effective: in September 1940, a picket line outside the Art Theater in New York "succeeded in reducing the attendance at each performance to little more than a score of persons." On December 2, 1942, only three hours after a picket line was established outside New York's 55th Street Playhouse, the theater management withdrew *The Birth of a Nation* from the screen. Less than two weeks later, Lowell Mellett, chief of Motion Pictures of the Office of War Information (OWI) effectively promised that *Birth* would be prohibited for the remainder of the war. "We are assured," he wrote to the NAACP,

> that the War Activities Committee will take up the matter with any theatre already showing or contemplating the showing of this picture, and there is reason to believe that representations by the Committee will be sufficient in most cases to prevent showings.[92]

In the Second World War, as in the First, *Birth*'s theme of racial conflict invited official suppression because it challenged the dominant public discourses of national unity and social solidarity.

Once the Second World War was over, *The Birth of a Nation* was occasionally revived at art house and other theaters. As soon as it was advertised, however, as Roy Aitken despondently recalled, minority groups organized against it and their protests were often "very effective."[93] It was banned by both the Maryland state board of censors and the city censor of Boston in 1952 and by the Atlanta censors in 1959 and 1961.[94] There would still be controversial showings of the film; it may not have been an entire coincidence that it was playing at a downtown movie house in Little Rock, Arkansas, when the riots against school integration broke out there in 1957.[95] According to Pete Daniel, a typical Klan rally of January 1958 still featured a screening.[96] But an attempted revival at the Lansdowne Theater in Philadelphia in 1965 was greeted by pickets carrying placards insisting "We shall overcome 'The Birth of a Nation'" and asking "Is this Pennsylvania or Alabama?"[97] From the late 1940s on, the main audience for *Birth* would be members of specialist film societies and college students taking courses in art, drama, film, or American history.[98]

The Birth of a Nation and the Social Impact of Cinema

Behind the efforts of the NAACP and other organizations to suppress *The Birth of a Nation* from the very beginning lay the assumption that the film would have bad effects on its spectators, stimulating race hatred and even violence.

Protesters against the film in New York in 1947. (Library of Congress, Prints and Photographs Division, LC-USZ62-84505)

As already noted, May Childs Nerney, the national secretary of the NAACP, told many of her correspondents of a young Southern white man who, on emerging from a screening of *Birth* in New York, remarked that he would like to "kill every nigger I know."[99] This subjective and possibly apocryphal story was accompanied by a number of cases in which the film's exhibition actually did seem to trigger racial violence. In June 1916, for example, *The Crisis* highlighted the case of Henry Brocj, originally from Kentucky. Five weeks after arriving in Lafayette, Indiana, Brocj went to a performance of *The Birth of a Nation*. On leaving the movie house and apparently without any provocation or prior knowledge of his victim, he "fired three bullets into the body of Edward Manson, a Negro high school student, fifteen years old." When the boy died, Brocj was charged with murder.[100] Such random violence seemed to confirm the view of *Birth*'s opponents that the film had terrible effects on audiences. One NAACP observer later noted that "some of the investigators at East St. Louis [a major Illinois race riot of May 1918] found its influence." "I also heard," wrote the same correspondent, "that the mob and lynching at Springfield, M[iss]o[uri], coincided with the exhibit of the film."[101]

Worries about the impact of viewing *The Birth of a Nation* on its spectators fitted well with wider anxieties voiced since the opening of the first nickelodeon in 1905 on the challenge to social order and traditional moral standards of behavior posed by the cinema generally. Many of the movements for censoring or otherwise controlling the movies during the Progressive Era were based on the assumption that films encouraged criminal acts or sexual irresponsibility. In 1916, Harvard psychologist Hugo Münsterberg published a pioneering study analyzing the powerful influences of feature films on their audiences. The techniques used by filmmakers (such as close-ups and cutting), he believed, gave their films great powers of suggestion so far as spectators were concerned. Münsterberg insisted that "the intensity with which the [photo]plays take hold of the audience cannot remain without strong social effects."[102]

Reformers' concerns in this period were focused mainly on children, who were regarded as the most impressionable and therefore the most vulnerable part of the movie audience. During the 1910s and 1920s, a number of surveys attempted to establish the impact of films on children who viewed them.[103] Some tried to establish a straightforward statistical connection between children's attendance at the movies and criminal activity of varying kinds. In 1926, for example, Alice Miller Mitchell conducted a survey of over 10,000 Chicago children drawn from three groups: children attending high schools and the last four years of grade schools, juvenile delinquents, and boy and girl scouts. The Mitchell study included one young subject, the inmate of a reformatory, who had committed a series of holdups to pay for his habit of daily movie attendance. This young man's favorite films included *The Birth of a Nation*.[104]

There was an ironic footnote to the demonization of mulattoes in *The Birth of a Nation*. In 1932, Harvard sociologist Caroline Bond Day published a study of 2,537 individuals belonging to mixed-race families in the United States. She found that—making a real contrast with white-only families—only one of her subjects had ever been in trouble with the police. The individual involved was Edward Franklin Frazier who, as a young sociologist, had been arrested for picketing a performance of *Birth of a Nation* outside New York's Capitol Theater in 1921.[105] The early 1930s also saw the completion of an ambitious sociological/psychological project: the series of studies financed by the Payne Fund investigating moviegoing and its effects on young people. Eleven of these studies were published between 1933 and 1935. Their initiator, William H. Short of the National Committee for Study of Social Values in Motion Pictures (later the Motion Picture Research Council), was a fervent advocate of censorship, and the purpose of the studies, as Robert Sklar has commented, was "to get the goods on the movies, to nail them to the wall."[106] In 1933, popular journalist Henry James Forman published *Our Movie-Made Children*, a book in which he summarized the findings of the studies as a whole. As Forman recounted it, impartial scientific research had now finally established what critics of the movies had long asserted: that children were inspired by the films they viewed to embrace anti-social behavior. Moving pictures, Forman argued, especially crime movies, demonstrated criminal techniques in action and helped propel many young people "toward acts of delinquency and crime."[107] The movies not only predisposed some young people toward crime, however. The Payne Fund studies also stressed that they gave their youthful spectators strong and influential stereotypes of certain individuals or racial/ethnic groups. "The depiction of certain characters, nationalities, races, forms of life, etc., in motion pictures," wrote sociologist Herbert Blumer in one of the studies, "is particularly likely to leave an impression on imagery because of their vivid visual presentations... They are likely, further, to be simple and unambiguous, and to be clothed with certain emotional and sentimental qualities which, one calculates, make their appeal somewhat irresistible."[108]

As part of one of the Payne Fund studies, sociologists Ruth C. Peterson and L. L. Thurstone investigated the effect of showing *The Birth of a Nation* on the social attitudes of 434 schoolchildren from Crystal Lake, Illinois. The children, who were drawn from grades six through twelve, were asked in May 1931 to fill out a questionnaire designed to ascertain their attitudes toward African Americans. A week later, they were shown the newly released sound version of *The Birth of a Nation*. The day after viewing the film, they filled out the same questionnaire. The children's attitude had changed enormously by the time of the second survey: they were now far more hostile to, and prejudiced against, black people. Nor did the influence of the film, which provided the most dramatic effect of all those measured by the researchers in their various experiments, prove short-lived. A follow-up survey suggested that much of the changed attitude persisted some five months after the film was first shown.[109] The strength and longevity of this changed attitude, of course, may have reflected not simply the racist power of the film but also the children's lack of knowledge about blacks generally. Little attention was paid to the race issue in (Northern) public discourse of the Depression era, and since there were no blacks among the 3,700 residents of Crystal Lake in 1931, it was probable, the investigators concluded, that very few children "had known or even seen Negroes" before viewing *The Birth of a Nation*.[110] The dramatic impact of the film on the children in the study may be explained at least partly by their earlier lack of knowledge of individual blacks and of the race issue as a whole.

However flawed it may have been, the Peterson and Thurstone study for the first time offered what William H. Short, in a letter to W. E. B. Du Bois, referred to as "scientific and convincing evidence of the harm that has been done to the colored race by the showing of the film 'The Birth of a Nation.'" Short, a former member of the NAACP, argued that the organization's long campaign against the film had been "comparatively ineffective" because the NAACP had been unable to prove the damaging psychological and social effects it alleged. The impending publication of the Peterson and Thurstone book, Short promised Du Bois, would remedy this situation and "put a weapon of considerable value into your hands." Clearly, Short was following his own agenda.

The NAACP appeared to him a possible ally in his censorship campaign. He promised to send the organization a copy of the published study. In return, the NAACP agreed to "make the book known through our press service" and to use the material on *The Birth of a Nation* when protesting against future screenings of the film.[111]

"The studies of the Payne Fund," wrote black scholar Lawrence Reddick a few years later, "document what we have all guessed from our own impressions; namely, that ideas of love, clothes, manners and heroism among adolescents (and others, of course) are directly traceable to movies...It is, therefore, important to inquire into what such a powerful instrument for influencing the attitudes and behavior of so many persons has had to say about the Negro." Reddick set out to explore what he called "the social function of the movie in the realm of race relations."[112] He analyzed 100 films, determining that seventy-five were anti-black, thirteen neutral, and only twelve "definitely pro-Negro." Hollywood's anti-black bias seemed to Reddick a major social and cultural problem, given the emphasis of the Payne Fund studies on the impact of motion pictures on their audiences. He was particularly troubled by *The Birth of a Nation*. Although he recognized the film's aesthetic merits—it was, he declared, "a masterpiece of conception and structure"—he still criticized it for being, "without question, the most vicious anti-Negro film that has ever appeared on the American screen."[113]

As Reddick, in 1944, saw *Birth* still posing a threat to black Americans by stimulating feeling against them, it is worth mentioning that social science would eventually suggest that this threat had virtually disappeared. One of the most fascinating and far-reaching effects of the Peterson and Thurstone Payne Fund study occurred nearly four decades later, after a vast migration of blacks to the North and all the heightened consciousness of racial matters that had been produced by the civil rights movement. A sociological researcher returned to the very same school in Crystal Lake, Illinois, that Peterson and Thurstone had investigated and repeated their survey of the impact of *The Birth of a Nation*, albeit with a somewhat different methodology. This time, using a control group and a revised attitude scale and allowing only three hours between the pre-screening and post-screening questionnaires, the researcher found that the power of the film to instill racial prejudice in children had largely disappeared. Little change was reflected in the children's attitudes before and after they viewed the film: if anything, there was a slight shift toward a more *favorable* perception of African Americans in the later survey.[114]

Communists and Anti-communists Fight over *The Birth of a Nation*

During the late 1930s, as Janet Staiger has shown, *The Birth of a Nation* became caught up in an ongoing argument among members of the American extreme left.[115] This controversy had its origins in the drive of the Committee on Industrial Organization (from 1937, the Congress of Industrial Organization [CIO]) to unionize steel and textile workers in the South. Many of the CIO organizers were either associated or were believed to be associated with communism. Moreover, black support for this new brand of unionization meant that left-wing activists were increasingly drawn to take a position on civil rights issues. During the 1930s, as Thomas Cripps has observed, "blacks became the darlings of the Communist party so that NAACP picket lines regularly drew white radicals who gave an unwarranted Marxist identity" to black protests and attempted to submerge them into their own struggle. At the same time, a much-weakened Ku Klux Klan attempted to revive its fortunes by reinventing itself primarily as an anti-union and anti-communist movement.[116]

The continuing significance of *The Birth of a Nation* for the NAACP, the film's strong associations with the revived Klan, and the Marxist belief in the manner in which the economic base determined a society's superstructure (what Marx referred to as its "social, political and intellectual life")[117] meant that it was almost inevitable, sooner or later, that the film would become a target for communist writers. Beginning in December 1939, David Platt published a series of articles in *The Daily Worker*, the main newspaper organ of the communist party, advancing the thesis that *The Birth of a Nation* had been part of a deliberate attempt by Hollywood, in collaboration with capitalist interests, to rule both whites and blacks by dividing them. However, the timing of this assault—only a few months after the signing of the Hitler-Stalin pact in August 1939—meant that *The Birth of a Nation* would now become both a symbol and a focus of the wider disagreements among American communists and ex-communists. Platt's attempt to use the film to demonstrate a link between racism and class exploitation was challenged in the *New Leader* by filmmaker and writer Seymour Stern. Almost certainly motivated by anti-Stalinism (the agreement with Hitler laying the foundations for the dismemberment of Poland had been preceded by the revelations of the purges and failure in the Spanish Civil War), Stern took issue with this view of the film, arguing that Griffith had been neither reactionary nor racist in making his film and attacking its critics such as Platt as "totalitarians."[118]

Stern's engagement with *The Birth of a Nation* did not end with his articles of 1940. In subsequent decades, as the world changed, he effectively appointed himself chief defender of both Griffith and his most controversial film. In the fall 1946 issue of the British film journal *Sight and Sound*, Peter Noble, an early student of the representation of blacks on film, published an article attacking Griffith as an "idol" with "feet of clay." According to Noble, as well as being a pioneer of cinema, Griffith had been "a pioneer of prejudice" because of "his anti-Negro bias." For all its artistic and aesthetic merits, *The*

Birth of a Nation was guilty of "sheer vicious distortion" that made it the leader among those American movies "which have consciously maligned the Negro race." It had been the first film to dwell (not once but twice) on the theme of the rape of white women by black men. It had offered "monstrous caricatures" of black politicians and servants. It also presented the Ku Klux Klan as the "heroic" rescuers of whites threatened by "black terror." Noble suggested that Griffith later tried to make amends for his treatment of blacks by inserting a shot of a white man kissing a dying black soldier in *Hearts of the World* (1918); but in the immediate postwar period, as the number of lynchings in the South rose and 13 million blacks anxiously waited to see if they were to be allowed to escape "persecution and injustice," he insisted that it was crucial to acknowledge "Griffith's contribution to past prejudice."[119] In the following issue of *Sight and Sound*, responses to Noble from both Griffith and Stern appeared. According to Griffith, his attitude toward blacks had "always been one of affection and brotherly feeling." Still a master of invention, the former director reinvented his own past, complete with mammy figure, to back up this claim. He had, he declared, been "partly raised by a lovable old Negress down in old Kentucky."[120]

While Griffith tried to defend himself by manipulating nostalgia for the past, closely associating himself with the plantation myth and the legend of the "Lost Cause," Stern's defense was carefully crafted to fit with the emerging realities of the Cold War. At the beginning of the 1930s, Stern had been linked with Lewis Jacobs, Harry Platt, and Harry Potamkin as co-founders of *Experimental Cinema*, a left-wing film journal. Potamkin died in 1934, shortly before the final issue of the journal, but the ideas and careers of the surviving three had already begun to diverge by this point. Jacobs would remain an independent left-wing figure. In 1939, he published *The Rise of the American Film*, in which *inter alia* he argued that *The Birth of a Nation* constituted "a passionate and persuasive avowal of the inferiority of the Negro."[121] Platt joined the Communist Party, whose main newspaper published his own attack on Griffith's film. Stern first became a socialist anti-Stalinist before, in the 1940s, staking out a position as a strident anti-communist. Nineteen forty-seven, of course, was a crucial year in both the development of the Cold War and American domestic anti-communism. In March, President Truman requested $400 million in military and economic assistance for Greece and Turkey to help their anti-communist governments and proclaimed what became known as the "Truman Doctrine," offering American aid to all nations threatened by communist aggression or subversion. Meanwhile, the House Committee on Un-American Activities (HUAC) began its investigation into communist subversion in Hollywood. In May, HUAC interviewed its first "friendly" witnesses in secret session; in September, it began the public hearings that led to the identification and later prosecution of the "Hollywood Ten."

Stern, anointed by Griffith around this time as his preferred biographer, would later be dismissed by Richard Schickel as the director's "half-mad acolyte."[122] However, there was nothing half-mad about his attack on Peter Noble in the spring of 1947. Stern's fervid anti-communism, the product of his own political trajectory from left to right, blended well with the atmosphere of the time. He began his defense of Griffith's reputation in *Sight and Sound* with a deliberate attempt to depict Noble as a "red." His criticisms of *The Birth of a Nation*, Stern argued, echoed the "anti-Griffith libel [that before World War II] issued periodically, and often in…identical phrases, from certain publications in the U.S.A. and the U.S.S.R." Elsewhere in his article, he accused Noble of "merely echoing in strangely familiar accents and phrases the astounding false-hoods and unbelievable nonsense on this subject which already have poured in volume from the presses of the N.Y. 'Daily Worker,' the 'New Masses,' the defunct 'Friday' and 'New Theatre.'" Stern paid off another old score by accusing Noble of being greatly influenced by the "errors, falsehoods and fanci-ful misinterpretations" of Griffith to be found in *The Rise of the American Film* by his former colleague on the left, Lewis Jacobs. Much of his article covered ground that was already very familiar to Griffith and the film's defenders: he contended that *Birth* was historically accurate and that it depicted good as well as bad African Americans. He also took the somewhat condescending position that Noble, as a non-American, could not be expected to know very much about American modes of film production. Two aspects of Stern's argument, however, were new. He justified the Klan as a rejection of the "totalitarianism" of radical Northern Republicans, comparing their activities to the resistance movements against the Nazis in France and Norway during the war. In using the term "totalitarianism," of course, he was clearly rejecting Stalinism as much as fas-cism. Finally, Stern contradicted the notion that movies such as *The Birth of a Nation* have effects: films, he maintained, "do not start attitudes or trends in political or social relations; they merely *reflect* them."[123]

While Noble did not deign to reply to Stern directly,[124] his point of view was championed by E. L. Cranstone in the fall 1947 issue of *Sight and Sound*. Cran-stone rejected Stern's argument that the South after the Civil War had been "occupied territory" and that the Ku Klux Klan—"that vile body of terrorists"—had functioned as a "partisan movement." He insisted that Stern's (and Grif-fith's) view of history was eccentric and recommended Howard Fast's novel *Freedom Road* as offering an alternative view of the Reconstruction period. He demolished the argument that because Griffith had made a major contribution to cinematic art, his ideological view of the past was necessarily correct. Cran-stone pointed out that *Birth* had incited riots, its exhibition had been banned by the Museum of Modern Art in New York, and that "tests carried out in Ameri-can schools confirmed that it creates racial bias." Finally, he defended Noble for criticizing Griffith's "anti-racial bias" and his "obvious glorification" of the "loathsome" Klan, and he accused Stern of "red-baiting" through his mentioning that Noble had once acted in a play by communist writer Clifford Odets.[125]

Stern replied to Cranstone, supposedly on behalf of both Griffith and himself, in the spring 1948 issue of *Sight and Sound*. If, in his earlier article, he had at times been subtle in criticizing communist assaults on *Birth of a Nation* and attempting to link Noble with them, he now abandoned all restraint. As the Cold War worsened (there was a communist coup in Czechoslovakia in February 1948), Stern's own anti-communism became irrational and obsessive. Cranstone was accused of vilifying Griffith using "Communist smear tactics." Stern denied that *The Birth of a Nation* exemplified the "'wrong-doing' which Communist fanatics and their partisans have imputed to it." He rejected the idea that anything could be learned from Fast's *Freedom Road*, which he dismissed as "an 'account' of the Reconstruction Period, based on isolated and obscure incidents, by...an American writer recently cited by Congress for concealing the records of a Communist-front group." According to Stern, the riots against *The Birth of a Nation* had often been politically motivated (he cited an attempt by communists to provoke a riot during a recent revival of the film in New York). The refusal of the Museum of Modern Art Film Library to circulate the movie was easily explained by the fact that "almost everyone today knows where the political sympathies of the Film Library lie" and its attempts at political propaganda "are as well known to film students as they are to the Federal Bureau of Investigation." Disingenuously, Stern refused to accept his "reference to Peter Noble as an actor in one of Clifford Odets' rabble-rousing plays" as "Red-baiting." He accused Cranstone of libeling *him* by insisting that he had a "hatred of anything savoring of the progressive." Stern finished by outlining his own beliefs and his opposition to Stalinism, which he described as "loathsome to true democrats" in both the United States and the rest of the world. Clearly, especially by the end of his long letter, Stern was drifting away from the discussion of Griffith and his film toward simple red-baiting and a defense of his own acquired antipathy to communism. The editor of *Sight and Sound* must have thought so too; he followed Stern's piece with a curt note that "This correspondence must now cease."[126]

The war of words fought out between communists and anti-communists over *The Birth of a Nation* did not end there, however. Communist writer V. J. Jerome criticized Griffith's depiction of African Americans again in *The Negro in Hollywood Films* (1950).[127] Stern returned to his attack on communism as the major source of Griffith's problems over *Birth* in articles in the *American Mercury* in 1949 and *Films in Review* in 1956. In the latter, he upped the ante by explaining not only why communists had sought to destroy Griffith but why, in more general terms, they were trying to dominate film scholarship. "Since the Communist movement is as much an ideological and cultural conspiracy as it is an economic, military and political one," he argued, "it is not surprising

that Communists the world over devote considerable time and energy to influencing, and controlling, film criticism and history."[128] It was not simply that
communists identified *The Birth of a Nation* intellectually as a source of racial
and class oppression. They continued to attack it physically, at least until the
late 1970s, most especially when it was screened in association with the hated
Ku Klux Klan.

The Remake Illusion

The Birth of a Nation was so successful in financial terms that inevitably over
time many people would be drawn to the idea of a remake. Roy Aitken recalled
that sometime in the late 1920s, he and his brother, Harry, met Griffith by accident in the lobby of the Algonquin Hotel in New York. The conversation, on the
part of Harry Aitken and Griffith, quickly turned to the possibility of a remake.
The careers of both men by this point were in sharp decline and, reluctantly,
they finally agreed on the impossibility of raising the million dollars Griffith
estimated would be necessary.[129] In early 1933, the *New York Times* printed a
statement by Thomas Dixon that he was trying to have a "talking picture version" of *Birth* made. In response to an anxious letter from the NAACP, Carl
E. Milliken of the MPPDA reported that so far as he was aware, none of the
companies involved in the association had shown any interest in such a film.
When similar anxieties had emerged over the synchronized sound version,
Milliken pointedly added, the NAACP had "wisely refrained from agitation that
might have directed public attention to the picture, with the result that it proved
unsuccessful and received very limited distribution."[130]

Dixon was back in the news four years later with a report in the *News
and Observer* of Raleigh, North Carolina, that he was planning a sequel to *The
Clansman*. The new book, Dixon asserted, would "bring the romance of the
South from Reconstruction days down to 1937." He also added, ominously,
"that various incidents of interracial import since 1900 would be incorporated
into the plot." The title of the new novel, *The Flaming Sword*, was taken from
W. E. B. Du Bois's 1935 book on Reconstruction, which savaged the "Tragic
Era" legend in which Dixon believed. (A major theme of Dixon's book, it was
claimed, would be "the development of communism" among blacks as a consequence of Du Bois's leadership.) Dixon touted the idea that the new story would
be made into a film and the report finished with the vague remark that "some
effort has been made to reproduce 'The Birth of a Nation' as a sound picture."
The NAACP's first reaction to the news was to think of making a formal protest
to Will Hays over any attempt to film a story by Dixon, but it also contacted Jonathan Daniels, editor of the *News and Observer*, for more information. Daniels
explained that Dixon was desperate to raise money, as he had lost a good deal
in real estate speculations, and hinted that the story probably originated with

his new agent, Virginia Nowell of Raleigh, whom he described as "a promoter somewhat extraordinary." Thus reassured, the NAACP decided not to take any action.[131] In reality, the final sentence in the *News and Observer*'s report had been more accurate than either Daniels or the NAACP realized. In the fall of 1937, Dixon, Griffith, and the Aitkens had begun seriously to discuss remaking *The Birth of a Nation* as a sound picture. Dixon asked for $10,000, plus royalties, for writing a new screenplay. Griffith and Harry Aitken agreed that Griffith would direct the remake and have responsibility for hiring the actors; Aitken's job would be to raise enough money for filming to begin. After several weeks of "intensive selling," however, Harry had promises of only $100,000. With Griffith believing that the minimum necessary to begin work was $400,000, or about half the estimated final cost, the project had to be abandoned for the time being.[132]

Rumors of a remake continued. In January 1938, Louella Parsons reported that Griffith would direct a new version "financed by Eastern capital" with Wally Ford as the "Little Colonel." A few weeks later, Cecil B. DeMille announced over the radio that he proposed to produce his own revised *Birth of a Nation* for Paramount. In July, as part of his court case against the Stone Film Library, Dixon said he was preparing a new talking version "to be produced by an independent company."[133] In 1940, the original producers seem to have made another attempt to get a remake under way. The principal catalyst—as Harry Aitken admitted on his way to see Dixon in North Carolina—was the enormous popularity of David O. Selznick's movie production of Margaret Mitchell's best-selling novel, *Gone With the Wind*. Aitken obviously hoped that the success of *Gone With the Wind* would create interest in the remake; he even suggested that *Birth* was "in effect" a sequel to Selznick's film, dealing in more detail "with the Carpetbag era that was only briefly touched on in 'Gone With the Wind.'" But his announcement of the planned remake "in technicolor and sound" provoked a fierce reaction from the NAACP. Walter White wrote to Will Hays on March 21 urging him to "use the full power of your office as President of the Motion Picture Producers-Distributors of America to prevent the remaking of this film." Over the next few weeks, the MPPDA was deluged with letters of protest from a large number of organizations, including the American Jewish Congress, the Commission on Interracial Cooperation, the Catholic Interracial Council, the Methodist Federation of Social Service, the Society of Friends' Committee on Race Relations, the National Council of Women, and the Descendants of the American Revolution.[134]

Critics of the proposed remake attacked both the idea itself and its timing. "The power of the silent version to arouse bitterness against...the Negro has been amply demonstrated," declared one writer. "The sound version would multiply that power many times." The fact that the Second World War had begun just over six months earlier was also very much in the minds of protestors. One wrote of being "unspeakably shocked and horrified by the brutalities of national and racial intolerance conspicuous of late in certain countries." The threat to democracy, both abroad and at home, suggested that "national unity" and "good will"—not a new version of a racist, socially divisive film—were what the times required.[135]

MPPDA officials replied to such protests by emphasizing that no proposal for a remake of *The Birth of a Nation* had been made by any member of their Association and that any such movie would have to conform to the Production Code of 1930 and consequently be approved by the Production Code Administration set up in 1934. Carl Milliken, now going much further than he had in response to the sound version of 1930, also assured the National Council of Women that although *Birth* had been "acclaimed a masterpiece in its day" it "could not at the present time be approved" by the PCA "without very far-reaching changes." Without such a seal of PCA approval, no film could be shown in a theater owned by any member of the MPPDA, effectively excluding it from most of the best "first-run" movie theaters in the United States. While MPPDA spokesmen qualified their comments by explaining that they had no control over the actions of nonmembers of the association, the assurances they had given were convincing enough for Walter White a few weeks later to claim that the protests of the NAACP and its allies had effectively "scotched" the idea of a remake.[136]

What really seems to have happened in 1940 is that Harry Aitken was floating a trial balloon. After the failed attempt at a remake in 1937, he had concluded that the only way such a remake might now happen would be for him to persuade some independent producer to finance it. The popularity of *Gone With the Wind* had already stimulated interest in the Civil War era and Aitken obviously hoped that his own announcement would create sufficient public controversy (and hence publicity) to suggest to such a producer that the project, while risky, was potentially very profitable. The behind-the-scenes tactics of the NAACP and its allies frustrated this hope. The closest the remake issue came to becoming a public controversy occurred with the publication on May 20 of a Walter Winchell gossip column. Winchell claimed that "communists are behind the artificial flood of protests sent directly or indirectly to the Hays Office. They object to the reissuing of 'The Birth of a Nation' film. The real squawk is that it is 'too patriotic.'" Denying that any of the protestors were "communists," Walter White summarized NAACP strategy by informing Winchell that

> We have given no publicity to the protests against the remaking of the picture because we have learned that the mysterious forces who are trying to get the film remade want just the kind of publicity that you have given them in your column today in order to build up a "demand" for the film by Kluxers, Nazis and potential anti-Semites, anti-Catholics and anti-Negroes.[137]

The kind of independent producer Harry Aitken was looking for would have had to be strong enough—and brave enough—to stand up to both the MPPDA and the PCA. One of the few who might have done so was David O. Selznick. Completely unknown to the Aitken brothers, a few months before buying the film rights for *Gone With the Wind*, Selznick had apparently considered remaking *Birth*. He abandoned the idea in the end because he became convinced it "would be difficult, if not impossible, to clarify for audiences the difference between the old Klan and the Klan of our times." Both as a Jew and as someone with no desire to produce an anti-black film, Selznick balked at key elements of *Birth*'s narrative.[138] He would insist, during the filming of *Gone With the Wind*, on asking the NAACP for advice to avoid exactly the kind of controversy associated with Griffith's earlier film. Yet as late as October 1941, he commented to story editor Katherine Brown that remaking *The Birth of a Nation* "isn't a bad idea!"[139]

Although Dixon died in 1946 and Griffith in 1948, the Aitken brothers lived out their retirement in Waukesha, Wisconsin, still dreaming of the day when *Birth* would be remade. In 1954, they were approached by Phil A. Ryan acting on behalf of a syndicate of banks and movie executives put together by financier Ted Thal to see if they would sell their rights to the picture. The Aitkens appear to have believed that they were about to be offered anything up to a million dollars. They agreed (for a nominal price) to an option on their rights to the *silent* version of the movie. The syndicate then approached Dixon's widow in an attempt to negotiate an option on her rights. Nothing happened for several months. Then, on December 2, 1954, *Film Daily* announced the planned remake: it was to be widescreen, in color, with a cast of 15,000. The new film, it was estimated, would cost $8,000,000 and the screenplay would be written by Dudley Nichols, whose writing credits included *The Informer* (1935), for which he received an Academy Award; *Stagecoach* (1939); and *Pinky* (1949). The Aitkens were worried that the story claimed (wrongly) that the rights to *Birth* had already been acquired from them and Dixon's widow for $750,000. They were even more dismayed by the "avalanche of publicity," much of it unfavorable, that followed. Roy Wilkins of the NAACP fired off a telegram claiming that the remake was "an effort...to encourage the 1876 rather than the 1955 view of Negroes as American citizens." Walter Winchell had obviously changed his mind since 1940: he "deplored" the planned remake of a film that had "exploited bigotry" and "deserves to be buried." Trade sources emphasized the difficulties of the project: to make a film about the Klan (which was now "thoroughly discredited") would alienate large elements of the moviegoing audience—Jews and Catholics as well as African Americans. It would have problems both getting a Production Code seal and passing state censorship boards. In any event, Dudley Nichols could not be persuaded to try his hand at producing a workable screenplay, and facing a storm of adverse publicity and with no major studio or director lined up, the Thal deal fell apart.[140]

The failure of the 1954 project was a major disappointment for the Aitken brothers. They continued to promote the original *Birth of a Nation* as actively as they could, hoping that someday someone would buy their rights and remake the picture. In 1956, at the age of seventy-eight, while discussing a showing of the film with a theater manager in Chicago, Harry had a fatal heart attack. In 1959, another Hollywood syndicate approached Roy with an offer for his rights in the film, but he thought the offer derisive and rejected it.[141] Five years later, Raymond Rohauer, who had made a specialty of acquiring the rights to old movies, persuaded Dixon's second wife and widow to permit him to approach Roy Aitken on her behalf to demand an accounting of the revenues from *The Birth of a Nation*.[142] Essentially, by threatening Roy with legal action, Rohauer managed to blackmail him into selling Epoch to Jay Ward Enterprises, a company hitherto known mainly for its cartoon series ("Rocky," "Bullwinkle"). At this point, the formal involvement of the Aitken family with *Birth*—an involvement that had lasted half a century—finally came to an end.[143]

For Rohauer, it was by no means the end of the story. He now sued Paul Killiam, who had bought the claims to the Griffith estate at an auction in 1959, and the Museum of Modern Art for infringing Epoch's copyright in *Birth of a Nation*.[144] The suit, heard in 1975 in New York's Foley Square courthouse, essentially revolved around the issue of who owned the rights to the film. (*Birth* had been copyrighted twice, once by Griffith and later by Epoch.) The defense attempted to prove that Griffith had been the author of the film and consequently "the only one with a legal right to copyright and renew that copyright." They called as witnesses Lillian Gish (Elsie Stoneman), Joseph Henabery (Abraham Lincoln), and film critic Andrew Sarris, then a leading exponent of the so-called "auteur theory" of film production. The jury, unimpressed, decided that Epoch owned the rights to the film. Rohauer's triumph, however, was very brief: two months later, in August 1975, the U.S. Circuit Court of Appeals overturned the verdict and decided that Griffith was both the creator and legal "author" of his film. Epoch had no right to the copyright; its renewal of the copyright was consequently invalid; and because Griffith had failed to renew his copyright, the film was now in the public domain. A few months later, the U.S. Supreme Court refused to review the decision of the lower court.[145]

Since 1975, therefore, with all rights in *The Birth of a Nation* reverting to the American public, it has theoretically been possible for anyone to remake the film. Practically, however, in today's more pluralistic—and at the same time more politically correct—world, a new version of so controversial and racist a film is almost inconceivable. Thus, although "director" Dalton Freed (Maurice Sonnenberg) in Woody Allen's *Celebrity* (1998) claims he is planning to remake *The Birth of a Nation* in "an all-black version," Manthia Diawara has linked the chase sequence in Steven Spielberg's *The Color Purple* (1985) to Gus's chase of Flora in *Birth of a Nation*,[146] and Michael Moore appropriated actual images of Gus and Flora in *Bowling for Columbine* (2002) to reinforce his argument that the media fomented fear of blacks, the closest to any kind of remake is likely to remain the simulated footage of some of the Ku Klux Klan sequences from *Birth* in Robert Zemeckis's *Forrest Gump* (1994).

After-lives

For David W. Griffith, *The Birth of a Nation* marked a clear turning point in his career. Before *Birth*, he had directed 460 films in seven years. After *Birth*, in the sixteen years of active filmmaking that remained to him, he would produce only twenty-seven. One reason for the disparity in numbers, of course, was that most of the films from the early part of his career were Biograph one-reelers. Griffith had already started to produce longer films before 1915, but his shortest film after *The Birth of a Nation* was six reels. His final fourteen films, released between 1921 and 1931, were all between nine and twelve reels.[147] *Birth* created expectations, both for Griffith and his audiences, that helped make it impossible to go back to the Biograph style of filmmaking.

Judith of Bethulia (1913) had already demonstrated Griffith's fondness for the epic and spectacular; *Birth* encouraged this taste. The immense commercial success of the film, moreover, fostered Griffith's faith that his way of doing things was the right one: he would seek to preserve as much as possible of his directorial independence in the years ahead, he would try for as long as he could to make films using a company of actors rather than individual stars, he would continue to see big pictures as the way to big profits, and he would consider road shows the most direct means of realizing such profits. All these views would put him significantly at odds with the way the film industry was developing after 1915 and in combination with other errors of judgment on his part would weaken his reputation so much that he would make no more films for the last seventeen years of his life.

The initial evidence of the impact of *Birth of a Nation* on Griffith's output came with the fate of *The Mother and the Law*, a short feature he had begun work on before *Birth* was released. When it was completed, sometime in mid-1915, it already seemed a throwback to an earlier time: Lillian Gish, present at a screening for Griffith and members of his team, remembered that "we all agreed with him that the film was too small in theme and execution to follow *The Birth*."[148] During the fall of 1915, Griffith tentatively began to revise *The Mother and the Law* and subsume it into a wider work: a study of prejudice and bigotry in four distinct historical epochs. *Intolerance* (1916), as a French critic noted, "evoked the fall of Babylon, the death of Christ, Saint Bartholomew's [massacre] and the life of an American worker all at the same time."[149] With its spectacular sequences, including Belshazzar's feast, the new film cost almost four times as much as *Birth*. In the beginning, it seemed likely to follow the same path as *Birth*: previewed in Riverside, shown at the Liberty Theater in New York, for the first three or four months it was successful at the box office. Then audiences began to fall away, and in the end, the film was a commercial failure. (Wark Productions, the company Griffith had formed to produce and distribute *Intolerance*, would go bankrupt six years later in 1921.) Ultimately, *Intolerance*, whatever its impressive spectacular effects, was too fragmented a film to appeal to the kind of mass audience *Birth* had attracted. Louis Delluc, the French critic quoted above, put his finger very accurately on Griffith's failure to unite the four stories into any coherent artistic narrative when he irreverently observed that for many people, the picture "quickly turned into an inexplicable chaos in which Catherine de Medici visited the poor of New York just as Jesus was baptizing the courtesans of Balthazar and Darius' armies were beginning to assault the Chicago elevated."[150]

In 1917, Griffith finally deserted the Aitkens to sign up with their principal adversary, Adolph Zukor. His contract obliged him to direct six feature films for Zukor's Paramount-Artcraft distribution company, each to cost a maximum of $175,000. The contract also allowed him to make a "big picture" which Zukor would finance, in return for the general distribution rights after Griffith's own company organized the initial road show release. Griffith opted to make this larger picture straight away. A few months earlier, he had been approached by the British government with an invitation to make a feature film about the war: the result would be *The Hearts of the World* (1918). The director spent six months in Europe, mostly in England but with two trips to France, including a visit to the trenches. He was fêted by the British literary and political establishment, including Prime Minister David Lloyd George. He was even permitted to film Queen Alexandra and various society ladies, including Lady Diana Manners and Elizabeth Asquith, and this footage would appear in his next Artcraft release, *The Great Love* (1918).[151] *The Hearts of the World*, like *The Birth of a Nation*, was structured around the wartime experiences of two American families, in this case expatriate neighbors in a small French town. Again, like *Birth*, the battles scenes came in the middle of the film and Lillian Gish, as the heroine, was once again threatened by rape (this time the would-be rapist was a German spy).[152] Griffith's biographer has underlined the main problems with this film: it does not really offer "any realistic sense of this war as it was actually fought" and its final part was little more than "a creaky and unpersuasive" melodrama. On the other hand, it did quite well at the box office, making a profit of more than $600,000 on its initial release.[153]

Of the six "normal" Artcraft films Griffith delivered under his contract with Zukor, two—*The Great Love* and *The Greatest Thing in Life* (1918)—have been lost. At least one other—*Scarlet Days* (1919), his final Western—according to Scott Simmon is "best forgotten."[154] But three of the other films are worthy of note. *A Romance of Happy Valley* (1919) and *True Heart Susie* (1919) were both simple, well-made rural romances demonstrating that Griffith could still produce intimate, more personal films as well as spectacular epics. *The Girl Who Stayed at Home* (1919), by contrast, is perhaps the least convincing of all Griffith's war movies. It is important, however, because it is the first film in which Carol Dempster replaces Lillian Gish (who had influenza) as the leading lady. Dempster, who was Griffith's lover, would be the heroine of many of his films up to 1926. She was neither especially beautiful nor an especially good actress. The moviegoing public never seems to have warmed to her and so Griffith's insistence on using her for so long helped weaken his own position.

Gish might have been replaced as Griffith's personal favorite but the two continued to work together until 1921. Immediately after *The Girl Stayed Home* they collaborated on *Broken Blossoms* (1919), in some respects the most remarkable film Griffith ever made. A story of implicit (but not actual) miscegenation between a Chinese man and a young white girl brutalized by her father, the movie ended tragically with the death of all three. It showed a rare sensibility that impressed both critics and filmgoers, who made it Griffith's most profitable film after *The Birth of a Nation*. This commercial success was all the more welcome because in February 1919, Griffith joined with Mary Pickford, Charlie Chaplin, Douglas Fairbanks, and William S. Hart to form United Artists (UA). *Broken Blossoms* became the first Griffith film to be distributed by UA. At this stage UA was *only* a distribution agency, and its founders needed to raise the money if they were to make their films themselves; so shortly thereafter Griffith also signed an agreement with First National—founded to check Zukor's growing power over the movie industry—to finance and distribute his next three films.[155]

In 1920, Griffith moved temporarily with most of his company to Florida, where he produced *The Idol Dancer* (1920) for First National and *The Love Flower* (1920) for United Artists. Both were essentially old-fashioned melodramas, as was *Way Down East* (1920), a film based on a highly popular classic of the legitimate stage. With its nostalgia for a simpler time and marvelous storm sequence at the end, *Way Down East* provided Griffith "with his last major box office success." That success, Richard Schickel argues, would in the end prove very much a mixed blessing as it concealed fatal flaws in the Griffith approach to filmmaking. For 1920 was also the year in which Griffith acquired his own studio by buying the Henry Flagler estate near Mamaroneck, New York, and converting it for his uses. While in some ways a logical development of Griffith's "company" approach to filmmaking, establishing an independent studio solely for producing films was significantly out of step with the way much of the American movie industry was now evolving. By the early 1920s, Famous Players-Lasky, Fox, and Universal were well on their way to being vertically integrated industrial conglomerates. They produced sufficient numbers of films to sign exclusive contracts with movie houses to provide with "blocks" of movies, and they were beginning to build up their own theater chains. Griffith's studio was outside this system—as, at this stage, was also United Artists. With the profits of his earlier films tied up in buying and setting up the studio itself, his only hope of long-term survival, as Schickel points out, "was to produce cheaply and quickly, using the cash flow from one production to finance the next." The profitability of *Way Down East* managed to hide this reality for a time.[156]

Between the première of *Way Down East* in September 1920 and the summer of 1924, Griffith released five more films. All were distributed by United Artists. None gave Griffith the profits he needed to break free from his increasing mountain of debt. All either lost money or failed to make money fast enough to help Griffith's increasingly desperate struggle to keep his studio going. *Dream Street* (1921), a picture dealing with a romantic triangle, lost around $150,000. *Orphans of the Storm* (1921), which featured Lillian Gish for the last time in a Griffith film, was essentially the story of a lost child set against the background of the French Revolution. It cost almost a million dollars to produce, and although it did quite well at the box office, the profits it accrued were slow in arriving. *One Exciting Night* (1922), a mystery film with elements of comedy, included a hugely expensive storm sequence that doomed the film's financial prospects. *The White Rose* (1923), which brought Mae Marsh temporarily back into the Griffith orbit, was the mildly sensational story of a clergyman's sexual transgressions. It made back more than double its production costs, although again the profits were slow to arrive. Finally, Griffith was drawn to make *America* (1924), a spectacle set against the backcloth of the American Revolution, which cost nearly $900,000 to produce. When the film was released to tepid reviews, it rapidly became clear that Griffith's own studio was doomed and the Mamaronek estate would need to be sold.[157]

The game of "what if …?" is always intriguing to play. Griffith might have kept his studio if he had been less drawn to the spectacular. This quality, first seriously in evidence with *Judith of Bethulia*, had been encouraged by *Birth of a Nation*. It was a major influence on the making of *Intolerance*, *Orphans of the Storm*, and disastrously, *America*. Griffith might have kept his studio if he had been less profligate as a director; his wish, particularly after the success of *Birth*, to spend whatever was necessary to achieve the effect he wanted meant that the budgets for his pictures were rarely adhered to. (Robert W. Chambers, the scenarist for *America*, wrote an amusing "playlet" that focused on Griffith's lack of concern for costs as part of his growing megalomania; at one point, he had Griffith's assistants gold-plating the Woolworth building in case the director needed to shoot there).[158] Griffith might have kept his studio if he had been less committed, in light of the experience with *Birth*, to road showing. Road shows were expensive to organize, slow to produce income for less spectacular or well-publicized pictures, and ultimately cut profits by delaying general release. Griffith might have kept his studio if he had been less loyal to Carol Dempster and less determined to force her on an unwilling moviegoing public. By the same token, his films might have made more money if he had been willing to develop or use more recognizable "stars." Griffith might also have kept his studio if he had been prepared to increase his output by collaborating with another small studio; he twice turned down such offers from William Randolph Hearst, who had founded Cosmopolitan Productions to showcase the acting talents of his mistress, Marion Davies.[159] Finally, Griffith might have kept his studio if United Artists had been able, as it was much later, to help more in financing its own productions.

"What if …?"—but in 1924, Griffith was confronted with pressing financial realities. Secretly, in June he abandoned UA to sign a contract to direct four films for Zukor's Famous Players-Lasky. Zukor even guaranteed a bank loan so that Griffith could produce a last, contractually required film for UA. This film, *Isn't Life Wonderful* (1924), shot partly on location in Europe, was a simple, unaffected study of a family's struggle to survive in postwar Germany. In the end, for Griffith to cut his links with UA proved harder than he expected, until the still-obliging Zukor agreed that UA would distribute the first film made under his new contract. This was *Sally of the Sawdust* (1926), a fairground comedy starring W. C. Fields in his first major screen role. It was, notes Richard Schickel, Griffith's "first quickly and distinctly profitable picture since *Way Down East.*" Griffith, however, was now a studio contract director and Famous Players compelled him, against his will, to direct *That Royle Girl* (1925), revolving around the story of a Chicago flapper who solves a murder case. The picture failed to make a profit, mainly because its cost had been inflated by an expensive storm sequence Griffith insisted on adding. When his next film, *The Sorrows of Satan* (1926), also came in $300,000 over budget and rapidly proved a commercial disaster, Zukor decided to cancel Griffith's contract.[160]

Although the Famous Players experience had demonstrated that Griffith did not fit easily into the disciplined world of studio production—and, to an extent, film critics had started to turn against him—his career did not end in 1926. In early 1927, he accepted an invitation from Joseph Schenck to rejoin United Artists. Unfortunately for Griffith, none of his first three films for UA could really be accounted a success. *Drums of Love* (1928), a depressing "love triangle" story, did poorly at the box office. *The Battle of the Sexes* (1928), essentially a plagiarism of Griffith's own 1914 film of the same title, was a curious combination of comedy and tragedy. Reviewers found it confused and amateurish.[161] *Lady of the Pavements* (1929), based on a scenario by Sam Taylor,[162] explored the themes of love, faithlessness, and revenge. Reviewers on the whole liked the star of the film, "Whoopee Lupe" Velez, much better than they liked the film itself. By this point, Schenck had probably decided to get rid of Griffith, yet he still allowed him, though with much more stringent financial conditions, to make his first "talkie": *Abraham Lincoln* (1930).[163]

Based on a script by young poet Stephen Vincent Benét, this project allowed Griffith to revisit for the last time *Birth of a Nation*–style territory. The actual making of the picture, however, involved a nightmarish war between Benét and Griffith on the one hand and UA producer John Considine Jr. on the other. In the end, Griffith virtually withdrew from the film, leaving its editing, dubbing, and scoring primarily in the hands of Considine. Instead of fighting for his film, Griffith preferred to concentrate on shooting a trailer for the new synchronized version of *Birth of a Nation*—a film in which both he and Walter Huston (who had played Lincoln in the 1930 film) appeared. Reviewers, who Schickel suggests may have felt guilt over their treatment of Griffith in recent years, tended to be highly positive in their treatment of *Abraham Lincoln*. Some suggested that Griffith had now returned to a position of leadership in the movie industry. In reality, the conclusion Griffith had drawn from the experience and the film's uneven performance at the box office was that he should withdraw completely from the studio system of production. He had no intention, ever again, of trying to satisfy studio factions. Henceforth, he would make a film only if he controlled the whole process, and he was prepared to wait until the right project came along.[164]

Griffith's attitude might have been realistic in 1914, with *The Birth of a Nation* just around the corner. It was deeply unrealistic in 1930. What destroyed his career finally, however, was the selection of his next film. About as far from *Birth of a Nation* as it was possible to get, *The Struggle* (1931) was an old-fashioned melodrama about alcoholism. Griffith borrowed heavily to finance it and the film was a commercial and critical disaster. Although Griffith would be honored by filmmakers (he received a special Oscar in 1936) and directors such as George Cukor, Preston Sturges, and Jean Renoir paid homage to him, he would never make another film. David O. Selznick did think privately of hiring Griffith as an adviser to George Cukor on *Gone With the Wind*. He also considered asking him to direct the second-unit shooting of "the evacuation of Atlanta and other episodes of the war and Reconstruction period." In the end, however, he seems to have decided that Griffith was simply too controversial a figure to associate with his greatest production.[165] During the last seventeen years of his life (he died in July 1948), Griffith was a virtual exile from the movies he had done so much to pioneer. Looking back over the rest of his career, he must have known that he had never succeeded in reproducing the kind of success he had enjoyed with *The Birth of a Nation* in 1915–16.

The vast profits generated by *The Birth of a Nation* also inspired Thomas Dixon to make films of his own, and at least in the short run, they provided him with the resources to gratify this ambition. During the summer of 1915, the novelist moved to Los Angeles where he established the "Dixon Studios" at Sunset Boulevard and Western Avenue. Most of Dixon's films over the next few years would have a clear didactic purpose. His first, *The Fall of a Nation* (1916), a clear attempt to cash in on the success of *Birth*, was a warning against pacifism and a plea for American military preparedness. An original feature of the film was that it was accompanied by a completely original musical score by Victor Herbert.[166] Almost superstitiously, Dixon followed the traditions set by *The Birth of a Nation*. He filmed battle scenes (at a cost of $31,000) where those for *Birth* had been staged (Universal Field, now part of the Forest Lawn Cemetery).

The film premièred at Clune's Auditorium and had its East Coast opening at the Liberty Theater. The trade press was enthusiastic and the movie made a total profit of $120,000, but it never became a runaway success in the way that Griffith's film had done.[167] The next three film projects Dixon was associated with were all versions of novels he had written. *The Foolish Virgin* (1915), dealing with modern womanhood, was made into a film in 1917. (It proved so successful, it was remade in 1924.) *The One Woman* (1903) examined the links between socialism and the "new woman"; it was released in 1918. *Comrades* (1909), a novel attacking communism, became the film *Bolshevism on Trial* (1919), which despite its topicality—it came out in the same year as the "Red Scare"—was not very successful.

In February 1921, Dixon's own production company, which had actually produced only one film, *The Fall of a Nation*, went bankrupt. Curiously, this seems to have had a liberating effect on Dixon. Although he would direct only one more film, he had already written the screenplay for *Wing Toy*, a film about white-oriental miscegenation released in January 1921. In the next five years, he would write screenplays for ten more movies (one of which, *The Mark of the Beast*, 1923, he would also produce and direct). Some of these, such as *Thelma* (1923), were melodramas. Others were Westerns: *Where Men Are Men* (1921), *Bring Him In* (1921), *The Trail Rider* (1925), and *The Gentle Cyclone* (1926). All but two were adaptations of stories by other authors. In the history of the cinema, the most interesting of Dixon's 1920s films was *The Mark of the Beast*. An intense psychological drama, involving just five characters, it looked forward in many respects to 1940s Hollywood films such as *Lady in the Dark* (1944) dealing with psychoanalysis. It also featured high-contrast lighting of the kind that would also come to be associated with noir films of the 1940s (Dixon was attempting, he thought, to bring the movies "up to date"). The film, which may simply have been too different for audiences of 1923 to appreciate, failed at the box office.[168]

Essentially, Dixon's involvement in the movie industry had ended by early 1926, though he would also contribute to the story that was the basis for *Nation Aflame* (1937), an anti-Klan picture made with the encouragement of the PCA's Joseph Breen.[169] The arrival in 1927 of the era of the "talkies" spelled the finish of Dixon's screenwriting career: his novels had already shown that he was rather mediocre at reproducing dialogue. In the first half of the 1920s, despite his film work, Dixon had continued to produce a steady succession of novels that reworked earlier writings on the Civil War (*A Man of the People: A Drama of Abraham Lincoln*, 1920, and *The Man in Gray: A Romance of North and South*, 1921), or Reconstruction (*The Black Hood*, 1924), or modern relationships (*The Love Complex*, 1925). In the summer of 1925, however, the deaths within a few weeks of one another of his elder and younger brothers made him eager to occupy himself with something new. Soon afterward he became involved in a plan to develop Wildacres, a beautiful area in western North Carolina, into a colony for creative people. By 1928, this real estate project, into which Dixon had sunk most of his money, was going well. Then came the collapse of the property boom, the stock market "Crash" of 1929, and the beginning of the Depression. Dixon lost nearly all his fortune and had to sell his home on Riverside Drive, New York; by 1934 he was describing himself as "penniless."[170]

Being Dixon, he turned to writing and lecturing as a way of making ends meet. In 1929, he published *The Sun Virgin*, a romance set against the background of the Inca civilization in Peru. It did poorly. In 1932, together with Harry M. Daugherty, he produced *The Inside History of the Harding Administration*, a defense of the late president.[171] Working on this book rekindled Dixon's old interest in politics. In the 1932 presidential election, he campaigned for Franklin D. Roosevelt and for the next two years was a strong supporter of the New Deal. By 1936, however, his politics had changed: believing the New Deal had been infiltrated by communists, he supported Roosevelt's Republican opponent. A year later, he was rewarded by being given the sinecure clerkship of a federal court for the eastern district of North Carolina by a Republican judge.[172] In February 1939, Dixon had a stroke. He made a partial recovery and with the help of his second wife, Madelyn (whom he had first met when she played the lead in *The Mark of the Beast*), he finished his last novel, *The Flaming Sword* (1939). This curious work was intended as a sequel to *The Clansman*. The heroine, Angela Cameron Henry, is the daughter of Ben Cameron and Elsie Stoneman, both now deceased. Angela at one point is hired, in a splendid piece of self-reflexivity, to promote *The Birth of a Nation*! Although this novel, together with *Birth* and Dixon's earlier novels, has a black rapist, the main story revolves around the successful attempt of black communists (led by W. E. B. Du Bois) to take over the United States by force. *The Flaming Sword* was a critical and financial failure. In the last years of his life, Dixon was an invalid, frequently wracked by pain. He was also poor and largely forgotten by an American public that had once flocked to read his novels or see his plays. He died in April 1946.[173]

Harry and Roy Aitken's careers were pretty much all downhill after *Birth of a Nation*. Even though the board of the Mutual Company had declined to finance the making of *The Birth of a Nation*, it resented the fact that the Aitkens had organized a separate company (Epoch) to handle the distribution of what had turned out to be an immensely profitable film. This grievance helped bring other long-simmering disputes to a head and led to a board-room coup in which first Roy and then Harry Aitken were removed as directors of the company. With his usual prescience, Harry, seeing which way the wind was blowing, had already taken the precaution of organizing the Triangle Picture Corporation with himself as chairman.[174] As its name indicated, Triangle brought together the three leading directors in America at this time: Griffith, Thomas Ince, and Mack Sennett. On the basis of the contracts he made with the three, Harry was able to sign up 600 theaters in Triangle's first three months: in a pioneering version of the block-booking system, theater owners committed themselves to take all their pictures from Triangle's exchanges.[175] As Richard Koszarksi notes, however, this early move toward vertical integration of the movie industry "began to unravel almost immediately." To get the Triangle scheme under way, Harry—who had little available money, since he had invested $200,000 in Griffith's *Intolerance*—was obliged to borrow from the banks. Griffith seems never to have directed a picture for Triangle, limiting himself to a "nominal supervision" of his assistants. Harry also made a major error of judgment when, in imitation of Adolph Zukor's Famous Players strategy of 1912, he began to sign up prominent stage stars to act in pictures for Triangle. The movies did not do very well and Harry was obliged to cancel almost all the contracts. The affair did not help Triangle's reputation and cost the company several hundred thousand dollars. Worse, it created pressure from the banks toward greater consolidation of the movie business. This, in turn, led Harry to make a fatal mistake: he drew up a plan for a merger of Triangle with the Zukor and Goldwyn interests.[176]

Harry Aitken's main problem, as a movie magnate, was that he was good at launching ventures, not consolidating them. His modus operandi also revolved around borrowing large amounts of money at high interest rates to underwrite the costs of expansion.[177] Moreover, even after years in the cutthroat movie business, Harry and his brother Roy still retained a certain naivety. As part of the merger negotiations, he allowed Zukor and Goldwyn to examine Triangle's books. Once aware of Triangle's weaknesses and high indebtedness, Harry's competitors not only withdrew from the proposed merger; they began actively to plot the Aitkens' downfall.[178] Joined together without Triangle, as the Paramount Pictures Corporation, they started to lure away Triangle's stars with offers of higher salaries. By late 1916, the Aitkens were forced to sell the twenty-five Triangle film exchanges, in the process relinquishing the movie theaters that had agreed to show only Triangle pictures. Clearly, by this point, Harry was resorting to creative accounting, using dividends from Epoch and another non-Triangle company to keep Triangle afloat. Finally, in May 1917, Zukor lured Griffith away with an offer to distribute films that Griffith would produce himself. Over the next two months, Ince and Sennett also left. Triangle temporarily resorted to a strategy of producing low-cost movies without big-name directors or stars. Although Harry disapproved of this strategy, it might have been made to work, but in May 1919, the banks finally stepped in to take over active management of the company. Abandoning film production, the new managers began to sell off the company's assets at a knock-down price, including the studio lot at Culver City (bought by Sam Goldwyn, it would eventually become the home of Metro-Goldwyn-Mayer). Harassed by legal actions from Triangle shareholders accusing them of stock manipulation and conspiracy to defraud, the Aitkens went back to their home town in Waukesha, Wisconsin, where they could lick their wounds, handle the distribution of a small number of their old films, and dream of the day when they would recover all their losses by financing the remake of their greatest success. It was not to be.[179]

Among the investors in *Birth*, it was not only Harry and Roy Aitken who ultimately suffered for their early success. One of the larger shareholders in the film after the Aitkens, according to the accounts of the Epoch Producing Corporation, was Robert Goldstein. Goldstein's firm provided costumes and uniforms for the production. Rather than paying money for this service, Griffith seems to have persuaded Goldstein to accept payment in the form of $6,250 of shares in the picture (and Goldstein personally subscribed a further $1,000 in cash).[180] The commercial success of *The Birth of a Nation* not only made Goldstein wealthy. It inspired him to produce and direct a film that would be a spectacular epic on the same lines as Griffith's. It would be set against the background not of the Civil War but of the American Revolution. Shortly before the United States entered World War I in April 1917, Goldstein finished work on his fourteen-reel film. During the eighteen months of production, he had had to deal with unscrupulous partners, seemingly endless financial problems, repeated efforts to remove him from the picture, and continuous attempts at sabotaging the whole project (which he blamed principally on Griffith and his agents).[181] His film's opening in Chicago in May was delayed for three weeks by legal and censorship wrangles. It was alleged that the movie would "arouse bitterness and sectional feeling" against Britain (now a U.S. ally, since the American entry into the First World War in April 1917) and that the battles it showed would discourage recruitment into the armed forces.[182]

The controversy in Chicago was nothing compared to what awaited Goldstein in Los Angeles, where his film, *The Spirit of '76*, had its West Coast première on November 28, 1917, in Clune's Auditorium (where *The Birth of a Nation* had premièred nearly three years earlier). The melodrama was set against a variety of backgrounds—France, Canada, England, Massachusetts (Paul Revere's ride and the battle of Lexington were shown), western New York, Pennsylvania (for the Declaration of Independence in Philadelphia and Washington's base at Valley Forge) and Virginia (for Lord Cornwallis's surrender at Yorktown).[183] *The Spirit of '76* apparently also contained a sequence in which British troops carried out a massacre of Americans. Sequences "showing British soldiers dragging women by the hair, carrying off girls and stabbing a woman" were now apparently objectionable since the United States and Britain were fighting on the same side against Germany in the war.[184]

After the first two showings of the film, District Judge Benjamin Franklin Bledsoe issued a warrant for the seizure of the film. Next day, when Goldstein filed a motion demanding the return of the film, Bledsoe not only denied the motion but ordered Goldstein's arrest for violating the Espionage Act passed in June 1917.[185] On December 4, 1917, a federal grand jury indicted Goldstein on two counts in relation to the Espionage Act and one under the Selective Service Act.[186] Once the case—with the deeply ironic name *The United States vs. The*

Spirit of '76—got under way, it rapidly became clear that in the atmosphere of the time Goldstein had very little chance of being acquitted. A procession of witnesses attested to his real or supposed anti-British sentiments and claimed (although this was untrue) that his film had been partially financed by Germans.[187] On April 15, 1918, after a trial that according to one later scholar was "an exemplary case of the suppression of civil liberties," Goldstein was convicted on the first two counts of his indictment. Two weeks later, Bledsoe sentenced him to ten years in prison and fined him $5,000. Although his sentence would later be commuted by President Wilson to just three years, Goldstein remains the only film director ever to have been sent to jail for producing a spectacular and patriotic epic on the subject of the American Revolution.[188]

To say that a curse followed those who helped make *Birth of a Nation* would probably be going much too far. Unquestionably, however, some of those involved had a tragic destiny. Bobby Harron (Tod Stoneman) collaborated with Griffith on several other films, including *Intolerance, Hearts of the World* (1918), *A Romance of Happy Valley* (1919), *The Girl Who Stayed Home* (1919) and *The Greatest Question* (1919). By 1920, he was feeling an increasing threat from the competition of Richard Barthelmess for major roles, and at twenty-six, he was too old to go back to the juvenile leads in which he had originally come to fame. Harron died in September 1920 of a gunshot wound; it would always be unclear if this was an accident or a botched (if ultimately successful) suicide attempt. Wallace Reid had already appeared in scores of one- and two-reelers before he accepted the role of Jeff the blacksmith in *The Birth of a Nation*. But the publicity he gained as a result of his stripped-to-the-waist exposure for a few minutes in Griffith's hugely successful film catapulted him into movie stardom. He acted in a series of films for the Famous Players-Lasky (later Paramount) Studio, doing particularly well in several films directed by Cecil B. De Mille. For half a decade he was the number one male box-office star in Hollywood. But in 1919, he was injured in an accident. Prescribed morphine for the pain, he swiftly degenerated into a drug addict. A pale shadow of his former self, he died in a clinic while trying to kick the habit in 1923.

The main actresses in *The Birth of a Nation* had movie careers of varying success and longevity. Josephine Crowell (Mrs. Cameron), already sixty-six when *Birth* was released, continued to appear in supporting roles until 1929. Miriam Cooper (Margaret Cameron) was the leading lady in many films until the mid-1920s, but her career did not survive the coming of sound. Mary Alden (Lydia Brown), although best known for her films with Griffith, continued as a character actress until the 1930s. Mae Marsh (Flora Cameron), cast once again as a "desperate" woman in the modern section of *Intolerance* (1916), subsequently left Griffith and starred in several Sam Goldwyn movies of the late teens. Although she reunited with Griffith in 1923 for *The White Rose* (1923), in which she starred with Ivor Novello, she made relatively few films in the early 1920s and retired in 1926. She was lured back in the 1930s, usually in supporting rather than starring roles, and worked continually—if intermittently—until the early 1960s. She became a particular favorite of John Ford, appearing in several of his films, including *The Sun Shines Bright* (1953), *The Searchers* (1956), and *Donovan's Reef* (1963).

Of all the Griffith "creations," Lillian Gish was the most successful and the most enduring. She was the girl rocking the cradle in *Intolerance* (1916) and starred in later Griffith films such as *Broken Blossoms* (1919), *Way Down East* (1920), and *Orphans of the Storm* (1921). Although beginning to detach herself personally from Griffith (who was increasingly enamored with the somewhat wooden charms of Carole Dempster) by 1919 and breaking with him professionally (over a money dispute) in 1921, Gish would remain a loyal defender of the director until the end of her life.[189] She made a number of memorable films for M-G-M in the late 1920s, including *The Wind* (1928), but fell victim to internal studio politics. After starring in two films in the early 1930s, she spent many years working solely in the theater. Gish returned to the movies in the 1940s as a character actor and had regular roles in films for most of the next half-century. Among many other films, she appeared in King Vidor's *Duel in the Sun* (1946), Charles Laughton's *The Night of the Hunter* (1955), and Robert Altman's *A Wedding* (1978). Her last appearances were in *Sweet Liberty* (1986) and *The Whales of August* (1987), when she was in her nineties.

Henry Walthall's performance as the "Little Colonel" made him one of the first "stars" of the movie industry. He left the Griffith company after *Birth of a Nation*, however, and as his stardom faded played a series of major roles in rather minor productions. As time went by, he found himself increasingly in demand as a character actor in supporting roles. His discreet and subtle style of acting and fine speaking voice made him equally at home in silent films and talkies; for example, he played the wronged husband in both the 1926 silent and the 1934 sound version of *The Scarlet Letter*. Walthall was reunited with Griffith in the latter's production of *Abraham Lincoln* (1930). He reprised his "Little Colonel" role in the final sequences of *Judge Priest* (1934), a Will Rogers vehicle. He died while filming *China Clipper* in 1936, just as he was about to film his character's death scene. Spottiswoode Aitken (Dr. Cameron) was a character actor who specialized in playing benign old men; he appeared in almost a hundred silent-era films. Two actors in *Birth* became typecast as villains: Ralph Lewis (Austin Stoneman) and Walter Long (Gus). Long, however, appeared in much better pictures; he played a convict in Laurel and Hardy's *Pardon Us* (1931) and was also in *I Am a Fugitive from a Chain Gang* (1932) and *The Thin Man* (1934). He finished his career playing in Westerns. Among actors with more minor roles in *Birth*, Elmo Lincoln was "White Arm Joe," blacksmith Jeff's main opponent in the fight in the saloon. Lincoln, whose real name was Otto Elmo Linkenhelter, later (in 1918) became the first movie Tarzan and continued playing played small film roles until his death in 1952. One of the extras paid to be a fallen Union soldier was Eugene Pallette, later a well-known character actor who appeared in over 200 films, including *Shanghai Express* (1932), *My Man Godfrey* (1936), *Mr. Smith Goes to Washington* (1939), and *The Lady Eve* (1941).

An astonishing number of those involved in making *The Birth of a Nation* would later carve out successful careers as movie directors. Joseph Henabery (Abraham Lincoln) became the director of many silent-era movies. Elmer Clifton (Phil Stoneman) would be a prolific director of (mostly) second features, and Raoul Walsh (John Wilkes Booth), in a career that lasted until the early 1960s, of many action films, including *Objective Burma* (1945) and *White Heat* (1949). Walsh would make his own Civil War "epic" in 1957: *Band of Angels*, starring Clark Gable. Donald Crisp (Ulysses S. Grant) would also have a long career on both sides of the camera. During the 1920s, he directed a series of silents, in some of which he also acted. Less comfortable with directing in the sound era, he thereafter concentrated entirely on acting in films such as *How Green Was My Valley* (1941), for which he won an Oscar as best supporting actor; *Lassie, Come Home* (1943); and *The Man from Laramie* (1955). According to Anthony Slide, one of the group of men surrounding Jeff the blacksmith in *Birth* was David Butler, later to be director of many films including *Road to Morocco* (1942) and *Calamity Jane* (1953).[190] Perhaps the two most significant names of all do not appear in most credit lists for *Birth*. The anonymous man who fell from the roof during the Confederate raid on Piedmont in the first part was Erich von Stroheim, who would direct *Greed* (1925), *The Wedding March* (1927), and *Queen Kelly* (1928) before resuming an acting career that climaxed with the part of the butler, ex-husband, and ex-director of Norma Desmond (Gloria Swanson) in Billy Wilder's *Sunset Boulevard* (1950). And if his own later recollection is true, somewhere among the masked riders of the Ku Klux Klan was John Ford. Knocked from his horse by the branch of a tree, Ford would survive to direct over 120 feature films, winning, in the process, four Oscars.[191]

Conclusion

In the first years of the twenty-first century, *The Birth of a Nation* seemed to be experiencing what the *Los Angeles Times* called "a mini-renaissance." In 2002, Kino on Video produced a DVD box set of Griffith's works, including *Birth*. In 2004, on the eve of the film's ninetieth anniversary, Paul D. Miller, a New York-based musician, conceptual artist, and filmmaker better known as DJ Spooky, used "footage from the film, graphics, special effects and an original score" to "remix" Griffith's movie. Miller's "Rebirth of a Nation" was premièred at the Lincoln Center in New York in July, before setting off on a tour of selected U.S. and European cities. In August 2004, Charlie Lustman, owner of the Silent Movie Theater on Fairfax Avenue in Los Angeles, announced plans to show *Birth* as part of a program of "rare and important silent films." Lustman, who had tried to screen the movie during the Democratic Convention four years earlier, had withdrawn the film on that occasion because of pressure from pro-black organizations. Local NAACP president Geraldine Washington, conscious of the Rodney King case and the riots of 1992 that had followed the acquittal of the police charged with beating him, had underscored the danger that showing the film might encourage some "to go out and get involved in some of these racist actions." History repeated itself in 2004: Lustman, confronted with protests, personal threats, and "warnings that his theater would be destroyed if he showed the film," canceled the screening at the last moment, prompting furious arguments outside the theater between protestors and would-be moviegoers.[1]

Two weeks after the aborted screening, the *Los Angeles Times* attempted to discover for itself why the film was still so controversial by arranging a showing followed by a round table discussion. For *Times* writers, watching the film was a deeply uncomfortable experience. They found many scenes of the film offensive because of their racism. "And yet," they reported, "the filmmaking craft is undeniable. There are moments of great emotional tenderness as well as masterfully choreographed battle scenes and thrilling action editing." Earl Ofari Hutchinson, community activist, radio host, and member of the round table, put the matter succinctly when he declared, "If this had been a third-rate film, a 10th-rate film...we wouldn't be sitting here now talking about it." According to Hutchinson, *The Birth of a Nation* broke new ground in cinematic terms, yet at the same time it helped disseminate Southern white views of race and the Civil War and propagated negative stereotypes of African Americans that had never disappeared. Aaron McGruder, author of *The Boondocks* cartoon strip and another member of the round table, criticized the ways in which *Birth* not only degraded blacks but also encouraged "delusions of grandeur" on the part of whites. He insisted that the film, by showing threatening black rapists, helped justify lynching: "A lot of people got killed because of this movie." David Shepard, the producer of the DVD edition of *Birth*, made a very old point when he insisted that the campaign against the film's screening had proved "a huge backfire": many more people had seen the film on video and DVD because of the publicity created by the suppression at the Silent Movie Theater than the 220 who actually had tickets. More subtly, UCLA historian Ellen Dubois suggested that the screening might have been used by the NAACP to instruct people on its own history and its long struggle against both *The Birth of a Nation* and lynching.[2]

Those watching or writing about *The Birth of a Nation* have always faced a classic dilemma. That dilemma was summarized in 1976 by black writer James Baldwin. Griffith's film, Baldwin remarked, "is known as one of the great classics of the American cinema: and indeed it is." At the same time, however, it is unrelentingly racist: Baldwin described it as "an elaborate justification of mass murder."[3] Baldwin, of course, was neither the first nor the last to distinguish between the politics of *The Birth of a Nation* and its reputation as a triumph of filmmaking art. Much the same distinction was made by the Los Angeles members of the NAACP who first protested the movie in early 1915—and by some of those who joined the debate over the withdrawal of the film in the same city some eighty-nine years later.

It was contemporaries of 1915 who first hailed *Birth* as a major contribution to the emergence of a new art. "This is the greatness of the motion picture, at last realized," commented George D. Proctor in the *Motion Picture News*. To Mark Vance in *Variety*, it was "a great epoch in picturemaking." The same issue of the show-business journal also described it as "a new milestone in film artistry."[4] "I am a film fan," declared Dorothy Dix, "but I never had the slightest conception of what could be done with the moving picture as an art until I saw 'The Birth of a Nation.'" "A wonderful art, this, the marriage of music and spectacle," commented Harlow Hare enthusiastically in the *Boston*

American.[5] It was not only professional critics who recognized the quality of the film. "Educationally, dramatically and artistically," observed the National Board of Censorship in its final statement approving the film, "this should prove a great step forward in motion picture production." Even the executive committee of the Boston NAACP, while deploring its "insidious" influence upon audiences, recognized it as "a most clever combination of spectacular and musical art."[6]

The perception that *The Birth of a Nation* had been crucial to cinema's development as the newest of the arts was taken up and propagated by later commentators. *Birth*, to Lewis Jacobs in 1931, "propelled the film into a new artistic level." Together with *Intolerance*, argued Herman G. Weinberg at the end of the 1930s, it "established the art of the film in America." "To watch his [Griffith's] work," asserted James Agee in 1948, "is like being witness to...the birth of an art." "Whether loved or hated," declared Arthur Knight in 1957, "*The Birth of a Nation* established once [and] for all that the film was an art in its own right." *Birth*, declared French film historian Georges Sadoul in 1952, "was a key film in the history of the cinematic art." "It is an undeniable fact," asserted Jean Mitry on similar lines in 1963, "that the cinema *as an art* was born in 1915...with *Birth of a Nation*...the cinema's first masterpiece." Michael Rogin concurred, writing in the 1980s that *Birth* "established film as a legitimate art."[7]

In the decades following *Birth*'s first release, many of its specific shots would become famous. Griffith's re-creation of the hall of the South Carolina legislature led to what Bruce Chadwick calls "one of the most gasp-inspiring shots in the film...of the empty chamber suddenly filling with people in a camera's millisecond."[8] The homecoming scene in which the Confederate son, played by Henry Walthall, returns from the war in Griffith's *In Old Kentucky* (1909) evolved, in *Birth*, into the sequence in which the Little Colonel (also played by Walthall) arrives back at Cameron Hall. Walthall, with his tattered clothes and hat, arrives at the gate of his home and dawdles as he inspects the wartime damage. He is met by his young sister, Flora, who has decorated her last good dress with shards of raw cotton. After hugging and kissing her brother, she goes back into the house where her mother, father, and sister are waiting. All the audience then sees of the family reunion, in a scene that would become a byword for cinematic self-discipline, are the arms of Flora and his mother reaching out through the doorway to embrace him and pull him into the house. As Leger Grindon notes, this sequence "embellishes the emotional encounter until it achieves the scope of spectacle."[9] Griffith showed himself equally talented with scenes of mass action. In 1948, critic James Agee described the battle charge sequence in *Birth of a Nation* as the "most beautiful single shot I have seen in any movie." To film historian and theorist Siegfried Kracauer, writing in 1960, the battle scenes of *The Birth of a Nation*—in spite of subsequent technical innovations—had never been surpassed.[10]

While some of Griffith's favorite camera techniques, such as artificial masking, iris framing, and dissolves, would over the years come to seem outdated and passé,[11] they often produced remarkable effects in *Birth*. In one of the more evocative sequences in the film, an iris shot shows a mother comforting three crying children. The camera pans slowly to the right and the iris opens up to show a detachment of infantry marching in battle formation across a plain (shots 318–322, 325). Shots of the family and the marching men then alternate. "The effect," observed Georges Sadoul, "is striking, just as easily because of the contrast of shots created by the panoramic view as because of the contrast between the distress of the woman and the implacable machinery of war."[12] The whole sequence demonstrated Griffith's skill at editing alternate shots sequentially, later known as cross-cutting or intercutting. It was a technique that could help create great dramatic tension—as Griffith switched between, on the one hand, shots of Elsie Stoneman under threat and later the beleaguered whites in the log cabin, and, on the other hand, the Klansmen riding to the rescue. At times, it could be used to do the opposite, injecting lightness of touch into a particular sequence (an early reviewer noted that Griffith at times "relieves the tension of emotions with a timely humorous incident"). Importantly, it could also tie together scenes of crowd action with individual experiences, offering an appealing personal perspective on the "history" it recounted. As Leger Grindon writes of one of the early sequences of the film:

> Griffith celebrates the dispatch of Piedmont's soldiers with street bonfires, an all-night ball, and finally a parade of the troops from the town. The director balances the scale of these social ceremonies with Ben's goodbye to his little sister, Flora. The cutting from the mass scenes to the intimate encounter maintains an emotional association between the collective experience and the private farewell.[13]

What distinguished *The Birth of a Nation* from Griffith's earlier films was not simply its length and scale or its critical and commercial success[14]: it was also the contribution it made to the development of American moviemaking. It used to be believed, notes William Rothman,

> that Griffith single-handedly invented what is loosely called the "grammar of film"—continuity editing, close-ups, point-of-view shots, iris shots, expressive lighting, parallel editing, and the other techniques and formal devices that movies have employed for over seventy years.[15]

In practice (as suggested in Chapter 3), precedents have been found for his so-called inventions. Rather than seeing Griffith as a lone pioneer, it would be far more accurate to regard him as engaging in skillful cinematic bricolage—taking the ideas and techniques of others and reworking them for his own purposes.

His own most distinctive contribution was in the realm of editing. Even Karl Brown, Bitzer's assistant, who had been present at all the filming (and whose job it was to keep a record of all the shots made), was astonished at the way Griffith managed to bring together so many disparate sequences into a flowing, coherent narrative.[16] In *The Birth of a Nation*, argued Lewis Jacobs, he "brought to maturity the editing principle begun with Méliès and furthered by Porter." *Birth*, Kevin Brownlow asserted, "was the first feature film to exploit fully the extraordinary power of editing. In the truest sense of the word, this was a masterpiece; it served as an example for the rest of the industry."[17] With his alternation of objective and subjective shots, the former conveying the action of a scene and the latter illustrating a particular character's point of view, Griffith's editing in *Birth of a Nation* made him, according to Harry M. Benshoff and Sean Griffin, "a key figure in the standardization of Hollywood storytelling form."[18]

If early reviewers of *The Birth of a Nation* were quick to point out its artistic qualities, a small minority also drew attention to its racism. W. Stephen Bush, writing for *The Moving Picture World*, noted that the New York audience responded not only with applause but also at times with hisses. These hisses, he insisted,

> were not, of course, directed against the artistic quality of the film. They were evoked by the undisguised appeal to race prejudices. The tendency of the second part is to inflame race hatred. The negroes are shown as horrible brutes, given over to beastly excesses, defiant and criminal in their attitude toward the whites, and lusting after white women.[19]

Even Ned Mackintosh, in the *Atlanta Constitution*, observed that this was a film that "makes you love *and hate* [my italics]."[20] The hatred, of course, was for the mulattoes and blacks depicted in the film. As Donald Bogle points out, Griffith took the demeaning stereotypes of blacks which were already present in American films (the mammy, Uncle Tom, mulatto, and coon) and added to them the much more threatening figure of the "brutal black buck," intent on forcing his attentions on white women.[21] Griffith always insisted that he was not racially prejudiced; he had shown "the old-time faithful servant" and the progress made by modern blacks (in the Hampton Epilogue) as well as Gus and Silas Lynch.[22] But as well as patronizing the "faithful souls," he failed to understand that in creating the black buck on screen he was helping to shape how white Americans perceived blacks in general. "Griffith's Negroes," argues Maurice Yacowar,

> were not just individual rotters ...; to the general audience they were the metaphors that expressed Griffith's limitation upon the Negro possibility. Where Griffith thought he meant "one or two

negroes at the time," the image suggested "The Negro—Everywhere and Always."[23]

Many of the earliest critics of the anti-black tone of *The Birth of a Nation* were blacks themselves. "A new art was used, deliberately, to slander and vilify a race," claimed W. E. B. Du Bois. "D. W. Griffith was the reason I got into film production," black actor and filmmaker William Greaves would later recall. *Birth* was so offensive to Greaves in its representation of African Americans that he determined to "start making films that would correct this image." To black sociologist Lawrence Reddick, it was still (Reddick was writing in 1944) "the most vicious anti-Negro film that has ever appeared on the American screen."[24] Perhaps the most vituperative critic of Griffith's film, however, was a white film writer. In 1948, Peter Noble observed, "Thirty years ago it constituted an incitement to race riot, and seeing it today still tends to leave a nasty taste in one's mouth." Although Griffith was born in Kentucky, according to Noble, "his understandable partisanship [toward the South] provides no real excuse for…his almost malevolent disregard of the real historical facts." In treating race relations of the Civil War and Reconstruction era, Noble observed, "Griffith concentrated all his patronizing sympathy upon…'Uncle Tom' characters while showing all other black men as vicious rebels and killers." His film not only was deeply critical in its treatment of full-blooded blacks—Noble referred to the "plundering, raping, and looting of…subhuman exslaves" and the "monstrous caricatures of colored politicians, officials, army officers, soldiers, and servants"—but it was even more vehement in its hostility to mixed-race characters (Lydia Brown, Silas Lynch). Indeed, by devoting "much of its content to Negro villainy," Noble insisted, Griffith had produced a deeply racist film of "almost unbelievable viciousness" that "deserves all the protests made against it, then and now."[25]

Despite the storm of criticism leveled at his best-known film, Griffith has never lacked defenders. According to James Agee, he "went to almost preposterous lengths to be fair to the Negroes as he understood them." (Lillian Gish, a lifelong champion of her former director, made clear in her autobiography just *how* Griffith understood blacks. She quoted him as saying "they were our children, whom we loved and cared for all our lives.") William Everson also claimed that "Griffith displayed considerable restraint in controlling Southern prejudices and in being fair to the Negro."[26] One of the more detailed attempts to play down the racism of Griffith in recent decades has been made by his biographer, Richard Schickel. According to Schickel, Griffith shared with most of his white contemporaries an "unconscious racism" that was "not especially passionate or vicious." Most of the racism in *Birth*, he argues, came not from Griffith but from Dixon's story. Indeed Griffith, Schickel argues, managed to limit the racism in the Gus/Flora chase sequence by having Gus played by a white man whose makeup and "weird less-than-human movements" made it impossible in any real sense to perceive him as black.

Schickel concedes that *Birth* does display a degree of "moral insensitivity," but he blames this on a series of extraneous reasons: much of the shooting schedule was improvised at the last moment rather than planned in advance; Griffith bore enormous burdens of logistics and finance; he was isolated in California and distant from organizations such as the NAACP and the black press; and his very independence meant there was nobody present on set to criticize what he was doing. Schickel also argues that once "he became aware of the (to him) surprising objections" to *Birth of a Nation*, "Griffith busied himself with the shears, trying to modify those sequences that had raised the greatest outcry." Finally, concluding his defense of Griffith's film, Schickel maintains that "there appears to have been no visible upsurge of *conscious* racism in the film's wake."[27]

Although Schickel's biography of Griffith is still the best available, his defense of his subject's role over *The Birth of a Nation* is far from convincing. Griffith may have been expressing an "unconscious racism" he shared with millions of white Americans, but it was a mistake to do so in a mass cultural form for which Griffith himself had such high aspirations. Everett Carter argued that *Birth*, far from encouraging the development of a cinematic art that would elevate those it touched, "served the ugliest purposes of pseudoart—giving people a reflection of their own prejudices, sentimental at best, vicious at worst."[28] It is true that the second and most controversial part of *Birth of a Nation* was based on Dixon's fiction and that Griffith *did* tone down Dixon's racism in some respects (for example, there is no outright mention of rape in *Birth*, whereas blacks rape white girls in both of Dixon's novels *The Leopard's Spots* and *The Clansman*). It is also the case, however, that Griffith shared some of Dixon's racial attitudes (he was opposed, for example, to miscegenation).[29] The argument that having Gus played by a white actor in makeup somehow diminishes the racial character of his pursuit of Flora is dismissed by Scott Simmon, who notes that "audiences today usually find the blackface casting intensifying, not mitigating, the sequence's racism."[30] The notion that Griffith revealed "moral insensitivity" because he was working under too many pressures and isolated in California—essentially that afflicted by strain and remoteness on the West Coast, he resorted to lazy racial stereotypes and failed to challenge comfortable received ideas—is unconvincing at best. He chose the project himself and, since he was so much in control of bringing it to the screen, must be assigned most of the blame for the final product. His remoteness in California does not wipe out the fact that, since 1899, he had lived mainly in the North and must have been aware that a race problem now existed there as well as in the South, a race problem his film could only exacerbate. To suggest that Griffith willingly cut the most controversial scenes is simply not correct: in reality, as discussed in Chapter 6, he was usually slow and reluctant to respond to censorship pressures, attempting to avoid, delay, or minimize changes wherever possible. Asserting, finally, that *Birth* produced no upsurge in "conscious racism" is to ignore the actions of the revived Ku Klux Klan and the increased number of lynchings that coincided with the film's initial release.[31]

With some notable exceptions, film scholars and critics, rather than confronting directly the racism expressed in *The Birth of a Nation*, have traditionally preferred to concentrate their attention on the aesthetics of the film. This tendency to privilege style over substance proved infuriating to the NAACP, which resented the growing tendency, from the 1930s onward, to ignore the ideological dimension of Griffith's masterpiece by constructing it as a film "classic." Preferring form over content also angered Sergei Eisenstein. In the early 1940s, as American left-wingers quarreled over *Birth*,[32] the Soviet filmmaker made his own position clear. "The disgraceful propaganda of racial hatred toward the colored people which permeates this film," he wrote in 1940, "cannot be redeemed by the purely cinematographic effects of this production."[33]

Only within the last few years have scholars begun to follow Eisenstein's lead by criticizing the artificial style–substance dichotomy. In an article of 1982, Brian Gallagher argued that *Birth*'s "ideologically determined montage" was "not a distraction from its endorsement of mass murder, but instead a demonstration of the kind of illogical reasoning that makes mass murder appear reasonable."[34] In 1985, in an extended essay on Griffith and his most notorious film, Michael Rogin observed that the two strategies pursued by most scholars and critics were "either [to] minimize the film's racialist content or separate its aesthetic power from negrophobia." Rogin, declining to separate form from content, set out to investigate the close relationship between the two by placing the film in its social and political context.[35] Clyde Taylor, in an article published in 1989, similarly questioned what he saw as the divorcement between the aesthetics of *Birth* and the ideological approach adopted by the film in its very negative social construction of blacks. The two, he argued, were closely connected: *The Birth of a Nation*'s aesthetic strategies had really been used to reinforce the film's ideological stance, in reality helping to normalize racism.[36] More recently, other writers have attempted to implicate *Birth*'s aesthetics in the film's politics, in effect rejecting the notion that its racist substance was somehow separate from its artistic and technical style. "We see the two as interdependent," argued Penny Starfield in 2000: "the form is placed at the service of the content and the innovations are largely necessitated by the construction of the racist discourse."[37] In 2004, two scholars blamed Griffith personally. Donato Totaro saw *Birth*'s form as subordinate to "Griffith's racist ideology" and Charlie Keil described the film as "the product of a mind determined to use style for racist ends."[38]

The Birth of a Nation has now remained fairly constant across more than nine decades as a signifier of racist attitudes. The film itself has not changed; once in the vanguard of cinematic innovation, it now, in spite of sections of surpassing visual appeal, seems creaky and antiquated when viewed by modern audiences.[39] This in fact is the key: the film has not changed; what *has* changed is the world around it. In 1915, it was recognized by the NAACP and other organizations as a racist attack on black people. At the same time, there can be little doubt that the attitudes expressed in the film were unexceptional to the vast majority of the white American population. Most critics who viewed the film could not understand why it generated such controversy, and it is probable that ordinary spectators reacted in much the same way. As the twentieth century moved on, however, racial attitudes began to change: the increasing success of the obsessive NAACP campaign against the film functioned as a barometer of this evolution. In reality, by the 1930s screening *The Birth of a Nation* was no longer commercially profitable, and by the 1940s and 1950s, the prospect of protests and picketing was sufficient to deter all but the most determined of theater managers from the attempt to do so. Over the years also, support for the film declined: the fact it was *The Birth of a Nation* weakened the position of those who, like the ACLU in the late 1930s, might otherwise have been tempted to defend the right to show the movie in terms of civil liberties. During the course of the twentieth century, what had been mainstream acceptance of the racism on which the film was based turned to mainstream rejection. In the early years of the twenty-first century, the film stands as a monument to once-dominant cultural attitudes over race and, in terms of most people's reaction to it, as a reminder of just how much has changed since 1915.

Notes

1. There are no accurate figures available either on the profits of the film or the size of its audience. In 1960, *Variety* estimated that it had grossed more than $50 million since 1915. In 1977, it revised that figure downward to $5 million. Russell Merritt estimated that the film had made $18 million by 1931. Seymour Stern, self-appointed Griffith "expert," claimed the film had earned $48,000,000 by 1948. Richard Schickel, in his biography of Griffith (1984), suggested total profits from the film's first run of $60 million. Audience figures are equally unreliable. Everett Carter estimated that 3 million people had seen it in the Greater New York area by January 1916. Carl E. Milliken, secretary of the MPPDA, estimated that "probably" 50 million people in all had seen it by 1930. The 200 million figure (by 1946) is given by Russell Merritt. *Variety*, April 13, 1960, cited in Anthony Slide, *American Racist: The Life and Films of Thomas Dixon* (Lexington: University Press of Kentucky, 2004), 198; Russell Merritt, "Dixon, Griffith, and the Southern Legend," *Cinema Journal* 12, no. 1 (Fall 1972): 27 and note 2; Seymour Stern, "D. W. Griffith: An Appreciation," *Sight and Sound* 17, no. 67 (Autumn 1948): 109; Richard Schickel, *D. W. Griffith and the Birth of Film* (London: Pavilion, 1984), 281; Everett Carter, "Cultural History Written with Lightning: The Significance of *The Birth of a Nation*," *American Quarterly* 12 (Fall 1960): 347–57, reprint in *Focus on "The Birth of a Nation,"* ed. Fred Silva (Englewood Cliffs, N.J.: Prentice-Hall, 1971): 133–43, citation from 133–34; Carl E. Milliken to Will W. Alexander (Director of the Commission on Interracial Cooperation), August 9, 1930, National Association for the Advancement of Colored People Papers, Library of Congress, henceforth NAACPP); Merritt, op. cit.

2. See Martin M. Marks, *Music and the Silent Film: Contexts and Case Studies, 1895–1924* (New York: Oxford University Press, 1997), 65–68, 71.

3. See Russell Merritt, "Nickelodeon Theaters, 1905–1914: Building an Audience for the Movies," in *The American Film Industry*, ed. Tino Balio (Madison: University of Wisconsin Press, 1976), 59–79; Robert C. Allen, "Motion Picture Exhibition in

Manhattan, 1906–1912: Beyond the Nickelodeon," *Cinema Journal* 18, no. 2 (Spring 1979): 2–15, reprint in *Film before Griffith*, ed. John L. Fell (Berkeley: University of California Press, 1983), 162–75.

4. Eileen Bowser, *The Transformation of Cinema 1907–1915* (New York: Scribner's, 1990), 125–29, 131–32; Richard Koszarski, *An Evening's Entertainment: The Age of the Silent Feature Picture, 1915–1928* (Berkeley: University of California, 1990), 10.

5. W. Stephen Bush in the *Moving Picture World*, 23 (March 13, 1915), reprinted in Silva, *Focus*, 25; George D. Proctor in *Motion Picture News*, 11, no. 10 (March 13, 1915), reprinted in Anthony Slide, ed., *Selected Film Criticism, 1912–1920* (Metuchen, N.J.: Scarecrow Press, 1982), 21; Mark Vance in *Variety*, March 12, 1915, reprinted in Silva, *Focus*, 22; "W," in the *New York Dramatic Mirror*, 73, no. 1890 (March 10, 1915), reprinted in Slide, *Selected Film Criticism*, 24.

6. Lewis Jacobs, *The Rise of the American Film: A Critical History* (New York: Harcourt, Brace, 1939), 175; Proctor review, op. cit., 18; "W" review, op. cit., 21; anonymous review in *The Moving Picture World*, 23 (March 13, 1915), reprinted in Silva, *Focus*, 29; Ned McIntosh, *The Constitution* [Atlanta], December 7, 1915, reprinted in Silva, *Focus*, 34; Harlow Hare, *The American* [Boston], July 18, 1915, reprinted in Silva, *Focus*, 37.

7. Graham Greene, "A History of the Film, 1896–1936: [The Birth of a Nation]. The Trail of the Lonesome Pine. Secret Agent," *Spectator* (May 15, 1936), in David Parkinson, ed., *Mornings in the Dark: The Graham Greene Film Reader* (Manchester: Carcanet Press, 1993), 101; Anthony Lejeune, ed., *The C. A. Lejeune Film Reader* (Manchester: Carcanet Press, 1991), 125; Christopher Cook, ed., *The Dilys Powell Film Reader* (Manchester: Carcanet Press, 1991), 357; James Agee, *Agee on Film: Reviews and Comments by James Agee* (New York: McDowell, Obolensky, 1958), 314.

8. Terry Ramsaye, *A Million and One Nights: A History of the Motion Picture*, 1 vol. ed., (London: Frank Cass, 1964, first pub. 1926), vol. 1, 641–42; Benjamin B. Hampton, *A History of the Movies* (New York: Covici, Friede, 1931), 129, 137; Jacobs, *The Rise of the American Film*, 187.

9. Georges Sadoul, *Histoire Générale du Cinéma: Tome III: Le Cinéma Devient un Art (1909–1920): Deuxième Volume: La Première Guerre Mondiale* (Paris: Editions Denoël, 1952), 24–25; Arthur Knight, *The Liveliest Art:A Panoramic History of the Movies* (New York: Macmillan, 1957, rev. ed. 1978), 23; Jean Mitry, "Naissance d'une Nation," in "Griffith," Supplement to *L'Avant Scène du Cinéma*, 45 (February 1, 1965): 89; Kevin Brownlow, *The Parade's Gone By* (London: Secker and Warburg, 1968), 281, 26.

10. Marjorie Rosen, *Popcorn Venus: Women, Movies and the American Dream* (New York: Coward, McCann and Geoghegan, 1973), 35; Thomas Cripps, *Slow Fade to Black: The Negro in American Film, 1900–1942* (New York: Oxford University Press, 1977), 41; William K. Everson, *American Silent Film* (New York: Oxford University Press, 1978), 87.

11. For a detailed study of attempts to censor *The Birth of a Nation*, see Nickieann Fleener-Marzec, *D. W. Griffith's "The Birth of a Nation": Controversy, Suppression, and the First Amendment as It Applies to Filmic Expression, 1915–1973* (New York: Arno Press, 1980), passim.

12. On early demands for movie censorship in the United States see Kathleen D. McCarthy, "Nickel Vice and Virtue: Movie Censorship in Chicago, 1907–1915," *Journal of Popular Film* 5, no. 1 (1976): 37–55; Stephen Vaughan, "Morality and Entertainment: The Origins of the Motion Picture Production Code," *Journal of American History* 77, no. 1

(June 1990): 40–42; Gregory D. Black, *Hollywood Censored: Morality Codes, Catholics, and the Movies* (Cambridge: Cambridge University Press, 1994), 8–12; Lee Grieveson, *Policing Cinema: Movies and Censorship in Early-Twentieth-Century America* (Berkeley: University of California Press, 2004), passim.

13. Donald Bogle, *Toms, Coons, Mulattoes, Mammies, and Bucks: An Interpretive History of Blacks in American Films* (Oxford: Roundhouse Press, 1994), 16–18 ; Bruce Chadwick, *The Reel Civil War: Mythmaking in American Film* (New York: Vintage, 2002), 8.

14. Gerald Mast, ed., *The Movies in Our Midst: Documents in the Cultural History of Film in America* (Chicago: University of Chicago Press, 1982), 213, 333. Only in 1956, when the Production Code was revised, was the prohibition on showing miscegenation dropped.

15. Daniel A. Lord, *Played by Ear: The Autobiography of Father Daniel A. Lord, S. J.* (New York: Image Books/Doubleday, 1959), 250.

16. Roy E. Aitken (with Al P. Nelson), *The "Birth of a Nation" Story* (Middleburg, Va.: Denlinger, 1965), 4.

17. Matthew Bernstein, ed., *Controlling Hollywood: Censorship and Regulation in the Studio Era* (London: Athlone Press, 2000), 12.

18. Richard Maltby, "*The King of Kings* and the Czar of All the Rushes: The Propriety of the Christ Story," in Bernstein, *Controlling Hollywood*, 80–81.

19. Charles Lyons, *The New Censors: Movies and the Culture Wars* (Philadelphia: Temple University Press, 1997), 14–15, 18–19, 53–80.

20. Lyons, *The New Censors*, 20–23, 81–145.

21. Lyons, *The New Censors*, 23–25, 146–82.

22. "Bollywood's Most Unwanted," www.rediff.com/entertai/2002/sep/11fil.htm website [November 5, 2005].

23. "Listmania! 25 Most Controversial Films of all Time," www.amazon.com website [November 5, 2005].

24. Fleener-Marzec, *D. W. Griffith's "The Birth of a Nation,"* 483, 518, 533; cf. Edward de Grazia and Roger K. Newman, *Banned Films: Movies, Censors, and the First Amendment* (New York: R. R. Bowker, 1982), 5–6.

25. See Janet Staiger, *Interpreting Films: Studies in the Historical Reception of American Cinema* (Princeton: Princeton University Press, 1992), 139–53; reprint in *The Birth of a Nation: D. W. Griffith, Director*, ed. Robert Lang (New Brunswick, N.J.: Rutgers University Press, 1994), 195–213.

26. Goodwin Berquist and James Greenwood, "Protest against Racism: *The Birth of a Nation* in Ohio," *Journal of the University Film Association* 26, no. 3 (1974): 39; Slide, *American Racist*, 199. Slide also notes that showings of the film at the Richelieu Cinema in San Francisco in June 1980 had to be abandoned when the theater was vandalized. Slide, *American Racist*, 199.

27. Gladwin Hill, "Polyglot City Is in Shock after a Melee," *New York Times*, August 3, 1978, A-14, quoted in Staiger, *Interpreting Films*, 139; Mark I. Pinsky, "Racism, History and Mass Media: Birth of a Nation, Gone With the Wind, The Greensboro Massacre," *Jump Cut* no. 28 (1983): 66–67.

28. "Cancellation of a 'Nation,'" *Variety*, May 31–June 7, 1989: 7; Jane M. Gaines, "Political Mimesis," in *Collecting Visible Evidence*, ed. Jane M. Gaines and Michael Renov (Minneapolis: University of Minnesota Press, 1999), 96–97.

29. Gibson, as quoted in Peter McDonald, "Birth of a Nation Award 'Is Racist,' " *Evening Standard* [London], December 9, 1992. There were protests a year later when *Birth* was screened at the Library of Congress. J. Hoberman, "We Must Remember This," *Village Voice*, November 30, 1993, 2–4.

30. Slide, *American Racist*, 201. Previously, PBS and WNET had withdrawn a new Photoplay Productions version of the film from its planned showing in the "American Masters" series. Channel Four television in Britain *did* broadcast the film, but only between the hours of 11 P.M. and 3 A.M. David Gill, "*The Birth of a* Nation: Orphan or Pariah?", *Griffithiana*, 60/61 (October 1997): 27.

31. Robert Edwards, "Turner Pulls Plug on Silent Classic," *Classic Images* no. 246 (December 1995): 14; Jill Jordan Sieder, "Within our Grasp...The Legend of Micheaux," *Oscar Micheaux Society Newsletter* 9 (Spring 2001): 10.

32. "Time to Move On," *Los Angeles Times*, December 15, 1999, F2; "DGA Blundered by Removing Griffith's Name from Award," *Los Angeles Times*, December 18, 1999, F4; "Putting the Historical Spin in Defense of D. W. Griffith Award," *Los Angeles Times*, January 10, 2000, F3. I owe special thanks to Denise Warren for bringing these reports to my attention.

33. Robert W. Welkos, "Debating an Icon's Genius, Racism," *Los Angeles Times*, February 1, 2000, A19; Philip J. Ethington, "D. W. Griffith," *Los Angeles Times*, February 6, 2000, M4; Ted Elliott, "The DGA Is Right, D. W. Griffith Was Wrong," *Los Angeles Times*, December 27, 1999, F3.

34. What follows does not pretend to be a complete accounting of scholarly writing about *Birth of a Nation*. It is intended only to draw attention to some of the more significant contributions.

35. Carter, "Cultural History Written with Lightning"; Raymond A. Cook, "The Man Behind *The Birth of a Nation*," *North Carolina Historical Review* 29 (October 1962): 519–40; Russell Merritt, "Dixon, Griffith, and the Southern Legend," 26–45.

36. Norman Kagan, "Two Classic War Films of the Silent Era: *Birth of a Nation* and *Shoulder Arms*," *Film and History* 4, no. 3 (September 1974): 1–5, 18.

37. John Hope Franklin, "*The Birth of a Nation*: Propaganda as History," *Massachusetts Review*, 20 (Autumn, 1979): 417–33, reprinted in *Race and History: Selected Essays 1938–1988*, ed. John Hope Franklin (Baton Rouge: Louisiana State University Press, 1989), 10–23.

38. John Hammond Moore, "South Carolina's Reaction to the Photoplay *The Birth of a Nation*," *Proceedings of the South Carolina Historical Association* 33 (1963): 30–40; Berquist and Greenwood, "Protest against Racism: 'The Birth of a Nation' in Ohio," 39–44.

39. Thomas Cripps, "The Reaction of the Negro to the Motion Picture, *Birth of a Nation*," *The Historian* 25, no. 3 (May 1963): 344–62, reprinted in Silva, *Focus*, 111–24; Cripps, *Slow Fade to Black*, 41–69.

40. Maxim Simcovitch, "The Impact of Griffith's *Birth of a Nation* on the Modern Ku Klux Klan," *Journal of Popular Film* 1, no. 1 (Winter 1972): 45–54.

41. Bogle, *Toms, Coons, Mulattoes, Mammies and Bucks*, first pub. in 1973, esp. 10–18; Robert M. Henderson, *D. W. Griffith: His Life and Work* (New York: Oxford University Press, 1972), especially 141–65; Everson, *American Silent Film*, especially 72–89.

42. Theodore Huff, *A Shot Analysis of D. W. Griffith's "The Birth of a Nation"* (New York: Museum of Modern Art, 1961); John Cuniberti, *"The Birth of a Nation":*

A Formal Shot-by-Shot Analysis Together with Microfiche (Woodbridge, Conn.: Research Publications, 1979).

43. Silva, *Focus*. Some material on *The Birth of a Nation* was also included in Harry M. Geduld, ed., *Focus on D. W. Griffith* (Englewood Cliffs, N.J.: Prentice-Hall, 1971).

44. Pierre Sorlin, *The Film in History: Restaging the Past* (Totowa, N. J.: Barnes and Noble, 1980), 83–115; Mimi White, "*The Birth of a Nation*: History as Pretext," *Enclitic* 5 (Fall 1981/Spring 1982): 17–24, reprinted in Lang, *The Birth of a Nation*, 214–24.

45. Fleener-Marzec, *D. W. Griffith's "The Birth of a Nation"*; de Grazia and Newman, *Banned Films*, 3–6, 180–83.

46. Nickie Fleener, "Answering Film with Film: The Hampton Epilogue, A Positive Alternative to the Negative Black Stereotypes Presented in *The Birth of a Nation*," *Journal of Popular Film and Television* no. 4 (1980): 400–25.

47. Martin Williams, *Griffith: First Artist of the Movies* (New York: Oxford University Press, 1980), especially 61–78; Schickel, *D. W. Griffith*, especially 206–302.

48. Michael Rogin, "'The Sword Became a Flashing Vision': D. W. Griffith's *The Birth of a Nation*," *Representations* 9 (Winter 1985): 150–95, reprint in Lang, *The Birth of a Nation*, 250–93, quotation from 251. Rogin also engaged in a detailed psychoanalytical reading of Griffith himself.

49. Clyde Taylor, "The Re–Birth of the Aesthetic in Cinema," *Wide Angle* 13, nos. 3 and 4 (July–October 1991): 12–30, reprinted in *The Birth of Whiteness: Race and the Emergence of U. S. Cinema*, ed. Daniel Bernardi (New Brunswick, N.J.: Rutgers University Press, 1996), 15–37.

50. Scott Simmon, *The Films of D. W. Griffith* (Cambridge: Cambridge University Press, 1993), 104–105.

51. Richard Dyer, "Into the Light: The Whiteness of the South in *The Birth of a Nation*," in *Dixie Debates: Perspectives on Southern Cultures*, ed. Richard H. King and Helen Taylor (London: Pluto Press, 1996), 165–76.

52. Jane Gaines and Neil Lerner, "The Orchestration of Affect: The Motif of Barbarism in Breil's *The Birth of a Nation* Score," in *The Sounds of Early Cinema*, ed. Richard Abel and Rick Altman (Bloomington: University of Indiana Press, 2001), 252–68. For more on *Birth*'s musical score, see Marks, *Music and the Silent Film: Contexts and Case Studies*.

53. Vincent F. Rocchio, *Reel Racism: Confronting Hollywood's Construction of Afro-American Culture* (Boulder, Colo.: Westview Press, 2000), 29–54, quotations from 36, 39.

54. James Chandler, "The Historical Novel Goes to Hollywood: Scott, Griffith, and Film Epic Today," in *The Romantics and Us: Essays on Literature and Culture*, ed. Gene W. Ruoff (New Brunswick, N.J.: Rutgers University Press, 1990), 237–73, reprinted in Lang, *The Birth of a Nation*, 225–49. Chandler intended his essay as an alternative thesis to that advanced earlier by Soviet filmmaker Sergei Eisenstein that Griffith's view of the world had been heavily influenced by Dickens. See Sergei Eisenstein, "Dickens, Griffith and the Film Today," in *Film Form: Essays in Film Theory*, ed. and trans. Jay Leyda (New York: Harcourt, Brace and World, 1949), 195–255.

55. Jane Gaines, "*The Birth of a Nation* and *Within Our Gates*: Two Tales of the American South," in *Dixie Debates*, 177–92.

56. Linda Williams, *Playing the Race Card: Melodramas of Black and White from Uncle Tom to O. J. Simpson* (Princeton, N.J.: Princeton University Press, 2001), 96–132;

Susan Courtney, *Hollywood Fantasies of Miscegenation: Spectacular Narratives of Gender and Race, 1903–1967* (Princeton: Princeton University Press, 2005), xvi, 5, 26, 40, 61–99, quotation from 19. Both Williams and Courtney (like Chandler) trace melodramatic elements in *Birth of a Nation* to earlier cultural forms: the "Tom" tradition in Williams's case and a prior tradition of films dealing with racial exchanges and misidentifications in Courtney's.

57. John Inscoe, "*The Clansman* on Stage and Screen: North Carolina Reacts," *North Carolina Historical Review* 64, no. 2 (April 1987): 139–61; Staiger, *Interpreting Films*; Jane M. Gaines, *Fire and Desire: Mixed-Race Movies in the Silent Era* (Chicago: University of Chicago Press, 2001), 219–57, quotation from 235; Anna Everett, *Returning the Gaze: A Genealogy of Black Film Criticism, 1909–1949* (Durham, N. C.: Duke University Press, 2001), 59–106.

58. Russell Merritt, "D. W. Griffith's *The Birth of a Nation*: Going After Little Sister," in *An Anthology of New Film Criticism*, ed. Peter Lehman (Tallahassee: Florida State University Press, 1990), 215–37, quotation from 219; Lang, *The Birth of a Nation*; Chadwick, *The Reel Civil War*, 107–50; Kris Jozajtis, "'The Eyes of All People Are upon Us': American Civil Religion and the Birth of Hollywood," in *Representing Religion in World Cinema: Filmmaking, Mythmaking, Culture Making*, ed. S. Brent Plate (London: Palgrave/St. Martin's, 2003), 239–61, quotation from 247; Paolo Cherchi Usai, ed., *The Griffith Project*, Vol. 8, *Films Produced in 1914–15* (London: British Film Institute/Le Giornate del Cinema Muto, 2004). In 2006, Michael R. Hurwitz published a revised version of his MA thesis on the film as *D. W. Griffith's "The Birth of a Nation": The Film that Transformed America* (North Charleston, S.C.: BookSurge, 2006).

59. Jesionowksi, "Performance and Characterization," in Usai, *The Griffith Project*, Vol. 8, p. 73

60. For example, David Mayer—in an otherwise excellent essay on the theatrical sources of *Birth of a Nation*—is apparently unaware of the existing scholarship on the reception of Thomas Dixon's play *The Clansman*. Mayer, "Theatrical Sources," in Usai, *The Griffith Project*, Vol. 8, 85.

61. Sorlin, *The Film in History*, 106–107; Bowser, "Production," in Usai, *The Griffith Project*, Vol. 8, 60.

62. Kaufman, "Distribution and Reception," in Usai, *The Griffith Project*, Vol. 8, 92.

CHAPTER 1

1. Schickel, *Griffith*, 246–47. The injunction granted was narrowly drawn. It forbade *only* the matinée performance and neither the evening nor any later showing. Ibid.

2. William H. Clune, the owner/manager of Clune's Auditorium, had contributed $15,000 toward the cost of completing the film. Billy Bitzer, the main cameraman on the film, had invested $7,000. Lillian Gish with Ann Pinchot, *The Movies, Mr. Griffith and Me* (London: W. H. Allen, 1969), 144; G. W. Bitzer, *Billy Bitzer: His Story* (New York: Farrar, Straus and Giroux, 1973), 111.

3. William De Mille, elder brother of director Cecil B. De Mille, probably expressed the conventional wisdom inside the movie industry when he wrote to producer Sam Goldwyn that "even if it's a hit, which it probably will be, it cannot possibly make any money. It would have to gross over a quarter of a million dollars for Griffith to get his

cost back and, as you know, that just isn't being done. *The Clansman* certainly establishes Griffith as a leader and it does seem too bad that such a magnificent effort is doomed to financial failure." Quoted in Chadwick, *The Reel Civil War*, 105.

4. Schickel, *Griffith*, 247.

5. Karl Brown, assistant cameraman on *Birth of a Nation*, recalled that Joseph Carl Breil conducted the orchestra playing the score he had composed at the Los Angeles première. But Brown was wrong: the Breil score would not be performed until the New York opening in March. At Clune's Auditorium, the orchestra on the opening night was led by Carli Elinor, playing a score he himself had compiled. Joseph Henabery ["Lincoln" in the film] considered the Elinor score—"an arrangement of popular music, well-known standard music and semiclassical work"—to be much more effective than the later Breil score. Karl Brown, *Adventures with D. W. Griffith*, Kevin Brownlow, ed. (London: Secker and Warburg, 1973), 87–88; Marks, *Music and the Silent Film*, 131–35; Anthony Slide, ed., *Before, In and After Hollywood: The Autobiography of Joseph E. Henabery* (Lanham, Md.: Scarecrow Press, 1997), 82.

6. Brown, *Adventures*, 88.

7. In 1979, in the aftermath of the Paul Killiam-Raymond Rohauer affair discussed in Chapter 8 below, Killiam presented further *Birth of a Nation* materials to the Library of Congress, including "more than 8,000 feet of 1915 negative, cut apart for the 1921 reissue." Until the work of film reconstruction can be completed, notes J. B. Kaufman, "there remains the breathtaking possibility that those long-lost 1915 scenes may have survived after all." Kaufman in Usai, *The Griffith Project*, Vol. 8, 112.

8. Cuniberti, *The Birth of a Nation*, 11.

9. Cited in Cuniberti, *The Birth of a Nation*, 15.

10. The number of such changes made by Griffith himself after the original première at Clune's was, according to Cuniberti, "ultimately incalculable." Cuniberti, *The Birth of a Nation*, 16. Moreover, according to Billy Bitzer, further film footage was shot *after* the première in Los Angeles. Bitzer, *Billy Bitzer*, 112.

11. Brown remembered a sequence with Lillian Gish running across a battlefield from body to body looking for her lover that was actually from Griffith's Allied propaganda film, *Hearts of the World* (1918). Brown also recalled that the hospital shots had been in the second part of the film (which made no sense, since they clearly had to precede Lincoln's grant of a pardon and his later assassination) and that the scene in which Flora Campbell died followed Stoneman's refusal to let his daughter marry Silas Lynch, the black leader (whereas it actually came much earlier in the film's narrative). Brown, *Adventures*, 80, 89, 91–93.

12. Lang, *The Birth of a Nation*, 37. As Karl Brown pointed out, there was simply one original negative: "The rule was to shoot with one camera, cut one negative, and that was that." Cuniberti, *The Birth of a Nation*, 17. When it came to assembling release prints, girls working at Epoch spliced together sequences by scraping the nitrate free of emulsion with a razor blade and then joining the two pieces of film together. Since it was not possible to remove all the emulsion, the joint of the two sections of film was never completely welded together and had a tendency to curl up at the edges and, later, often to break in the projector. "With production methods of this kind," comments Cuniberti, "it is inconceivable that any two release prints would ever be exactly identical." Ibid., 17.

13. For an assessment of this print in comparison with the Museum of Modern Art (MOMA) 16mm circulating print, see Cuniberti, *The Birth of a Nation*, 8–20. Cuniberti himself uses the Library of Congress print as the basis for his shot-by-shot analysis of the film, whereas Robert Lang based his reconstructed continuity script on the MOMA print. In view of the relatively small number of differences between the two and the greater availability of Lang's work, references to shots in this book are taken from the analysis in Lang's book. When Cuniberti's book was published in 1979, he was probably unaware of the existence of a print owned by private Minneapolis collector Lawrence R. Landry, a tinted version of the 1921 reissue. This would become the principal basis of Photoplay Productions' new version of the film, prepared by Kevin Brownlow, Patrick Stanbury, John Allen, and the late David Gill during the 1990s. J. B. Kaufman in Usai, *The Griffith Project*, Vol. 8, 111–12; David Gill, "*The Birth of a Nation*: Orphan or Pariah?" *Griffithiana* 60–61 (1997): 16–29.

14. In the New York *American*, March 5, 1916, the Reverend Thomas B. Gregory observed that the opening part of this shot depicted a Dutch slave ship arriving in James-town, Virginia. Karl Brown later confirmed the existence of this sequence. There was probably also a shot in which it was made clear that Northern traders had been mainly responsible in the first place for bringing black slaves to America and selling them. Cuniberti, *The Birth of a Nation*, 36; W. Stephen Bush, review from *The Moving Picture World*, 23 (March 13, 1915), reprinted in Lang, *The Birth of a Nation*, 176.

15. This shot is in neither the Library of Congress nor the MOMA print but was attested to by two of the film's earliest reviewers. See Francis Hackett, "Brotherly Love," *The New Republic*, 7 (20 March 1915) and W. Stephen Bush, *Moving Picture World*, 23 (March 13, 1915), both reprinted in Lang, *The Birth of a Nation*, 162, 176.

16. According to reviewer W. Steven Bush, the original version of the film had Stoneman kissing the mulatto. Lang, *The Birth of a Nation*, 176–77. Karl Brown, however, contended that no such kiss took place. Cuniberti, *The Birth of a Nation*, 49.

17. There is evidence that some early versions of the film cut away from the battle to show two parallel scenes: one of a "Northern lady waiting," the other of an African depicted in the jungle. Cuniberti, *The Birth of a Nation*, 72. Cuniberti points out that if the shot of the black man in the jungle had occurred earlier in the film, it might perhaps have been a reference to raids on African villages by Yankee slave owners. Since it was located in the midst of the Petersburg battle sequences, it is unclear what Griffith's purpose actually was. Ibid.

18. Seymour Stern contends that three Civil War actions besides Petersburg were shown in the earliest prints: the firing on Fort Sumter and the battles at Cold Harbor and Antietam. Stern, "Griffith: I—*The Birth of a Nation*," *Film Culture*, 36, Special Griffith Issue (Spring–Summer 1965): 82.

19. The earliest prints showed Lee trying to find a pencil to make some notes on the papers of the surrender document and finding that none of his officers had one. Cuniberti, *The Birth of a Nation*, 82. The incident was based on fact. Wanting, with Grant's agreement, to add a word to the surrender document, Lee "felt for a pencil, but could not find one. [Union] Colonel Horace Porter stepped forward and offered his." Douglas Southall Freeman, *R. E. Lee: A Biography* (New York and London: Charles Scribner's Sons, 1934), vol. IV, 138.

20. Brown, *Adventures*, 88–89.

21. Brown, *Adventures*, 92–93.

22. Brown, *Adventures*, 90–91.

23. Carpetbaggers were postwar Northern immigrants to Southern states. The term had its origins in the widespread belief of Southern whites that Northerners of this type were all unscrupulous adventurers carrying their scanty possessions in a single carpetbag. This stereotype was untrue: the carpetbaggers included, for example, many idealistic Northerners, such as men and women who came to teach in the South.

24. Seymour Stern claimed that the original print of the film also contained the actual rape of Flora by Gus. This is extremely unlikely. Although rape sequences were fairly common in films by 1915 [see Sarah Projansky, "The Elusive/Ubiquitous Representation of Rape: A Historical Survey of Rape in U.S. Film, 1903–1972," *Cinema Journal* 41, no. 1 (Fall 2001): 63–90], the program summary of *Birth of a Nation* for Clune's asserted that Flora jumped off the rock to "escape with honor intact." Karl Brown later insisted that there was no such rape sequence. Cuniberti, *The Birth of a Nation*, 125. For a detailed and subtle analysis of the Flora-Gus chase sequence, suggesting a much less malevolent, alternative reading of Gus's motivations, see Merritt, "D. W. Griffith's *The Birth of a Nation*: Going After Little Sister": 215–37.

25. According to Stern, the original prints depicted Gus's castration by Klansmen. Karl Brown insists that this was untrue. Cuniberti, *The Birth of a Nation*, 131–32.

26. A scalawag was a local Southern white man who collaborated with blacks and the radical Republican regimes.

27. According to Stern, shots "of screaming white women being whisked by Negro rapists into doorways in the back alleys of the town were omitted after the initial showings." Stern, 'Griffith: I—*The Birth of a Nation*': 66. Evidence from a local Californian newspaper supports this assertion. Cuniberti, *The Birth of a Nation*, 151.

28. It is very likely, according to Cuniberti, that the version of the film shown at its première at Clune's had the Klan rescue the party in the cabin first and then afterward set off to save Elsie—the opposite order of rescue to that shown in all other surviving prints. Cuniberti, *The Birth of a Nation*, 159–60.

29. It seems clear that the final part of the original print of the film also included a shot referring to the possible "solution" of the race "problem" through a mass deportation of blacks. While this sequence was later lost, its existence was remarked on by several critics. Francis Hackett, for instance, observed that the reference to Christ was preceded by "a suggestion of 'Lincoln's solution'—back to Liberia" and W. Stephen Bush noted that *The Birth of a Nation* "suggests as a remedy of the racial question the transportation of the negroes to Liberia, which Mr. Griffith assures us was Lincoln's idea." Hackett, "Brotherly Love," Bush, "*Birth of a Nation*," both in Lang, *The Birth of a Nation*, 162, 178. Also see Rolfe Cobleigh, "Why I Oppose *The Birth of a* Nation," in Silva, *Focus*, 82. Although there was seemingly no actual "deportation scene," one historian has cited hearsay evidence of a sequence in which the entire black population was lined up in New York harbor for transportation. Merritt, "Dixon, Griffith, and the Southern Legend," 42.

30. Silent movie star (and former Griffith actress) Mary Pickford remembered getting "so excited I stood up in my seat." Pickford, quoted in "Tribune Tip Brings Crowds," *Daily Tribune* [Chicago], June 24, 1915, *David W. Griffith Papers, 1897–1954,*

microfilm edition (Frederick, Md.: University Publications of America, 1982), Manuscript Division, Library of Congress (henceforth DWGP).

31. Hackett, "Brotherly Love," in Lang, *The Birth of a Nation*, 162.

32. Brown, *Adventures*, 94. Several other sources claimed that during the Klan's final ride to the rescue, a shot was made of their horses jumping over the camera. See Aitken, *The Birth of a Nation Story*, 53; Gish, *The Movies, Mr. Griffith and Me*, 146; Bitzer, *Billy Bitzer*, 109. There is no shot of this kind in any of the surviving prints.

33. Brown, *Adventures*, 95. For another recollection of the enthusiasm of the première audience, see the recollections of Joseph Henabery in Slide, *Before, In and After Hollywood*, 82.

CHAPTER 2

1. North Carolina had been one of the last states to secede from the Union. Only with the firing on Fort Sumter and Lincoln's call for volunteers in April 1861 had the state—together with three other slave states (Virginia, Arkansas, and Tennessee)—finally chosen between the Union and the new Confederacy. At that point, with considerable reluctance and by fairly narrow margins, all four states passed ordinances of secession and threw in their lot with the South's bid for independence.

2. Raymond A. Cook, *Thomas Dixon* (New York: Twayne, 1974), 143, n. 1. Cook had earlier produced a longer biography of Dixon: *Fire from the Flint: The Amazing Careers of Thomas Dixon* (Winston-Salem, N.C.: John F. Blair, 1968). I have preferred to rely on Cook's two volumes in reference to Dixon's earlier life. Anthony Slide's recent, well-received study of Dixon, *American Racist: The Life and Films of Thomas Dixon*, summarizes Dixon's early career very briefly before concentrating its attention "on Dixon as a member of the film community" (11).

3. Cook, *Thomas Dixon*, 21–22.

4. Hugh Talmadge Lefler and Albert Ray Newsome, *North Carolina: The History of a Southern State* (Chapel Hill: University of North Carolina Press, 1973), 460.

5. Cook, *Thomas Dixon*, 22–23.

6. The only ex-Confederate state to avoid radical Reconstruction in 1867 was Tennessee, which had already accepted the Fourteenth Amendment defining former slaves for the first time as citizens of the United States. Eric Foner, *Reconstruction: America's Unfinished Revolution, 1863–1877* (New York: Harper and Row, 1988), 261, 276.

7. Foner, *Reconstruction*, 273–77.

8. Cited in Cook, *Fire from the Flint*, 12.

9. Lefler and Newsome, *North Carolina*, 491–92, 495–99; Foner, *Reconstruction*, 440–41. Thomas Dixon would later assert that his uncle, Colonel Lee Roy McAfee, had moved the motion for Holden's impeachment. According to Lefler and Newsome, this was actually done by Frederick M. Strudwick. See *North Carolina*, 498. Dixon also claimed that during his own short career as a lawyer, Holden had requested his help (which Dixon refused) in petitioning the legislature for the restoration of his state citizenship. Cook, *Thomas Dixon*, 37.

10. Cook, *Thomas Dixon*, 23–24.

11. Ibid., 25–26.

12. Ibid., 26–28.

13. Ibid., 28–31.

14. Ibid., 32–34.

15. Richard T. Ely, *Ground under Our Feet: An Autobiography* (New York: Macmillan, 1938), 99.

16. Shaw, *Diary (D-4)*, January 11, 1882, Shaw Papers, New York Public Library. On Adams and his views in general, see *Historical Scholarship in the United States, 1876–1901: As Revealed in the Correspondence of Herbert B. Adams*, ed. W. Stull Holt, Johns Hopkins University Studies in Historical and Political Science, 56:4 (Baltimore: Johns Hopkins University Press, 1938).

17. Cook, *Thomas Dixon*, 34–35.

18. Ibid., 35.

19. Ibid., 36–38.

20. Ibid., 38–39.

21. Ibid., 40–41.

22. Ibid., 41–44.

23. Ibid., 44–50.

24. Joel Williamson, *The Crucible of Race: Black-White Relations in the American South since Emancipation* (New York: Oxford University Press, 1984), 157–58. F. Garvin Davenport Jr. argues that Dixon's defense of the South was part of his wider sense of "mission": to save white Anglo-Saxon civilization in America. Davenport, "Thomas Dixon's Mythology of Southern History," *Journal of Southern History* 36, no. 3 (August 1970): 350–67.

25. Cook, *Thomas Dixon*, 51.

26. "The key to the novel's convulsive power," Linda Williams has written, "is Stowe's interweaving of a conventional sentimental story of youthful female suffering on the model of Dickens (Little Eva's death by consumption) with a more distinctively American story of a racialized Christlike passion ([Uncle] Tom's death by beatings from his white master)." Williams, *Playing the Race Card*, 47.

27. Thomas F. Gossett, *Uncle Tom's Cabin and American Culture* (Dallas: Southern Methodist University Press, 1985), 164–65, 183–84, 339, 341. The quotation from Lincoln is on 314 and 344. The Harriet Beecher Stowe website, in slightly different phrasing, has Lincoln greeting Mrs. Stowe with the words "So you're the little woman who wrote the book that started this Great War!" (http://www.harrietbeecherstowecenter.org/life/#war [accessed April 2, 2007]). The quotation, which may be apocryphal, apparently came from Mrs. Stowe's daughter (who was not present at the meeting with Lincoln) and who was "probably repeating what her mother said to her." Gossett, *Uncle Tom's Cabin*, 314.

28. Gossett, *Uncle Tom's Cabin*, 260–62, 266, 268, 269–70, 272, 275, 277, 283. Also see Williams, *Playing the Race Card*, 82–83.

29. Gossett, *Uncle Tom's Cabin*, 367–68, 370–71.

30. Ibid., 268–69, 274–75, 278–79, 368–69, 372, 377–78.

31. Ibid., 260.

32. Cook, *Thomas Dixon*, 65–66; Williamson, *Crucible of Race*, 157–58. The story of the acceptance of *The Leopard's Spots* may have been more complicated than this. Page apparently sent the manuscript to be read by novelist Frank Norris, who urged that it not be published. It is unlikely that Page allowed his friendship with Dixon (they had both been members of the Watauga Club in Raleigh, dedicated to the establishment of a state

industrial school) to influence his decision. *The Leopard's Spots*, with its combination of melodrama, sex, and racism, had clear commercial possibilities. But Page, according to his biographer, did not have a high opinion of Dixon's abilities as a writer and would later be embarrassed that he had subordinated his own moral principles to the desire for profit. John M. Cooper, Jr., *Walter Hines Page: The Southern as American, 1855–1918* (Chapel Hill: University of North Carolina Press, 1977), 69–70, 168–69.

33. Thomas Dixon Jr., *The Leopard's Spots: A Romance of the White Man's Burden, 1865–1900* (London: Doubleday, Page, 1902), 84–91, 109, 113–17, 132–33, 144–50, 161–62. The University of North Carolina at Chapel Hill has republished *The Leopard's Spots* and Dixon's later novel, *The Clansman* as part of its digitization project, *Documenting the American South*.

34. Dixon, *The Leopard's Spots*, 86–88, 105–106, 138, 144–46, 151–52, 154.

35. Because Augustine St. Clare and his only child, the saintly Eva, both die in *Uncle Tom's Cabin*, Bob St. Clare would have to be the son (or grandson) of Augustine's harsher brother, Alfred. See Dixon, *The Leopard's Spots*, 211, 312–13.

36. Ibid., 309–11, 385–96.

37. Ibid., 5, 33, 63, 80, 93, 100–103.

38. Ibid., 32, 63, 73, 120–21, 104, 107–108.

39. Ibid., 118–19, 123.

40. Ibid., 89, 113–14, 122–28, 145–52, 159–61.

41. Ibid., 195–96, 241–42, 320, 335, 349–50, 365–75, 377–80, 404, 410–16, 423–29, 433–43, 455, 459.

42. Ibid., 13, 219; Cook, *Thomas Dixon*, 19–20. Dixon gave his great-grandfather's name, Hambright, to the principal town in *The Leopard's Spots*.

43. Williamson, *The Crucible of Race*, 158–61; Dixon, *The Leopard's Spots*, 14, 30–32, 52, 284, 254.

44. Ibid., 288–89, 354–60, 404–405, 417–21, 431–32.

45. Ibid., 8, 328–36. Durham's desperate ride to the local head of the Klan, Major Stuart Dameron (modeled on Dixon's uncle, Colonel McAfee), for help in restraining some drunken Klansmen is derived from the experience of Dixon's father. Ibid., 165–68.

46. Ibid., 95, 97, 242, 333, 459. Also see 198, 241, 331, 335, 383, 460.

47. Cook, *Thomas Dixon*, 25; Cook, *Fire from the Flint*, 17–19.

48. Cook, *Thomas Dixon*, 58, 59, 62.

49. Dixon, *The Leopard's Spots*, 405–408.

50. Maxwell Bloomfield, "Dixon's *The Leopard's Spots*: A Study in Popular Racism," in *The Negro in the South Since 1865: Selected Essays in American Negro History*, ed. Charles E. Wynes (Montgomery: University of Alabama Press, 1965), 89–90. Charles Gaston, in his speech in *The Leopard's Spots*, establishes a correlation between the two (435): "In this hour of crisis, our flag has been raised over ten millions of semi-barbaric black men in the foulest slave pen of the Orient. Shall we repeat the farce of '67, reverse the order of nature, and make these black people our rulers? If not, why should the African here, who is not their equal, be allowed to imperil our life?"

51. Williamson, *Crucible of Race*, 5–6, 111, 116, 118, 113–15.

52. For an analysis of the nature of this interracial alliance, see Lawrence Goodwyn, *Democratic Promise: The Populist Movement in America* (New York: Oxford University Press, 1976), 276–306.

53. Williamson, *Crucible of Race*, 229, 224–25, 164.

54. Dixon, *The Leopard's Spots*, 262; M. B. Wharton, "The Leopard's Spots," *Atlanta Journal*, April 20, 1902, 9, cited in Cook, *Fire from the Flint*, 114.

55. Nordau to Dixon, June 10, 1902, cited in Cook, *Fire from the Flint*, 114. Nordau, whose book *Degeneration* had been published in America in 1894, was probably particularly sympathetic to Dixon's anxieties over retrogression.

56. At one point in his novel, Dixon has Charles Gaston set forth his own idealized view of women: "Every woman is something divine to me. I think of God as a woman, not a man—a great loving Mother of all Life." Dixon, *The Leopard's Spots*, 245.

57. Mrs. Stowe saw Eva and Topsy as highly representative of their respective races. Harriet Beecher Stowe, *Uncle Tom's Cabin; or, Life Among the Lowly* (1852; reprint, London: David Campbell, 1995), 275–76.

58. Ibid., 187, 314–15, also see 201–202, 349; Dixon, *The Leopard's Spots*, 310, 385–95, also see 313–14, 395–403.

59. Stowe, *Uncle Tom's Cabin*, 8, 203, 476–79, 491; Dixon, *The Leopard's Spots*, 438–39, 459.

60. Dixon, *The Leopard's Spots*, 46, 95, 97, 242, 262–63, 308, 335, 382–83, 437, 460; Stowe, *Uncle Tom's Cabin*, 8, 239–40, 260, 277, 299, 363, 490–93.

61. Bloomfield, "Dixon's *The Leopard's Spots*," 100; Cook, *Fire from the Flint*, 112.

62. Bloomfield, "Dixon's *The Leopard's Spots*," 101. Perceiving the "Negro problem" as a national rather than purely sectional one was easier because of the huge migration of Southern blacks to Northern cities that began after Reconstruction and accelerated over time. The first really major commentator to observe that the North as well as the South now had a race problem was "muckraking" journalist Ray Stannard Baker in a series of articles for the *American* Magazine beginning in April 1907. The articles were later republished as Baker, *Following the Color Line: An Account of Negro Citizenship in the American Democracy* (New York: Doubleday, Page, 1908).

63. Dixon, *The One Woman: A Story of Modern Utopia* (New York: Doubleday, Page, 1903); Cook, *Fire from the Flint*, 122–26

64. Thomas Dixon, *The Clansman: An Historical Romance of the Ku Klux Klan* (New York: Doubleday, Page, 1905), 3–4, 6–8. Phil Stoneman is not only impressed by Cameron's bravery in leading a doomed Confederate attack on superior Union forces but also by the way the wounded Southerner resembles Stoneman himself ("He is so much like me I feel as if I had been shot myself!"). Ibid., 8

65. Dixon, *The Clansman*, 6, 8–9, 12–14, 18–55. Besides expressing Dixon's own fear of a "mulatto citizenship," Lincoln addresses Stoneman (improbably) by quoting directly from the words of the Gettysburg Address and his second inaugural. Additionally, he refers back to, or expands upon, phrases originally used in the Lincoln-Douglas debates of 1858. At one point, indeed, Dixon's Lincoln offers an updated version of his famous "house divided" speech: "The Nation cannot now exist half white and half black, any more than it could exist half slave and half free." Ibid., 39–55, quotation from 47.

66. Ibid., 56, 60, 61–65, 68–69, 71–79, 82–85, 87–89.

67. Ibid., 90–92, 57–58, 93–94. Dixon hints that Lydia Brown and Lynch, unknown to Stoneman, have a secret relationship. Ibid., 94, 99–100.

68. Ibid., 98–99, 101–14, 120–35.

69. Ibid., 136–37, 139–51, 162–63, 152, 156, 165–86.

70. Anthony Slide points out that Dixon changed the Southern setting from North Carolina in *The Leopard's Spots* to South Carolina in *The Clansman* to emphasize the evils of "black" Reconstruction. South Carolina was the only Southern state to have a legislature with a black majority. Slide, *American Racist*, 37.

71. Dixon, *The Clansman*, 188–89, 204–36, 247–52, 258, 268, 284, 288–89, 297–99, 302–308.

72. Ibid., 311–36.

73. Ibid., 337–41, 344–46, 349–50, 355–57, 359–61, 365–74.

74. Dixon was criticized, among other things, for his fictional account of Thaddeus Stevens (as Stoneman) and for his unacknowledged borrowings from Walt Whitman. Cook, *Fire from the Flint*, 126–29, 131. On Dixon and Whitman, see Francis Oakes, "Whitman and Dixon: A Strange Case of Borrowing," *Georgia Review* 11, no. 3 (Fall 1957): 333–40.

75. Cook, *Fire from the Flint*, 131–33, 136.

76. Dixon would later assert that while his novel might eventually have five million readers, "the play if successful would reach ten millions and with an emotional power ten times as great as in cold type." Cited in Cook, *Thomas Dixon*, 102.

77. Cook, *Fire from the Flint*, 136–37.

78. Thomas Dixon, "The Clansman," manuscript in D. W. Griffith Papers, Act I, 1–3, 6, 9–13, 18–24, 29, 32–41.

79. Ibid., Act II, 1–2, 8–25.

80. Ibid., Act III, 1, 7–9, 13–31.

81. Ibid., Act IV, 2–4, 7, 10–11, 13–17, 19–29.

82. Cook, *Fire from the Flint*, 139–45.

83. *News and Observer* [Raleigh], October 3, 5, 1905, quoted in Cook, *Fire from the Flint*, 141.

84. *Montgomery Advertiser*, November 5, 1905, quoted in Cook, *Fire from the Flint*, 144; *News and Courier* [Charleston], October 21, 1905, quoted in ibid., 142–43; *The State* [Columbia], October 23, 1905, quoted in Moore, "South Carolina's Reaction to the Photoplay, *The Birth of a Nation*," 32–33. Even Dixon's father criticized the play's highly disparaging view of African Americans. Cook, *Fire from the Flint*, 149.

85. *Virginian-Pilot* [Norfolk], September 23, 1905, quoted in John C. Inscoe, "*The Clansman* on Stage and Screen: North Carolina Reacts," 144; *Twin City Sentinel* [Winston], September 30, 1905, quoted in ibid., 146; *Charlotte Daily Observer*, October 12, 1905, quoted in ibid., 146; *Chattanooga Daily Times*, quoted in Cook, *Fire from the Flint*, 144.

86. John Dittmer, *Black Georgia in the Progressive Era, 1900-1920* (Urbana: University of Illinois Press, 1977), 66–67.

87. Pete Daniel, *Standing at the Crossroads: Southern Life in the Twentieth Century* (Baltimore: Johns Hopkins University Press, 1996), 59; Walter White, *A Man Called White: The Autobiography of Walter White* (London: Victor Gollancz, 1949), 8. Just over a year earlier (May–June 1905), James R. Gray had serialized Dixon's novel, *The Clansman*, on the editorial pages of the Atlanta *Journal*. Gregory Mixon, *The Atlanta Riot: Race, Class and Violence in a New South City* (Gainesville: University Press of Florida, 2005), 21.

88. Cook, *Fire from the Flint*, 144–46, 148–49. There were, of course, some severe criticisms of Dixon's output outside the South. Muckraking journalist Ray Stannard

Baker, for example, attacked Dixon's "incendiary and cruel books and plays" for their encouragement of racial hatred. See Baker, *Following the Color Line*, 111, 266, 298.

89. Cook, *Fire from the Flint*, 149. Evelyn Ehrlich noted that in 1908 *The Clansman* "ran for a respectable 51 performances." Ehrlich, "The Civil War in Early Film: Origin and Development of a Genre," *Southern Quarterly* 19, nos. 3–4 (Spring–Summer 1981): 71.

90. Schickel, *Griffith*, 80–81; Russell Merritt, "Rescued from a Perilous Nest: D. W. Griffith's Escape from Theatre into Film," *Cinema Journal* 21, no. 1 (Fall 1981): 27; Mrs. D. W. Griffith [Linda Arvidson], *When the Movies Were Young* (New York: Dover, 1969), 21–22.

91. Cook, *Fire from the Flint*, 150–53.

92. Reversing his usual practice, Dixon later published a novel based on the play: *The Sins of the Father: A Romance of the South* (New York: D. Appleton, 1912).

93. Cook, *Fire from the Flint*, 153–56.

94. The first filmed version was directed by Edwin S. Porter for the Edison Company in 1903. A fourteen-shot "feature," it introduced each scene by a title on film. The film's meaning ultimately came from the cultural competence of its audience. It was not, Janet Staiger has argued, as fragmentary and disconnected as it might later appear. The fourteen discrete tableaux, to spectators familiar with the novel and play, "must have called up a whole causal chain of events, fully motivated in psychologies of characters, and complexly ordered into a story that involved a simultaneity of events as well as sequentiality." Staiger, *Interpreting* Films, 105–18, quotation from 118. Shortly afterward, another (slightly shorter) version was produced by Sigmund Lubin. In 1910, a Vitagraph version, released in three reels, played its own part in encouraging the move toward longer films. Charles Musser, *The Emergence of Cinema: The American Screen to 1907* (New York: Charles Scribner's Sons, 1990), 349, 361; Bowser, *The Transformation of Cinema*, 198, 203; Williams, *Playing the Race Card*, 87–94.

95. Cook, "The Man behind *The Birth of a Nation*," 525, n. 24.

96. On early attempts at innovating sound, see J. Douglas Gomery, "The Coming of the Talkies: Invention, Innovation, and Diffusion," in Balio, *The American Film Industry*, 192–211.

97. Jack Spears, *The Civil War on the Screen and Other Essays* (South Brunswick: A. S. Barnes, 1977), 32. For an alternative view of the difficulties facing Kinemacolor and the eventual collapse of the company, see Gorham Kindem, "The Demise of Kinemacolor: Technological, Legal, Economic, and Aesthetic Problems in Early Color Cinema History," *Cinema Journal* 20, no. 2 (Spring 1981): 3–14.

98. Spears, *The Civil War on the Screen*, 32–33.

99. Cook, "The Man behind *The Birth of a Nation*," 525.

CHAPTER 3

1. Schickel, *Griffith*, 16–17; James Hart, ed., *The Man Who Invented Hollywood: The Autobiography of D. W. Griffith* (Louisville, Ky.: Touchstone, 1972), 24.

2. Schickel, *Griffith*, 17–18.

3. Hart, *The Man Who Invented Hollywood*, 36; Schickel, *Griffith*, 18.

4. Schickel, *Griffith*, 18–19; Hart, *The Man Who Invented Hollywood*, 24.

5. Schickel, *Griffith*, 19.

6. Ibid., 19–20.

7. Ibid., 19–23.

8. Hart, *The Man Who Invented Hollywood*, 26; Schickel, *Griffith*, 16, 23.

9. Schickel, *Griffith*, 24; Hart, *The Man Who Invented Hollywood*, 25–27.

10. Hart, *The Man Who Invented Hollywood*, 26; Schickel, *Griffith*, 30–31.

11. Rogin, "The Sword Became a Flashing Vision," in Lang, *The Birth of a Nation*, 275; Hart, *The Man Who Invented Hollywood*, 28–30, quotation from 30.

12. Hart, *The Man Who Invented Hollywood*, 32, 34, 35; Schickel, *Griffith*, 31–32.

13. Hart, *The Man Who Invented Hollywood*, 34–38.

14. Ibid., 32–33.

15. Ibid., 39.

16. Hart, *The Man Who Invented Hollywood*, 41–42; Schickel, *Griffith*, 39–40, 44.

17. Schickel, *Griffith*, 25, 31–32, 41; Hart, *The Man Who Invented Hollywood*, 42–43.

18. Schickel, *Griffith*, 40–43, 46; Hart, *The Man Who Invented Hollywood*, 43–44, 48, 52–53. While Griffith does not seem to have committed himself finally to an acting career until the spring of 1896, he appeared in a testimonial benefit in Louisville at the end of July 1895. For this, as well as the most complete chronology of Griffith's career on the stage, see Merritt, "Rescued from a Perilous Nest," 19–27.

19. Schickel, *Griffith*, 46; Hart, *The Man Who Invented Hollywood*, 48–49.

20. Hart, *The Man Who Invented Hollywood*, 38–39; Gerrie Griffith Reichard, interviewed in *D. W. Griffith: Father of Film*, documentary film, produced by Kevin Brownlow and David Gill (1993).

21. Schickel, *Griffith*, 43–44, 47, 82.

22. Schickel, *Griffith*, 47–49; Hart, *The Man Who Invented Hollywood*, 49–51.

23. Hart, *The Man Who Invented Hollywood*, 53; Schickel, *Griffith*, 49–51; Merritt, "Rescued from a Perilous Nest," 22.

24. Hart, *The Man Who Invented Hollywood*, 53; Schickel, *Griffith*, 51–52.

25. Schickel, *Griffith*, 53, 55–56, 58–59; Hart, *The Man Who Invented Hollywood*, 53–55.

26. Hart, *The Man Who Invented Hollywood*, 37, 53, 58, 68.

27. Schickel, *Griffith*, 62.

28. Mrs. D. W. Griffith, *When the Movies Were Young*, 12; Merritt, "Rescued from a Perilous Nest," 26–27; Schickel, *Griffith*, 63–70; Hart, *The Man Who Invented Hollywood*, 59.

29. Hart, *The Man Who Invented Hollywood*, 69; Walter Whiteside, 1915, quoted in Merritt, "Rescued from a Perilous Nest," 5; Mrs. D.W. Griffith, *When the Movies Were Young*, 14.

30. Hart, *The Man Who Invented Hollywood*, 68; Merritt, "Rescued from a Perilous Nest," 23–24, 26; Schickel, *Griffith*, 60, 65, 67–68, 71–75.

31. Mrs. D. W. Griffith, *When the Movies Were Young*, 21–22.

32. Hart, *The Man Who Invented Hollywood*, 69–70; Schickel, *Griffith*, 82–90.

33. Hart, *The Man Who Invented Hollywood*, 73; Schickel, *Griffith*, 51–52. In 1904, Griffith had appeared in a play, *Winchester*, which blended together a film with live stage action. Merritt, "Rescued from a Perilous Nest," 25.

34. On Davidson, see Robert Farr, "Hollywood Mensch: Max Davidson," *Griffithiana* 55/56 (September 1996): 107–25 (on his relations with Griffith, see 109).

35. Mrs. D. W. Griffith, *When the Movies Were Young*, 29–30; Hart, *The Man Who Invented Hollywood*, 73.

36. Eileen Bowser, "Griffith's Film Career before *The Adventures of Dollie*," in *Film before Griffith*, ed. John L. Fell (Berkeley: University of California Press, 1983), 367.

37. Iris Barry, *D. W. Griffith—American Film Master* (New York: Museum of Modern Art, 1940), 11; Bowser, "Griffith's Film Career before *The Adventures of Dollie*," 368; Mrs. D. W. Griffith, *When the Movies Were Young*, 41. According to his wife, Griffith also approached Kalem, Lubin, and other studios, but did not find work there. Ibid.

38. Mrs. D. W. Griffith, *When the Movies Were Young*, 31, 34, 40; Bowser, "Griffith's Film Career before *Dollie*," 368–69, 371–73.

39. Bitzer, *Billy Bitzer*, 63.

40. Mrs. D. W. Griffith, *When the Movies Were Young*, 42, 45–48

41. Schickel, *Griffith*, 107–11; Hart, *The Man Who Invented Hollywood*, 75–75; Mrs Griffith, *When the Movies Were Young*, 51–52.

42. In practice, his productivity was highest at the beginning of the period, declining toward the end. He directed 60 films in 1908, 141 in 1909, 87 in 1910, 70 in 1911, 67 in 1912, and 31 in 1913. Figures based on the filmography in Schickel, *Griffith*, 637–43. For the most detailed listing of Griffith's Biograph films, see Cooper C. Graham, Steven Higgins, Elaine Mancini, and João Luiz Vieira, *D. W. Griffith and the Biograph Company* (Metuchen, N.J.: Scarecrow Press, 1985).

43. Hart, *The Man Who Invented Hollywood*, 74.

44. Michel Ciment, *Le crime à l'écran: une histoire de l'Amérique* (Paris: Gallimard, 1992), 17.

45. Spears, *The Civil War on the Screen*, 11.

46. Ibid., 12, 21–23, 29–30.

47. Robert Lang, "D. W. Griffith: A Biographical Sketch," in Lang, *The Birth of a Nation*, 29.

48. Although it was not a Civil War film, *The Girls and Daddy* (1909) anticipated the threat posed to Elsie and Flora by Lynch and Gus by showing a blackface burglar threatening two young white girls. See Daniel Bernardi, "The Voice of Whiteness: D. W. Griffith's Biograph Films (1908–1913)," in *The Birth of Whiteness: Race and the Emergence of U.S. Cinema*, ed. Daniel Bernardi (New Brunswick, N.J.: Rutgers University Press, 1996) , 122–23; Courtney, *Hollywood Fantasies of Miscegenation*, 20, 31–32.

49. Bowser, *Transformation of Cinema*, 22.

50. Tom Gunning, *D. W. Griffith and the Origins of American Narrative Film: The Early Years at Biograph* (Urbana: University of Illinois Press, 1991), 60–64.

51. Gunning, *D. W. Griffith and the Origins of American Narrative Film*, 64–65.

52. Schickel, *Griffith*, 122; Gunning, *D. W. Griffith and the Origins of American Narrative Film*, 143–45; Henderson, *D. W. Griffith*, 31–32.

53. Gunning, *D. W. Griffith and the Origins of American Narrative Film*, 144–45; Henderson, *Griffith*, 49–50.

54. Gunning, *D. W. Griffith and the Origins of American Narrative Film*, 145–48, 155–58, 160–62.

55. Schickel, *Griffith*, 111. His wife remembered the salary as $45. Mrs. D. W. Griffith, *When the Movies Were Young*, 52.

56. Schickel, *Griffith*, 115–16.

57. Bitzer, *Billy Bitzer*, 8–9, 20, 53; Karl Brown, *Adventures*, 18–19; Schickel, *Griffith*, 118.

58. Schickel, *Griffith*, 103; Mrs. D. W. Griffith, *When the Movies Were Young*, 62–65.

59. Mrs. D. W. Griffith, *When the Movies Were Young*, 95–97.

60. Schickel, *Griffith*, 137, 141, 153, 167.

61. Gish, *The Movies, Mr. Griffith and Me*, 63.

62. Bowser, *Transformation of Cinema*, 196–97. Other longer films included *Buffalo Bill's Wild West Show* (three reels, 1910), which was distributed outside the normal exchange system, and *Drink* (a two-reel adaptation of Zola's *L'Assommoir*), which was probably exhibited by special arrangement between Pathé Frères, its producer, and the MPPC. Ibid., 192, 197.

63. Henderson, *Griffith*, 97–98; Hart, *The Man Who Invented Hollywood*, 87; Graham, Higgins, Mancini, and Vieira, *D. W. Griffith and the Biograph* Company, 102.

64. Gish, *The Movies, Mr. Griffith, and Me*, 63; Schickel, *Griffith*, 160.

65. Graham, Higgins, Mancini, and Vieira, *D. W. Griffith and the Biograph Company*, 145, 160, 162.

66. Schickel, *Griffith*, 185, 196, 199–200; Williams, *Griffith: First Artist of the Movies*, 54–55; Henderson, *Griffith*, 119–20, 124, 132.

67. Henderson, *Griffith*, 119.

68. Schickel, *Griffith*, 188–89; Henderson, *Griffith*, 124. Blanche Sweet later recalled that she had seen *Quo Vadis* with Griffith in New York. Slide, *American Racist*, 83.

69. Since Griffith himself was supposedly supervising two other Biograph directors, Dell Henderson and Anthony O'Sullivan, for part of the time, the attribution of some of the films is not absolutely clear. See Graham, Higgins, Mancini, and Vieire, *D. W. Griffith and the Biograph Company*, 171–211.

70. Richard Schickel points out that it was a historical epic, based in fact on the biblical Apocrypha, and the author of the play used as the basis for the film, Thomas Bailey Aldrich, had at least as high a literary reputation as Henryk Sienkiewicz, who had written *Quo Vadis*. Schickel, *Griffith*, 191.

71. Henderson, *Griffith*, 126–27, 131. Griffith himself later recalled that the film took two weeks to shoot, cost $13,000, and as a consequence led to his "getting in Dutch with the bosses again." Hart, *The Man Who Invented Hollywood*, 83–84.

72. Gish, *The Movies, Mr. Griffith, and Me*, 108.

73. Hart, *The Man Who Invented Hollywood*, 87; Henderson, *Griffith*, 115–16, 131–32.

74. This ad is reproduced in Jacobs, *The Rise of the American Film*, 117.

75. Biograph would finally release all four films between February and April 1914. Graham, Higgins, Mancini, and Vieira, *D. W. Griffith and the Biograph Company*, 160, 210–11.

76. Griffith repeated his claims to have invented techniques such as the close-up, the flashback, the fade-out, and the iris shot both in later interviews and in his autobiography. See David W. Griffith, "The Miracle of Modern Photography," *The Mentor* 9, no. 6 (July 1921), 67; Hart, *The Man Who Invented Hollywood*, 84–86.

77. Williams, *Griffith: First Artist of the Movies*, 27.

78. Edward Wagenknecht, "Griffith's Biographs: A General View," *Films in Review* 26, no. 8 (October 1975), 465.

79. Bitzer, *Billy Bitzer*, 54.

80. Bitzer recalled that Cuddebackville could easily be used as "a mountainous locale" since "the sloping hills looked like mountains when photographed against the sunset." Bitzer, *Billy Bitzer*, 68

81. Bowser, *Transformation of Cinema*, 171.

82. Ibid., 162–65, 171–72. Biograph was the third major film company to arrive in California. The Selig studio and the New York Motion Picture Company had already established themselves there in 1909. Ibid., 151–52.

83. Williams, *Griffith: First Artist of the Movies*, 34.

84. Williams, *Griffith: First Artist of the Movies*, 39; cf. Iris Barry, *D. W. Griffith: American Film Master*, 16.

85. Mrs. D. W. Griffith, *When the Movies Were Young*, 128–31.

86. Hart, *The Man Who Invented Hollywood*, 82; Bitzer, *Billy Bitzer*, 84–85.

87. Bitzer, *Billy Bitzer*, 54. Later, to boost Griffith's reputation at Bitzer's expense, Griffith partisans, including Lillian Gish and Linda Arvidson, asserted that Bitzer had at times dragged his feet over some of Griffith's suggestions. See Gish, *The Movies, Mr. Griffith and Me*, 61–62; Mrs. D. W. Griffith, *When the Movies Were Young*, 128–29.

88. Bowser, *Transformation of Cinema*, 54

89. "Before his arrival," Bitzer later reflected on Griffith as a director, "I, as cameraman, was responsible for everything except the immediate hiring and handling of the actor. Soon it was his say whether the lights were bright enough, or if the make-up was right." Bitzer, *Billy Bitzer*, 69.

90. Gunning, *D. W. Griffith and the Origins of American Narrative Film*, 42–43. Much the same point was made by Edward Wagenecht. See Wagenecht, "Griffith's Biographs," 465.

91. Williams, *Griffith: First Artist of the Movies*, 34–35. Griffith himself later claimed that Bitzer had resisted the notion of shooting close-ups. Hart, *The Man Who Invented Hollywood*, 85–86. The management of the Biograph were even more skeptical: manager Henry Marvin argued that audiences had paid to see actors and might object if they could see only part of them, and that they would be unable to follow the changes between long or medium shot and close-up. Williams, *Griffith: First Artist of the Movies*, 35.

92. Gunning, *D. W. Griffith and the Origins of American Narrative Film*, 108–109.

93. Quoted in Bowser, *Transformation of Cinema*, 88.

94. Roberta E. Pearson, *Eloquent Gestures: The Transformation of Performance Style in the Griffith Biograph Films* (Berkeley: University of California Press, 1992), 4, 20, 23, 28, 36, 51, 120.

95. Pearson, *Eloquent Gestures*, 79–80; Bitzer, *Billy Bitzer*, 63.

96. Barry, *D. W. Griffith—American Film Master*, 15; cf. Gunning, *D. W. Griffith and the Origins of American Narrative Film*, 97.

97. Bowser, *Transformation of Cinema*, 62.

98. Bowser, *Transformation of Cinema*, 58–59.

99. According to Tom Gunning, parallel editing was the "linch-pin" of the new narrator system for film introduced by Griffith in his first eighteen months at Biograph. Gunning, *D. W. Griffith and the Origins of American Narrative Film*, 80.

100. Iris Barry, *D. W. Griffith—American Film Master*, 16–17.

101. Gunning, *D. W. Griffith and the Origins of American Narrative Film*, 41–42.

102. Bowser, *Transformation of Cinema*, 269. Harrison's article, "The Art Director and His Work," appeared in *Moving Picture World*, November 22, 1913, 847–48.

103. Bowser, "Griffith's Film Career before *The Adventures of Dollie*," 373.

104. Bowser, *Transformation of Cinema*, 105; Everson, *American Silent Film*, 51.

105. Schickel, *Griffith*, 203.

106. Bowser, *Transformation of Cinema*, 221–22: Aitken, *The Birth of a Nation Story*, 20–21; Robert Lang, "Biographical Sketch," in Lang, ed., *The Birth of a Nation*, 29; Henderson, *Griffith*, 137–38.

107. Barry, *American Film Master*, 20 (cf. Gish, *The Movies, Mr. Griffith and Me*, 123); Bowser, *Transformation of Cinema*, 258.

108. Bowser, *Transformation of Cinema*, 164–65.

109. Gish, *The Movies, Mr. Griffith and Me*, 109–11; Bitzer, *Billy Bitzer*, 89–90.

110. Gish, *The Movies, Mr. Griffith and Me*, 112–113; Brown, *Adventures*, 31; Williams, *Griffith: First Artist of the Movies*, 57–60; Everson, *American Silent Film*, 76–77. Part of the intertitle language may be derived from Poe's poem "Annabel Lee."

111. Comparatively recent as his memories of the abortive 1912 color film were, Woods's recollection of the project may have been prompted still further by the fact that when Griffith arrived in Los Angeles to work for Majestic he took over the old Kinemacolor lot at 4500 Sunset Boulevard as his studio. Brown, *Adventures*, 9.

112. Spears, *The Civil War on the Screen*, 33. According to Griffith's wife, he was already familiar with the play "as he had heard from his friend Austin Webb, who had played the part of the mulatto Silas Lynch, about all the exciting times attending the performance of the play—the riots and all—and more he had heard from Claire McDowell, who was also in the show, and more still from Mr. Dixon himself." Mrs. D. W. Griffith, *When the Movies Were Young*, 251.

113. Hart, *The Man Who Invented Hollywood*, 88–89.

114. Aitken, *The Birth of a Nation Story*, 26.

115. Cook, *Fire from the Flint*, 163.

116. Aitken, *The Birth of a Nation Story*, 26, 31; Hart, *The Man Who Invented Hollywood*, 89.

117. Aitken, *The Birth of a Nation Story*, 31. According to Roy Aitken, his brother Harry gave Dixon a personal check for the $2,000. Dixon's biographer believes he settled just for the 25 percent. Ibid., 35; Cook, *Fire from the Flint*, 164.

118. Aitken, *The Birth of a Nation Story*, 36; Gish, *The Movies, Mr. Griffith and Me*, 132.

119. Aitken, *The Birth of a Nation Story*, 27, 29–38.

120. Bernardi, "The Voice of Whiteness," 103–28. Although Bernardi is not discussing *The Birth of a Nation*, the implication of his essay is that Griffith, at Biograph, was already working through technologies and ideologies he would use in *Birth*.

121. While Griffith made a number of films in which Indians were depicted as violent savages (*Fighting Blood*, 1911; *The Last Drop of Water*, 1911; and *The Battle at Elderbush Gulch*, 1913), Kim Newman points out that he "also made the significantly-titled *The Redman's View* (1909) and *A Mohawk's Way* (1910), [and] was reasonably sympathetic to the Indians in *The Squaw's Love* (1911), *The Chief's Daughter* (1911), *The Indian Brothers* (1911) and *The Chief's Blanket* (1912)." Among other Griffith films that were "sympathetic

to Native Americans," Michael Hilger lists *The Redman and the Child* (1908), *The Broken Doll* (1910), and *Ramona* (1910). As Hilger notes, in fact, Griffith veered between depicting Indians as "savages" and as "noble red men." Sometimes, as in *Iola's Promise* (1912), he included both. Kim Newman, *Wild West Movies, or, How the West Was Found, Won, Lost, Lied About, Filmed and Forgotten* (London: Bloomsbury, 1990), 67; Michael Hilger, *From Savage to Nobleman: Images of Native Americans in Film* (Lanham, Md.: Scarecrow Press, 1995), 2, 17–19, 23, 40, 44.

CHAPTER 4

1. According to Cook, the loft was owned by the Epoch Producing Company. However, Epoch was not itself organized until the beginning of March 1915. Cook, *Fire from the Flint*, 164.

2. Cuniberti, *The Birth of a Nation*, 16. Seymour Stern later claimed that Dixon and Woods had collaborated on a scenario for the film. Ibid., n. 17.

3. D. W. Griffith, "What I Demand of Movie Stars," *Moving Picture Classic*, 3 (February 1917), 40–41, 68, reprinted in Geduld, *Focus on D. W. Griffith*, 54. Cuniberti observes that Griffith on other occasions either contradicted this or insisted that there had never been a scenario. Cuniberti, *The Birth of a Nation*, 16, n. 20.

4. On this aspect of Griffith's work, see Michael Allen, *Family Secrets: The Feature Films of D. W. Griffith* (London: BFI Publishing, 1999).

5. Flora *Camp*, of course, had been the name of the young girl raped by Dick in *The Leopard's Spots*.

6. Henderson, *Griffith*, 146; Gish, *The Movies, Mr. Griffith, and Me*, 131–32. The reason for such secrecy, Gish explained, was to try to prevent another film company from rushing out a competing version.

7. Hart, *The Man Who Invented Hollywood*, 90; Schickel, *Griffith*, 216; Gish, *The Movies, Mr. Griffith and Me*, 135.

8. Lillian Gish, *The Movies, Mr. Griffith and Me*, 6–7, 9–12, 14, 16, 20–21, 29–39.

9. Anthony Slide, *The Griffith Actresses* (South Brunswick: A. S. Barnes, 1973), 112–16.

10. Bitzer, *Billy Bitzer*, 68.

11. Slide, *The Griffith Actresses*, 127–31

12. Quoted in Schickel, *Griffith*, 218.

13. Ibid., 219.

14. Gish, *The Movies, Mr. Griffith, and Me*, 133; Slide, *The Griffith Actresses*, 99–100.

15. Richard Dyer, "A White Star," *Sight and Sound* 3, no. 8 (August 1993): 22–24.

16. Schickel, *Griffith*, 217.

17. Hart, *The Man Who Invented Hollywood*, 90; Slide, *The Griffith Actresses*, 112, 116–17. The very earliest scenes of the film had Flora as a child played by Violet Wilkie.

18. Slide, *The Griffith Actresses*, 131–32.

19. Beringer, who also functioned as an assistant director for the film, later changed his name to André Beranger and became a character actor of some note in the 1920s. Cuniberti, *The Birth of a Nation*, 12, n. 7.

20. Griffith, as quoted by Henry Stephen Gordon, "D. W. Griffith Recalls the Making of *The Birth of a Nation*," in *The Photoplay Magazine* 10 (October 1916), 86–94, reprinted in Silva, *Focus*, 58.

21. Leon F. Litwack, *"The Birth of a Nation,"* in *Past Imperfect: History According to the Movies*, Mark C. Carnes, Ted Mico, John Miller-Monzon, and David Rubel, eds. (London: Cassell, 1996), 140.

22. Gish, *The Movies, Mr. Griffith, and Me*, 134.

23. Gish, *The Movies, Mr. Griffith, and Me*, 134–35. Sul-Te-Wan appeared as a woman on the sidewalk jeering a dead white victim in the wartime raid on Piedmont, as one of the spectators in the South Carolina House of Representatives, and as the woman taunting Dr. Cameron when he is brought in front of his former slaves in chains. Cuniberti, *The Birth of a Nation*, 59. It would be interesting—but completely unprofitable, since no evidence exists—to speculate on the precise nature of the relationship between Griffith and Sul-Te-Wan while he was making *The Clansman*, a film about miscegenation.

24. Schickel, *Griffith*, 233; Gish, *The Movies, Mr. Griffith, and Me*, 134.

25. Brown, *Adventures*, 62.

26. Eric Lott has demonstrated the manner in which blackface minstrelsy both expressed and challenged white working-class culture. Sarah Meer has recently analyzed 1850s minstrelsy and the "Uncle Tom" phenomenon in an international perspective. Eric Lott, *Love and Theft: Blackface Minstrelsy and the American Working Class* (New York: Oxford University Press, 1993); Sareh Meer, *Uncle Tom Mania: Slavery, Minstrelsy, and Transatlantic Culture in the 1850s* (Athens: University of Georgia Press, 2005). For another study of blackface minstrelsy in historical perspective, see Michael Rogin, *Blackface, White Noise: Jewish Immigrants in the Hollywood Melting Pot* (Berkeley: University of California Press, 1996), especially chaps. 1 and 2.

27. Brown, *Adventures*, 71.

28. Slide, *Before, In and After Hollywood*, 75–77.

29. Gish, *The Movies, Mr. Griffith, and Me*, 136.

30. Walsh had made his own theatrical debut in a touring company of *The Clansman*. He was an expert rider and bit player who, at Biograph, had risen to become an assistant director. After shooting "Lincoln" in his box at the theater, like Booth he was required to leap onto the stage and—like Booth—injured himself in the process, limping off stage in a very convincing imitation of reality. Schickel, *Griffith*, 221.

31. Brown, *Adventures*, 28, 57; cf. Gish, *The Movies, Mr. Griffith, and Me*, 91, 93; Slide, *Before, In and After Hollywood*, 76, 105.

32. Schickel, *Griffith*, p. 222. According to von Stroheim's biographer, it took two takes to get the shot of the fall off the roof right. Cuniberti, *The Birth of a Nation*, 61. Joseph Henabery contested Stroheim's role in the production, implying that he had only met Stroheim once *Birth of a Nation* had been completed. After reviewing the evidence available, Richard Koszarski is inclined to accept the case for Stroheim's participation in *Birth*. Slide, *Before, In and After Hollywood*, 88; Richard Koszarski, "'So Long, Master …': Stroheim, Griffith, and the Griffith Studio," *Griffithiana* 71 (2001): 47–53.

33. Gish, *The Movies, Mr. Griffith and Me*, 139.

34. Slide, *Before, In and After Hollywood*, 81, 74–75.

35. Gish, *The Movies, Mr. Griffith and Me*, 145; cf. Cuniberti, *The Birth of a Nation*, 68.

36. Slide, *Before, In and After Hollywood*, 122; Schickel, *Griffith*, 226.

37. Gish, *The Movies, Mr. Griffith, and Me*, 142.

38. Schickel, *Griffith*, 216; Hart, *The Man Who Invented Hollywood*, 91.

39. Brown, *Adventures*, 28.

40. Slide, *Before, In and After Hollywood*, 78–80.

41. Brown, *Adventures*, 28; Bitzer, "D. W. Griffith," DWGP.

42. Brown, *Adventures*, 28–29; Slide, *Before, In and After Hollywood*, 79–80.

43. Bitzer, "D. W. Griffith," DWGP.

44. Schickel, *Griffith*, 212. The one outline of scenes in Griffith's handwriting that has survived seems to have been something of an aide-mémoire from the editing process. Cuniberti, *The Birth of a Nation*, 170–75.

45. Slide, *Before, In and After Hollywood*, 139.

46. Gish, *The Movies, Mr. Griffith, and Me*, 133.

47. Gish, *The Movies, Mr. Griffith and Me*, 138; Bitzer, untitled recollections, DWGP.

48. Gish, *The Movies, Mr. Griffith and Me*, 138.

49. There is a list of interiors and exteriors in the Epoch accounts for March 13, 1915. It is impossible to say when it was written; since it includes scenes that are missing from the final film, this might have been done at an early stage, possibly even before filming started. See "Birth of a Nation Budget," DWGP.

50. Gish, *The Movies, Mr. Griffith and Me*, 137–38; Schickel, *Griffith*, 224. Brown remembered that Wortman and his gang of long-seasoned stage carpenters had no need to think very long about "what the town should look like or how it should be dressed." All the gang had worked at some point for "Tommer" shows—traveling companies playing the stage version of *Uncle Tom's Cabin*. The "Southern" town they created in California was based on this earlier experience. Moreover, Brown claimed, force of habit made them build scenery in sections that could be folded up and shipped (in reality, of course, most would simply be destroyed when filming was over). Brown, *Adventures*, 63–64. Linda Williams uses the background of the carpenters on *Birth of a Nation* in "Tom" shows to introduce her own discussion of "the strange confluence of the most popular and influential play of the nineteenth century with the most popular and influential film of the early twentieth century." Williams, *Playing the Race Card*, 96–98.

51. Brown, *Adventures*, 63–64.

52. Gish, *The Movies, Mr. Griffith and Me*, 136–37; Brown, *Adventures*, 74. Bitzer also claimed that Griffith relied on documents to a very great extent. Bitzer interview, 1940, DWGP.

53. Brown, *Adventures*, 58–59, 64–65.

54. Ibid., 65.

55. Ibid., 57–58.

56. Schickel, *Griffith*, 224.

57. Brown, *Adventures*, 65.

58. Bitzer, *Billy Bitzer*, 107; Raoul Walsh, *Each Man in His Time: The Life Story of a Director* (New York: Farrar, Straus and Giroux, 1974), 106.

59. Gish, *The Movies, Mr. Griffith, and Me*, 137; Brown, *Adventures*, 55–56.

60. Gish, *The Movies, Mr. Griffith and Me*, 139–40: cf. Bitzer, *Billy Bitzer*, 107.

61. Walsh, *Each Man*, 107; Brown, interviewed in *D. W. Griffith: Father of Film*.

62. Brown, *Adventures*, 75–76; Gish, *The Movies, Mr. Griffith and Me*, 140. This technique of using assistant directors to control groups of extras would later become known as the nucleus system. Henderson, *Griffith*, 150.

63. Walsh, *Each Man*, 106.

64. Brown, *Adventures*, 56; Gish, *The Movies, Mr. Griffith and Me*, 140.

65. Schickel, *Griffith*, 225; Cuniberti, *The Birth of a Nation*, 11.

66. Henderson, *Griffith*, 149; Miriam Cooper with Bonnie Herndon, *Dark Lady of the Silents: My Life in Early Hollywood* (Indianapolis: Bobbs-Merrill, 1973), 77–78.

67. Brown, *Adventures*, 66–74. As Brown was trying to push the dummy off the rock, he almost fell. He just managed to keep his footing, denying Griffith the shot—as he sardonically noted—"of not one but two dummies making the drop." Ibid., 73–74.

68. Slide, *Before, In and After Hollywood*, 186.

69. Billy Bitzer, "Our Neighbor Mrs. Thoren Almost Became a Stockholder," DWGP.

70. Gish, *The Movies, Mr. Griffith and Me*, 138–39.

71. Cooper, *Dark Lady of the Silents*, 67.

72. Gish, *The Movies, Mr. Griffith and Me*, 139, 141.

73. Brown, *Adventures*, 17; Gish, *The Movies, Mr. Griffith and Me*, 139.

74. Bitzer, *Billy Bitzer*, 107; Cuniberti, *The Birth of a Nation*, 69; Billy Bitzer, "On Camera," DWGP. The only times Bitzer recalled his own camera not being used was when it was an elevated platform "as in the distant battlefield shots where it would require a little time in hoisting it up and placing it." On these occasions, a second camera—which Griffith would call Bitzer off the platform to operate—was used instead. Ibid.

75. Bitzer, *Billy Bitzer*, 86, 112. Bitzer's assistant, Karl Brown, later suggested that Bitzer also had a Swiss-made lens that was the best of the lot. Cuniberti, *The Birth of a Nation*, 69.

76. Cuniberti, *The Birth of a Nation*, 69; Bitzer, *Billy Bitzer*, 108.

77. Brown, *Adventures*, 59. Griffith's language may have been derived from the live theater. Connecticut actor-author-director William Gillette pioneered the development of the "fade-out," involving a gradual dimming of the lights before the curtain was lowered. Griffith had once appeared in a play of Gillette's. Kenneth S. Lynn, *Charlie Chaplin and His Times* (1997; reprint, London: Aurum Press, 2002), 76.

78. Cuniberti, *The Birth of a Nation*, 26.

79. "Billy Bitzer on Photography," Conversation with Beaumont Newhall, January 30, 1940, DWGP; Cuniberti, *The Birth of a Nation*, 26, 45.

80. Bitzer, *Billy Bitzer*, 107; Gish, *The Movies, Mr. Griffith and Me*, 141. In handwritten notes on making *The Birth of a Nation*, not dated but probably around 1940, Bitzer commented, "There were flares used in some battle scenes." Bitzer, "No Electric Light All Sun Photography," DWGP.

81. Bitzer, "No Electric Light All Sun Photography," DWGP. Karl Brown, Bitzer's assistant, remembered that "the day ended when the light became yellow." Brown, *Adventures*, 17.

82. Cuniberti, *The Birth of a Nation*, 52; Gish, *The Movies, Mr. Griffith and Me*, 141.

83. Bitzer, "One Camera," DWGP; Bitzer, *Billy Bitzer*, 108. Some sources identify the explosives expert for the film as Walter "Slim" Hoffman. According to Karl Brown, however, he was a one-armed man pockmarked by powder burns called "Fireworks" Wilson. Since Griffith and Bitzer already had experience in shooting Civil War pictures, it was Bitzer—Brown claimed—who finally told Wilson how to create the effect required of something that *looked* like a big explosion by making the "bombs" themselves out of

mainly sawdust and very little powder. Cuniberti, *The Birth of a Nation*, 68; Schickel, *Griffith*, 227–28; Brown, *Adventures*, 52–53, 55.

84. Aitken, *The Birth of a Nation Story*, 40.

85. Gish, *The Movies, Mr. Griffith and Me*, 146–47; Bitzer, *Billy Bitzer*, 108–109; Bitzer, "One Camera," DWGP; Bitzer, "In the Rides of the Clansmen," DWGP. This shot does not appear in versions of the film available today.

86. Brown, *Adventures*, 75.

87. Bitzer, "The Old Film in Half Tones," DWGP. Karl Brown remembered that while directing the shot of Lee's surrender, Griffith was holding a historical picture of the scene in his hand—"a unique example," he commented, "of a picture being directed by a picture." Brown, *Adventures*, 75.

88. Bitzer, "The Old Film in Half Tones," DWGP; Bitzer, "No Electric Light All Sun Photography," DWGP; "Billy Bitzer on Photography," conversation with Beaumont Newhall, January 30, 1940, DWGP. Bitzer also implied that both he and Griffith had been familiar with Brady's photographs and had been trying consciously to imitate them. Ibid.

89. Aitken, *The Birth of a Nation Story*, 34, 39.

90. Bitzer, *Billy Bitzer*, 109; Billy Bitzer, "Money," DWGP.

91. Aitken, *The Birth of a Nation Story*, 37–41, 43.

92. Gish, *The Movies, Mr. Griffith and Me*, 142–43.

93. Schickel, *Griffith*, 239; Bitzer, *Billy Bitzer*, 110–11.

94. Gish, *The Movies, Mr. Griffith and Me*, 144; Schickel, *Griffith*, 240–41; Bitzer, *Billy Bitzer*, 110–11.

95. See "Investors and Amounts Invested," DWGP.

96. Ibid. Curiously, Bitzer's name does not appear on the list of investors in the movie.

97. Bitzer, "The Birth of a Nation," n.d., DWGP. The only offer to help finance the film Griffith actually turned down was that of Lillian Gish's mother, who attempted to invest her $300 savings. Ironically, of course, his principled refusal—he thought it too risky an investment—cost the Gishes a fortune. Gish, *The Movies, Mr. Griffith and Me*, 143.

98. Aitken, *The Birth of a Nation Story*, 45, 47–48.

99. In 1914, the Mutual Film Corporation filed suit to restrain the enforcement of an act of the Ohio legislature creating a state movie censorship board. Both Gerald Mast and Richard Koszarski wrongly state that this was in connection with the distribution in the state of *The Birth of a Nation*. Koszarski, *An Evening's Entertainment*, 199; Mast, *The Movies in Our Midst*, 136. In reality, since the Majestic Corporation had declined to finance *The Birth of a Nation*, the Aitkens decided not to distribute it through the Mutual company, and the Aitkens and Griffith created a separate organization, the Epoch Producing Company, to distribute the film. In 1915, the United States Supreme Court came down on the side of the Ohio Censorship Board, effectively deciding that film censorship would be permitted, a decision that stood until the Court reversed itself in the *Miracle* case of 1951. Later, in 1916, Mutual signed an exclusive contract with Charlie Chaplin to produce a series of twelve pictures. Lynn, *Charlie Chaplin and His Times*, 173–74.

100. Henderson, *Griffith*, 156; Aitken, *The Birth of a Nation Story*, 48–49; "ByLaws," Epoch Producing Company, March 13, 1915, 2–3, DWGP.

101. Bitzer, *Billy Bitzer*, 105–106. Neither Bitzer nor his assistant, Karl Brown, shared Griffith's enthusiasm for the project. Bitzer remembered thinking it "was just another sausage after all." Ibid., 106; Brown, *Adventures*, 31–33.

102. Bitzer, *Billy Bitzer*, 106; Slide, *Before, In and After Hollywood*, 66; Brown, *Adventures*, 65.

103. Bitzer, *Billy Bitzer*, 107, 109.

104. Schickel, *Griffith*, 61; Slide, *Before, In and After Hollywood*, 67.

105. Gish, *The Movies, Mr. Griffith and Me*, 123–24.

106. Slide, *Before, In and After Hollywood*, 67.

107. Gish, *The Movies, Mr. Griffith and Me*, 126; Brown, *Adventures*, 29.

108. Gish, *The Movies, Mr. Griffith and Me*, 126; Brown, *Adventures*, 29; Bitzer, *Billy Bitzer*, 70.

109. Slide, *Before, In and After Hollywood*, 67; Brown, *Adventures*, 29; Bitzer, "D. W. Griffith," DWGP; Gish, *The Movies, Mr. Griffith and Me*, 127–28.

110. Bitzer, "D. W. Griffith," DWGP; Brown, *Adventures*, 15, 30–31, 79–80; Gish, *The Movies, Mr. Griffith and Me*, 92, 126, 127–29; Schickel, *Griffith*, 229.

111. Bitzer, *Billy Bitzer*, 106, 110; Brown, *Adventures*, 14–16; Aitken, *The Birth of a Nation Story*, 39.

112. Slide, *Before, In and After Hollywood*, 140.

113. Karl Brown was terrified, as Henry Walthall slowly loitered, that the camera would run out of film before he reached the front door. Brown, *Adventures*, 81–82.

114. Brown, *Adventures*, 81 (also see 93).

115. Gish, *The Movies, Mr. Griffith and Me*, 141; Bitzer, "D. W. Griffith," DWGP; Bitzer, *Billy Bitzer*, 108.

116. Slide, *Before, In and After Hollywood*, 137–39. Henabery, later an experienced director, considered Walthall "the best silent picture actor who ever lived." Once told by Griffith what was needed, Walthall usually asked if it was a long shot or a close-up: "He varied his style and degree of exaggeration according to his distance from the camera. He even varied his action according to the focal length of the lens. He knew how differently action appeared with a very wide angle lens as compared to one with a narrow angle. He was a master of overplaying, sometimes valuable in long shots, and a master of underplaying, so important in close-ups. At times, without...apparent facial movement, Walthall expressed a character's innermost feeling to the audience." Ibid., 137–38.

117. Slide, *Before, In and After Hollywood*, 138; Gish, *The Movies, Mr. Griffith and Me*, 127.

118. Brown, *Adventures*, 18–19; Henderson, *Griffith*, 152; Gish, *The Movies, Mr. Griffith and Me*, 102.

119. Gish, *The Movies, Mr. Griffith and Me*, 153.

120. Bitzer, *Billy Bitzer*, 105. According to Henderson, the printing was done in Chicago. The accounts of the Epoch Producing Company, however, show that Bitzer's recollection of New York was correct. Henderson, *Griffith*, 152; Epoch Producing Company accounts, dated March 13, 1915, DWGP.

121. Brown interview, January 12, 1976, quoted in Cuniberti, *The Birth of a Nation*, 17.

122. Gish, *The Movies, Mr. Griffith and Me*, 125; Brown, *Adventures*, 20, 85.

123. Brown, *Adventures*, 16, 22–23.

124. Gish, *The Movies, Mr. Griffith and Me*, 147; Brown, *Adventures*, 20, 85.

125. Epoch Producing Corporation, Accounts dated March 13, 1915, DWGP.

126. For a discussion of the various claims made over the length of the final version, see Cuniberti, *The Birth of a Nation*, 20–22.

127. Schickel, *Griffith*, 242.

128. Brown, *Adventures*, 74; Gish, *The Movies, Mr. Griffith and Me*, 147.

129. A. R. Fulton, "Editing in *The Birth of a Nation*," reprinted in Silva, *Focus*, 145.

130. Brown, *Adventures*, 17, 20. "Final" here is in quotation marks to emphasize that Griffith, as noted in Chapter 1, continued to edit the film after its première at Clune's Auditorium: a number of shots were added, changed, or removed. Others were cut at a later stage as a result of protests, political pressure, and censorship.

131. Brown, *Adventures*, 74.

132. According to the scripts prepared by Theodore Huff and John Cuniberti, there are fifty-five shots in this sequence. Robert Lang identifies sixty-three. See Huff, *A Shot Analysis of D. W. Griffith's "The Birth of a Nation,"* 25–27; Cuniberti, *The Birth of a Nation*, 86–91; Lang, *The Birth of a Nation*, 88–92. The shot analysis that follows is based on Lang.

133. Fulton, "Editing in *The Birth of a Nation*," 151.

134. Brown, *Adventures*, 59.

135. Cuniberti, *The Birth of a Nation*, 20. See Huff, *A Shot Analysis of D. W. Griffith's "The Birth of a Nation."* Cuniberti comments that on the basis of both internal and external evidence, Huff prepared this work c. 1939. Cuniberti, *The Birth of a Nation*, 20, n. 38.

136. Cuniberti, *The Birth of a Nation*, 22; Lang, *The Birth of a Nation*, 43–156.

137. "Birth of a Nation Budget," DWGP; Griffith's autograph list of scenes reprinted in Cuniberti, *The Birth of a Nation*, 170–75.

138. *Nashville Banner*, January 25, 1916, and Brown in a 1975 letter, both cited in Cuniberti, *The Birth of a Nation*, 37. It may be, of course, that the *Nashville Banner's* description of the film beginning with a scene of slaves being sold is simply a longer version of the shot ("The bringing of the African to America planted the first seed of disunion") which is the opening scene that survives in today's versions of the film (shots 7–8). This also is a slave-selling scene.

139. W. Stephen Bush, "*The Birth of a Nation*," *Moving Picture World*, March 13, 1915, reprinted in Silva, *Focus*, 25–26; Cuniberti, *The Birth of a Nation*, 38. Francis Hackett also commented on the "smell" incident in his March 20, 1915 review of the film. See Lang, *The Birth of a Nation*, 162.

140. Cuniberti, *The Birth of a Nation*, 37–38, 151, 166–67.

141. Cuniberti, *The Birth of a Nation*, 125.

142. Brown, *Adventures*, 84–85; Cuniberti, *The Birth of a Nation*, 92; Schickel, *Griffith*, 242–43.

143. Gish, *The Movies, Mr. Griffith and Me*, 146; Cuniberti, *The Birth of a Nation* 19, n. 31. Brown also asserted that early prints were both tinted and *toned*, a claim "supported by others who have seen surviving remnants of the original." Cuniberti, *The Birth of a Nation*, 19, n. 31.

144. "The Clansman, Statement of Receipts and Disbursements," DWGP; Brown, *Adventures*, 120–21.

145. Russell Lack, *Twenty Four Frames Under: A Buried History of Film Music* (London: Quartet Books, 1997), 56.

146. Brown, *Adventures*, 30, 79; Gish, *The Movies, Mr. Griffith and Me*, 92. Griffith's secretary, Agnes Wiener, told Gish that he kept more than 1,000 classical records in his suite at the Alexandria Hotel. Gish, *The Movies, Mr. Griffith and Me*, 124.

147. *Moving Picture World*, March 13, 1909, quoted in Charles Hofmann, *Sounds for Silents* (New York: Drama Books Specialists, 1970), n. p.

148. *New York Daily Mirror*, October 9, 1909, quoted in Lack, *Twenty Four Frames Under*, 30.

149. Marks, *Music and the Silent Film*, 68. Also see Laurence E. MacDonald, *The Invisible Art of Film Music: A Comprehensive History* (New York: Ardsley House, 1998), 2; Kathryn Kalinak, *Settling the Score: Music and the Classical Hollywood Film* (Madison: University of Wisconsin Press, 1992), 51; Hofmann, *Sounds for Silents*, n. p.

150. Marks, *Music and the Silent Film*, 64–65, 100. The connection between film and theater was further emphasized by the new tendency of referring to films as "photoplays."

151. Charles Merrell Berg, *An Investigation of the Motives for and the Realization of Music to Accompany the American Silent Film, 1896–1927* (New York: Arno Press, 1976), 147–48; Marks, *Music and the Silent Film*, 99–101, 103–105.

152. Breil, quoted in Marks, *Music and the Silent Film*, 136.

153. Gish, *The Movies, Mr. Griffith and Me*, 152; Berg, *An Investigation*, 150.

154. Marks, *Music and the Silent Film*, 148, 143–44.

155. Marks, *Music and the Silent Film*, 208–209.

156. Hofmann, *Sounds for Silents*, n.p.; Marks, *Music and the Silent Film*, 148.

157. Marks, *Music and the Silent Film*, 140, 209.

158. Wagner's *Rienzi* overture was used as well as the "Ride of the Valkyries." Marks, *Music and the Silent Film*, 209.

159. Scott D. Paulin, "Richard Wagner and the Fantasy of Cinematic Unity: The Idea of the *Gesamtkunstwerk* in the History and Theory of Film Music," in *Music and Cinema*, ed. James Buhler, Caryl Flinn, and David Neumeyer (Hanover, N.H.: Wesleyan University Press, 2000), 58–84.

160. On the Wagnerian vogue and the composer's influence on U.S. culture generally, see Joseph Horowitz, *Wagner Nights: An American History* (Berkeley: University of California Press, 1994).

161. Paulin, "Richard Wagner and the Fantasy of Cinematic Unity," 66; Kalinak, *Settling the Score*, 63.

162. Paulin, "Richard Wagner and the Fantasy of Cinematic Unity," 70.

163. Marks, *Music and the Silent Film*, 101–102, 137–38, 142. The love/Elsie Stoneman theme from *The Birth of a Nation* proved highly successful when released as sheet music under the title "The Perfect Song." In the 1930s, it was also used as the theme of the extremely popular "Amos 'n' Andy" radio program. The Chappell Company in New York and London continued to publish new arrangements of the song until the 1950s. Ibid., 128. One of Breil's motifs was the "Negro theme," later referred to as the "Motif of Barbarism." According to Jane Gaines and Neil Lerner, this theme—"an insistent tom-tom beating underneath a mildly syncopated melody"—was used in a way that was both "systematic and extreme" to suggest that the black characters in the film were "barbaric." Gaines and Lerner, "The Orchestration of Affect," 252, 254, 257.

164. Jean Mitry, *The Aesthetics and Psychology of the Cinema*, trans. Christopher King (1963; reprint, London: Athlone Press, 1998), 67.

165. Marks, *Music and the Silent Film*, 166.

166. Some commentators almost from the beginning divided the film into "Griffith's" first half of the film (good) and "Dixon's" second half (bad). Vachel Lindsay was among the first to argue that "wherever the scenario shows traces of *The Clansman*, the original book, by Thomas Dixon, it is bad. Wherever it is unadulterated Griffith, which is half the time, it is good." To divide the film in this way, however, argues Linda Williams, "is to ignore both the power and excitement of the second part of the film with its last-minute rescues as well as the raid by 'black renegades' on the Cameron plantation in the first half of the film." Vachel Lindsay, *The Art of the Moving Picture* (1915: reprint, New York: Modern Library, 2000), 48; Williams, "Politics," in Usai, *The Griffith Project*, Vol. 8, 102.

CHAPTER 5

1. "News of the Trade," *Reel Life*, March 20, 1915; "President Witnesses Moving Pictures in the White House," *Post-Dispatch* [St. Louis], February 19, 1915; "President Sees Photo-Play," *Morning Telegraph* [New York], February 19, 1915; "President Acts in White House Movies," *Evening Globe* [Boston], February 19, 1915; "Feature Film Shown at the White House," *Public Ledger* [Philadelphia], February 19, 1915; "Wilson to See Moving Pictures," *Evening Star* [Washington, D.C.], February 19, 1915; all in DWGP. Also see Thomas Dixon Jr. to Joseph P. Tumulty, January 27, 1915, in Arthur S. Link, ed., *The Papers of Woodrow Wilson*, Vol. 32 (January 1–April 16, 1915) (Princeton: Princeton University Press, 1980), 142.

2. Cripps, *Slow Fade to Black*, 52.

3. On Wilson's attitudes toward race, see Kathleen L. Wolgemuth, "Woodrow Wilson and Federal Segregation," *Journal of Negro History*, 44, no. 2 (April 1959): 158–73; Henry Blumenthall, "Woodrow Wilson and the Race Question," *Journal of Negro History*, 48, no. 1 (January 1963): 1–21; Nancy J. Weiss, "The Negro and the New Freedom: Fighting Wilsonian Segregation," *Political Science Quarterly*, 84, no. 1 (March 1969): 61–79; Nicholas Patler, *Jim Crow and the Wilson Administration: Protesting Federal Segregation in the Early Twentieth Century* (Boulder: University of Colorado Press, 2004).

4. Link, ed., *The Papers of Woodrow Wilson*, Vol. 32, 267, n.1.

5. Program reproduced in Cuniberti, *The Birth of a Nation*, 185 (page itself unnumbered); D. W. Griffith to Woodrow Wilson, March 2, 1915, in Link, ed., *The Papers of Woodrow Wilson*, Vol. 32, 310–11. Griffith appears to have discussed with Wilson the possibility of making more "historical and political" films. Ibid.

6. "'The Birth of a Nation' Shown," *Evening Star* [Washington, D.C.], February 20, 1915, DWGP; "Chief Justice and Senators at 'Movie,'" *Herald* [Washington, D.C.], February 20, 1915, DWGP; "The Birth of a Nation," *Sun* [New York], February 22, 1915, DWGP; Eric F. Goldman, *Rendezvous with Destiny: A History of Modern American Reform* (New York: Vintage, 1977), 176–77.

7. "Griffith Highly Honored," *Motography*, March 6, 1915; "The Birth of a Nation," *Sun* [New York], February 22, 1915; "Chief Justice and Senators at 'Movie,'" *Herald* [Washington, D.C.], February 20, 1915; all in DWGP

8. Henderson, *Griffith*, p. 156; Chairman [Joel E. Spingarn]'s Report, Minutes of the Annual Meeting of Members of the NAACP, January 3, 1916, 14, National Association for the Advancement of Colored People Papers, Library of Congress (henceforth NAACPP).

9. At the Raleigh Hotel showing, Griffith formally requested that no review of the film appear before its New York première on March 3. "Movies at Press Club," *Washington Post*, February 20, 1915, DWGP.

10. Lack, *Twenty Four Frames Under*, 48–49.

11. Merritt, "Nickelodeon Theaters, 1905–1914: Building an Audience for the Movies," 59–79. Also see Robert C. Allen, "Motion Picture Exhibition in Manhattan, 1906–1912: Beyond the Nickelodeon," in Fell, ed., *Film before Griffith*, 162–75. For a summary of the later debates in the *Cinema Journal* on the social composition of early movie audiences, see Melvyn Stokes, "Introduction: Reconstructing American Cinema's Audiences," in Stokes and Richard Maltby, eds., *American Movie Audiences: From the Turn of the Century to the Early Sound Era* (London: BFI Publishing, 1999), 2–5.

12. Gunning, *D. W. Griffith and the Origins of American Narrative Film*, 6–7, 41–42.

13. Bowser, *Transformation of Cinema*, 203–204; Schickel, *Griffith*, 155.

14. Tim Anderson, "Reforming 'Jackass Music': The Problematic Aesthetics of Early American Film Music Accompaniment," *Cinema Journal*, 37, no. 1 (Fall 1997): 8.

15. Bowser, *Transformation of Cinema*, 127–31.

16. On the birth of the movie palace, see David M. Naylor, *American Picture Palaces: The Architecture of Fantasy* (New York: Van Rostrand Reinhold, 1981); idem, *Great American Movie Theaters* (Washington, D.C.: Preservation Press, 1987); Ben M. Hall, *The Best Remaining Seats: The Story of the Golden Age of the Movie Palace* (New York: Clarkson N. Potter, 1961); Ave Pildas, *Movie Palaces* (New York: Clarkson N. Potter, 1980).

17. Macdonald, *The Invisible Art of Film Music*, 2; Lack, *Twenty Four Frames Under*, 50; Victor Watson in the *New York Times* cited in Koszarski, *An Evening's Entertainment*, 20. The pattern of change may have been especially rapid in the bigger cities. In poverty-stricken Lowell, Massachusetts, the brand-new 350-seat Colonial Theater closed in 1911 after only two months. In Worcester, Massachusetts, Roy Rosenzweig has traced the opening of a series of new, cheap movie theaters and the creation of a working-class audience that as late as 1914 still dominated moviegoing in the city. Bowser, *Transformation of Cinema*, 129; Roy Rosenzweig, *Eight Hours for What We Will: Workers and Leisure in an Industrial City, 1870–1920* (Cambridge: Cambridge University Press, 1983), 192–213.

18. Bowser, *Transformation of Cinema*, 201, 204, 210–11, 255; Schickel, *Griffith*, 155; *Star* [Lincoln, Nebraska], March 14, 1915, DWGP.

19. Marks, *Music and the Silent Film*, 104.

20. Aitken, *The Birth of a Nation Story*, 47. Linda Arvidson also noted that the $2 admission was Harry Aitken's idea, and that both Griffith and Dixon had opposed it. Mrs. D. W. Griffith, *When the Movies Were Young*, 255. The idea of charging higher prices of admission for longer films was not new. Thomas Ince, for example, had charged extra for his five-reel *The Battle of Gettysburg* (1913). Spears, *The Civil War on the Screen*, 26.

21. Cook, *Fire from the Flint*, 145.

22. *World* [New York], June 6, 1915, DWGP.

23. Schickel, *Griffith*, 267–68. If this story of the film's renaming is true, the suggestion must have been made at one of the earliest of the New York screenings, since

the film shown at the White House on February 18 was entitled *The Birth of a Nation*. See "Preview Program" in Cuniberti, *The Birth of a Nation*, n.p.

24. Aitken, *The Birth of a Nation Story*, 51–52.

25. As discussed in Chapter 4, the film cost around $100,000 to produce. The battle scenes needed only a few hundred extras and the Klan rides a group of professional riders.

26. On alterations to the Liberty Theater to make it ready for the first performances, see *Globe* [New York], February 26, 1915, DWGP.

27. See the later account of the showing to three journalists from the New York *American* in February 1915. Despite the small size of the audience, all three found themselves (with some embarrassment) applauding the ride of the Ku Klux Klan. "'Birth of a Nation' Proved Gold Mine for Producers," *American* [New York], November 7, 1915, DWGP.

28. "The Birth of a Nation," *Brooklyn Times*, March 2, 1915, DWGP.

29. *Variety* [New York City], March 19, 1915, DWGP; Schickel, *Griffith*, 275–76; "Griffith Film Scores," *The Moving Picture World*, March 13, 1915, DWGP.

30. *The Moving Picture World*, March 13, 1915, DWGP; review in the *New York Times* as cited in Henderson, *Griffith*, 157; Schickel, *Griffith*, 277; "'The Birth of a Nation' at the Liberty Theater, Manhattan—Notes," *Standard Union* [Brooklyn], March 4, 1915, DWGP.

31. Schickel, *Griffith*, 277.

32. *New York Commercial*, March 13, 1915, DWGP; Bitzer, *Billy Bitzer*, 113.

33. *Evening Sun* [New York], March 8, 1915; "The Best Moving Pictures—'Birth of a Nation,'" *Globe* [New York], March 6, 1915; *New York Commercial*, March 6, 1915; all in DWGP.

34. *Journal of Commerce* [New York], April 3, May 15, 1915; *Evening Journal* [New York], June 9, 1915; "'Birth of a Nation' Souvenir," *Motion Picture World* [New York], July 3, 1915; *New York Press*, August 9, 1915; all in DWGP.

35. *Brooklyn Eagle* [New York], April 25, 1915; "At the Liberty Theatre," *New York Telegraph*, July 6, 1915; both in DWGP.

36. Merritt, "Dixon, Griffith, and the Southern Legend," p. 27, n. 2.

37. "Griffith's $2 Feature Film Sensation of Picture Trade," *Variety* [New York City], March 12, 1915, DWGP.

38. Figures based on "Income and Expenditure to March 13, 1915" and "Trial Balance, April 30, 1915," Accounts of the Epoch Producing Company, DWGP.

39. Aitken, *The Birth of a Nation Story*, 55; *New York Commercial*, March 29, 1915, DWGP; *New York Tribune*, March 29, 1915, DWGP; *Telegraph* [New York], March 29, 1915, DWGP.

40. Aitken, *The Birth of a Nation Story*, 58–59. On the Mayer syndicate, see "Mayor Will Hear Colored Citizens," *Enterprise* [Brockton, Massachusetts], August 12, 1915, DWGP.

41. Aitken, *The Birth of a Nation Story*, 59; "'Birth of a Nation' Advance Man Here," *St. Joseph Gazette* [Missouri], November 19, 1915, DWGP; "Takes Large Staff to Run 'Birth of a Nation,'" *Lansing Press* [Michigan], January 28, 1916, DWGP; "Heavy Sales for 'Birth of a Nation,'" *Evening Times* [Trenton], September 20, 1915, DWGP.

42. "'The Birth of a Nation' Draws Great Crowds," *Paragraph* [Akron, Ohio], September 14, 1915; "'Birth of a Nation' Advance Man Here," *St. Joseph Gazette* [Missouri], November 19, 1915; both in DWGP.

43. Epoch Producing Corporation, Balance Sheet, June 30, 1915, DWGP.

44. Epoch Producing Corporation, Comparative Statement of Gross Receipts for the Period ended February 29, 1916, DWGP; Epoch Producing Corporation, Profit and Loss Statement for the Period ended February 29, 1916, DWGP.

45. By February 29, 1916, income from the sale of city and state rights had reached $237,500 ($100,000 for the Western rights, $50,000 for New England, $40,000 for Canada, $20,000 for California, $11,000 for Wisconsin, $11,000 for Spokane and Seattle, Washington, and $5,500 for Portland, Oregon. Income from the percentages paid on operations in these areas amounted to $38,240.85. Epoch Producing Corporation, Sale of City and State Rights, February 29, 1916, DWGP.

46. Epoch Producing Corporation, Treasurer's Statement for February 1916, DWGP. On the foreign reception of *Birth*, see Michael Hammond, "'A Soul-Stirring Appeal to Every Briton': The Reception of *The Birth of a Nation* in Britain (1915–1916)," *Film History*, 11, no. 3 (1999): 353–70: Melvyn Stokes, "Fighting the Color line in Montmartre and Montparnasse: The Reception of *The Birth of a Nation* in France" (forthcoming).

47. Schickel, *Griffith*, 280–81; Henderson, *Griffith*, 159.

48. Musser, *Emergence of Cinema*, 417, 433; Bowser, *Transformation of Cinema*, 131.

49. Bowser, *Transformation of Cinema*, 210–12. Also see Cook, *Fire from the Flint*, 182.

50. In the same interview, Griffith claimed that people would eventually be willing to pay $5 to see a movie that had cost $2,000,000 to make. *Citizen* [Columbus, Ohio], April 2, 1915; *Republican* [Gloversville, New York], April 1, 1915; *Chronicle* [Augusta, Georgia], April 2, 1915; *Times* [Racine, Wisconsin], April 19, 1915; all in DWGP.

51. See, for example, *Times-Picayune* [New Orleans, Louisiana], March 31, April 4, 1915; "Seat Sale at Grand for 'Birth of a Nation' to Start Tomorrow," *Kansas City Post*, October 21, 1915; "Don't Miss This Chance to See Big Picture The Birth of a Nation," *Call* [Allentown, Pennsylvania], March 30, 1916; all in DWGP.

52. "D. W. Griffith's Great Idea and How He Worked Out Historically Accurate Battle Scenes with 18,000 Actors and 3,000 Horses," *Sunday Star* [Terre Haute, Indiana], January 2, 1916, DWGP; *Kansas City Journal*, October 26, 1915, DWGP.

53. "Virginians First to See the 'Birth of a Nation,'" *Sentinel* [Milwaukee, Wisconsin], July 14, 1915; "18,000 People in Film of First $2 Movie," *Sun* [Baltimore], March 7 [?], 1915; *St. Louis Republic*, September 5, 1915; "Seat Sale at Grand for 'Birth of a Nation' to Start Tomorrow," *Kansas City Post*, October 21, 1915; "Producing a Play on a Stage Five Miles Wide," *Sun*, April 25, 1915; "Surgeons Busy When Birth of a Nation Filmed," *Press* [Atlantic City], July 3, 1915; "'Birth of a Nation' to Be Shown Here," *Kansas City Post*, November 13, 1915; *Evansville Courier*, December 4, 1915; "What It Meant to Make the Picture," *Gettysburg Times*, April 29, 1916; all in DWGP.

54. "Seat Sale at Grand for 'Birth of a Nation' to Start Tomorrow," *Kansas City Post*, October 21, 1915, DWGP; *The Patriot* [Jackson, Michigan], February 10, 1916, DWGP. Other reports said that Lillian Gish, during the filming, wore several dresses that had earlier been worn by members of her family during the Civil War and Reconstruction eras. The Baltimore *Star* even asserted that one of these dresses was a family heirloom, once worn by her mother at a ball in Springfield, Ohio, that had been disrupted by Morgan's Raiders! "Great Picture Spectacle," *St. Joseph New Herald*, November 19, 1915, DWGP; "Foyer Chat and Footlight Gossip," *Star* [Baltimore], April 6, 1916, DWGP.

55. For hostile reactions to the film, see Chapter 6.

56. "Birth of a Nation—Ford's," *American* [Baltimore], March 28, 1916; "You Should See 'The Birth of a Nation,'" *Daily Times* [Huntsville, Alabama], February 8, 1916; "National—'The Birth of a Nation,'" *Washington Herald*, May 4, 1916; "'The Birth of a Nation' Draws Great Crowds," *Paragraph* [Akron, Ohio], September 14, 1915; "Social Ideas Anent [*sic*] 'The Birth of a Nation,'" *Daily Journal* [Quincy, Illinois], December 27, 1915; all in DWGP.

57. See, for example, *Chicago Tribune*, May 25, 1915; Neil G. Caward, "Griffith's 'The Birth of a Nation,'" *Chicago American*, June 10, 1915; *Journal* [Providence, Rhode Island], August 17, 1915; all in DWGP.

58. Dramatic Editor, "Philadelphia Takes a Look at the Heights of the Photoplay Art," *Evening Ledger* [Philadelphia], September 18, 1915, DWGP.

59. "Worth-While Feature Films Recommended by 'Wid': D. W. Griffith's Production of 'The Birth of a Nation,'" *Mail* [New York], March 6, 1915, DWGP.

60. *Evening Sun* [New York], March 20, 1915; "The Talk of New York," *Morning Telegraph* [New York], March 23, 1915; "Griffith Spectacle Birth of a New Art," *Press* [Atlantic City, New Jersey], August 12, 1915; *American* [Baltimore], April 11, 1916; "With the Photo Players," *Tribune* [San Diego, California], July 14, 1915; *Evening Post* [Charleston, Virginia], January 19, 1916; *Times-Picayune* [New Orleans], March 31, 1916; all in DWGP.

61. Lotte H. Eisner, *The Haunted Screen: Expressionism in the German Cinema and the Influence of Max Reinhardt*, trans. Roger Greaves (London: Thomas and Hudson, 1969), 39.

62. *Mail* [New York], March 6, 1915, DWGP. The anonymous reviewer moved on, in a foretaste of the "auteur theory" of the 1960s, to suggest a ranking of the best directors (he continued to refer to them as "producers") and their films.

63. Ironically, the Biograph Company itself—soon to disappear from the scene—attempted to capitalize on Griffith's new, post-*Birth* fame by rereleasing some of the films he had directed for them. "Biograph Plans to Re-issue 1912–1913 Griffith Films," *Motion Picture Weekly* [New York], May 15, 1915, DWGP.

64. "Griffith Spectacle Birth of a New Art," *Press* [Atlantic City], August 12, 1915; "National—'The Birth of a Nation,'" *Washington Post*, May 16, 1916; both in DWGP.

65. See, for example, "He Invented 'Switch-Back' in the Movies," *New York Herald*, March 28, 1915, DWGP.

66. *Evansville Courier*, December 8, 1915, DWGP.

67. "Return Engagement of 'The Birth of a Nation,'" *Evening Report* [Lebanon, Pennsylvania], May 11, 1916, DWGP. See Chapter 4 on Freeman.

68. Koszarski, *An Evening's Entertainment*, 222.

69. *Times* [Brooklyn, New York], April 17, 1915, DWGP. The same story appeared in the *Standard Union* [Brooklyn, New York], April 18, 1915, DWGP.

70. "'The Birth of a Nation' Draws Great Crowds," *Paragraph* [Akron, Ohio], September 14, 1915, DWGP. The estimate of 850 performances in Chicago was very high and may have been a misprint.

71. *Kansas City Star*, November 4, 1915, DWGP. The figure of 725 performances in New York by November 27 must have taken into account not just the Liberty Theater but also the Brighton Beach Music Hall in Brooklyn, where the film started its run on July 2. "Mayor to Greet 'Birth of a Nation,'" *Standard-Union* [Brooklyn], July 2, 1915, DWGP.

72. "Not to have seen it," commented one Western journalist, "becomes a mark of unprogressiveness. To hold no opinion, either 'for' or 'forninst [sic],' marks one as indifferent indeed." "Some Thoughts for Dog Days on Things Theatrical," *Chronicle* [Spokane, Washington], August 7, 1915, DWGP.

73. "'Birth of a Nation' Still Draws Well," *Mail* [New York], May 22, 1915, DWGP.

74. "N.E. Rights to Birth of a Nation," *Sentinel* [Fitchburg, Massachusetts], August 17, 1915; "Stay Home and Save $1.95 Each Jit Show," *Denver Times*, March 4, 1915; both in DWGP.

75. Advertisement in *Kansas City Post*, October 16, 1915; cf. "Birth of a Nation Drawing Well at Olympic Theater," *Globe-Democrat* [St. Louis], September 6, 1915; "Grant and Lee at Appomattox," *Labor Herald* [Kansas City], October 22, 1915; all in DWGP.

76. See "Art Goes on Road with New Success," *Galveston News* [Texas], August 8, 1915; "Seat Sale at Grand for 'Birth of a Nation' to Start Tomorrow," *Kansas City Post*, October 21, 1915; "'Birth of a Nation' to Open Here Tonight," *Daily Press* [Newport News, Rhode Island], January 6, 1916; all in DWGP.

77. "Mayor May Pass Birth of a Nation," *Evansville Press*, November 30, 1915; cf. "Seat Sales for 'Birth of a Nation' Have Broken Record in Every City in the South," *Selma Times* [Selma, Alabama], December 31, 1915, and "Crowds See 'Birth of a Nation' but Protest Brings No Clash," *Springfield New Record* [Springfield, Illinois], January 17, 1916; all in DWGP. Herrick, once a newspaper man, had previously spent three years on the road with Dixon's play, *The Clansman*. See "'Birth of a Nation' Advance Man Here," *St. Joseph Gazette* [St. Joseph, Missouri], November 19, 1915; "Here's More Advertising for Big Film," *Lansing Press* [Lansing, Michigan], February 3, 1916; both in DWGP.

78. "'Birth of a Nation' Music Is Effective," *Post* [New York], June 10, 1915, DWGP.

79. "Music Feature of Spectacle 'Birth of a Nation,'" *Enquirer* [Buffalo, New York], February 15, 1916, DWGP.

80. "Birth of a Nation Drawing Well at Olympic Theater," *Globe-Democrat* [St. Louis], September 6, 1915; cf. *Milwaukee News*, July 6, 1915; "New View of American History Shown on Film," *Oil City Blizzard* [Pennsylvania], April 11, 1916; "Seat Sale at Grand for 'Birth of a Nation' to Start Tomorrow," *Kansas City Post*, October 21, 1915; all in DWGP.

81. For its first showings in Brooklyn, an orchestra of fifty was organized. In Dallas, Texas, the orchestra had forty players. An ad in the *Kansas City Post* talked of a "Symphony Orchestra of Thirty." In Decatur, Alabama, it was only a "twenty-piece orchestra." "Special Music for 'Birth of a Nation,'" *Standard-Union* [Brooklyn, New York], July 11, 1915; "'Birth of a Nation' History in Motion," *Morning News* [Dallas, Texas], October 5, 1915; *Kansas City Post*, October 16, 1915; "'Birth of a Nation' is Revelation of Possibilities of Silent Drama," *Decatur Daily* [Alabama], April 16, 1916; all in DWGP.

82. "Dreadnought Orchestra for 'Birth of a Nation,'" *Examiner* [New York], August 1, 1915; "Music Is Strong Feature of 'Birth of a Nation,'" *Milwaukee Sentinel*, August 7, 1915; "J.O.L. Finds Thrill in Music of 'The Birth of a Nation,'" *Baltimore News*, March 16, 1915; "Music Feature of Spectacle 'Birth of a Nation,'" *Enquirer* [Buffalo, New York], February 15, 1916; "'Birth of a Nation' Throbs with Stirring Songs of War," *Indianapolis Star*, December 15, 1915; *Press* [Philadelphia], August 8, 1915; all in DWGP.

83. "N. E. Rights to Birth of a Nation," *Sentinel* [Fitchburg, Massachusetts], August 17, 1915; "Birth of a Nation Thrills Audience at Olympic," *Globe-Democrat* [St. Louis],

August 30, 1915; "Birth of a Nation—Ford's," *American* [Baltimore], March 28, 1916; "'Birth of a Nation' Wonder Spectacle," *Journal* [Martinsburg, West Virginia], May 4, 1916; "Last Times Today and Tomorrow, 'Birth of a Nation' at Lyric," *Allentown Democrat* [Pennsylvania], March 31, 1916; *Telegraph* [Philadelphia], August 10, 1915; "Don't Miss This Chance to See Big Picture The Birth of a Nation," *Call* [Allentown, Pennsylvania], March 30, 1916; "'All Seats Sold,' Is the Regular Sign at 'Birth of a Nation,'" *Chicago American*, July 24, 1915; "'The Birth of a Nation' Draws Great Crowds," *Paragraph* [Akron, Ohio], September 14, 1915; "National—'The Birth of a Nation,'" *Washington Herald* [DC], May 4, 1916; all in DWGP.

84. "'Birth of a Nation' Drawing Hundreds to the Decaturs," *New Decatur* [Alabama], April 16, 1916; H. C. Danforth, "Los Angeles Activities," *Star* [New York], March 3, 1915; *Review* [Atlantic City, New Jersey], July 24, 1915; "Picture in Fourth Week," *Times-Picayune* [New Orleans], April 2, 1916; "Central to Operate Special Train for 'Birth of a Nation,'" *Advertiser* [Montgomery, Alabama], February 18, 1916; "Amusements— Special Trains for Miracle Movie," *Daily Observer* [Charlotte, North Carolina], February 29, 1916; "Heavy Sales for 'Birth of a Nation,'" *Evening Times* [Trenton, New Jersey?], September 20, 1915; "Crowds See 'Birth of a Nation' but Protest Brings No Clash," *New Record* [Springfield, Illinois], January 17, 1916; "'Birth of a Nation' Wins Longer Time," *Post Intel* [Seattle, Washington], July 3, 1915; "Grand," *Daily Record* [Kansas City], November 20, 1915; "Seat Sales for 'Birth of a Nation' Have Broken Record in Every City in the South," *Selma Times* [Alabama], December 31, 1915; all in DWGP.

85. "'Birth of a Nation' Coming to Brighton Beach," *Brooklyn* Eagle [New York], June 21, 1915; *Oklahoma Oklahoman*, July 25, 1915; "Mayor to Greet 'Birth of a Nation,'" *Standard-Union* [Brooklyn, New York], July 2, 1915; "'The Birth of a Nation' Is Shown for First Time in South and Achieves Decided Success at Norfolk, Va.," *Morning News* [Dallas, Texas], September 29, 1915; *Herald* [Boston, Massachusetts], April 10, 1915; Kitty Kelly, "Flickerings from Filmland—Why Don't Chicago Managers Do This?," *Tribune* [Chicago], March 24, 1915; "Big Orchestra for Spectacle," *Review* [Atlantic City, New Jersey], July 4, 1915; "Special Maine Trains to Boston for 'Nation,'" *Mail* [New York], July 10, 1915; "Birth of a Nation—Special Car for Ayer after Saturday Evening Performance at the Cummings," *Sentinel* [Fitchburg, Massachusetts], September 9, 1915; "Amusements—Special Trains for Miracle Movie," *Daily Observer* [Charlotte, North Carolina], February 29, 1916; all in DWGP.

86. "Veterans from Soldiers' Home Parade for Manager," *Motion Picture News* [New York], July 3, 1915; "Veterans Will See 'Birth of a Nation,'" *Record* [Fort Worth, Texas], November 19, 1915; *Atlanta Constitution*, December 13, 1915; *Terre Haute Tribune* [Indiana], January 6, 1916; *Times-Picayune* [New Orleans], April 3, 1916; "Ad Men to Watch 'Birth of a Nation,'" *Journal* [Chicago], June 21, 1915; "Censor Board Made Permanent," *Evansville Courier* [Illinois], December 20, 1915; "Newsboys to See Birth of a Nation," *Scranton Republican* [Pennsylvania], May 31, 1916; *Evening Sun* [Baltimore], March 30, 1916; "Orphans' Parade at Brighton to See 'Birth of a Nation,'" *Times* [Brooklyn, New York], July 27, 1915; "Orphans Will See 'Birth of a Nation,'" *Louisville Herald*, February 20, 1916; "Orphans to See 'Movies,'" *San Antonio Express* [Texas], March 13, 1916; all in DWGP.

87. "'Birth of a Nation' Enters on Second Week at Olympic," *Star* [St. Louis], September 6, 1915; cf. "'Rebel Yell' Adds Realism to 'The Birth of a Nation,'" *Constitution* [Atlanta], December 14, 1915; *American* [Baltimore], April 11, 1916; all in DWGP.

88. "American Theater Notes," *Christian Science Monitor* [Boston], August 18, 1915; "'Birth of a Nation' at Grand Another Week," *Kansas City Post*, November 19, 1915; "Picture in Fourth Week," *Times-Picayune* [New Orleans], April 2, 1916; "Ford's," *Star* [Baltimore], April 11, 1916; all in DWGP.

89. Merritt, "Dixon, Griffith, and the Southern Legend," 27, n. 2.

90. Aitken, *The Birth of a Nation Story*, 59.

91. "The opening of 'The Birth of a Nation' in Los Angeles...," reported one newspaper, "brought out the first ticket speculators in the motion picture field. The demand for seats was so large that 75-cent seats were bought up and resold for $2.50." With tickets for the Liberty Theater being sold a month in advance, another paper observed that "ticket speculators—the bane of New York theatricals—are said to be reaping a harvest." *Evening Mail* [New York], February 22, 1915; *Times-Picayune* [New Orleans], April 4, 1915; both in DWGP; cf. James S. Metcalf, "Theatre Tales from New York," *Herald* [Washington, D.C.], March 14, 1915.

92. "Many "Repeaters" at 'Birth of a Nation,'" *Evening Sun* [New York], April 2, 1915; "See Picture Again," *News* [Baltimore], March 28, 1916; *Sentinel* [Milwaukee, Michigan], April 18, 1915; *Post* [Chicago], August 1, 1915; Boston *Record* [Massachusetts], August 17, 1915; *Kansas City Journal*, November 3, 1915; M. O. Marshall, *Higginsville Advance* [Oklahoma], November 5, 1915; *Patriot* [Jackson, Michigan], February 11, 1916; "Amusements—Special Trains for Miracle Movie," *Daily Observer* [Charlotte, North Carolina], February 29, 1916; "Newsboys to See Birth of a Nation," *Scranton Republican* [Pennsylvania], May 31, 1916;

93. *Kansas City Journal*, November 4, 1915; "A Real Work of Art," *Evansville Journal-News*, November 25, 1915; "Hundreds Brought to Atlanta by 'The Birth of a Nation,'" *Constitution* [Atlanta], December 13, 1915; *Courier-Journal* [Louisville, Kentucky], February 10, 1916; *Sun* [Baltimore], April 4, 1916; "'The Birth of a Nation' Drawing Capacity Houses," *Clearfield Progress*, May 23, 1916; all in DWGP. On the epic journey of one Minnesota family to see the film, see Hazel Jungquist, "Viewing D. W. Griffith's 'The Birth of a Nation': A First Hand Account," Robert K. Klepper, ed., *Classic Images*, no. 245 (November 1995): 36–37.

94. *Variety* [New York], March 19, 1915; "Birth of a Nation Sways Its Audience," *Evansville Press*, December 9, 1915; both in DWGP.

95. "The Clansman's Audience Cheers, Weeps and Sings," *Enquirer* [Oakland, California], May 11, 1915; cf. "Film, 'Birth of a Nation,' Grips Emotion of Audience," *Star* [Indianapolis, Indiana], December 14, 1915; "Audience Cheers and Weeps over 'Birth of a Nation,'" *Daily States* [New Orleans], March 13, 1916; all in DWGP.

96. M. O. Harshall, *Higginsville Advance* [Oklahoma], November 5, 1915; "'Rebel Yell' Adds Realism to 'The Birth of a Nation,'" *Constitution* [Atlanta, Georgia], December 14, 1915; "'Birth of a Nation' at Vendome To-Night," *Banner* [Nashville, Tennessee], January 24, 1916; all in DWGP.

97. *Star* [Terre Haute, Indiana], January 4, 1916, DWGP. The Hoosier audience also applauded the so-called Hampton Epilogue, discussed in Chapter 6.

98. Kitty Kelly, "Flickerings from Filmland—Why Don't Chicago Managers Do This?," *Tribune* [Chicago], March 24, 1915; "'Birth of a Nation' Justifies Praise," *Kansas City Journal*, October 25, 1915; M. O. Harshall, *Higginsville Advance* [Oklahoma], November 5, 1915; *Terre Haute Tribune* [Indiana], January 4, 1916; "Hosts of People Seeing 'The

Birth of a Nation,'" *Marrett Weekly*, January 27, 1916; "'Birth of a Nation' at Vendome To-Night," *Banner* [Nashville, Tennessee], January 24, 1916; G. B. D. "The Birth of a Nation," *Battle Creek Morning Journal* [Michigan], February 4, 1916; *Patriot* [Jackson, Michigan], February 11, 1916; *Star* [Baltimore], March 21, 1916; all in DWGP.

99. "Some Thoughts for Dog Days on Things Theatrical," *Chronicle* [Spokane, Washington], August 7, 1915; "This Movie Battle Just Like Real War," *Milwaukee Leader*, July 20, 1915; both in DWGP.

100. "Audience Cheers and Weeps over 'Birth of a Nation,'" *Daily States* [New Orleans], March 13, 1916; "National—'The Birth of a Nation,'" *Washington Herald*, May 11, 1916; *Sun* [Baltimore], March 14, 1915; all in DWGP.

101. See, for example, *Evening Sun* [New York], April 10, 1915, DWGP.

CHAPTER 6

1. The title of this chapter is derived from the work of the Boston branch of the NAACP which, in the spring of 1915, produced a forty-seven-page pamphlet bringing together criticism of *The Birth of a Nation* from many different sources. It was entitled *Fighting a Vicious Film: Protest against "The Birth of a Nation."*

2. May Childs Nerney to Butler R. Wilson, April 5, 1915, NAACPP. "We have reason to believe," Nerney observed, "that this committee must have been rather carefully selected to get such a judgement."

3. Lester F. Scott to Dr. J. E. Spingarn, April 12, 1915, NAACPP.

4. See Lester F. Scott, Vice-Chairman of the National Board of Censorship, to J. E. Spingarn, April 12, 1915, NAACPP.

5. *Moving Picture World*, April 24, 1915. Also see *Evening Sun* [New York], April 2, 1915; *New York Commercial*, April 2, 1915; *Journal of Commerce* [New York], April 2, 1915; *Brooklyn Times*, April 2, 1915, DWGP.

6. E. Burton Ceruti to May Childs Nerney, February 3, 1915, NAACPP; Dr. Chas. E. Locke and E. Burton Ceruti, "To the Honorable The City Council of Los Angeles, State of California," February 2, 1915, NAACPP; Schickel, *Griffith*, 246–47.

7. Dr. Chas. E. Locke and E. Burton Ceruti, "To The Honorable the City Council of the City of Los Angeles, State of California," February 2, 1915, 1–4, NAACPP.

8. Ibid., 3–4.

9. E. Burton Ceruti to May Childs Nerney, February 3, 1915, NAACPP.

10. Bowser, *Transformation of Cinema*, 51. By early March 1915, the NAACP national secretary was informed that bills for legal censorship were pending in seven more states: Iowa, Massachusetts, Michigan, Minnesota, Missouri, New York, and Tennessee. "RR," "Memorandum for Miss Nerney," March 9, 1915, NAACPP. On the censorship framework in the United States in 1915, see Fleener-Marzec, *D. W. Griffith's "The Birth of a Nation,"* 57–60.

11. U. S. Congress, House of Representatives, *Motion Picture Commission: Hearings before the Committee on Education . . . on Bills to Establish a Federal Motion-Picture Commission*, 63rd Congress, 2nd session, Nos. 1 and 2, 1914, Part 1, 3–4, 56–62; Part 2, 79.

12. Minutes of the Meeting of the NAACP Board of Directors, January 5, 1915, Box A-8, NAACPP.

13. "N.A.A.C.P. Notes," *The Crisis*, March 1915, 246; from the NAACP, Fifth Annual Report (1914), report of the Chairman of the Board of Directors, February 12, 1915, in *The Crisis*, April 1915, 293. If Congress passed "Jim Crow" laws for the District of Columbia, the NAACP worried, this might encourage imitation in the Border States and perhaps farther North.

14. "N.A.A.C.P. Notes," *The Crisis*, March 1915, 247.

15. John M. Cooper, *Pivotal Decades: The United States, 1900–1920* (New York: W. W. Norton, 1990), 208. "It is the purpose of the Association to bring a succession of cases to the Supreme Court until it has placed that Court on record on Jim Crow cars, segregation and the race question in general." *The Crisis*, August 1915, 200.

16. Cooper, *Pivotal Decades*, 78.

17. "The Movie Picture and the National Character," *Review of Reviews*, September 1910, quoted in Mast, *Movies in Our Midst*, 61.

18. On the stereotypes of blacks in early movies, see Cripps, *Slow Fade to Black*, chapter 1, especially 8, 10, 13–14. According to Cripps (especially 8, 11, 12–13, 18–19, 21–22), the earliest "nonfiction" American films did not represent blackness in a racist manner. It was only later, as scriptwriting, directing, and editing developed and greater emphasis was placed on producing fictional characters and narratives, that racist modes of representing blacks emerged. Both Daniel J. Leab and Jacqueline Najuma Stewart reject this notion that blackness was represented differently at first and that racism emerged only later. Stewart, in particular, argues that early cinema participated "in a larger effort on the part of a dominant and diverse white population to suppress and ignore rising Black voices of self-determination, politicization, and protest." She observes that "even these earliest images are heavily informed by Black representations in [white-dominated] literature, vaudeville, newspapers, and cartoons and by Black iconography on postcards and other commercial products." Moreover, Stewart argues, tropes of blacks washing babies in an attempt to make them white or eating watermelons were used "to demonstrate Blacks' natural inferiority and predictability." Equally, early films responded to increasing interracial contact in American society itself by foregrounding themes of race-based substitution and masquerade. Leab, *From Sambo to Superspade: The Black Experience in Motion Pictures* (London: Secker and Warburg, 1975), 8, 11; Stewart, *Migrating to the Movies: Cinema and Black Urban Modernity* (Berkeley: University of California Press, 2005), 51–53, 56, 66–90, quotations from 51, 67, and 78. On the rare attempts to criticize unfavorable African American stereotypes in a black newspaper (*Chicago Defender*), see Everett, *Returning the Gaze*, 56–57.

19. Cripps, *Slow Fade*, 25, 30.

20. Dan Streible, "Race and the Reception of Jack Johnson Fight Films," in *The Birth of Whiteness*, ed. Daniel Bernardi, 182–83, 185–86, 192–93; Everett, *Returning the Gaze*, 49, 51.

21. May Childs Nerney to Mrs. S. B. Henderson, May 24, 1915, NAACPP.

22. Russell, quoted in Everett, *Returning the Gaze*, 67. For contemporary attacks on the play in black newspapers such as the *Afro-American Ledger* [Baltimore] and the *Iowa State Bystander*, see ibid., 60–62, 65.

23. Garth Jowett, "'A Capacity for Evil': The 1915 Supreme Court Mutual Decision," *Historical Journal of Film, Radio and Television* 9, no.1 (1989): 59–78; John Wertheimer,

"Mutual Film Reviewed: The Movies, Censorship, and Free Speech in Progressive America," *American Journal of Legal History* 37, no. 2 (1993): 158–89.

24. "D. W. Griffith Speaks against Censorship Law Pending at Albany," *Clipper* [New York], March 13, 1915, DWGP. The bill to set up a censorship board for New York State had been introduced into the legislature by Assemblyman Mitchell. Ibid.

25. Captioned "A Plea for the Art of the Motion Picture," this intertitle—the longest in the entire film—grandiloquently insisted that "We do not fear censorship, for we have no wish to offend with improprieties or obscenities, but we do demand, as a right, the liberty to show the dark side of wrong, that we may illuminate the bright side of virtue—the same liberty that is conceded to the art of the written word—that art to which we owe the Bible and the works of Shakespeare (shot 3)."

26. Francis G. Couvares notes that white radicals such as Floyd Dell were embarrassed to find themselves allied with D. W. Griffith in defense of "free speech" and argues that in the long term their dislike of restraints on freedom of expression was correct. Not only would such restraints limit how racial and social issues were depicted on screen, but they would also finally lead to the Production Code (1930) and the Production Code Administration (1934). Couvares, "The Good Censor: Race, Sex, and Censorship in the Early Cinema," *Yale Journal of Criticism* 7, no. 2 (Fall 1994): 236–38, 247.

27. William L. Chenery, "The Guide Post," *Record Herald* [Chicago], April 13, 1915, DWGP. On this point, also see Staiger, *Interpreting Films*, 141; Cripps, *Slow Fade to Black*, 55.

28. May Childs Nerney to Joseph P. Loud, May 6, 1915; Mary White Ovington to May Childs Nerney, March 5, 1915; both in NAACPP. May Nerney sometimes signed herself "Mary Nerney," but used May as her Christian name on most occasions. She appears here, for the sake of consistency, only as May.

29. R. W. Stewart to May Childs Nerney, April 24, 1915, NAACPP.

30. Minutes of the Meeting of the Board of Directors, July 12, 1915, NAACP Board of Directors, Box A-8; Roberta J. Dunbar to May Childs Nerney, October 1, 1915; both in NAACPP.

31. "It is not speakers we need," wrote May Childs Nerney, drawing the appropriate conclusion from the experience of Kansas City, "but people who can organize, who can conciliate, who can get different cliques to work together. That is the immediate problem." May Childs Nerney to Dr. Charles E. Bentley, June 2, 1915, NAACPP.

32. May Childs Nerney to Mrs. Anna Gillis, July 27, 1915; Nerney to Rabbi Rudolph I. Coffee, June 7, 1915; both in NAACPP.

33. "Summary," Minutes of the Annual Meeting, January 3, 1916, 34–35, NAACP Board of Directors, Box A-8, NAACPP.

34. May C. Nerney to Charles S. Macfarland, March 26, 1915; May C. Nerney to D. W. Griffith, February 25, 1915; both in NAACPP.

35. May C. Nerney to E. Burton Ceruti, February 25, 1915; W. D. McGuire Jr. to J. E. Spingarn, April 12, 1915; May C. Nerney to the Reverend Charles F. Macfarland, March 26, 1915; Memo entitled "National Board of Censorship," February 27, 1915; all in NAACP.

36. See May C. Nerney to Miss Walters, secretary to Oswald Garrison Villard, March 1, 1915; May C. Nerney to Paul Kennaday, March 1, 1915, both in NAACPP. With

one member of the National Board of Censorship's general committee away from New York, McGuire sent his ticket to Holmes, an NAACP vice-president. W. D. McGuire to May C. Nerney, February 27, 1915, NAACPP. There were apparently ten supporters of the NAACP in the audience for the film's actual première on March 3. The Liberty Theater was refusing "to admit any colored people" but the NAACP hoped to have "at least two very fair colored people" present for this performance. May C. Nerney to Dr. Jacques Loeb, March 3, 1915, NAACPP.

37. May C. Nerney to E. Burton Ceruti, March 4, 1915, NAACP; May C. Nerney to the Reverend Charles S. Macfarland, March 26, 1915, NAACP; Frederic C. Howe, "Might Lead to Serious Race Riots," in *Fighting a Vicious Film*, p. 33.

38. May C. Nerney to E. Burton Ceruti, March 2, 1915, NAACPP.

39. May C. Nerney to the Reverend Henry S. Coffin, March 11, 1915; untitled note, signed May Childs Nerney, March 6, 1915; May C. Nerney to Stephen S. Wise, March 8, 1915; all in NAACPP.

40. NAACP to Moving Picture Firms, March 11, 1915; Kalem Company to NAACP, March 16, 1915; both in NAACPP.

41. NAACP to George H. Bell, Commissioner of Licenses, March 12, 1915, NAACPP.

42. Schickel, *Griffith*, 275. Chief Magistrate William McAdoo, though sympathetic to the NAACP's position, ruled against them since he believed nothing could be done to stop the film legally unless a breach of the peace had actually occurred. Ibid.; May C. Nerney to Lillian Wald, March 9, 1915, NAACPP.

43. W. D. McGuire Jr. to May C. Nerney, March 15, 1915; May C. Nerney to E. Burton Ceruti, March 18, 1915; May C. Nerney to Jane Addams, March 13, 1915; May C. Nerney to Caroline M. Dexter, March 13, 1915; all in NAACPP. The NAACP later was able to identify seven of the minority of committee members who had opposed the film's passing: Chairman Howe; Mrs. Howard S. Gans; Orlando P. Lewis of the Prison Commission; Dr. Charles S. Macfarland, general secretary of the Federal Council of the Churches of Christ in America; J. K. Paulding; Mrs. Miriam S. Price; and Dr. J. P. Warbasse of Brooklyn. "Memorandum on 'The Birth of a Nation' Founded on Dixon's 'Clansman,'" n.d.; secretary to Miss Nerney to J. Milton Sampson, October 25, 1915; both in NAACPP.

44. Osborne was appointed on the advice of Moorfield Storey, "who offered personally to contribute to the expense of the case," Oswald Garrison Villard of the New York *Post* and others. May C. Nerney to Members of the Board of Directors, March 17, 1915, NAACPP.

45. May C. Nerney to Members of the Board of Directors, March 17, March 18, 1915; National Association for the Advancement of Colored People to Mayor John Purroy Mitchel, March 19, 1915; both in NAACPP. On the attempt to influence the Mayor, see Cripps, "The Reaction of the Negro to the Motion Picture, *Birth of a Nation*," in Silva, *Focus*, 117–18.

46. May C. Nerney to Glesner Fowler, May 18, 1915, NAACPP.

47. May C. Nerney to Samuel R. Morsell, June 3, 1915, NAACPP.

48. "'The Birth of a Nation' Trial Set for Wednesday," *Call* [New York], March 20, 1915, DWGP; May C. Nerney to J. E. Spingarn, March 29, 1915, NAACPP; May C. Nerney to Helen Lansdowne, March 31, 1915, NAACPP; May C. Nerney to Frederic C. Howe,

April 1, 1915, NAACPP; "Film Play Hearing Adjourned," *Post* [New York], April 1, 1915, DWGP; May C. Nerney to Rosalie M. Jones, April 7, 1915, NAACPP; May C. Nerney to William H. Baldwin, April 12, 1915, NAACPP; "Anti-Negro Film Case Is Again Postponed," *Call* [New York], April 17, 1915, DWGP.

49. Minutes of the Special Meeting of the Board of Directors, March 23, 1915, NAACP Board of Directors files, Box A-8, NAACPP.

50. "Films and Births and Censorship," *Survey*, April 3, 1915; "Howe Objects to the Clansman Film," *Evening Post* [New York], March 24, 1915, DWGP; "Censorship Board Splits on Dixon's 'Clansman' Film," *World* [New York], March 24, 1915, DWGP; "Fears Riots from Movies," *Mail* [New York], March 24, 1915, DWGP.

51. May C. Nerney to George E. Wibecan, March 26, 1915, NAACPP; May C. Nerney to Dr. Stephen S. Wise, March 26, 1915, NAACPP; May C. Nerney to Major R. C. Wendell, March 27, 1915, NAACPP; May C. Nerney to J. E. Spingarn, March 29, 1915, NAACPP; May C. Nerney to Mayor John Purroy Mitchel, March 30, 1915, NAACPP; "Fighting Race Calumny," *The Crisis* (April 1915): 41.

52. Moore, as quoted in Alessandra Lorini, *Rituals of Race: American Public Culture and the Search for Racial Democracy* (Charlottesville: University Press of Virginia, 1999), 233.

53. See May C. Nerney to Lillian D. Wald, March 11, 1915; Nerney to Jane Addams, March 11, 1915; both in NAACP.

54. May C. Nerney to Berkeley G. Tobey of *New Republic*, March 31, 1915, NAACPP.

55. *The Crisis* (May 1915): 33.

56. Anderson was collector of internal revenue for the Second District of New York. When he left his post at the beginning of April 1915, one newspaper praised him for standing the test of occupying "the most important [office] every [sic] held by a colored man under the government." "By Their Fruits," Editorial, *New York World*, April 1, 1915, Booker T. Washington Papers—Library of Congress.

57. Charles W. Anderson to Booker T. Washington, March 31, 1915, Booker T. Washington Papers; Booker T. Washington to Charles W. Anderson, April 10, 1915, in *The Booker T. Washington Papers*, Vol. 13, *1914–1915*, ed. Louis R. Harlan and Raymond W. Smock (Urbana: University of Illinois Press, 1984), 259–60. Also on the meeting with the mayor, see May C. Nerney to G. Washington Butt, March 30, 1915, NAACPP; "May Tone Down Part of Anti-Negro Film," *World* [New York], March 31, 1915, DWGP; "Mayor Hears Film Protest," *Telegraph* [New York], March 31, 1915, DWGP; "Mayor Bars Brute as Negro on Film," *Tribune* [New York], March 31, 1915, DWGP; "Promise to Tone Down Two Scenes of Vicious Photo Play," *New York Age*, April 1, 1915, NAACPP.

58. "Fighting Race Calumny," *The Crisis* (April 1915): 42. "Of course," confessed the national secretary of the NAACP, "if these [two scenes] are eliminated we would have no case legally." May C. Nerney, Memo, March 31, 1915, NAACPP.

59. J. E. Spingarn, chairman, Board of Directors, NAACP, to Mayor John Purroy Mitchel, April 1, 1915, NAACPP.

60. "Negro Film Play Unfit, Mayor Says," *Tribune* [New York], April 2, 1915, DWGP; "Mayor Is Asked to Aid the 'Clansman' Film," *The World* [New York], April 2, 1915, DWGP; "Fight Negro 'Movie' Ban," *Press* [New York], April 2, 1915, DWGP; "Mayor Advises Change in Scenes in Photo Play," *The Herald* [New York], April 2, 1915; "Mayor Orders More Cuts in the 'Nation,'" *Sun* [New York], April 2, 1915, DWGP.

· 61. J. E. Spingarn to Mayor John Purroy Mitchel, April 6, 1915; Theodore Rousseau to J. E. Spingarn, April 6, 1915; May C. Nerney to George H. Bell, April 9, 1915; all in NAACPP. "I very much fear," Nerney declared on April 8, "that we cannot put any more pressure...on the Mayor than we are now." May C. Nerney to Verne E. Sheridan, April 8, 1915, NAACPP.

62. May C. Nerney to George Packard, April 17, 1915, NAACPP.

63. The controversy over *The Birth of a Nation* had a catalytic effect on the National Board of Censorship. Frederic C. Howe resigned as chairman, almost certainly because of the board's failure to support his stance on Griffith's film. The board, realizing that it was losing ground to demands for formal censorship (demands that were aided by the nationwide agitation surrounding *Birth*), embraced a new purpose (encouraging better film quality) and consequently, later in 1915, changed its name to the National Board of Review. May C. Nerney to Butler R. Wilson, May 1, 1915, NAACPP; May C. Nerney to Samuel R. Morsell, May 26, June 3, 1915, NAACPP; Bowser, *Transformation of Cinema*, 52.

64. "Still Showing Vicious Picture," *New York Age*, March 11, 1915, NAACPP; *Post* [Washington, D.C.], April 25, 1915, DWGP.

65. "Egg Negro Scenes in a Film Play," *Union* [Springfield, Massachusetts], April 15, 1915; *New York Times*, April 15, 1915; *Telegraph* [New York], April 15, 1915; *Telegram* [New York], April 15, 1915; all in DWGP. Schaeffle was charged and convicted of creating a disturbance but sentence was suspended on condition that he left New York for California. *Call* [New York], April 27, 1915, DWGP. See also Fleener-Marzec, *D. W. Griffith's "The Birth of a Nation,"* 176–77. For a provocative reflection on the significance of the egg-throwing incident, see Gaines, *Fire and Desire*, 219–22 and passim.

66. May C. Nerney to J. E. Spingarn, April 19, 1915, NAACPP; May C. Nerney, "Memorandum for Dr. Du Bois," dated May 7, 1915, NAACPP; "May Tone Down Part of Anti-Negro Film," *World* [New York], March 31, 1915, DWGP; "The Regulation of Films," *Nation* [New York] 100, no. 2601 (May 6, 1915), DWGP; Minutes of the Meeting of the Board of Directors, April 13, May 10, 1915, NAACP Board of Directors, Box A-8, NAACPP

67. "Dismiss Film Play Case," *Mail* [New York], May 24, 1915, DWGP.

68. S. S. Frissell to May C. Nerney, March 30, 1915, NAACPP.

69. "The press," commented the NAACP national secretary, "except papers like the New York Call, is closed to us." May C. Nerney to Verne E. Sheridan, March 24, 1915, NAACPP.

70. "Comments Heard at the Theatre," in "Memorandum on 'The Birth of a Nation' Founded on Dixon's 'Clansman,'" n.d., p. 2, NAACPP; Elizabeth D. White to May C. Nerney, March 11, 1915, NAACPP; *Fighting a Vicious Film*, 17–18.

71. May C. Nerney to Joseph P. Loud, May 6, 1915, NAACPP; Lester Walton, "Colored Citizens' Weakness Shown in Photo Play Incident," *New York Age*, March 23, 1915, cited in Anna Everett, *Returning the Gaze*, 75.

72. On Curley, see Jack Beatty, *The Rascal King: The Life and Times of James Michael Curley* (Reading, Mass.: Addison-Wesley, 1992). On the campaign against the film in Boston generally, see Cripps, "The Reaction of the Negro to the Motion Picture, *Birth of a Nation*," 118–22.

73. On Trotter and his background, see Stephen R. Fox, *The Guardian of Boston: William Monroe Trotter* (New York: Atheneum, 1970). The disagreement between

Wilson and Trotter ended, according to the late Arthur S. Link, with "the President accusing Trotter of trying to blackmail him and virtually ordering him from his office." Link, *Wilson: The New Freedom* (Princeton: Princeton University Press, 1956), 252; cf. Fox, *Guardian of Boston*, 179–86 and David L. Lewis, *W. E. B. Du Bois: Biography of a Race, 1868–1919* (New York: Henry Holt, 1993), 509–12.

74. Two comments by the national secretary of the NAACP emphasize the conservatism and elitism of NAACP tactics and the organization's dislike of large demonstrations. On the abortive parade to Mayor Mitchel's New York office, May C. Nerney wrote that "It is our object to have a very dignified procession of representative people. We feel that it is quality rather than quantity that counts." "Mass meetings," Nerney asserted in mid-March, "will only dissolve in rhetoric and in the end serve to advertise the picture." May C. Nerney to Major R. C. Wendell, March 26, 1915; Nerney to the Reverend William P. Hayes, March 17, 1915; both in NAACPP.

75. Fox, *Guardian of Boston*, 191; "In Reply to Mr. Storey," J. J. McCarthy to editor of the *Herald*, April 7, 1915, DWGP; "Defends 'Birth of a Nation' in Strong Reply," *Evening Record* [Boston], April 7, 1915, DWGP. Naively, the NAACP in New York appears to have no idea who McCarthy, one of the chief publicists of the film and its local business manager in Boston, actually was. See May C. Nerney to Joseph P. Loud [telegram], April 21, 1915; Joseph P. Loud to May C. Nerney, April 22, 1915; both in NAACPP.

76. Mary White Ovington to J. E. Spingarn, April 9, 1915, NAACPP; Fox, *Guardian of Boston*, 191.

77. "Hiss President Wilson at Race Film Hearing," *Traveller and Evening Herald* [Boston], April 8, 1915, DWGP; "Hissed Wilson's Name," *Transcript* [Boston], April 8, 1915, DWGP; Mary White Ovington to J. E. Spingarn, April 9, 1915, NAACPP.

78. "Hissed Wilson's Name," *Transcript* [Boston], April 8, 1915; "Photoplay, 'Birth of Nation,' All Right, Says Mayor," *Herald* [Boston], April 11, 1915; cf. *Telegraph* [Boston], April 12, 1915; all in DWGP.

79. "Picture Play Arouses Furore," *Herald* [Boston], April 10, 1915; Aitken, as quoted in "The Birth of a Nation," *Morning Globe* [Boston], April 12, 1915; both in DWGP.

80. "Calls Film an Outrage," *Evening Transcript* [Boston], April 12, 1915, DWGP; "Mayor Calls Film 'Outrage,'" *Herald* [Boston], April 13, 1915, DWGP; Joseph P. Loud to May C. Nerney, April 15, 1915, NAACPP; "Mayor Can Not Stop Film Play," *Evening Record* [Boston], April 12, 1915, DWGP.

81. Joseph P. Loud to May C. Nerney, April 15, 1915, NAACPP.

82. "Will Add New Film to 'The Birth of a Nation,'" *Herald* [Boston], April 15, 1915; "Will Improve Big Picture," *Evening Record* [Boston], April 15, 1915; "'Birth of a Nation' to Have New Film," *Traveler and Evening Herald* [Boston], April 15, 1915; all in DWGP.

83. "Added Film Depicts Progress of Negro," *Morning Herald*, April 17, 1915, DWGP. The new film was "heartily applauded" at both of its first performances. Ibid.

84. Philip J. Allston to Booker T. Washington, April 12, 1915, *Letters of Booker T. Washington*, 13, 1914–1915, eds. Harlan and Smock, 261–62. Washington was determined not to do anything that might be construed in any way as an endorsement of *The Birth of a Nation*, which he regarded as a "hurtful, vicious play." Booker T. Washington to Philip J. Allston, April 25, 1915, Booker T. Washington Papers. Also see Booker T. Washington to Florence E. Sewell Bond, June 30, 1915, *Letters of Booker T. Washington*, 13, 1914–1915, ed. Harlan and Smock, 335.

85. Fleener, "Answering Film with Film," 402–4; May C. Nerney to Desha Breckenridge, September 20, 1915, May C. Nerney to Huston Quin, September 20, 1915, both in NAACPP.

86. Fleener, "Answering Film with Film": 406–11, 404–405. Thomas Cripps argues that the adding of the new epilogue effectively "drove a wedge between Northern and Southern wings of black opinion." Cripps, "The Making of *The Birth of a Race*," p. 43.

87. Charles [A?]llason to Booker T. Washington, June 1, 1915, Booker T. Washington Papers, quoted in Fleener, "Answering Film with Film": 412. Fleener observes that the epilogue was shown during 1915–16 in Allentown, Pennsylvania; Richmond, Virginia; New Haven, Connecticut; and New York. Ibid. For other showings, see "The Birth of a Nation," *Battle Creek Morning Journal*, February 4, 1916, DWGP; "'Birth of a Nation' Here Again; Negro Views Added," *Post* [St. Louis], March 6, 1916, DWGP; Fleener-Marzec, *D. W. Griffith's "The Birth of a Nation,"* 367–70.

88. May C. Nerney to Dr. Charles E. Bentley, April 17, 1915, NAACPP. Nerney was referring to black boxer Jack Johnson's defeat by white pugilist Jess Willard in Cuba a few days earlier.

89. "'Birth of a Nation' Causes Near-Riot," *Morning Globe* [Boston], April 18, 1915, DWGP; "150 Patrolmen Guard 'Birth of a Nation,'" *Morning Herald* [Boston], April 18, 1915, DWGP; "Small Riot over Film," *Moving Picture World* [New York], May 1, 1915, DWGP; Schickel, *Griffith*, 294–95; Cripps, *Slow Fade to Black*, 59–60; Fox, *Guardian of Boston*, 192–93. On this and later incidents in Boston, see Fleener-Marzec, *D. W. Griffith's "The Birth of a Nation,"* 177–80.

90. "To Take Protest to Gov. Walsh," *Advertiser* [Boston], April 19, 1915, DWGP; "Mass Meeting in Boston to Ask Governor's Support in Prohibition," *Morning Union* [Springfield, Massachusetts], April 19, 1915, DWGP; Fox, *Guardian of Boston*, 193–94.

91. "No Race Film for Sundays," *Post* [Boston], April 17, 1915, DWGP; "Memorandum on 'The Birth of a Nation' Founded on Dixon's 'Clansman,'" n.d., 3, NAACPP.

92. "Race Issue in Old Bay State," *Morning Star* [Newark, New Jersey], April 26, 1915;"Walsh Acts on Photo-Play," *Post* [Boston], April 15, 1915; "Confer on Film Play," *Globe* [Boston], April 15, 1915; all in DWGP.

93. Schickel, *Griffith*, 295–96; Fox, *Guardian of Boston*, 194.

94. "Hundreds Flock to City Court," *Record* [Boston], April 20, 1915, DWGP; "Court to Rule on Photo-Play," *Globe* [Boston], April 20, 1915, DWGP; Schickel, *Griffith*, 296; Fox, *Guardian of Boston*, 194.

95. Samuel E. Courtney to Booker T. Washington, April 19, 1915, Harlan and Smock, eds., *The Booker T. Washington Papers*, 13, 1914–1915, 274.

96. "Hundreds Flock to City Court," *Record* [Boston], April 20, 1915, DWGP; "Resume Hearing on Film Protest," *American* [Boston], April 21, 1915, DWGP; "'Birth of a Nation' Can Continue Is Court's Ruling," *Journal* [Boston], April 22, 1915, DWGP; "Theatre Yields on Film Protest," *American* [Boston] April 22, 1915, DWGP; "Protested Film Scene Cut after Court Warning," *Christian Science Monitor* [Boston], April 22, 1915, DWGP; Schickel, *Griffith*, 296; Joseph P. Loud to Mae [sic] C. Nerney [night letter], April 28, 1915, NAACPP. Also on this, see Fleener-Marzec, *D. W. Griffith's "The Birth of a Nation,"* 107–109.

97. "Files Bill Aimed at Photo-Play," *Journal* [Boston], April 21, 1915; "Protested Film Scene Cut after Court Warning," *Christian Science Monitor* [Boston], April 22, 1915;

"Movies Hearing on Friday," *Evening Record* [Boston], April 22, 1915; "Fight for New Law in War on 'Birth of a Nation,'" *Traveler and Evening Herald* [Boston], April 22, 1915; all in DWGP. On the struggle for censorship legislation in Massachusetts, see Fleener-Marzec, *D. W. Griffith's "The Birth of a Nation,"* 332–38.

98. "Fight for New Law in War on 'Birth of a Nation,'" *Traveler and Evening Herald* [Boston], April 22, 1915, DWGP.

99. "Winnow Crop of 'Rush Order' Censor Bills," *American* [Boston], April 30, 1915, DWGP.

100. For these and other editorial condemnations of the threatened legislation, see "Kill the Sullivan Bill!," *Traveler and Evening Herald* [Boston], April 26, 1915, DWGP.

101. Thomas Dixon to the editor, *Journal* [Boston], April 26, 1915, DWGP.

102. "Race Question Moves Boston," *Public Ledger* [Philadelphia], April 24, 1915; "Film May Be a Factor in Mass. Politics," *Gazette* [Worcester, Massachusetts], April 24, 1915; both in DWGP.

103. "Eliot Protests 'Birth of a Nation,'" *Journal* [Boston], April 26, 1915; "Negro Women Offer to Die to Stop Film," *Morning Herald* [Boston], April 26, 1915; "Colored Women Form a League," *Morning Globe* [Boston], April 26, 1915; "500 in a Room Meant for 200," *Evening Globe* [Boston], April 26, 1915; "Negroes Hear Opponents," *Evening Transcript* [Boston], April 26, 1915; all in DWGP.

104. *American* [Boston], May 1, 1915, DWGP; "New Bill Provides 3 Censors," *Post* [Boston], May 1, 1915, DWGP; Butler R. Wilson to Dear Sir, April 27, 1915, NAACPP.

105. Joseph P. Loud to May C. Nerney, May 4, 1915, NAACPP; Butler R. Wilson to May C. Nerney, May 4, 1915, NAACPP; M. H. Loud to May C. Nerney, May 2, 1915 [telegram], NAACPP; "Pres. Eliot Scores 'Birth of a Nation,'" *Advertiser* [Boston], May 3, 1915, DWGP. On Governor Walsh's role in the controversy, see Fleener-Marzec, *D. W. Griffith's "The Birth of a Nation,"* 258–60.

106. Joseph P. Loud to May C. Nerney, May 10, May 13, 1915, NAACPP; Joseph P. Loud to May C. Nerney, May 18, 1915 [telegram], NAACPP; "'Birth of a Nation' Opponents Win Senate Fight," *Journal* [Boston], May 18, 1915, DWGP; "Opponents of 'Birth of a Nation' Win," *Post* [Boston], May 18, 1915, DWGP; "Film Censorship Bill Now Law," *Advertiser* [Boston], May 22, 1915, DWGP; "'Nation' Film Is Now Up to Censor Board," *Journal* [Boston], May 22, 1915, DWGP.

107. E. D. White to J. P. Tumulty, April 5, 1915, Woodrow Wilson Papers, here as cited in Link, *Woodrow Wilson: The New Freedom,* 253.

108. Warren F. Johnson to Woodrow Wilson, March 29, 1915, enclosing Margaret B. Damrosch to Joseph P. Tumulty, March 27, 1915, in Link, ed., *The Papers of Woodrow Wilson,* Vol. 32, 454–55; from Joseph P. Tumulty to Woodrow Wilson, April 24, 1915; Woodrow Wilson to Joseph P. Tumulty, April 24, 1915, including n. 1; Woodrow Wilson to Joseph P. Tumulty, April 28, 1915, including nn. 1 and 2, in Link, ed., *The Papers of Woodrow Wilson, Vol. 33, April 17-July 21, 1915* (Princeton: Princeton University Press, 1980), 68, 86. On Wilson's statement, also see "Says He Didn't O.K. Movie," *Blade* [Toledo], April 30, 1915; "Wilson Denies He O.K.D Film," *Sun* [New York], May 1, 1915; both in DWGP. Three years later, Wilson wrote to Tumulty, his secretary, of his strong disapproval of this "unfortunate production" and expressed his wish that its screening "might be avoided, particularly in communities where there are so many colored people." Wilson to Tumulty, c. April 22, 1918, in Link, ed., *The Papers of Woodrow*

Wilson, Vol. 47: *March 13—May 12, 1918* (Princeton: Princeton University Press, 1984), 388, n.3.

109. May C. Nerney to Joseph P. Loud, April 21, 1915 (also see George Foster Peabody, "Gross Caricatures of the Negro," reprinted in *Fighting a Vicious Film*, 32, and George Foster Peabody to the editor, *Herald* [Boston], April 15, 1915); Walter P. Eaton to May C. Nerney, April 23, 1915; May C. Nerney to Senator Wesley L. Jones, April 22, 1915; W. L. Jones to May C. Nerney, April 27, 1915; May C. Nerney, "Memorandum for Dr. Du Bois," dated May 7, 1915; all the above, except where indicated, from NAACPP.

110. "Demand Censors Act Immediately," *Post* [Boston], May 22, 1915, DWGP; Fox, *Guardian of Boston*, 196–97; Joseph P. Loud to May C. Nerney, May 21, 1915, NAACPP; "Trotter in Appeal for the Mayor," *Post* [Boston], May 24, 1915, DWGP.

111. "Protested Film Scene Cut after Court Warning," *Christian Science Monitor* [Boston], April 22, 1915; "Theatre Yields on Film Protest," *American* [Boston], April 22, 1915; both in DWGP.

112. "Censors 'Pass' Film Play that Stirred City," *Morning Herald* [Boston], June 3, 1915; "'Birth of a Nation' Wins," *Post* [Boston], June 3, 1915; "Race Film Foes Undaunted by Censors 'OK,'" *Boston Traveler*, June 4, 1915; "'Birth of a Nation' Wins," *Boston Transcript*, June 6, 1915; all in DWGP.

113. "Photo-Play Opponents Arrested," *Post* [Boston], June 8, 1915, DWGP; "Arrest Eight of Objectors," *Morning Globe* [Boston], June 8, 1915, DWGP; Fox, *Guardian of Boston*, 197.

114. "Resolutions of Executive Committee, Boston Branch, National Association for the Advancement of Colored People," June 8, 1915; May C. Nerney to Nettie J. Asberry, July 30, 1915; May C. Nerney to George W. Crawford, September 7, 1915; all in NAACPP.

115. Albert E. Pillsbury to Archibald Grimké, May 17, 1915, quoted in Fox, *Guardian of Boston*, 196.

116. "I wish you could have been here on Sunday," one Bostonian proudly observed; "you would never doubt the colored people in this part of the country. We have them with us…The colored people are fighting <u>superbly</u>. The whites agree, but are 'too busy'—with notable exceptions." Mrs. Mary H. Loud to May C. Nerney, May 5, 1915, NAACPP.

117. May C. Nerney to Dr. Charles E. Bentley, March 17, 1915, NAACPP; Celia Parker Woolley to editor, *Record Herald* [Chicago], April 1, 1915 (printed April 6, 1915), DWGP; May C. Nerney to Dr. Charles E. Bentley, April 5 [telegram], April 9, April 30, May 7, 1915, NAACPP.

118. "Mayor's Wife Censors 'The Birth of a Nation,'" *Tribune* [Chicago], March 20 [?], 1915, DWGP; "'The Birth of a Nation' Passed in Chicago," *Moving Picture World*, April 10, 1915, DWGP; George Packard to May C. Nerney, April 12, 1915, NAACPP; Alonzo J. Bowling to editor of *The Crisis*, November 1, 1916, NAACPP. Later, as the controversy over the film deepened, Mrs. Harrison changed her mind, describing it now as an "awful thing" that "would arouse racial feeling." "Mrs. Harrison Objects to 'Birth of a Nation,'" *Tribune* [Chicago], April 28, 1915, DWGP.

119. "Mayor Arouses Ire of Negroes," *Examiner* [Chicago], July 12, 1915, DWGP.

120. Dr. Charles E. Bentley to May C. Nerney, May 4, 1915, NAACPP.

121. Thomas W. Allinson to May C. Nerney, May 3, 1915, NAACPP; *The Crisis* (June 1915): 85–86; Booker T. Washington to Charles E. Mason, May 28, 1915, *Letters of Booker T. Washington*, 13, *1914–1915*, ed. Harlan and Smock, 296.

122. "Thompson Bars Griffith Film, Birth of a Nation," *Tribune* [Chicago], May 15, 1915, DWGP; May C. Nerney to Glesner Fowler, May 18, 1915, NAACPP; City Ordinances Governing the Exhibition of Moving Pictures [pamphlet], Department of Police, City of Chicago, n.d., NAACPP.

123. Joseph P. Loud to May C. Nerney, June 15, 1915, NAACPP; Booker T. Washington to William H. Thompson, June 3, 1915, *Letters of Booker T. Washington*, 13, *1914–1915*, ed. Harlan and Smock, 317–18.

124. "It will be a serious and grave mistake to wait until the pictures are actually being exhibited…and then attempt to close them up," observed Booker T. Washington. "The weakness of this plan has been clearly demonstrated in New York and Boston." Washington, as quoted in *Fighting a Vicious Film*, 35.

125. "Movie Gives Patriotic Thrills," *Examiner* [Chicago], May 24, 1915, DWGP; James Warren Currie, "The Turn of the Wheel," *Examiner* [Chicago], May 29, 1915, DWGP; the Hattons, "Mr. Griffith and Our Busy Censors," *Herald* [Chicago], May 30, 1915, DWGP; T. W. Allinson to May C. Nerney, June 5, 1915, NAACPP.

126. May C. Nerney to Dr. Charles E. Bentley, May 21, 1915; May C. Nerney to T. W. Allinson, May 24, 1915; both in NAACPP.

127. Charles Bentley, a member of the Board of the Chicago NAACP, tried to persuade national secretary May Nerney not to launch a major campaign against the state censorship bill. The bill, he wrote, "is being fought by every Church—social service and philanthropic organization, I believe, in Chicago. I can see no good of you expending your energy so long as so many splendid organizations are fighting it and are upon the ground." Charles E. Bentley to May C. Nerney, May 25, 1915, NAACP. On the Jackson bill, see *The Crisis*, April 1915, 269; May C. Nerney to Judge Robert McMurdy, May 24, NAACPP; "Race Film Bill Passes in House on Negro's Plea," *Tribune* [Chicago], May 19, 1915, DWGP; "Race Film Bill Passes House," *Billboard* [Chicago], May 29, 1915, DWGP.

128. "City Loses Fight to Bar 'The Birth of a Nation,'" *Journal* [Chicago], June 5, 1915; "'Birth of a Nation' Wins," *News* [Chicago], June 5, 1915; "'Nation's Birth' Film Is O. K.'D," *American* [Chicago], June 5, 1915; all in DWGP. On the legal background to the Chicago fight, see Fleener-Marzec, *D. W. Griffith's "The Birth of a Nation,"* 112–13.

129. "The Birth of a Nation," *Tribune* [Chicago], May 25, 1915; "There Is No Excuse for Stopping This Show," *Examiner* [Chicago], May 22, 1915; "Let It Stay Barred," *Herald* [Chicago], May 17, 1915; all in DWGP.

130. "Mayor to Pass on 'Birth of a Nation' Film," *American* [Chicago], May 27, 1915; "Colored Clergymen May Pass on a Film," *Herald* [Chicago], June 1, 1915; both in DWGP.

131. "Sue Mayor to Show 'Birth of a Nation' Pictures in Chicago," *American* [Chicago], June 2, 1915; "Backers of Photoplay Seek to Enjoin Mayor," *Journal* [Chicago], June 2, 1915; "Injunction Asked against City for 'Birth of a Nation,'" *Examiner* [Chicago], June 3, 1915; "'Birth of a Nation' at Crisis," *News* [Chicago], June 3, 1915; all in DWGP.

132. T. W. Allinson to May C. Nerney, June 5, 1915; Charles E. Bentley to May C. Nerney, June 10, 14, 1915; all in NAACPP.

133. "Opinion by Hon. William Fenimore Cooper, Superior Court of Cook County," in the case of *Joseph J. McCarthy vs. City of Chicago*, June 5, 1915, 1–3, DWGP.

134. "Society Puts Approval on Dixon Film," *Examiner* [Chicago], June 6, 1915, DWGP; "Crowds Get Thrill at 'Birth of a Nation,'" *News* [Chicago], June 7, 1915, DWGP; "Questions Motive of City in Fight on Birth of a Nation," *Tribune* [Chicago], June 8, 1915, DWGP. Griffith's gratitude to Cooper was long-lived: he sent members of his staff to help the judge (a Democrat) a year later in a difficult fight for reelection. See "Griffith and Film Houses Play Part in Chicago Politics," *Morning Telegraph* [New York], June 9, 1916; "News and Gossip of the Plays and Players," *Globe and Commercial Advertiser* [New York], June 9, 1916; both in DWGP.

135. "'Birth of a Nation' May Be Produced, Court Decides," *Examiner* [Chicago], June 6, 1915; "Censors to Report on 'Birth of a Nation' Today," *Tribune* [Chicago], June 7, 1915; "Censors Find against 'Birth of a Nation,'" *Herald* [Chicago], June 8, 1915; all in DWGP

136. "Censorship Loses Again," *Motography* [Chicago] 13, no. 25 (June 19, 1915); "'Birth of a Nation' Should Be Shown the Children," *Post* [Chicago], June 19, 1915; both in DWGP.

137. "Film Censors Are Censored," *Examiner* [Chicago], June 8, 1915, DWGP; "'Birth of a Nation' Appeal Is Up To-Day," *Examiner* [Chicago], June 10, 1915, DWGP; "Asks Quick Appeal in Birth of a Nation Suit," *Journal* [Chicago], June 21, 1915, DWGP; Charles E. Bentley to May C. Nerney, June 10, 14, 1915, NAACPP; May C. Nerney to Roger N. Baldwin, June 11, 1915, NAACPP.

138. "In Again, Out Again," *Tribune* [Chicago], July 16, 1915, DWGP; Thomas W. Allinson to May C. Nerney, July 19, 1915, NAACPP.

139. May C. Nerney to Dr. Stephen J. Lewis, September 11, 1915, NAACPP; "Movie Show Free for Legislators," *Evening Telegraph* [Philadelphia], March 12, 1915, DWGP; G. W. Bradenburgh to NAACP, March 12, 1915, NAACPP. Bradenburgh, a supporter of the independent filmmakers, was under the false impression that *Birth* was released by the General Film Company.

140. See, for example, Jennie M. Proctor to May C. Nerney, June 7, 1915; Stephen J. Lewis to May C. Nerney, September 8, 1915; both in NAACPP.

141. Jennie M. Proctor to May C. Nerney, June 15, August 13, 1915; S. R. Morsell to May C. Nerney [telegram], August 25, 1915; Jennie M. Proctor to NAACP [telegram], September 6, 1915; all in NAACPP.

142. May C. Nerney to Laetitia A. Graves, June 2, 1915, NAACPP.

143. "Philadelphia Authorities, Overzealous for Colored Brother's Safety, Fail in Court Attempt to Suppress 'Nation,'" *Motion Picture News* [New York], September 26 [?], 1915, DWGP; also see Fleener-Marzec, *D. W. Griffith's "The Birth of a Nation,"* 114.

144. "Seek Again to Ban 'Birth of a Nation,'" *Inquirer* [Philadelphia], September 8, 1915; "Colored Mob Starts a Riot over Film Play," *Press* [Philadelphia], September 21, 1915; "Negro Mob Clubbed from Film Theater," *Public Ledger* [Philadelphia], September 21, 1915; all in DWGP.

145. "Philadelphia Authorities, Overzealous for Colored Brother's Safety, Fail in Court Attempt to Suppress 'Nation,'" *Motion Picture News* [New York], September 26 [?], 1915; "Colored Mob Starts a Riot over Film Play," *Press* [Philadelphia], September 21, 1915; "Mayor to Review Row over 'Movie' on Friday," *Evening Bulletin* [Philadelphia], September 21, 1915;

"Threw Bricks into Box-Office," *The Billboard* [Philadelphia], October 2, 1915; all in DWGP. Also see Fleener-Marzec, *D. W. Griffith's "The Birth of a Nation,"* 180–81.

146. "Mayor to Review Row over 'Movie' on Friday," *Evening Bulletin* [Philadelphia], September 21, 1915; "Colored Leaders Protest to Mayor 'Attack by Police,'" *Telegraph* [Philadelphia], September 21, 1915; both in DWGP.

147. "Ministers Condemn 'Birth of a Nation,'" *Public Ledger* [Philadelphia], October 3, 1915, DWGP.

148. The NAACP also seems to have been involved in unsuccessful attempts to stop the film in the cities of Harrisburg and Easton. See Stephen J. Lewis to May C. Nerney, September 11, 1915; Burton Branch to May C. Nerney, October 26, 1915; secretary to Miss Nerney to Burton Branch, November 2, 1915; all in NAACPP.

149. S. P. Keeble to May C. Nerney, April 9, 11, 1915, NAACPP.

150. S. P. Keeble to May C. Nerney, April 9, 1915, NAACPP.

151. S. P. Keeble to May C. Nerney, April 16, 29, May 12 [telegram], 1915; M. Sula Butler to May C. Nerney, May 7, 1915; May C. Nerney to M. Sula Butler, May 11, 1915; May C. Nerney to S. P. Keeble, May 16, 1915; May C. Nerney to Minnie B. Mosby, May 24, 1915; May C. Nerney to Minnie B. Mosby, June 2, 1915; Chas. B. Williams, chairman, Ohio Board of Censors, to May C. Nerney, May 26, 1915; all in NAACPP.

152. S. P. Keeble to May C. Nerney, May 25, 1915; May C. Nerney to Our Ohio Branches, June 15, 1915; S. P. Keeble to May C. Nerney, July 9, 1915; all in NAACPP.

153. "Ohio Bars Dixon Play," *Times-Star* [Cincinnati], September 28, 1915, DWGP; "Birth of a Nation Can't Be Shown in Cleveland," *News* [Cleveland], September 28, 1915, NAACPP; S. P. Keeble to May C. Nerney, September 28, 1915, NAACPP; Robert B. Barcus to editor, *The Crisis*, September 28, 1915, NAACPP.

154. Untitled report of May C. Nerney on the Ohio situation, received November 1, 1915, 1, NAACPP.

155. Ibid; S. P. Keeble to May C. Nerney, April 9, September 28, 1915, NAACPP; Harry C. Smith to May C. Nerney, May 24, 1915, NAACPP; Minnie B. Mosby to May C. Nerney, May 26, 1915, NAACPP. Later, Nerney protested to Governor Willis that the Ohio traveling show known as the "Corn Boys" tour had included *The Birth of a Nation* on its program in Philadelphia. Willis contacted Thomas P. Riddle, the organizer of the tour and an employee of the state government, to express his disapproval. When *Birth* nonetheless still formed part of the entertainment, Riddle was dismissed. May C. Nerney to Governor Frank B. Willis, November 26, 1915; "Corn Tour Man to Be Ousted," *Times Star* [Cincinnati], December 6, 1915; Harry E. Davis to May C. Nerney, December 29, 1915; all in NAACPP. On the Ohio controversy, also see Fleener-Marzec, *D. W. Griffith's "The Birth of a Nation,"* 260–61.

156. "The Birth of a Nation," *Gazette* [Cleveland], October 28, 1916, NAACPP; *Star* [?] [Cincinnati], January 6, 1916, NAACPP; "Ohio Supreme Court Throws Out Film Suit," *Citizen* [Columbus], October 24, 1916, NAACPP. Also see Fleener-Marzec, *D. W. Griffith's "The Birth of a Nation,"* 96–97.

157. Untitled report of May C. Nerney on the Ohio situation, received November 1, 1915, 1–2, NAACPP.

158. William Stevenson to Hon. George Puchta [mayor of Cincinnati], February 15, 1916; William Stevenson to Roy Nash, acting national secretary, February 22,

1916; Roy Nash to the Honorable George Puchta, February 24, 1916 [telegram]; all in NAACPP.

159. One of the film's distributors in Kansas City, Missouri, complained to a journalist that the film would be kept out of Kansas because "the members of the appeal board and the official censor are afraid of the big colored vote." "'Birth of a Nation' Barred in State?," *Leavenworth Times* [Kansas], November 26, 1915, DWGP.

160. May C. Nerney to Arthur Capper, November 9, 1915; Arthur Capper to May C. Nerney, November 13, 1915; May C. Nerney to Arthur Capper, November 23, 1915; Arthur Capper to May C. Nerney, November 27, 1915; all in NAACPP. Capper was as good as his word. As he noted in October 1918, *Birth of a Nation* had still not been shown in Kansas. Arthur Capper to John R. Stilladay, October 17, 1918, NAACPP.

161. Governor Woodbridge N. Ferris of Michigan promised to do anything he could to help the NAACP but warned that state law "made it unlikely [he] could help much." Governor Hiram W. Johnson of California, asked to state his position on the film, responded that he had "never in any fashion" endorsed it (though he also described it as "a very remarkable and wonderful production"). Woodbridge N. Ferris to May C. Nerney, October 12, 1915; Hiram W. Johnson to W. A. Butler, May 8, 1915; both in NAACPP.

162. "Action against Production of 'The Birth of a Nation,'" undated memo, NAACPP; May C. Nerney to Judge William M. Dunn, July 27, 1915, NAACPP; May C. Nerney to R. L. Brokenburr, July 29, 1915, NAACPP; May C. Nerney to Cornelia F. Maury, June 10, 1915, NAACPP; Report of the Secretary, Miss Nerney, Minutes of the Meeting of the Board of Directors, June 14, 1915, NAACP Board of Directors, Box A-8, NAACPP; Eva B. Jones to Mr. Randolph, August 23, 1915, NAACPP; "'Birth of a Nation' Is Banned," *Review* [Atlantic City, New Jersey], August 14, 1915, DWGP; "Bartlett to Stop 'Birth of a Nation,'" *Press* [Atlantic City], August 14, 1915, DWGP; "Negro Protest Stops Film Play," *Public Ledger* [Philadelphia], August 14, 1915, DWGP; unsigned memorandum (on New Haven situation), dated August 13, 1915, NAACPP; George W. Crawford to May C. Nerney, September 11, 1915, NAACPP; "A Statement of Facts Regarding the photo play 'The Birth of a Nation,' by the Providence Branch of the NAACP," n. d., NAACPP; "Memorandum from Mr. [Butler R.] Wilson," November 5, 1915, NAACPP; Mary White Ovington to Butler R. Wilson, November 4, 1915, NAACPP; T. M. Brown to NAACP, November 8, 1915, NAACPP; "Censorship Bugbear Is Laid Low in Minneapolis; Mayor Has Confidence in National Board," *Motion Picture News* [New York], January 1, 1916, DWGP; Fleener-Marzec, *D. W. Griffith's "The Birth of a Nation,"* 104–107.

163. E. Marshall to May C. Nerney, August 9, 1915 [telegram]; Eva B. Jones to Mr. Randolph, August 23, 1915; "Politics in Censoring," *Motion Picture World* [New York], October 9, 1915; all in NAACPP.

164. Jessye E. McClain to May C. Nerney, April 12, 1915; May C. Nerney to S. Joe Brown, May 7, June 7, 1915; both in NAACPP. On the Des Moines ordinance, also see *The Crisis* (June 1915): 86.

165. On Tacoma, see Henrietta Sadler to May C. Nerney, August 11, 1915 [telegram]; copy of Tacoma Ordinance no. 6179; "Action against Production of 'The Birth of a Nation,'" undated memo; all in NAACPP. On Wilmington, see Report of the Secretary, Miss Nerney, Minutes of the Meeting of the Board of Directors, June 14, 1915, NAACP Board of Directors, Box A-8; "An Ordinance to Prohibit the Exhibition of Any Moving Picture Likely to Cause Ill-Feeling between the White and Black Races," June 18, 1915,

all in NAACPP. For Lansing, see Charles A. Campbell to May C. Nerney, December 30, 1915, February 10, 1916, NAACPP; "Photoplay Is All 'O.K.' Says Board of Censors," *The Lansing Press* [Michigan], January 29, 1916, DWGP. On Detroit, see "Defeat Effort to Restrict Film," *Morning Telegraph* [Detroit, Michigan], December 21, 1915, DWGP.

166. See copy of Joint Resolution proposed in the House of Representatives (64th Congress, 1st session, H. J. Res. 221, May 9, 1916), NAACPP. The following day, Congressman Benjamin K. Focht of Pennsylvania also introduced an unsuccessful resolution to suppress the film on the grounds that it insulted the memory of Pennsylvanian Thaddeus Stevens, a congressional Republican who had been a major supporter of radical Reconstruction. "Would Suppress 'Birth of a Nation,'" *Daily Item* [Sunbury, Pennsylvania], May 10, 1916, DWGP. A copy of the resolution itself (64th Congress, 1st session, H. J. Res. 222, May 10, 1916) is in the NAACPP.

167. "Police Won't Stop 'Birth of a Nation,'" *Post* [Terre Haute, Indiana], January 5, 1916; "Mayor Will Not Oppose Showing of Photodrama," *Times* [Louisville, Kentucky], February 9, 1916; "Declines to Interfere," *Louisville Herald*, February 9, 1916; "Show Photoplay in Present Form," *Chronicle* [Spokane, Washington], July 26, 1915; all in DWGP.

168. "'Clansman,' with One Scene Removed, Approved," *Bee* [Sacramento, California], May 28, 1915, DWGP; "'Nation' Is No Race Slanderer, Milwaukee Declares," *Motion Picture News* [New York], July 24, 1915, DWGP; "Action against Production of 'The Birth of a Nation,'" undated memo, NAACPP.

169. "Walter Sanford Is Acquitted," *Republic* [St. Louis], October 7, 1915; "Fear Race Feud; Arrest Manager," *Morning Telegraph* [New York], February 19, 1916; "Says Photoplay Has Stimulated Race Prejudice," *Times* [Louisville, Kentucky], February 18, 1916; "Bigelow Files Demurrer in 'Birth of a Nation' Suit," *Courier-Journal* [Louisville], February 20, 1916; "Writ against Film Play Denied by Judge Fields," *Courier-Journal* [Louisville], February 26, 1916; all in DWGP.

170. Carole Marks, *Farewell—We're Good and Gone: The Great Black Migration* (Bloomington: Indiana University Press, 1989), 121–22.

171. See "Negro Protest Stops Film Play," *Public Ledger* [Philadelphia], August 14, 1915; "Nixon to Make Fight for Suppressed Film," ibid.; "Court Says No Law Makes Him Picture Censor," *Evening Union* [Atlantic City?], August 24, 1915; all in DWGP.

172. "Negro Protest Stops Film Play," *Public Ledger* [Philadelphia], August 14, 1915, DWGP.

173. "Negroes Object to 'Birth of a Nation,'" *News Press* [St. Joseph, Missouri], November 20, 1915; "Negroes Protest Some 'Birth of a Nation' Scenes," *Gazette* [St. Joseph], November 21, 1915; both in DWGP.

174. "Evansville Must Be Protected Always," *Journal News* [Evansville, Kentucky], November 30, 1915; "Colored Citizens Denounce Lynching," *Courier* [Evansville], December 5, 1915; "Censor Board Made Permanent," *Courier* [Evansville], December 6, 1915; "Armed Officers Guard Theater," *Courier* [Evansville], December 8, 1915; all in DWGP.

175. May C. Nerney to Desha Breckinridge, September 16, 1915, NAACPP; cf. J. Mott Hallowell to Mayor James M. Curley, n.d., reprinted in *Fighting a Vicious Film*, 26.

176. Frederic C. Howe to Joseph P. Loud, April 6, 1915; May C. Nerney to Desha Breckinridge, September 16, 1915; both in NAACPP.

177. P. A. Goines to W. E. B. Du Bois, August 12, 1915. An article on Johnson's lynching by novelist James Oppenheim had appeared in the *New York Independent* on October 10, 1912. May C. Nerney to P. A. Goines, September 7, 1915; Nerney to R. Granville Curry, September 16, 1915; Nerney to Hudson Quin, September 16, 1915; all in NAACPP.

178. May C. Nerney to P. A. Goines, September 7, 1915, NAACPP.

179. J. Milton Sampson to May C. Nerney, October 16, 1915; J. Milton Sampson to R. G. Randolph, November 8, 1915; "Ainslie Authorizes Griffith's Big Photo Play," *News Leader* [Richmond, Virginia], November n.d., 1915; all in NAACPP.

180. "Hate of a Nation," *Afro-American* [Baltimore], March 18, 1916, DWGP.

181. J. Rivers Barnwell to W. E. B. Du Bois, August 16, 1915; May C. Nerney to the Reverend S. E. J. Watson, September 8, 1915; both in NAACPP.

182. "Protest Made against Showing of Picture," *Citizen* [Asheville, North Carolina], October 2, 1915, DWGP.

183. P. A. Goines to W. E. B. Du Bois, August 12, 1915, NAACPP; J. Rivers Barnwell to W. E. B. Du Bois, August 16, 1915, NAACPP; "Protest Made against Showing of Picture," *Citizen* [Asheville, North Carolina], October 2, 1915, DWGP; Joseph G. Attwell to May C. Nerney, November 6, 1915, NAACPP; D. B. Frazier to W. E. B. Du Bois, November 6, 1915, NAACPP; Dr. Wm P. Saunders to W. E. B. Du Bois, October 19, 1915, NAACPP; P. J. Clyde Randall to May C. Nerney, December 4, 1915, NAACPP; "Ainslie Authorizes Griffith's Big Photo Play," *News Leader* [Richmond, Virginia], November [?], 1915, NAACPP.

184. T. G. Nutter to W. E. B. Du Bois, December 9, 1915 [telegram], NAACPP; "Make Protest against Movie," *Charleston Post* [Charleston, Virginia], December 10, 1915, DWGP; T. G. Nutter to NAACP, December 13, 1915 [telegram], NAACPP; J. M. Reed to W. E. B. Du Bois, November 28, 1915, NAACPP; "'Birth of a Nation' Warmly Defended," *Sentinel-Record* [Hot Springs, Arkansas], December 3, 1915, DWGP; "Censorship by City Council," *Sentinel-Record* [?], December [?], DWGP.

185. P. J. Clyde Randall to May C. Nerney, December 4, 1915, NAACPP.

186. Cook, *Fire from the Flint*, 141–42; Moore, "South Carolina's Reaction to the Photoplay *The Birth of a Nation*": 30–40, quotation from 40.

187. Inscoe, "*The Clansman* on Stage and Screen: North Carolina Reacts: 139, 151–60.

188. Dan Leab, "Blacks in American Cinema," in *The Political Companion to American Film*, ed. Gary Crowdus (Chicago: Lake View Press, 1994), 42; Bogle, *Toms, Coons, Mulattoes, Mammies and Bucks*, 3–14, 17. Cedric J. Robinson criticizes Bogle's stereotyping, arguing, for example, that the "buck" had a history antedating black slavery in the Americas (he cites Shakespeare's Othello as an example). Robinson, "In the Year 1915: D. W. Griffith and the Whitening of America," *Social Identities* 3, no. 2 (1997): 162.

189. Koszarski, *An Evening's Entertainment*, 1–2.

190. May C. Nerney [?] to Dr. Stephen S. Wise, April 16, 1915, NAACPP; Mary White Ovington, memorandum marked "Confidential," June 1915, NAACPP. In this memorandum, Ovington identified Sterne as the instigator of the project.

191. May C. Nerney to Joseph P. Loud, May 6, 1915, NAACPP.

192. Ibid.; May C. Nerney to William English Walling, May 17, 1915, NAACPP.

193. May C. Nerney to Frederic C. Howe, June 10, 1915, NAACPP.

194. Minutes of the Meeting of the Board of Directors, June 14, 1915, NAACP Board of Directors, Box A-8; May C. Nerney to Dr. Charles E. Bentley, May 11, 1915; Nerney to William English Walling, May 13, 1915; all in NAACPP.

195. "Memorandum for Miss Stearne [sic]," dated April 26, 1915, enclosed with May C. Nerney to Rose Janowitz, April 26, 1915, NAACPP.

196. Minutes of the Meeting of the Board of Directors, May 10, 1915, NAACP Board of Directors, Box A-8; May C. Nerney to Joseph P. Loud, May 17, 1915; both in NAACPP.

197. May C. Nerney to Joseph P. Loud, May 15, 1915; Loud to Nerney, May 16, 1915; Nerney to Loud, May 17, 1915; all in NAACPP.

198. E. E. Bentley to May C. Nerney, May 13, 1915 [telegram]; postscript by Mary Hallowell Loud to Joseph P. Loud to May C. Nerney, May 19, 1915; May C. Nerney to Joseph P. Loud, May 17, May 21, 1915; all in NAACPP.

199. May C. Nerney to Dr. Charles E. Bentley, May 11, 1915, NAACPP.

200. Minutes of the Meeting of the Board of Directors, June 14, 1915, NAACP Board of Directors, Box A-8, NAACPP.

201. May C. Nerney to Esther Nelson, June 15, 1915, NAACPP; Cripps, *Slow Fade*, 72.

202. "Negroes to Produce Own 'Birth of a Nation,'" *Public Ledger* [Philadelphia], September 11, 1915, DWGP; Schickel, *Griffith*, 306–307; Harry C. Oppenheimer to Emmett Jay Scott, October 1, 1915, *Booker T. Washington Papers*, 13, 1914–1915, ed. Harlan and Smock, 374–75.

203. According to Thomas Cripps, Sterne "liked the idea of engaging white attention by defining black aspiration as *Lincoln's Dream*." Cripps, "The Making of *The Birth of a Race*," p. 44.

204. Report of the Scenario Committee, Minutes of the Meeting of the Board of Directors, October 11, November 8, 1915, NAACP Board of Directors, Box A-8, NAACPP; Thomas Cripps, 'The Making of *The Birth of a Race*,' 44; Cripps, *Slow Fade*, 73.

205. Cripps, *Slow Fade*, 73–74.

206. Cripps, 'The Making of *The Birth of a Race*,' 46–51. Cripps argues (45–46) that *The Birth of a Race* was originally intended to demonstrate that the history of African Americans could be integrated into a broader story of "universal…human progress," but that this idea began to unravel as the United States moved toward intervention in the First World War and the film's producers became increasingly focused on making a film that would appeal to a mass market.

207. *The Birth of a Nation* did prompt a number of responses from black filmmakers determined to critique its view of African Americans. According to Thomas Cripps, such productions included three films from the Lincoln Motion Picture Company: *The Realization of a Negro's Ambition* (c. 1917), *The Trooper of Troop K* (c. 1920) and *By Right of Birth* (1921). Similar productions from the Colored Players' Company were *A Prince of His Race* (1926), *Ten Nights in a Bar Room* (1926) and *The Scar of Shame* (1928). Thomas Cripps, *Black Film as Genre* (Bloomington: Indiana University Press, 1978), 17–19, 29–30. According to Jane Gaines, black "race" films were produced in direct response to Griffith's *The Birth of a Nation*. Her examples include three films produced by the Frederick Douglass Company: *The Colored American Winning His Suit* (1917), *The Scapegoat* (1917), and *Heroic Negro Soldiers of the World War* (1919). Gaines, *Fire and Desire*, 6, 97–98, 263. While the films so far cited by Cripps and Gaines did

critique aspects of the unflattering view of blacks presented in *Birth*, they did not engage directly with the principal themes of Griffith's movie. The one film that did was black filmmaker Oscar Micheaux's *Within Our Gates* (1919), which presented questions of rape and lynching from a very different perspective to Griffith's. J. Roland Green has argued that *Within Our Gates* was deliberately designed and structured by Micheaux as an attempt to contradict Griffith's film. See Gaines, *"The Birth of a Nation* and *Within Our Gates,"* 177–92; J. Roland Green, "Micheaux v. Griffith," *Griffithiana,* 60–61 (1997): 32–49.

208. W. E. Burghardt Du Bois, *The Souls of Black Folk: Essays and Sketches* (New York: A. C. McClurg, 1903), 3.

209. Will (Juli Jones) Foster founded the first black filmmaking company in Chicago in 1912. His films, all shorts, "indirectly contested the one-dimensional black stereotypes portrayed in such popular productions as the Lubin Company's 'Rastus' series." Mark A. Reid, "African-American Filmmakers," in *The Political Companion to American Film,* 3. Haynes tried to compel the big white companies to recognize the importance of "Negro comedies" starring black (instead of blacked-up white) actors. His Haynes Photoplay Company also attempted to sell the idea of a film about black businesses to Booker T. Washington's National Negro Business League. "Biggest Motion Picture Deal," *The Freeman* [Indianapolis], March 4, n.y., clipping; H. C. Haynes to Emmett J. Scott, March 18, 1915; both in Booker T. Washington Papers, Library of Congress. Veteran black filmmaker William Greaves explained to a 1994 symposium on *The Birth of a Nation* that he had first become actively involved in films specifically to challenge Griffith's view of the world. Craig D'Ooge, ed., *"The Birth of a Nation:* Symposium on Classic Film Discusses Inaccuracies and Virtues," *Library of Congress Information Bulletin* 53, no. 13 (June 27, 1994): 265.

210. W. E. B. Du Bois, "Memorandum to Dr. Spingarn and Miss Nerney of the Moving Picture Committee," May 12, 1915, NAACPP.

211. Lorini, *Rituals of Race,* 219–224; Cripps, *Slow Fade,* 42–43, 69; "The Slanderous Film," *The Crisis* (December 1915): 76–77; "Negroes Subscribe $1000 to Give Pageant Here," *North American* [Philadelphia], October 13, 1915, NAACPP; Lewis, *Du Bois,* 459–61, 509. Also see David W. Blight, *Race and Reunion: The Civil War in American Memory* (Cambridge, Mass.: Harvard University Press, 2001), 374–77. While it did not involve Du Bois, another example of protest by pageant occurred in Chicago in August 1915, when the Lincoln Jubilee Exposition at the Coliseum put on a show depicting black history since Emancipation at the same time as *The Birth of a Nation* was running at the Chicago Opera House. "From Our Western Window," *The Congregationalist,* September 9, 1915, NAACPP.

212. Secretary's Report, Minutes of the Annual Meeting, January 3, 1916, NAACP Board of Directors, Box A-8, NAACPP; Lewis, *Du Bois,* 498–500.

213. All these scenes were objected to by the Censorship Board of San Francisco. Mary Ashe Miller to "Gentlemen," March 2, 1915; cf. May C. Nerney to Gilbert D. Lamb, April 13, 1915 (on the New York cuts); untitled, undated memorandum on the cuts made in New Haven, Connecticut; Jose H. Sherwood to May C. Nerney, October 31, 1915 (on the cuts in St. Paul, Minnesota); all in NAACPP.

214. According to May Nerney, the Boston cuts left the film "so mutilated as to be almost unintelligible." Nerney to George W. Crawford, September 7, 1915, NAACPP.

215. Du Bois, as quoted in Lorini, *Rituals of Race*, 225; cf. S[?] Kenwood to May C. Nerney, August 31, 1915, NAACPP. Although Booker T. Washington had criticized *The Birth of a Nation* in a letter to the *Chicago Defender*, he had also been very concerned that attempts to stop the film might in the end only serve to publicize it. Washington to the editor, *Chicago Defender*, May 22, 1915, cited in Fleener-Marzec, *D. W. Griffith's "The Birth of a Nation,"* 430; Washington to Samuel E. Courtney, April 23, 1915, in *The Booker T. Washington Papers*, 13, *1914–1915*, ed. Harlan and Smock, 277. Lexington, Kentucky, provided a good example of what a failed campaign against the film could do. It helped make *Birth's* six-day engagement at the Opera House, according to its manager, "by far the most largely attended of any production ever billed at a Lexington theatre," attracting more than 16,000 spectators. *Lexington Leader*, March 26, 1916, 1, cited in Gregory A. Waller, "Another Audience: Black Moviegoing, 1907–16," *Cinema Journal*, 31, no. 2 (Winter 1992): 20.

216. Cripps, *Slow Fade*, 64; "Spokane Censor Praises 'Birth of a Nation,'" *Motion Picture News* [New York], August 14, 1915, DWGP.

217. Gaines, *Fire and Desire*, 263. On this point, also see Cripps, *Slow Fade to Black*, 58, 61, 63, 64, 66.

218. Chas. A. Gird to W. E. B. Du Bois, August 20, 1915, NAACPP.

219. See, for example, P. A. Goines to W. E. B. Du Bois, August 12, 1915; Samuel E. Brown to NAACP, October 25, 1915; both in NAACPP.

220. Minutes of the Meeting of the Board of Directors, January 5, May 10, November 8, December 13, 1915, NAACP Board of Directors, Box A-8, NAACPP.

221. Cripps, "The Making of *The Birth of a Race*," 41.

CHAPTER 7

1. Gish, *The Movies, Mr. Griffith, and Me*, 131–32.

2. Thomas Dixon Jr., "Civil War Truth," *New York Times*, May 8, 1921, reprinted in *Encyclopedia of Film*, n.p; "Mayor Orders More Cuts in the Nation," *Sun* [New York], April 2, 1915, DWGP. According to Seymour Stern, Griffith did "considerable" research for his film. See Stern, "Griffith: 1—'The Birth of a Nation,'" *Film Culture* 36 (Spring–Summer 1965): 34–36.

3. Henry Stephen Gordon, "D. W. Griffith Recalls the Making of *The Birth of a Nation*," in Silva, *Focus*, 59; "Five Dollar Movies Prophesied," *Encyclopedia of Film*, March 28, 1915.

4. Griffith, "The Rise and Fall of Free Speech in America," in Mast, *The Movies in Our Midst*, 132. In terms of numbers, Griffith had a point. Academic historians could reach only a small percentage of the population with their ideas. In 1890, only 157,000 Americans were enrolled in institutions of higher education, some 3.04 percent of the population aged 18 to 21. By 1910, the comparable figures were 355,000 and 5.12 per cent of the 18–21 age group. Only a minority of these, of course, would have taken history courses. See U.S. Bureau of the Census, *Historical Statistics of the United States—Colonial Times to 1957* (Washington, D.C.: U. S. Government Printing Office, 1960), 211.

5. "When We Have 'Movie Books,'" *Post* [Washington, D.C.], March 28, 1915; "A Prophecy," *Journal* [Columbus, Ohio], April 4, 1915; "At the Majestic," *Sentinel* [Fort Wayne, Indiana], January 28, 1916; "At the Post," *Moon-Journal* [Battle Creek, Michigan],

February 3, 1916; all in DWGP. Griffith was quoted in each of these stories as claiming that by this stage, "the operation of a motion picture machine will be as familiar as putting a record on a gramophone."

6. Grieveson, *Policing the Cinema*, 195, 199–202 and passim; "*Mutual Film Corporation v. Industrial Commission of Ohio* (1915), United States Supreme Court," in Mast, ed., *Movies in Our Midst*, 136–43, quotation 142. The Supreme Court's decision was also apparently based on the notion that movies could not convey ideas—something strongly refuted by *The Birth of a Nation* itself.

7. "Capitalizing Race Hatred," *Globe* [New York], April 6, 1915, D. W. Griffith, "Reply to the *New York Globe*," *Globe*, April 10, 1915, both reprinted in Silva, *Focus*, 73–75, 77–79.

8. Michael Rogin, "The Sword Became a Flashing Vision," in Lang, *The Birth of a Nation*, 287.

9. "D. W. Griffith's Great Idea and How He Worked Out Historically Accurate Battle Scenes with 18,000 Actors and 3,000 Horses," *Sunday Star* [Terre Haute], January 2, 1916, DWGP; "The Birth of a Nation," *Sight and Sound* 16, no. 61 (Spring 1947): 32. Comments by those who viewed the film attested to the effectiveness of Griffith's strategy of re-creating history visually. One observer, for example, recalled that "I had never seen a plantation, but now I could imagine I was walking in one." Jungquist, "Viewing D. W. Griffith's *The Birth of a Nation*: A First Hand Account," 36.

10. Richard J. Evans, *In Defence of History* (London: Granta Books, 1997), 17–18.

11. See John Higham, *History: Professional Scholarship in America* (Baltimore: Johns Hopkins University Press, 1983), 16, 18–20.

12. Such historians in the first part of the nineteenth century included George Bancroft, William Lothrop Motley, Francis Parkman, and William H. Prescott. In the last quarter of the century, Henry Adams, John Ford Rhodes, John Bach McMaster, Theodore Roosevelt, and Moses Coit Tyler can broadly be included in this category.

13. White, "*The Birth of a Nation*: History as Pretext," in Lang, *The Birth of a Nation*, 214.

14. Stevens's Lydia Smith was transformed in the film into Lydia Brown.

15. Francis B. Simkins and Robert H. Woody, *South Carolina during Reconstruction* (Chapel Hill: University of North Carolina Press, 1932), 130. Also see John Hope Franklin, "*The Birth of a Nation*: Propaganda as History," 19.

16. Spears, *The Civil War on the Screen*, 38. Some reviewers commented on the resemblance of the film's historical characters to their originals. See G. B. D., "The Birth of a Nation," *Moon Journal* [Battle Creek, Michigan], February 4, 1916, DWGP.

17. Griffith's treatment of Charles Sumner as a moderate and in some respects a racist (he clearly disdains Stoneman's mulatto housekeeper) is both strange and inaccurate. Perhaps the best known of the "radical" Republican leaders after Stevens, Sumner was presented in the film as a brake on Stoneman/Stevens's radicalism. In reality, Sumner's approach to Reconstruction was very similar to Stevens's. He advocated the "state suicide" theory (the view that by seceding, the Southern states had lost all their constitutional rights) whereas Stevens believed that the old states of the Confederacy should be treated as "conquered provinces." Sumner remained a strong supporter of black rights until his death in 1874: Congress passed the Civil Rights Act of 1875 very

largely as a tribute to his memory. See David H. Donald, *Charles Sumner and the Rights of Man* (New York: Alfred A. Knopf, 1970), passim.

18. Brian Gallagher points out that "no other silent film relies so heavily or so intricately on words." Griffith used titles as a means of signing his work, as a way of including the audience in the narrative fiction, and "as a device for setting up a quasi-historical discourse which will be reified by that much larger portion of the film which is visual." By using intertitles in this way, Gallagher argues, Griffith turned "what otherwise would be an exciting racist photo-drama into an ideological project whose aim is no less than the reformulation of a major segment of American history." Gallagher, "Racist Ideology and Black Abnormality in the Birth of a Nation," *Phylon* 43, no. 1 (1st. qrt., 1982): 73.

19. These facsimiles, Gallagher notes, play a role similar to that of the intertitles: they "root the film's quasi-historical discourse in a realm that combines the 'reasonableness' of written history with the believability of 'seen' events." Ibid., 75.

20. John Nicolay and John Hay's ten-volume *Abraham Lincoln: A History* (New York: Century, 1890) was cited as the source for the shots of Lincoln's call for volunteers and Ford's Theatre. The shot of Grant and Lee was attributed to Colonel Horace Porter's *Campaigning with Grant* (New York: Century, 1897) and that of the South Carolina House of Representatives to a photograph in a local paper, the Columbia *State*.

21. *Kansas City Journal*, October 26, 1915; "Facts on the Screen," *Sun* [New York], May 23, 1915; both in DWGP.

22. "Ford's," *Star* [Baltimore], March 21, 1916; "'Birth of a Nation' Story of History," *Sentinel* [Milwaukee], July 27, 1915 (cf. "A Reconstruction Story," *New York Times*, March 21, 1915A, in *Encyclopedia of Film*); "One Point of Detail in 'The Birth of a Nation,'" *Post* [Chicago], June 22, 1915; "Grant and Lee at Appomattox—in 'The Birth of a Nation'—Grand," *Labor Herald* [Kansas City], October 22, 1915; all in DWGP.

23. Stern, "Griffith: I—*The Birth of a Nation*," 34–35; Brown, *Adventures*, 64–65.

24. Brown, *Adventures*, 57–59, 64—65.

25. Bitzer, "The Old Film in Half Tones," DWGP; Bitzer, "No Electric Light All Sun Photography," DWGP; "Billy Bitzer on Photography," Conversation with Beaumont Newhall, January 20, 1940, DWGP.

26. Rogin, "The Sword Became a Flashing Vision," in Lang, *The Birth of a Nation*, 286.

27. "'The Birth of a Nation': Griffith's Superb Spectacle," *The Muncie Post*, January 14, 1916; "Greatest of All Movies at Bijou for a Week," *Evansville Courier*, November 28, 1915; both in DWGP.

28. Ehrlich, "The Civil War in Early Film: Origin and Development of a Genre," 80.

29. Williams, *Playing the Race Card*, 100. For Williams's discussion of "what is melodramatically familiar in Griffith and Dixon's film," see ibid., Chapter 3.

30. Chadwick, *The Reel Civil War*, 21. Gordon had been a Grand Dragon of the Georgia Ku Klux Klan. Later, in 1889, he became the first commander-in-chief of the United Confederate Veterans. Chalmers, *Hooded Americanism*, 15; Blight, *Race and Reunion*, 127, 272.

31. Gordon, as one of Lee's divisional commanders, had fought an action around Appomattox Court House early on April 9, 1865. Gordon's message to Lee saying that he had "fought my corps to a frazzle" and could now "do nothing" unless supported by

Longstreet's corps (which was already heavily committed defending Lee's rear) was the decisive factor—since Gordon had a reputation as "one of the most daring leaders in the Army of Northern Virginia"—in convincing Lee to surrender. Freeman, *R. E. Lee*, vol. 4, 120.

32. Griffith himself used the term "Lost Cause" in a newspaper interview in 1915. Asked what he thought constituted the "great appeal" of *Birth of a Nation*, the director replied "Because it's the story of a lost cause." Other examples of appealing "lost cause" stories cited by Griffith included Napoleon's exile on the island of Elba [he probably meant St. Helena] and Christ's crucifixion. "David W. Griffith Tells How He Entered 'Movie' Business," *Tribune* [Chicago], May 30, 1915, DWGP.

33. David W. Blight, *Beyond the Battlefield: Race, Memory, and the American Civil War* (Amherst: University of Massachusetts Press, 2002), 102.

34. Blight, *Race and Reunion*, 272.

35. Blight, *Beyond the Battlefield*, 103; Blight, *Race and Reunion*, 211, 216–17, 221–27; Chadwick, *The Reel Civil War*, 8.

36. Blight, *Beyond the Battlefield*, 103. The stories told by these writers reprised, in some ways, the "plantation" novels of the antebellum period that had been written to contradict impressions based on *Uncle Tom's Cabin*. Twenty-seven of these works, according to Linda Williams, had been published between 1852 and 1861. Williams, *Playing the Race Card*, 101.

37. Blight, *Beyond the Battlefield*, 103.

38. Chadwick, *The Reel Civil War*, 19, 21; Blight, *Race and Reunion*, 215–16; Blight, *Beyond the Battlefield*, 121.

39. Chadwick, *The Reel Civil War*, 21, 19, 22.

40. Cripps, *Slow Fade*, 26.

41. Alan T. Nolan, "The Anatomy of the Myth," in *The Myth of the Lost Cause and Civil War History*, ed. Gary W. Gallagher and Alan T. Nolan (Bloomington: Indiana University Press, 2000), 15–19.

42. Bowser, *Transformation of Cinema*, 178; Ehrlich, "The Civil War in Early Film," 77–78.

43. Bowser, *Transformation of Cinema*, 177.

44. This intertitle also puts *Birth of a Nation* in the same tradition as the Nationalist school of American history (Ford, Burgess, Rhodes) in assuming that slavery was the issue that started the war. Other historians would later advance different arguments: Charles and Mary Beard, for example, saw the conflict as an economic war between capitalists and agrarians. See Charles A. Beard and Mary R. Beard, *The Rise of American Civilization* (New York: Macmillan, 1937, 2 vol. in one ed., originally published in 1927), especially chapters 14, 15, and 17.

45. Stern, "Griffith: 1—The Birth of a Nation," 66; cf. W. Stephen Bush, "*The Birth of a Nation*," in Silva, *Focus*, 25.

46. Bush, op. cit, 25–26; cf. Francis Hackett, "Brotherly Love," *The New Republic*, 7 (March 20, 1915), 185, in Silva, *Focus*, 85.

47. "*Birth of a Nation*," *News-Press* [St. Joseph, Missouri], November 20, 1915, DWGP.

48. In the second part of the film, the house servants, Mammy and Jake, are shown as even closer to the Camerons, sharing their postwar misfortunes out of loyalty and

affection. They even play a major part in rescuing Dr. Cameron when on Lynch's orders he is arrested as a suspected member of the Klan.

49. Sorlin, *The Film in History*, 89.

50. On this point, see Frederic Merk, *Slavery and the Annexation of Texas* (New York: Knopf, 1972); Robert E. May, *John A. Quitman: Old South Crusader* (Baton Rouge: Louisiana State University Press, 1985); Robert E. May, *The Southern Dream of a Caribbean Empire, 1854–1861* (Gainesville: University Press of Florida, 2002, first published 1973); Robert E. May, *Manifest Destiny's Underworld: Filibustering in Antebellum America* (Chapel Hill: University of North Carolina Press, 2002).

51. Nolan, "The Anatomy of the Myth," 19–27, 29, 31.

52. Ibid., 12.

53. Jean-Louis Comolli and Jean Narboni, "Cinema/ideology/criticism (1)," originally published in *Cahiers du cinéma*, no. 216 (October 1969), 11-15, trans. Susan Bennett, in Nick Browne, ed., *Cahiers du cinema, Vol. 3, 1969-72: The Politics of* Representation (London: Routledge/BFI, 1990), 58-67; "John Ford's *Young Mr Lincoln*, a Collective Text by the Editors of *Cahiers du Cinéma*," originally published in *Cahiers du cinéma*, no. 223 (August 1970), 29-47, trans. Helen Lackner and Diana Matias, *Screen* 13, no. 3 (Autumn 1972): 5–44.

54. On the construction of Lincoln's historical reputation, see Merrill D. Peterson, *Lincoln in American Memory* (New York: Oxford University Press, 1994) and Barry Schwartz, *Abraham Lincoln and the Forge of National Memory* (Chicago: University of Chicago Press, 2000).

55. Eric F. Goldman, *The Tragedy of Lyndon Johnson* (New York: Dell, 1969), 13.

56. John G. Nicolay and John Hay, *Abraham Lincoln: A History*, 10 vols. (New York: Century, 1890).

57. William Henry Herndon and Jesse William Weik, *Herndon's Lincoln: The True Story of a Great Life…The History and Personal Recollections of Abraham Lincoln by William Henry Herndon* (Chicago: Belford, Clarke, 1889).

58. Cornelius Regier, *The Era of the Muckrakers* (Chapel Hill: University of North Carolina Press, 1932), 17.

59. Regier, *Era of the Muckrakers*, 13–14, 20–21.

60. Ray Stannard Baker, *American Chronicle: The Autobiography of Ray Stannard Baker* (New York: C. Scribner's Sons, 1945), 96–97; Mary E. Tomkins, *Ida M. Tarbell* (Boston, Mass.: Twayne, 1974), 38; Ida M. Tarbell, *All in the Day's Work: An Autobiography* (New York: Macmillan, 1939), 161; Harold S. Wilson, *"McClure's Magazine" and the Muckrakers* (Princeton: Princeton University Press, 1970), 73–74.

61. Spears, *The Civil War on the Screen*, 65, 67–70; Robert C. Roman, "Lincoln on the Screen," *Films in Review* 12, no. 2 (February 1961): 87–90; Schwartz, *Abraham Lincoln and the Forge of National Memory*, 180.

62. Roman, "Lincoln on the Screen," 89–90.

63. Robert Lang, "*The Birth of a Nation*: History, Ideology, Narrative Form," in Lang, *The Birth of a Nation*, 23.

64. In the original film, indeed, as cited above, African Americans were shown being deported *en masse* back to Africa (this sequence, titled "Lincoln's Solution," was cut after protests at an early stage in the film's exhibition). Cuniberti, *Birth of a Nation*, 166–67.

65. Spears, *The Civil War on the Screen*, 75; Schickel, *Griffith*, 551.

66. Vlada Petric, "Two Lincoln Assassinations by D. W. Griffith," *Quarterly Review of Film Studies* 3, no. 3 (Summer 1978): 347–48, 350.

67. The fact that Northern and Southern whites in the film take refuge together against the marauding blacks in what Michael Rogin terms a "Lincoln log cabin" is clearly a conscious attempt to link national (white) unity with perhaps the most famous icon associated with the Lincoln legend. Rogin, "The Sword Became a Flashing Vision," in Lang, *The Birth of a Nation*, 281.

68. Peter Noble, "A Note on an Idol," *Sight and Sound* 15, no. 59 (Autumn 1946): 81–82; "The Birth of a Nation," *Sight and Sound* 16, no. 61 (Spring 1947): 32.

69. William Archibald Dunning, *Essays on the Civil War and Reconstruction and Related Topics* (New York: Macmillan, 1897); William Archibald Dunning, *Reconstruction, Political and Economic, 1865–1877* (New York: Harper and Brothers, 1907). On Dunning, see Philip R. Muller, "Look Back without Anger: A Reappraisal of William A. Dunning," *Journal of American History* 61 (1974): 325–38. On the Dunning/Bowers view of Reconstruction, see Kenneth M. Stampp, *The Era of Reconstruction 1865–1877* (New York: Alfred A. Knopf, 1965), 3–23.

70. E. Merton Coulter, *The South during Reconstruction 1865–1877* (Baton Rouge: Louisiana State University Press, 1947), xi.

71. Stern, "Griffith: 1—'The Birth of a Nation,'" 35–36; Woodrow Wilson, *A History of the American People*, Vol. V, *Reunion and Nationalization* (New York: Harper and Brothers, 1902); Albion Winegar Tourgée, *A Fool's Errand and the Invisible Empire* (New York: Fords, Howard, and Hulbert, 1880); Walter L. Fleming, *The Prescript of [the] Ku Klux Klan* (an undated pamphlet); J. C. Lester and D. L. Wilson, *The Ku Klux Klan: Its Origins, Growth and Disbandment*, intro. by Walter L. Fleming (New York: Neale, 1905, originally published 1884); John S. Reynolds, *Reconstruction in South Carolina, 1865–1877* (Columbia, S.C.: State Company Publishers, 1905); *Testimony Taken by the Joint Committee on Reconstruction to Inquire into the Condition of Affairs in the Late Insurrectionary States* (Washington, D.C.: Government Printing Office, 1972).

72. Stern, "Griffith: 1—'The Birth of a Nation,'" 35–36. According to Stern (36), the books by Tourgée, Lester, and Wilson, and Reynolds, together with the Ku Klux Klan Report, and Fleming's pamphlet, also came from Dixon. Anthony Slide comments that Dixon provided Griffith "with a trunkful of books from his library" before shooting started on *Birth of a Nation*. Slide, *American Racist*, 74.

73. This could in fact have been either Fleming's 1905 book on *Civil War and Reconstruction in Alabama* (1905) or, more likely, the 64-page untitled pamphlet he had published a year before dealing with "Public Fraud in South Carolina" and other matters, including the local constitution of the Klan (Morgantown, W. Va.: n.p., 1904).

74. James S. Pike, *The Prostrate State: South Carolina under Negro Government* (New York: D. Appleton, 1874); J. J. McCarthy to editor of the News, in *Indianapolis News*, December 10, 1915, DWGP.

75. Gettysburg (July 1–3, 1863) was the greatest battle of the Civil War, with total casualties on both sides of 51,000. See James M. McPherson, *Battle Cry of Freedom: The Civil War Era* (London: Penguin, 1990), 664. Though many, both blacks and whites, were the subject of Klan violence during Reconstruction, it is unlikely that the death toll came anywhere near this figure. The congressional "Ku Klux" Committee, for example,

estimated that there had been seventy-four murders by the Klan in Georgia and 109 in Alabama. Albion W. Tourgée, *A Fool's Errand by One of the Fools; Part II, The Invisible Empire, A Concise Review of the Epoch on Which the Tale Is Based* (New York: Fords, Howard and Hulbert, 1880), 436–37.

76. Otto H. Olsen, *Carpetbagger's Crusade: The Life of Albion Winegar Tourgée* (Baltimore: Johns Hopkins University Press, 1965), 1–2, 14–21, 23–24, 26–28, 73–74; John Hope Franklin, "Editor's Introduction," to Albion W. Tourgée, *A Fool's Errand* (Cambridge, Mass.: Harvard University Press, 1961), x.

77. Olsen, *Carpetbagger's Crusade*, 35–37, 41–51, 56–57, 61–72, 74, 79, 86, 90–91, 93–115, 118, 121, 146–48, 159, 167–68, 172–73, 179, 184–87, 191, 208, 220–21.

78. See Tourgée, *A Fool's Errand* (1961), Chapter 36.

79. See, for example, Tourgée, *A Fool's Errand* (1961), Chapter 28.

80. Stern, "Griffith: 1—'The Birth of a Nation,'" 35.

81. Tourgée, *A Fool's Errand* (1961), 183–88, 190.

82. Tourgée, *A Fool's Errand* (1880), 385–86, 394.

83. Tourgée, *A Fool's Errand* (1880), 414–17. The battle, Tourgée noted, "was almost always Shiloh," a fact reflecting the Southwestern roots of the Klan. Ibid., 397.

84. Tourgée, *A Fool's Errand* (1880), 407. Another source used by Griffith in preparing the film observed that Klansmen not only wore robes to disguise themselves, but that they also covered their horses to make them harder to recognize as well. This too was done in the film. Lester and Wilson, *Ku Klux Klan*, 93–94.

85. Tourgée, *A Fool's Errand* (1880), 425, 428.

86. Ibid., 422–23.

87. Tourgée, *A Fool's Errand* (1880), 419–22; Lester and Wilson, *Ku Klux Klan*, facing 58 and 97. In both cases, the uniforms had been captured by federal forces. Walter L. Fleming, "Introduction," ibid., 43–44.

88. Stern, "Griffith: 1—'The Birth of a Nation,'" 35–36.

89. The uniforms of the Klansmen in *Birth of a Nation* are very similar to those worn by the night riders in Griffith's *The Rose of Kentucky* (1911).

90. Robert F. Durden, *James Shepherd Pike: Republicanism and the American Negro, 1850–1882* (Durham, N.C.: Duke University Press, 1957), vii–viii, 3, 13–14, 16–19, 30–31, 37–38, 45–46, 51, 161–62, 167–68, 185–86, 195–97, 201, quotation 31.

91. Pike, *Prostrate State*, 4, 11–12, 56–57, 67, 89.

92. Durden, *Pike*, 205–206.

93. Cook, *Fire from the Flint*, 126. On Dixon's tendency to "borrow" without attribution, see Frances Oakes, "Whitman and Dixon: A Strange Case of Borrowing," *Georgia Review* 11, no. 3 (Fall, 1957): 333–40.

94. Pike, *The Prostrate State*, 44, 180, 183–86, 222–24, 266.

95. Curiously, although an intertitle specified that the film would deal with the session of 1871, the very next title claimed that the facsimile of the House was actually based on a photograph of 1870 in the *Columbia State* newspaper (shot 839). Mimi White emphasizes the importance of this "gap between the source and the filmic representation." White, "*The Birth of a Nation*," in Lang, *The Birth of a Nation*, 218.

96. Pike, *The Prostrate State*, 12; Dixon, *The Clansman*, 263; *The Birth of a Nation*, shot 839.

97. Pike, *Prostrate State*, 15–16, 42.

98. Pike, *Prostrate State*, 10; Dixon, *The Clansman*, 264–65.

99. Pike, *Prostrate State*, 13, 94; Dixon, *The Clansman*, 264, 267; *The Birth of a Nation*, shots 839, 859–60.

100. Pike, *Prostrate State*, 20; Dixon, *The Clansman*, 266; *The Birth of a Nation*, shot 844.

101. Pike, *Prostrate State*, 10, 17, 20, 226; Dixon, *The Clansman*, 265–66; *The Birth of a Nation*, shots 845–54. On the chicken-eating cliché, see, for example, Cripps, *Slow Fade to Black*, 13–14; Bogle, *Toms*, 7–8.

102. Dixon, *The Clansman*, 268; *The Birth of a Nation*, shots 866–74. South Carolina indeed passed a law banning interracial marriage in 1865. This law would not be repealed (by referendum) until 1998. See Joel Williamson, *New People: Miscegenation and Mulattoes in the United States* (Baton Rouge: Louisiana State University Press, 1995), 91–92.

103. Pike, *Prostrate State*, 14, 44; Dixon, *The Clansman*, 264; *Birth of a Nation*, shot 839.

104. Wilson, *A History of the American People, vol. 5, Reunion and Nationalization*, 7, 17–18.

105. Wilson, *History*, 47; Pike, *Prostrate State*, 252–53.

106. Wilson, *History*, 48–49, 89–92, 95–96; cf. Stampp, *Era of Reconstruction*, 177–80.

107. Wilson, *History*, 38, 49–52.

108. Ibid., 59–60, 62–64, 74–76. On October 12, 1871, Grant issued a proclamation that singled out nine counties of South Carolina where Klan activity was at its worst and calling on members of all illegal organizations there to give up their guns and disguises within five days. When his proclamation was ignored, he suspended *habeas corpus* rights in the counties concerned and 200 arrests were made—arrests that were "promptly" followed by prosecutions and convictions in federal courts. Ibid., 75–76.

109. Cook, *Fire from the Flint*, 13–14; Cook, *Thomas Dixon*, 23–24.

110. Henry Stephen Gordon, "D. W. Griffith Recalls the Making of *The Birth of a Nation*," *Photoplay Magazine* 10 (October 1916), reprinted in Silva, *Focus*, 57.

111. Allen W. Trelease, *White Terror: The Ku Klux Klan Conspiracy and Southern Reconstruction* (London: Harper and Row, 1971), 89.

112. Hart, *The Man Who Invented Hollywood*, 88.

113. Schickel, *Griffith*, 21.

114. Hart, *The Man Who Invented Hollywood*, 27.

115. Merritt, "Dixon, Griffith, and the Southern Legend," 38.

116. Linda Williams points out that in *Uncle Tom's Cabin*, black characters Cassy and Emmeline take revenge on Simon Legree for the murder of Tom by wearing white sheets (suggesting they are ghosts) around Legree's house. *Playing the Race Card*, 63–64.

117. Dixon, *The Clansman*, 318–26.

118. Publicity for *The Birth of a Nation* insisted that the Klan had been founded by the descendants of Scottish highlanders and that the "St. Andrew's cross" had been "the conventional sign of Scottish clans." "Scottish Clans Revived in Carolinas," *Record* [Boston], May 13, 1915, DWGP.

119. David M. Chalmers, *Hooded Americanism: The History of the Ku Klux Klan* (Chicago: Quadrangle, 1968), 8–9.

120. William P. Randel, *The Ku Klux Klan: A Century of Infamy* (Philadelphia: Chiltern Books, 1965), 53.

121. Chalmers, *Hooded Americanism*, 10, 9.

122. Chalmers, *Hooded Americanism*, 18–19; Stanley F. Horn, *Invisible Empire: The Story of the Ku Klux Klan, 1866–1871* (Boston: Houghton Mifflin, 1939), 232, 238–41; Randel, *The Ku Klux Klan*, 55; Trelease, *White Terror*, 71, 369–70, 373, 378, 388–89; Simkins and Woody, *Reconstruction in South Carolina*, 509.

123. Trelease, *White Terror*, xxviii.

124. Ibid., xx.

125. Wyn Craig Wade, *The Fiery Cross: The Ku Klux Klan in America* (New York: Simon and Schuster, 1987), 146.

126. In reality, the burning of white owners' barns, stables, and saloons by African Americans seems to have been a protest against the far more numerous aggressions committed by whites against blacks. Trelease, *White Terror*, 363–64, 366.

127. Chalmers, *Hooded Americanism*, 9. Other battles were sometimes cited. Shiloh (Pittsburgh Landing, April 6–7, 1862), however, reflected the Southwestern origins of the Klan, since the battle had taken place approximately eighty miles to the west of the Klan's birthplace in Pulaski, Tennessee.

128. The Klan's main strength was in the nine counties of the South Carolina piedmont in which President Ulysses S. Grant later (October 12, 1871) suspended habeas corpus: Spartanburg, Laurens, Union, Newberry, York, Chester, Fairfield, Lancaster, and Chesterfield. Horn, *Invisible Empire*, 217, 235; Chalmers, *Hooded Americanism*, 10, 16; Trelease, *White Terror*, 115, 353.

129. Horn, *Invisible Empire*, 218–21, 230; Trelease, *White Terror*, 350–52.

130. Horn, *Invisible Empire*, 225–27; Randel, *The Ku Klux Klan*, 54–55; Chalmers, *Hooded Americanism*, 13; Trelease, *White Terror*, 356–58.

131. Trelease, *White Terror*, 364–5; Horn, *Invisible Empire*, 222.

132. Horn, *Invisible Empire*, 227.

133. Trelease, *White Terror*, 371–72.

134. *Sun* [Baltimore], March 25, 1916, DWGP; Schickel, *Griffith*, 277; Rogin, "The Sword Became a Flashing Vision," in Lang, *The Birth of a Nation*, 277.

135. Schickel, *Griffith*, 286; the Reverend Dr. Charles H. Parkhurst, "*The Birth of a Nation*," in Silva, *Focus*, 102-103. "New York accepted it [*Birth*] in the light of an educational entertainment," Griffith claimed. "Fifteen schools came to see the picture in lieu of a history lesson." "Seen on the Screen," *Herald* [Chicago], May 27, 1915, DWGP.

136. The first black regiments raised were in Louisiana and Kansas. The first black regiment to be formed in the North was the 54th Massachusetts. See McPherson, *Battle Cry of Freedom*, 84 n, 500, 563–65.

137. Lang, *The Birth of a Nation*, 9. The first Africans to arrive in the British colonies in America were allegedly the twenty blacks who landed at Jamestown in 1619 from a Dutch frigate. John Hope Franklin and Alfred A. Moss Jr., *From Slavery to Freedom: A History of African Americans*, 7th ed. (New York: Alfred A. Knopf, 1994), 56. One month earlier, the Virginia colonists had been granted the right to hold an annual general assembly. To Philip S. Foner, the conjunction of the two events emphasized "the contradictory nature of American democracy: the establishment of representative government on the one hand, and the institution of forced labor on the other." Foner, *History of Black*

Americans: From Africa to the Emergence of the Cotton Kingdom (Westport, Conn.: Greenwood Press, 1975), 186–87.

138. D'Ooge, "'The Birth of a Nation': Symposium on Classic Film Discusses Inaccuracies and Virtues," *Library of Congress Information Bulletin* 53, no. 13 (June 27, 1994): 264, 266.

139. For Pennsylvania protests at the depiction of Stevens/Stoneman in the film, see "Stoneman Was Stevens," *Franklin Repository* [Chambersburg, Pennsylvania], May 2, 1916, DWGP; "Would Suppress 'Birth of a Nation,'" *Sunbury Daily Item* [Sunbury, Pennsylvania], May 10, 1916, DWGP; Joint Resolution (H.J. Res. 222), "The Birth of a Nation" Picture, introduced by Congressman Benjamin K. Focht, 64th Congress, 1st Session, May 10, 1916, copy in NAACPP.

140. Stevens's Lydia Smith was transformed in the film into Lydia Brown.

141. For Dixon's highly critical view of Stevens, see Dixon, "Reply to the *New York Globe*," April 10, 1915, reprinted in Silva, *Focus*, 76.

142. Franklin, "*The Birth of a Nation*: Propaganda as History," 20. For a contemporary criticism of the film's view of Stevens, see "*The Birth of a Nation*: An Editorial," *The Crisis*, 10 (May–June 1915), reprinted in Silva, *Focus*, 64–65.

143. Fawn M. Brodie, *Thaddeus Stevens: Scourge of the South* (New York: W. W. Norton, 1959), 92, 365. The estate was initially left to his nephew with the condition that he give up drinking—a condition Stevens shrewdly judged would not be met.

144. G. B. D. "The Birth of a Nation," *The Moon Journal* [Battle Creek, Michigan], February 4, 1916, DWGP.

145. Schickel, *Griffith*, 555.

146. On Phillips, see John D. Smith and John C. Inscoe, eds., *Ulrich Bonnell Phillips: A Southern Historian and His Critics* (Athens: University of Georgia Press, 1993).

147. Franklin, "*The Birth of a Nation*: Propaganda as History," 23. Franklin seemed just as convinced of the influence of Griffith's film fifteen years later. See D'Ooge, "*The Birth of a Nation*: Symposium on Classic Film Discusses Inaccuracies and Virtues," 266.

148. W. E. B. Du Bois, "Reconstruction and Its Benefits," *American Historical Review* 15, no. 4 (July 1910): 781–99. Du Bois extended this argument a quarter of a century later in W. E. B. Du Bois, *Black Reconstruction: An Essay toward a History of the Part Which Black Folk Played in the Attempt to Reconstruct Democracy in America, 1860–1880* (New York: Russell and Russell, 1935).

149. John R. Lynch, *The Facts of Reconstruction* (New York: Neale Publishing, 1913). Lynch, who had served as a U.S. senator from his state during Reconstruction, was later described by Kenneth Stampp as "an able Mississippi Negro politician." *Era of Reconstruction*, 218.

150. For one protest against the insult to ex-Senator Lynch, see Dr. Chas. E. Locke and E. Burton Ceruti, "To the Honorable the City Council of the City of Los Angeles, State of California," February 2, 1915, 1–4, NAACPP. Lynch himself wrote to the Chicago *Tribune* criticizing *The Birth of a Nation* as being "grounded on historical misrepresentation, without having a single actual fact as the basis of its existence. It is fiction pure and simple, painted from a diseased and prejudiced imagination." John R. Lynch to editor, *Tribune*, May [?], 1915, printed in "Voice of the People—'The Birth of a Nation,'" *Tribune* [Chicago], June 1, 1915, DWGP.

151. For the original story, see Ramsaye, *A Million and One Nights*, 641 (also Jacobs, *The Rise of the American Film*, 174–75); Merritt, "Dixon, Griffith, and the Southern Legend," 39, n. 32; Schickel, *Griffith*, 268.

152. "D. W. Griffith, Producer of the World's Biggest Picture, Interview with D. W. Griffith," *American* [New York], February 28, 1915, 9, reprinted in Geduld, *Focus on D. W. Griffith*, 28.

153. Joseph Smith, *The Spanish-American War: Conflict in the Caribbean and the Pacific 1895–1902* (London: Longman, 1994), 102; Frank Freidel, *The Splendid Little War* (Boston: Little, Brown, 1958), 33.

154. Thomas Cripps, "The Absent Presence in American Civil War Films," *Historical Journal of Film, Radio and Television* 14, no. 4 (1994): 371; Cripps, *Slow Fade to Black*, 26.

155. Maldwyn A. Jones, *The Limits of Liberty: American History, 1607–1980* (New York: Oxford University Press, 1983), 412.

156. See John Higham, *Strangers in the Land: Patterns of American Nativism, 1860–1925* (New Brunswick, N.J.: Rutgers University Press, 1955), 204–207, 212–19; John F. McClymer, "The Federal Government and the Americanization Movement, 1915–24," *Prologue: The Journal of the National Archives* 10, no. 1 (Spring 1978): 22–41; Frederick C. Luebke, *Bonds of Loyalty: German-Americans and World War I* (DeKalb: Northern Illinois University Press, 1974).

157. "Seen on the Screen," *Herald* [Chicago], May 27, 1915, DWGP.

158. Kagan, "Two Classic War Films of the Silent Era," 1.

159. Rogin, "The Sword Became a Flashing Vision," in Lang, *The Birth of a Nation*, 271. Rogin also points out that Griffith omitted "the greatest destruction at Petersburg, the one suffered by black troops sent into the crater opened up by Northern mining under Southern lines." Ibid.

160. Kagan, "Two Classic War Films," 1.

161. Tara McPherson, "'Both Kinds of Arms': Remembering the Civil War," *Velvet Light Trap* no. 35 (Spring 1995): 7.

162. Benedict R. O'G. Anderson, *Imagined Communities: Reflections on the Origins and Spread of Nationalism*, rev. ed. (London: Verso, 1991).

163. Jane Gaines comments that *Birth* was "perhaps the first successful example of the mass media production of a group identity through exclusion and scapegoating." Gaines, *Fire and Desire*, 265.

164. David R. Roediger, *The Wages of Whiteness: Race and the Making of the American Working Class* (London: Verso, 1991); Alexander Saxton, *The Rise and Fall of the White Republic: Class, Politics and Mass Culture in Nineteenth-century America* (London: Verso, 1990).

165. Rachel F. Moran, *Interracial Intimacy: The Regulation of Race and Romance* (Chicago: University of Chicago Press, 2001), 4–5. I am grateful to Dr. Arlene Hui for bringing this point to my attention.

166. Reginald Horsman, *Race and Manifest Destiny: The Origins of American Racial Anglo-Saxonism* (Cambridge, Mass.: Harvard University Press, 1981), 32–36, 68.

167. Jean Boissel, *Gobineau biographie: mythes et réalité* (Paris: Berg International, 1993), 119; Paul A. Fortier, "Gobineau and German Racism," *Comparative Literature* 19,

no. 4 (Fall 1967): 341–42; Richard Hofstadter, *Social Darwinism in American Thought, 1860–1915* (Philadelphia: University of Pennsylvania Press, 1944), 147.

168. Edward A. Freeman's *Comparative Politics* (1874) provides a good illustration of the first of these tendencies and John W. Burgess's *Political Sciences and Comparative Constitutional Law* (1890) of the second. See Hofstadter, *Social Darwinism*, 148–50.

169. Horsman, *Race and Manifest Destiny*, 9–10, 12–23.

170. Ibid., 12, 16–17.

171. George M. Frederickson, *The Black Image in the White Mind: The Debate on Afro-American Character and Destiny, 1817–1914* (New York: Harper and Row, 1971), 98–99; Horsman, *Race and Manifest Destiny*, 160–61, 182–85.

172. On Adams, see Holt, ed., *Historical Scholarship in the United States, 1876–1901: As Revealed in the Correspondence of Herbert B. Adams.*

173. Hofstadter, *Social Darwinism*, 149.

174. For Dixon's "decidedly muddled" thinking on race, see Slide, *American Racist*, 144.

175. Horsman, *Race and Manifest Destiny*, 44, 62–6, 77, 128, 131, 159, 174, 179.

176. Ibid., 165, 172, 179, 184–85, 209–10, 213, 215.

177. Ibid., 178–79.

178. Horsman, *Race and Manifest Destiny*, 65, 156, 168, 172–73, 230, 243, 290–91, 294; Hofstadter, *Social Darwinism*, 148, 152–56.

179. Smith, *The Spanish-American War*, 195, 198; David Healy, *U.S. Expansionism: The Imperialist Urge in the 1890s* (Madison: University of Wisconsin Press, 1970), 241–42; Eric T. L. Love, *Race over Empire: Racism and U.S. Imperialism, 1865–1900* (Chapel Hill: University of North Carolina Press, 2004), 190–91.

180. See Brian McAllister Linn, *The Philippine War, 1899–1902* (Lawrence: University Press of Kansas, 2000); Higham, *Strangers in the Land*, 145–46.

181. Henry Adams to Charles M. Gaskell, April 28, 1894, in *The Letters of Henry Adams*, Vol. IV: *1892–1899*, ed. J. C. Levenson, Ernest Samuels, Charles Vandersee, and Viola Hopkins Winner (Cambridge, Mass.: Harvard University Press, 1988), 185.

182. Edward A. Ross, "The Causes of Racial Superiority," in *Annals of the American Academy of Political and Social Science* 18 (1901): 67–89; Julius Weinberg, *Edward Alsworth Ross and the Sociology of Progressivism* (Madison: State Historical Society of Wisconsin, 1972), 156; David M. Kennedy, *Birth Control in America: The Career of Margaret Sanger* (New Haven: Yale University Press, 1970), 42; Higham, *Strangers in the Land*, 172.

183. Madison Grant, *The Passing of the Great Race; or the Racial Basis of European History* (New York: C. Scribner, 1916); Higham, *Strangers in the Land*, 156–57.

184. John W. Blassingame, *The Slave Community: Plantation Life in the Antebellum South* (Oxford: Oxford University Press, 1979), 231.

185. Natalie Zemon Davis, *Slaves on Screen: Film and Historical Vision* (Cambridge, Mass.: Harvard University Press, 2000), 17. According to Brian Gallagher, "the film's black characters are defined and limited by their inevitable and inherent excesses." In terms of whites, they always appear as the "other," and this otherness is presented in the first half of the movie as "comic relief." In the second half, however, it can no longer be contained and—in "the morally inverted world of Reconstruction"—is depicted as "the motive force of tragedy." Gallagher, "Racist Ideology and Black Abnormality in the Birth of a Nation," 68, 71.

186. Allen W. Trelease points out that the program of black legal and political equality "was rendered all the more noxious [to many Southern whites] by the common assumption that it would lead inevitably to social mixing." Trelease, *White Terror*, xxxviii.

187. Williamson, *The Crucible of Race*, 253.

188. J. Morgan Kousser, *The Shaping of Southern Politics: Suffrage Restriction and the Establishment of the One-Party South, 1880–1910* (New Haven: Yale University Press, 1974).

189. Precise estimates of the number of lynchings vary. *Thirty Years of Lynching in the United States 1889–1918* (New York: Negro Universities Press, 1919; reprint 1969), 29, gives a comparatively high figure. Stewart E. Tolnay and E. M. Beck, *A Festival of Violence: An Analysis of Southern Lynchings, 1882–1930* (Urbana: University of Illinois Press, 1995), 271, has slightly lower figures. On the phenomenon of lynching generally, see Philip Dray, *At the Hands of Persons Unknown: The Lynching of Black America* (New York: Random House, 2002).

190. Sorlin, *The Film in History*, 108.

191. Edward L. Ayers, *The Promise of the New South: Life after Reconstruction* (New York: Oxford University Press, 1992), 155.

192. Baker, *Following the Color Line*, 30–31.

193. C. Vann Woodward, *Origins of the New South 1877–1913* (Baton Rouge: Louisiana State University Press, 1951), 354–55; Williamson, *Crucible of Race*, 253, 255.

194. On the riot and the founding of the NAACP, see Charles F. Kellogg, *NAACP: A History of the National Association for the Advancement of Colored People* (Baltimore: Johns Hopkins University Press, 1967), vol. 1, 9–30.

195. Roger Daniels, *Asian America: Chinese and Japanese in the United States since 1850* (Seattle: University of Washington Press, 1988), 9, 10, 12, 15, 19–20, 29–66, 100–43.

196. Jones, *Limits of Liberty*, 321.

197. Anon., *White American* (San Francisco, n.p., 1914); Higham, *Strangers in the Land*, 186.

198. Higham, *Strangers in the Land*, 173.

199. Ibid., 164–69, 171, 175, 191.

200. Wilson vetoed the second of these bills exactly ten days after watching *The Birth of a Nation* at the White House. See Wilson to the House of Representatives, January 28, 1915, Link, ed., *The Papers of Woodrow Wilson*, Vol. 32, 142–44.

201. *The Crisis* (January 1915); Chairman [Joel E. Spingarn]' Report, Minutes of the Annual Meeting of the NAACP, January 3, 1916, 4, NAACPP.

202. Robinson, "In the Year 1915: D. W. Griffith and the Whitening of America," 174.

203. "Miscegenation" was a word coined by two Democratic party publicists, David G. Croly (the father of Herbert Croly) and George Wakeman, during the presidential election campaign of 1864. Attempting to undermine support for the Republican Party, Croly and Wakeman suggested that its leaders, including Lincoln, supported intermarriage between the races. See David G. Croly, George Wakeman, and E. C. Howell, *Miscegenation: The Theory of the Blending of the Races, Applied to the American White Man and Negro* (London: Trübner, 1864); Sidney Kaplan, "The Miscegenation Issue in the Election of 1864," *Journal of Negro History* 34, no. 3 (July 1949): 274–343.

204. David H. Fowler, *Northern Attitudes towards Interracial Marriage: Legislation and Public Opinion in the Middle Atlantic States and the States of the Old Northwest,*

1780–1930 (New York: Garland, 1987), 273. On the basis of Fowler's information, there were actually forty-two attempts, all of which failed. Ibid., 271, n.1.

205. If anti-miscegenation laws were oldest in the South, they were most complicated in the West. See Arlene Hui, "Miscegenation in Mainstream American Cinema: Representing Interracial Relationships, 1913–1956" (Ph.D. diss., University of London, 2006), 28–29.

206. Tacitus, as quoted in Horsman, *Race and Manifest Destiny*, 12.

207. Horsman, *Race and Manifest Destiny*, 210, 213, 215.

208. Higham, *Strangers in the Land*, 109–10, 144–45; Horsman, *Race and Manifest Destiny*, 295–96. Interbreeding between black men and white women, it was suggested, would have exactly the opposite effect, encouraging racial deterioration. Ibid.

209. The depiction of Lydia and Silas Lynch on screen seems to suggest that women and men of mixed race are both less in control of their passions and more dangerous than "pure" blacks. In the film's distinct hierarchy of races, mulattoes inherit their brutality and primitivism from their black inheritance, but their white blood is responsible for endowing them with political and organizational skills. Michael Rogin points out that the liaison between Stoneman and Lydia foregrounds the idea of the mulatto, born of interracial relationships. Rogin, "The Sword Became a Flashing Vision," in Lang, *The Birth of a Nation*, 269. Some contemporary critics of *Birth* commented that while the film presented blacks preying on white women as the main avenue to interracial relationships, most mulattoes—as the product of such relationships—had been born because Southern white men had sexually exploited their female slaves. Letter by Ross D. Brown, published in "People"s Forum—The Birth of a Nation," *Muncie Star* January 18, 1916, DWGP; Francis H. Rowley, "A Reproach to Our City," *Fighting a Vicious Film*, 36–37.

210. States proposing laws against intermarriage included California, Colorado, Illinois, Iowa, Kansas, Michigan, Nebraska, New York, Ohio, Pennsylvania, Washington, and Wisconsin. NAACP Sixth Annual Report, 1915, *The Crisis* (March 1916), 248. Also see minutes of the Meeting of the NAACP Board of Directors, February 2, 1916, and Annual Meeting of the Members of the NAACP, February 12, 1915, both in NAACPP.

211. See Chairman [Joel E. Spingarn]'s Report, Minutes of the NAACP Annual Meeting, January 3, 1916, 4, NAACPP; *The Crisis* (March 1915), 246.

212. On this fight sequence, see Melvyn Stokes, "Structuring Absences: Images of America Missing from the Hollywood Screen," *Revue Française d'Études Américaines* no. 89 (June 2001): 47–50.

213. As reviewer Mark Vance commented: "Griffith struck it right when he adapted the Dixon story for the film. He knew the South and he knew just what kind of picture would please all white classes." *Variety*, March 12, 1915, reprinted in Silva, *Focus*, 23.

214. Williamson, *Crucible of Race*, 111–33, 178–79, 306–9; Frederickson, *The Black Image in the White Mind*, 273–81; Ayers, *The Promise of the New South*, 158.

215. Jack S. Blocker Jr., *Retreat from Reform: The Prohibition Movement in the United States 1890–1913* (Westport, Conn.: Greenwood Press, 1976), 214, 216, 239.

216. McKelway, as quoted in Hugh C. Bailey, *Liberalism in the New South: Southern Social Reformers and the Progressive Movement* (Coral Gables, Fla.: University of Miami Press, 1969), 65.

217. Musser, *Emergence of Cinema*, 200.

218. Dan Streible, "Race and the Reception of Jack Johnson Fight Films," in *The Birth of Whiteness*, ed. Daniel Bernardi, 170–90; Grieveson, "Fighting Films," 44. On Johnson's career, also see Al-Tony Gilmore, *Bad Nigger! The National Impact of Jack Johnson* (Port Washington: Kennikat Press, 1975) and Randy Roberts, *Papa Jack: Jack Johnson and the Era of White Hopes* (New York: Free Press, 1983).

219. Quoted in Streible, "Race and the Reception," 173.

220. Streible, "Race and the Reception," 192–93; Grieveson, "Fighting Films," 45–46. On the background to the Sims Act, also see Gilmore, *Bad Nigger!*, 75–93.

221. Alternatively, Richard Maltby has argued in more symbolic terms that "The Great White Hope longed for in saloons across the country finally appeared in 1915...[as] Henry B. Walthall, D. W. Griffith's Little Colonel." Maltby, "The Social Evil, the Moral Order, and the Melodramatic Imagination, 1890–1915," in *Melodrama: Stage, Picture, Screen*, ed. Jacky Bratten, Jim Cook, and Christine Gledhill (London: BFI, 1994), 226, n. 23.

222. George Kibbe Turner, "The City of Chicago: A Study of the Great Immoralities," *McClure's Magazine* 28 (April 1907): 575–92; Turner, "Tammany's Control of New York by Professional Criminals," *McClure's Magazine* 33 (June 1909): 117–34; Turner, "The Daughters of the Poor," *McClure's Magazine* 34 (November 1909): 45–61. The first and last of these articles were reprinted in Arthur and Lila Weinberg, eds., *The Muckrakers* (New York: Simon and Schuster, 1961), 389–429.

223. On the white slave panic, see Frederick K. Grittner, *White Slavery: Myth, Ideology, and American Law* (New York: Garland, 1990); Ben Brewster, "*Traffic in Souls*," *Cinema Journal* 31, no. 1 (Fall 1991): 37–56.

224. David J. Langum, *Crossing over the Line: Legislating Morality under the Mann Act* (Chicago: University of Chicago Press, 1994), 48, 75.

225. Langum, *Crossing over the Line*, 48–49.

226. Gilmore, *Bad Nigger!*, 95–96, 105–106.

227. Prosecutor, as cited in Langum, *Crossing over the Line*, 185. Johnson fled to Europe to escape his sentence but eventually, in 1920, gave himself up to federal authorities and served his sentence.

228. Roberts, *Papa Jack*, 159–160; also see Gilmore, *Bad Nigger!*, 106–13.

229. Williams, *Playing the Race Card*, 100.

230. There has been little investigation of such spectatorship. For exceptions to this, see Gregory A. Waller, "Another Audience: Black Moviegoing, 1907–1916," 3–25; Mary Carbine, "'The Finest Outside the Loop': Motion Picture Exhibition in Chicago's Black Metropolis, 1905–1928," *Camera Obscura* 23 (May 1990): 9–41; Stewart, *Migrating to the Movies*, passim.

231. Cripps, *Slow Fade*, 11.

232. Walker, interviewed in Brownlow and Gill, *D. W. Griffith—Father of Film* (1993).

233. African American writer Ida B. Wells mentioned the visit of "two [black?] women friends [who] came in to tell me that they had just been to see *The Birth of a Nation* and agreed with me that it was an outrage which ought never to have been perpetrated, nor allowed to be shown here [in Chicago]." Wells, quoted in Stewart, *Migrating to the Movies*, 24. The *Chicago Defender* reported that black women had led the stone-throwing inside the theater that escalated into the September 1915 anti-*Birth* riot

in Philadelphia (discussed in Chapter 6 above). It also printed a response to *Birth* from Mrs. K. J. Bills, a black woman who had lived in the South during Reconstruction. Bills had no quarrel with the first half of the film, which she thought to contain "historical facts which hold a person almost spellbound." But citing her own memories, she dismissed much of the so-called history of the second part as fiction. As Bills remembered it, Klansmen had ridden round "very quietly, like thieves" to intimidate black neighbors. They had not engaged in romantic group charges on horseback. Everett, *Returning the Gaze*, 94, 90–92.

234. bell hooks, "The Oppositional Gaze: Black Female Spectators," in *Black American Cinema*, ed. Manthian Diawara (New York: Routledge, 1993), 292, 295.

235. Samuel Edward *Courtney to Booker T. Washington, April 19, 1915, Letters of Booker T. Washington*, 13, *1914–1915*, ed. Harlan and Smock, 274–75. Also see *Advertiser* [Boston], April 19, 1915, and *Post* [Boston], April 24, 1915, both in DWGP. It was also suggested that William Lewis, a black former U.S. assistant attorney general, agreed with the proposed endorsement. Cripps, "The Reaction of the Negro to the Motion Picture, *Birth of a Nation*," in Silva, *Focus*, 120–21.

236. Berquist and Greenwood, "Protest against Racism: 'The Birth of a Nation' in Ohio," 43.

237. Quoted in Everett, *Returning the Gaze*, 81.

238. Berquist and Greenwood, "Protest against Racism: 'The Birth of a Nation' in Ohio," 43; "Unwanted advertising," *Chicago Defender*, November 13, 1915, 8.

239. Brown, *Adventures*, 94; Schickel, *Griffith*, 247.

240. *Forum* [Dayton, Ohio], reprinted in *The Crisis* 14, no. 1 (May 1917): 25–26.

241. Maurice Yacowar, "Aspects of the Familiar: A Defense of Minority Group Stereotyping in the Popular Film," *Literature/Film Quarterly* 2, no. 2 (Spring 1974): 134.

242. Fleener. "Answering Film with Film," 400–25.

243. See, for example, Janice A. Radway, *Reading the Romance: Women, Patriarchy and Popular Literature* (Chapel Hill: University of North Carolina Press, 1984); Ien Ang, *Watching Dallas: Soap Opera and the Melodramatic Imagination*, trans. Della Couling (London: Methuen, 1985).

244. Diawara, "Black Spectatorship: Problems of Identification and Resistance," in *Black American Cinema*, ed. Diawara, 211.

CHAPTER 8

1. Elijah Hodges, "Another Protest against Picture," *Press* [Atlantic City], July 26, 1915; cf. Uriah N. Murray, M.D., to editor of the *Traveler* and *Evening Herald* [Boston], April 15, 1915; both in DWGP.

2. Marvin Fletcher, *The Black Soldier and Officer in the United States Army, 1891–1917* (Columbia: University of Missouri Press, 1974), 53–59; W. E. B. Du Bois to International Committee, YMCA, September 7, 1916, NAACPP.

3. Mark Meigs makes the point that many World War I American soldiers "first saw battle" in *The Birth of a Nation*. He notes that among countless references in their diaries and letters to watching movies, the only film actually mentioned by name is *Birth*. Meigs, *Optimism at Armageddon: Voices of American Participants in the First World War* (Basingstoke: Macmillan, 1997), 20–21.

4. NAACP Secretary [John R. Shillady] to Mayor John F. Hylan, February 21, 1918, NAACPP; "Colored People Aroused at Film," *Daily Alaska Dispatch*, October 9, 1918, clipping in NAACPP.

5. "Resolution," signed by Houston G. Young, secretary of state and secretary of the Executive State Council of Defense, West Virginia, June 18, 1918; Chas. E. Morris, secretary to the governor, to Harry C. Smith, editor of the *Gazette* [Cleveland, Ohio], October 12, 1918, clipping; both in NAACPP. Also see Fleener-Marzec, *D. W. Griffith's "The Birth of a Nation,"* 275, 257.

6. Olie V. Gregory to James Weldon Johnson, February 23, 1918; "War Dept. Urged to Ban Vicious Film," letter from Negro Civic League of Marshall, Texas, to Newton D. Baker, secretary of war, printed in the *Age* [New York], May 18, 1918; "Birth of a Nation Is Barred" and "Victory Won" in *Supreme Circle News* [Albany, Georgia], May 18, 1918; "'Birth of a Nation' May Not Appear," the *Lincoln [word missing]*, June 26, 1918; all in NAACPP.

7. "Particularly at this time," asserted the governor, "we should be careful to preserve the utmost cordiality between all classes of American citizens. The negroes are doing their share in the war and should be treated with the respect shown the whites." The mayor stressed the "self sacrifice and devotion to the cause of the nation" demonstrated by local blacks and "the noble sacrifices which their brethren are making on the battle fronts." Governor Thomas Riggs to U.S. Marshall J. M. Tanner, October 9, 1918; Mayor E. Valentine to W. D. Grosse, October 8, 1918; cf. "Governor Suppresses 'Birth of a Nation,'" and "Suppression of Picture Pleases Colored People," *Daily Alaska Dispatch*, October 10, 1918, clippings; Charles W. Mosby et al. to Thomas Riggs, October 11, 1918; Mrs. C. Mosby et al. to John R. Shillady, October 12, 1918; all in NAACPP.

8. See John R. Shillady to Dear Sir, October 10, 1918; John R. Shillady to All Branches, October 10, 1918; Minutes of Meeting of the NAACP Board of Directors, October 14, 1918, Box A-8; Press Release, October 14; all in NAACPP.

9. Governor Arthur Capper to John R. Shillady, October 17, 1918; Governor James Withycombe to John R. Shillady, October 16, 1918; H. E. Samuelson to John R. Shillady, October 14, 1918; Governor R. Livingston Beechman to John R. Shillady, October 12, 1918; governor of North Dakota to David W. Griffith Corporation, October 15, 1918; Governor Thomas W. Bickett to John R. Shillady, October 14, 1918; all in NAACPP.

10. Governor Theo G. Bilbo to John R. Shillady, October 15, 1918; Dorrice B. Cowie to John R. Shillady, October 15, 1918; Governor Walter E. Edge to John R. Shillady, October 16, 1918; Governor Sidney J. Catts to John R. Shillady, October 15, 1918; Rolph Duff to John R. Shillady, October 14, 1918; O. J. Grimes to John R. Shillady, October 16, 1918; Governor Emanuel L. Philipp to John R. Shillady, October 16, 1918; all in NAACPP.

11. Arch M. Thurman, secretary of council of defense, to John R. Shillady, October 24, 1918; Henry M. Wriston to John R. Shillady, October 15, 1918; Director Chas. C. Moore to NAACP, October 24, 1918; all in NAACPP.

12. Dr. A. C. McIntyre to John R. Shillady, November 17, 1918 [telegram]; Geo. Weissinger Smith to John R. Shilliday [*sic*], November 20, 1918; "Action against Production of 'The Birth of a Nation,'" 1922 file, n.p.; all in NAACPP.

13. "'Birth of a Nation' May Not Be Shown," *Daily Register* [Richmond, Virginia], n.d. but from internal evidence late November 1918; "Great Picture Won't Be Shown," *Daily Register* [Richmond, Virginia], n.d. but from internal evidence November 29,

1918; both in NAACPP. Also see Fleener-Marzec, *D. W. Griffith's "The Birth of a Nation,"* 218.

14. Robert J. Nelson to Governor William C. Sproul, n.d. but from internal evidence early February 1919 [copy]; Governor William J. Sproul to Robert J. Nelson, February 5, 1919; also see Mary White Ovington to Governor William C. Sproul, January 27, 1919; S. H. Kelly and S. E. Beach to Governor William C. Sproul, January 25, 1919; Robert J. Nelson to John R. Shillady, February 11, 1919; all in NAACPP.

15. Untitled report by J. C. Gilmer, Charleston, West Virginia, dated February 26, 1919; "The Birth of a Nation," n.d. memorandum; both in NAACPP.

16. See Langston Hughes, *Fight for Freedom: The Story of the NAACP* (New York: W. W. Norton, 1962), 60–62; Minnie Finch, *The NAACP: Its Fight for Justice* (Metuchen, N.J.: Scarecrow Press, 1981), 55–56.

17. The film continued, however, to be banned in a number of places: for example, Marshall, Texas, passed a local ordinance in 1920 to prevent its screening. Cindy Patton, "White Racism/Black Signs: Censorship and Images of Race Relations," *Journal of Communication* 45, no. 2 (Spring 1995): 65.

18. Koszarski, *An Evening's Entertainment*, 201–206.

19. See Charles Musser, *Before the Nickelodeon: Edwin S. Porter and the Edison Manufacturing Company* (Berkeley: University of California Press, 1991), 302–303, 307, 309, 392, 530, n. 14; cf. Wade, *The Fiery Cross*, 114–15, 220.

20. Scott Simmon observes that one of the possible inspirations for *The Rose of Kentucky* may have been the "Black Patch War" of 1904–1910 between tobacco farmers in the west of Kentucky, which featured Klan-style night riders. Simmon, *The Films of D. W. Griffith*, 124.

21. See Cook, *Fire from the Flint*, 196–97; Slide, *American Racist*, 16. After the publication of *The Clansman*, Dixon had rejected suggestions that he lead some kind of Klan revival. Chalmers, *Hooded Americanism*, 27.

22. Leonard Dinnerstein, *The Leo Frank Case* (New York: Columbia University Press, 1968), 1, 11, 125–26, 136–37, 139–41; Wade, *The Fiery Cross*, 143–44. For a concise overview of the history of the Frank case, see Matthew Bernstein, "Oscar Micheaux and Leo Frank: Cinematic Justice across the Color Line," *Film Quarterly* 57, no. 4 (Summer 2004): 8–21, especially 8–11. On the case itself and its significance, also see Steve Oney, *And the Dead Shall Rise: The Murder of Mary Phagan and the Lynching of Leo Frank* (New York: Pantheon Books, 2003); Nancy MacLean, "The Leo Frank Case Reconsidered: Gender and Sexual Politics in the Making of Reactionary Populism," *Journal of American History* 78, no. 3 (December 1991): 917–48.

23. Wade, *The Fiery Cross*, 144.

24. Wade, *The Fiery Cross*, 144. At least one newspaper of the time equated the men who lynched Leo Frank with Dixon's Klansmen. "The Clansman of 1915," *Press* [Akron, Ohio], August 19, 1915, DWGP.

25. Wade, *The Fiery Cross*, 140–43; Chalmers, *Hooded Americanism*, 28–30.

26. Although the presence of members of the Knights of Mary Phagan at the ceremonial reorganization of the Klan has generally been accepted by historians (see Dinnerstein, *The Leo Frank Case*, 150, for example), Nancy Maclean argues that "no one has ever documented a direct connection between the two." Maclean, *Behind the Mask of Chivalry: The Making of the Second Ku Klux Klan* (New York: Oxford University Press, 1994), 12.

27. Wade, *The Fiery Cross*, 144–45.

28. Ibid., 138.

29. Maxim Simcovitch, "The Impact of Griffith's *Birth of a Nation* on the Modern Ku Klux Klan," *Journal of Popular Film* 1, no. 1 (Winter 1972): 46–48; Wade, *The Fiery Cross*, 146–47.

30. A rival Klan briefly appeared in San Francisco. Wade, *The Fiery Cross*, 146.

31. Simcovitch, "The Impact of Griffith"s *Birth of a Nation* on the Modern Ku Klux Klan," 48–51.

32. Chalmers, *Hooded Americanism*, 3; Simcovitch, "The Impact of Griffith's *Birth of a Nation* on the Modern Ku Klux Klan," 49, 51. Also see Robert Alan Goldberg, *Hooded Empire: The Ku Klux Klan in Colorado* (Urbana: University of Illinois Press, 1981), 52, 153–54.

33. Chalmers, *Hooded Americanism*, 3–4, 31–33; Simcovitch, "The Impact of Griffith's *Birth of a Nation* on the Modern Ku Klux Klan," 52.

34. Mrs. S. E. F. Rose, "The Ku Klux Klan and *The Birth of a Nation*," *Confederate Veteran* 24, no. 4 (April 1916): 157; Maclean, *Behind the Mask of Chivalry*, 13; William G. Shepherd, "How I Put Over the Klan," *Collier's Magazine*, July 14, 1928, quoted in Simcovitch, "The Impact of Griffith's *Birth of a Nation* on the Modern Ku Klux Klan," 46.

35. Chalmers, *Hooded Americanism*, 31–33, 35–38; Maclean, *Behind the Mask of Chivalry*, 5, 10.

36. L. D. Reddick, "Educational Programs for the Improvement of Race Relations: Motion Pictures, Radio, the Press, and Libraries," *Journal of Negro Education* 13, no. 3 (Summer, 1944): 372.

37. Walter F. White to S. L. Rothafel [*sic*], April 26, 1921; S. F. Rothapfel to Walter F. White, April 29, 1921; JWJ [James Weldon Johnson] to Richard E. Enright, Commissioner of Police, May 4, 1921; all in NAACPP. The principal argument used by the NAACP to these officials, it was later claimed, was that *The Birth of a Nation* "was returning to New York, first, to offset the expose of conditions in Jasper County, Georgia, and second, to aid the Ku Klux Klan in its propaganda in New York." James W. Johnson to Lester A. Walton, May 20, 1921, NAACPP.

38. James W. Johnson to Governor Nathan L. Miller, April 30, 1921 [telegram]; James W. Johnson to Lester A. Walton, May 20, 1921; both in NAACPP.

39. "N.A.A.C.P. Issues Statement on 'Birth of a Nation' Protest," NAACP Press Release, May 7, 1921; "Negroes Oppose Film," *Times* [New York], May 7, 1921; "Negroes Picket 'Birth of a Nation,'" *World* [New York], May 7, 1921; "Negroes Protest Film Play," *Tribune* [New York], May 7, 1921; "Arrest Negroes at 'Birth of a Nation,'" *Herald* [New York], May 7, 1921; all in NAACPP.

40. "Stop the Ku Klux Propaganda in New York," n.d., leaflet in NAACPP. Also see Fleener-Marzec, *D. W. Griffith's "The Birth of a Nation,"* 188–89.

41. "Arrest Negroes at 'Birth of a Nation,'" *Herald* [New York], May 7, 1921; "Film Protestants Arraigned in Court," *Globe* [New York], May 9, 1921; "Defends Film Production," *Times* [New York], May 9, 1921; "Negro Pickets in Court," *Times* [New York], May 10, 1921; "Negro Pickets Found Guilty by City Court," *Call* [New York], May 13, 1921; "N.A.A.C.P. Makes Test Case of Protest against 'Birth of a Nation'—Several Pickets Arrested," *Michigan State News* [Grand Rapids], May 19, 1921; Opinion, *State of New York against Kathryn Johnson, Helen Curtis, Laura Pollock, Edward Frasier and Llewellyn Pollock,*

Court of General Sessions of the Peace in and for the County of New York, November 3, 1921, 3, copy in James Weldon Johnson to National Urban League, November 9, 1921; all in NAACPP. Also see Fleener-Marzec, *D. W. Griffith's "The Birth of a Nation,"* 189–92.

42. "'Birth of a Nation' Pickets Freed by Higher Court," *Call* [New York], November 5, 1921; "Convicted N.A.A.C.P. Pickets Freed," NAACP Press Release, n.d. but early November 1921; James Weldon Johnson to National Urban League, November 9, 1921; HJS [H. J. Seligman], director of publicity, NAACP to Fred R. Moore, May 14, 1921; Lester A. Walton to James W. Johnson, May 25, 1921; all in NAACPP.

43. Butler R. Wilson to James W. Johnson, May 16, 1921; "Boston Closes Theater to Stop 'Birth of a Nation,'" *Tribune* [New York], May 17, 1921; "'Birth of a Nation' Closes Boston House," *Herald* [New York], May 17, 1921; all in NAACPP. Also see Fleener-Marzec, *D. W. Griffith's "The Birth of a Nation,"* 243–44.

44. Fox, *Guardian of Boston*, 261. Catholics fought back by making anti-Klan movies. In 1922, Creston Pictures, a Catholic production company, released *Knight of the Eucharist* and Hopp Hadley's *The Mask of the Ku Klux Klan* appeared in 1923. I am indebted to Tom Rice for information on these pictures.

45. Butler R. Wilson to James W. Johnson, May 17, 1921, NAACPP.

46. "'Birth of a Nation' Film Stopped in Boston," NAACP Press Release, May 20, 1921; Emery T. Morris and Albert G. Wolff to NAACP, May 21, 1921; both in NAACPP.

47. Walter F. White, George W. Harris, and Henri W. Shields to Motion Picture Commission of the State of New York, November 27, 1922; "The Birth of a Nation," n.d. memorandum; both in NAACPP.

48. Charles Alexander to James W. Johnson, June 26, 1921 [telegram]; "Birth of a Nation Film Barred in California," NAACP Press Release, July 8, 1921; both in NAACPP. Whatever Clune's assurances, *The Birth of a Nation* did not disappear from the State of California. In 1922, the City Council of Sacramento passed an ordinance to prohibit its showing there. "The Birth of a Nation," n.d. memorandum, NAACPP.

49. Walter F. White to James Hallinan, state director, Knights of Columbus, November 27, 1922, NAACPP.

50. Walter F. White to the Reverend John Roach Straton, December 18, 1922, NAACPP.

51. Hays's efforts proved successful. As Richard Koszarski notes: "After 1922 no more states established censorship boards, and the MPPDA successfully lobbied against all bills for federal regulation." *An Evening's Entertainment*, 206.

52. Will Hays, *The Memoirs of Will H. Hays* (New York: Doubleday, 1955), 467.

53. Walter F. White, George W. Harris, and Henri W. Shields to Motion Picture Commission of the State of New York, November 27, 1922; "The Birth of a Nation," memorandum dated 1922, 1–3; Walter F. White to the Reverend John Roach Straton, December 18, 1922; "Statements made at conference on Birth of a Nation before New York State Censorship Commission," n.d.; all in NAACPP.

54. Opinion of Commissioner Joseph Levenson on protest filed by the NAACP against the picture entitled "The Birth of a Nation," December 8, 1922, NAACPP. The letter from the state censorship board outlining the required cuts (dated December 20, 1922) was reprinted in Aitken, *The Birth of a Nation Story*, 84–85.

55. See George H. Cobb to Walter F. White, January 3, 1923; H. M. Smith to Walter F. White, January 11, 1923; George H. Cobb to Walter White, January 18, 1923

(including a list of the cuts ordered by the commission with White's handwritten assessment of whether the cuts had been made); all in NAACPP.

56. "Klansmen on Screen Cheered by Audiences," *World* [New York], December 5, 1922, clipping in NAACPP. One press agent informed several reviewers in the lobby of the theater that the Klan itself had caused this revival of the film. Ibid.

57. Walter F. White to the Reverend H. M. Smith, January 8, 1923; "Theatre Owners Condemn 'Birth of a Nation' as Klan Aid," *World* [New York], n.d. but from internal evidence December 23, 1922; both in NAACPP. The New York *World* itself was a committed opponent of the Klan, and in October 1921 had published a series of articles exposing the hooded order.

58. "Topeka, Kansas White Newspaper Endorses N.A.A.C.P. Protest," Press Release, dated June 29, 1923, NAACPP.

59. Walter White to the Honorable Jonathan M. Davis, December 4, 1923 [telegram]; Arthur Capper to Walter White, December 4, 1923; both in NAACPP.

60. "To His Excellency, Jonathan M. Davis, Governor of the State of Kansas, Greetings," n.d.; C. W. Comagor to Walter F. White, December 14, 1923 [misdated 1924 in original]; Walter F. White to C. W. Comagor, December 17, 1923; all in NAACPP.

61. Chalmers, *Hooded Americanism*, 143–48.

62. Chalmers, *Hooded Americanism*, 4–5; Wade, *The Fiery Cross*, 257.

63. Aitken, *The Birth of a Nation Story*, 84–86.

64. "The Birth of a Nation," n.d. memorandum, NAACPP.

65. "Virginia Amusement Company vs. W. W. Wertz, Mayor, and John Britton, Chief of Police of Charleston," n.d. memorandum; "The Birth of a Nation," n.d. memorandum; "Ohio Bars 'Birth of a Nation,'" NAACP Press Release, June 12, 1925; "'Birth of a Nation' Refused License by Supreme Court," *Herald* [Cleveland], June 6, 1925; all in NAACPP.

66. Aitken, *The Birth of a Nation Story*, 88–89.

67. Ibid., 90–92.

68. Will W. Alexander to Will Hays, July 23, 1930, NAACPP.

69. Carl E. Milliken to Will W. Alexander, August 9, 1930, NAACPP.

70. Walter F. White to John H. Butler, September 2, 1930, NAACPP. The NAACP branch in San Francisco, where the new version of the film was advertised to be shown for the first time, was similarly split over what tactics to use. See John H. Butler to Walter White, September 5, 1930, NAACPP.

71. "To the Branches: Re Revival of 'The Birth of a Nation,'" circular signed by Walter White, September 9, 1930, NAACPP.

72. "Pressure from Negroes Too Strong for 'Birth': Taken Off in Detroit," *Variety*, February 18, 1931, 24; Acting Secretary to the Honorable Frank Murphy, February 19, 1931; Herbert J. Seligman to John P. Fletcher, April 2, 1931; "'Birth of a Nation' Film Barred by Philadelphia Mayor," clipping dated September 4, 1931; Roy Wilkins to Governor Harry H. Woodring, October 13, 1931; Roy Wilkins to Mrs. Myers, Kansas State Board of Motion Picture Reviews, November 5, 1931; Governor Harry H. Woodring to Roy Wilkins, November 23, 1931; all in NAACPP. Also see Fleener-Marzec, *D. W. Griffith's "The Birth of a Nation,"* 219–21, 262, 267–68.

73. Walter White to Dr. James H. Gillespie, June 15, 1931; Dr. H. Cicero Edwards to Walter White, June 22, 1931; Walter White to Police Commissioner Mulrooney, September 18, 1931; all in NAACPP.

74. Aitken, *The Birth of a Nation Story*, 89, 92–93; Wade, *The Fiery Cross*, 257. Some years later, a British critic commented that the speeding up of the sound version of the film "renders ineffective a number of scenes, and particularly damages the beautiful performance of Mae Marsh, the delicacy and nervous excitability of whose playing become ludicrous when thus arbitrarily galvanised." L.G.A., *"The Birth of a Nation," Monthly Film Bulletin* 20, no. 228 (January 1953): 4; cf. Lindsay Anderson, "Birth of a Nation," *Sight and Sound* 22, no. 3 (January–March 1953): 129.

75. "'Birth of a Nation' Seen on Way Out," *Tribune* [Washington, D.C.], August 6, 1938, NAACPP.

76. Walter White to Estelle Sternberger, September 5, 1935; Jack Nadel to Walter White, September 6, 1935; both in NAACPP.

77. "Film Course for Adults Will Be Given at N.Y.U.," *Herald-Tribune* [New York], August 30, 1937; Walter White to Dean Ned H. Dearborn, September 8, 1937; both in NAACPP. Mob violence and lynching were major issues during the Depression, when Hollywood produced a cycle of anti-lynching films, including *Fury* (1936). The Black Legion was an organization resembling the Klan that attacked immigrants in the Midwest during the 1930s. See Melvyn Stokes, "The Ku Klux Klan as Good and Evil in American Film," in *Les Bons et les Méchants dans le Cinéma Anglophone*, ed. Francis Bordat and Serge Chauvin (Paris: University of Paris 10-Nanterre), 224.

78. E. George Payne to Walter White, September 16, 1937, NAACPP; Walter White to Dean E. George Payne, September 17, 1937, NAACPP; Chalmers, *Hooded Americanism*, 313–16.

79. "New York U. Drops Plan to Use 'Birth of a Nation,'" NAACP press release, September 24 [1937]; Robert R. Gessner to Walter White, September 30, 1937; Class Notes, "History and Appreciation of the Cinema, Session II: October 4, 1937, The Movies Come of Age"; Archer Winsten, "'The Birth of a Nation' Surprises Old Admirer," *Post* [New York], October 5, 1937; all in NAACPP.

80. "Birth of a Nation," NAACP Press Release, October 8, 1937; Charles H. Houston to the Board of Education, City of New York, October 5, 1937; Memorandum from Roy Wilkins to Charles H. Houston, December 8, 1937; all in NAACPP.

81. Gertrude E. Ayer to Walter White, February 10, 1938; "Birth of a Nation," circular dated January 17, 1938, the Stone Film Library, Inc.; David H. Moskowitz to Roy Wilkins, October 14, 1937; Roy Wilkins to Henry C. Turner, president, Board of Education, February 11, 1938; Harold G. Campbell, superintendent of schools, to Roy Wilkins, March 23, 1938; all in NAACPP.

82. "Author of 'Birth of a Nation' Sues to Stop Showing of His Own Film," *Call* [Kansas City], July 16, 1938; "'Birth of Nation' Seen on Way Out," *Guardian* [Boston], August 13, 1938; both in NAACPP.

83. W. A. Robinson to Walter F. White, January 12, 1939; Walter White to W. A. Robinson, January 15, 1939; Walter White to Jackson Davis, General Education Board, January 16, 1939; Walter White to Fanning Hearon, Association of School Film Libraries, January 18, 1939; all in NAACPP.

84. "Riotous Film Costs Exhibitor $1,400 Fine," *Rocky Mountain News* [Denver], April 20, 1939 [transcript]; W. F. Turner to Thurgood Marshall, October 4, 1939; "City Right to Ban 'Racial Hatred' Movies Is Upheld," *Post* [Denver], February 1, 1940; "Denverite Is Fined $200 for Showing 'Birth of a Nation,'" *Post* [Denver], February 28, 1940;

"Denver Movie Censorship Law to Be Fought in State Court," NAACP press release, n.d.; Roger Baldwin to Walter White, April 25, 1939; all in NAACPP. Also see Fleener-Marzec, *D. W. Griffith's "The Birth of a Nation,"* 192–98. *Birth* was banned by the Milwaukee board of censors in 1939. Ibid., 245.

85. Arthur Garfield Hays to Nate Goldstick, Corporation Counsel's Office, Detroit, May 1, 1939, copy in NAACPP.

86. Roger Baldwin to editor, *The Crisis*, April 17, 1940; Morris Fine [The American Jewish Committee] to Thurgood Marshall, May 25, 1939; "Theatre Man Arrested for Showing 'Birth of a Nation,'" NAACP Press Release dated May 20, [1939?]; all in NAACPP. Also see Fleener-Marzec, *D. W. Griffith's "The Birth of a Nation,"* 185–86.

87. Roger Baldwin to editor, *The Crisis*, April 17, 1940, NAACPP.

88. Irwin Esmond, director, Motion Picture Division, to Thurgood Marshall, October 31, 1938, NAACPP.

89. Dr. James J. McClendon ("Mac") to Walter White, May 1, 1939 (White wrote to RR on this letter "Show to B[oar]d. in its discussion on Roger Baldwin's letter"); Walter White to RR [Richetta Randolph?], "Memorandum Re 'The Birth of a Nation,'" June 13, 1939; Roger Baldwin to Walter White, June 17, 1939; all in NAACPP.

90. R. B. Eleazer to Will Hays, March 25, 1940; Charles C. Webber to Will Hays, March 26, 1940; Will H. Hays to Dr. Stephen S. Wise, March 29, 1940; all in NAACPP.

91. Walter White to Will Hays, March 21, 1940; Carl E. Milliken to Walter White, March 25, 1940; both in NAACPP.

92. "Excerpts from NAACP Press Releases Re 'Birth of a Nation,'" n.d., 1–2, NAACPP; Peter Noble, "The Negro in *The Birth of a Nation*," reprinted in Silva, ed., *Focus*, 132. On the OWI, see Clayton R. Koppes and Gregory D. Black, *Hollywood Goes to War: Patriotism, Movies and the Second World War from "Ninotchka" to "Mrs. Miniver"* (London: Tauris Parke Paperbacks, 2000), passim, and Robert Fyne, *The Hollywood Propaganda of World War II* (Lanham, Mass.: Scarecrow Press, 1997), 9–10, 42, 48–49, 52–53, 56, 58, 64, 97, 159.

93. Aitken, *The Birth of a Nation Story*, 92. In October 1947, for example, the film was revived at Harry Brandt's Republic Theater in New York. The NAACP began to picket the theater and, after one week, the film—which was losing money—was withdrawn. "Excerpts from NAACP Press Releases Re 'Birth of a Nation,'" 3, NAACPP.

94. Slide, *American Racist*, 199; Fleener-Marzec, *D. W. Griffith's "The Birth of a Nation,"* 102–104, 245, 273–74.

95. Robert J. Landry, "'Race': Boxoffice But Booby-Trapped," *Variety*, January 8, 1958, p. 15. I am very grateful to Tom Doherty for bringing this article to my attention.

96. Pete Daniel, *Lost Revolutions: The South in the 1950s* (Chapel Hill: University of North Carolina Press for the Smithsonian National Museum of American History, 2000), 242.

97. Fleener-Marzec, *D. W. Griffith's "The Birth of a Nation,"* 385.

98. Roy Aitken commented that he and his brother Harry had made many 16mm prints of the film since most university projectors could not handle the 35mm size of film used in ordinary movie theaters. Aitken, *The Birth of a Nation Story*, 92. Screenings of the film on college campuses also attracted intense controversy. In 1959, for example, the University of Cincinnati planned to show *Birth* as part of a silent film festival. The film was withdrawn after protests from the local NAACP. After would-be viewers

and newspapers complained at this suppression, the movie was reinstated. *Film Daily*, March 30, 1959, cited in Aitken, *The Birth of a Nation Story*, 8.

99. May C. Nerney to Desha Breckinridge, September 16, 1915, NAACPP; cf. J. Mott Hallowell to James Michael Curley and Stephen O'Meara, n.d., reprinted in *Fighting a Vicious Film*, 26.

100. *The Crisis* 12, no. 2 (June 1916): 87.

101. Duncan C. Milner to Dr. [Charles E.] Bentley, April 13, 1918, NAACPP. On East St. Louis, see "The Massacre of East St. Louis" in *The Crisis*, September 1917.

102. Hugo Münsterberg, *The Photoplay: A Psychological Study* (New York: D. Appleton, 1916), 87–90, 94–111, quotation from 221.

103. A survey of 37,000 high school students in 1923 revealed that *The Birth of a Nation* was still the favorite movie for Southern boys. Koszarski, *An Evening's Entertainment*, 28.

104. Alice Miller Mitchell, *Children and Movies* (Chicago: University of Chicago Press, 1929), 141.

105. Caroline Bond Day, *A Study of Some Negro-White Families in the United States*, foreword and notes on the anthropometric data by Earnest A. Hooton, Harvard African Studies, no. 10 (Cambridge, Mass.: Peabody Museum of Harvard University, 1932), 126.

106. Robert Sklar, *Movie-Made America: A Cultural History of American Movies* (New York: Vintage Books, 1994), 134. Sklar's view of the Payne Fund studies reflects the critique of them by Raymond Moley and the Motion Picture Producers and Distributors Association, a view that was politically motivated. For a more recent, balanced assessment of the studies, see Garth S. Jowett, Ian C. Jarvie, and Kathryn H. Fuller, *Children and the Movies: Media Influence and the Payne Fund Controversy* (Cambridge: Cambridge University Press, 1996). Also see Shearon A. Lowery and Melvin L. DeFleur, *Milestones in Mass Communications Research: Media Effects* (New York: Longman, 1995), Chapter 2.

107. Henry James Forman, *Our Movie Made Children* (New York: Macmillan, 1933), 196–213, quotation from 212.

108. Herbert Blumer, *Movies and Conduct* (New York: Macmillan, 1933), 150. Blumer pointed out, however, that "the meanings which movie-goers may get from the same picture are diametrically opposite." To support this proposition, he cited two very different reactions to *The Birth of a Nation*: one female subject of his survey admitted that the film increased her racism while another remembered "crying because the poor colored people were so mistreated." Ibid., 180–81.

109. Ruth C. Peterson and L. L. Thurstone, *Motion Pictures and the Social Attitudes of Children* (New York: Macmillan, 1933), 35, 38, 60–61, 64–65

110. Peterson and Thurstone, *Motion Pictures and the Social Attitudes of Children*, 35.

111. William H. Short to [W. E.] Burghardt Du Bois, October 27, 1927; "Memorandum to Mr. White from Mr. Seligmann," dated November 16, 1932; both in NAACPP.

112. Reddick, "Educational Programs for the Improvement of Race Relations," 368, 380.

113. Ibid., 368–69, 370.

114. Douglas Cameron Moore, "A Study of the Influence of the Film *The Birth of a Nation* on the Attitudes of Selected High School White Students toward Negroes" (Ph.D. diss., University of Illinois, Urbana-Champaign, 1971).

115. Staiger, *Interpreting Films*, 139–53.

116. Rick Halpern, "Organized Labor, Black Workers, and the Twentieth Century South: The Emerging Revision," in *Race and Class in the American South since 1890*, ed. Melvyn Stokes and Rick Halpern (Oxford: Berg, 1994), 61–64, 67–72; Cripps, *Slow Fade to Black*, 68; Chalmers, *Hooded Americanism*, 5, 316.

117. Karl Marx, *A Contribution to the Critique of Political Economy*, in Karl Marx and Friedrich Engels, *Selected Works*, I (Moscow: Progress Publishers, 1969), 503.

118. Seymour Stern, "Suppression of Showing Marks 25th Year of *Birth of a Nation*," *New Leader*, March 16, 1940, 3; Staiger, *Interpreting Films*, 139, 146–48.

119. Peter Noble, "A Note on an Idol," *Sight and Sound* 15, no. 59 (Autumn 1946): 81–82.

120. D. W. Griffith, "*The Birth of a Nation*," *Sight and Sound* 16, no. 61 (Spring 1947): 32.

121. Jacobs, *The Rise of the American Film*, 177.

122. Schickel, *Griffith*, 602. Stern labored unsuccessfully on the projected biography for almost two decades. All that finally appeared were a series of notes on the production of *Birth of a Nation*. See Stern, "Griffith: 1—*The Birth of a Nation*," 1–210.

123. Seymour Stern, "Griffith Not Anti-Negro," *Sight and Sound* 16, no. 61 (Spring 1947): 32–35.

124. He reiterated much the same critique of *The Birth of a Nation* in a book published the following year. See Noble, "The Negro in *The Birth of a Nation*," *The Negro in Films* (London: Skelton Robinson, 1948), 33–43.

125. E. L. Cranstone, "The 'Birth of a Nation' Controversy," *Sight and Sound* 16, no. 63 (Autumn 1947): 119.

126. Seymour Stern, "The Griffith Controversy," *Sight and Sound* 17, no. 65 (Spring 1948): 49–50. In its preceding issue, the journal had published "without comment" a translated article by Sergei Eisenstein criticizing *The Birth of a Nation* as an "ultra-reactionary" picture "which celebrated the formation of the Ku Klux Klan, a fascist organisation." S. M. Eisenstein, "Purveyors of Spiritual Poison," *Sight and Sound* 16, no. 63 (Autumn 1947): 103.

127. V. J. Jerome, *The Negro in Hollywood Films* (New York: Masses and Mainstream, 1950), 19–20.

128. Seymour Stern, "D. W. Griffith and the Movies," *American Mercury* 68, no. 303 (March 1949): 308–19; Stern, "The Cold War against David Wark Griffith," *Films in Review* 7, no. 2 (February 1956): 49–59.

129. Aitken, *The Birth of a Nation Story*, 87–88. The meeting seems to have occurred in 1926, with Aitken remembering it as happening six months *before* the emergence of "rumors of sound pictures." Ibid, 88.

130. Roy Wilkins to MPPDA, February 10, 1933; Carl E. Milliken to Roy Wilkins, February 11, 1933; both in NAACPP.

131. "'Birth of a Nation' Will Have Sequel," *News and Observer* [Raleigh, North Carolina], October 22, 1937; Jonathan Daniels to Walter White, November 15, 1937; Walter White to Jonathan Daniels, November 22, 1937; all in NAACPP.

132. Aitken, *The Birth of a Nation Story*, 93–95. Harry Aitken apparently paid Dixon $2,500 out of his own pocket for his work on the screenplay. Ibid, 95.

133. Louella O. Parsons, "Griffith to Remake 'The Birth of a Nation,'" *Herald* [Washington], January 4, 1938; Walter A. Gordon to Walter White, February 16, 1938; "Author

of 'Birth of a Nation' Sues to Stop Showing of His Own Film," *Call* [Kansas City], July 16, 1938; all in NAACPP.

134. Carol Frink, "'Birth of a Nation' Movie to Be Remade as Talkie," *Times-Herald* [Washington, D.C.], March 13, 1940; Walter White to Will Hays, March 21, 1940; Stephen S. Wise to Will Hays, March 26, 1940; R. B. Eleazer to Will Hays, March 25, 1940; George K. Hunten to Will Hays, April 3, 1940; Charles C. Webber to Will Hays, March 26, 1940; Mrs. Bernard G. Waring to Will Hays, March 28, 1940; Carl E. Milliken to Dr. Alice V. Keliher, April 10, 1940; Sylvia Wilcox Razey to Will Hays, April 1, 1940; all in NAACPP.

135. Charles C. Webber to Will Hays, March 26, 1940; R. B. Eleazer to Will Hays, March 25, 1940; both in NAACPP.

136. Francis S. Harmon to R. B. Eleazer, March 29, 1940; Francis S. Harmon to Frank R. Crosswaith, March 29, 1940; Francis S. Harmon to Mary Fox, May 2, 1940; Carl E. Milliken to Dr. Alice V. Keliher, April 10, 1940; Walter White to Dr. Everett R. Clinchy, April 22, 1940; all in NAACPP.

137. Walter White to Walter Winchell, May 20, 1940, NAACPP.

138. David O. Selznick to Sidney Howard, January 6, 1937, Rudy Behlmer, ed., *Memo from David O. Selznick* (New York: Modern Library, 2000), 162. Selznick also made sure that the references to the Klan in Margaret Mitchell's novel were removed from the film version of *Gone With the Wind*.

139. On Selznick's relations with the NAACP during the filming of *Gone With the Wind*, see Ronald Haver, *David O. Selznick's Hollywood* (London: Secker and Warburg, 1980), 250–51 and *The Making of a Legend: Gone With the Wind*, 1989 documentary; David O. Selznick to Katherine Brown, October 7, 1941, *Memo from David O. Selznick*, 274. Spectators of *Gone With the Wind* often found themselves comparing its spectacular effects to those of *The Birth of a Nation*. "The street scenes," commented Sue Myrick to Margaret Mitchell, "are so fine I think the thing is a *Birth of a Nation*." See Myrick to Mitchell, June 2, 1939, quoted in Ann Edwards, *The Road to Tara: The Life of Margaret Mitchell* (London: Hodder and Stoughton, 1983), 280. One member of the preview audience for *Gone With the Wind* simply described it as "the greatest picture since *Birth of a Nation*." Ibid., 281.

140. Aitken, *The Birth of a Nation Story*, 4–5, 11, 13–19, 96.

141. Aitken, *The Birth of a Nation Story*, 96. Aitken may have confused the precise year of this final remake bid. Anthony Slide writes of King Bros. Productions launching such a project in 1960. Slide, *American Racist*, 198.

142. Slide, *American Racist*, 203, 205. After the mid-1920s, with screenings infrequent and expenses of promotional efforts still high, Epoch apparently never declared dividends. Al P. Nelson and Mel R. Jones, *A Silent Siren Song: The Aitken Brothers' Hollywood Odyssey, 1905–1926* (New York: Cooper Square Press, 2000), 185.

143. Slide, *American Racist*, 206. Roy Aitken died in 1976.

144. John Belton, "The Birth of a Nation," *Sight and Sound* 45, no. 2 (Spring 1976): 85; Slide, *American Racist*, 206. The American Film Institute (AFI) had also acquired film materials relating to *The Birth of a Nation*. These were deposited with the Library of Congress. In 1972, Epoch launched a suit for copyright infringement against the AFI and dispatched federal marshals with a warrant to the Library of Congress in an (unsuccessful) attempt to seize the materials. Two years later, the suit was settled for $250. Slide,

American Racist, 206. On the Killiam-Rohauer conflict, also see J. B. Kaufman, "Non-Archival Sources," in Usai, *The Griffith Project: Vol. 8*, 108–10.

145. Belton, "The Birth of a Nation," 85; Slide, *American Racist*, 205–207.

146. See Tommy L. Lott, "Aesthetics and Politics in Contemporary Black Film Theory," in *Film Theory and Philosophy*, ed. Richard Allen and Murray Smith (Oxford: Oxford University Press, 1997), 293.

147. These statistics are based on "A Checklist of D. W. Griffith's Film," in Schickel, *Griffith*, 637–47.

148. Gish, *The Movies, Mr. Griffith, and Me*, 166.

149. Louis Delluc, "Prologue" (1923), in Richard Abel, *French Film Theory and Criticism: A History/Anthology 1907–1939*, Vol. 1: *1907–1929* (Princeton: Princeton University Press, 1988), 290.

150. Schickel, *Griffith*, 326, 330–31, 334–35, 447; Delluc, "Prologue," in Abel, *French Film Theory and Criticism*, 290.

151. Schickel, *Griffith*, 340–41, 344–50.

152. So much did Gish "suffer" as a Griffith heroine that one critic would eventually facetiously suggest creating a Society for the Prevention of Cruelty to Lillian Gish. Schickel, *Griffith*, 393.

153. Ibid., 353, 356, 360.

154. Simmon, *The Films of D. W. Griffith*, 12.

155. In any event, only two films were made under this contract. Neither was at all memorable: *The Greatest Question* (1919) and *The Idol Dancer*.

156. Schickel, *Griffith*, 415–17, 419–22, 428, 448.

157. Ibid., 450, 460–61, 464, 472–74, 482, 491, 494, 498.

158. Robert W. Chambers, "The Sacrifice," reprinted in *Film Comment* 21, no. 4 (July–August 1985): 72.

159. Schickel, *Griffith*, 458–59, 491.

160. Ibid, 495, 498, 506, 514–17, 524–25.

161. Ibid, 529–31, 537–43.

162. Taylor would achieve an immortality of sorts in one line of the credits for the Douglas Fairbanks/Mary Pickford sound version of *The Taming of the Shrew* (1929): "By William Shakespeare. Additional dialogue by Sam Taylor." Ibid., 544.

163. Ibid., 544–45, 551–52.

164. Ibid., 553–57, 559.

165. David Thomson, *Showman: The Life of David O. Selznick* (London: Abacus, 1993), 235; Selznick to Wm. Wright, January 5, 1937, in *Memo from David O. Selznick*, 158.

166. Slide, *American Racist*, 93. By contrast, Breil's score for *The Birth of a Nation* had been compiled from already existing musical pieces, with some original pieces by Breil himself.

167. Slide, *American Racist*, 92–93, 96, 101–102; Cook, *Fire from the Flint*, 184–88.

168. Slide, *American Racist*, 157–61; Cook, *Fire from the Flint*, 197–98.

169. Anthony Slide emphasizes the irony of Dixon's film career: beginning with a pro-Klan picture (*The Birth of a Nation*), it ended by vilifying the Klan. Slide, *American Racist*, 183.

170. Cook, *Fire from the Flint*, 206–12, 222; Slide, *American Racist*, 185; "Dixon Penniless: $1,250,000 Gone," *Times* [New York], April 17, 1934, 19.

171. Thomas Dixon, *The Sun Virgin* (New York: Horace Liveright, 1929); Slide, *American Racist*, 165–66; Cook, *Fire from the Flint*, 212–13; Thomas Dixon and Harry M. Daugherty, *The Inside Story of the Harding Tragedy* (New York: Churchill, 1932). Dixon also wrote a book on a boy's colony in Portugal, published in 1934.

172. Cook, *Fire from the Flint*, 216–17, 219–21. Black historian John Hope Franklin, working on his Ph.D. in Raleigh, was regularly greeted with "a warm smile" from "a courtly gentleman outside the courthouse." Later, having discovered that the old gentleman was Thomas Dixon, Franklin wondered whether his welcoming smile "was more a reflection of his secret delight at keeping 'the likes of me' out of any governmental office more influential than 'a Jim Crow cubby-hole in the State Archives.'" D'Oogle, "*The Birth of a Nation*: Symposium on Classic Film Discusses Inaccuracies and Virtues," 265.

173. Cook, *Fire from the Flint*, 223–26; Slide, *American Racist*, 186–88. Dixon might have been pleased to know that he was buried in the same cemetery as another well-known commentator on the South: W. J. Cash.

174. "Mutual Co. Fight Is On and Aitken May Be Deposed," *Telegraph* [New York], June 17, 1915; "Aitken Out of Mutual Films," *Sun* [New York], June 24, 1915; "Three Film Men in Big Combine," *Herald* [New York], June 18, 1915; all in DWGP.

175. "Triangle Film Formed," *New York Times*, July 21, 1915; Nelson and Jones, *A Silent Siren Song*, 165.

176. Koszarski, *An Evening's Entertainment*, 68; Nelson and Jones, *A Silent Siren Song*, 162, 166–69.

177. Nelson and Jones, *A Silent Siren Song*, 160–61, 163, 182.

178. Ibid., 169–70. It has also been suggested that the negotiations failed because Harry refused to put two other Aitken companies—Epoch (distributing *The Birth of a Nation*) and the Western Import Company (distributing films in Europe)—into the new combination. Ibid., 170.

179. Ibid., 171–72, 174, 176–77, 180–81, 183–85.

180. Accounts of the Epoch Producing Corporation, March 13, 1915, DWGP.

181. Robert Goldstein, "The True Story of the Making of a Motion Picture and Its Maker, Written in Narrative Form, Comprising the Facts," in *Robert Goldstein and "The Spirit of '76,"* ed. Anthony Slide (Metuchen, N.J.: Scarecrow Press, 1993), especially 7–51. Griffith's version of the story of the American Revolution, *America*, was released in 1924.

182. *Motion Picture News* 15, no. 21 (May 26, 1917), 3300, reprinted in Slide, *Robert Goldstein*, 203.

183. For a summary of the film's complex plot, see Slide, *Robert Goldstein*, 30–35.

184. Ibid., 34, 95–96, quotation on 104.

185. G. P. Harleman, "'Spirit of '76' Confiscated by Government," *The Moving Picture World*, December 22, 1917, 1786, reprinted in Slide, *Robert Goldstein*, 212; Michael Selig, "United States v. Motion Picture Film *The Spirit of '76*: The Espionage Case of Producer Robert Goldstein (1917)," *Journal of Popular Film and Television* 10, no. 4 (Winter 1983): 170–71.

186. "*Spirit of '76* Film Called Part of Plot: Picture Incites to Mutiny Is Allegation—Producer May Be Given Penitentiary Sentence," *Movie Picture World*, December 29, 1917, 1947, reprinted in Slide, *Robert Goldstein*, 214–15.

187. Anthony Slide, "*The Spirit of '76*," and the Strange Case of Robert Goldstein," *Films in Review* 27, no. 1 (January 1976): 4.

188. Selig, "United States v. Motion Picture Film *The Spirit of "76*," 169, 173; G. P. Harleman, "Goldstein Is Sentenced to Ten Years: Producer of *The Spirit of '76* Is Sent to the Federal Penitentiary and Fined $5,000," *Moving Picture World*, May 25, 1918, 145, reprinted in Slide, *Robert Goldstein*, 219. Also see ibid., xxi–xxii.

189. Gish's 1969 autobiography was revealingly entitled *The Movies, Mr. Griffith and Me*. In her will, she made a bequest to the Museum of Modern Art "so they could protect the work of Mr. Griffith." David Thomson, "Lillian Gish," in *The New Biographical Dictionary of Film* (London: Little, Brown, 2002), 340.

190. Slide, *American Racist*, 78.

191. Thomas Quinn Curtiss, *Von Stroheim* (London: Angus and Robertson, 1971), 37–39; John Ford, interview with Richard Schickel, n.d., cited in Schickel, *Griffith*, 231.

CONCLUSION

1. Greg Braxton, "Controversy Reborn," *Los Angeles Times*, August 7, 2004, E1, E4; Greg Braxton, "Showing of 'Birth of a Nation' canceled," ibid., August 10, E2; Martin Miller, "No canceling the 'Birth' debate," ibid., August 11, 2004, E6. My thanks to Denise Warren for drawing these articles to my attention.

2. "The Worth of 'A Nation,'" *Los Angeles Times*, September 19, 2004, E1, E24–25.

3. James Baldwin, *The Devil Finds Work* (London: Michael Joseph, 1976), 43, 45.

4. George D. Proctor, "The Birth of a Nation," *Motion Picture News* 11, no. 10 (March 13, 1915), 49-50, reprinted in Slide, *Selected Film Criticism, 1912–1920*, 18; Mark Vance, *Variety*, March 12, 1915, reprinted in Silva, *Focus*, 25; *Variety*, March 12, 1915, quoted in Jacobs, *The Rise of the American Film*, 175.

5. Dorothy Dix, "The Birth of a Nation," *Journal* [New York], March 5, 1915, quoted in Schickel, *Griffith*, 278; Harlow Hare, *Boston American*, July 18, 1915, reprinted in Silva, *Focus*, 37.

6. *Washington Post*, April 11, 1915, DWGP (cf. *Journal of Commerce*, March 18, 1915, DWGP); Resolutions of the Executive Committee, Boston Branch, NAACP, June 8, 1915, NAACPP.

7. Jacobs, *Rise of the American Film*, 187; Herman G. Weinberg, "American Film Directors and Social Reality," *Sight and Sound* 7, no. 28 (Winter 1938–39): 168; Agee, *Agee on Film*, 313; Knight, *The Liveliest Art*, 23; Sadoul, *Histoire Générale du Cinéma*, Tome III: *Le Cinéma Devient un Art*, 25; Jean Mitry, *The Aesthetics and Psychology of the Cinema*, trans. Christopher King (London: Athlone Press, 1998), 67; Rogin, "The Sword Became a Flashing Vision," in Lang, *The Birth of a Nation*, 257.

8. Chadwick, *The Reel Civil War*, 103. This shot, as Chadwick points out, would be copied in many later films.

9. Leger Grindon, *Shadows on the Past: Studies in the Historical Fiction Film* (Philadelphia: Temple University Press, 1994), 17–18. Both Grindon and William K. Everson suggest that it is his mother's arms that draw Ben Cameron into the house. What is shown, however, on the left of the back of the "Little Colonel" is the slender arm of Flora, with the ruche of her dress sleeve showing; on the right is a broader arm and the plainer

sleeve of his mother's dress. See Grindon, *Shadows on the Past*, 17; Everson, *American Silent Film*, 80.

10. Agee, *Agee on Film*, 313; Siegfried Kracauer, *Theory of Film: The Redemption of Physical Reality* (New York: Oxford University Press, 1960), viii. In much the same way that the homecoming sequence shows a further evolution in a shot from an earlier film, the battle scenes in *The Birth of a Nation* often grew out of shots in Griffith Biograph films about the Civil War, such as *The Battle* (1911).

11. Andrew Sarris, however, pointed out that "Welles reintroduced the iris dissolve as an expression of nostalgia in *The Magnificent Ambersons* in 1942, and Ophuls reinvented artificial masking and framing in *Lola Montez* in 1955 to make CinemaScope more supple, and Godard expressed his fleeting narrative instinct with an iris fadeout in *Breathless* in 1960. With everything again possible, nothing seems antiquated, Griffith least of all." Sarris, "BIRTH OF A NATION or White Power Back When," *Village Voice*, July 17 and 24, 1969, reprinted in Silva, *Focus*, 107.

12. Sadoul, *Histoire Générale du Cinéma*, Tome III: *Le Cinéma Devient un Art*, 18; cf. Everson, *American Silent Film*, 79–80.

13. Ned Mackintosh, "The Birth of a Nation," *Atlanta Constitution*, December 7, 1915, reprinted in Silva, *Focus*, 34; Grindon, *Shadows on the Past*, 17 (cf. Sadoul, *Histoire Générale du Cinéma*, Tome III: *Le Cinéma Devient un Art*, 23).

14. Lary May points out that it "became the most widely acclaimed and financially successful film of the entire silent era." May, *Screening Out the Past: The Birth of Mass Culture and the Motion Picture Industry* (Chicago: University of Chicago Press, 1983), 67.

15. William Rothman, *The "I" of the Camera: Essays in Film Criticism, History, and Aesthetics* (Cambridge: Cambridge University Press, 1988), 11.

16. Brown, *Adventures*, 74, 76, 88–90, 95–96. "The heart of his craft," Brown recalled, "was in what we fumblingly called cutting, or editing." Ibid., 96.

17. Jacobs, *The Rise of the American Film*, 187; Brownlow, *The Parade's Gone By*, 281.

18. Harry M. Benshoff and Sean Griffin, *America on Film: Representing Race, Class, Gender, and Sexuality at the Movies* (Oxford: Blackwell, 2004), 235. Benshoff and Griffin illustrate this point by noting that "Griffith continually cuts from Ben Cameron gazing romantically or Silas Lynch gazing threateningly to shots of Elsie Stoneman." Ibid.

19. W. Stephen Bush, "The Birth of a Nation," *The Moving Picture World*, March 13, 1915, reprinted in Silva, *Focus*, 27.

20. Ned Mackintosh, *Atlanta Constitution*, December 7, 1915, reprinted in Silva, *Focus*, 34.

21. Bogle, *Toms, Coons, Mulattoes, Mammies and Bucks*, 3–18.

22. Louella Parsons, "D. W. Griffith in Plea for His Greatest Film," *Herald* [New York], May 30, 1915, DWGP.

23. Yacowar, "Aspects of the Familiar," 133.

24. W. E. B. Du Bois, "Memorandum to Mr. White of the N.A.A.C.P. on 'The Birth of a Nation,'" n.d., NAACPP; D'Ooge, "*The Birth of a Nation*: Symposium on Classic Film Discusses Inaccuracies and Virtues," 265; Reddick, "Educational Programs for the Improvement of Race Relations," 370.

25. Noble, "The Negro in *The Birth of a Nation*," in Silva, *Focus*, 125–32.

26. Agee, *Agee on Film*, 314; Gish, *The Movies, Mr. Griffith and Me*, 162; Everson, *American Silent Film*, 83–87.

27. Schickel, *Griffith*, 29, 213, 233—37, 299.

28. Carter, "Cultural History Written with Lightning," in Silva, *Focus*, 141.

29. For Griffith's views of miscegenation ("The negro should be as much opposed to this as the white man"), see Louella Parsons, "D. W. Griffith in Plea for His Greatest Film," *Herald* [New York], May 30, 1915, DWGP.

30. Simmon, *The Films of D. W. Griffith*, 107. Griffith, as noted in Chapter 4, declined to have any "black blood" among the major players in *Birth*. Russell Merritt, although not thinking primarily in racial terms, argues that the Gus-Flora chase sequence is far more complex than it might first appear because of Gus's previously more sympathetic appearances in the film and his hesitancy and nervousness during the chase itself. Merritt, "D. W. Griffith's *The Birth of a Nation*: Going after Little Sister," 227–28, 232–33.

31. According to W. E. B. Du Bois, the number of African Americans lynched increased from sixty in 1914 to ninety-nine in 1915, the year of *The Birth of a Nation*. The main "alleged excuse" for such lynchings, Du Bois noted, "was the attacks upon white women by colored men," an issue highlighted in the film by Gus's pursuit of Flora and Lynch's wish for a "forced marriage" with Elsie. W. E. B. Du Bois, "Memorandum to Mr. White of the N.A.A.C.P. on 'The Birth of a Nation,'" n.d., NAACPP.

32. See Chapter 8.

33. S. Eisenstein, "To the Editors of *International Literature*," in David Platt, *Celluloid Power: Social Film Criticism from "The Birth of a Nation" to "Judgement at Nuremberg"* (Metuchen, N.J.: Scarecrow Press, 1992), 81.

34. Gallagher, "Racist Ideology and Black Abnormality in the Birth of a Nation," 75.

35. Michael Rogin, "The Sword Became a Flashing Vision," in Lang, *The Birth of a Nation*, 251. [This essay was first published in 1985.]

36. Clyde Taylor, "The Re-birth of the Aesthetic in Cinema," in *The Birth of Whiteness*, ed. Bernardi, 15–37.

37. Penny Starfield, "Le racisme dans le cinéma américain: entre exclusion et expression," in Michel Prum, ed., *Exclure au nom de la race (États-Unis, Irlande, Grande Bretagne)* (Paris: Editions Syllepse, 2000), 51 [my translation].

38. Donato Totaro, "*Birth of a Nation*: Viewed Today," http://www.horschamp.qc.ca/new_offscreen/birthofnation.html, accessed on 29 March 2007; Keil, "Style and Technique," in Usai, *The Griffith Project: Vol. 8*, 69.

39. Other work in reception studies parallels this way of perceiving *Birth*. For example, in *Melodrama and Meaning: History, Culture, and the Films of Douglas Sirk* (Bloomington: Indiana University Press, 1994), Barbara Klinger shows how films in a body of 1950s melodramas directed by Sirk do not change but are interpreted differently by different institutions (including academia, film critics, the stardom "industry" and mass media) at different times.

Bibliography

Abel, Richard. *French Film Theory and Criticism: A History/Anthology 1907–1939*, Vol. 1: *1907–1929*. Princeton: Princeton University Press, 1988.

Abel, Richard and Rick Altman. *The Sounds of Early Cinema*. Bloomington: University of Indiana Press, 2001.

Agee, James. *Agee on Film: Reviews and Comments by James Agee*. New York: McDowell, Obolensky, 1958; originally published in 1941.

Aitken, Roy E. (with Al P. Nelson). *The Birth of a Nation Story*. Middleburg, Va.: Denlinger, 1965.

Allen, Michael. *Family Secrets: The Feature Films of D. W. Griffith*. London: BFI Publishing, 1999.

Allen, Richard and Murray Smith, eds. *Film Theory and Philosophy*. Oxford: Oxford University Press, 1997.

Allen, Robert C. "Motion Picture Exhibition in Manhattan, 1906–1912: Beyond the Nickelodeon." *Cinema Journal* 18, no. 2 (Spring 1979): 2–15. Reprinted in *Film before Griffith*, 162–75, ed. Robert L. Fell. Berkeley: University of California Press, 1983.

Anderson, Benedict R. O'G. *Imagined Communities: Reflections on the Origin and Spread of Nationalism*. Rev. ed. London: Verso, 1991.

Anderson, Lindsay. "*Birth of a Nation*." *Sight and Sound* 22, no. 3 (January–March 1953): 129–30.

Anderson, Tim. "Reforming 'Jackass Music': The Problematic Aesthetics of Early American Film Music Accompaniment." *Cinema Journal* 37, no. 1 (Fall 1997): 3–22.

Ang, Ien. *Watching Dallas: Soap Opera and the Melodramatic Imagination*. Trans. Della Couling. London: Methuen, 1985.

Anon. *White American* (pamphlet). San Francisco: n.p., 1914.

L'Avant-Scène, Spécial Griffith: Naissance d'une Nation no. 193–94 (October 1–15, 1977): 3–80.

Ayers, Edward L. *The Promise of the New South: Life after Reconstruction*. New York: Oxford University Press, 1992.

Bailey, Hugh C. *Liberalism in the New South: Southern Social Reformers and the Progressive Movement*. Coral Gables, Fla.: University of Miami Press, 1969.

Baker, Ray Stannard. *American Chronicle: The Autobiography of Ray Stannard Baker*. New York: Charles Scribner's Sons, 1945.

———. *Following the Color Line: An Account of Negro Citizenship in the American Democracy*. New York: Doubleday, Page, 1908.

Baldwin, James. *The Devil Finds Work*. London: Michael Joseph, 1976.

Balio, Tino, ed. *The American Film Industry*. Madison: University of Wisconsin Press, 1976.

Barry, Iris. *D. W. Griffith: American Film Master*. New York: Museum of Modern Art, 1940.

Beard, Charles A. and Mary Beard. *The Rise of American Civilization*, 1-vol. ed. New York: Macmillan, 1937; originally published in 1927.

Beatty, Jack. *The Rascal King: The Life and Times of James Michael Curley*. Reading, Mass.: Addison-Wesley, 1992.

Behlmer, Rudy, ed. *Memo from David O. Selznick*. New York: Modern Library, 2000.

Belton, John. "*The Birth of a Nation*." *Sight and Sound* 45, no. 2 (Spring 1976): 85–86.

Benshoff, Harry M. and Sean Griffin. *America on Film: Representing Race, Class, Gender, and Sexuality at the Movies*. Oxford: Blackwell, 2004.

Berg, Charles Merrell. *An Investigation of the Motives for and the Realization of Music to Accompany the American Silent Film, 1896–1927*. New York: Arno Press, 1976.

Bernardi, Daniel, ed. *The Birth of Whiteness: Race and the Emergence of U.S. Cinema*. New Brunswick, N.J.: Rutgers University Press, 1996.

———. "The Voice of Whiteness: D. W. Griffith's Biograph Films (1908–1913)." In *The Birth of Whiteness*, 103–28, ed. Daniel Bernardi. New Brunswick, N.J.: Rutgers University Press, 1996.

Bernstein, Matthew, ed. *Controlling Hollywood: Censorship and Regulation in the Studio Era*. London: Athlone Press, 2000.

———. "Oscar Micheaux and Leo Frank: Cinematic Justice across the Color Line." *Film Quarterly* 57, no. 4 (Summer 2004): 8–21.

Berquist, Goodwin and James Greenwood. "Protest against Racism: *The Birth of a Nation* in Ohio." *Journal of the University Film Association* 26, no. 3 (1974): 39–44.

Bitzer, G. W. *Billy Bitzer: His Story*. New York: Farrar, Straus and Giroux, 1973.

Black, Gregory D. *Hollywood Censored: Morality Codes, Catholics, and the Movies*. Cambridge: Cambridge University Press, 1994.

Blassingame, John W. *The Slave Community: Plantation Life in the Antebellum South*. New York: Oxford University Press, 1979.

Blight, David W. *Beyond the Battlefield: Race, Memory and the American Civil War*. Amherst: University of Massachusetts Press, 2002.

———. *Race and Reunion: The Civil War in American Memory*. Cambridge, Mass.: Harvard University Press, 2001.

Blocker, Jack S. Jr. *Retreat from Reform: The Prohibition Movement in the United States 1890–1913*. Westport, Conn.: Greenwood Press, 1976.

Bloomfield, Maxwell. "Dixon's *The Leopard's Spots*: A Study in Popular Racism." In *The Negro in the South since 1865: Selected Essays in American Negro History*, 83–102, ed. Charles E. Wynes. Montgomery: University of Alabama Press, 1965.

Blumer, Herbert. *Movies and Conduct*. New York: Macmillan, 1933.

Blumenthal, Henry. "Woodrow Wilson and the Race Question." *Journal of Negro History* 48, no. 1 (January 1963): 1–21.

Bogle, Donald. *Blacks in American Films and Television: An Encylopedia*. New York: Garland, 1988.

———. *Toms, Coons, Mulattoes, Mammies and Bucks: An Interpretive History of Blacks in American Films*. 4th ed. Oxford: Roundhouse Press, 1994.

Boissel, Jean. *Gobineau biographie: mythes et réalité*. Paris: Berg International, 1993.

"Bollywood's Most Unwanted." www.rediff.com/entertai/2002/sep/11fil.htm, accessed on November 5, 2005.

Bowser, Eileen, "Griffith's Film Career before *The Adventures of Dollie*." In *Film before Griffith*, 367–73, ed. John L. Fell. Berkeley: University of California Press, 1983.

———. *The Transformation of Cinema 1907–1915*. New York: Charles Scribner's, 1990.

Brewster, Ben. "*Traffic in Souls*." *Cinema Journal* 31, no. 1 (Fall 1991): 37–56.

Brodie, Fawn M. *Thaddeus Stevens: Scourge of the South*. New York: W. W. Norton, 1959.

Brown, Karl. *Adventures with D. W. Griffith*, ed. Kevin Brownlow. London: Secker and Warburg, 1973.

Browne, Nick, ed. *Cahiers du cinéma, Vol. 3, 1969–1972: The Politics of Representation*. London: Routledge/BFI, 1990.

Brownlow, Kevin. *The Parade's Gone By*. London: Secker and Warburg, 1968.

Burnett, Ron, ed. *Explorations in Film Theory: Selected Essays from Ciné-Tracts*. Bloomington: Indiana University Press, 1991.

Carbine, Mary. "'The Finest Outside the Loop': Motion Picture Exhibition in Chicago's Black Metropolis, 1905–1928." *Camera Obscura* 23 (May 1990): 9–41.

Carter, Everett. "Cultural History Written with Lightning: The Significance of *The Birth of a Nation*." *American Quarterly* 12 (Fall 1960): 347–57. Reprinted in *Focus on "Birth of a Nation*," 133–43, ed. Fred Silva. Englewood Cliffs, N.J.: Prentice-Hall, 1971.

Casty, Alan. "The Films of D. W. Griffith: A Style for the Times." *Journal of Popular Film* 1, no. 2 (Spring 1972): 67–79.

Chadwick, Bruce. *The Reel Civil War: Mythmaking in American Film*. New York: Vintage Books, 2002.

Chalmers, David M. *Hooded Americanism: The History of the Ku Klux Klan*. Chicago: Quadrangle, 1968.

Chambers, Robert W. "The Sacrifice." *Film Comment* 21, no. 4 (July–August 1985): 72–73.

Chandler, James. "The Historical Novel Goes to Hollywood: Scott, Griffith, and Film Epic Today." In *The Romantics and Us: Essays on Literature and Culture*, 237–73. Ed. Gene W. Ruoff. New Brunswick, N.J.: Rutgers University Press, 1990. Reprinted in *The Birth of a Nation*, 225–49, ed. Robert Lang. New Brunswick, N.J.: Rutgers University Press, 1994.

Ciment, Michel. *Le crime à l écran: une histoire de l Amérique*. Paris: Gallimard, 1992.

Combs, Richard. "*The Birth of a Nation*." *Monthly Film Bulletin* 46, no. 544 (May 1979): 105–106.

Comolli, John-Louis and Narboni, Jean. "Cinema/ideology/criticism (1)." *Cahiers du cinéma*, no. 216 (October 1969): 11–15. Trans. Susan Bennett, in *Cahiers du cinéma, Vol. 3, 1969–1972: The Politics of Representation*, 58–67, ed. Nick Browne. London: Routledge/BFI, 1990.

Conn, Peter. *The Divided Mind: Ideology and Imagination in America, 1898–1917.* Cambridge: Cambridge University Press, 1983.

Cook, Christopher, ed. *The Dilys Powell Film Reader.* Manchester: Carcanet Press, 1991.

Cook, Raymond A. *Fire from the Flint: The Amazing Careers of Thomas Dixon.* Winston-Salem, N.C.: John F. Blair, 1968.

———. "The Man behind *The Birth of a Nation.*" *North Carolina Historical Review* 29 (October 1962): 519–40.

———. *Thomas Dixon.* New York: Twayne, 1974.

Cooper, John Milton Jr. *Pivotal Decades: The United States, 1900–1920.* New York : W. W. Norton, 1990.

———. *Walter Hines Page: The Southerner as American, 1855–1918.* Chapel Hill: University of North Carolina Press, 1977.

Cooper, Miriam, with Bonnie Herndon. *Dark Lady of the Silents: My Life in Early Hollywood.* Indianapolis: Bobbs-Merrill, 1973.

Coulter, E. Merton. *The South during Reconstruction 1865–1877.* Baton Rouge: Louisiana State University Press, 1947.

Courtney, Susan. *Hollywood Fantasies of Miscegenation: Spectacular Narratives of Gender and Race, 1903–1967.* Princeton: Princeton University Press, 2005.

Couvares, Francis G. "The Good Censor: Race, Sex, and Censorship in the Early Cinema." *Yale Journal of Criticism* 7, no. 2 (Fall 1994): 233–51.

Cranstone, E. L. "The 'Birth of a Nation' Controversy." *Sight and Sound* 16, no. 63 (Autumn 1947): 119.

Cripps, Thomas. "The Absent Presence in American Civil War Films." *Historical Journal of Film, Radio and Television* 14, no. 4 (1994): 367–76.

———. *Black Film as Genre.* Bloomington: Indiana University Press, 1978.

———. "The Death of Rastus: Negroes in American Films since 1945." *Phylon* 28, no. 3 (3rd qrt., 1967): 267–75.

———. "The Making of *The Birth of a Race*: The Emerging Politics of Identity in Silent Movies." In *The Birth of Whiteness*, 38–55, ed. Daniel Bernardi. New Brunswick, N.J.: Rutgers University Press, 1996.

———. "The Reaction of the Negro to the Motion Picture, *Birth of a Nation.*" *The Historian* 25, no. 3 (May 1963): 344–62. Reprinted in *Focus on "The Birth of a Nation,"* 111–24, ed. Fred Silva. Englewood Cliffs, N.J.: Prentice-Hall, 1971.

———. *Slow Fade to Black: The Negro in American Film, 1900–1942.* New York: Oxford University Press, 1977.

The Crisis.

Croly, David G., George Wakeman, and E. C. Howell. *Miscegenation: The Theory of the Blending of the Races, Applied to the American White Man and Negro.* London: Trübner, 1864.

Crowdus, Gary, ed. *The Political Companion to American Film.* Chicago: Lake View Press, 1994.

Cuniberti, John. *"The Birth of a Nation": A Formal Shot-by-Shot Analysis Together with Microfiche.* Woodbridge, Conn.: Research Publications, 1979.

Curtiss, Thomas Quinn. *Von Stroheim.* London: Angus and Robertson, 1971.

Daniel, Pete. *Lost Revolutions: The South in the 1950s.* Chapel Hill: University of North Carolina Press for the Smithsonian National Museum of American History, 2000.

———. *Standing at the Crossroads: Southern Life in the Twentieth Century*. Baltimore: Johns Hopkins University Press, 1996.

Daniels, Roger. *Asian America: Chinese and Japanese in the United States since 1850*. Seattle: University of Washington Press, 1988.

Davenport, F. Gavin Jr. "Thomas Dixon's Mythology of Southern History." *Journal of Southern History* 36, no. 3 (August 1970): 350–67.

Davis, Natalie Zemon. *Slaves on Screen: Film and Historical Vision*. Cambridge, Mass.: Harvard University Press, 2000.

Day, Caroline Bond. *A Study of Some Negro-White Families in the United States*, foreword and notes on the anthropometric data by Earnest A. Hooton. Harvard African Studies, no. 10. Cambridge, Mass.: Peabody Museum of Harvard University, 1932.

Diawara, Manthia, ed. *Black American Cinema*. London: Routledge, 1993.

———. "Black Spectatorship: Problems of Identification and Resistance." In *Black American Cinema*, 211–20, ed. Manthia Diawara. London: Routledge, 1993.

Dinnerstein, Leonard. *The Leo Frank Case*. New York: Columbia University Press, 1968.

Dittmer, John. *Black Georgia in the Progressive Era, 1900–1920*. Urbana: University of Illinois Press, 1977.

Dixon, Thomas Jr. *The Clansman: An Historical Romance of the Ku Klux Klan*. New York: Doubleday, Page, 1905.

———. *The Leopard's Spots: A Romance of the White Man's Burden*. London: Doubleday, Page, 1902.

———. *The One Woman: A Story of Modern Utopia*. New York: Doubleday, Page, 1903.

———. *The Sins of the Father: A Romance of the South*. New York: D. Appleton, 1912.

Donald, David H. *Charles Sumner and the Rights of Man*. New York: Alfred A. Knopf, 1970.

D'Ooge, Craig, ed. "*The Birth of a Nation*: Symposium on Classic Film Discusses Inaccuracies and Virtues." *Library of Congress Information Bulletin* 53, no. 13 (June 27, 1994): 263–66.

Dray, Philip. *At the Hands of Persons Unknown: The Lynching of Black America*. New York: Random House, 2002.

Du Bois, W. E. B. *Black Reconstruction: An Essay toward a History of the Part which Black Folk Played in the Attempt to Reconstruct Democracy in America, 1860–1880*. New York: Russell and Russell, 1935.

———. "Reconstruction and Its Benefits." *American Historical Review* 15, no. 4 (July 1910): 781–99.

———. *The Souls of Black Folk: Essays and Sketches*. New York: A. C. McClurg, 1903.

Dunning, William Archibald. *Essays on the Civil War and Reconstruction and Related Topics*. New York: Macmillan, 1897.

———. *Reconstruction, Political and Economic, 1865–1877*. New York: Harper and Brothers, 1907.

Durden, Robert F. *James Shepherd Pike: Republicanism and the American Negro, 1850–1882* (Durham, N.C.: Duke University Press, 1957).

Dyer, Richard. "Into the Light: The Whiteness of the South in *The Birth of a Nation*." In *Dixie Debates: Perspectives on Southern Culture*, 165–76, ed. Richard H. King and Helen Taylor. London: Pluto Press, 1996.

———. "A White Star." *Sight and Sound* 3, no. 8 (August 1993): 22–24.

Edwards, Ann. *The Road to Tara: The Life of Margaret Mitchell*. London: Hodder and Stoughton, 1983.

Edwards, Robert. "Turner Pulls Plug on Silent Classic." *Classic Images* no. 246 (December 1995): 14.

Ehrlich, Evelyn. "The Civil War in Early Film: Origin and Development of a Genre." *Southern Quarterly* 19, nos. 3–4 (Spring–Summer 1981): 70–82.

Eisenstein, Sergei. "Dickens, Griffith and the Film Today." In *Film Form: Essays in Film Theory*, 195–255, ed. and trans. Jay Leyda. New York: Harcourt, Brace, 1949.

Eisenstein, S. M. "Purveyors of Spiritual Poison." *Sight and Sound*, 16, no. 63 (Autumn 1947): 103–105.

Eisner, Lotte H. *The Haunted Screen: Expressionism in the German Cinema and the Influence of Max Reinhardt*. Trans. Roger Greaves. London: Thames and Hudson, 1969.

Ely, Richard T. *Ground under Our Feet: An Autobiography*. New York: Macmillan, 1938.

Evans, Richard J. *In Defence of History*. London: Granta Books, 1997.

Everett, Anna. *Returning the Gaze: A Genealogy of Black Film Criticism, 1909–1949*. Durham, N.C.: Duke University Press, 2001.

Everson, William K. *American Silent Film*. New York: Oxford University Press, 1978.

Farr, Robert. "Hollywood Mensch: Max Davidson." *Griffithiana* no. 55–56 (September 1996): 107–25.

Feldman, Charles M. *The National Board of Censorship (Review) of Motion Pictures, 1909–1922*. New York: Arno Press, 1977.

Fell, Robert L., ed. *Film before Griffith*. Berkeley: University of California Press, 1983.

"Fighting a Vicious Film—Protest against *The Birth of a Nation*." Pamphlet published by the Boston Branch of the NAACP, spring 1915.

Finch, Minnie. *The NAACP: Its Fight for Justice*. Metuchen, N.J.: Scarecrow Press, 1981.

Fleener, Nickie. "Answering Film with Film: The Hampton Epilogue, A Positive Alternative to the Negative Black Stereotypes Presented in *The Birth of a Nation*." *Journal of Popular Film and Television*, no. 4 (1980): 400–25.

Fleener-Marzec, Nickieann. *D. W. Griffith's "The Birth of a Nation": Controversy, Suppression, and the First Amendment as It Applies to Filmic Expression, 1915–1973*. New York: Arno Press, 1980.

Fletcher, Marvin. *The Black Soldier and Officer in the United States Army, 1891–1917*. Columbia: University of Missouri Press, 1974.

Foner, Eric. *Reconstruction: America's Unfinished Revolution, 1863–1877*. New York: Harper and Row, 1988.

Foner, Philip S. *History of Black Americans*, Vol. 1: *From Africa to the Emergence of the Cotton Kingdom*. Westport, Conn.: Greenwood Press, 1975.

Forman, Henry James. *Our Movie Made Children*. New York: Macmillan, 1933.

Fortier, Paul A. "Gobineau and German Racism." *Comparative Literature* 19, no. 4 (Autumn 1967): 341–50.

Fowler, David H. *Northern Attitudes towards Interracial Marriage: Legislation and Public Opinion in the Middle Atlantic and the States of the Old Northwest, 1780–1930*. New York: Garland, 1987.

Fox, Stephen R. *The Guardian of Boston: William Monroe Trotter*. New York: Atheneum, 1970.

Franklin, John Hope. *"Birth of a Nation*—Propaganda as History." *The Massachusetts Review* 20 (Autumn, 1979): 417–33. Reprinted in *Race and History: Selected Essays 1938–1988*, 10–24, ed. John Hope Franklin. Baton Rouge: Louisiana State University Press, 1989.

Franklin, John Hope and Alfred A. Moss Jr. *From Slavery to Freedom: A History of African Americans*. 7th ed. New York: Alfred A. Knopf, 1994.

Frederickson, George M. *The Black Image in the White Mind: The Debate on Afro-American Character and Destiny, 1817–1914*. New York: Harper and Row, 1971.

Freeman, Douglas Southall. *R. E. Lee: A Biography*. Vol. IV. New York and London: Charles Scribner's Sons, 1934.

Freidel, Frank. *The Splendid Little War*. Boston: Little, Brown, 1958.

French, Philip. "Black and White Movie Turns Grey." *Observer* [London], September 5, 1993.

Fulton, A. R. "Editing in *The Birth of a Nation*." In Fulton, *Motion Pictures: The Development of an Art from Silent Films to the Age of Television*, 89–101. Norman: University of Oklahoma Press, 1960. Reprinted in *Focus on "The Birth of a Nation,"* 144–53, ed. Fred Silva. Englewood Cliffs, N.J.: Prentice-Hall, 1971.

Fyne, Robert. *The Hollywood Propaganda of World War II*. Lanham, Md.: Scarecrow Press, 1997.

Gaines, Jane. "*The Birth of a Nation* and *Within Our Gates*: Two Tales of the American South." In *Dixie Debates: Perspectives on Southern Culture*, 177–92, ed. Richard H. King and Helen Taylor. London: Pluto Press, 1996.

Gaines, Jane. "White Privilege and Looking Relations: Race and Gender in Feminist Film Theory." *Cultural Critique* no. 4 (Fall 1986): 59–79.

Gaines, Jane and Neil Lerner. "The Orchestration of Affect: The Motif of Barbarism in Breil's *The Birth of a Nation* Score." In *The Sounds of Early Cinema*, 252–68, ed. Richard Abel and Rick Altman. Bloomington: University of Indiana Press, 2001.

Gaines, Jane M. *Fire and Desire: Mixed-Race Movies in the Silent Era*. Chicago: University of Chicago Press, 2001.

Gaines, Jane M. and Michael Renov, eds. *Collecting Visible Evidence*. Minneapolis: University of Minnesota Press, 1999.

Gallagher, Brian. "Racist Ideology and Black Abnormality in the Birth of a Nation." *Phylon* 43, no. 1 (1st qrt. 1982): 68–76.

Gallagher, Gary W. and Alan T. Nolan. *The Myth of the Lost Cause and Civil War History*. Bloomington: Indiana University Press, 2000.

Geduld, Harry M., ed. *Focus on D. W. Griffith*. Englewood Cliffs, N.J.: Prentice-Hall, 1971.

Gill, David. "*The Birth of a Nation*: Orphan or Pariah?" *Griffithiana* no. 60–61 (October 1997): 16–29.

Gilmore, Al-Tony. *Bad Nigger! The National Impact of Jack Johnson*. Port Washington: Kennikat Press, 1975.

Gish, Lillian, with Ann Pinchot. *The Movies, Mr. Griffith and Me*. London: W. H. Allen, 1969.

Goldberg, Robert Alan. *Hooded Empire: The Ku Klux Klan in Colorado*. Urbana: University of Illinois Press, 1981.

Goldman, Eric F. *Rendezvous with Destiny—A History of Modern American Reform*. New York: Vintage, 1977.

————. *The Tragedy of Lyndon Johnson*. New York: Dell, 1969.

Gomery, Douglas J. "The Coming of the Talkies: Invention, Innovation, and Diffusion." In *The American Film Industry*, 192–211, ed. Tino Balio. Madison: University of Wisconsin Press, 1976.

Goodwyn, Lawrence. *Democratic Promise: The Populist Movement in America*. New York: Oxford University Press, 1976.

Gossett, Thomas F. *Uncle Tom's Cabin and American Culture*. Dallas: Southern Methodist University Press, 1985.

Graham, Allison. *Framing the South: Hollywood, Television, and Race during the Civil Rights Struggle*. Baltimore: Johns Hopkins University Press, 2001.

Graham, Cooper C., Steven Higgins, Elaine Mancini, and João Vieira. *D. W. Griffith and the Biograph Company*. Metuchen, N.J.: Scarecrow Press, 1985.

Grant, Madison. *The Passing of the Great Race; or the Racial Basis of European History*. New York: Charles Scribner's, 1916.

Grazia, Edward de and Roger K. Newman. *Banned Films: Movies, Censors, and the First Amendment*. New York: R. R. Bowker, 1982.

Green, J. Roland. "Micheaux v. Griffith." *Griffithiana*, 60–61 (1997): 32–49.

Grieveson, Lee. "Fighting Films: Race, Morality, and the Governing of Cinema, 1912–1915." *Cinema Journal* 38, no. 1 (Fall 1998): 40–72.

————. *Policing Cinema: Movies and Censorship in Early-Twentieth-Century America*. Berkeley: University of California Press, 2004.

Griffith, David W. "The Miracle of Modern Photography." *The Mentor* 9, no. 6 (July 1921): 67.

David W. Griffith Papers, 1897–1954 (DWGP). Frederick, Md.: University Publications of America, 1982. Microfilm in Library of Congress.

Griffith, David W. "The Rise and Fall of Free Speech in America." Los Angeles: n. p., 1916. Partly reprinted in *The Movies in Our Midst*, 132–35, ed. Gerald Mast. Chicago: University of Chicago Press, 1982.

Griffith, D. W. "The Birth of a Nation." *Sight and Sound* 16, no. 61 (Spring 1947): 32.

D. W. Griffith: Father of Film, documentary film directed by Kevin Brownlow and David Gill (1993).

Griffith, Mrs. D. W. [Linda Arvidson]. *When the Movies Were Young*. New York: Dover, 1969.

Grindon, Leger. *Shadows on the Past: Studies in the Historical Fiction Film*. Philadelphia: Temple University Press, 1994.

Grittner, Frederick K. *White Slavery: Myth, Ideology, and American Law*. New York: Garland Press, 1990.

"G.T." "*The Birth of a Nation*: G. W. 'Billy' Bitzer." *American Cinematographer* 80, no. 3 (March 1999): 118.

Guerrero, Ed. *Framing Blackness: The African American Image in Film*. Philadelphia: Temple University Press, 1993.

Gunning, Sandra. *Race, Rape and Lynching: The Red Record of American Literature, 1890–1912*. New York: Oxford University Press, 1996.

Gunning, Tom. *D. W. Griffith and the Origins of American Narrative Film: The Early Years at Biograph*. Urbana: University of Illinois Press, 1991.

Hackett, Francis. "Brotherly Love." *The New Republic* 7 (March 20, 1915). Reprinted in *The Birth of a Nation*, 161–63, ed. Robert Lang. New Brunswick, N.J.: Rutgers University Press, 1994.

Hall, Ben M. *The Best Remaining Seats: The Story of the Golden Age of the Movie Palace*. New York: Clarkson N. Potter, 1961.

Halpern, Rick. "Organized Labor, Black Workers, and the Twentieth Century South: The Emerging Revision." In *Race and Class in the American South since 1890*, 43–76, ed. Melvyn Stokes and Rick Halpern. Oxford: Berg, 1994.

Hammond, Michael, "'A Soul-stirring Appeal to Every Briton': The Reception of *The Birth of a Nation* in Britain (1915–1916)." *Film History* 11, no. 3 (1999): 353–70.

Hampton, Benjamin B. *A History of the Movies*. New York: Covici, Friede, 1931.

Harlan, Louis R. and Raymond W. Smock. *The Booker T. Washington Papers*, Vol. 13: *1914–1915*. Urbana: University of Illinois Press, 1984.

Hart, James, ed. *The Man Who Invented Hollywood: The Autobiography of D. W. Griffith*. Louisville, Ky.: Touchstone, 1972.

Haver, Ronald. *David O. Selznick's Hollywood*. London: Secker and Warburg, 1980.

Hays, Will. *The Memoirs of Will H. Hays*. New York: Doubleday, 1955.

Healy, David F. *U. S. Expansionism: The Imperialist Urge in the 1890s*. Madison: University of Wisconsin Press, 1970.

Heath, Stephen. "Questions of Property: Film and Nationhood." In *Explorations in Film Theory: Selected Essays from Ciné-Tracts*, 180–90, ed. Ron Burnett. Bloomington: Indiana University Press, 1991.

Henderson, Robert M. *D. W. Griffith: His Life and Work*. New York: Oxford University Press, 1972.

———. *D. W. Griffith: The Years at Biograph*. New York: Farrar, Straus and Giroux, 1970.

Herndon, William Henry and Jesse William Weik. *Herndon's Lincoln: The True Story of a Great Life...The History and Personal Recollections of Abraham Lincoln by William Henry Herndon*. Chicago: Belford, Clarke, 1889.

Higham, John. *History: Professional Scholarship in America*. Baltimore: Johns Hopkins University Press, 1983.

———. *Strangers in the Land: Patterns of American Nativism, 1860–1925*. New Brunswick, N.J.: Rutgers University Press, 1955.

Hilger, Michael. *From Savage to Nobleman: Images of Native Americans in Film*. Lanham, Md.: Scarecrow Press, 1995.

Hoberman, J. "We Must Remember This." *Village Voice*, November 30, 1993, 2–4.

Hofmann, Charles. *Sounds for Silents*. New York: Drama Books Specialists, 1970.

Hofstadter, Richard. *Social Darwinism in American Thought, 1860–1915*. Philadelphia: University of Pennsylvania Press, 1944.

Holt, W. Stull, ed. *Historical Scholarship in the United States, 1876–1901: As Revealed in the Correspondence of Herbert B. Adams*. Johns Hopkins Studies in Historical and Political Science, 56, no. 4. Baltimore: Johns Hopkins University Press, 1938.

hooks, bell. *Black Looks: Race and Representation*. Boston, Mass.: South End Press, 1992.

———. "The Oppositional Gaze: Black Female Spectators." In *Black American Cinema*, 288–302, ed. Manthia Diawara. London: Routledge, 1993.

———. *Reel to Real: Race, Sex, and Class at the Movies*. London: Routledge, 1996.

Horn, Stanley F. *Invisible Empire: The Story of the Ku Klux Klan, 1866–1871*. Boston, Mass.: Houghton Mifflin, 1939.

Horowitz, Joseph H. *Wagner Nights: An American History.* Berkeley: University of California Press, 1994.

Horsman, Reginald. *Race and Manifest Destiny: The Origins of American Racial Anglo-Saxonism.* Cambridge, Mass.: Harvard University Press, 1981.

Huff, Theodore. *A Shot Analysis of D. W. Griffith's "The Birth of a Nation."* New York: Museum of Modern Art, 1961.

Hughes, Langston. *Fight for Freedom: The Story of the NAACP.* New York: W. W. Norton, 1962.

Hui, Arlene. "Miscegenation in Mainstream American Cinema; Representing Interracial Relationships, 1913–1956." Ph.D. diss., University of London, 2006.

Hurwitz, Michael R. *D. W. Griffith's "The Birth of a Nation": The Film that Transformed America.* North Charleston, S.C.: BookSurge, 2006.

Inscoe, John. "*The Clansman* on Stage and Screen: North Carolina Reacts." *North Carolina Historical Review* 64, no. 2 (April 1987): 139–61.

Jacobs, Lewis. *The Rise of the American Film: A Critical History.* New York: Harcourt, Brace, 1939.

Jerome, V. J. *The Negro in Hollywood Films.* New York: Masses and Mainstream, 1950.

Jesionowski, Joyce E. *Thinking in Pictures: Domestic Structures in D. W. Griffith's Biograph Films.* Berkeley: University of California Press, 1987.

"John Ford's *Young Mr. Lincoln,* a Collective Text by the Editors of *Cahiers du cinéma.*" *Cahiers du cinéma,* no. 223 (August 1970): 29–47. Trans. Helen Lackner and Diana Matias in *Screen* 13, no. 3 (Autumn 1972): 5–44.

Jones, Maldwyn A. *The Limits of Liberty: American History, 1607–1980.* New York: Oxford University Press, 1983.

Jowett, Garth. "'A Capacity for Evil': The 1915 Supreme Court Mutual Decision." *Historical Journal of Film, Radio and Television* 9, no. 1 (1989): 59–78.

Jowett, Garth, Ian C. Jarvie, and Kathryn H. Fuller. *Children and the Movies: Media Influence and the Payne Fund Controversy.* Cambridge: Cambridge University Press, 1996.

Jozajtis, Kris. "'The Eyes of All People Are Upon Us': American Civil Religion and the Birth of Hollywood." In *Representing Religion in World Cinema: Filmmaking, Mythmaking, Culture Making,* 239–61, ed. S. Brent Plate. London: Palgrave/St. Martin's, 2003.

Jungquist, Hazel. "Viewing D. W. Griffith's *The Birth of a Nation:* A First Hand Account," ed. Robert K. Klepper. *Classic Images* no. 245 (November 1995): 36–37.

Kagan, Norman. "Two Classic War Films of the Silent Era: *Birth of a Nation* and *Shoulder Arms.*" *Film and History* 4, no. 3 (September 1974): 1–5, 18.

Kalinak, Kathryn. *Settling the Score: Music and the Classical Hollywood Film.* Madison: University of Wisconsin Press, 1992.

Kaplan, Sidney. "The Miscegenation Issue in the Election of 1864." *Journal of Negro History* 34, no. 3 (July 1949): 274–343.

Keil, Charlie. "Transition through Tension: Stylistic Diversity in the Late Griffith Biographs." *Cinema Journal,* 28, no. 3 (Spring 1989): 22–40.

Kellogg, Charles F. *NAACP: A History of the National Association for the Advancement of Colored People,* Vol. 1: *1909–1920.* Baltimore: Johns Hopkins University Press, 1967.

Kennedy, David M. *Birth Control in America: The Career of Margaret Sanger*. New Haven: Yale University Press, 1970.

Kindem, Gorham. "The Demise of Kinemacolor: Technological, Legal, Economic, and Aesthetic Problems in Early Color Cinema History." *Cinema Journal* 20, no. 2 (Spring 1981): 3–14.

King, Richard and Helen Taylor, eds. *Dixie Debates: Perspectives on Southern Culture*, London: Pluto Press, 1996.

Kirby, Jack Temple. "D. W. Griffith's Racial Portraiture." *Phylon* 39, no. 2 (1978): 118–27.

Klinger, Barbara. *Melodrama and Meaning: History, Culture, and the Films of Douglas Sirk*. Bloomington: Indiana University Press, 1994.

Knight, Arthur. *The Liveliest Art: A Panoramic History of the Movies*, rev. ed. New York: Macmillan, 1978; originally published in 1957.

Koppes, Clayton R. and Gregory D. Black. *Hollywood Goes to War: Patriotism, Movies and the Second World War from "Ninotchka" to "Mrs Miniver."* London: Tauris Parke Paperbacks, 2000.

Koszarski, Richard. *An Evening's Entertainment: The Age of the Silent Feature Picture, 1915–1928*. Berkeley: University of California Press, 1990.

———. "'So Long, Master …': Stroheim, Griffith, and the Griffith Studio." *Griffithiana*, no. 71 (2001): 45–81.

Kousser, J. Morgan. *The Shaping of Southern Politics: Suffrage Restriction and the Establishment of the One-Party South, 1880–1910*. New Haven: Yale University Press, 1974.

Kracauer, Siegfried. *Theory of Film: The Redemption of Physical Reality*. New York: Oxford University Press, 1960.

Lack, Russell. *Twenty Four Frames Under: A Buried History of Film Music*. London: Quartet Books, 1997.

Landry, Robert J. "'Race': Box Office but Booby Trapped.'" *Variety* (January 8, 1958): 15.

Lang, Robert, ed. *The Birth of a Nation: D. W. Griffith, Director*. New Brunswick, N.J.: Rutgers University Press, 1994.

Langum, David J. *Crossing over the Line: Legislating Morality and the Mann Act*. Chicago: University of Chicago Press, 1994.

Leab, Dan. "Blacks in American Cinema." In *The Political Companion to American Film*, 41–50, ed. Gary Crowdus. Chicago: Lake View Press, 1994.

Leab, Daniel J. *From Sambo to Superspade: The Black Experience in Motion Pictures*. London: Secker and Warburg, 1975.

Lefler, Hugh Talmadge and Albert Ray Newsome. *North Carolina: The History of a Southern State*. Chapel Hill: University of North Carolina Press, 1973.

Lejeune, Anthony, ed. *The C. A. Lejeune Film Reader*. Manchester: Carcanet Press, 1991.

Lester, J. C. and D. L. Wilson. *Ku Klux Klan: Its Origin, Growth and Disbandment*, intro. by Walter L. Fleming. New York: Neale Publishing, 1905.

Levenson, J. C., Ernest Samuels, Charles Vandersee, Viola Hopkins Winner, eds. *The Letters of Henry Adams*, Vol. IV: *1892–1899*. Cambridge, Mass.: Harvard University Press, 1988.

Lewis, David L. *W. E. B. Du Bois: Biography of a Race, 1868–1919*. New York: Henry Holt, 1993.

L.G.A. *Birth of a Nation, Monthly Film Bulletin* 20, no. 228 (January 1953): 3–4.

Lindsay, Vachel. *The Art of the Moving Picture*. New York: Modern Library, 2000; reprint of 1915 ed.

Link, Arthur S., ed. *The Papers of Woodrow Wilson*, Vol. 32: *January 1–April 16, 1915*. Princeton: Princeton University Press, 1980.

———, ed. *The Papers of Woodrow Wilson*, Vol. 33: *April 17–July 21 1915*. Princeton: Princeton University Press, 1980.

———, ed. *The Papers of Woodrow Wilson*, Vol. 47: *March 13–May 12, 1918*. Princeton: Princeton University Press, 1984.

———. *Woodrow Wilson*: Vol. 2, *The New Freedom*. Princeton: Princeton University Press, 1956.

Linn, Brian McAllister. *The Philippine War, 1899–1902*. Lawrence: University Press of Kansas, 2000.

'Listmania! 25 Most Controversial Films of All Time,' www.amazon.com, accessed on November 5, 2005.

Litwack, Leon F. *"The Birth of a Nation."* In *Past Imperfect: History According to the Movies*, 136–41, ed. Mark C. Carnes, Ted Mico, John Miller-Monzon, and David Rubel. London: Cassell, 1996.

Lord, Daniel A. *Played by Ear: The Autobiography of Daniel A. Lord, S. J.* New York: Image Books/Doubleday, 1959.

Lorini, Alessandra. *Rituals of Race: American Public Culture and the Search for Racial Democracy*. Charlottesville: University Press of Virginia, 1999.

Lott, Eric. *Love and Theft: Blackface Minstrelsy and the American Working Class*. New York: Oxford University Press, 1993.

Louvish, Simon. "Burning Crosses." *Sight and Sound* 10, no. 9 (September 2000): 12–13.

Love, Eric T. L. *Race over Empire: Racism and U.S. Imperialism, 1865–1900*. Chapel Hill: University of North Carolina Press, 2004.

Lowery, Shearon A. and Melvin L. DeFleur. *Milestones in Mass Communication Research: Media Effects*. New York: Longman, 1995.

Luebke, Frederick C. *Bonds of Loyalty: German-Americans and World War I*. DeKalb: Northern Illinois University Press, 1974.

Lynch, John R. *The Facts of Reconstruction*. New York: Neale Publishing, 1913.

Lynn, Kenneth S. *Charlie Chaplin and His Times*. London: Aurum Press, 2002.

Lyons, Charles. *The New Censors: Movies and the Culture Wars*. Philadelphia: Temple University Press, 1997.

MacDonald, Laurence E. *The Invisible Art of Film Music: A Comprehensive History*. New York: Ardsley House, 1998.

MacLean, Nancy. *Behind the Mask of Chivalry: The Making of the Second Ku Klux Klan*. New York: Oxford University Press, 1994.

———. "The Leo Frank Case Reconsidered: Gender and Sexual Politics in the Making of Reactionary Populism." *Journal of American History* 78, no. 3 (December 1991): 917–48.

The Making of a Legend: "Gone With the Wind," documentary film directed by David Hinton (1989).

Malcolm, Derek. "The Art of the States." *Guardian* [London], November 25, 1999, 11.

Maltby, Richard. "*The King of Kings* and the Czar of All the Rushes: The Propriety of the Christ Story." In *Controlling Hollywood: Censorship and Regulation in the Studio Era,* 60–86, ed. Matthew Bernstein. New Brunswick, N.J.: Rutgers University Press, 2000.

———. "The Social Evil, the Moral Order, and the Melodramatic Imagination, 1890–1915." In *Melodrama: Stage, Picture, Screen,* 214–30, ed. Jacky Bratten, Jim Cook, and Christine Gledhill. London: BFI, 1994.

Marks, Carole. *Farewell—We're Good and Gone: The Great Black Migration.* Bloomington: Indiana University Press, 1989.

Marks, Martin M. *Music and the Silent Film: Contexts and Case Studies, 1895–1924.* New York: Oxford University Press, 1997.

Martin, Jeffrey B. "Film Out of Theatre: D. W. Griffith, *Birth of a Nation* and the Melodrama *The Clansman.*" *Literature/Film Quarterly* 18, no. 2 (1990): 87–95.

Marx, Karl. *A Contribution to the Critique of Political Economy.* In Karl Marx and Friedrich Engels, *Selected Works,* 1 (Moscow: Progress Publishers, 1969).

Mast, Gerald, ed.. *The Movies in Our Midst: Documents in the Cultural History of Film in America.* Chicago: University of Chicago Press, 1982.

May, Lary. *Screening Out the Past: The Birth of Mass Culture and the Motion Picture Industry.* Chicago: University of Chicago Press, 1983.

May, Robert E. *John A. Quitman: Old South Crusader.* Baton Rouge: Louisiana State University Press, 1985.

———. *Manifest Destiny's Underworld: Filibustering in Antebellum America.* Chapel Hill: University of North Carolina Press, 2002.

———. *The Southern Dream of a Caribbean Empire, 1854–1861.* Gainesville: University Press of Florida, 2002; originally published in 1973.

McCarthy, Kathleen D. "Nickel Vice and Virtue: Movie Censorship in Chicago, 1907–1915." *Journal of Popular Film* 5, no. 1 (1976): 37–55.

McClymer, John F. "The Federal Government and the Americanization Movement, 1915–24." *Prologue: The Journal of the National Archives* 10, no. 1 (Spring 1978): 22–41.

McGee, Brian R. "Thomas Dixon's *The Clansman*: Radicals, Reactionaries, and the Anticipated Utopia." *Southern Communications Journal* 65, no. 4 (Summer 2000): 300–17.

McPherson, James M. *Battle Cry of Freedom: The Civil War Era.* London: Penguin, 1990.

McPherson, Tara. "Both Kinds of Arms: Remembering the Civil War." *Velvet Light Trap,* no. 35 (Spring 1995): 3–18.

Meer, Sarah. *Uncle Tom Mania: Slavery, Minstrelsy, and Transatlantic Culture in the 1850s.* Athens: University of Georgia Press, 2005.

Meigs, Mark. *Optimism at Armageddon: Voices of American Participants in the First World War.* Basingstoke: Macmillan, 1997.

Merk, Frederick. *Slavery and the Annexation of Texas.* New York: Knopf, 1972.

Merritt, Russell. "Dixon, Griffith, and the Southern Legend." *Cinema Journal* 12, no. 1 (Fall 1972): 26–45.

———. "D. W. Griffith's *The Birth of a Nation*: Going after Little Sister." In *Close Viewings: An Anthology of New Film Criticism,* 215–37, ed. Peter Lehman. Tallahassee: Florida State University Press, 1990.

———. "Nickelodeon Theaters, 1905–1914: Building an Audience for the Movies." In *The American Film Industry*, 59–79, ed. Tino Balio. Madison: University of Wisconsin Press, 1976.

———. "Rescued from a Perilous Nest: D. W. Griffith's Escape from Theatre into Film." *Cinema Journal* 21, no. 1 (Fall 1981): 2–30.

Miller, James A. "The Case of Early Black Cinema." In "Race and Cultural Production: Responses to *The Birth of a Nation*," ed. Linda Steiner. *Critical Studies in Mass Communication*, 10, no. 2 (June 1993): 181–84.

Mitchell, Alice Miller. *Children and Movies*. Chicago: University of Chicago Press, 1929.

Mitry, Jean. *The Aesthetics and Psychology of the Cinema*, trans. Christopher King. London: Athlone Press, 1998; originally published in 1963.

———. "Naissance d'une Nation," in "Griffith." Supplement to *L'Avant Scène du Cinéma*, no. 45 (February 1, 1965): 83–89.

Mixon, Gregory. *The Atlanta Riot: Race, Class and Violence in a New South City*. Gainesville: University Press of Florida, 2005.

Moore, Douglas Cameron, "A Study of the Influence of the Film *The Birth of a Nation* on the Attitudes of Selected High School White Students toward Negroes," Ph.D. diss., University of Illinois, Urbana-Champaign, 1971.

Moore, John Hammond. "South Carolina's Reaction to the Photoplay *The Birth of a Nation*." *Proceedings of the South Carolina Historical Association* 33 (1963): 30–40.

Moran, Rachel F. *Interracial Intimacy: The Regulation of Race and Romance*. Chicago: University of Chicago Press, 2001.

Mueller, Matt. "Birth of an Industry." *Empire* no. 51 (September 1993): 64–67.

Muller, Philip R. "Look Back without Anger: A Reappraisal of William A. Dunning." *Journal of American History* 61 (1974): 325–38.

Münsterberg, Hugo. *The Photoplay: A Psychological Study*. New York: D. Appleton, 1916.

Musser, Charles. *Before the Nickelodeon: Edwin S. Porter and the Edison Manufacturing Company*. Berkeley: University of California Press, 1991.

———. *The Emergence of Cinema: The American Screen to 1907*. New York: Charles Scribner's Sons, 1990.

NAACP Papers (NAACPP), Microfilm and Paper. Library of Congress, Washington, D.C.

Naylor, David. *American Picture Palaces: The Architecture of Fantasy*. New York: Van Rostrand Reinhold, 1981.

———. *Great American Movie Theaters*. Washington, D.C.: Preservation Press, 1987.

Nelson, Al P. and Mel R. Jones. *A Silent Siren Song: The Aitken Brothers' Hollywood Odyssey, 1905–1926*. New York: Cooper Square Press, 2000.

Newman, Kim. *Wild West Movies, or, How the West Was Found, Won, Lost, Lied About, Filmed and Forgotten*. London: Bloomsbury, 1990.

New York Times Encyclopedia of Film, 1896–1928, ed., Gene Brown. New York: Times Books, 1984.

The New York Times Film Reviews 1913–1968, Vol. 1: *1913–1931*. New York: New York Times and Arno Press, 1970.

Nicolay, John G. and John Hay. *Abraham Lincoln: A History*, 10 vols. New York: Century, 1890.

Niver, Kemp R. *David W. Griffith: His Biograph Films in Perspective*. Los Angeles: Niver, 1974.

Noble, Peter. "The Negro in *The Birth of a Nation*." In Noble, *The Negro in Films*, 33–43 (London: Skelton Robinson, 1948). Reprinted in *Focus on "Birth of a Nation,"* 125–32, ed. Fred Silva. Englewood Cliffs, N.J.: Prentice-Hall, 1971.

———. "A Note on an Idol." *Sight and Sound* 15, no. 59 (Autumn 1946): 81–82.

Oakes, Francis. "Whitman and Dixon: A Strange Case of Borrowing." *Georgia Review* 11, no. 3 (Fall 1957): 333–40.

O'Dell, Paul, with Anthony Slide. *Griffith and the Rise of Hollywood*. New York: A. S. Barnes/A. Zwemmer, 1970.

Olsen, Otto H. *Carpetbaggers Crusade: The Life of Albion Winegar Tourgée*. Baltimore: Johns Hopkins University Press, 1965.

Oney, Steve. *And the Dead Shall Rise: The Murder of Mary Phagan and the Lynching of Leo Frank*. New York: Pantheon Books, 2003.

Parkinson, David, ed. *Mornings in the Dark: The Graham Greene Film Reader*. Manchester: Carcanet Press 1993.

Pascoe, Peggy. "Miscegenation Law, Court Cases, and Ideologies of 'Race' in Twentieth-Century America." In *Sex, Love, Race: Crossing Boundaries in North American History*, 464–90, ed. Martha Hodes. New York: New York University Press, 1999.

Patler, Nicholas. *Jim Crow and the Wilson Administration: Protesting Federal Segregation in the Early Twentieth Century*. Boulder: University of Colorado Press, 2004.

Patton, Cindy. "White Racism/Black Signs: Censorship and Images of Race Relations." *Journal of Communication* 45, no. 2 (Spring 1995): 65–77.

Paulin, Scott D. "Richard Wagner and the Fantasy of Cinematic Unity: The Idea of the *Gesamtkunstwerk* in the History and Theory of Film Music." In *Music and Cinema*, 58–84, ed. James Buhler, Caryl Flinn, and David Neumeyer. Hanover, N.H.: University Press of New England, 2000.

Pearson, Roberta E. *Eloquent Gestures: The Transformation of Performance Style in the Griffith Biograph Films*. Berkeley: University of California Press, 1992.

Pease, Donald E., ed. *National Identities and Post-Americanist Narratives*. Durham, N.C.: Duke University Press, 1994.

Peterson, Merrill D. *Lincoln in American Memory*. New York: Oxford University Press, 1994.

Peterson, Ruth C. and Louis L. Thurstone. *Motion Pictures and the Social Attitudes of Children*. New York: Macmillan, 1933.

Petric, Vlada. "Two Lincoln Assassinations by D. W. Griffith." *Quarterly Review of Film Studies* 3, no. 3 (Summer 1978): 345–69.

Phillips, Mike. "White Lies." *Sight and Sound* 4, no. 6 (June 1994): 69.

Pike, James S. *The Prostrate State: South Carolina under Negro Government*. New York: D. Appleton, 1874.

Pildas, Ave. *Movie Palaces*. New York: Clarkson N. Potter, 1980.

Pinsky, Mark I. "Racism, History and Mass Media: Birth of a Nation, Gone With the Wind, The Greensboro Massacre." *Jump Cut*, no. 28 (1983): 66–67.

S. Brent Plate, ed. *Representing Religion in World Cinema: Filmmaking, Mythmaking, Culture Making*. London: Palgrave/St. Martin's, 2003.

Platt, David. *Celluloid Power: Social Film Criticism from "The Birth of a Nation" to "Judgement at Nuremberg."* Metuchen, N.J.: Scarecrow Press, 1992.

Porter, Horace. *Campaigning with Grant.* New York: Century, 1897.

Projansky, Sarah. "The Elusive/Ubiquitous Representation of Rape: A Historical Survey of Rape in U.S. Film, 1903–1972." *Cinema Journal* 41, no. 1 (Fall 2001): 63–90.

Radway, Janice A. *Reading the Romance: Women, Patriarchy, and Popular Culture.* Chapel Hill: University of North Carolina Press, 1984.

Randel, William P. *The Ku Klux Klan: A Century of Infamy.* Philadelphia: Chilton Books, 1965.

Ramsaye, Terry. *A Million and One Nights: A History of the Motion Picture,* 1 vol. ed. London: Frank Cass, 1964, originally published in 1926.

Reddick, L. D. "Educational Programs for the Improvement of Race Relations: Motion Pictures, Radio, the Press, and Libraries." *Journal of Negro Education* 13, no. 3 (Summer 1944): 367–89.

Reid, Mark A. "African-American Filmmakers." In *The Political Companion to American Film,* 3–9, ed. Gary Crowdus. Chicago: Lake View Press, 1994.

———. *Redefining Black Film.* Berkeley: University of California Press, 1993.

Regier, Cornelius C. *The Era of the Muckrakers.* Chapel Hill: University of North Carolina Press, 1932.

Rhines, Jesse A. *Black Film, White Money.* New Brunswick, N.J.: Rutgers University Press, 1996.

Roberts, Randy. *Papa Jack: Jack Johnson and the Era of White Hopes.* New York: Free Press, 1983.

Robinson, Cedric. "In the Year 1915: D. W. Griffith and the Whitening of America." *Social Identities* 3, no. 2 (June 1997): 161–92.

Rocchio, Vincent F. *Reel Racism: Confronting Hollywood's Construction of Afro-American Culture.* Boulder, Colo.: Westview Press, 2000.

Roediger, David R. *The Wages of Whiteness: Race and the Making of the American Working Class.* London: Verso, 1991.

Rogin, Michael. *Blackface, White Noise: Jewish Immigrants in the Hollywood Melting Pot.* Berkeley: University of California Press, 1996.

———. "'The Sword Became a Flashing Vision': D. W. Griffith's *The Birth of a Nation.*" *Representations* 9 (Winter 1985): 150–95. Reprinted in *The Birth of a Nation,* 250–93, ed. Robert Lang. New Brunswick, N.J.: Rutgers University Press, 1994.

Roman, Robert C. "Lincoln on the Screen." *Films in Review* 12, no. 2 (February 1961): 87–101.

Rose, Mrs. S. E. F. "The Ku Klux Klan and *The Birth of a Nation.*" *Confederate Veteran* 24, no. 4 (April 1916): 157.

Rosen, Marjorie. *Popcorn Venus: Women, Movies and the American Dream.* New York: Coward, McCann and Geoghegan, 1973.

Rosenzweig, Roy. *Eight Hours for What We Will: Workers and Leisure in an Industrial City, 1870–1920.* Cambridge: Cambridge University Press, 1983.

Ross, B. Joyce. *J. E. Spingarn and the Rise of the NAACP, 1911–1939.* New York: Atheneum, 1972.

Ross, Edward A. "The Causes of Race Superiority." *Annals of the American Academy of Political and Social Science* 18 (July 1901): 67–89.

Rothman, William. *The "I" of the Camera: Essays in Film Criticism, History, and Aesthetics.* Cambridge: Cambridge University Press, 1988.

Sadoul, Georges. *Histoire Générale du Cinéma: Tome III: Le Cinéma Devient Un Art (1909–1920): Deuxième Volume: La Première Guerre Mondiale.* Paris: Editions Denoël, 1952.

Sarris, Andrew. "BIRTH OF A NATION or White Power Back When." *Village Voice,* July 17 and 24, 1969, 45; 37, 45. Reprinted in *Focus on "The Birth of a Nation,"* 106–110, ed. Fred Silva. Englewood Cliffs, N.J.: Prentice-Hall, 1971.

Saxton, Alexander. *The Rise and Fall of the White Republic: Class, Politics and Mass Culture in Nineteenth-century America.* London: Verso, 1990.

Schickel, Richard. *D. W. Griffith and the Birth of Film.* London: Pavilion, 1984.

Schwartz, Barry. *Abraham Lincoln and the Forge of National Memory.* Chicago: University of Chicago Press, 2000.

Scott, Ian. *American Politics in Hollywood Film.* Edinburgh: Edinburgh University Press, 2000.

Selig, Michael. "United States v. Motion Picture Film *The Spirit of '76:* The Espionage Case of Producer Robert Goldstein (1917)." *Journal of Popular Film and Television* 10, no. 4 (Winter 1983): 168–74.

Sieder, Jill Jordan. "Within Our Grasp...The Legend of Micheaux." *Oscar Micheaux Society Newsletter* 9 (Spring 2001): 10–12.

Silber, Nina. *The Romance of Reunion: Northerners and the South.* Chapel Hill: University of North Carolina Press, 1993.

Silva, Fred, ed. *Focus on "The Birth of a Nation."* Englewood Cliffs, N.J.: Prentice-Hall, 1971.

Simcovitch, Maxim. "The Impact of Griffith's *Birth of a Nation* on the Modern Ku Klux Klan." *Journal of Popular Film* 1, no. 1 (Winter 1972): 45–54.

Simmon, Scott. *The Films of D. W. Griffith.* Cambridge: Cambridge University Press, 1993.

Simkins, Francis B. and Robert H. Woody. *South Carolina during Reconstruction.* Chapel Hill: University of North Carolina Press, 1932.

Sklar, Robert. *Movie-Made America: A Cultural History of American Movies.* New York: Vintage Books, 1994.

Slide, Anthony. *American Racist: The Life and Films of Thomas Dixon.* Lexington: University Press of Kentucky, 2004.

———, ed. *Before, In and After Hollywood: The Autobiography of Joseph E. Henabery.* Lanham, Md.: Scarecrow Press, 1997.

———. *The Griffith Actresses.* South Brunswick: A. S. Barnes, 1973.

———, ed. *Robert Goldstein and "The Spirit of '76."* Metuchen, N.J.: Scarecrow Press, 1993.

———, ed. *Selected Film Criticism, 1912–1920.* Metuchen, N.J.: Scarecrow Press, 1982.

———. *"The Spirit of '76* and The Strange Case of Robert Goldstein." *Films in Review* 27, no. 1 (January 1976): 1–4.

Smith, John D. and John C. Inscoe, eds. *Ulrich Bonnell Phillips: A Southern Historian and His Critics.* Athens: University of Georgia Press, 1993.

Smith, Joseph. *The Spanish-American War: Conflict in the Caribbean and the Pacific 1895–1902.* London: Longman, 1994.

Smith, Valerie, ed. *Representing Blackness: Issues in Film and Video*. London: Athlone Press, 1997.

Snead, James A. *White Screens, Black Images: Hollywood from the Dark Side*. New York: Routledge, 1994.

Sorlin, Pierre. "The American Civil War." In Sorlin, *The Film in History: Restaging the Past*, 83–115. Totowa, N.J.: Barnes and Noble, 1980.

Spears, Jack. *The Civil War on the Screen and Other Essays*. South Brunswick: A. S. Barnes, 1977.

Spehr, Paul C. *The Civil War in Motion Pictures—A Bibliography of Films Produced in the United States since 1897*. Washington, D.C.: Library of Congress, 1961.

Staiger, Janet. *Interpreting Films: Studies in the Historical Reception of American Cinema*. Princeton: Princeton University Press, 1992.

———. "*The Birth of a Nation*: Reconsidering Its Reception." In Staiger, *Interpreting Films*, 139–53. Princeton: Princeton University Press, 1992. Reprinted in *The Birth of a Nation*, 195–213, ed. Robert Lang. New Brunswick, N.J.: Rutgers University Press, 1994.

Stampp, Kenneth M. *The Era of Reconstruction 1865–1877*. New York: Alfred A. Knopf, 1965.

Starfield, Penny. "Le racism dans le cinéma américain: entre exclusion et expression." In *Exclure au nom de la race (États-Unis, Irlande, Grande-Bretagne)*, 37–57, ed. Michel Prum. Paris: Editions Syllepse, 2000.

Steiner, Linda, ed. "Race and Cultural Production: Responses to *The Birth of a Nation*." *Critical Studies in Mass Communication* 10, no. 2 (June 1993): 179–97.

Stern, Seymour. "*The Birth of a Nation*." Special Supplement to *Sight and Sound*, Index Series, No. 4 (July 1945): 2–16.

———. "*The Birth of a Nation*: An Assessment." *American Classic Screen* 5, no. 1 (November–December 1980): 26–31.

———. "The Cold War against David Wark Griffith." *Films in Review* 7, no. 2 (February 1956): 49–59.

———. "D. W. Griffith: An Appreciation." *Sight and Sound*, 17, no. 67 (Autumn 1948): 109–10.

———. "D. W. Griffith and the Movies." *American Mercury* 68, no. 303 (March 1949): 308–19.

———. "Griffith: I—*The Birth of a Nation*." *Film Culture* 36, Special Griffith Issue (Spring–Summer 1965): 1–210.

———. "The Griffith Controversy." *Sight and Sound* 17, no. 65 (Spring 1948): 49–50.

———. "Griffith Not Anti-Negro." *Sight and Sound* 16, no. 61 (Spring 1947): 32–35.

———. "Suppression of Showing Marks 25thYear of *Birth of a Nation*." *New Leader* (March 16, 1940): 3.

Stewart, Jacqueline Najuma. *Migrating to the Movies: Cinema and Black Urban Modernity*. Berkeley: University of California Press, 2005.

Stoddart, Patrick. "*Birth of a Nation*: Racist but Still Riveting." *Broadcast*, no. 1138 (December 14, 1981): 17.

Stokes, Melvyn. "The Endless Re-birth of *The Birth of a Nation*?" *Interdisciplinary Journal for German Linguistics and Semiotic Analysis* 5, no. 2 (Fall 2000): 199–212

———. "Fighting the Color Line in Montmartre and Montparnasse: The Reception of *The Birth of a Nation* in France," forthcoming

———. "The Ku Klux Klan as Good and Evil in American Film." In *Le Bons et les Méchants dans le Cinéma Anglophone*, 215–28, ed. Francis Bordat and Serge Chauvin. Paris: University of Paris X—Nanterre, 2005.

———. "Race, Nationality and Citizenship: The Case of *The Birth of a Nation*." In *Federalism, Citizenship, and Collective Identities in U.S. History*, 107–19, ed. Cornelis A. van Minnen and Sylvia L. Hilton. Amsterdam: VU University Press, 2000.

———. "Structuring Absences: Images of America Missing from the Hollywood Screen." *Revue Française d Études Américaines* no. 89 (June 2001): 43–53.

Stokes, Melvyn and Rick Halpern, eds. *Race and Class in the American South since 1890*. Oxford: Berg, 1994.

Stokes, Melvyn and Richard Maltby, eds. *American Movie Audiences: From the Turn of the Century to the Early Sound Era*. London: BFI Publishing, 1999.

Stowe, Harriet Beecher. *Uncle Tom's Cabin; or, Life Among the Lowly*. London: David Campbell, 1995; reprint of 1852 edition.

———, website. http://www.harrietbeecher stowecenter.org/life/#war, accessed on March 29, 2007

Streible, Dan. "A History of the Boxing Film, 1894–1915." *Film History* 3, no. 3 (1989): 235–57.

———. "Race and the Reception of Jack Johnson Fight Films." In *The Birth of Whiteness*, 170–200, ed. Daniel Bernardi. New Brunswick, N.J.: Rutgers University Press, 1996.

Tarbell, Ida M. *All in the Day's Work: An Autobiography*. New York: Macmillan, 1939.

Taylor, Clyde. "The Re–Birth of the Aesthetic in Cinema." *Wide Angle* 13, nos. 3 and 4 (July–October 1991): 12–30. Reprinted in *The Birth of Whiteness*, 15–37, ed. Daniel Bernardi. New Brunswick, N.J.: Rutgers University Press, 1996.

Thirty Years of Lynching in the United States 1889–1918. New York: Negro Universities Press, 1918; reprint 1969.

Thomson, David. "Lillian Gish." In Thomson, *The New Biographical Dictionary of Film*, 4th ed., 338–40. London: Little, Brown, 2002.

———. *Showman: The Life of David O. Selznick*. London: Abacus, 1993.

Tolnay, Stewart E. and E. M. Beck. *A Festival of Violence: An Analysis of Southern Lynchings, 1882–1930*. Urbana: University of Illinois Press, 1995.

Tomkins, Mary E. *Ida M. Tarbell*. Boston, Mass.: Twayne, 1974.

Totaro, Donato. "Birth of a Nation: Viewed Today," http://www.horschamp.qc.ca/new_offscreen/birthofnation.html, accessed on March 29, 2007.

Tourgée, Albion W. *A Fool's Errand*, ed. John Hope Franklin. Cambridge, Mass.: Harvard University Press, 1961.

Tourgée, Albion W. *A Fool's Errand by One of the Fools; Part II, The Invisible Empire, A Concise History of the Epoch on Which the Tale Is Based*. New York: Fords, Howard and Hulbert, 1880.

Trelease, Allen W. *White Terror: The Ku Klux Klan Conspiracy and Southern Reconstruction*. London: Harper and Row, 1971.

Turner, George Kibbe. "The City of Chicago: A Study of Great Immoralities." *McClure's Magazine* 28 (April 1907): 575–92. Reprinted in *The Muckrakers*, 389–407, ed. Arthur and Lila Weinberg. New York: Simon and Schuster, 1961.

———. "The Daughters of the Poor." *McClure's Magazine*, 34 (November 1909): 45–61. Reprinted in *The Muckrakers*, 408–429, ed. Arthur and Lila Weinberg. New York: Simon and Schuster, 1961.

———. "Tammany's Control of New York by Professional Criminals." *McClure's Magazine* 33 (June 1909): 117–34.

Usai, Paulo Cherchi, ed. *The Griffith Project*: Vol. 8, *Films Produced in 1914–15*. London: British Film Institute/Le Giornate del Cinema Muto, 2004.

U.S. Bureau of the Census. *Historical Statistics of the United States—Colonial Times to 1957*. Washington, D.C.: U.S. Government Printing Office, 1960.

Van Minnen, Cornelis and Sylvia L. Hilton, eds. *Federalism, Citizenship, and Collective Identities in U.S. History*. Amsterdam: VU University Press, 2000.

Vaughan, Stephen. "Morality and Entertainment: The Origins of the Motion Picture Production Code." *Journal of American History* 77, no. 1 (June 1990): 39–65.

Wade, Wyn Craig. *The Fiery Cross: The Ku Klux Klan in America*. New York: Simon and Schuster, 1987.

Wagenknecht, Edward. "Griffith's Biographs: A General View." *Films in Review* 26, no. 8 (October 1975): 449–67.

Waller, Gregory A. "Another Audience: Black Moviegoing, 1907–1916." *Cinema Journal* 31, no. 2 (Winter 1992): 3–25.

Waller, Signe. *Love and Revolution: A Political Memoir: People's History of the Greensboro Massacre and Its Aftermath*. Lanham, Md.: Rowman and Littlefield, 2002.

Walsh, Raoul. *Each Man in His Time: The Life Story of a Director*. New York: Farrar, Straus and Giroux, 1974.

Booker T. Washington Papers, Microfilm and Paper, Library of Congress, Washington, D.C.

Weinberg, Herman G. "American Film Directors and Social Reality." *Sight and Sound* 7, no. 28 (Winter 1938–39): 168–69.

Weinberg, Julius. *Edward Alsworth Ross and the Sociology of Progressivism*. Madison: State Historical Society of Wisconsin, 1972.

Weiss, Nancy J. "The Negro and the New Freedom: Fighting Wilsonian Segregation." *Political Science Quarterly* 84, no. 1 (March 1969): 61–79.

Wertheimer, John. "Mutual Film Reviewed: The Movies, Censorship, and Free Speech in Progressive America." *The American Journal of Legal History* 37, no. 2 (April 1993): 158–89.

White, Mimi. "*The Birth of a Nation*: History as Pretext." *Enclitic*, 5 (Fall 1981/Spring 1982): 17–24. Reprinted in *The Birth of a Nation*, 214–224, ed. Robert Lang. New Brunswick, N.J.: Rutgers University Press, 1994.

White, Walter. *A Man Called White: The Autobiography of Walter White*. London: Victor Gollancz, 1949.

"Will Reservoir Dogs Be Next? After 80 years *The Birth of a Nation* Gets a Video Certificate …" *Empire* no. 63 (September 1994): 13.

Williams, Linda. *Playing the Race Card: Melodramas of Black and White from Uncle Tom to O. J. Simpson*. Princeton: Princeton University Press, 2001.

Williams, Martin. *Griffith: First Artist of the Movies*. New York: Oxford University Press, 1980.

Williamson, Joel. *After Slavery: The Negro in South Carolina during Reconstruction, 1861–1877*. Chapel Hill: University of North Carolina Press, 1965.

———. *The Crucible of Race: Black-White Relations in the American South since Emancipation*. New York: Oxford University Press, 1984.

———. *New People: Miscegenation and Mulattoes in the United States*. Baton Rouge: Louisiana State University Press, 1995.

Wilson, Harold S. *"McClure's Magazine" and the Muckrakers*. Princeton: Princeton University Press, 1970.

Wilson, Woodrow. *A History of the American People*, Vol. V, *Reunion and Nationalization*. New York: Harper and Brothers, 1902.

Wolgemuth, Kathleen L. "Woodrow Wilson and Federal Segregation." *Journal of Negro History* 44, no. 2 (April 1959): 158–73.

Woodward, C. Vann. *Origins of the New South 1877–1913*. Baton Rouge: Louisiana State University Press, 1951.

Yacowar, Maurice. "Aspects of the Familiar: A Defense of Minority Group Stereotyping in the Popular Film." *Literature/Film Quarterly* 2, no. 2 (Spring 1974): 129–39.

Index